PENGUIN BOOKS

LONDON: A SOCIAL HISTORY

'There are surprisingly few good general histories of London, New York or Paris concerned with where and how people worked, amused themselves, prayed, or raised families ... Roy Porter has a novelist's eye for telling details about everyday life, and a scholar's care for evidence. The book comes to life politically at the end, when he discusses the impact of the Thatcher years on London's social fabric; Porter sees deeply engrained habits, survival strategies and street-wise pleasures which have marked the social history of Londoners rich and poor suddenly corroded within the space of a decade' – Richard Sennett in *The Times Literary Supplement*, Books of the Year

'It should be read by every Londoner of whatever political persuasion; by every Briton who lives north of Watford or south of Croydon; and by anyone, anywhere, who is concerned about the current problems and future prospects of the world's great conurbations. For cities, like nations, can only be understood in an historical perspective. It is that perspective which this book so brilliantly provides. In more senses than one, it is a capital history' – David Cannadine in the *Independent on Sunday*

'One of the virtues of this account is the range of contemporaneous quotation which Porter provides, giving full weight to that period when London was the wonder and the mystery of the world. But he is also very good on those details which mark the city's true and enduring identity' – Peter Ackroyd in *The Times*

'A fascinating trawl through its colourful past' – Clare Colvin in the *Sunday Express*

ABOUT THE AUTHOR

Dr Roy Porter is Professor in the Social History of Medicine at the Wellcome Institute for the History of Medicine, London. He is currently working on a general history of medicine, on the history of Bethlem Hospital and on the Enlightenment in Britain. Recent books include *Mind Forg'd Manacles: Madness in England from the Restoration to the Regency* (Athlone, 1987); *A Social History of Madness* (Weidenfeld and Nicolson, 1987); *In Sickness and in Health: The British Experience 1650–1850* (Fourth Estate, 1988) and *Patient's Progress* (Polity, 1989), both co-authored with Dorothy Porter; *Health for Sale: Quackery in England 1660–1850* (Manchester University Press); *Doctor of Society: Thomas Beddoes and the Sick Trade in Late Enlightenment England* (Routledge, 1991); and *London: A Social History* (Hamish Hamilton, 1994). He has also edited, with Jeremy Black, *The Penguin Dictionary of Eighteenth-Century History.*

LONDON

A Social History

ROY PORTER

PENGUIN BOOKS

PENGUIN BOOKS

Published by the Penguin Group
Penguin Books Ltd, 27 Wrights Lane, London w8 5TZ, England
Penguin Books USA Inc., 375 Hudson Street, New York, New York 10014, USA
Penguin Books Australia Ltd, Ringwood, Victoria, Australia
Penguin Books Canada Ltd, 10 Alcorn Avenue, Toronto, Ontario, Canada M4V 3B2
Penguin Books (NZ) Ltd, 182–190 Wairau Road, Auckland 10, New Zealand

Penguin Books Ltd, Registered Offices: Harmondsworth, Middlesex, England

First published by Hamish Hamilton 1994
Published in Penguin Books 1996
1 3 5 7 9 10 8 6 4 2

Acknowledgement is made to the following for permission to use extracts from: *The Waste Land* by T. S. Eliot, reprinted by permission of Faber & Faber; *Something in Linoleum* by Paul Vaughan, reprinted by permission of Sinclair-Stevenson; *The Girls of Slender Means* by Muriel Spark, published by Penguin Books, reprinted by permission of David Higham Associates; 'Summoned by Bells' and 'Thoughts on the Diary of a Nobody', from *Collected Poems*, and *Betjeman's London*, edited by Pennie Denton, all by John Betjeman, reprinted by permission of John Murry (Publishers) Ltd.
    Acknowledgement is also made for permission to use the following illustrations: Fotomas Index, pp. iii, 33, 50, 59, 67, 77, 84, 88, 101, 108, 111, 117, 128, 129, 139, 145, 163, 174, 191, 193, 206, 219, 266, 301, 314; Mary Evans Picture Library, pp. 35, 39, 195, 286; Hulton Deutsch Collection, pp. 44, 57, 265, 360; The Bridgeman Art Library, pp. 47, 71, 81, 107, 130, 258; Guildhall Library, pp. 137, 161, 223, 252, 340; London Transport Museum, pp. 226, 316, 318; Paul Middleton, p. 378; LDDC, p. 380; Port of London Authority, p. 189; Popular Atlas of the British Isles (Bacon), p. 230; The Abercrombie Plan, p. 350; Greater London Record Office, p. 256; The Ashmolean Museum, p. 1.

Set in 10/13.75 Linotype Janson
Typeset by Selwood Systems, Midsomer Norton
Printed in Great Britain by Butler & Tanner Ltd, Frome and London

PREVIOUS PAGE View of London from Richard Pynson's *Cronycle of Englande*, 1510

To my parents

Contents

Illustrations

When I grow rich,
Say the bells of Shoreditch

CHILDREN'S SONG, 'Oranges and Lemons'

From the bones of extinct monsters and the coins of Roman emperors in the cellars to the name of the shopman over the door, the whole story is fascinating and the material endless. Perhaps Cockneys are a prejudiced race, but certainly this inexhaustible richness seems to belong to London more than to any other great city.

VIRGINIA WOOLF, Review of E. V. Lucas's *London Revisited* (1916)

I have often amused myself with thinking how different a place London is to different people. They, whose narrow minds are contracted to the consideration of some one particular pursuit, view it only through that medium. A politician thinks of it merely as the seat of government in its different departments; a grazier, as a vast market for cattle; a mercantile man, as a place where a prodigious deal of business is done upon 'Change; a dramatick enthusiast, as the grand scene of theatrical entertainments; a man of pleasure, as an assemblage of taverns, and the great emporium for ladies of easy virtue. But the intellectual man is struck with it, as comprehending the whole of human life in all its variety, the contemplation of which is inexhaustible.

JAMES BOSWELL, *Journal* (1763)

Jerusalem Athens Alexandria
Vienna London
Unreal

T. S. ELIOT, *The Waste Land* (1922)

Preface

Maybe it's because I'm a Londoner, but when Peter Carson and Andrew Franklin invited me, more years ago than I can recall without shame, to write a social history of London, I leapt at the opportunity. I grew up in south London just after the war. Three miles from London Bridge, New Cross Gate was not exactly the Bethnal Green beloved of Young and Willmott, but it was a stable if shabby working-class community completely undiscovered by sociologists. In many ways, that past now seems another country: bomb-sites and prefabs abounded, pig-bins stood like pillboxes on street corners, the Co-op man came round with a horse and cart delivering the milk, everybody knew everybody. Some of the houses in Camplin Street still had gas lighting, as did my infant school; clanking trams are a vivid memory, and it was fun creeping to school through pea-soupers, a torch vainly held out in front. In those years of austerity – ration-book coupons taught me my sums – locals grumbled about how run-down and old-fashioned the area was, hemmed in by the railway sidings, canal and docks that had long provided secure employment but which imparted a grimy, dingy feel. The three-up, three-down council house that my parents shared with my grandparents and an uncle had an outside lavatory; a tin bath was hauled in once a week from the bottom of the garden, set down on the scullery floor, and filled from kettles and a wheezing Ascot gas water-heater. Domestic overcrowding was worsened but redeemed by the sanctity of the front room, used only at Christmas, though unlocked once a week so that the Rexine three-piece suite could be polished with Ronuk.

People wanted to get out of New Cross. We were on the London County Council housing list, but that was regarded as an unfunny joke ('You'll be dead before they'll offer you a place'). Eventually, in 1959, Dad had finally saved enough to get a mortgage on a house, in Norwood, five miles out into the suburbs. It cost £3,000. Its walls were pebble-dash; it had a bathroom, an inside toilet, french windows and plumbed-in hot water. It was heaven. The Porters were a classic upward-social-mobility statistic in the era that had never had it so good.

Before then, when I was a kid we went visiting hordes of uncles and aunts, all of whom also lived in council houses a short walk or a threepenny bus-ride away – though some relatives had been rehoused at Harold Hill, the new LCC estate in south Essex, where there were still bluebells to pick in the spring in what was left of Harold Wood, though no corner shop to buy sherbet dips. We rarely travelled far. A couple of Sundays a year we'd pile into a cheap special-excursion train lumbering from London Bridge to Brighton, armed with buckets and spades and bottles of Tizer. There'd be an annual Christmas shopping spree to Gamage's at Holborn, with – treat of treats – lunch out at Lyons; and a summer trip to see the Crazy Gang, or Al Read at the Palladium, and perhaps a pleasure steamer up to Kew. Who needed to travel far? There were plenty of things to do around home. The Gaumont, ABC and Astoria all lay within easy walking distance. There were municipal parks and swimming-baths. Millwall Football Club was only five minutes away at the Den, Cold Blow Lane; there were also greyhounds on Thursdays and Saturdays, and speedway on Wednesdays. In the summer there was the Oval, and that magical Surrey cricket team.

Nobody liked living in New Cross Gate. Yet there was much to be said for that kind of respectable working-class inner-city neighbourhood that is now pretty much a thing of the past. My parents had seen serious poverty around them when they were growing up in Bermondsey in the twenties, but all that had disappeared by 1950. Only a few kids got free school dinners – my class looked on them with a mix of pity and envy. All the men were in work, many with big local employers such as the council, Surrey Commercial Docks, the railways, London Transport, Borough market or Peek Frean's biscuit factory; women kept house and raised children. Husbands had wives, housewives had breadwinners, and children had parents (and aunts, in-laws and grandparents round the corner). Families stuck together. Menfolk slipped down to the Royal Archer, but there were no notorious drunks or wife-beaters. Nor was there violence or crime. Girls skipped, and we boys kicked a tennis ball in the street, and mothers didn't worry too much: there was little backstreet traffic – no one we knew owned a car – and no fear of child-molesters.

Mine was a happy childhood. And though living was cramped and people had to be careful with money, the feeling was that, with the war over, with full employment and the NHS, life was secure; within limits, you could get on, be neighbourly, be respectable, grow tomatoes, save for a washing-machine and afford a week's holiday at Jaywick Sands with candyfloss and cockles.

How different are things in SE14 now? Camplin Street's terraces have changed remarkably little: even some of the privet hedges look familiar. In the fifties the talk was of bulldozing the area and redeveloping it with council flats. About flippin' time too, neighbours grumbled: the houses were dark and damp and never looked clean. In the event, nothing happened. Now many of them are privately owned, and the monotony of Deptford Borough Council's bottle-green and cream paint has yielded to rainbow hues, Regency doors and louvre windows, and kerbsides crammed with cars. Certain bits look more tacky now, but it is also livelier, brighter, less regimented. There must be fewer nuclear families with 2·4 children and grandparents and in-laws living round the block. What lives are led behind the front doors and the permanent lace curtains? Five minutes' walk away, however, change hits you in the face. Millwall Football Club boasts a brand-new stadium with a multimillion-pound entertainment complex. Surrey Docks are closed, the canal is filled in, the railway a ghost of its former self. The local sweet factory and dressmakers have closed down. New Cross Road, which once wore an air of faded early Victorian elegance, is now a ceaseless roar of lorries hurtling down to the Channel ports. The big houses near the Marquis of Granby pub, once admired, are slums, squats or boarded-up, like many of the shops. Dossers and drunks litter the gardens, and some students of mine were mugged there last year. South London has gained a mean name for drug-dealing, racial violence, gangland crime and contract killing.

Things endure, things change: improvement, deterioration, adjustment – all respond to the deep pulse of the city. And in that respect the south London community where I grew up forms a cameo of London at large: the physical fabric engages in endless dialogue with the inhabitants; the townscape shapes them, while they reconstruct it. Factories and flats, railways and roads outlive individuals. People make their own cities, but never under conditions of their own choosing. That is why telling the story of a city presents special challenges, demanding a collective biography strung out on a prolonged time-line, rather as with a family history in which each generation is different but recognizably of the original stock.

On rereading my text I am profoundly aware of all that is left out. I can only plead that this is a consequence of what I have above all tried to put in: that is, a substantial account and analysis of the making of the metropolis in terms of its people, economy and buildings. I hope that what I have written will lead readers to think about *their* own London.

I claim little originality for the facts and interpretations that follow. Mine is a work of synthesis in which I have drawn heavily and gratefully on the work of hundreds of experts who know far more than I about West Ham and West Hampstead, Barnes and Barnsbury, sweatshops and sewers, mews and zoos. I have not festooned my text with references to them by name, but have tried to detail if not discharge my huge intellectual debts in the Further Reading section.

Over the years of writing this book I have benefited enormously from the help of a multitude of friends, historians and Londoners. For reading drafts, I am particularly grateful to W. F. Bynum, Christine Stevenson, David Feldman, Vanessa Harding, Anne

Hardy, Rob Iliffe, Lara Marks, and Hamish Hamilton's referees. I also wish to thank all those at, and working for, Hamish Hamilton who have made the production of this book such a pleasure, in particular Keith Taylor, Sally Abbey, Bob Davenport, Bela Cunha, Helen Dore and the indexer, Douglas Matthews.

I am above all indebted to the patient staffs of the Wellcome Library, the British Library, the Guildhall Library and the Museum of London for their helpfulness and expertise. As always, the Wellcome Institute (housed tellingly in a central London building flanking what was, 200 years ago, London's first bypass) has been a wonderfully supportive environment. For all their help I wish to thank in particular Caroline Overy, London's best research assistant; and Frieda Houser, Michelle Johnson, Jan Pinkerton, Tracey Wickham, Jo Lane and Sally Bragg, who have corrected wave upon wave of drafts.

For reasons that will already be clear, I would like to dedicate this volume to my mother and my late father, Londoners both, whose experience it was to have the worst day of the Blitz, 10 May 1941, as their wedding day. To them I owe the happy London childhood already referred to, and so much else besides.

CHAPTER ONE

Introduction

London is not the eternal city; it had its hour upon the stage. Between the two Elizabeths, between 1570 and 1986 to be more precise, it was to become the world's greatest city. Those dates are convenient benchmarks. In 1570, twelve years after ascending the throne, Henry VIII's daughter opened the Royal Exchange, proudly erected in Cornhill by the millionaire merchant prince Sir Thomas Gresham; through that arcaded and four-storeyed Renaissance bourse the City told the world it was now a great commercial and financial mart. In 1986 Prime Minister Margaret Thatcher abolished the Greater London Council, leaving the metropolis the only Western 'world city' without its representative government. The GLC, it must be admitted, had been a failure for the twenty-odd years of its existence; but the abandonment of the idea that London deserved a democratic government of its own, like Paris, Berlin, New York and every other major city in the civilized world, marked the moment when the doctor decided the case was incurable and abandoned the patient. London's recent decline has been so precipitate, and roads to recovery would now have to be so radical and costly, that late twentieth-century administrations prefer to avert their eyes from the deteriorating megalopolis and let nature, or international financiers and the multi-nationals, take their course.

London's current crisis as an ageing, ailing city suffering from hardening of the arteries – though patched up here and there with replacement surgery – is hardly unique. Babylon disappeared, Rome and Venice declined. In our days the dilemmas of urban deindustrialization and the obsolete inner city are as universal as Coca-Cola. But London's difficulties are worse than most, because in its time London has been so inordinately great, because its fortunes were built on an imperial glory now departed, and because of the crazy chronicles of the capital's government.

This book charts London's rise to a greatness that carried with it the seeds of its present disintegration. London grew because it became the headquarters of the world's hugest empire. Since the First World War, and especially since 1945, industrial and imperial decline have posed readjustment problems that successive ministries never remotely faced head-on – partly because the blessings of empire sustained London in prosperity long after it was showing all the symptoms of hypertrophy. Enormous postwar New Commonwealth immigration is one of the more conspicuous consequences of Britain's former imperial mission. Such an influx has brought problems, but new life as well.

The key to the capital is the British Empire. London became a city of 1 million, 2 million, 5 million, 10 million citizens not because the United Kingdom had 10, 20, or 40 million inhabitants but because the Empire consisted of ten times as many – 400 million souls by 1900. As capital and port, finance and manufacturing centre all in one, London was the beneficiary-in-chief from the British Empire – while it lasted.

With imperial twilight and the trivialization of the Commonwealth, London desperately needed to reconstitute itself as a new global city, both strategically and physically. Yet it has lacked the three elements necessary to do this effectively: resources, vision and will. And this lack has followed from the peculiarities of London's administration. The Greeks celebrated the city-state: according to Aristotle, man is a political animal who lives in the *polis*, or city, which provides not just life but the good life. Paul was proud to be a citizen of no mean city. In the Middle Ages, city air made free: Renaissance art and politics flourished in city-states such as Venice, Florence, Milan and Geneva. Municipality still retains proud traditions: it means something to be Mayor of New York or Chicago, of Paris or Berlin. But the Lord Mayor of London is, and long has been, a nobody, a ceremonial stuffed-shirt glimpsed for a few minutes a year on the day of the mayoral parade: how many mayors of London can anyone name apart from Dick Whittington? I doubt if anyone thinks of themselves today as *citizens* of London.

Not since the Romans has London possessed a unified government, a government relevant to all its needs. Administration has been fragmented, often deliberately. In days of copper-bottomed expansion this proved no insuperable obstacle: the fact that the capital was never under royal or parliamentary thumb was probably a blessing in disguise, facilitating unfettered growth. London, however, has ceased to be a boom town cashing in on the military-economic might of the *Pax Britannica* and the sterling area, with buoyant business readily creating solutions to its problems, albeit often in makeshift and inequitable ways. Constructive statecraft and munificent funding are now required to bale it out, renew its fabric, and restore its morale. These have not been forthcoming, for reasons endemic to Britain's larger economic and international malaise.

Does this smack of ritual doom-mongering, yet another premature obituary on a city that has often confounded its critics down the generations? In former centuries London was pronounced sick because it was seen as too swollen, too luxurious, too hectic for the nation's good. This diagnosis proved mistaken, for urban pathology lies not in growth but in collapse, emigration, impoverishment, idleness. It is these symptoms that are evident today. Whether anything will restore London's former vigour is unclear, though millions of tourists buzzing round the patient will certainly provide a stimulus, or an irritant.

London is not about to be abandoned to the dogs, as Londinium was in the fifth century once the Romans left. But statistics may be suggestive. Since the Second World War, Greater London's population has plunged by over 20 per cent, from 8,196,000 in 1951 to 6,393,000 in 1991. An ever-rising proportion of today's population is unproductive, unemployed and chronically dependent on income support and social services. Many – a percentage that might have shocked Charles Booth a century ago – are 'problem people': the aged and disabled, lone-parent families, children in care, delinquents, drop-outs, dossers. For so long a fully employed city, remarkably successful at integrating newcomers via the world of work, London now has an unemployment rate of 17 per cent, and in some inner-city boroughs it is over 25 per cent. The capital today harbours huge concentrations of the unskilled, the long-term unemployed, new migrants, drifters, offenders and others caught in the poverty trap and excluded from the mainstream. In the Thatcher years the number of homeless shot up from 8,000 to 80,000. Council-housing waiting-lists now stand at 400,000, and in 1990 barely 300 public-authority dwellings were built (5,000 were erected in Rotterdam). In 1990 London's recorded crimes totalled 800,000 – you might say that every tenth person either committed a crime or was the victim of one. And so forth. The point is clear: London has critical and intensifying problems, and is no longer routinely offering all its citizens the elementary benefits that Aristotle thought were the city's *raisons d'être*: shelter, safety, society, support. Divested of a government of its own, and suffering year after year of punitive rate-capping from Downing Street, it is on a downward spiral of infrastructural and human problems that will prove hard to halt.

London's difficulties are not unique: the wounds of Washington, downtown Detroit and riot-torn Los Angeles afford perhaps even worse instances of what happens when inner-city problems are nobody's business and private affluence condones public squalor. Yet certain European cities are battling more effectively to cope with the crises of the post-industrial city: Barcelona, Copenhagen and Lyons are just a few of the places where transportation systems have been revitalized, moribund industrial or dock areas imaginatively redeveloped, and civic pride rekindled.

Dismal diagnoses for London, some will say, are overdramatic; for is there not the City? High finance doubtless remains a success story, but the future of the City today, unlike at the imperial high noon, depends upon factors primarily beyond London's control: upon Tokyo and Wall Street, and the wheelings and dealings of European

Union politics. What will happen once the European Central Bank is located in Frankfurt, once the European Parliament at Strasbourg grows in powers? What if sterling becomes viewed as the currency of an inveterately second-division economy?

This book tracks London's rise and decline, plotting that path against various back-grounds that cannot be investigated here but which must not be ignored. One, it goes without saying, is the history of Europe and the wider world. Londinium was founded by Italians; it arose as the trading post and administrative headquarters of a far-flung province of the Roman Empire. Throughout the medieval centuries England was a significant actor in Europe's dynastic dramas and a producer of primary products sited towards its economic periphery. From Tudor times, and particularly after 1650, Britain expanded as a global military and maritime power, and her economy blossomed alongside. Of trading and colonial conquests in the West and East Indies, in India, Africa and the Pacific, London was the supreme beneficiary, becoming the powerhouse of an unprecedented empire. Without Marlborough, Wolfe and Clive, Wellington and Nelson, without the Royal Navy, London would doubtless have become impressive – a match for Bordeaux, Rotterdam and Hamburg – but it would not have become the marvel of the world, as it did in the nineteenth century when, in 1862, *Routledge's Popular Guide to London and Its Suburbs* could patriotically but almost incontrovertibly declare:

London is the political, moral, physical, intellectual, artistic, literary, commercial and social centre of the world ... no other city possesses the wealth, importance and abounding population which distinguish it. To London, as the true centre of the world, come ships from every clime, bearing the productions of nature, the results of labour and the fruits of commerce ... Its merchants are princes; the resolves of its financiers make and unmake empires and influence the destiny of nations.

The history of cities cannot be detached from human affairs at large, and this applies above all to the city that became the sun of suns, a fact confirmed when international bureaucracy fixed the zero meridian at Greenwich in 1884: the longitude took its law from London.

Another backdrop to this story – one about which I shall say little – is the theory of urbanism. Social scientists and urban geographers struck it lucky in the postwar years. Especially in the sixties, planning proliferated, architects and sociologists set about changing the world, and campuses and town halls echoed with theories about zonal morphology, modernization, space management and the rival virtues of 'central places' and 'networks'. Such concepts, it was confidently believed, would provide the key to creating the city of the future, a wholly planned environment.

Whether such doctrines have built better towns I leave to others to decide. I doubt whether they have contributed much to the better grasp of urban history. Certain urban thinkers have, without a doubt, proved immensely stimulating. With his visionary urban pathologies culminating in parasitopolis and necropolis, Lewis Mumford may have been mistaken, but he had the great merit of trying to set the city in history. Rayner Banham and Peter Hall have never lost sight of nitty-gritty particularity. But the enterprise of urban theorizing as such seems to be a blind alley. Its aim has been to generalize about variables like communications, wealth, social zoning and power systems in the pre-industrial, industrial and post-industrial city. Yet great cities tend to be the singular products of unique geographical, social, economic and political ecosystems. No two cities are alike, and metropolises do not match planners' models. And so if the remainder of this book makes little explicit reference to the postulates of urbanists, it is because their abstractions cannot throw much light upon the municipality which the Danish architect and humanist Steen Eiler Rasmussen aptly dubbed 'the unique city'. For several centuries, nowhere *could* be quite like London: its very existence precluded peers, at least in Europe. Readers fascinated by urbanist castles in the air are invited to sample the relevant literature cited in the Further Reading section.

If attempts to theorize 'the city' require caution, the importance of understanding the lives of cities is crystal-clear. For ours is an urban world. A century ago only 4 per cent of the earth's population lived in towns of over 20,000 people; today a quarter do, and the proportion is rising. Less than two centuries ago, only one city in the West, maybe in the world, had more than a million inhabitants. Now there are over 100 such cities, and London is a fading star in this firmament, where the nebulae are Asia and the Americas. We must swallow any lingering chauvinism and remember that the metropolitan areas of Tokyo and Mexico City are already about twice as large as London; in population, London is no longer even in the world's top dozen cities.

Cities have been called social laboratories in the making of modernity, experiments in social chemistry, where nature, communities and artefacts interact, where the past shapes the present and the present moulds the future – a future more unintended than planned. Change is the essence.

Take Covent Garden. This entered history as some pasturage belonging to the abbey (or convent) of St Peter at Westminster. Henry VIII's dissolution of the monasteries led to Crown seizure of the estate and its bestowal upon John Russell, 1st Earl of Bedford. One of his successors built Bedford House on ground north of the Strand, the site of the present Southampton Street. Anxious to turn his property to profit, in the 1630s the 4th Earl obtained a licence to build residences there 'fitt for the habitacions of *Gentlemen* and men of ability'. Brought in as architect, Inigo Jones built a piazza for the Earl, consisting of St Paul's church (rebuilt) and three blocks of noble terraced houses (demolished). These gained quality tenants, and the piazza became a classy address. In time, however, the fruit and vegetable market also operating in the square sapped its smartness and the aristocracy quit, migrating to Mayfair.

The square was taken over by taverns, coffee-houses, gambling-dens and brothels – 'one would imagine that all the prostitutes in the kingdom had picked upon the rendezvous', observed the magistrate Sir John Fielding. John Cleland's heroine Fanny Hill naturally took lodgings there, and it became a haunt of artists and writers like Henry Fielding (Sir John's brother) and Oliver Goldsmith. By the Regency even the market had declined, infiltrated by knick-knack dealers. Deploring the 'total want of … arrangement, neatness and accommodation', in 1813 the 6th Duke of Bedford secured an Act of Parliament for regulating the market; and, to cajole tradesmen into conducting their business in an orderly manner, a new building was erected in the early 1830s – the handsome centre-piece familiar today. This in turn became inadequate and was reconstructed and given annexes, and further market buildings were run up – for instance, the Floral Hall (1860), south of the Royal Opera House, which itself had been opened in 1732.

If fashion no longer dwelt in Covent Garden, it still visited the opera. The odd juxtaposition of vegetables and Verdi struck Virginia Woolf, a great lover of London but one acutely sensitive to its distinct social 'beats'. 'Men and women in full evening dress were walking along the pavement,' she observed in *The Years*:

They looked uncomfortable and self-conscious as they dodged between costers' barrows, with their high-piled hair and their evening cloaks with the buttonholes and their white waistcoats, in the flare of the afternoon sun. The ladies tripped uncomfortably on their high-heeled shoes; now and then they put their hands to their heads. The gentlemen kept close beside them as though protecting them. It's absurd, Kitty thought … Covent Garden porters, dingy little clerks in their ordinary working clothes, coarse-looking women in aprons stared at her. The air smelt strongly of oranges and bananas. But the car was coming to a standstill. It drew up under the archway; she pushed through the glass doors and went in.

In the Victorian era Covent Garden thrived as London's chief fruit and vegetable market, employing nearly 1,000 porters. It was, however, incorrigibly chaotic; the Bedfords decided to give it up. After the First World War it was finally disposed of to a private company, the Covent Garden Estate Co. Ltd, which in turn tried to sell it to the London County Council. Although condemned by the Ministry of Food as 'altogether inadequate to the necessities of the trade', the congested market lingered for a further half-century, finally moving in 1974 to a sixty-acre site on disused railway land at Nine Elms, Vauxhall, allowing the GLC to come forward with comprehensive redevelopment plans that involved multi-level roads, high-rise offices, walkways and shops. Locals rose against the scheme, and won. Preserved and pedestrianized, Covent Garden became London's prime tourist playground, one of the very few parts of the capital providing traffic-free urban space. A centre for strolling and diversion, it has unexpectedly recaptured some of the spirit of the eighteenth century.

From pasture to piazza; a den of vice, and then a hive of trade; still later the planners' dream almost come true; and now the picturesque delight of tourists – Covent Garden has worn numerous guises, some planned, some accidental. Its history has been shaped by the Crown, by grandees, by commerce, by local government and by the will of the people. In *Little Dorrit* Dickens documented all the different Covent Gardens:

Courtly ideas of Covent Garden, as a place with famous coffee-houses, where gentlemen wearing gold-laced coats and swords had quarrelled and fought duels; costly ideas of Covent Garden, as a place where there were flowers in winter at guineas a-piece, pine-apples at guineas a pound, and peas at guineas a pint; picturesque ideas of Covent Garden, as a place where there was a mighty theatre, showing wonderful and beautiful sights to richly-dressed ladies and gentlemen, and which was forever far beyond the reach of poor Fanny or poor uncle; desolate ideas of Covent Garden, as having all those arches in it, where the miserable children in rags among whom she had just now passed, like young rats, slunk and hid, fed on offal, huddled together for warmth, and were hunted about (look to the rats young and old, all ye Barnacles, for before God they are eating away our foundations, and will bring the roofs on our heads!); teeming ideas of Covent Garden, as a place of past and present mystery, romance, abundance, want, beauty, ugliness, fair country gardens, and foul street-gutters; all confused together ...

It has rarely been just one thing at a time. Despite everyone from Inigo Jones to the GLC, it has never remained what its planners desired – and who can predict what it will be next? And such is the story not just of Covent Garden but of the metropolis at large. Everywhere continuity and change coalesce; forms and functions mutate; past buildings and townscapes enhance but inhibit the present; the future refashions the debris of the past.

People make cities, and cities make citizens. The townscape each generation inherits is a support but sometimes also a strait-jacket. The great city is a wonder of nature, or rather of civilization. In a castle or camp, living-patterns may be stringently controlled. Lord and priest, soil and crops dictate rules of life to villages, regulating activities, policing peasants. But the giant city knows no great dictator. It has a varied cast – magistrates, landlords and property-owners, markets, migrants, manufacturers – who improvise the urban drama – conflicting, competing, creating new scenes. And all such human players collaborate with great impersonal forces: rivers, climate, soil, trading opportunities, population pressures, market forces. Not least, cities function within force fields determined by distance, communications systems and layout, and are shaped by exogenous factors – regional, national, continental, global. They possess internal topographies, part spontaneous, part planned, zonings for homes and markets, for rich and poor. And all the time, as noted with Covent Garden, the elements fluctuate. Cities are not machines, built once and for all, but remarkable organisms. Like a coral reef, the city is always becoming a product, but that is because, first of all, it is a process.

Cities thus afford special fascination for the historian, being outgrowths of human aims but also the effects of a concatenation of activities beyond central control. The great city assumes a life of its own, and super-cities such as London are always spilling beyond their limits, by eating up not just the countryside but also the imagination – transcending ideas about what a city should, or even could, be. London grew bigger than any imagined city, provoking observers to call it a cancer, fatal to itself, lethal to its citizens, mortal to the kingdom.

London was above all the uncontrolled city. What a paradox! The vastest city in the nation, in the world – the one which, above all, one might think most would need governing – long had Bumbledom. Within the Square Mile the Corporation lorded it over soaring wealth and a vanishing population. From Tudor times the City washed its hands of responsibility for governing the swelling metropolis as a whole, while also frustrating moves by Parliament to rule the capital. And sometimes, as has twice happened within the last thirty years, agencies established by Westminster to administer the capital have been dismantled when they proved too independent and threatened to wag the dog. The fact that, alone of the world's great cities, London has no unifying municipal government is not only symptomatic of the crisis of the metropolis today: it is also a clue to its history.

There are countless books on London's history. Is another needed? I believe so. Urban history has now rooted itself as a thriving academic discipline. It has produced a huge research harvest during the last twenty years, in scholarly journals, PhD theses and academic monographs. Each year *Urban History* (formerly the *Urban History Yearbook*) – around 300 pages long – publishes a bibliography of new work that runs to nearly 2,000 items. Old orthodoxies have been demolished, landscapes of ignorance explored, new findings accumulated. But little of this has permeated into the wider histories of London readily available to readers at large. I cannot pretend to have read all that has recently been written on London, or more than a fraction of writings about the urban experience the world over, but I have aimed to produce an up-to-date synthesis.

I have also beaten a particular path. Histories of London have been of two sorts. Most have concentrated on buildings – above all, the forty-two volumes that have so far appeared of the magisterial and indispensable *Survey of London*, set up in the late 1890s by the LCC and still lovingly documenting architraves and architects. Others, by contrast, give pride of place to goings-on in the metropolis: for example, beheadings at the Tower, coronations at Westminster Abbey, or the General Strike. Architecture and events are both, of course, essential, but concentration on them may be a distraction to city history. If buildings take precedence over people we get heritage, not history. And we must make the distinction between the city as stage for public events and the city as actor.

I have tried to make the city itself my hero, focusing on the interaction of its people, its economy and its physical fabric. I have, in other words, tried to explore urbanization, the evolution of the metropolis itself. Consigning princes and palaces to the background, I have sought to probe the play of built environment with inhabitants: what made London tick? And, in creating a sense of place, I have paid attention to the local as well as the total, to the modest as well as the mighty – not just Westminster but West Norwood; not just Piccadilly but Pinner – heeding Samuel Johnson's advice to James Boswell that 'if you wish to have a just notion of the magnitude of this city, you must not be satisfied with seeing its great streets and squares, but must survey the innumerable little lanes and courts. It is not in the showy evolutions of buildings, but in the multiplicity of human habitations which are crowded together, that the wonderful immensity of London consists.' Grist to the urban historian's mill, Johnson's counsel was reformulated in slightly different terms over a century later by Ford Madox Ford in *The Soul of London*, where he implied that the true London was not the flashy public edifices:

A brilliant, wind-swept, sunny day, with the fountains like hay-cocks of prismatic glitter in the shadow of Nelson's Column, with the paving stones almost opalescent, with colour everywhere ... is that 'London'? Does that rise up in your Londoner's mind's eye, when, in the Boulevard Haussmann, or on the Pyramids, he thinks of his own places?

Or is it the chaotic crowd, like of baggage wagons huddled together after a great defeat, blocked in the narrow ways of the City, an apparently indissoluble muddle of grey wheel traffic, of hooded carts, or 'buses drawing out of line, of sticky mud, with a pallid church wavering into invisibility towards the steeple in the weeping sky, or grimy upper windows through which appear white faces seen from one's level on a 'bus-top ... is this again 'London', the London we see from a distance?

Or do we see it in the glare of kerosene lamps, the diffused blaze of shop fronts, the slowly moving faces ... They will be carrying string bags, carrying paper parcels, carrying unwrapped green stuff, treading on layers of handbills, treading on the white scrolls of orange peels, on small heaps of muddy sawdust, standing in shawled groups round the glare of red joints in butchers' shops, standing in black groups round the carts of nostrum sellers, round the cards of Dutch auctioneers; with ears deafened by the cries of the vendors of all things meet for a Saturday night, by the incessant whistle of trams looming at a snail's pace through the massed humanity, by the incessant, as if vindictively anvil-like, peals of notes of barrel organs. In a patch of shadow left in a vacant space, you will hardly make out the figure of a forlorn man standing still ... Is this again the London that comes to one at a distance?

*

9

As Ford suggested, there are many Londons; I have tried to explore some, concentrating on the town itself and working from street level.

Urban history has made great strides since the war, thanks above all in Britain to the inspiration of Professor H. J. Dyos. Dyos wrote a study of Victorian Camberwell, which is where I went to school. Accustomed to reading about St Paul's and Piccadilly, it came as a revelation to me that it was possible to write the biography of an ordinary suburb. In this book I have tried to follow Dyos's example, building up a jigsaw out of lots of localities. London is a cluster of communities, great and small, famous and unsung; a city of contrasts, a congregation of diversity. Some may sense a surfeit of Shadwell or of Marylebone minutiae. I demur. For me the key to London lies in metropolitan heterogeneity, the sense of local habitations and their names.

A few final words of explanation. Without, I hope, loss of precision, I have tried to avoid pedantry about terminology. Till the setting up of the London County Council in 1888, London was officially the City of London (that is, the area administered by the Corporation) and nothing else. Beyond London properly so called, there were also Westminster, boroughs like Southwark, and parishes like Chelsea; but technically these were not London. I have ignored such legal niceties. Henceforth in this book London or the city means the town as a whole; the City (capitalized), on the other hand, either means the City of London – the traditional Corporation area largely within the walls – or stands as shorthand for the business and financial operations centred on the Square Mile. While not everyday terms, 'intramural' and 'extramural' are useful ways of referring to parts within and beyond the walled area. Terms like Greater London are defined in the text as appropriate.

CHAPTER TWO

Formation to Reformation

A late medieval poet praised London thus:

> Soveraign of cities, semeliest in sight,
> Of high renoun, riches, and royaltie;
> Of lordis, barons, and many a goodly knyght;
> Of most delectable lusty ladies bright;
> Of famous prelatis in habitis clericall;
> Of merchauntis full of substaunce and of myght:
> London, thou art the flour of Cities all.

Poetic licence no doubt – Rome and Byzantium had been no mean cities – but it is true that during its first 1,500 years London became one of Europe's prize blooms. The Romano-British city and its medieval successor have left extensive archaeological remains and chronicles, but we have no full visual record from before the Tudor age. It took the Renaissance to create the city portrait; thereafter London parades itself in a profusion of maps and bird's-eye views, one of the earliest being a panorama executed by the Flemish artist Anthonis van den Wyngaerde around 1544.

Wyngaerde's London is a resplendent scene, with its wall, palaces and castles, and its urban forest surmounted by the spires and towers of over 100 parish churches. Not a map but a vista, Wyngaerde's work captures the living city, showing the size and style of its renowned buildings and suggesting its variegated life.

Wyngaerde chose a spot south of Southwark High Street to display the sweep of the Thames. Southwark is shown forming the highway to London Bridge; on the right is the squat tower of St George's church, on the left the cupolas of Suffolk House, and in the middle ground St Olave's tower and the town houses of the Bishops of Winchester and Rochester.

Like its Continental cousins, mid-Tudor London was still defined by its walls and gates, though, unlike many of them, London had long been spared a siege. Thirty feet high, London Wall added medieval crenellations to the Roman defences and was pierced by seven gateways. Five hundred yards north-west of the Tower was Aldgate, and Bishopsgate was a similar distance farther on. Then the wall turned west for half a mile to Moorgate and nearby Cripplegate and Aldersgate. Rebuilt in the fifteenth century out of Sir Richard (Dick) Whittington's bequest to the City, Newgate led out to Holborn and the leper-house at St Giles. Finally came Ludgate, through which Westminster traffic poured into Fleet Street and the Strand, which, as its name indicates, was the route north of the boggy Thames bank, curving towards Westminster Hall and the abbey. (Or, on a modern map, Aldgate issues into Whitechapel Road, Bishopsgate into Shoreditch High Street, Moorgate into City Road, Cripplegate from Wood Street, Aldersgate towards Goswell Road, Newgate into Holborn and Ludgate into Fleet Street.) Beyond the walls the Middlesex woodlands stretched away to St John's Wood and beyond.

London's profile around 1500 was much as it was at the peak of Roman power, twelve centuries earlier. The chief alteration in medieval times lay within the wall. With military precision the Romans laid out their streets in grid-iron fashion. After their departure, however, and with the abandonment of the settlement by the conquering Saxons, the old rectangular street lines were lost; when the city recovered, it happened haphazardly rather than by design. (Today's antipathy to planners may reflect Anglo-Saxon attitudes!) The Roman wall remained, however, though the Thames-side was allowed to decay, replaced by a street with alleys descending to the jetties. Trade came first: unlike many European sites, London's *raison d'être* was as a market, not a fortress.

London Bridge, begun in 1176, was one of the marvels of Christendom in Wyngaerde's day. Built on nineteen stone arches sprouting from broad boat-shaped piles, its roadway was flanked by tall houses, the ground-floor premises doubtless tourist shops. One arch towards its southern end contained a drawbridge to let big shipping through. Stuck on pikes, traitors' skulls stared out, reminders that London was the stage of treason, not just trade.

Wyngaerde's south bank hints at the local colour Shakespeare dramatized, though the Bankside theatres had not yet been built. Southwark High Street dominates, with its half-timbered, lattice-windowed houses. Business and pleasure meet: a man with a dog leads his packhorse towards the bridge, while a courtly rider canters by; a fellow carries an enormous harp, heralding the cultural glory of the Elizabethan city, while, as signs of low life, there are the Bankside brothels. Across Lambeth marsh in the foreground a track leads to the Westminster horse ferry.

The Thames, London's chief highway, commands the middle distance. A barge with fluttering pennants is being rowed upstream from Old Palace Yard, Westminster. Another is in front of Baynard's Castle, surrounded by wherries and sloops plying between the banks. A timber-laden barge is being punted downstream; a raft of logs is at anchor. The north bank is dissected by the Fleet, rippling down from the hills of Hampstead and Highgate, skirting London Wall to the west and emptying into the Thames by Bridewell Palace. Up-river, princely power is displayed: lining the north bank are the nobility's town houses – Somerset Place, Durham House, York House and the royal palace of Whitehall, each with its riverside mooring. Down-river, beyond the precincts of the just-dissolved Black Friars and the glowering bulk of Baynard's Castle, trade is king, with quays such as Queenhithe and Broken Wharf and the cranes at Dowgate, near where the Walbrook, splitting the City's two hills, Ludgate Hill and Cornhill, trickles into the Thames.

Below Dowgate is the Steelyard, stronghold of the Hanseatic League. Jam-packed with lodgings, counting-houses and warehouses, this three-acre plot was a little Hong Kong, granted to the Hanse by Henry III as an enclave where Germanic traders might live under their own laws. The League brought London business but also provoked fierce resentment until, capitalizing on the foreigners' unpopularity, Edward VI revoked the Steelyard's privileges and the Baltic merchants were finally evicted by Elizabeth. Henceforth it was London that would assume the imperial role.

Above London Bridge the Thames is unruffled, for the piles supporting the arches almost dam the stream. By the bridge, however, the glassy surface breaks into rapids, and boats approaching too close risk being sucked through the narrow arches and cast into the pool below. Shooting the rapids was a daredevil sport: London Bridge, the saying ran, was made for wise men to pass over and for fools to pass under. Prudent boatmen took the wider channel under the drawbridge towards the south bank. Down-river in the Pool of London, Wyngaerde reveals the key to London's prosperity: sea-going vessels are unloading at St Botolph and Billingsgate wharves with the aid of man-powered cranes. Cannon guard the waters by the double archway of Traitors' Gate.

Beyond the river stretches the City, a tangle of tiled roofs speared by church steeples, matching the great cities of Lombardy and the Low Countries. From Wyngaerde's vantage point, the houses already appear sardine-packed, and crowding was to worsen: the invisible gardens, bowers and orchards that had let the City breathe were soon to be built over in a riot of development.

At the west end of the walled City soars St Paul's, boasting the longest nave in Europe, topped by a tower and a splendid spire dwarfing everything else. (A few years later, in 1561, the spire was struck by lightning and had to be demolished.) Adjacent to Cheapside market, St Paul's had long been infiltrated by Mammon. Vegetables were hawked in its precincts; in the porch, journeymen offered themselves for hire and lawyers bilked clients; the font was a place for clinching deals, while in the dim chapels pickpurses and whores lurked. St Paul's had become sacred to commerce, harbinger of the shopping mall.

East from St Paul's, Wyngaerde shows Cheapside, or Westcheap, the City's handsome thoroughfare. Derived from the Saxon *ceap* (to barter), 'cheap' means market.
Lined with booths and warehouses, Cheapside was the market street of the west part
of the City. Eastcheap, Falstaff's drinking haunt, forms a similar focus to the east,
running towards the Tower from Cannon Street.

Other landmarks loom, including the Guildhall, nucleus of the City's courts and
chambers, radiating civic pride and power. East of Cornhill is the enclosed rectangle
of Leadenhall Market, endowed with a granary by a noted citizen, Simon Eyre. With
its cloth and wheat warehouses, it forms London's merchandizing centre. At the eastern
end is the Tower, with its grisly execution site, a rostrum on an open space adjoining
the church of All Hallows Barking.

Thus stood the City on the eve of the Elizabethan age, girdled by its wall, a square
mile of higgledy-piggledy houses, 100-plus churches, a busy river and thronging
markets. Royal Westminster is distantly in the picture, but the citizens' city, with its
shipping, markets and workshops, holds centre stage. Almost all that Wyngaerde drew
is now gone: most medieval dwellings, churches and warehouses were razed in the
Great Fire of 1666: by contrast to Siena, Bruges or perhaps still Dubrovnik, London's
fabric is modern. At Elizabeth's accession in 1558 London was poised to expand both
in size and in stature; but its future had already been cast by its past.

Geography was destiny. From prehistoric times, Britain's grandest river ran through a
broad valley, fed by streams from the wooded hills now called Highgate and Hampstead
and from higher ground beyond Camberwell, down to the North Sea. The Thames
was wider and shallower than now; marshes and mud-flats abounded, and islands
appeared at low tide – names like Battersea and Bermondsey commemorate former
islands. (The Anglo-Saxon *ea* means island, so Battersea is Peter's Island.) The Thames
valley offered hospitable terrain for pastoralists, and neolithic sites sprang up; but
though settlements have been discovered – at Runnymede, Staines and Heathrow, for
instance – there is no proof that central London was permanently settled by the Celts
before the Romans. Nevertheless, geology and geography foreordained that it would,
in time, become a choice place of habitation.

Strategic considerations and physical features marked this spot as suitable for civilization. It was the lowest point where the Thames could be forded and bridged. Here,
forty miles from the sea, the river was blessed with a gravel bed. In contrast to
treacherous mud-banks, gravel subsoil provided safe landings for trading craft crossing
the Channel and venturing up the Thames.

Attempting to stabilize Gaul, Julius Caesar felt the need to make a show of strength
north of the Channel. After a brief reconnaissance the previous year, he set sail in
54 BC, beaching near Deal. His invading force of five legions and 2,000 cavalry met

skirmishing from the tribes who harried his march. It was against forces led by Cassivellaunus, whose rule stretched north and west of the Thames, that Caesar concentrated his onslaught. No match for the disciplined Roman troops, the natives enjoyed the natural advantage of the Thames, which, Caesar recorded in his *Gallic Wars*, 'can be forded only at one place and that with difficulty'. The British forces waited north of the river. Caesar made the crossing, and, overwhelmed, the Britons 'abandoned the banks and took flight'.

The scene of this engagement has been hotly debated. Caesar does not name it, making no mention of the location his successors called Londinium. It is quite possible that he crossed around Westminster or somewhat upstream, where lay the firm gravel foundations upon which, at low tide, the river could safely be forded.

Did Caesar plant the seed of London? It is conceivable that, on returning to Gaul in the autumn of 54 BC, he left a bridge, which formed the nucleus of a community. Yet, despite later legends, no evidence exists for 'Caesar's London' any more than for the London of King Brutus (a supposed descendant of Aeneas), who, according to medieval legends, founded the city of Troynovant (New Troy), later fortified by the mythic King Lud as the first London.

The island was then left in peace by the Empire; cross-Channel trade blossomed, and the Celts acquired a taste for the trappings of Roman civilization. Almost a century after Caesar's departure, however, Rome unleashed a second invasion. In AD 43, in the reign of Claudius, an army of 40,000 was dispatched. The Thames again formed the Celts' chief defensive line. Some legionaries swam across, and a bridge was built. The Roman infantry 'assailed the barbarians from several sides at once and cut down many of them'. It was this invasion that precipitated the planting of London. Within a decade it was a flourishing settlement. Writing in the second century AD, Tacitus called this first settlement a place 'filled with traders and a celebrated centre of commerce'. The city began as it was to continue: trade was to prove its lifeblood.

London afforded the ideal colonial centre-point. The Romans needed a route from near Deal, in Kent, to Colchester and to their far-flung military outposts. A Thames bridge at London killed two birds with one stone. London's tidal river made it a port with handy Continental access. It also became the centre of a spider's web of highways: Watling Street, threading in from the south-east (along the line of the Old Kent Road) and absorbing traffic from Stane Street (coming up through modern Clapham), which connected with another key Roman town, Chichester, led to the wooden bridge that spanned the Thames some fifty yards east of the modern London Bridge. Roads radiated out to Colchester and the east, and to Silchester (north of Winchester) and the west. Watling Street continued north (the modern Edgware Road) to Verulamium (St Albans), Chester and the north-west frontier. Ermine Street linked London with Lincoln, York, Hadrian's Wall and the savage Scots.

Barely born, Roman London suffered a calamity that indirectly ensured its lasting greatness. In AD 61 a band of East Anglian tribes known as the Iceni revolted under their Queen, Boudicca (Boadicea). On her husband's death his lands had been despoiled, Boudicca had been flogged, and her daughters had been ravished. She took revenge on the imperial overlords. Her insurrection caught the Governor, Suetonius Paulinus, on the hop, for he was busy suppressing uprisings on the frontier. With a host of Iceni and the neighbouring Trinovantes, the Queen sacked Colchester and descended unchecked on London. The barely defended town was doomed. Boudicca fired its buildings, and the inhabitants, according to Tacitus, were 'massacred, hanged, burned and crucified'. The carnage in Colchester, St Albans and London is given as 70,000 (read: 'a large number'). Coins found by London Bridge have been fused by the flames, suggesting a ferocious inferno in this, the first of London's many terrible fires.

Boudicca's attack wrought havoc – it is the only occasion London has ever been completely destroyed, ironically by a Briton. But, already thriving as a port and market, it was rapidly rebuilt after her revolt had been crushed, and it assumed imperial rank in the next century, with a basilica and forum, temples and an amphitheatre, and shops and residences laid out in the formal piazza patterns of Roman townscaping. And this time London's defences were secured.

A fortress 200 yards square was built in the north-west of the city, by Cripplegate, at the north end of today's Wood Street, to guard against raiders from the north. And then, probably after AD 160, work was started on a defensive wall, built of Kentish ragstone interspersed with brick courses. The wall, which was surrounded by a ditch, had a circumference of nearly three miles, enclosed about 330 acres, and was some fifteen feet high and eight feet thick.

Only fragments survive, generally in the foundations of later buildings, but the wall's course has been traced. It started east of what is now the Tower of London. It then ran northwards to Aldgate, north-west near Camomile Street to Bishopsgate, then west along London Wall to Cripplegate (the Romans had no Moorgate). Here it turned south and south-west to Aldersgate and Newgate, then, at the foot of Ludgate Hill, along the River Fleet to the Thames east of today's Blackfriars Bridge. At a later date a wall was built along the river front, where Upper and Lower Thames Streets run today.

Despite ups and downs, the Roman colony flourished and London enjoyed growth and prosperity, its intramural area a medley of villas, workshops, public buildings, warehouses, shops and temples. Eclipsing Colchester, it became the largest city in Britain and the fifth most populous Roman centre north of the Alps, with some 30,000 inhabitants by the year 250, and even more in the next century, the halcyon days of Roman London. It enjoyed the confident civic life of the *Pax Romana*, almost a foretaste

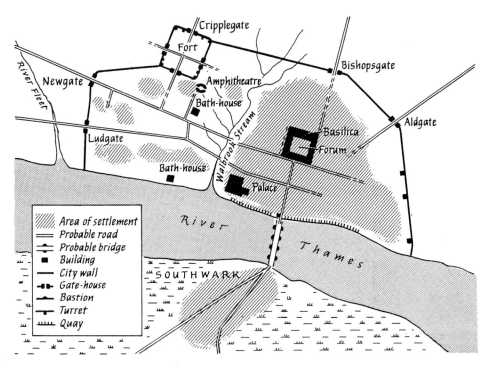

Roman London. A wall was built around the city *c.* A.D. 200 to enclose a dwindling population

of Belgravia or Kensington. Fine mosaic pavements and courtyard pools graced handsome villas. Excavations have unearthed elaborate goblets and drinking flagons, red-glazed Rhineland Samian ware, and precious *objets d'art*, including carved figurines used in household worship. Finds of cosmetic items like glass beads, silver armbands, bronze brooches and tweezers attest feminine luxury. Better-off citizens enjoyed a civilization not a whit inferior to that of Wyngaerde's day. And, when their days of *otium et negotium* drew to a close, they were cremated and their remains preserved in urns, sometimes carved out of porphyry. Numerous burial-places have been found, mostly west of the walls, including one at Westminster.

The capital's centre-pieces were the basilica and the forum. The commercial and administrative headquarters, the basilica crowned the higher, easterly, slope of Cornhill. Comprising a lengthy, aisled hall tripling as town hall, law courts and exchange, it was over 500 feet long from east to west (as long as the present St Paul's) and 150 feet wide, which probably made it the largest Roman building north of the Alps.

South of the basilica was a colonnaded temple, standing in the forum and skirted by shopping arcades. Built probably during the third century, the temple was dedicated to Mithras, the Persian god of light. Introduced into the Empire by soldiers from the eastern provinces, Mithraism, which promised life after death, was popular. Exclusive to males, the faith valued fortitude and honour, and so became prestigious, rather like freemasonry, among the military. Exquisite marble heads of Mithras and of Serapis, the Graeco-Egyptian god of the underworld, have been found, as have moulded heads of Minerva and a group including the Roman god Bacchus and Cautopates, Mithras's torch-bearer. Some of these were perhaps carved by native craftsmen. More awaits discovery: a second-century amphitheatre was recently dug up at Guildhall; the area was presumably the Piccadilly of the day.

As a mark of distinction, in the reign of the Emperor Gratian London was granted the honorary title 'Augusta'. Towards the end of the third century, however, cracks appeared in the Empire. In 286, during the reign of Diocletian, Marcus Carausius, commander of the Channel fleet, mutinied, declaring himself Emperor of Britain and establishing a London mint from which he produced coins bearing his head (the equivalent, in ancient *coups d'état*, of commandeering the radio station). Carausius's reign lasted six years, before he was slain in 293 by his lieutenant, Allectus, who, backed by British legions, in turn styled himself Emperor. In 296 the Empire struck back; the Emperor Constantius Chlorus crossed from Gaul and began reconquest, killing Allectus and rescuing London.

Constantius did more than return London and the province to Roman rule: he sought to make the city safe against barbarian raids. With foreign invasion endangering the peace for the first time since Boudicca's revolt, twenty-one bastions were added to the defences. (The bastions near St Giles Cripplegate and the portion of the wall preserved nearby, though rebuilt in medieval times, show their solidity.)

Constantius died in Britain. He was succeeded by his son Constantine ('the Great'), whose mother, Helena, was a Briton. In 313 Constantine issued a proclamation making Christianity the Empire's official religion. What impact the edict had in England is unclear.

Half a century later the province was menaced by Picts and by Germanic pirates. Sent to help, the commander Theodosius arrived at Richborough to find the southern counties overrun. Hastening through Kent, his troops subdued the raiders, and he reached the beleaguered capital in the nick of time. 'Joyful and triumphant', writes a contemporary chronicler, Theodosius 'made his entry into the city which had just before been overwhelmed with disasters'. Theodosius strengthened the defences of various British cities. But, when danger later threatened Rome itself, from Alaric the Goth, distant provinces could no longer be garrisoned and in 410 the Emperor Honorius warned Britain it must protect itself. Soon after, troops were withdrawn and Roman London's days were numbered.

*

The legions departed and thick fog descends over London. Marauding from the mid fifth century, Angles and Saxons were peasant warriors who initially had no use for towns. North Sea raiders killed Roman trade, and the city lost its *raison d'être*, dwindling into a ghost town. For a century there is little evidence that the new settlers had any real contact with it at all. Early Saxon settlements – for instance, at Mitcham and Croydon – are eight miles and more from London Bridge; and the sole early-Saxon cemetery excavated closer to the city is at Greenwich, five miles downstream. The migrants were inevitably familiar with the shell of the city, but there is no proof of positive urban living. The city may have fallen into ruin, occupied by squatters among the mouldering baths and basilica. The *Anglo-Saxon Chronicle*, written centuries later, speaks of the invaders burning down Romano-British townships 'so that the flames could be seen from the east coast to the west', but there is no sign they fired London.

During the sixth century, however, Anglo-Saxon settlement took root – though recent excavations suggest that the area initially colonized (Lundenwic) may not have been the old Roman city but a zone around the Strand and Covent Garden. In 604, at the time of the conversion of the East Saxons, London was sufficiently important to warrant a Christian mission. Mellitus, a monk from Rome, was ordained as Bishop of London, founding a wooden cathedral dedicated to St Paul. But he was soon driven out, and the seat of the Primate of England, intended for London, became established at Canterbury, where it was to remain. Not till 650 did the East Saxons officially embrace Christianity.

Despite this reverse, once converted the Anglo-Saxons started to erect churches. One early structure existed on Cornhill – St Peter's, perhaps first founded in Roman times – and two churches were set up on Ludgate Hill, one dedicated to St Gregory and the other to St Augustine, the latter associated with the papacy's first effort to convert the heathen Anglo-Saxons. And succeeding centuries saw the establishment of the churches that became the nucleus of the hundred parishes networking Norman London – one for every three acres.

Commerce rekindled urban life. The Thames attracted foreign trade to the city which Bede, writing around 730 from Northumbria, called 'the mart of many nations resorting to it by land and sea'. Merchants from France, Italy and the Low Countries were drawn to London, offering as it did ready access to the raw materials of an underdeveloped country. In the tenth century Rouen wine merchants settled in the precinct of the present Vintners' Place; German dealers set up at nearby Dowgate; while, after Londoners accepted the Danish leader Cnut (Canute) as their king in 1016, Danes established themselves in the City and beyond Ludgate to the west, where St Clement Danes now links Fleet Street and the Strand. Before London became the nation's capital – the dominant West Saxons had their headquarters at Winchester – it had become England's foremost mart, its prosperity guaranteed by the wool trade.

Flanked by the pastures of the Downs and the Chilterns, London suited wool-producers and Flemish dealers alike.

Commercial rebirth was interrupted from 834, however, when England was once more overrun, this time by the Norsemen. London proved a valuable and vulnerable target, and for nearly two centuries the Vikings remained a deadly threat. In 841 the *Anglo-Saxon Chronicle* records 'great slaughter in London', and in 851 the Danes left the city a ruin.

England's fortunes began to turn with King Alfred of Wessex (r. 871–99), who may have grasped London's strategic significance. For some years the city remained in Viking hands, who were sufficiently entrenched to mint coins. But in 886 Alfred regained it, the walls were rebuilt, his capable son-in-law, Aethelred, was appointed its governor, and its citizens were organized into a fighting force. With hindsight Alfred's recapture of London seems a turning-point: thereafter, no invader succeeded in taking it by storm.

By 900 the Viking onslaught had waned, and for the next hundred years London prospered. And when the second tide of Norse invasions came in the late tenth century, this time principally Danish, London fought back. In 984 an attack was repulsed and, according to the *Anglo-Saxon Chronicle*, the invaders 'suffered more harm and injury than they ever thought any citizens could do to them'. The Scandinavian threat spurred the formation of an organized defence system and perhaps the division of the city into wards, land being parcelled out to lordlings with local power. In times of emergency, such elders (in later parlance, aldermen) furnished men and arms. Their wards later formed the building-blocks of the City's administration.

Renewed assaults followed. In 994, alone of English towns, London resisted Sweyn, King of Denmark. The next decades saw confusion, and in 1013 London fell under enemy control; but the invaders were dislodged, and London was soon recaptured by King Aethelred. In 1016 Aethelred was succeeded by the young Cnut, who was proclaimed King of All England; but the city was powerful enough to be able to treat with the conqueror and thus 'welcome' him rather than surrender. London was made to pay a vast tribute (one-eighth of the entire nation's), but under Cnut the city effectively supplanted Winchester as England's capital, an eminence it was never to lose.

London revived in the eleventh century; ward and parish communities developed within the City, and religious establishments were planted, despite the destruction by fire in 961 of the second St Paul's. In 982 another fire raged, proving, once again, the acute vulnerability of timbered towns: 'the only pests of London,' wrote a Norman chronicler, 'are the immoderate drinking of fools and the frequency of fires'.

London's religious history was decisively altered by Edward the Confessor (r. 1042–66), who concentrated his efforts on rebuilding Westminster Abbey. Three centuries earlier, King Offa had founded a Benedictine monastery, the West Minster, on the desolate Thorney Island ('Isle of Brambles'), formed by the forking of the Tyburn near the present St James's Park Underground station. The first abbey had never flourished, and Westminster had been sacked by the Danes and the site abandoned. Edward's plans for a new Benedictine abbey of Peter at Westminster were altogether grander, as can be seen from the Bayeux tapestry. The Romanesque style reflected the monarch's Norman tastes, and surviving foundations show it was as long as today's abbey.

To oversee the project, Edward quit the Wardrobe palace near St Paul's, and moved between the abbey and the river. This migration to Westminster had profound repercussions: it was the first step towards the planting of royal government at Westminster, drawing expansion westward, and setting up potential polarities between Crown and City, government and trade. Royal Westminster permitted the City to develop relatively autonomously – a luxury denied to many medieval cities.

Edward apparently envisaged that his abbey should be both a royal burial-place and a coronation chapel; and his death in January 1066, days after the consecration of the chancel, enabled it to fulfil both purposes without delay, for his successor William, Duke of Normandy, had himself crowned in the abbey, which remained thereafter identified with the throne.

The Anglo-Saxon epoch left a mixed legacy. The settlers became townees by the way, and the city grew largely thanks to the stimulus of overseas merchants. Now through trade, now through invasion, London was sucked into Europe. Saxon influence on the city proved great, however, and parish and ward organization and the city's very street plan derive from pre-Conquest times – as hundreds of place-names testify. Defence against raiders galvanized communal government. By 1066 London had become too mighty to be crushed even by the Conqueror, and was set to shape the nation's future in an uneasy dialogue of power with the Crown.

On the Confessor's death, the Witan, the national assembly, nominated Earl Harold as King. Protesting that Edward, his cousin, had promised him the crown, William, Duke of Normandy, invaded with an army of 10,000 and crushed Harold at Hastings. He then took his time. Judging London would not easily fall, William marched only as far as Southwark, burning it but then circling west to foment terror. Crossing the Thames at Wallingford, he laid waste the countryside supplying London's food. Its elders and the Witan accepted the inevitable: a deputation rode out to offer him the throne. On Christmas Day 1066, before the high altar, William was crowned at Westminster. Taking the royal oath, he vowed, not entirely unambiguously, to treat his English subjects with the same justice as those of Normandy.

Terror would work elsewhere, but the Conqueror recognized the need to win London over. Early in his reign he granted the City a charter:

William, King, greets William, Bishop, and Godfrey, Portreeve, and all the burghers within London, French and English, friendlike. And I will that both be worthy of all the rights of which ye both were worthy in King Edward's day. And I will that every child be his father's heir after his father's day. And I will not suffer that any man offer you any wrong. God keep you.

Ostensibly for defence against Danish invasion but surely to guard himself against the populace, William raised three citadels: Baynard's Castle, built by one of his henchmen, Ralph Baynard, on the river, by the Fleet; Montfichet, a moated keep, near Ludgate (this did not survive long); and the White Tower, at the eastern edge of the Roman wall, begun in 1078 on William's orders by Gundulph, Bishop of Rochester. The immense keep of white Caen stone, ninety-two feet tall and with walls up to fifteen feet thick, was designed to house the King, his household and his treasury, and also garrisoned the royal guard. Later kings made additions to what became known as the Tower of London. The inner curtain wall with its dozen supporting towers was mainly the work of Henry III; his son, Edward I, added Traitors' Gate in St Thomas's Tower, the Middle Tower screening the outer entrance, and the moat; together, these turned it from a tower into a concentric walled fortress, a little city in itself. William built soundly. From time to time the Tower changed hands through perfidy, but it was never taken by storm.

The cautious Conqueror also hedged his bets. As a bolt-hole, he erected another castle a day's march away, at Windsor. And the Normans signalled their independence – and also perhaps their fear – of the locals by establishing their main domicile at Westminster, which became a kind of eleventh-century Versailles. Between 1097 and 1099 the Conqueror's son, William II (Rufus), replaced Edward the Confessor's structure with something entirely grander. Westminster Hall, the only part of Rufus's palace to survive, was its main feature. Though the prodigal expressed dissatisfaction at this 'mere bedchamber', in truth Westminster Hall was a superb galleried edifice, nearly 240 feet long and almost forty feet high. By the time Hugh Herland designed his extraordinary hammer-beam roof in the late fourteenth century, Westminster Hall had become the centre of administration and justice. The kingdom's government was significantly being conducted beyond London walls: monarch and municipality were at arm's length. Westminster was the King's domain, two miles away from the citizenry to the east. Later dissensions between Crown and City, or Parliament and Corporation, were thus rooted in medieval realities. Such tensions are with us still.

Early Norman London remained essentially the walled city of the Anglo-Saxons. Between 1077 and 1136, however, devastating fires raged through the precincts with their timber-framed cottages. Four times in sixty years rebuilding was undertaken. London Bridge proved peculiarly vulnerable, suffering fire damage on ten occasions. In 1176 work began to replace the wooden structure which, repeatedly patched up, had perhaps done duty since the Romans – or had fallen into total disrepair. The new stone bridge was completed in 1209, four years after the death of its designer, Peter of Colechurch, a parish priest. Though continually needing repair, the new bridge proved almost as tough as the Tower. Until the eighteenth century the only bridge downstream from Kingston, it lasted till 1830: another nine years and it would have been immortalized by daguerreotype.

London pride grew. The city 'pours out its fame more widely, sends to farther lands its wealth and trade, lifts its head higher than the rest', boasted the monk William Fitz-Stephen in his *Descriptio Londiniae* (1183):

It is happy in the healthiness of its air, in the Christian religion, in the strength of its defences, the nature of its site, the honour of its citizens, the modesty of its matrons; pleasant in sports; fruitful of noble men.

We can take this with a pinch of salt; what is clear, however, is that London grew strong, secure and successful. Crude drawings from the thirteenth century give a first glimpse of 'the most noble city' of which the tonsured patriot wrote.

Ecclesiastical edifices commanded the skyline. 'As concerns Christian worship,' boasted Fitz-Stephen, 'there are both in London and the Suburbs thirteen great Conventual Churches and one hundred and twenty-six lesser Parochial.' Medieval figures are notoriously fictive, but there were certainly about 100 parish churches within the wall. The thirteen monastic houses Fitz-Stephen counted included two founded before the Conquest: the abbey of St Peter (Westminster) and St Martin's-le-Grand, within the wall by Aldersgate – not large, but important as a sanctuary, beyond City jurisdiction. From the late eleventh century others were planted across the river, on open ground within the perimeter, or just beyond the walls. Austin (Augustinian) canons established themselves at Holy Trinity (Aldgate), St Mary Overie across the river (to which the hospital of St Thomas was attached) and St Bartholomew-the-Great, Smithfield. This last was aptly named, for it rose on a massive scale: the majestic church surviving today is but the choir of the original monastic edifice. The present churchyard gateway was once the west end of the church, and the stumps of the former nave's columns still protrude. At the Reformation the choir alone was preserved for parish use.

Nunneries were established too – Holywell, Shoreditch; St Mary's Clerkenwell; St Helen's Bishopsgate. In 1148 St Katharine's was planted just east of the Tower by Matilda, Stephen's queen, as a hospital for female lepers. Refounded by Henry III's wife, Eleanor, it remained under the wing of succeeding queens, and, thanks to Anne Boleyn's intercession, escaped the Reformation – being finally closed after 1800 to make way for the docks!

St Paul's was rebuilt. The second cathedral had been razed by fire in 961; its successor, the sepulchre of early kings, was burnt down in 1087; Maurice, the Bishop of London, began replacement. The fourth St Paul's was built of stone and built to last. A stupendous cruciform cathedral, the marvel of London, it measured 585 feet, conspicuously longer than the present St Paul's. The wooden spire, soaring to 450 feet (Wren's dome is a puny 365 feet high), dominated medieval London, and its profile leaps up from early maps. Building crept forward as funds permitted, and it was two centuries before St Paul's stood in the finished form that survived until the seventeenth century, when Inigo Jones gave it a classical cladding shortly before its devastation in the Great Fire.

Two of London's thirteen monasteries had crusading links: one, founded in Clerkenwell about 1100, belonged to the Order of St John of Jerusalem; the other, established in Holborn some thirty years later, to the Knights Templar. These military orders had been created to regain the Holy Land. Named after Solomon's Temple in Jerusalem, in about 1160 the Templars moved to the Strand, where they housed a royal treasury. The corruption of Templar values of austerity by filthy lucre provided a pretext for suppression in 1307 by papal order. The site was appropriately taken over by lawyers, but Temple Church still stands, its circular nave modelled on the rotunda of the Church of the Holy Sepulchre in Jerusalem.

London's spiritual life was transformed in the thirteenth century by the arrival of the mendicant friars as popular preachers. From the 1220s the former Montfichet site housed the Dominican Black Friars. The Carmelite White Friars also settled there after Edward I granted riverside land east of the Temple, their gardens stretching over today's Bouverie Street, White Friars Street and Carmelite Street. The exemption from secular jurisdiction enjoyed by the Black Friars and White Friars survived long after the Dissolution, and the plot from Fleet Street down to the river, bought up by speculative builders, became the haunt of rogues and outlaws and one of London's worst slums, being known as 'Alsatia', after the province long disputed between France and Germany. Not until 1697 was the right revoked.

The Crutched or Crossed Friars – a crucifix formed part of their habit – existed from 1298 near the Tower. The Grey or Franciscan Friars (1223) had their house in Stinking Lane, just inside Newgate by the butchers' shambles. After the heart of Queen Eleanor, Henry III's wife, was buried there, royal patronage followed: in 1306 Margaret, the second Queen of Edward I, began rebuilding the church, which became inferior in size only to St Paul's.

Overall, the friars enhanced the city's religious presence, particularly where they performed pious works among the poor. Hospitals also developed. As today, medieval hospitals tended the sick, but they were primarily travellers' hostels and refuges for the unfortunate. They received pious donations from aristocrats and aldermen for the salvation of their souls. Leading early hospitals included St Bartholomew's, next to the priory, and St Thomas's in Southwark.

Meanwhile Henry III was rebuilding the abbey church of Westminster into one of the glories of European Gothic. Demolition of Edward's old abbey began in 1245, and within a generation the east end of Henry's vision was complete, though work ceased after his death, to be resumed more than a hundred years later by Richard II, and finally completed in 1517. The early sixteenth century also brought the building in Perpendicular style of the abbey's greatest glory, the Henry VII Chapel at the east end. Till 1760 the abbey served as the burial-place of English sovereigns.

The City led a double life: it was self-governing but also under royal rule. Around 1200 a new office emerged, that of the Mayor, combining both aspects of governance, the Mayor being the City's voice in dealings with the Crown but also the King's agent within the City. The first Mayor was Henry FitzAilwin, a prosperous City merchant resident beside Walbrook. Appointed in 1192 – there is no evidence that he was elected – FitzAilwin held office for some twenty years; in 1193 he was active in collecting ransom money for Richard I, then held captive in Germany.

The Mayor wore several hats. He was the royal deputy, he was the spokesman of the City's élite, and he also became a popular symbol, proof of London's kinship with the communes so powerful in Italy and parts of Germany. 'Londoners,' a citizen supposedly exclaimed in 1193, 'shall have no king but their Mayor.' The Mayor came to be chosen annually from among the aldermen, who, as head men of the wards, independently possessed great personal power. In war they organized defence; in peace they administered justice, sitting as the Court of Aldermen.

Norman kings were strong, but, needing the City's support, prudently made concessions. It is widely believed that Henry I (r. 1100–1135) granted London the right to collect its own taxes and choose its sheriffs – a notable concession, since the Sheriff ('shire reeve', the King's representative in a county) was the local agent of royal authority. London paid the treasury £300 a year for the privilege of making its own appointments. Wise kings knew London was more effectively cajoled than crushed.

Times of royal weakness gave leverage to the City. During the civil war following Henry I's death, London took Stephen's part against Matilda, contributing to his coffers. On one occasion when Matilda was in the ascendancy, the citizens, 'like thronging swarms from bee-hives', chased her from the City, thus frustrating her hopes of the Westminster coronation she sought to bolster her regal claims. A domineering sovereign, Henry II (r. 1154–89) issued a charter acknowledging citizens' rights, and reaped the reward by securing London's support at a critical juncture in his son's rebellion of 1181. His successor, Richard I (r. 1189–1199), sapped the Crown's strength, squandering his subjects' wealth to further his crusading tastes. 'If I could have found a buyer,' a malicious chronicler has him boasting, 'I would have sold London itself.' Under John (r. 1199–1216), discontented citizens joined the barons in enforcing the signing of Magna Carta; the Mayor was the only commoner whose name appeared among the signatories. Recognizing he could not browbeat the citizens, John granted them the Right of Commune, a privilege guaranteeing a measure of self-government.

Royal financial demands bred enduring tensions between Crown and City, monarchs tending to look upon the kingdom's wealthiest town as a milch cow. When the City held out against the demands of Henry III (r. 1216–72), he responded by suspending privileges, repeatedly setting aside the Mayor and aldermen and imposing direct royal rule. But in 1255, after years of harassment, the City was still refusing to pay him a compulsory 'tallage' – as free men, its leaders asserted, they were liable only for voluntary 'aids' – and he had to give way. The truth was, the Plantagenets needed Londoners' loans too urgently to risk a showdown.

Crown/town struggles followed predictable patterns. Powerful kings, such as Edward I (r. 1272–1307), could usually compel the Mayor to respect their authority. But the Plantagenet line oscillated between the forceful and the feeble, and the interludes of Edward II (r. 1307–27), Richard II (r. 1377–99) and the Wars of the Roses offered the City breathing-spaces and bargaining powers. Yet anarchy and war were hardly in the City's interests: they disrupted trade and drew away the Court and all its expenditure. Kings and the City were thus trapped like the partners in a bickering marriage, finding it hard to live with each other but impossible to do without.

The Domesday Book (1086) omitted London itself – that may have been an astute silence on William I's part – but gives the impression that the city was already smiling in the midst of plenty. Riverside settlements like 'Fuleham' had fishing rights on the Thames, and 'Stebenhede' (Stepney) and 'Chenesitun' (Kensington) were villages with arable land and grazing for pigs and cattle. Produce was sent to London markets, to feed the 10,000 to 15,000 residents – still perhaps only a quarter of the population at the height of the Roman era. London exerted a growing pull over local farming.

Within the crenellated walls, manufactures and markets developed and street-life buzzed, enlivened with the cries of hawkers and pedlars. As in all traditional towns, people worked, talked, haggled and relaxed in the streets, and Fitz-Stephen speaks of taverns and 'a public cook shop' selling 'viands, dishes roast, fried and boiled, fish great and small'. Craftsmen lived where they worked, nestling trade by trade in their distinctive quarters – tanners, fullers, cordwainers and saddlers, bell-founders and cloth-dressers, tailors and dyers all had their patch or market, often perpetuated in street names. Today's Fish Street Hill marks where the fishmongers set up shop; Sea Coal Lane, near the Fleet, was where the coal merchants settled from 1250. Cannon Street derives from Candlewick Street, once home of the candlemakers and wax-dealers (the old form 'Candle wick' survives as a ward name). Cordwainer ward recalls the cordwainers (shoemakers), who clustered round St Mary-le-Bow, while Vintry

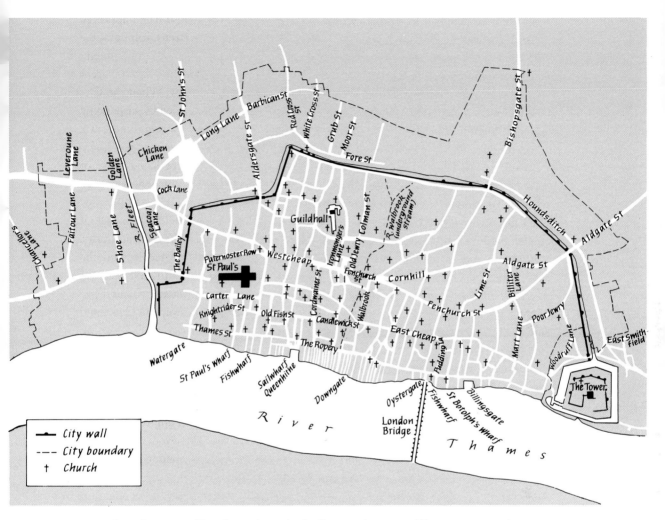

A modern map of London as it was in the fourteenth century. The street pattern is
firmly established and all the medieval parish churches and most of the religious houses
are in place

ward was the centre for wine merchants. In Bread Street were bakers, and tailors in
Threadneedle Street. The streets branching off Cheapside – Wood Street, Milk Street,
Ironmonger Lane, Poultry – indicate the stalls of divers trades. The corn market was
on Cornhill, and the wool market near St Mary Woolchurch in Lombard Street.

London lured foreign traders. 'Many natives of the chief Norman cities, Rouen and
Caen,' explained a chronicler, 'settled in London as the foremost town in England,
because it was more suited to commerce and better stored with the goods in which

they were accustomed to trade.' Weavers flowed in from Flanders. London had no formal ghetto, but foreigners kept themselves to themselves. By the twelfth century the 'men of Cologne' had a 'house' by the Thames as a fixed trading post. The Jewish financiers who flocked to England set up shop at what became known as 'Jews' Street' (Old Jewry). Although many English towns had Jewish residents, only in London were they allowed a cemetery, outside Cripplegate, and all Jews dying in England were brought there for burial.

As resident aliens, Jews were not integrated into English society – indeed, as mere 'chattels of the King' they possessed no legal rights, being dependent upon royal protection. Monarchs were always finding excuses to siphon money from them, and they were exposed to outbursts of pious anti-Semitism. In 1189 an incident at Richard I's coronation triggered a riot in which thirty Jews were killed. The arrival of Italian bankers from Lucca, Florence and Venice enabled Edward I to turn the screw, forbidding Jews to practise usury on pain of death; and a few years later, to finance Caernarvon and Conway castles, he bled them for money. Persecution intensified: on a charge of coin-clipping, nearly 300 Jews were put to death and their possessions seized. Then all the Jews in the kingdom were imprisoned and ransomed for £20,000. Finally, in 1290, came their expulsion, when between 15,000 and 16,000 were forced to leave the country, their houses being confiscated and mortgages forfeit to the Crown. The Italians, who had settled in Lombard Street, replaced them as the City's money-dealers. There was as yet no way of avoiding a rankling dependency upon foreign financiers.

Manufactures created pollution. Breweries and tanneries, established by the banks of the Fleet, made for a fetid, messy town; close-packed houses, their gables oversailing till they almost touched, excluded light and air. Attempts were made to clean the streets through rakers attached to each ward and 'laystalls' (refuse heaps) set up outside the walls. But as London boomed, its population perhaps exceeding 80,000 by the mid fourteenth century, a darker threat loomed: pestilence. In 1348 plague reached southern England, and by September its offensive symptoms ('sweat, excrement, spittle, breath, so fetid as to be overpowering') were plain throughout the City. In early 1349 200 victims a day were being shovelled into the Smithfield pits, and in the next two years up to half the City's population died. Nevertheless, like other plague-devastated cities, London recovered, and its population had risen to around 50,000 by 1380, though it stagnated during the fifteenth century.

But labour shortages after the plague threatened feudal ties, creating tensions between lords and men that culminated in the Peasants' Revolt of 1381, led by Wat Tyler. Professing loyalty to the King, Richard II, the rebels avenged themselves against rich landlords and fat clerics; a key target was the King's chief minister, the Archbishop of Canterbury, Simon Sudbury. Tyler rallied his forces on Blackheath and descended on London, making a beeline for Lambeth and setting fire to the Archbishop's palace. Crossing the river, the insurgents sacked the Savoy Palace on the Strand, home of the detested John of Gaunt. Their cause was supported by bands of London's citizenry, who opened the gates. The mighty mob rampaged unchecked, and soon 'hardly was there a street ... in which there were no bodies lying of those who had been slain'. The rebels were even admitted by sympathizers within the Tower, where they murdered the Archbishop and many of his entourage, spiking their heads on London Bridge. As ever, foreigners provided sitting targets, and thirty-five Flemings were slain in Cheapside alone.

The King went to parley with the peasants, meeting them at Mile End. Richard shrewdly proclaimed himself their true leader and promised redress of grievances. They followed him to Clerkenwell, where they were dispersed by the City militia, Wat Tyler being badly wounded. Thereafter London was long extraordinarily free of serious public disorder – probably a token of its broad-based prosperity and the socio-economic cohesion created by its guilds.

Gravitating to specific localities, craftsmen found brotherhood and strength in guilds. Linking with parish churches and adopting patron saints, guilds fulfilled pious, charitable and social functions, but their prime rationale was occupational, for trade promotion and protection. Self-governing and proud of their traditions, ceremonies and regalia, guilds policed the crafts. Admission was ordinarily by apprenticeship – a system designed to uphold skills, prevent undercutting, and limit entry. Indentured for seven years to a master craftsman to learn the 'mistery', on completing his apprenticeship a craftsman became a freeman of his guild, permitted to serve a master as a journeyman or to set up on his own.

Guilds proliferated: by 1423 there were over 100. New ones formed, and amalgamations occurred. The leather-sellers absorbed the glovers, pursers, curriers (leather-workers) and pouchmakers; the haberdashers affiliated with the hatters; and the clothworkers were formed from the union of the fullers and shearmen. By no means all freemen actually practised the business of the guild they represented: many acquired their wealth from foreign trade, mainly in wool, cloth and corn, but sought a guild like a club. Exponents of trades without a guild would join one for the legal and social advantages it offered. (Only guild membership could confer citizenship.)

Guilds spawned fraternities, clubs within clubs. In the 1340s the Skinners, for example, had a Fraternity of Corpus Christi consisting of some fifty to seventy brethren. These had a religious purpose, but they also formed an exclusive élite within the craft, including the top men of the trade and other dignitaries besides: the Skinners' Fraternity of Corpus Christi enjoyed the patronage of Edward III and Queen Philippa, the Black Prince, Richard II and Queen Anne, and enrolled noblemen and great merchants. At first fraternities were informal bodies, but as the leading guilds bought charters to clarify their legal status they obtained in the process legal recognition for their ruling fraternity.

The first to gain a charter were the Weavers, from Henry I in 1155. The Bakers obtained a charter from Henry II, who charged eighteen guilds – among them, the Butchers, Pepperers and Goldsmiths – with having formed without permission as a pretext for fining them. In time, all guilds became corporate bodies, acquiring royal charters entitling them to hold property in perpetuity. The Merchant Taylors were one of the first guilds to erect a hall (their Threadneedle Street premises include stonework from the original fourteenth-century building). By 1500 almost thirty guilds – nearly a third – owned halls, many on sites that have proved permanent. The Skinners, for instance, have been on Dowgate Hill, south of Cannon Street, for nearly seven centuries, and the Saddlers are still off Foster Lane.

Disparities of wealth and influence created tensions, especially once the guild super-league emerged – the Mercers, Grocers, Drapers, Fishmongers, Goldsmiths, Skinners, Merchant Taylors, Haberdashers, Salters, Ironmongers, Vintners and Clothworkers. In the fifteenth century the Mayor and aldermen generally emerged from the Mercers, the Grocers or the Drapers.

The Mercers had existed from the reign of Henry II, receiving their charter in 1393 from Richard II. At first they were general dealers in linen, haberdashery, and imported goods; later they specialized in fine textiles. Their first London site was on the north of Cheapside, where their hall was later built. Gilbert à Becket, father of Thomas, had been a mercer, and some twenty years after Thomas's martyrdom (in 1170) his sister built the chapel and hospital of St Thomas of Acre close to Ironmonger Lane, off Cheapside, bestowing it upon the guild. Henry III later granted the Mercers land there that had belonged to wealthy Jews, upon which they built their first hall and chapel.

The Grocers were first known as Pepperers, that being their principal commodity. They appeared in the reign of Henry II, but not till 1428 were they incorporated by charter. After several temporary homes, they built their hall in Old Jewry, on the site of a friary which had originally been the Jewish synagogue. First mentioned towards the end of the twelfth century, the Drapers were granted Arms in 1439, soon after they had erected their first hall, in Throgmorton Street. The Fishmongers, fourth in precedence and one of the wealthiest, received their charter from Edward I. Salters grew wealthy on the huge quantities of salt used for salting fish, eaten on fast days. They received their first privileges from Edward III and built their first hall, with six almshouses adjoining, in about 1454, in Bread Street, near the Fishmongers in Knightrider Street.

Unlike the polar divisions between employers' organizations and trade unions typical of industrial capitalism, guilds professedly united all practitioners of a craft. But internal differentiation emerged. Initially, the guild's whole membership had been entitled to wear the distinctive uniforms or 'liveries'; by the fifteenth century this privilege was becoming restricted to an élite, the 'liverymen', who gave their name to the livery companies, as the guilds eventually became known. Thus socio-occupational hierarchies hardened, normally elevating merchants above craftsmen, wholesalers above retailers. Inter-company rivalry also raged, to calm which the Court of Aldermen ruled an order of precedence for the big twelve companies, based on political influence.

Forming robust lobbies, the crafts naturally carried clout in City politics, sometimes engaging in infighting with the plutocrats heading the aldermanic élite. As top men of the twenty-four wards (twenty-five from 1396), aldermen wielded great power, acting as magistrates in ward courts (the wardmotes) and collectively choosing the Mayor, as well as 'guarding the walls and gates' and exercising legal jurisdictions. Though aldermen were nominally elected by their wards, in fact the system operated through self-selection among people with pull.

City government was headed by a band of intermarried families, especially mercers and grocers, whose wealth and overseas connections enabled them to dominate the key wool, cloth and wine trades. But, despite these oligarchic tendencies, there was room at the top and circulation of élites. Because rich merchants aimed to quit trade and buy into land, newcomers had the opportunity of filling the gaps. The most famous merchant of all, Richard Whittington, Mayor four times between 1397 and 1420, came from a Gloucestershire family which, like many of the landed gentry, provided for younger sons by apprenticing them in the City. Later legend has the disheartened young Whittington, resting at the foot of Highgate Hill, being given fresh heart by the (inaccurate) message of Bow Bells:

> Turn again Whittington,
> Thrice Lord Mayor of London Town.

Whittington grew immensely wealthy through wool exports. Urban society was fluid: few late medieval Londoners could claim more than two or three generations' residence, and aldermanic dynasties were exceptional.

Just north of the commercial thoroughfare of Cheapside in Aldermanbury – an area, as the name suggests, long associated with London's government – work started in 1411 on a building incorporating City power. 'In this yere,' wrote the chronicler Robert Fabyan, 'was ye Guyld Halle of London began to be new edyfied, and an olde and lytell cottage made into a fayre and goodly house as it now appereth.' The name Guildhall – rather than some variant on City Hall – is itself suggestive. It was in operation by 1425; the original Gothic porch was finished in 1430 and provided with statues in niches (now in the Museum of London). The main structure, over 150 feet long, and the chapel were completed shortly after. In 1501 kitchens were added, so that aldermen could enjoy their geese and capons. The entrance was rebuilt in the eighteenth century and the roof has been restored, but the walls are still largely fifteenth-century work, which makes it London's oldest civic building (and the large medieval crypt survives). The erection of a Guildhall was a landmark in City politics.

Tensions sometimes ran high between the aldermanic élite and the citizenry. Election to high offices – Mayor, Sheriff and Chamberlain – lay in aldermanic hands, and, sitting in the Guildhall, the Court of Aldermen formed an august executive body, empowered to maintain law, order and public morals, fix prices, and execute countless other regulations. But alongside the Mayor and the Court of Aldermen, the City also developed from the late thirteenth century (and, more formally, from 1346) a Court of Common Council consisting of men elected by the wards, which sent totals of representatives in proportion to their size.

In the fourteenth century appointment of common councillors became a bone of contention. The guilds asserted that they, not the wards, had the right to elect them. This was a populist move, aimed to wrench control away from the aldermanly patriciate into the hands of craftsmen at large. The guilds' victory proved short-lived, however. From 1384 the ward was restored as the electoral unit (permanently as it turned out); thereafter common councilmen were annually elected by citizens at wardmotes held on St Thomas's Day (21 December). The élite consolidated itself without the bloodshed and vendettas common in Italian communes: London never had Montagues and Capulets.

The post-Conquest centuries proved favourable for London. The monarchy was generally strong; England was safe from invasion; war and territorial possessions in France put business in the way of London's merchants and purveyors; the wool trade boomed (London Bridge, the saying ran, had been built upon woolpacks). Yet not all was rosy. Amidst dynastic and military conflicts, relations between Crown and City had their fluctuations. At war with the Scots, the first two Edwards made York their headquarters, and Crown servants duly followed them there, leaving Westminster something of a ghost town. Its fortunes revived with the Hundred Years War, once Edward III ordered the Exchequer back to Westminster 'so that it might be near to him in the parts beyond the sea'. More importantly in the long run, Parliament, initially itinerant, began to meet somewhat more regularly at Westminster. Sessions of Lords and Commons together were held in the painted chamber in Westminster Palace, and the emergent Commons would convene in the abbey Chapter House. These gatherings of grandees were a windfall, and when Richard II summoned Parliament to Gloucester the City found it worthwhile to stump up £600 to lure it back.

During the Wars of the Roses London's prosperity for a time hung in the balance, because the Lancastrians had a major power-base in the Midlands. London aided the Yorkist victory, which proved a godsend, as Edward IV re-established Westminster as the seat of government. Once the Tudors were in the saddle, London never looked back, and gradually the monarchy itself grew less itinerant, helping the consolidation of Westminster. By Chaucer's day, bishops' inns stretched like a necklace along the south side of the Strand from Temple Bar to Charing Cross, with John of Gaunt's Savoy Palace as its gem. To the north, a ribbon of houses had been built from the City to near the present church of St Mary-le-Strand. But until Elizabeth's reign the zone west of Chancery Lane and north of the Strand, all the way to the isolated hamlet of St Giles-in-the-Fields, with its leper hospital, remained pasture.

The route from the Strand to Westminster wound through the village of Charing, where, on the site of the present Trafalgar Square, stood the royal mews. Nearby, in 1291, Edward I had erected the last of his memorial crosses to his beloved Queen Eleanor. From there, the main road to the right led through fields to Knightsbridge, over the Tyburn; a track on the left – later to be called Whitehall – went to Westminster. In Chaucer's day, fields and gardens belonging to the Abbot of Westminster lay on the site of the present Admiralty. On the left at Charing Cross the traveller would pass the Augustinian House of St Mary, which belonged to Roncesvalles, or Roncevaux, in the Pyrenees. After St Mary Rouncewell the traveller to Westminster passed virgin soil stretching down to the river, called 'Scotland' – hence Scotland Yard – after one Adam Scot, who had owned it in Edward I's day. Next to Scotland was York Palace, the impressive residence of the Archbishop of York, whose gardens extended down to the Thames. Westminster, however, was still a moon, whereas the real City of London had already established itself as one of Europe's foremost commercial stars. This dual identity was to prove momentous.

View of London from Richard Pynson's *Cronycle of Englande*, 1510

CHAPTER THREE

Tudor London

The courtly splendour and national pride of the Tudor age owed much to the phenomenal expansion of the capital. Hitherto London had been, by European standards, in the second division – smaller in 1400 than not just Paris, Milan, Venice, Florence and Naples, but also perhaps Granada, Genoa and Prague, and not very much larger than Louvain, Brussels, Ypres, Barcelona, Rouen, Ghent, Seville, Cordova, Cologne or Lübeck. By 1600, however, London was one of Europe's top five cities, exciting the envy of startled foreigners, and spurring civic patriotism, if also perplexity.

Hub of court, councils and Parliament, London provided the backdrop for the momentous dynastic events following Richard III's overthrow in 1485 and the founding of the upstart Tudor line. From Westminster Hall issued the Acts and proclamations decreeing the dissolution of the monasteries and Henry VIII's 'divorce'; from there the Protestant Reformation was promulgated under Edward VI and Elizabeth, interrupted by the bloody Marian reaction. Citizens were witness to ghastly tragedies touching the fate of Christendom itself: the beheadings on Tower Hill of Thomas More and Thomas Cromwell; of two queens, Anne Boleyn and Katherine Howard; of the Duke of Somerset, Protector under Edward VI; of John Dudley, Duke of Northumberland, in 1553 and of Lady Jane Grey the year after. They attended the burnings of Mary's almost 300 'Smithfield martyrs' (at East Smithfield, by the Tower) in a reign of terror on the foolish Queen's part that decisively stiffened support for the Reformers.

London was, however, more than a stage-set for the Reformation: it played a major part in its triumph, thanks to its astute, articulate trading community with close links in the Low Countries and the Rhineland, those springs of early Protestantism. Merchants and lawyers had long grumbled against the parasitic priests swarming in the capital, whose locust appetite for fees and malversations of canon law and Church courts were all the more resented as the clergy themselves appeared so proud and pompous. Small wonder London had become an early nursery of Lollardy, that anti-

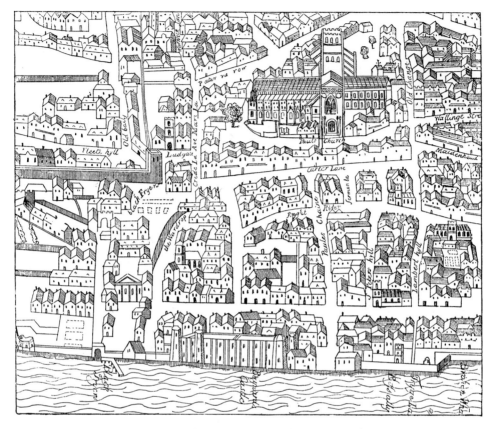

Map of St Paul's area, *c.* 1550–60, from 'Agas's Plan'

clerical evangelical movement inspired in the late fourteenth century by the heretic John Wyclif. In such well-prepared tilth, Lutheran teachings rooted and shooted. Circles of citizens clamoured to read smuggled Bibles in William Tyndale's translation; they held prayer meetings and gave sanctuary to brave gospellers fleeing persecution. From the 1540s the fervent proselytizings of Calvinist preachers were popular among the 'godly sort', though satirized in Ben Jonson's image of Zeal-Of-The-Land-Busy. If, as historians nowadays believe, much of England, especially those 'dark corners of the land' in the north-west, were tenaciously loyal to Roman Catholicism, or at least to the 'old ways', Londoners leaned towards the Reformed faith largely independently of dynastic designs and acts of state.

The new teachings found eager metropolitan ears, and many sympathized with the first Protestant evangelicals' denunciations of purgatory and pardons and supported doctrines like salvation by faith. Reformed beliefs would be reinforced by the astonishing physical transformation of the Church and its clergy from the late 1530s. Altars, images and rood screens were hacked down, desecrated or burnt, while the calm cloisters of the priories were profaned through requisition as warehouses, workshops and taverns. Holy London underwent unparalleled sacrilege. Destruction of shrines and effigies, and the dispersal of monks, nuns and friars helped to undermine belief in the tenets they had personified – the magic of transubstantiation, intercession for souls in purgatory, the invocation of saints, and numerous other solemn observances. Transformation in the visible Church fabric, in services and liturgy, doubtless left many bewildered or aghast. Yet however momentous the doctrinal upheaval wrought by the Reformation, among citizens the passage of faiths proved remarkably smooth. Rising literacy spread the Protestant gospel; alongside the Scriptures, the presses poured forth spiritual literature, catechizing was a serious matter, and the pulpit played a key role in re-education – there were as many as three sermons a week in some parishes. Up from the benighted provinces, ministers reported, 'here the word of God is plentifully preached'. London was preached, not pummelled, into Protestantism.

It was fortunate for the capital that its faith changed through gradual adjustment of minds and habits, in step with the judicious, middle-of-the-road Anglican doctrines promoted through Elizabeth's *via media*. By contrast, many of Europe's other great cities were devastated by the holy wars waged between Catholics, Lutherans, Calvinists, Anabaptists and sectaries. Antwerp, Ghent, Paris and other key Netherlandish, French and German cities were ravaged time and again from Luther's first witness (1517), through the Wars of Religion and the Dutch Revolt, to the conclusion of the Thirty Years War (1648), suffering bloodbaths and the trials, torture and burning of thousands of heretics, traitors and witches. Münster in Westphalia was torn apart in the 1550s; in 1572 the St Bartholomew's Day massacre rocked Paris; the twelve-day sack of Antwerp in 1576 by mutinous Spanish troops (the Spanish Fury) resulted in 6,000 deaths and 800 houses being burnt down. But while in many Continental cities violence reigned between princes and peoples battling over the true faith, London escaped civil crisis and, after Mary's death, serious religious persecution. Elizabeth's softly-softly policies gave citizens time to adjust: piecemeal Reformation proved peaceful Reformation.

Doctrinal controversies naturally persisted among zealots; but, as Elizabeth's reign progressed, the City consolidated with a Protestant voice. And as the grave and godly tightened their grip on government, they stole the thunder of Presbyterian firebrands, the would-be 'saints' whose militant tendency rarely proved a truly disruptive force. Moderate on this as on other matters, City fathers were concerned more with practical godliness and discipline than with radical restructuring of the Church, and, in the absence of grass-roots sectarianism or the fanatical tradition of religious assassination that proved so catastrophic in the Netherlands and France, London's parishioners escaped massacre and mayhem. Indeed, the new teachings rapidly proved a source of ideological confidence and cohesion: for many citizens the spread of the gospel, the progress of trade, and England's deliverance from popish Spain's Armada were all manifestations of divine Providence. The new faith created not division but a heightened sense of destiny, through the shared vision of a chosen citizenry living under godly rule.

The Reformation revolutionized the face of the medieval city. Launched by Henry VIII and completed under Edward VI, the dissolution of the monasteries and chantries brought unprecedented confiscations of ecclesiastical estates, treasure, vestments, plate, sculpture and furniture, and nowhere in the kingdom was the impact so astonishing as in the capital. At a stroke, priories, hospitals, chapels and shrines changed hands. Church lands and properties were, formally speaking, nationalized, but in effect most were privatized, being sold off or dished out by the Crown to its courtiers and cronies. London acquired a new breed of parvenu landlords, who felt free to do as they pleased with their windfall wealth. A hectic property market followed, encouraging opportunistic redevelopment comparable perhaps to the speculative fever following the Second World War. And this real-estate boom occurred just when population was soaring and the economy was hotting up. With the buyers' market in land and property created by the Dissolution promoting new workshops and housing, the Reformation fuelled London's economic expansion.

Imagination is needed to envisage the Church's domination of London's traditional townscape: the Tower and Guildhall apart, all the towering buildings in the medieval capital belonged to the Church. On the eve of the Reformation the north bank of the river between Blackfriars and Westminster was one string of ecclesiastical palaces – then known as 'inns', though that term belies their splendour. At the east end rose the riverside residences of the Bishop of Exeter and the Bishop of Bath and Wells; then, beyond the Savoy Palace, built in the thirteenth century for the uncle of Eleanor, wife of Henry III, but after 1505 converted into a charity for the 'destitute and disorderly', were the inns of the Bishops of Carlisle, Durham and Norwich, the hospital of St Mary Rouncewell and, approaching Westminster, the majestic manor of the Archbishop of York.

Much as in Edward the Confessor's day, Westminster in 1500 was still an ecclesiastical enclave. The estates of the mighty Abbot of Westminster extended west to the horse ferry and north to the May fair. Bloomsbury Manor belonged to the Prior of the Charterhouse; and today's Soho and Piccadilly were divided between Abingdon Abbey and the hospitals of St Giles, St James and Burton Lazars. On the south bank the story was the same: Bermondsey Abbey stretched towards Lambeth, including the hospital of St Thomas, while the Bishops of Winchester and Rochester and the Prior of Lewes controlled bankside acres. We remember the churches and cloisters within the walls; we tend to forget that pre-Reformation London was encircled by Church estates.

An asset-stripping exercise unleashed by a destitute and opportunist regime, the Dissolution transformed this situation in an orgy of wrecking and looting. A handful of religious houses survived. Virtually on his deathbed, Henry permitted the City to establish or renew five institutions vital to welfare services. These included the hospital of St Bartholomew in Smithfield and St Thomas's Hospital, which, commemorating St Thomas à Becket, had been founded by the canons of St Mary Overie and the monks of Bermondsey Abbey. On its surrender to Henry VIII in 1538, St Thomas's had a master, six brethren, and three lay sisters who tended forty poor people. The City bought it back from the Crown for £647 4s 1d, and in 1553 Edward VI granted it a charter, appointing the City as its governors (though mention of 'Thomas Becket' prudently ceased, the dedication being transferred to St Thomas the Apostle).

The hospital of St Mary of Bethlehem outside Bishopsgate, used from the fourteenth century for 'distracted people', was also spared, becoming the notorious Bethlem Hospital (Bedlam). The madhouse was twinned with Bridewell, which became a workhouse for delinquents. Finally, Greyfriars, with its church – excepting St Paul's, London's largest place of worship – became Christ's Hospital orphanage and school, an institution favoured by Londoners in charitable bequests: it was where Samuel Coleridge and Charles Lamb later learned their letters.

These apart, however, pious foundations were abolished and plundered for booty. Thames-side episcopal inns went to courtiers for a song. The houses of the Bishops of Exeter, Bath and Wells, and Carlisle became respectively the seats of the Pagets, the Earl of Southampton and the Earl of Bedford. Durham House passed into Crown hands, and by 1553 the Duke of Northumberland was ensconced in it. His son, Lord Guildford Dudley, was married there to Lady Jane Grey two months before she was fatally escorted to the Tower, ready to be proclaimed Queen. Elizabeth later gave Durham House to Sir Walter Ralegh, though after his downfall part was demolished to make way for the New Exchange, a bourse with ground-floor arcades and shops above: thus the altar soon made way for the counter. The Savoy, formerly a hospital for the poor, was parcelled out between industry and idleness: a glass factory, the first in England, was started there, while suites were provided for the Chancellor of the Duchy of Lancaster.

Belying his epithet, Protector Somerset flattened the houses of five bishops to build his own residence, scrounging materials from the charnel-house at St Paul's and the church of the Knights Hospitaller in Smithfield, which, complained the septuagenarian antiquarian John Stow in his *Survay of London* (1598), 'was undermined and blown up with gunpowder'. The Protector never lived to enjoy the first Somerset House, being executed in 1552. The most resplendent of all the Strand palaces, it survived as

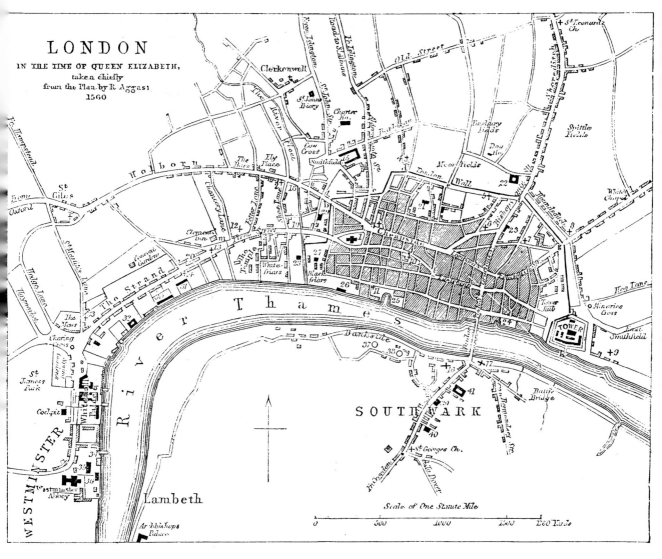

LONDON

IN THE TIME OF QUEEN ELIZABETH,
taken chiefly
from the Plan by R. Aggas;
1560

a. Ludgate.	4. St. Giles', Cripplegate.	17. St. Towles (or St. Olaves).	30. Savoy Palace.
b. Newgate.	5. All-Hallows-in-the-Wall.	18. Holborn Bridge.	31. Somerset Place.
c. Aldersgate.	6. St. Anthony.	19. Fleet Bridge.	32. Durham House.
d. Cripplegate.	7. St. Andrew-under-Shaft	20. Strand Bridge.	33. St. Martin's-in-the-Fields.
e. Moorgate.	8. St. Botolph.	21. Guildhall.	34. Star Chamber.
f. Bishopsgate.	9. St. Katherine.	22. Bethlehem Hospital.	35. Westminster Hall.
g. Aldgate.	10. St. Thomas Apostle.	23. Crosby Place.	36. Parliament House.
h. Postern Gate.	11. St. Mary Somerset.	24. Billingsgate.	37. Bull-baiting Ring.
k. Traitors' Gate.	12. St. Dunstan.	25. Queenhithe.	38. Bear-baiting (afterwards
m. Temple Bar.	13. St. Clement Danes.	26. Baynard's Castle.	the Globe Theatre).
1. St. Paul's Church.	14. St. Mary-le-Strand.	27. Blackfriar's Theatre.	39. The Tabard Inn.
2. St. Andrew's.	15. St. Bartholomew's Priory.	28. Bridewell Palace.	40. Marshalsea Prison.
3. St. Martin's.	16. St. Mary Overy.	29. Old Bailey.	41. Hospital of St. Thomas.

London, 1560

39

Crown property, Princess Elizabeth living there before her accession. There, James I's Queen, Anne of Denmark, held her court; under Charles I it was made over to Queen Henrietta Maria; and Charles II's Catherine of Braganza withdrew there after he installed his mistress, Lady Castlemaine, at Whitehall Palace. It was finally demolished in 1775, when William Chambers built the present Somerset House.

Thus peers replaced prelates along the Strand. Some stayed – Northumberland House, rebuilt in the seventeenth century, survived long enough to be photographed – but after the Restoration in 1660 grandee palaces were demolished in their turn, to make room for new speculations, and street names are now the only reminders of those Thames mansions – Arundel Street, Savoy Place, Northumberland Avenue, and so forth.

Amidst this largesse to its henchmen, the Crown retained one palace, that of the Archbishop of York, which Cardinal Wolsey had tactlessly begun to fashion finer than the King's. Predictably piqued, on Wolsey's ruin Henry seized York Palace, which was renamed Whitehall. This acquisition formed part of a grandiose Henrician expansion, which included the palaces at Greenwich, Nonsuch, Ham, Eltham and Hampton Court. Elizabeth, pennywise and strapped for cash, later vacated many of her father's mansions, making Whitehall and Greenwich her settled residences.

If the Dissolution unleashed royal looting in Westminster, its impact within and around the walls was yet more dramatic, loosing a frenzy of demolition, conversions and rebuilding. Within years, almost all the twenty-three medieval religious houses in the City were razed or requisitioned. Many of them were architectural gems, including those of the Austin canons at St Martin's-le-Grand, the Dominican Black Friars and the Carmelite White Friars east of the Temple. Token churches were preserved for parish use – for instance, the former Austin priory of St Bartholomew-the-Great in Smithfield (one of only two Norman churches still extant in the City – the other being the Temple; though there is also the crypt of St Mary-le-Bow). The choir alone was saved, and even that had a narrow escape in 1563 when the Bishop of London tried to pilfer its roof leads for St Paul's. Other Austin priories (Holy Trinity Aldgate and St Mary Spital) were vandalized and their hospitals redeveloped.

Not untypical was the fate of the Austin Friars house by London Wall. This was granted to the Marquess of Winchester, who built an imposing house on the site, but soon afterwards, perhaps sensing the City was losing residential cachet, sold it for £5,000 to the Lord Mayor. The church furniture was meanwhile sold for £100 and the roof lead stripped; in 1550 the nave was given by Edward VI to Dutch refugees (it survived until the Second World War), while the rest was used for warehousing coal, wine and corn.

Another Austin Friars property underwent a drastic redevelopment that stuck in the elderly Stow's gullet. The mighty Thomas Cromwell appropriated their buildings north of Throgmorton Street, and ran up a handsome dwelling:

this house finished, and having some reasonable plot of ground left for a garden he caused the pales of the gardens adjoining to the north part thereof on a sudden to be taken down; twenty-two feet to be measured forth right into the north of every man's ground; a line there to be drawn, a trench to be cast, a foundation laid, and a high brick wall to be built. My father had a garden there, and a house standing close to his south pale; this house they loosed from the ground, ere my father heard thereof; no warning was given him, nor other answer, when he spake to the surveyors of that work, but that their master Sir Thomas commanded them so to do; no man durst go to argue the matter, but each man lost his land. Thus the sudden rising of some men causeth them to forget themselves.

The stop-at-nothing developer evidently has an eminent pedigree.

Men of rank bought up City property. The Herberts, Earls of Pembroke, established themselves in Baynard's Castle, and some Tudor courtiers, like Walsingham and Lumley, dwelt in Church buildings within the walls. But, faced by the rising tide of population, they tended to quit for more spacious and salubrious quarters, pocketing the proceeds. The house of the Earl of Ormond in Knightrider Street, Stow noted in the 1590s, had been 'lately taken down and divers fair tenements are builded there'; the hall of the Berkeleys was 'all in ruin, and letten out in several tenements', while the Percys' London home had given way to bowling-alleys, gambling-haunts and 'small cottages for strangers and others' – bedsit land, we would say.

Courtiers capitalized on windfall gains. The church of the Crutched Friars near the Tower had been bestowed upon Sir Thomas Wyatt: he ripped it down and replaced it (grumbled Stow) with a 'carpenter's yard, a Tennis Court and such the like': the friars' hall was made into a glasshouse, worked by glass-blowers from Venice and then by Jean Carré, an Antwerp glass-maker.

The order of the Franciscan Minoresses, just north of the Tower, suffered humili-ation: 'in place of this house of nuns,' lamented Stow, 'is now built divers fair and large storehouses for armour and habiliments of war'; next it became a gunpowder works! The Bishop of Hereford's inn stood service as a sugar-mill; the Cistercian abbey of Eastminster was replaced by a ship's-biscuit bakery; and Dutch watchmakers, to evade City jurisdiction, set up shop in St Martin's-le-Grand. Sites like these were ideal for industrial or recreational purposes: the exemption from City jurisdiction granted to religious houses being thrown in with their sale, former monastic properties were exempt from many City restrictions. That is why Coldharbour, once the residence of Cuthbert Tunstall, Bishop of London, ended up as a warren inhabited by debtors seeking immunity from the law, and St Martin's-le-Grand became a haunt of hucksters. England's first indoor theatre, established in Blackfriars where the City's writ did not run, derives from the 1540s, when Sir Thomas Carwarden, Master of the Revels, turned the convent into a store for props from court revels. By shaking up the property world, the Reformation released dramatic economic possibilities.

*

This landlords' bonanza went hand in hand with demographic and economic growth. Like all contemporary cities, London was a death-trap; any population rise depended wholly upon an influx from outlying regions. With plague and other epidemics worsening, Tudor London required an inflow of around 5,000 migrants per year – over 10 per cent of its initial population – to sustain expansion. Absorbing such masses posed huge problems, but promised rewards.

Young, single males above all flocked in, hoping to make their fortunes, or at least earn their bread. London's streets were hardly El Dorado, but such teenagers passed through service or apprenticeship to rise into the ranks of the shopkeepers, master craftsmen and merchants whose enterprises in turn created further business. Tudor London had an insatiable appetite for new workshops, yards and stores, comfortable habitations for the better-off, and makeshift quarters for needy labourers.

At Henry VIII's accession in 1509 London was still playing a subaltern role within the trading systems of the Low Countries and the Mediterranean. By the Restoration in 1660 its population had increased tenfold and it presided over an economic empire of its own – indeed, it was fast achieving European eminence. This growth entailed heavy costs for rural hinterlands, for provincial towns and countless expendable workers; it also paved the way for world leadership. All was change: 'The population of London is immense,' observed a Venetian in 1531; soon after, a traveller estimated 70,000 denizens, while in 1557 another visitor thought London had 185,000 inhabitants a wild overstatement, but clearly the city was making an impression as a mushroom metropolis.

With no censuses, gauging London's numbers is a matter of informed guesswork. Historians reckon that the city's population in 1500 was under 50,000; by mid-century it had perhaps 70,000 inhabitants, one in twenty of the nation as a whole; by 1565 there were some 85,000 Londoners; and by Elizabeth's death, in 1603, 140,000 may have been living within and without its ancient walls and another 40,000 in its spreading suburbs – almost a threefold leap in a century. Confronting this astounding surge – 'Soon London will be all England,' quipped James I – jaundiced contemporaries judged London's cancerous spread would be fatal alike for itself and for the nation. This prognosis proved false. What was true, however, was that the city was a killer, for burials far exceeded baptisms, at least till around 1780. Had not newcomers 'congregated there from all parts of the island, from Flanders and from every other place', filling the shoes of those felled by pestilence, London would certainly have proved self-destructive.

How were these swarms of migrants accommodated? Before 1600 the great majority of Londoners lived within the bars – that is, within the twenty-six wards. These chiefly lay within the walls, though some wards spilled over into extramural precincts, westwards to Temple Bar and Holborn Bar, and east to Whitechapel Bar and the Minories. The earliest extant map – it appears in a German atlas of 1572 – depicts the city in about 1550; except for Westminster, it shows hardly any built-up areas on the north bank beyond the wards and hence outwith the City's jurisdiction. The great majority of households south of the river also lay within the City's bounds, for the built-up zone on the south bank fell within the ward of Bridge Without, formerly the borough of Southwark; the rights to this neighbourhood were purchased by the City from Edward VI in 1550.

Swelling proportions of Londoners – ultimately the majority – were to dwell in the suburbs 'without the bars' (that is, beyond the wards) and thus beyond the writ of the Guildhall and the guilds. But under the Tudors most lived and worked within the wards, leading to sardine packing, especially towards Aldgate and in the eastern suburbs. The Dissolution had freed building-lots; but within a generation the spaces gained by seizure and demolition had grown congested, and landlords resorted to throwing up hovels in side-alleys, crowding the poor into cellars, and dividing up properties for multiple occupation. Southwark, Whitechapel and Houndsditch had declined into 'nurseries and seminary places of the begging poor that swarm with the City', griped Stow.

Ancient Stow was appalled by the press of lodgings, stables and stores, especially in and around the City's east end where he lived. Once a green, Tower Hill had been 'greatly diminished by building of tenements and garden plots'. Beyond Bishopsgate, dwellings had been knocked up 'with alleys backward, of late time too much pestered with people (a great cause of infection)' – back alleys were always a bane, harbouring slums and rubbish heaps. The Lime Street residence of the Earls of Oxford had first been 'letten out to Powlters for stabling of horses and stowage of poultrie', and then it was 'builded into a number of small tenements, letten out to strangers [foreigners] and other meane people'. Scores of other sites had suffered the same fate – that is, if we read between the lines, they had become part of the thriving economy of landlordism and trade that was to give the City the distinctive flavour it retained at least until Dickens's day.

The three major routes east out of the city attracted low-grade housing. The southernmost skirted the river from the Tower, through recently reclaimed mud-flats to Wapping, populated mostly by sailors and shipyard workers, especially after the East India Company's Blackwall dockyard was created in 1614. Further north, Ratcliff Highway ran east from Tower Hill to Shadwell, south of the village of Stepney, this built-up thoroughfare replacing (Stow regretted) 'a large highway, with Elme trees on both sides'. The very first buildings there had been a school and almshouses, 'but of late yeares ship-wrights and . . . other marine men have builded many large and strong houses for themselves and smaller for Saylers from thence almost to Poplar and so to Blakewall'. The northern route, Whitechapel Street, ran from Aldgate East. 'Both the sides of the streete,' Stow growled,

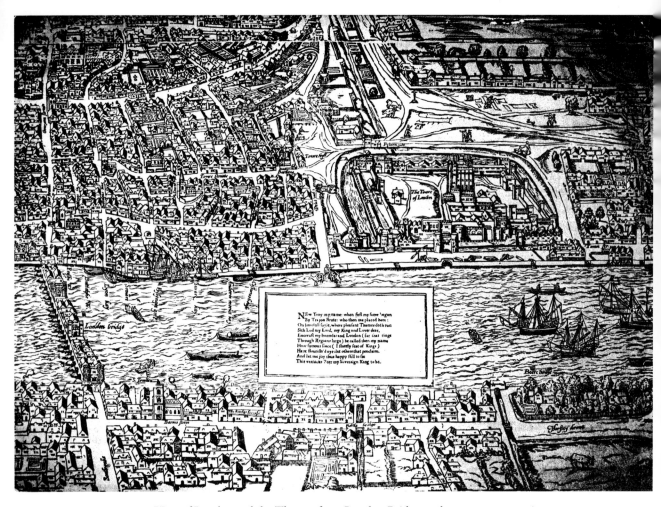

View of London and the Thames from London Bridge to the tower, *c.* 1550–60,
from 'Agas's Plan'

bee pestered with buildings, with Cottages, and Allies, even up to White chappel church; and
almost halfe a myle beyond it, into the common field ... which ... being sometime the beauty
of this City on that part, is so incroched upon by building of filthy Cottages ... that in some
places it scarce remaineth a sufficient high way for the meeting of Carriages and droves of
Cattell, much lesse is ther any faire, pleasant or wholsome way for people to walke on foote.

Business before beauty. Had Stow lived to be 100 he would have grown yet more
disgruntled. A new edition of his *Survay*, published in 1633, long after his death, noted
the stink of a new Wapping alum works.

Expansion also nosed westward. Beyond Temple Bar, gracious residences arose, and elegant tailors' and silkware shops. Though the City strove to restrict goldsmiths and silversmiths to Lombard Street, some sprang up in Fleet Street and the Strand. Aldermen denounced the migration of fashion, and the City protested when the Earl of Salisbury proposed his 'New Exchange' on the Durham House site in the Strand – 'Britain's Bourse', a rival to Gresham's Royal Exchange, was actually built in 1609. But the westward drift of superior crafts was unstoppable: the court proved a magnet. Spared the proliferation of yards and passages that drew the poor and trapped the stench, parts of Westminster grew more exclusive than the City. The Strand could boast the residences of Lord Burghley (Exeter House, also known as Burghley House or Cecil House), the Earl of Bedford and the Lord Chancellor; and Robert Cecil was soon to create St Martin's Lane. Attractive speculations rose to the west, while manufacturers and mariners squeezed into the east.

The City itself remained a social mishmash, wealthy, middling and poor jostling wherever mazes of backyards and blind alleys led off main streets. Aldermen and a few aristocrats still lived within the walls; yet within spitting distance dwelt butchers, bakers and candlestick-makers with their stores and stables, fires and furnaces, and rowdy apprentices under the eaves.

Unchecked growth sparked alarm: slums were festering – would not crime, riot and pestilence follow? Noting 'the great number of dissolute loose and insolent people harboured in such and like noisome and disorderly houses as namely poor cottages and habitants of beggars and people without trade, stables, inns, ale houses, taverns, garden houses, converted to dwellings, ordinaries, dicing houses, bowling allies and brothel houses', the Privy Council acted. In 1580, 'moved by the considerate opinions of the Lord Mayor, Aldermen and other grave wise men in or about the City', a proclamation was issued prohibiting new building within three miles of the gates, except upon existing foundations (a foretaste of the Green Belt!). A ban was also slapped on multi-occupation: owners were to 'forebear from letting ... any more families than one only to be placed or to inhabit from henceforth in any house that heretofore hath been inhabited'. These proved the first of numerous futile efforts by Crown and City to prevent intramural overcrowding and freeze extramural suburbs. Commendable in its intention of averting slums and plague, the decree, like most building controls, was hopelessly unworkable – indeed, had it been enforced, the building ban would have created worse overcrowding or mass homelessness. In the event, the legislation possibly proved counter-productive, tempting lessees to jerry-build lath-and-plaster premises in case they had to demolish. Then as later, legislation did not get to the root of the problem. So long as business boomed, housing freezes were a nonsense. Nevertheless, the precedent set, further decrees followed: in 1598 the Privy Council warned JPs about landlords renting out tenements in Shoreditch and Clerkenwell to 'base people and to lewd persons that do keep evil rule, and harbour thieves, rogues and vagabonds'.

Perhaps this legislation was but paper pieties. Elizabeth was soon making exceptions for 'the better sort', and the Stuarts characteristically went one step further, granting immunities to those paying through the nose for the privilege. The Earl of Bedford, for example, had to shell out £2,000 for a licence to build in Covent Garden: small wonder he fell out with the Stuarts.

Tudor London boomed and was the making of many a fortune: the Dick Whittington rags-to-riches myth, which became popular around 1600, sometimes came true. The capital, of course, also had masses of the working poor. Nevertheless, work was available, no permanent underclass formed, and few starved to death or rebelled. Elizabethan London was a success. On what was that success based?

London's place in Europe's intricate trading network was improving. Ideally sited on the Thames, the capital had always enjoyed ready access to the entrepôts of the Netherlands, to Rhineland cloth markets, and to the Baltic towns of the Hanse. At first a dependent economy, medieval England had exported such raw materials as grain, hides, wool, tin and lead, reimporting the wool as finished cloth, woven around Ghent and Bruges, along with wine, spices, silk and fineries. Change began when Edward III brought in Flemish weavers and the kingdom started exporting not just wool but coarse woollen cloth. Cloth export leapt eighteen-fold between 1350 and 1500, becoming England's prime export. Thanks to cloth, London's share of the nation's trade increased by 1550 to nearly 90 per cent, mainly in the hand of the Merchant Adventurers, a consortium founded in 1407, drawing its 100 active members from several companies but controlled by the Mercers. The dominance of cloth-making and finishing is evident from guild membership: around 1550 the cloth guilds had about two out of five freemen.

London was perfectly placed to capitalize on overseas trading opportunities. Its growing role in international exchanges owed something to the fall of Constantinople to the Turks in 1453 and the subsequent tilting of trade away from the Mediterranean towards the Atlantic. It later benefited from other rivals' woes. For a while, Antwerp was the sun of European trade and London its satellite: outstripping Venice, Antwerp was sending up the Thames all manner of necessities and luxuries: silver bullion, silks, sugar, cotton, linen, tapestry, glass, swords, firearms and furniture, eastern spices and perfumes. But with the closing of Antwerp to the English in 1568, the Spanish sack of that town in 1576 and the religious wars raging across the Netherlands and France, London, so peaceful and stable by Continental standards, was well placed to profit. 'A man would say, that seeth the shipping there,' boasted William Camden of the Pool of London in 1586, 'that it is, as it were, a very wood of trees disbranched to make glades and let in light, so shaded it is with masts and sails.'

The Royal Exchange, opened in 1570 by Queen Elizabeth. This engraving *c.* 1750

London's rise was epitomized by the career of Thomas Gresham and his establishment of the Royal Exchange as a commercial headquarters. Himself a merchant's son, by the early 1560s Gresham had fingers in many pies, dealing with international financiers and shipping vast cargoes of cloth to the Italian merchants in Antwerp in exchange for Italian silk. London's merchants felt the lack of a prestigious exchange like that of Venice or Antwerp for trading their commodities. Gresham offered to build one at his own cost; the clearance of eighty houses in Cornhill, near the Stocks market, provided a site; and the resulting Exchange was the City's first and finest dip into Renaissance architecture – a four-storeyed brick building (later stuccoed), built around a courtyard with covered arcades and dominated by a bell-tower. Above the arcades were haberdashers, armourers, goldsmiths, drapers and glass-sellers. Opened by Queen Elizabeth in 1570, the Exchange advertised the status of London, after the 'Spanish fury', as northern Europe's chief entrepôt.

Widening horizons overseas afforded fresh opportunities. Chartered in 1555, the

47

Russia Company was the first of numerous new London trading enterprises that included the Levant Company (1581), the East India Company (1600), the Virginia Company (1606) and various African and American ventures. These new joint-stock companies, encouraging risk capital, were more enterprising than the guilds. The voyages they financed, like those of the comparable privateering and plantation syndicates, in which sea dogs like Sir Walter Ralegh played a large part, were highly risky but commonly returned colossal profits. They opened a gap between big international businessmen and domestic traders, while also leading to new links between City and court, for such ventures attracted noblemen and hangers-on with an eye to profit, as did the tax-collectorships and concessions offered by the Crown under Elizabeth and the early Stuarts to courtiers in cahoots with London merchants and syndicates. Monopolies forged ties between trade and politics as financiers promoted state business under Crown protection. Following in the steps of the great Elizabethan merchant princes like Gresham and Sir Thomas Smythe (who served as a governor of the Levant and Russia Companies) came the great Stuart projectors: Sir William Cockayne made a fortune out of a cloth monopoly, while Sir Lionel Cranfield, a mercer's apprentice who married his master's daughter, rose through handling royal patents to become Lord High Treasurer and Earl of Middlesex. Commercial achievement brought social advancement, as families like the Garveys and the Sandys made their way from counting-house to court.

Under Elizabeth and James I the City was thus emerging as a finance capital, with a new cadre of merchant princes; yet it chiefly remained a hive of handicrafts and trading, wholesale and retail, swarming with masters and their journeymen active in manufacturing, merchandising and processing. Traders dominated the inner precincts – mercers, drapers, haberdashers and furriers occupied the central thoroughfares, Cheapside and East Cheap – but most of the messy, smelly trades had migrated towards the rim. Brewers, millers and dyers lined the riverside; carpenters and curriers, founders and printers were crowded to the north by Aldersgate and Cripplegate; and glass-makers, basket-makers and wire-drawers bunched around Aldgate. This tendency for dealers to hog the centre while craftsmen scattered towards the more spacious periphery was emphasized by the settling of brickmakers, armourers and shipwrights beyond the walls in the emergent industrial suburb to the east.

Markets remained the heartbeat of city business. Four great food markets straddled the central axis from Newgate to Aldgate: Newgate (for corn and flesh), Cheap (for vegetables and dairy produce), the Stocks (by today's Mansion House: for fish and flesh), and Leadenhall (for butcher's meat and hides – it also served as a granary). The fish markets were along Old Fish Street and in Bridge Street near the river – indeed, London's favourite fish was caught in the Thames and its tributaries: 'What should I speak of the fat and sweet salmon daily taken in this stream,' drooled Stow, 'and that in

48

such plenty ... as no river in Europe is able to exceed it? But what store also of barbels, trouts, chevens, perches, smelts, breams, roaches, daces, gudgeons, flounders, shrimps, eels etc. are commonly to be had therein?' Blackwell Hall, the cloth exchange, was situated near Guildhall. Though the livestock market, Smithfield, lay beyond the walls, the concentration of markets within the walls is striking: London long remained a market.

Bakers and cookshops were emerging in the suburbs, north-east of the Tower near the Navy Victualling Office, and ships' victuallers hugged Wapping riverside; but, as in the medieval city, street trading and handicrafts remained densely packed within the walls. Dives and Lazarus still rubbed shoulders there, and there was little segregation as yet between home and shop.

London was a bustling, bursting city; a new merchant-prince élite was emerging; there were multitudes of migrants and the 'meaner' sorts, and all ranks and stations in between. All were fighting to survive and thrive. Stresses and strains were inevitable, but what is remarkable is the city's ability to cope with them. This was largely due to the concentric structures of community government inherited and evolving.

The City had a dual framework of institutions, overlapping and interlocking. There were the guilds. Though the freedom (the right to trade and participate as a citizen) was inheritable or purchasable, the main entry to it remained the seven-year apprenticeship. Being 'free' of a guild and thus a citizen was a coveted privilege, conferring superiority over foreigners, provincials and the *hoi polloi* – all the porters, potboys, carters, watermen and other menials. In early Tudor times no more than a quarter of the City's male population belonged to this citizen class. Recent research has suggested that, with relaxation of entry requirements, this fraction rapidly increased, until by the mid sixteenth century almost three-quarters of the City's adult male population were probably sworn to the freedom, creating remarkable social cohesion.

Conferring status and opportunities, citizenship was a prize to set one's sights upon, and guild membership the escalator of advancement. It assured assimilation for tens of thousands of youthful newcomers to the big city, while, for younger sons of country gentlemen, initiation into the 'art or mistery' offered prospects of soaring into the civic hierarchy to enjoy business contacts, perquisites and pomp. It might even lead to a fortune sufficient to buy into land.

From the late fourteenth century the guilds had acquired charters; by 1500 the more prosperous had erected sumptuous halls, and high status accrued to those known as the Twelve Great – the Mercers, Grocers, Drapers, Haberdashers, Fishmongers, Goldsmiths, Skinners, Merchant Taylors, Salters, Ironmongers, Vintners and Cloth-workers. In Tudor times the Grocers, Drapers, Haberdashers, Merchant Taylors and Mercers supplied nearly half of London's aldermen and common councillors, thus forming an élite within the élite.

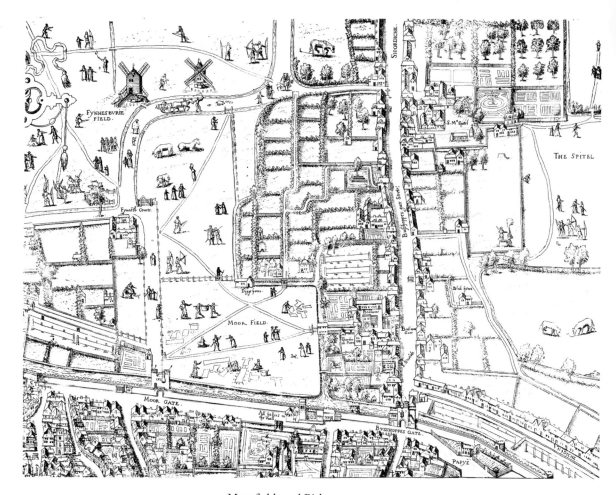

Moorfields and Bishopsgate, 1559

Meanwhile divisions continued to harden between those privileged members authorized to wear the livery and the lesser 'yeomanry' – mainly craftsmen. From the livery came the masters, wardens and Court of Assistants (past masters and wardens) who controlled guild affairs. Guilds exercised strict membership control. The wardens and the Court of Assistants undertook professional supervision, policing production and marketing and settling trades disputes. The prime guild function was apprenticeship regulation. Guilds examined candidates, drafted indentures, and enforced discipline in cases of dishonesty, disorder and drunkenness. A professional status ladder involving initiation ceremonials and rites of passage gave members promotion prospects. Few got to the top, but most journeymen might hold intermediate office or serve on committees, and all could savour the pleasures of belonging, and benefit from the trade protection offered through the guilds' hounding of outsiders and unlicensed traders.

Guilds basked in City prestige thanks to their religious, fraternal and charitable functions. They made provision for members' widows and orphans and their own pensioners. On religious holidays the 'whole company of the fellowship' – the masters, wardens, assistants, livery, clerks, beadles and yeomen – would stage parades, dressed up in full regalia, the Lord Mayor's pageant being the year's solemn climax. Public pageantry consolidated occupational allegiances, fostered civic chauvinism, and upheld traditions and customs. By requiring deference and conformity among lower ranks, in return for prospects of promotion for those prepared to toe the line and work within the system, guilds proved a powerful civic cement.

Complementing the guilds were the institutions of civic government proper, centred on the Guildhall, which served as court, debating-chamber, banqueting-hall and civic chapel. These formed a pyramid. At the apex stood the Lord Mayor and the Court of Aldermen, the City's executive governing body. Beneath the Bench sat the Court of Common Council, a legislative assembly of roughly 200 members, six or eight from each ward. Members were elected by all freemen at an annual December wardmote assembly; custom guaranteed that it was liverymen, the richer sort, who were chosen. The Court of Common Council cooperated with the Court of Aldermen in civic legislation and levying taxes.

At the base (and meeting only rarely) lay the Court of Common Hall. London's largest assembly, Common Hall had lesser functions, meeting mainly to elect City officials, or rather to rubber-stamp nominations by the aldermanic élite. Every year Common Hall would advance the names of two candidates for Lord Mayor – usually hand-picked senior aldermen; the aldermen themselves then made the final decision. Common Hall also participated in the election of London's two sheriffs and the City's four Members of Parliament.

The aldermanic committee was the powerhouse. Aldermen held office for life; when vacancies arose, candidates were selected by the Court of Aldermen, though officially put forward by the ward. Together with the Mayor and sheriffs – ordinarily chosen from among their ranks – the aldermen thus *de facto* formed a self-perpetuating oligarchy. Elevation came only after long service on the ladder of office, and hinged upon a reputation for prudence and upon meeting wealth qualifications that grew stiffer over the years.

City fathers wielded wide-ranging powers. Aldermen were responsible for order in their wards, and senior aldermen, as justices of the peace, presided over London's many courts and jails. They issued licences, heard grievances and frequently served as Members of Parliament. Aldermen also controlled the City's chest and charities. City income came from many sources, including properties and bequests; but the most useful source of corporate revenue was the Orphans' Fund. The City was the official guardian for all children whose citizen-fathers died before they married or came of age. Executors responsible for maintaining such orphans might transfer into the City's coffers the sums involved, these then being invested, loaned out, or drawn upon to cover current expenses.

Aldermen formed a redoubtable clique, reinforced through kinship and inter-marriage, and by life tenure. But it was a fluid élite, constantly replenished by an influx of young men from the countryside; for aldermanic dynasties rarely lasted very long (the City was run by institutions rather than by individuals). And checks and balances were provided by lesser bodies operating at parish and ward level.

Divided into wards (themselves split into precincts) and a separate patchwork of around 100 parishes, this profusion of local jurisdictions encouraged impressive levels of neighbourly participation. Attendance at the December wardmotes, at which elections took place, was compulsory. Prominent residents were appointed to ward offices like the alderman's deputy, who played a key role in settling squabbles; and the ward decided which householders served on the watch. To make up for these burdens, the December wardmote was the occasion for a binge.

Alongside the ward, parishes formed active communities, secular as well as ecclesiastical. Small by Continental standards, London's parishes handled local affairs and fostered a sense of identity. Usually a number of substantial parishioners formed an executive committee; meeting in the church's vestry, it soon adopted that name. Parish clerks registered baptisms and burials, while churchwardens and vestrymen handled the finances, dealt with nuisances and moral offences, and managed collective resources. The vestry of St Olave Southwark, for instance, owned property leased to parishioners, ranging from shacks let out to the poor to desirable buildings leased, not surprisingly, by vestrymen themselves. The Southwark vestry managed common land for grazing, maintained the parish pumps, and kept the butts in good repair for archery practice. Thanks to parochial bequests, St Olave's had acquired its own school, 'to teche the cheldarne of the sayd parryshe to wrete and rede and caste accoumptes'. (Was spelling on the curriculum?)

Parishes disbursed poor relief (as did livery companies), and the indigent received annual hand-outs of bread, fuel and sometimes clothing. Most parishes sent foundlings out to nurse to villages out of town – Hounslow, Walthamstow or Brentford – the country air being thought more wholesome. Sizeable sums were sometimes given to those in need. Peter Hartly, an elderly man in St Bartholomew Exchange, was paid a yearly pension of £2 3s 4d. In addition, the parish paid his rent, and when he fell sick an extra £2 10s was found for a nurse and a doctor. The parish bought him a shirt and two pairs of shoes at a cost of 9s 2d – a total of £7 2s 6d in one year, a sum roughly equivalent to a workman's wage.

The City's multilayered government, involving guilds, wards and parishes, created loyalties that gave Londoners, or at least citizens, feelings of fellowship and dignity. Householders belonged to nests of communities – neighbourhoods, parishes, wards and livery companies – that offered security in return for conformity and deference. Naturally, some belonged more than others. City fathers lorded it over civic parades and company feasts; they were running the show. Liverymen took their seats on the barges accompanying the Mayor to his oath-taking at Westminster. Mere house-holders, by contrast, participated largely by waiting on their betters, while recipients of charity were expected to bow and scrape. All the same, appeals to civic pride seem to have struck a chord. Tudor London was doubtless ruled by a hierarchy, but City fathers exercised their stewardship judiciously, avoiding gross profiteering and aggran-dizement and heedful of the prime need for stability. London escaped the sale of office and nepotism that corrupted local government in Spain and France. City fathers upheld what has been called the 'moral economy', preferring the old ways and prudent paths of consensus. Prerogative was thus curtailed by custom.

Respect between City and Crown helped maintain stability. (It may be no accident that Elizabeth's maternal great-great-grandfather had himself been a Lord Mayor.) After Henry VIII, Tudor monarchs abstained from opportunistic meddling, never imposing Crown governors in the manner of the *corregidores* in Castile. In return the City staged lavish displays of loyalty, exalting their monarch's generosity. With pardonable patriotic exaggeration, one author noted that London was governed

not by cruell viceroyes, as in Naples or Millaine, neither by proude Podesta, as be most cities in Italie, or insolent Lieutenantes or presidentes, as are sundry Cities in France ... but by a man of trade or a meere marchant, who notwithstanding, during the time of his magistracie, carieth himselfe with ... honourable magnificence in his port, and ensignes of estate.

The dynastic and ecclesiastical stabilization of Elizabeth's reign clearly worked to London's benefit, and institutional resilience was also important: civic bodies proved adequate to the administrative and financial challenges the growing metropolis posed.

The absence of grass-roots rebellion suggests that, though run by the rich, City institutions were experienced not as alien and despotic but as in some measure respon-sible and responsive. Young men could aspire to office in a system with a graded power hierarchy stressing reciprocal obligations and expectations. And not least, London was conspicuously governed by Londoners, by an élite recruited from within the freemen body – 'an incouragement,' judged Recorder Croke, mouthing the pieties of the times, 'to the one to governe well, a provocacion to the other to obey well, the band of love &

societie knitting both together, banishing discord, the poison of all commen weales'. Having risen through the ranks, aldermen showed solicitude towards fellow citizens, hearing their grievances, if not always remedying them.

Such prudence proved its worth in difficult times, notably the 1590s, when inflation, unemployment and plague created tensions exploited by the Earl of Essex in his turbulent court feud with Robert Cecil. Essex had a London following that he hoped to stir up in his attempted coup in 1601, when he paraded down Fleet Street with his followers. His failure shows the resilience of London's governing system. Over the next centuries, London was to prove remarkably proficient at riding out storms.

The City's success was, however, partly due to turning its back on a problem that in time became a festering sore. Settlement was expanding beyond the walls and even the wards. Those outside lay under no real government or economic regulation at all. And there loomed a further anomaly. A weak link in City government had been the liberties – that is, the private concessions held by lay and particularly ecclesiastical proprietors, where the Guildhall's writ did not normally run. Beyond the walls, Whitefriars, St Katharine's east of the Tower, the priories and nunneries in Clerkenwell, and St Bartholomew's Hospital; across the river, St Mary Overie in Southwark; and, within the walls, the Black Friars, the Austin Friars, the sanctuary of St Martin's-le-Grand, the priory of Holy Trinity Aldgate – all these and more had enjoyed liberties which passed into various hands after the Dissolution. There were also non-monastic liberties and precincts: the Duchy of Lancaster in the Savoy, the liberty of the Rolls, Ely House or Rents, and the Inns of Court. All these precincts were, in significant respects, exempt from mayoral jurisdiction, and were feared as breeding-grounds for blackguards – and plague:

> The city's sure in progress, I surmise,
> Or going to revel it in some disorder,
> Without the walls, without the liberties,
> Where she need fear nor Mayor nor Recorder.

City fathers chose to turn a blind eye to the suburbs. This expedient avoided direct confrontation, but in time it created the most bizarre paradox: the fact that a majority of the inhabitants lay (by aldermanic preference) beyond municipal government, in effect ungoverned. London was on the road to becoming a small, highly regulated, corporate City lapped by a turbulent metropolitan sea. The predicament was tricky. If the City fathers had sought to control those purlieus, the burdens would have proved onerous. On the other hand, if peace and prosperity were to prevail, stability was essential.

This dilemma surfaced in the writings of the time. A lurid literature arose teeming with low-life characters: rogues and frauds, cheats and bawds. Chock-full of wealthy blockheads readily parted from their money, the capital, it was claimed, was very heaven for cutpurses and 'cony-catchers'. *A Manifest Detection* reported in 1552 that pickpockets and swindlers had parcelled up the town, some working St Paul's, others Westminster, some Cheapside, others Southwark. Robert Greene, Thomas Dekker and other journalists dashed off 'penny-dreadful' pamphlets itemizing the wicked ways of underworld London. The cony-catchers, explained Greene in *A Notable Discovery of Cozenage*, were 'apparelled like honest civil gentlemen or goodfellows, with a smooth face, as if butter would not melt in their mouths'; but

after dinner when the clients are come from Westminster Hall and are at leisure to walk up and down Paul's, Fleet Street, Holborn, the Strand and such common-haunted places, where these cozening companies attend only to spy out a prey ... as soon as they see a plain country fellow, well and cleanly apparelled, either in a coat of homespun russet or of frieze, as the time requires and a side-pouch at his side – 'There is a cony' saith one.

Their revelations of vice and crime find some echo in official records. A Bridewell inmate reported in 1576 that thieves gathered on Saturday nights in a barn in Tothill Street, Westminster; a gang met with 'diverse whores' in a Lambeth cowshed; and Lord Burghley was informed in 1585 of forty-five 'masterless men and cut-purses, whose practice is to rob gentlemen's chambers and artificers' shops'.

Did the capital really sport a picturesque brotherhood of malefactors (like the one 'Deformed', of whom the watchmen in *Much Ado About Nothing* had heard tell), or was this but the tabloid journalism of the day? And what about the tales of growing hordes of 'masterless men' – vagrants, aliens, Anabaptists and other heretics, huddling in secret conventicles?

Court records afford no proof of organized crime, and little sign of uproar and riot. One serious incident flared early in the century, the 'Evil May Day Riots' in May 1517, targeted against foreigners. A mob of apprentices was stirred to action by a certain Dr Beal, preaching at St Paul's Cross. The authorities overreacted. The Lieutenant of the Tower let off guns, and the Earls of Surrey and Suffolk brought in troops, quelling the outburst and taking 400 prisoners. Some of the leaders were hanged, drawn and quartered, and their remains gibbeted.

Thereafter Tudor London was remarkably disturbance-free; most subsequent ruckuses involved little more than juvenile pranks and drunken loutishness. For instance, after a 'disorder' in March 1576, householders were warned that their apprentices must not 'misuse, molest, or evil treat any servant, page, or lackey of any nobleman, gentleman, or other going in the streets'. Apprentices were involved in a fracas with noblemen's attendants in 1581, and twelve months later 'an affray' arose among watermen at Lion Key, by London Bridge. As always, aliens made prime targets: 'They care little for foreigners,' the Duke of Würtemberg grumbled in 1592, 'but scoff and laugh at them; and moreover one dare not oppose them, else the street-boys and apprentices collect together in immense crowds and strike to the right and left unmercifully without regard to person.' Then as now, football spelt trouble. Youths were barred from playing in January 1586, and again in April 1590, when three journeymen were imprisoned for 'outrageously and riotously behaving themselves at football play in Cheapside'.

A traditional apprentice holiday, Shrove Tuesday sometimes got out of hand. In 1578 assemblies were banned during Shrovetide, to prevent 'great disorders, uncomely and dangerous behaviours ... in the fields and elsewhere and especially in Moorfields and Finsbury Fields' (significantly beyond the City). Five youths were imprisoned in 1595 after Shrove Tuesday disturbances on Bankside. From time to time Southwark's brothels were attacked – the London waterman-poet John Taylor noted that on Shrove Tuesday 'youths arm'd with cudgels, stones, hammers, rules, trowels and hand-saws, put playhouses to the sack and bawdy-houses to the spoil'.

On the south bank, disorderly behaviour, if not exactly licensed, was borne with a certain resignation. Safely outside the City's jurisdiction, Bankside had emerged as the prime site for bull- and bear-baiting and whoring. Like their Continental colleagues, London's magistrates had taken the view that prostitution, though sinful, was, like sin, ineradicable and a money-spinner. Hence 'stews' (brothels) ought to be licensed and located where they would cause least trouble. Traditionally they had to be painted white and carry a distinctive mark; one of the most celebrated was the 'Cardinal's Hat', for most were on lands owned by the Bishop of Winchester (hence the whores were known as Winchester geese).

In the light of the syphilis wave, the closing of Southwark's stews was ordered in 1546 by, of all people, Henry VIII (himself a sufferer). The decree lapsed on his death, and the bordellos reopened under Edward. Mary Tudor then once more closed them, but they reopened on Elizabeth's accession and prospered. Both Philip Henslowe, the theatre impresario, and his son-in-law, the actor Edward Alleyn, engaged in the trade – by tradition, whoring and acting went together. Alleyn also ran a bear-garden. Bawds and strumpets were occasionally prosecuted, the whores being committed to Bridewell.

Southwark saturnalia were doubtless stoked by the inns and hostelries that had gathered there because it was beyond City limits – and also the spot where the roads from Sussex, Surrey and Kent converged. Chaucer immortalized the Tabard, the departure-point for Canterbury-bound pilgrims, but along Southwark High Street there were also the Spurre, the Christopher, the Bull, the Queen's Head, the George, the Hart, the King's Head, and the Anchor, not to mention the Gun, Castle, Bullhead, Crane, Beerpot, Vine, Elephant, Sugar Loaf, Three Tuns, Bear and Barge. And, to handle trouble from its bear-pits, stews, taverns and (later) playhouses, Southwark sported no fewer than five prisons – the Clink, the Compter, the King's Bench, the Marshalsea (immortalized by Dickens) and the White Lyon. First mentioned in 1509, the Clink was for revellers who broke the peace; it survived into the eighteenth century as a debtors' prison, to be burnt down in the Gordon Riots.

Bankside, 1560, showing bear-baiting arenas in the foreground (Guildhall Library)

Holiday scuffles, football hooliganism, brawls with whores – these are the frolics of urban youth. What records of such incidents highlight is the law-abiding if raucous tenor of workaday London life, the infrequency of serious crime and strife, and the effectiveness of the agencies of law and order. Shakespeare might pillory the watch as dull Dogberry and vacuous Verges, but in truth London possessed a thorough policing apparatus. Assisted by constables and beadles, aldermen maintained order in their wards through the wardmote inquest, which handled local matters from health hazards to family feuds. Within the wards, a grid of over 200 tiny precincts (averaging 120 square yards) was policed by constables and the watch. Clergy and churchwardens investigated drunkenness, fornication, bastardy and other moral offences. Godly Protestants accepted that they were their brothers' keepers. Persistent offenders could be sent to Bridewell.

Beggars, however, were growing more troublesome with the tidal wave of migration. In his *Description of England*, written in the 1570s, William Harrison guessed there might be 'above ten thousand' beggars. Things were worse in the troubled 1590s. St Botolph Aldgate, for example, recorded the burials between 1593 and 1598 of:

> Edward Ellis a vagrant who died in the street.
> A young man not known who died in a hay-loft.
> A cripple that died in the street before John Awsten's door.
> A maid, a vagrant, unknown, who died in the street
>   near the Postern.
> A young man in a white canvas doublet . . .
>   being vagrant and died in the street near Sparrow's
>   corner being in the precinct near the Tower.
> A young man vagrant having no abiding place . . .
>   who died in the street before the door of Joseph Hayes,
>   a brazier dwelling at the sign of Robin Hood in the High
>   Street. . . . He was about 18 years old. I could not
>   learn his name.

Such mentions of the unknown and homeless show that some of the metropolitan masses were adrift and falling through the elaborate relief nets. Bridewell attests increasing vagrancy. Sixty-nine vagrants were handled by the Court of Governors in 1560/61, but 815 in 1624/5 – almost a twelvefold rise. Even so the totals are hardly huge, and overall Tudor London proved remarkably effective in assimilating migrant workers and teenagers, thanks to a buoyant labour market, mechanisms for betterment, and parochial policing. Despite rising numbers of the needy, respectable artisans remained in a majority: there was no violent polarization between rich and poor, but a graded community of stations, for most males could hope to join a guild and thus get a foot on the civic ladder. In any year, about one in ten of London's householders was holding some kind of local office, and the world of petty capitalism was open, because start-up costs were low: 'for the man who sweated out his years of apprenticeship and then journey work,' writes Steve Rappaport of craftsmen gaining the freedom in 1551–3, 'the odds were seven to one that he would become a householder and have his own shop and then were roughly one in three that one day, if he remained alive and in London, he would wear the livery and thus enter the élite of his company'. While never forgetting the sufferings of the silent, a combination of economic opportunities and energetic paternalism seems to have headed off any looming crisis of destitution or disorder.

*

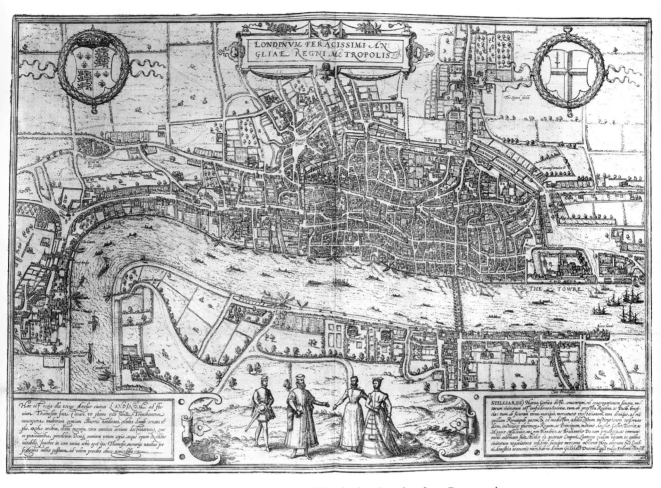

One of the best contemporary maps of Elizabethan London from Braun and
Hohenberg's *Civitates Orbis Terrarum*, 1575

As London grew and grew rich, it also assumed European stature in culture. Contemporaries made play of the symbiosis between city and civilization; it was, one Tudor
writer opined, 'through the monuments of writing' that men were 'moved ... to build
cities'; bards, thought the poet Thomas Lodge, were the 'first raisers of cities'. Thanks
to the Renaissance, literary forms derived from antiquity and Italian humanists gave
Londoners new cultural tools for fashioning themselves and carving out careers.
Literacy rose rapidly, alongside the expansion of schools and printed books. St Paul's
School, reorganized by John Colet, Dean of St Paul's, in 1509 for 'little Londoners
especially', introduced the humanistic curriculum to England and became the flagship
in a flotilla of schools, including Merchant Taylors', Charterhouse and Christ's Hospital

in Newgate Street. Founded as an orphanage in 1553, this last soon acquired its school, with a grammar master, writing master and music master. Westminster School evolved from a school for clerks attached to the Benedictine abbey of Westminster. At the Dissolution, the school continued under the humanist headmaster Alexander Nowell. City merchants collaborated with godly preachers in establishing parish grammar schools. Taking time off from his interests in the stage, bear-baiting and brothels, Edward Alleyn founded Dulwich College; in nearby Camberwell, the Puritan vicar Edward Wilson obtained a charter from James I to set up a parish grammar school for village boys to learn Latin and the Scriptures. Civic pride and Protestant piety spurred educational foundations.

By the early seventeenth century, up to three-quarters of London's tradesmen and artisans could sign their name, as could half of a sample of craftsmen and shopkeepers in Stepney and Whitechapel. Nearly half of those sentenced to death by Middlesex juries between 1612 and 1614 pleaded benefit of clergy (that is, gave proof of literacy) – and got off with lesser punishment. Female literacy came later, rising from about 10 per cent in 1650 to nearly 50 per cent in the 1690s.

London was the cradle of printing. In 1485 William Caxton, governor of the Merchant Adventurers at Bruges, set up his press at the Red Pale in Westminster. He paid tribute to the City in one of his first books: 'my mother, of whom I have received my nurture and living'. His apprentice, Wynkyn de Worde, moved to Fleet Street at the sign of the Sun near Shoe Lane, with another shop at St Paul's Churchyard. He printed nearly 800 books. With the incorporation in 1557 of the Company of Stationers – a measure designed to strengthen censorship – printing became a virtual London monopoly. In 1585 twenty-four printers were operating in town; by 1649 there were sixty. Stationers and booksellers gathered round St Paul's Churchyard and Paternoster Row. (The Row was named after the old trade of bead-making, for use in rosaries: with the Reformation, the trade became obsolete. The book thus literally and figuratively displaced the bead.) Demand was brisk for devotional and doctrinal works, and print promoted Protestantism. The remarkable diaries of Nehemiah Wallington, a London shoemaker, born in 1598, give some idea of the craving for spiritual reading among avid Puritans. But a lowbrow printed culture also emerged – broadsides, folk-tales, improving fables and fairy stories, ballads at a penny, almanacs at twopence, chap-books threepence.

Humanist education raised the status of the professions. Though London lacked a university, learned institutions were set up like the Royal College of Physicians (founded 1518) and Gresham College (1579), the latter, created by Thomas Gresham, offering public lectures in divinity, law, astronomy, music, geometry, rhetoric and physic. London, judged Sir Donald Lupton, had become the 'gallimaufry of all the sciences, arts, and trades'.

London grew renowned, or notorious, for its lawyers, trained in the four Inns of Court – the Inner and Middle Temples, Lincoln's Inn and Gray's Inn – or in the lesser Inns of Chancery: Clifford's Inn in Fleet Street, Serjeant's Inn in Chancery Lane and Thavies, Furnival's, Barnard's and Staple Inns, all in Holborn. The oft-restored timber Tudor façade of Staple Inn survives, opposite the end of Gray's Inn Road (it just escaped the Great Fire of 1666).

Evolving from the twelfth century, the Inns reached their apogee in Elizabeth's day, comprising, in Stow's words, 'a whole university, as it were, of students, practisers and pleaders, and judges of the laws of this realm'. Organized on university lines, with courts and halls, the Inns had up to 1,000 students in residence during term-time, for studying law was thought the right grounding for public life – and, in any case, in a litigious age, legal know-how was essential to the landed gentry.

Bristling with learned jurists and ambitious gentlemen, the Inns transformed the Fleet Street and Holborn areas into a lively gentleman's quarter. The benchers stimulated luxury trades and spiced intellectual life, imparting wit, eloquence and style. The Inns' location between the City and Westminster – marking the situation of law between business and politics – created a neighbourhood with an air of its own, nurturing writers, poets and wits: town thereby became the nursery of the intellectual class.

The court, meanwhile, attracted talent. The roughly 1,500 members of the royal household itself, located first in St James's and later in Whitehall Palace, represented only the tip of the employment and excitement generated by the court. The pursuit of patronage, contacts and matrimonial alliance induced the ambitious to flock to Westminster – alongside the aristocracy, some half of whom owned London houses, a few on the sites of old Strand episcopal palaces. Their presence generated conspicuous consumption, thriving on luxury goods imported by merchants or wrought by craftsmen. The fopperies of the age required countless jewellers, hat-trimmers, button-makers, collar-makers, starch-makers, ruff-makers and others.

The court and the noble houses offered patronage to poets, musicians, secretaries, tutors, chaplains and toadies. Sir Philip Sidney's literary circle at Leicester House included Edmund Spenser, a journeyman's son from Merchant Taylors' School. A more *outré* clique formed around the Earl of Northumberland and Sir Walter Ralegh, including Christopher Marlowe and George Chapman, translator of Homer. Between them, Westminster and the Inns of Court thus attracted the wits and created an audience for the arts. Street culture, for its part, upheld plebeian traditions of jest, quips and fable, while songs and ditties were peddled in markets and chorused in alehouses, where low and high cultures often met: the Mermaid Inn in Bread Street numbered among its clientele the likes of Ralegh, Donne, Jonson, Beaumont and Shakespeare.

Theatre flourished. Entertainments had long been performed at the Clerkenwell pump; passion plays were enacted at St Peter upon Cornhill; and the City's galleried inn-yards housed wandering mummers. But, stimulated by the formation of companies of players under court patronage, the drama came of age under Elizabeth, when eleven theatres were opened in the unregulated liberties and suburbs, including the Rose, the Swan and the Globe.

In 1576 the actor James Burbage, whose patron was the Earl of Leicester, borrowed money to erect London's first theatre. To escape the strait-laced City fathers, he put it up in Shoreditch, on the site of the former Holywell Priory. Close by, where Curtain Road now lies, a second theatre rose, the Curtain (supposedly so named because it was the first theatre to use one). Playwrights migrated to Shoreditch – Robert Greene, Thomas Nashe, George Peele and Thomas Kyd; in 1587 Christopher Marlowe, just down from Cambridge, offered *Tamburlaine the Great* to Philip Henslowe, manager of the Curtain. That same year Henslowe acquired the Rose theatre on Bankside (partially excavated in recent years). A typical entrepreneur of the day, as well as deriving part of his income from the Bankside stews he also traded in goatskins and dabbled as a pawnbroker and moneylender.

At the time of the Armada, the young William Shakespeare reached London, joining the Chamberlain's men and giving performances at court. Some years earlier James Burbage had built a theatre in the precincts of the Black Friars, where sanctuary still existed. Here Burbage's company prospered, despite City attempts to uproot them, and Shakespeare joined them for a time. In 1599 Shakespeare's company was playing at Burbage's Shoreditch theatre, and then Burbage moved to Bankside, near the Rose, and set about building the Globe. The Burbage family owned half that property, and Shakespeare and four other associates each received a tenth. The Globe saw Shakespeare's greatest triumphs.

Of the other Bankside theatres, the Swan was briefly successful but then decayed; its swansong came in 1613. After 1600 Henslowe and Alleyn, stung by the Globe's success, built the Fortune just outside Aldersgate. A popular venue, it burnt down in 1621 but was rebuilt, surviving till 1649, when the Zeal-Of-The-Land-Busys finally had their way. Also destroyed by fire, in 1613, the Globe was quickly rebuilt, standing until the Commonwealth, when all the London theatres were closed in the name of religious correctness and for fear of sedition.

The City was itself a theatre in its own right, a scene of conflicting voices, styles and purposes; the streets sometimes became pure pageant, with the Corporation, guilds and parishioners combining in ceremony and song to celebrate civic events and calendar customs – festivities that were still going strong under the Georges, and even into the Victorian age. Shrove Tuesday had its rowdy side, but it was also a day when Londoners engaged in harmless merriment. In his *Jack a Lent* (1620), John Taylor described the day as a feast of 'boiling and broiling . . . roasting and toasting . . . stewing and brewing'. London apprentices guzzled pancakes and amused themselves in the sport of whipping cocks.

The Reformation notwithstanding, many old religious festivals continued, with parochial parades and feastings. Ascension Day involved beating the bounds, processions and jollifications: churchwardens' accounts record payments for ribbons and decorations, bread, cheese and ale. May Day was celebrated with dancing and maypoles, especially in the Strand. Walking to Westminster on 1 May 1667, Pepys recorded 'meeting many milkmaids with their garlands upon their pails dancing with a fiddler before them'. There was also a May Fair, held around what would become Curzon Street, with dancing and puppet-shows. At Midsummer the Mayor and his entourage walked through the City; processions were held, with 'great and ugly giants marching as if they were alive and armed at all points'; Londoners decked their houses with fennel; and in 1694 John Aubrey spied a score of young women 'in the pasture behind Montague House . . . looking for a coal under the root of a plantain, to put under their heads that night, and they should dream who would be their husbands'. St Bartholomew's Day, 25 August, was celebrated at Bartholomew Fair, Smithfield, with rope-dancers, puppets, farces and the gargantuan gorging of roast pork. Permitting apprentices to let off steam, such holidays also provided occasions for spontaneous social mixing. At a time when educated culture was becoming more élitist and courtly, street culture remained inclusive, glorying in the City itself.

A remarkable window on to, and elegy for, Shakespeare's London is offered by John Stow's *Survay of London*. An antiquarian in his seventies, Stow had spent years strolling the lanes and poring over old records and manuscripts for his tome in which he 'attempted the discovery of London, my native soil and country'. A tailor's son, born in 1525 in the parish of St Michael Cornhill, young Stow had gossiped with greybeards who remembered Richard III; he lived to see James I ascend the throne. He recorded a London shedding its medieval face and taking modern shape. As we have already noted, he did not like what he saw. Painstakingly documented, the *Survay* was the work of one who rued the destruction of a noble city by greed.

Relics of the fair city of his youth survived, Stow maintained, and he could admire certain developments, including splendid merchant houses from Baynard's Castle to Coldharbour, in Limestreet and Basinghall wards, and in commercial Candlewick, Fenchurch and Lombard Streets. From 'Crosby place up to Leadenhall corner, and so down Gracechurch Street', he reported, lay 'fair and large-built houses for merchants and such like'. At the City's north-western confines, from Cripplegate out to the Barbican and east along Beech Lane, nestled 'summer houses for pleasure' and 'beautiful houses of stone, brick, and timber'; Stow was probably having a chuckle when he complained that such summerhouses were 'like Midsummer pageants, with towers, turrets, and chimney tops, not so much for use of profit as for show or pleasure, betraying the vanity of men's minds'.

But the London Stow painted had suffered from speculators. Once spacious and dignified, it was being vandalized, he alleged, by rapacious landlords, profiteering out of jerry-built dwellings and foul industrial premises. East of the Tower, the area around St Katharine's was 'pestered with small tenements and homely cottages, having inhabitants, English and strangers, more in number than some cities in England'. Further north, Petty France on the banks of Houndsditch was built by sharks 'that more regarded their own private gain than the common good of the city'.

Stow's lament might be put less moralistically. London was expanding at a phenomenal rate. Densification within the walls was matched by explosive suburban growth. The river economy, aided by royal shipyards at Deptford and Woolwich, was tugging development eastward, and buildings were crowding the river from the Tower to Wapping, especially nearest the walls. Open spaces remained in the northern suburbs – the Artillery Yard near Spitalfields, the archery ground in Finsbury Field, and Moorfields, a former fen laid out in 1607 with walks – but development had surged north to Hoxton, to Old Street, along the unsavoury Turnmill Street to Clerkenwell, and out of Holborn toward St Giles-in-the-Fields (still in the fields). And beyond these built-up areas, hamlets and shanties were beginning to ring the metropolis.

Stow read change as decay: more meant worse. Troubles were indeed brewing. Population rise was producing shocking price inflation, especially in foodstuffs. The immigrant tide increased demand for produce while keeping wages down. By 1600, food prices had increased fourfold while wages had fallen in real terms, and the mixed blessings of London's growth were evident in a harvest of poverty, unemployment, unrest and disease.

Expansion posed further problems, for example with water supply. In 1572 Pieter Morice, a German, using a wheel turned by the tidal rush through London Bridge, impressed the Mayor and aldermen by shooting a water jet over St Magnus church. Granted a 500-year lease of an arch of the bridge, he had water pumped up to Leadenhall, the highest ground in the City, where he installed a standard, 'plentifully serving to the commodity of the inhabitants near adjoining in their houses'. Soon these pumps became inadequate, and recourse was had to constructing a forty-mile canal to bring water from Hertfordshire. Likewise in the 1590s poor harvests and short supplies required the City to lay in vast corn stocks in the municipal granaries. Coal was replacing the dwindling wood supply, but both were dear. Salubrity was threatened. The Walbrook and the Fleet rivers had become sewers; waste littered the streets; epidemics like the sweating sickness took a heavy toll, and bubonic plague visited regularly: it is estimated that 17,500 died in 1563, 23,000 in 1593, 30,000 in 1603, and

40,000 in 1625. None, however, was as disastrous as the great onset of 1665, which took perhaps 80,000 lives.

Ironically, Stow himself became a victim of the bitter times he deplored. At seventy-nine he was forced to seek a royal licence to beg. Issued by James I, this described him as 'a very aged and worthy member of our city of London, who hath for forty-five years to his great charge and with neglect of his ordinary means of maintenance, for the general good as well as posterity of the present age, compiled and published divers necessary books and chronicles'. Dying in 1605, he was buried in St Andrew Undershaft, where every year the monument depicting him writing is provided with a new quill pen, *pour encourager les autres*.

If Stow, like all antiquaries, was nostalgic and no enthusiast for 'the most scoffing, respectless and unthankful age that ever was', for another contemporary antiquarian London's rise could be related with pride. In the eyes of William Camden, London, 'the epitome or breviary of all Britain, the seat of the British Empire, and the king of England's chamber', had become a glory:

A long time it would ask to discourse particularly of the good laws and the orders of the laudable government, of the port and dignity of the mayor and aldermen, of their forward service and loyalty to their prince, of the citizens' courtesy, the fair building and costly furniture, the breed of excellent and choice wits, their gardens in the suburbs full of dainty arbours and banqueting rooms, stored also with strange herbs from foreign countries, of the multitude, strength, and furniture of their ships, the incredible store of all sorts of merchandise (two hundred thousand broad cloths, beside other Antwerp alone hath received from hence every year) and of the superabundance of all things which belong to the furniture or necessity of man's life.

CHAPTER FOUR

War, Plague and Fire

Writing under Charles I, the courtier-historian Peter Heylin protested that London 'is grown at last too big for the Kingdom', developing a simile doomed to become the great cliché:

Great Towns in the body of a State are like the *Spleen* or *Melt* in the body natural; the monstrous growth of which impoverisheth all the rest of the Members, by drawing to it all the *animal* and *vital* spirits, which should give nourishment unto them; And in the end cracked or surcharged by its own fulness, not only sends unwholsom fumes and *vapours* unto the *head* and heavy *pangs* unto the *heart*, but draws a *consumption* on it self.

Anxieties ran high about the metropolitan 'spleen' and its distension; London was perceived as a parasite, or as poisoning the kingdom. 'Certainly the overgrowth of great Cities is of consequence,' Heylin continued, 'not only in regard of famin ... but in respect of the irreparable danger of insurrections.' Such fears had a basis in demographic fact: the capital was ballooning out of all proportion to its sister cities. In 1500 London had been around three or four times the size of the largest provincial town at that time, Norwich; two centuries later it was *fifteen* times bigger – beyond comparison the key market, manufactory and port. London shot up the European urban league from a position of seventh or eighth biggest in 1550 to third in 1600 (exceeded by Paris and Naples) and second in 1650, behind Paris alone. From 1700 the monster city had no superior in Christendom.

The capital was not merely expanding; it was bursting out of its shell, ceasing to be the familiar old walled city. The line of the walls was becoming a historical monument. Stretching down-river, the east side was assuming a character all of its own, as an industrial suburb dominated by shipping, wharves and boat-building, with swarms of artisans, mariners and migrants. And Westminster too was coming into its own as a town, as distinct from being greensward planted with an abbey, a royal precinct and a

Old London Bridge, 1624

lustrous border of palaces. Indeed, regarding developments west, West End begins to be an apter term than Westminster.

In 1560 three-quarters of London's population had lived within the City. But the balance was shifting. Just over a century later, only a quarter of the metropolis lived within the bars – the jurisdiction of the wards – a third were settled in the eastern suburbs, while the northern and southern suburbs and Westminster could each claim about an eighth. In the emergent metropolis the City-within-the-bars was ceasing to be the indisputable heartland. It no longer made sense to think of London proper (within the walls or wards) and London peripheral: the quarters of the new metropolis were less inner and outer than east, central and west, north and south, distinguished by different manufacturing, commercial, residential and political complexions. In short, the town which, as drawn by Wyngaerde, had still around 1550 been a walled medieval municipality, with a castle standing guard at either end, was becoming dispersed – not a head and body but a federation of zones.

Population rise was due solely to migration: this was provoked by economic aspirations but also by the political and courtly allure of Westminster. London's combination of economic and political pre-eminence was uncommon in *ancien régime* Europe, for capital and commercial cities rarely coincided – witness Valladolid, Madrid and Seville, or Paris, Lyons and Bordeaux. London's exceptional economic role will be examined later; here its political pull will be explored – London as the nerve-centre of administration and the law courts, and as a magnet for magnates.

The civil service made a sizeable but, at least before 1700, not a huge impact upon Westminster's growth, for, unlike France and Spain, the English state was not maggoty with functionaries and sinecurists. Under Elizabeth, senior officials totalled somewhat over 400, and Charles I had roughly as many in Whitehall, with a comparable number of subalterns. Including the private staffs of top men like the Cecils, the tally of bureaucrats directly involved in state affairs could scarcely have exceeded 1,500. The civil service expanded after 1650, however, and especially after the Glorious Revolution of 1688, when military and colonial expansion demanded far more administrators; by 1725 there were around 3,000 career officials in Westminster, and Georgian politics proved a bonanza for sinecurists. Parliamentary sessions also drew the élite to town: between 300 and 500 MPs needed to live on and off in the capital, after 1640 (and especially after 1688) on an increasingly regular basis.

There was also the court, which was bigger than the civil service and growing appreciably under the early Stuarts. Approaching 1,000 in Elizabeth's reign, the monarch's household and entourage more than doubled under Charles I. And the body of peers with a toe-hold in London rose correspondingly, from about thirty in the 1560s to ninety in the 1630s; by then the resident gentry ran to several hundred. Many of these had links to the Inns of Court, which experienced a fivefold leap in admissions between 1550 and 1650, housing in term-time over 1,000 lawyers and students. Legal business boomed – pleas at King's Bench rose tenfold during the sixteenth century – and the legal profession expanded to meet the taste for litigation. In view of the abnormally centralized nature of the politico-legal system – unlike France, England had no provincial *parlements* – only in London were there rich pickings for lawyers and career opportunities for notaries, scriveners, secretaries, chaplains, ushers, heralds, minstrels, grooms, agents and others whose job it was to wait upon the great.

The presence of the Quality was making the West End a happy hunting-ground for all manner of professionals. By the early seventeenth century there were already some 500 medical practitioners in London – a century later courtly physicians such as Sir Hans Sloane (after whom the square is named) could expect incomes running into thousands. Specialized needs were catered for by tutors, musicians and painters, and London was acclaimed for its astrologers such as Simon Forman and William Lilly. As the single city where (before 1695) commercial publishing was lawful, London drew the nation's professional writers, who congregated around Fleet Street. Ambitious clergymen loitered in the capital, courting prelates, seeking preferment. Jewellers, engravers, heralds, peruke-makers, booksellers, art-dealers and other experts and luxury dealers aimed to satisfy sophisticated tastes, in turn sucking in a country clientele – the gentleman wanting his portrait painted, a new suit of armour, or some theological tracts to chew on during the winter. Squires weary of the idiocy of rural life rode up to town for business and pleasure – to dabble in politics, beg favours from the great, sell acres, borrow gold, arrange marriages for daughters, purchase fine fabrics, see the sights, and sup with boon companions in the dozens of hostelries, inns and (from mid-century) coffee-houses. Such men required eligible lodgings, eating-houses, elegant tailors, streetwise gentlemen's men, and cooks, tradesmen, shop-keepers, menials and porters, to say nothing of hangers-on, clients and visitors.

With families and retainers included, by the late seventeenth century there were at least 25,000 people resident (permanently or temporarily) west of the walls by reason of public affairs, professional business, the pursuit of fashion, and all the employment these created.

Westminster grew more regal, fit for a king. Charles Stuart loved stateliness, restyling Whitehall in Continental taste with the aid of the brilliant Royal Surveyor General Inigo Jones, a clothworker's son and devoted disciple of Palladio who was England's first outstanding native architect. Jones's first architectural commission had been a lodge outside London, in Greenwich, for James I's Queen – the Queen's House (now part of the Maritime Museum). Designed in the Palladian manner, its exquisite classicism marked a radical break with the fussy, irregular vernacular prevalent in the Elizabethan era.

Jones's masterpiece was the Banqueting House, completed around 1622 – now the sole survivor of a suite of new buildings erected, or for the most part merely envisaged, in Whitehall to replace an Elizabethan construction that James dismissed as an 'old, rotten, slight-builded shed'. Jones used a Palladian double cube for the galleried hall (110 feet long, and half that height and breadth), with spacious windows. The ceiling was covered with pictures by Rubens – a mark of England's continuing dependence on foreign masters. London's first purely Palladian building, the Banqueting House is still a revelation.

Jones planned the rebuilding of Whitehall as a magnificent Italianate palace that, if completed, would have stood comparison with the Escorial and provided competition for the later Versailles. It proved a pipedream. Nevertheless, the court grew in éclat. Whereas Elizabeth's entourage had been largely peripatetic, serviced by assorted aristocratic seats, the early Stuarts made Whitehall the permanent nucleus of state occasions, royal entertainments and diplomacy. Magnificent masques and Charles I's superior artistic patronage established the court as the fount of conspicuous con-sumption, ringed by grandees and all their demands for luxury services.

In 1662 William Petty wrote that London was reaching westwards to escape 'the fumes, steams and stinks of the whole easterly pyle'. He was right, and the east–west axis, the mile from St Paul's to Westminster, assumed supreme symbolic significance.

Immediately beyond the wall by Ludgate, the banks of the Fleet river presented squalid overspill, tenements and squats from Holborn bridge south to Fleet Street, while down to the Thames spread the infamous liberty of 'Alsatia', long disreputable, the London no one owned and everyone feared. Ever after, the valley of the Fleet, from Blackfriars right up to St Pancras, was to remain at best unfashionable and at worst squalid. But, once this slum strip was negotiated, things steadily improved as one cantered west. There was the Temple and, to its north, Gray's Inn. Haunt of lawyers and leisured gentry, High Holborn and Chancery Lane had a stylish, raffish air. And the atmosphere grew better still upon reaching the Strand, with its mansions dominating the river. Linking City and court, the Strand was the top spot for the beau monde deserting a walled city increasingly dismissed as dilapidated and pestilential. Landowners began to espy the profit and prestige of speculative Strand-side building. High-class property development was given the nod by James I. Elizabeth had banned building in the suburbs; James sold licences for otherwise illegal projects, justifying his actions with his famous comparison of London with Rome:

As it was said of the first Emperor of Rome that he had found the city of Rome of Brick and left it of marble, so Wee, whom God hath honoured to be the first of Britaine, might be able to say in some proportion, that we had found our Cities and suburbs of London of sticks, and left them of bricke, being a material farre more durable, safe from fire and beautiful and magnificent.

Around 1609 Robert Cecil, Earl of Salisbury and Viscount Cranborne, received James's consent to develop Swan Close east of Leicester Fields. Over the next ten years, Salisbury developed properties around St Martin's Lane, substantial residences occupied by the Quality, today remembered by Cecil Court, New Row and the Marquis of Salisbury pub in St Martin's Lane and, to the north, by Cranbourn Street. Great Newport Street was an offshoot, built after 1612 when Salisbury granted a builder a lease to 'sett up severall substantiall and well built dwelling houses'. Their tenants, however, allowed them to 'go to ruine', and the Earl soon had to replace them with new buildings that retained their cachet through the eighteenth century – Sir Joshua Reynolds lived there.

In 1631 Francis Russell, 4th Earl of Bedford, whose forebears had had the foresight to acquire from Henry VIII the magnificent Covent ('convent') Garden from the abbey of Westminster, decided to develop the site. Charles I instructed the Earl to maintain Long Acre on his land. Bedford bargained: he would 'pave and keep it as well as any street in London', provided that the King granted him 'leave to build'. The Earl duly received a licence, though the scope of Bedford's plans led the Privy Council to insist on the involvement of the Royal Surveyor, Inigo Jones. Constructed probably with Paris's Place des Vosges in mind, the Piazza – surely Jones's brainchild – was surrounded by arcaded housing and a Tuscan church, spectacular not least for its plainness. Money perhaps had the last word. Eager to maximize returns, the 5th Earl of Bedford did not leave Jones's square as a residential oasis but obtained a licence to hold a fruit and vegetable market on the site. A hundred years later the gross invasion of trade into a sophisticated square would not have made commercial, let alone aesthetic or social, sense. As pioneering aristocratic estate-developers, however, the Bedfords were anxious to recoup their outlays (the 4th Earl had sunk about £13,000 in the project).

The Piazza proved a great success, and Great Queen Street (named after Henrietta Maria), King Street, Henrietta Street, Russell Street, Bedford Street, Maiden Lane and James Street followed as part of the development of the forty-acre estate, bounded by Long Acre, Drury Lane, the Strand and St Martin's Lane. Bedford's boast that it would be 'fit for the habitations of gentlemen and men of ability' was vindicated, for courtiers coveted the gracious houses overlooking the square. Chandos Street maintained the area's avant-garde character by incorporating England's first balcony.

A view under the portico, Covent Garden, 1766. Print by J. Sandby and E. Rooker (Guildhall Library)

These developments north of the Strand were echoed further east in the laying-out of Lincoln's Inn Fields, perhaps to Inigo Jones's design (architectural historians, however, rarely resist the temptation of attributing each and every Caroline development to Jones). This had been a traditional recreation field for the benchers of Lincoln's Inn, whose property flanked the site. They protested; nevertheless, in 1638 a speculator named William Newton obtained permission to erect thirty-two houses. Within five years, the west of the square had been run up, with as its centre-piece the majestic Lindsey House, handsome with its Ionic pilasters and entablature.

This rising neighbourhood between the two cities draws our attention to new political trends and tensions – not least because in the 1630s the Earl of Bedford grew notoriously alienated from Charles's court. Shifting urban topography hints at fluctuating relations between Crown, Parliament and City. The consequences proved catastrophic.

The accord between Elizabeth and the City was delicate. Under the early Stuarts, acrimony arose between Crown and Parliament, and relations between the City fathers and Whitehall also became tense. The City itself was under stress: was it to continue as the champion of crafts and trades, traditionally represented by the guilds and Common Council, or would new alliances between merchant princes, monopolists and courtiers skew City loyalties in the direction of big money and court intrigue? Could the Guildhall still speak for craftsmen citizens while serving new gentlemanly capitalists? And what of the mass, soon a majority, living beyond City jurisdiction – who would stand up for them? Or would they have their own say?

Storm clouds gathered, dispersed, then gathered again over Westminster. Elizabeth's relations with her Parliaments had never been balmy, but the coming of the new Stuart dynasty, fresh from Scotland and green in English politics, created friction between King and Commons, often over money matters dear to City hearts, such as excise and taxation. It would, recent historians have insisted, be rank hindsight to imply that early Stuart rule was rushing unstoppably down the rapids towards the Niagara of the Civil War – a disaster in which London was destined to be ranged against the King, representing, as vulgar Marxists might put it, bourgeois revolution against feudal monarchy. Nevertheless the metropolis was becoming so populous and powerful, so indispensable to royal solvency and the nation's prosperity, that the days had long passed when the White Tower terrorized the citizenry, or rebel leaders would meekly be led off to Mile End by a Richard II: things soon turned out quite the reverse, with a King being led to the scaffold, ironically in front of Inigo Jones's Banqueting House. Relations between court and City demanded tact on both sides.

Much would hinge on the adaptability and resilience of London's own corporate government. The sturdy representative framework of wards, parishes and guilds had long secured metropolitan stability. The participation of thousands of citizens in this wheels-within-wheels machinery proved a stabilizing force. Thousands of ordinary freemen participated in assemblies or held unpaid and rotating office. There were about 1,400 parish officials at any one time, or one for every twenty-one households. In the 1640s in a small ward like Cornhill no fewer than 118 different appointees (beadles, scavengers, constables, watchmen and jurymen) were annually elected to serve a population of around 1,800 – that is, one officer for about sixteen people or one for every three householders. Overall, London had around 3,000 elected officials, not to mention guild officials. All this ordinarily made for cast-iron stability, since it gave so many a stake in the status quo. It was for this reason that London's government was applauded by John Graunt, that pioneer of political arithmetic, who drew attention in 1662 to London's remarkably low crime rate, even during the Civil War. This, he believed, was due to participation in self-government: 'The Government and Guard of the City was by Citizens themselves and that alternately; no man settling into a trade for that employment.' James Howell, who, having written a history of Venice, knew all about urban order, emphasized the virtue of face-to-face rule. London's excellence, he wrote, lay in 'her strict and punctual government ... there's no City goes beyond her, nor indeed equals her, take night or day together; for there is not the least misdemeanour or inconvenience that can be, but there be officers in every corner of the City to pry unto them and find them out'. But if that 'strict and punctual government' normally made for stability, it also afforded a magnificent training in political activism to London's householders – citizens who, in dire straits, would prove a vociferous and confident opposition.

London's official voice, broadcast from the bench, was that of its merchant oligarchy. Historians disagree about the politics of this clique: was it essentially united or divided? Were its expressed loyalties heartfelt or just the expedient views of men with money at stake? Broadly speaking, London's oligarchs in the early seventeenth century were behind the Crown; many, after all, were concessionaries of projects and monopolies floated under Crown licence or were fishing for royal favour. The monopolists who managed the new East India and Levant Companies were specially dependent upon royal patronage, but scores of merchants profited from privileges and exemptions which the Stuarts disbursed through their favourites. Self-interest taught venture capitalists to see eye to eye with the King and his ministers, and City and Crown had all to gain by pulling together, for the fragile royal finances depended upon City prosperity. Even bishops could see that. 'When I behold that forest of masts upon your river for trafficke,' declared the Bishop of London, preaching in St Paul's in 1620, buttering up the City fathers, your Royall Exchange for Merchants, your Halls and Companies, your Gates for defence, your markets for victuals, your aqueducts for water, your granaries for provision, your hospitalls for the poore, your Bridewells for the idle, your Chamber for orphans and your Churches for holy assemblies; I cannot denie them to be magnificent workes, and your Citty to deserve the name of an Augustious and majesticall Citty.

Yet Stuart folly sorely tried the loyalty of those spearheading the 'commercial revolution'. Though enmeshed with royal interests, by the 1620s London's merchants were disabused, resentful of the Crown's myopic meddling with business. Too many commercial crises seemed to be precipitated by hare-brained royal schemes. Some excluded merchants resented the monopolies held by joint-stock enterprises like the Russia, Muscovy, and East India Companies. For their part, investors in these chartered companies fumed at stop-go support and the mixed messages emitted by the Crown. A blow to City confidence was dealt by the Cockayne project of 1614 (a cloth export patent granted to courtiers), which alienated established traders merely to line certain courtiers' pockets. In the 1630s, royal backing for Courteen's East India Association – undercutting the East India Company – provided a vivid reminder of the Cockayne fiasco. Distrust of court machinations led to parleyings around 1628 between chartered-company heads and Commons leaders; what Robert Brenner has called the 'new merchant group' in the City, promoting new North American colonial developments and the tobacco trade, showed parliamentary leanings.

With its failure to intervene in the Thirty Years War and its soft line on Spain, Stuart foreign policy was objectionable to London's Puritans – and, they claimed, detrimental to overseas trade. Exaction of tonnage and poundage (customs duties), abuse of monopolies, royal attempts to legislate for the suburbs and thus fiddle with the City's freedoms – a succession of ham-fisted actions of James and Charles tended to alienate merchants from Crown policies, fuelling criticism amongst the citizenry at large, already enraged at Archbishop Laud's High Church religious policies, which seemed to be bringing Catholicism in again by the back door.

The City began to show divergences of interest: between courtier merchants and the directors of the great chartered companies, between regular merchants and dabblers in concessions and tax-collectorships. Under James these generally swallowed their differences to support the Crown – in part to head off a hostile House of Commons – but from the late 1620s disenchantment grew more open. From this, a zealous Marxist might assume that the City, representing 'bourgeois capitalism', would have led an assault upon the 'feudal' Crown. But City politics were more labyrinthine. Frustrations and anger did not preclude the City from continuing to lend the Crown support, and even money – business remained dominated by men whose investments, leanings and offices bound them closely, if exasperatingly, to Crown and court. Between 1625 and

1638 the City raised loans for the King, and even at the beginning of the crack-brained Scottish war (1637) it made a formal agreement with Charles: business was business. By the time of the 1640 confrontations between King and Parliament the City itself would no longer risk raising cash for the Crown, but even then individual aldermen were keen to lend as tax-collectors. Doubtless money talked, but so presumably did gut loyalties.

In the event, the City's hand was forced – by the momentum of national events, but largely by popular passions in churches and taverns and on the streets. Religious dis-affection boiled up. London had become a stronghold of evangelical Protestantism, associated among the 'godly' – always a minority, if a vociferous and often wealthy one – with strenuous religious activities – sermons, fasts, Bible-reading – and with vehement anti-French, anti-Spanish and anti-Catholic opinions. From the 1620s such Puritan ministers, and the 'lecturers' or unofficial preachers installed in many parishes, increas-ingly identified Archbishop Laud with popery or even Antichrist. A succession of *causes célèbres* during the 1630s drew the religious battle lines, and anti-Catholicism was easily whipped up, because Charles's Queen, Henrietta Maria, had brought over from France such a huge foreign entourage. Puritan preachers made common cause with discontented merchants and craftsmen, while a rhetoric of religious wrath arose in the 1630s among apprentices and journeymen, anxious about the growth under Charles and Laud of such sins (as the Puritan shoemaker Nehemiah Wallington put it) as

idolatry, superstition, woeful profaning of the names, titles, attributes, creatures, and of God himself, with the perfect language of hellish swearers in every child's mouth, whoredoms, adulteries, fornication, murders, oppressions, drunkenness, cozening, lying, the contempt of the Gospel with slandering, mocking, flouting, chiding, silencing and stopping the mouths of God's prophets and servants, and other gross secret sins.

Street demonstrations, public prayers, fasts and petitions multiplied – targeted not against the Guildhall but against Laud, Strafford (the chief minister) and the King. Only in extremity did London's citizenry turn against its own governors.

Grass-roots anger did not immediately find support in the Guildhall. The Court of Common Council showed no consistent opposition to the aldermen or Crown until 1639, when it drew up a petition of grievances for presentation to the King. But in 1640 Common Council gave no corporate support to John Pym and the parliamentary opposition, and as late as November 1641 Common Council backed the feasting of Charles at a City banquet and his being presented with £20,000.

Confusion turned to polarization. But as protests rose from below, as sermons got shriller and the citizens protested on the streets against ministers who seemed to favour foreign, popish interests above the Protestant cause, aldermen wavered, and, swallowing their criticisms of the King, many looked once more to Charles as the lesser evil, the only pillar of stability. Terrified by the spectre of anarchy, the Mayor and bench stood by the Crown almost up to the outbreak of war. But national crisis deepened, 'men of a mean or middle quality', hitherto sidelined from City councils, seized the initiative, and all the while Puritan preachers whipped up disfranchised suburbanites into a frenzy which eventually toppled the Mayor and precipitated rebellion.

Popular muscle first became menacing in May 1641 when Parliament presented Charles with a Bill for the execution of his chief minister, the Earl of Strafford. The King hesitated, but Londoners seized the streets and made up his mind for him (he became, a contemporary reported, 'so frighted with these burghers'). Parliament soon grew no less 'frighted' than the King. Its Westminster sittings were assailed by hordes of apprentices and labourers who began to recognize their own strength and cowed dithering MPs into measures precluding compromise with Charles. The turning-point came on 4 January 1642, when Charles tried to arrest five House of Commons opponents and they fled into the City, thereby sealing a Parliament/London bond. The King pursued. At the Guildhall his reception was mixed, but in the streets a howling mob of tradesmen, apprentices and mariners cried 'privilege of Parliament, privilege of Parliament'. 'The good king,' reported the Venetian ambassador, 'was somewhat moved and I believe was glad when he was at home.' That night the City dreaded royal reprisal, but the King lost his nerve; on 11 January he quit Whitehall: the slide into civil war led to the King raising his standard in Nottingham in August.

Charles's flight left the way open for radicals to take over the City they had browbeaten for the previous year. Having whipped up the citizenry in churches and taverns, they overthrew the City's government through seizing control of its militia and help from the Commons. The aldermanic right to veto Common Council proposals was abolished. In July 1642 the royalist Lord Mayor was impeached in Parliament, dismissed, and clapped in the Tower. A radical was appointed in his place, and London armed for war.

Civil war would have been unthinkable without the City's provision of men and money for the parliamentary side. These flowed, because the radicals who had seized the Guildhall had burned their boats: only victory would save their skins. Charles's first priority was to capture the unruly City – that would have won the war at a stroke – and his chance came early, before the parliamentary army was organized. On 12 November 1642 royalists overwhelmed the parliamentary troops at Brentford; to parry the inescapable attack, London gathered its trained bands in a force of 24,000 at Turnham Green, by Chiswick Common; Charles hesitated, retired to Reading, and missed his golden chance of seizing the mutinous capital. For London then threw up an impressive defence system, ringing the City with ditches and fortifications. By May 1643 the Venetian ambassador reported 'the forts completed and admirably designed. They are now beginning the connecting lines.' Uniting for the first time the cities of

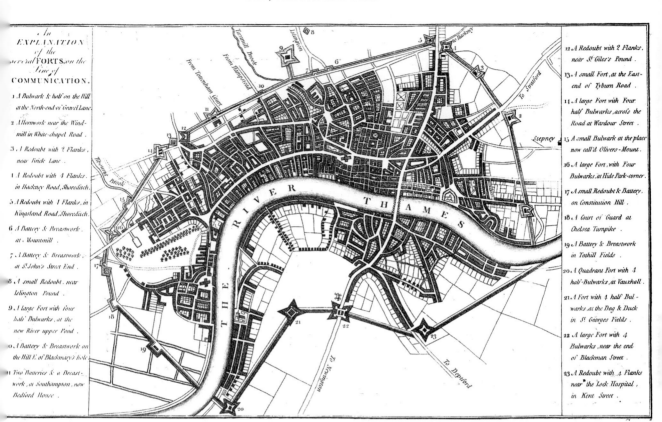

Civil War defences, 1642

London and Westminster, Mayor and Parliament, the shield reached from beyond Hyde Park in the west to the Tower in the east, from Hoxton in the north to Newington in the south. Danger had, fleetingly, united all London.

The fortifications were never put to the test, however, largely because City coffers kept the New Model Army paid, while the royalists went bankrupt. Once Charles failed to win fast, he was condemned to slow defeat. 'If posterity shall ask who pulled the Crown from the King's head,' a royalist remarked, 'say, 'twas the proud, unthankful, schismatical, rebellious, bloody City of London.' Parliamentary victory also owed much to high morale among ordinary citizens, whose radical energies galvanized Cromwell's army. Londoners at large – literate folk long accustomed to holding positions in parish and precinct and listening to morale-boosting sermons – gave backbone to the parliamentary effort. War released unprecedented articulacy among the citizens. Guild, parish and ward membership had, after all, given the citizenry an apprenticeship in ideas and organization, while suburbanites and outsiders for their part felt deep-seated grievances and so were easily mobilized to bulk out the forces. Civic rhetorics of law and liberties were ignited by Puritan messianism: 'Behold now this vast city,' wrote the London merchant's son John Milton, born in Bread Street, 'city of refuge, the mansion-house of liberty, encompassed and surrounded with His protection.'

Long before William Blake, zealots saw City streets as the New Jerusalem. Dissent found fertile soil in wartime and interregnum London. Separatist congregations had existed before 1641 – there had been Baptist cells in Spitalfields, Southwark and Wapping: all, significantly, beyond the walls – but during the war they came out into the open and blossomed. Quakers and Ranters recruited followings from tailors, shoemakers, weavers, carpenters and other artisans, while the Fifth Monarchists, hostile to all forms of imposed religious authority, included a master cooper, a ribbon-weaver and a bricklayer among their leaders. Many separatist preachers were laymen, so-called mechanic preachers, such as Samuel How, a Southwark cobbler, Praise-God Barbon, a Baptist leather-seller of Fleet Street, Lodowicke Muggleton, a London tailor who founded his own sect, and Thomas Lamb, a soap-boiler who headed a Baptist congregation off Coleman Street. Women were prominent as separatists, among them the visionary Anna Trapnel. Literacy, citizen democracy and gospel Protestantism produced an extraordinary populist religious awakening. Such self-expression peaked in the 1640s and 1650s, but religious heterodoxy and radicalism remained forces to be reckoned with for many generations, despite fierce post-Restoration persecution, which forced some underground and into quietism. London's Puritan legacy proved lasting. In 1711 there were 26 Presbyterian meeting-houses in London and its suburbs, 23 for the Baptists, 14 for the Quakers and 12 for the Independents: ordinary people were determining their religious affiliation in a manner unthinkable in 1600. The only great European city offering similar liberty and extensive if incomplete tolerance was Amsterdam. As the life and views of the visionary poet and painter William Blake attest, as late as 1800 radical religious streams that had flowed partly over- and partly underground since the 1640s could still be forces to be reckoned with.

How deeply the Civil War and even the execution of the King at Whitehall on 30 January 1649 – an awesome moment in British history – changed everyday London life is difficult to assess. The City escaped siege or sack, and in many respects things carried on as normal. But under the strain of heavy taxation on the City and the Dutch wars the emergency wartime accord between Parliament, City and Army did not last, and Londoners soon resented military or Presbyterian interference and attempts to enforce godliness – for instance, the empowering of soldiers to enter houses to ensure Sabbath observance as decreed by Parliament. The banning of the celebration of Christmas – it was condemned as an idle papist superstition – irked many. Attending a private Christmas service at Exeter House, John Evelyn noted that, just as 'the service was ended, and the Sacrament about to be administered, the chapel was surrounded by soldiers, and all the communicants and assembly surprised and kept prisoners'. Evelyn was detained for several hours. London's theatres were pulled down and Sunday sports were banned. Many citizens decided they no more wanted saints or synods breathing down their neck than they wanted Laud.

Significantly, despite the King's execution and the abolition of the bishops and the House of Lords, no revolution followed in the City's constitution. The oligarchical institutions survived, as did other props of the old order, like the Royal College of Physicians. Having seized power, London's radicals had no wish to saw off the bough they were sitting on. Nor, despite the symbolic fortifications, was any attempt made to establish a government for the whole of the metropolis. This halting of change proved momentous: the chance never recurred. Yet monarchs would henceforth have to ensure that their policies heeded the commercial, financial and manufacturing interests of the metropolis, for the Civil War had shown London a match for the King, if only thanks to the power of the purse. If not quite an urban tail wagging the national dog, London had at least become a force no future King or Parliament could afford to slight.

'A triumph of above 20,000 horse and foote' accompanied the returning Charles II, recorded John Evelyn,

brandishing their swords and shouting with inexpressible joy; the wayes strewed with flowers, the bells ringing, the streets hung with tapistry, the fountaines running with wine; the Major, Aldermen, and all the Companies in their liveries, chaines of gold, and banners; Lords and Nobles clad in cloth of silver, gold and velvet; the windowes and balconies well set with ladies.

It was perhaps ominous that the City bestowed such a pointedly gracious welcome on the King in 1660. Landing at Dover, Charles and his retinue were greeted by General Monck accompanied by civic dignitaries. And, having taken the old pilgrim route up through Canterbury, the Martyr's son passed over London Bridge and was, as Evelyn recorded, solemnly greeted by the City with pealing bells and cheering crowds, before proceeding to Whitehall Palace. The King had thus first found it necessary to make his peace with rebellious London. 'It is no exaggeration to say,' reflected Macaulay in the nineteenth century, 'that but for the hostility of the City, Charles I would never have been vanquished, and that without the help of the City, Charles II could never have been restored.'

During the first halcyon months and years, Charles seemed to justify the high hopes vested in him. Whatever his shortcomings, he was the ruler Restoration London needed, almost an ambassador for a new era of urbanity. A natural man about town, his easy accessibility around Whitehall and St James's Park gave a fillip to fashionable

London after his father's frigid pomp and the interregnum's military austerity – no other royal personage imparted tone to town until the Prince Regent. The Merrie Monarch encouraged writers and wits; he licensed two playhouses, the King's Theatre in Drury Lane and the Duke of York's in Lincoln's Inn Fields; and in 1662 leading scientists including Christopher Wren, Robert Boyle and Robert Hooke obtained a charter setting up the Royal Society of London for Improving Natural Knowledge, among the earliest public scientific societies in Europe. The King seemed eager to patronize metropolitan improvements. The early years of his reign were a honeymoon period, hinting at a happy coexistence between Crown and town.

Terrible times lay ahead. Five years after the Restoration, one in five Londoners died; the following year the very fabric of the City was largely destroyed. With a *Schadenfreude* they could not resist, the godly linked the Great Plague of 1665 and the Great Fire of 1666: were not both divine judgements on Restoration Sodom, Old Rowley's reign of pleasure? In reality, however, London had become so huge and heterogeneous that the Plague and Fire struck largely separate quarters, leaving certain districts (including rakish St James) relatively unscathed. The plague-ravaged parts – extramural settlements like Holborn, Shoreditch, Finsbury, Whitechapel and Southwark that housed the most squalid slums – were, sadly, little touched by the Fire (burning down was what they needed). And all these precincts had higher death rates in 1665 than the City itself, however dreadful the slaughter within the walls: not for nothing was the visitation known as 'the poor's Plague'. The extramural slums suffered worst from pestilence because, with their sheds and stores and pigs and poultry, they provided an ideal city for the black rat.

The 1665 outbreak was the appalling finale of a long history of epidemics. Marked by its tell-tale soft black swellings (buboes), bubonic plague had been a regular visitor to London in the three centuries since the Black Death, causing major disasters every so often and persisting in a milder, endemic form. In 1563 London suffered an appalling proportional loss, with 17,500 people dying, perhaps a fifth of the capital's population. Moderate outbreaks followed in 1578 and 1582, with 6,000 and 7,000 deaths respectively, and a further serious epidemic in 1593 carried off 18,000 in the intramural parishes alone. Plague then gave a surly greeting to James I's accession in 1603 by massacring 30,000. 'Imagine then that Death (like the Spanish Leaguer, or rather like Stalking Tamberlaine) hath pitcht his tents (being nothing but a heape of winding cheets tackt together) in the sinfully polluted Suburbs,' the pamphleteer Thomas Dekker told his frightened readers:

Feare and Trembling (the two Catch-polles of Death) arrest every one: no parley will be graunted, no composition stood upon, but the Allarum is strucke up, the Toxin ringes out for life, and no voyce heard but *Tue, Tue*, Kill, Kill; the little Belles onely (like small shot) doe yet goe off, and make no great worke for wormes, a hundred or two lost in every skirmish, or so:

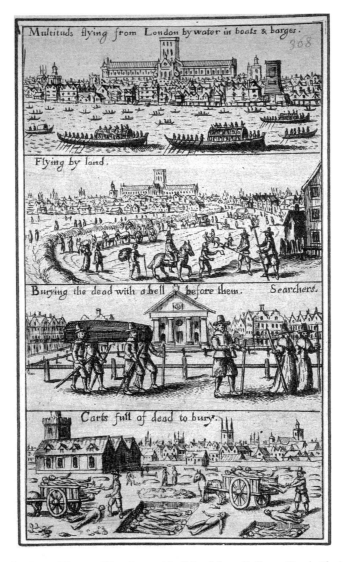

The Great Plague of London, 1665 (Magdalene College, Cambridge)

but alas, that's nothing: yet by those desperat sallies, what by opan setting upon them by day, and secret Ambuscadoes by night, the Skirts of London were pittifully pared off, by little and little: which they within the gates perceiving, it was no boot to bid them take their heels, for away they troop thick and threefold; some riding, some on foote: some without bootes, some in their slippers, by water, by land, in shoales swam they West-ward, many to Gravesend: none went unless they be driven, for whosoever landed there never came back again: Hacknies, Water-men & Wagons, were not so terribly imployed many a yeare: so that within a short time, there was not a good horse in Smithfield, nor a Coach to be set eye on.

In 1625 Charles I's accession was marked by another visitation, causing some 40,000 deaths. The 1665 outbreak predictably started in what was soon to be the slum of slums: St Giles. This suburban parish (immediately to the south of the modern New Oxford Street) was already notorious for epidemics. So when plague erupted in early 1665 alarm bells did not immediately ring in the Guildhall. To the end of May the plague death rate for the capital as a whole was nothing exceptional: of forty-three deaths in early June, thirty-one were in St Giles parish.

The outbreak was spreading to St Clement Danes, St Margaret Westminster, St Dunstan-in-the-West, St Andrew Holborn, St Giles Cripplegate; cases occurred in Islington and Whitechapel; and in late May there had been a death in the City near Cornhill. Yet things seemed under control till June brought a heatwave: 'The hottest day that ever I felt in my life', recorded Pepys on the 7th. On that very same day he saw red crosses springing up on houses in Drury Lane, with the words 'Lord, have mercy upon us.' On the 17th the hackney coachman driving him along Holborn suddenly grew delirious. In the final week of June the toll was 267, but, to preclude panic, people reassured themselves: 'but 4 in the City – which is a great blessing to us', recorded Pepys, instinctively expressing the citizens' distinction between Us and Them.

But then infection spread like wildfire, and the wealthy couldn't get out fast enough. 'All the town almost going out of town,' the diarist noted, 'the coaches and waggons being all full of people going into the country.' Clergymen abandoned their flocks, doctors fled their patients, even the lawyers left. Early in July, King, court and judges joined the stampede (the next six months were uniquely execution-free). Parliament was prorogued. Not for the last time, the town was in effect abandoned by its ruling class, though, to his credit, George Monck, Duke of Albemarle, stayed at the helm, establishing himself at the Cockpit at St James's Park in his office of *custos rotulorum* for Middlesex, dictating orders to JPs. Though frightened, Pepys stayed too, evacuating his wife to Woolwich and his mother to the country, putting his affairs in order, making out a new will ('for a man cannot depend on living two days'), and locking his valuables away – and, it seems, taking the opportunity to indulge his taste for extramarital dalliance more than usual.

Though for a time the City had remained relatively immune – a contemporary related that 'so few of the religious sort were taken away that (according to the mode of many such) they began to be puffed up and to boast the great difference that God did make' – that did not last. By mid-July more than 1,000 were dying each week. In early August the death toll increased to 2,020; a month later, it peaked at 7,000 a week.

As so often, official action came slowly. The Lord Mayor ordered lodgers and visitors to quit the City. When plague was diagnosed in a house, all residents were locked inside for forty days, by when, it was assumed, the infected had either died or recovered. Watchmen kept guard to enforce this quarantine. Trade was disrupted, production halted, tens of thousands were out of work, grass sprouted in the streets, and the numbed town echoed to the cry 'Bring out your dead!' Many citizens took to the Thames, living on vessels moored in mid-river. Nearby towns that had earlier welcomed refugees (they were profitable) began turning them away: in Oxford a nightwatch was set on the city entrances to exclude them.

Panic and disaster grew so great that victims allegedly leapt from their beds and stood 'crying and roaring at their windows'; others ran naked into the streets, crazed and foaming at the mouth. JPs built new pest-houses in Marylebone, Soho Fields and Stepney, and the Lord Mayor ordered the eradication of all dogs and cats, in the belief that they spread pestilence. Pepys reckoned 40,000 dogs and perhaps five times as many cats were killed: it must, alas, have been the perfect recipe for safeguarding the rats! In despair the Court of Aldermen resorted in September to an old remedy, lighting bonfires to break up pestilential air. Pepys conveyed the melancholy terror of continually 'meeting dead corps's of the plague, carried to be buried close to me at noon-day through the City in Fanchurch-street':

To see a person sick of the sores, carried close to me by Gracechurch in a hackney-coach – My finding the Angel tavern, at the lower end of Tower-hill, shut up, and more than that, the alehouse at the Towerstairs; and more than that, that the person was then dying of the plague when I was last there, a little while ago at night ... To hear that poor Payne, my water[man], hath buried a child and is dying himself. To hear that a labourer I sent but the other day to Dagenhams to know how they did there, is dead of the plague; and that one of my own watermen, that carried me daily, fell sick as soon as he had landed me on Friday morning last ... is now dead of the plague ... doth put me into great apprehensions of melancholy, and with good reason.

Corpses posed terrible problems, as churchyards overflowed and the air reeked of death. The authorities ordered mass graves, lined with quicklime. It was impossible to bury all immediately, and bodies piled up in the streets. Pepys came across a body in a coffin in an open yard, with nobody to bury it, 'the plague making us as cruel as dogs one to another'. In his *Journal of the Plague Year*, written fifty years later, Daniel Defoe portrayed a poor man from Blackwall, reporting on the plight of locals:

'Alas! Sir,' says he, 'almost desolate: all dead or sick. Here are very few families in this part, or in the village' (pointing at Poplar), 'where half of them are not dead already, and the rest sick.' Then he, pointing to one house, 'There they are all dead,' said he ... Then he pointed to several other houses. 'There,' says he, 'they are all dead, the man and his wife and five children. There,' says he, 'they are shut up; you see a watchman at the door'; and so of other houses.

With the cooler weather the epidemic waned and people trickled back to the stricken City with its deathly stillness. But it was still paralysed. 'I to Lumbard Streete,' Pepys wrote on 16 October, 'but can get no money. So upon the Exchange, which is very empty.' London remained a ghost town:

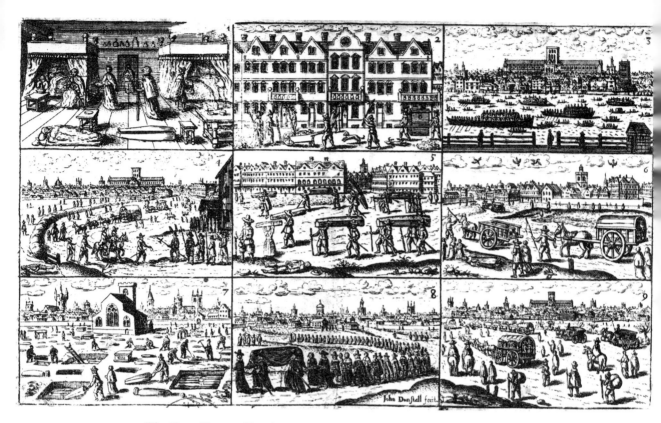

The Great Plague of London, 1665. As the plague died down, people took a morbid interest in recalling aspects of the horror

Lord, how empty the streets are and melancholy, so many poor sick people in the streets, full of sores: and so many sad stories overheard as I walk, everybody talking of this dead, and that man sick, and so many in this place, and so many in that.

Not till February 1666 did the King feel it safe to return to St James's, to the peal of bells. London recovered its usual bustle – though not for long. The weekly Bills of Mortality, which from the sixteenth century collated death statistics from 109 London parishes, attributed about 68,000 deaths to plague, but modern historians incline towards 80,000 or more. Maybe a fifth of London's inhabitants had died in 1563, the greatest mortality rate: in 1665 about one in six died, equivalent to the total inhabitants of the next five towns in the kingdom – Norwich, Bristol, Newcastle, York and Exeter. It was a disaster of nuclear proportions.

Providence was not yet placated, however. In the early hours of Sunday 2 September 1666, Thomas Farrinor (or Farynor), a baker in Pudding Lane, just north of Billings-gate fish market, failed to put out the fire under his oven. His house caught light.

Flying sparks fired the Star Inn on Fish Street Hill. A Thames Street tallow-chandler's went up in flames, which were fanned by a strong east wind. The Lord Mayor, Sir Thomas Bludworth, was awakened, but judged it a typical minor outbreak, observing, 'Pish! A woman might piss it out!' before going back to bed. Roused from sleep in his house in Seething Lane, near the Tower, Pepys did not trouble to watch the flames for long: fires were nothing new. But before the night was out fire was sweeping across the tight-packed streets, devouring all in its path; by morning 300 houses and the north end of London Bridge were alight.

Once it reached Thames Street, with its warehouses piled with oil, tallow, pitch and spirits, the fire took deep root, mocking the buckets, hand-squirts, long-handled fire-hooks and other crude equipment trained against it. By morning, Pepys found pandemonium:

Everybody endeavouring to remove their goods, and flinging into the River or bringing them into lighters that lay off. Poor people staying in their houses as long as till the very fire touched them, and then running into boats or clambering from one pair of stair by the waterside to another.

From Southwark, John Evelyn could view the whole conflagration as it engulfed the City. On Monday 3 September he described 'the whole south part of the Citty burning from Cheape Side to the Thames, and all along Cornehill. Tower-streete, Fen-church-streete, Gracious-streete [Gracechurch Street] and so along to Bainard Castle, and was now taking hold of St Paules-church to which the scaffalds contributed exceedingly'. By then the blaze covered the riverfront west of London Bridge and north as far as Cannon Street, reaching Baynard's Castle (Blackfriars) in the morning. By mid-afternoon all Lombard Street and the Royal Exchange were ablaze. On Monday morning Pepys moved his valuables again, to a colleague's at Bethnal Green, and ferried his furniture downstream, burying his wine and Parmesan cheese in the garden before taking his wife back to Woolwich. (In the event, his house was spared.)

Tuesday 4 September was the worst day. The fire had got north beyond Thread-needle Street; Cheapside was destroyed. St Paul's blazed. At long last systematic demolition was organized, to stop the spread, but too late to save the Guildhall. Flames burst through the City wall by way of Ludgate, leaping over the Fleet ditch. Prisoners in the Fleet were released. Salisbury Theatre and the Inner Temple, St Bride's Church and Bridewell took fire. 'All Fleetstreete, Old baily, Ludgate hill, Warwick lane, Newgate, Paules chaine, Wattling-streete, now flaming, and most of it reduc'd to ashes,' Evelyn reported: 'the stones of St Paules flew like grenados, the Lead mealting down the streetes in a streame and the very pavements of them glowing with fiery rednesse, so as no horse, nor man, was able to tread on them.'

On Wednesday 5 September Cripplegate and the Temple burnt; but fortunately the wind dropped and demolition work – long resisted – finally proved effective, and the

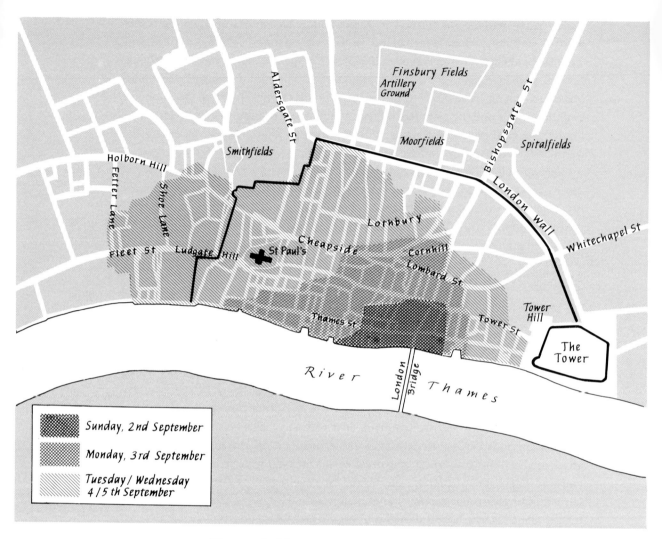

The spread of the Great Fire from 2 to 5 September 1666

fire was checked by midnight. Pepys climbed the steeple of All Hallows Barking and reconnoitred the desolation: 'Everywhere great fires. Oyle cellars and brimstone and other things burning.' The wind had dropped but still there was a blaze at the Temple, Holborn and Cripplegate, where the King himself was seen helping the soldiers. On Thursday the fire was decisively halted at Fetter Lane, Cock Lane and All Hallows Barking.

Various factors exacerbated the devastation. One was the early spread of the flames to the warehouses and cellars of Thames Street. Another was the gusty east wind. The plague had spread east, but the flames were driven westward. It was not till Monday night that the blaze reached Billingsgate, only 150 yards east from Pudding Lane, although by then it was already licking Baynard's Castle on the City's western extremity.

A third was the ineptitude of the Mayor. Houses should have been pulled down in the fire's path, but Bludworth lost his nerve. He had money on his mind: 'who shall pay the cost of rebuilding the houses?' he asked Pepys. Looking 'like a man spent, with a handkerchief about his neck', he complained to the diarist, 'Lord, what can I do?' – 'people will not obey me.' Appalled, Pepys had dashed to Whitehall on Sunday morning to post the King and his brother, the Duke of York, neither of whom had apparently heard of the fire – if true, a telling indication of the isolation of the two districts. Only royal intervention had coordinated fire-fighting attempts, Charles ordering streets in the fire's path to be blown up to act as fire-breaks, supervising the campaign in person, and refreshing exhausted fire-fighters with cascades of coins. Evelyn was put in charge of a party deputed to save the part of Holborn by Fetter Lane (the timber-framed houses of Staple Inn have survived to this day):

The clowds also of smoke were dismall and reach'd upon computation neer 56 miles in length. Thus I left it this afternoone burning, a resemblance of Sodom, or the last day. It forcibly call'd to my mind that passage – *non enim hic habemus stabilem civitatem*: the ruines resembling the picture of Troy.

Today's 55 Fleet Street marks the westerly limit of the fire's progress.

Huge camps of refugees gathered in Moorfields and other open spaces north of London Wall; Evelyn guessed some 200,000 were encamped in Highgate and Islington. The King organized relief, and contributions poured in. But the City had suffered grievously: 'I went againe to the ruines,' Evelyn noted a week later, 'for it was now no longer a citty.' Though there were only eight deaths, for the tens of thousands of homeless Evelyn's sentence would have rung true: 'London was, but is no more.' Yet he was also curiously out of date: it was not *London* that was destroyed, but only the *City*.

The City the Fire destroyed had worn a medieval face. The wall still existed almost in its entirety, and several monastic edifices remained, though put to new uses – Greyfriars as Christ's Hospital school, the refectory of the Austin Friars as the Pinners' Company hall. The City's 100 medieval parish churches still dazzled in Wenceslaus Hollar's superb panorama of 1647. Even without its spire, St Paul's dwarfed all else, though the cathedral was crumbling and under Cromwell only the east end was reserved for religion, troops being quartered in the nave. Old St Paul's epitomized the City it shadowed – awesome from a distance, but alarmingly decayed. About four-fifths of this medieval city had been razed within three days. Around 87 parish churches, 44

The Great Fire, 1666. The church in the centre is the original St Paul's Cathedral

livery-company halls, 13,200 houses, the Royal Exchange and the Custom House had been destroyed completely, and extensive damage had been done to St Paul's, Bridewell and the Fleet prison, the western gates (Ludgate, Newgate and Aldersgate), much of the Inner Temple and Christ's Hospital. The devastated area extended over 373 acres within the City itself, and 63 acres extramurally. Four hundred streets lay smoking; 100,000 were homeless. It was, reflected Pepys, 'the saddest sight of desolation that I ever saw'.

The first priority was to restore business as usual. The Court of Common Council and the Court of Aldermen secured quarters at Gresham College, a Custom House was set up in Mark Lane, the Excise Office in Southampton Fields, the Hearth Tax Office in Leadenhall Street, and the Post Office in Brydges Street. It was essential to start collecting revenues without delay.

Rebuilding schemes flooded in. Within days Christopher Wren presented his master plan, recommending that the entire burnt area should be cleared and a fresh start be made with wide streets and large open spaces, with a new Royal Exchange and St Paul's serving as the principal of several focal points – including a huge Fleet Street piazza and the embanking of the Fleet. He was soon followed by John Evelyn and Robert Hooke with comparable schemes for squares and vistas: geometrical, fit for a king. But the decision did not rest with the King or with architects. The City needed business to resume pronto, whereas the imagined rebuilding would have taken years, destroying many of London's traditional markets and thoroughfares. Not least, whatever their merits as townscapes, conceptions like Wren's were Utopian: who would foot the bill? The only practical scheme was one that would get each property-owner to rebuild as fast as possible. Rebuilding districts holistically would have necessitated the dragooning of innumerable independent householders: Charles I had lost his head for less. Not for the last time, neither Crown nor Corporation interfered with capital.

Commissioners were appointed, however, who enacted certain public improvements. Hitherto the waterfront had been a jungle of yards, landing-places, water-steps and narrow lanes obstructed with sheds. Now an open quayside was decreed from Black-friars to the Tower, with warehouses pitched back from the waterfront. And though the ancient street plan was retained, some streets were widened, including Cheapside, Poultry and Cornhill, while the creation of New Queen Street, just east of Queenhithe, attempted an imposing approach from the river up to the Guildhall.

To prevent architectural bedlam and ensure safety, building regulations and safety standards were stipulated. Brick and stone were required. 'In high and principal streets' structures had to be four storeys high; in secondary streets three storeys; and in side-streets two storeys. A major improvement was a Sewage and Paving Act (1671), which introduced the cambering of roads into a side-drain, flanked by a raised pavement, in place of the old 'kennel', the central drainage ditch. Later Building Acts restricted wood use, particularly in the newly popular sash windows. Wooden door and window frames, previously flush with the outer wall, were required to be set back at least four inches, and wooden eaves and cornices were prohibited, all to reduce fire risk. Oversailing (upper floors jutting outward over a street) was prohibited. Side-streets had to be at least fourteen feet wide and alleys ten feet: London was to become a city of vehicles.

Finance presented problems. Much of the initial cost, especially for warehouses, wharves, markets and prisons, was met by a shilling per ton coal levy – later trebled to finance City churches and the new St Paul's, for which 50,000 tons of Portland stone had to be shipped. A special court was set up to settle the myriad lawsuits resulting from the disputes of tenants and landlords.

Rebuilding gathered pace, as laws against stonemasons, bricklayers and builders from outside the City, so long jealously maintained by the guilds, were waived. Four new buildings were put up, large enough to take the markets off the streets. Leaden-hall – the biggest market in Europe – absorbed into four courtyards the street sellers from Gracechurch Street, Cornhill and Eastcheap. By 1668 the Cutlers and Butchers had finished their new halls, and the Custom House, the Royal Exchange and Blackwell Hall (Cloth Hall) were soon ready. By the early 1670s most private houses were occupied and trade had revived.

The Fire was commemorated in the Monument, designed by Wren's colleague and friend Robert Hooke and standing 202 feet high – its distance from the site of the Pudding Lane baker's house where the fire started – its inscription truly boasting 'London rises again.' Another legend, added later, blamed Roman Catholics for allegedly starting the fire 'in order for carrying on their horrid plott for extirpating the Protestant and old English liberty, and introducing Popery and slavery'. This inscription was removed in 1685 under James II, reinstated in 1689, and then not erased till 1830.

The truly noble rebuilding lay in the churches. Christopher Wren received the commission; fifty-two were rebuilt, nearly all to his designs or under his care. Of the rebuilt churches, around St Paul's lie St Vedast Foster Lane and a little to the west Christ Church Newgate Street, with its superb tower. Immediately east of the cathedral is the tower of St Augustine Watling Street, now incorporated into the choir school. Then there are St Nicholas (largely rebuilt after the Second World War) and, south of the cathedral, the brick church of St Benet Paul's Wharf. North-west, by St Andrew's Hill, is St Andrew-by-the-Wardrobe, also rebuilt after the Blitz damage. The unique spire of St Bride, Fleet Street, is 200 yards west of Ludgate Hill, beyond St Martin Ludgate.

Two groups of Wren churches lie east of St Paul's in the heart of the City. The more westerly includes St Mary-le-Bow (of Bow bells fame); north of Mansion House stands Wren's Gothic experiment – St Mary Aldermary. Near the Guildhall is St Lawrence Jewry, severely damaged during the Blitz. Further south are two more – St James Garlickhythe, on the western side of Queen Street, and St Michael Paternoster Royal, on the east, just north of Upper Thames Street.

North-east is St Margaret Lothbury, another Wren church, while behind the Mansion House stands St Stephen Walbrook. Up Abchurch Lane, off Cannon Street, is one of the smallest: St Mary Abchurch. St Clement Eastcheap, just off King William Street, and St Edmund the King, in Lombard Street, east of St Mary Woolnoth, are also Wren's; Cornhill contains two more, St Michael and St Peter upon Cornhill.

Towering over all was St Paul's Cathedral, which Wren erected as 'an ornament to His Majesty's most excellent reign, to the Church of England, and to the Great City'. Wren's son described his father's laying of the first stone in 1675 on the ruins of the old cathedral as involving 'a memorable omen':

When the SURVEYOR in Person had set out, upon the Place, the Dimensions of the great Dome, and fixed upon the centre; a common Labourer was ordered to bring a flat stone from the Heaps of Rubbish ... to be laid for a Mark and Direction to the Masons; the Stone happened to be a Piece of Grave-stone, with nothing remaining of the Inscription but this simple word in large capitals, RESURGAM.

The word was emblazoned on the south transept of the new cathedral above the figure of a phoenix rising from the ashes, though after the cathedral's completion in 1710 Wren was stripped of his job in an infamous piece of political skulduggery. Trade resurrected the City, but thanks to Wren the reborn City was left more attractive. Alongside Nash and Bazalgette, he stands as one of London's noblest builders.

The seventeenth-century poet Thomas Freeman predicted:

> Hogsden will to Highgate ere't be long
> London has got a long way from the streame,
> I think she means to go to Islington
> To eat a dish of strawberries and creame.

Though Evelyn lamented that 'London was, but is no more', in truth a new London, the London Evelyn forgot but Freeman glimpsed, had been growing up east of the City and, through the accident of the fierce east wind, escaped the fire. Notwithstanding Privy Council bans, suburban building had raced ahead, much going up in Wapping in the 1620s and 1630s. A list of illegal buildings drawn up in 1638 recorded 188 houses newly erected there, mainly around the vacant mud-flats – suggesting that the inner suburbs, around St Katharine's, were chock-full. In Shadwell, to the east, nearly 700 houses were built in the 1630s and 1640s; and thirty years later Spitalfields saw similar growth. By 1680 most of Wapping and Shadwell and some of Spitalfields had been filled in. By 1700 building had spread to Mile End, an extension of Spitalfields; to Goodman's Fields, already hemmed in by building; and around Wapping Marsh.

In old districts like St Katharine's, houses were wedged into a maze of courts, and sometimes even put up on refuse tips. In the new areas, however, where space was available, building was generally more orderly, with streets in Shadwell running straight between Ratcliff Highway and Wapping Wall. In the 1650s Sir William Wheler made Wheler Street, and John Pennington laid out Pennington Street on the north edge of Wapping Marsh – now notorious as the site of Rupert Murdoch's News International. Spitalfields developed a grid pattern, paralleling contemporary developments in the West End.

Some landowners tried to control building – in 1681 Lady Ivie, owner of part of Wapping Marsh, let a plot along Old Gravel Lane to a builder on condition that he build houses three storeys high with cellars – but builders were generally left to their own devices. Only the larger buildings were brick-built, the smaller being lath-and-plaster ('paper work' as the phrase went). A proclamation of 1661 recommended brick; Bridewell Hospital, owning land in Wapping, claimed that its tenements there had to be rebuilt with timber because (ominously) the ground was too marshy to bear anything heavier. It duly got a licence, though after a fire in 1673 the next rebuilding was in brick.

Serving as artisans' and mariners' cottages, East End houses were small, with frontages around twelve feet. A Shadwell survey (1650) shows that, out of 701 houses, 195 had a single storey, 473 had two storeys and 33 had three storeys. Many became subdivided. The inventory of the possessions of a certain Samuel Jackman of Stepney mentioned only one room, containing a bed, a chest of drawers, a table and some chairs. John Fernew occupied a tenement in Whitechapel consisting of two chambers, with a bed, kitchen utensils, tables and chairs. Inventories suggest some superior occupants. A certain Isaac Howe, evidently a tobacconist, had one of the larger houses; its ground floor had a kitchen (containing grates, spits, a table and cupboards), a carpet, leather chairs, and a shop with stores of tobacco and sugar and weighing apparatus. On the first floor there were three chambers with chairs, beds, chests and looking-glasses, and on the second floor two similar chambers. There obviously was, as there remained, solid bourgeois prosperity in the East End. A new London was developing, beyond City jurisdiction, beyond the punishment of the Fire, responding to London's booming role in world trade.

CHAPTER FIVE

The Triumph of Town:
From Restoration to Regency

My first business was to acquire some knowledge of the place whereof I am now become an inhabitant. I began to study the plan of London, though dismayed at the sight of its prodigious extent, – a city a league and [a] half from one extremity to the other, and about half as broad, standing upon level ground. It is impossible ever to become thoroughly acquainted with such an endless labyrinth of streets; and, as you may well suppose, they who live at one end know little or nothing of the other.

ROBERT SOUTHEY, Letters from England (1807)

Writing soon after the Fire, John Dryden was inspired to dedicate his *Annus Mirabilis: The Year of Wonders 1666* to 'the Metropolis of Great Britain, the most renowned and late flourishing City of London'. Reflecting that he was the first to dedicate a poem to a city, Dryden apostrophized the capital that had survived sword, pestilence and fire: 'You, who are to stand a wonder to all Years and Ages ... a *Phoenix* in her ashes.' He was right to sense something special in the air, for the 'long eighteenth century' – the years from Restoration to Regency – proved epochal for London, involving the birth of a residential quarter, the West End, which decisively shaped the capital's future. Hitherto people had settled in the metropolis because that was where they earned their livelihood – masters dwelling above the shop on Garlick Hill or Bread Street, artisans in Shadwell, pettifogging lawyers poring over precedents in Chancery Lane, and even courtiers simpering at Whitehall. After the Restoration, however, thousands took up residence in the West End because that was the finest place to live – a place to spend money, to entertain or just to bask in being. With the rise of finance in the City, bankers trickled out of Cornhill and the Cheap into the splendid squares shooting up further west, and fine folks flooded from the shires. 'London,' pronounced the Revd Thomas Gisborne around 1800,

is the centre to which almost all the individuals who fill the upper and middle ranks of society are successively attracted. The country pays its tribute to the supreme city. Business, interest, curiosity, the love of pleasure, the desire of knowledge, the thirst for change, ambition to be deemed polite, occasion a continual influx into the metropolis from every corner of the Kingdom.

New metropolitan elegance was eye-catching. Around 1700 Celia Fiennes was impressed to find 'London joyned with Westminster ... it makes up but one vast building with all its suburbs.' 'New squares and new streets rising up every day to such a prodigy of buildings that nothing in the world does, or ever did equal it, except old Rome in Trajan's time,' enthused Daniel Defoe twenty years later. Soon the novelist Tobias Smollett had his country character Matt Bramble quite boggled. 'London is literally new to me,' he gasped,

new in its streets, houses, and even in its situation; as the Irishman said, 'London is now gone out of town.' What I left open fields, producing hay and corn, I now find covered with streets and squares, and palaces, and churches ... Pimlico and Knightsbridge are now almost joined to Chelsea and Kensington, and if this infatuation continues for half a century, I suppose the whole county of Middlesex will be covered with brick.

In the 1750s Charles Jenner said it all in verse:

> Where'er around I cast my wand'ring eyes
> Long burning rows of fetid bricks arise,
> And nauseous dunghills swell in mould'ring heaps
> While the fat sow beneath their covert sleeps.

Perhaps for the first time, foreign tourists flocked in to view the 'monster city', with that surge of anticipation, awe and apprehension felt by newcomers today approaching New York. Sophie von La Roche, the first notable German woman novelist, could hardly contain herself on first seeing London: it meant 'more to me than Paris and France'. Continentals never used to pay compliments like that. Sophie was a starry-eyed Anglophile, but others too were thrilled. 'At last I am in my beloved London, for which I have longed and schemed and pined,' the German *philosophe* Georg Christoph Lichtenberg told a Göttingen friend in 1775.

'London is a giant,' remarked the Swiss-American Louis Simond at the dawn of the nineteenth century. It had a pulse of its own: 'Shut up in our apartments ... we have full leisure to observe its outward aspect and general movements, and listen to the roar of its waves ,,, like the tides of the ocean.' The mass and medley of people, the hurly-burly, were breathtaking, like a force of nature. The traffic jams on the river astonished César de Saussure, a Swiss visitor, who guessed that 'round about London there are at least 15,000 boats for the transport of persons, and numbers of others for that of merchandise' – 'the Thames below the bridge,' he gasped, 'is almost hidden by merchant vessels from every country.'

London was becoming *different*, unique. In 1785 a German traveller, J. W. von Archenholz, found that in the West End 'the houses are mostly new and elegant; the squares are superb, the streets straight and open'. It amounted to an innovation in urban living. Accustomed to cities in which wealth and squalor were all mixed together like bubble and squeak, people were intrigued to find a new social segregation, in which the hierarchy of ranks was stamped upon the topography of town. The *Spectator* magazine, appealing to the *bon ton*, highlighted this conspicuous social polarization: 'The inhabitants of St James's, notwithstanding they live under the same laws and speak the same language, are a distinct people from those of Cheapside' – London was thus becoming 'an aggregate of various nations distinguished from each other by their respective customs, manners and interests'.

Addresses assumed great weight. Craftsmen stuck to the City, while the *hoi polloi* were elbowed into the extramural East End, which gained notoriety as an exotic nation of its own. Dr Johnson 'talked today a great deal of the wonderful extent and variety of London,' James Boswell recalled, 'and observed, that men of curious enquiry might see in it such modes of life as very few could even imagine. He in particular recommended us to explore *Wapping*.' (The dutiful disciple obeyed the doctor's orders, though in the event he was 'disappointed'.) The West End, for its part, was Quality Street.

The West End/East End divide became definitive. 'London is more remarkable for the distribution of its inhabitants than any city of the continent,' explained Robert Southey around 1800:

there is an imaginary line of demarcation which divides them from each other. A nobleman would not be found by any accident to live in that part which is properly called the City … whenever a person says that he lives at the West End of the Town, there is some degree of consequence connected with the situation: For instance, my tailor lives at the West End of the Town, and consequently he is supposed to make my coat in a better style of fashion: and this opinion is carried so far among the ladies, that if a cap was known to have come from the City, it would be given to my lady's woman, who would give it to the cook, and she perhaps would think it prudent not to inquire into its pedigree.

Yet the new West End did not exude imperiousness, like baroque St Petersburg or Dresden: it was *sui generis*. For it was the work not of princes or popes but of aristocratic capitalism, its driving force noblemen building for profit and prestige. The result, of course, was awfully superior – raising the tone raised the rentals: for a mid-eighteenth-century developer to have littered Mayfair with markets would have been mad. But it was not just exclusive: it was particularly intimate and private.

Turin, Berlin, Mannheim, Lisbon and Washington radiated pomp. With its grand boulevards, piazzas and obelisks, its vistas of cathedrals and citadels and other scenic climaxes, the baroque or neoclassical capital enshrined the aesthetics of absolutism: monumentality and wide open spaces bespoke power unopposed. Nothing remotely like that appeared in London, at least not until the Prince Regent. (Georgian London owed nothing to the first three Georges, whose taste was for rural Richmond, Windsor and Kew.) The West End was not imposed from on high as an ensemble; it grew through piecemeal development of self-contained aristocratic estates, forming individual building-blocks. The coherence of the mosaic was due not to dictated vision but to shared values, strengthened by matrimonial alliances.

The West End grandee estate created a character of its own; its inward-looking squares formed self-sufficient classy quarters – almost pastoral idylls. Bloomsbury, Bedford and Russell Squares in west-central London, and, above all, Hanover, Berkeley and Grosvenor Squares in Mayfair and Cavendish, Portman and Manchester Squares in Marylebone, made the emergent West End an accumulation of units, detached from each other, lacking stately connecting boulevards and panoramas. But this 'defect' (to conventional aesthetic eyes) imparted a unique flavour, indeed a classical Whig political message: here was a town not dictated by despots and their architect toadies, but true to the principles of propertied patricians.

This is reflected in a remarkable fact. Over the centuries various addresses rose and fell in eligibility. West Cheap, Chancery Lane, the Strand, Covent Garden – each had its day, and then slid downmarket or was redeveloped. But the great Georgian estates have remained (with their clones, such as Belgravia and Kensington) the chic places to live, shop, saunter and dine. Town remained tops. Unlike Birmingham's Edgbaston and Manchester's Didsbury, no Victorian suburb eclipsed the West End.

Why did so many grandees and gentry, judges and generals, flock to the West End? Why did it attract writers, artists, visitors? This chapter will explore the triumph of town, but something must first be said about the Georgian metropolis as a whole, for the West End could never have been sustained without overall vitality and growth.

Rebuilding after the Fire might have given the city éclat. That did not happen. Thrown up on its archaic street plan, the new City was made of vermin- and fire-proof brick and stone; thoroughfares were wider, paving and drainage were improved, and very agreeable residences were put up like those on Laurence Pountney Hill. Yet the new City flaunted no residential glory; the housing style was vernacular and solid, built for burgesses – there was nothing like the new West End. The most attractive Fire replacement took place west of the walls – for instance, New Court in Middle Temple.

Of course St Paul's Cathedral, completed in 1710, was peerless. And the City acquired other handsome public buildings, like the new Bethlem lunatic asylum, built in the 1670s at Moorfields to Robert Hooke's designs. In 1734 George Dance the Elder embarked on the Wren-influenced but rather clumsy Lord Mayor's Mansion

House on the site of the old Stocks market. And about the same time the governors of the Bank of England commissioned George Sampson's Palladian building in Threadneedle Street. Overall, however, James Ralph was right to lament in his *Critical Review of the Public Buildings ... in and about London and Westminster* (1734) that the phoenix City displayed little that was grand or gorgeous – '*Porticos* and *Piazzas* are not now to be expected in the City,' complained Joseph Massie. The City lacked unity and dignity; all was commonplace and confusion – in fact, complained a critic, it remained a 'Babel ... with the Hotch-Potch of half-moon and serpentine narrow Streets, close, dismal, long Lanes, stinking Allies, dark, gloomy Courts and suffocating Yards'. Trade was a leveller: 'Here lives a Personage of high Distinction; next Door, a Butcher with his stinking Shambles.'

Not the least drawback of the City was its pall of smoke. John Evelyn's *Fumifugium* (1661) railed against the 'impure and thick mist', due to the burning of sea coal in grates, in the brewing, baking and boiling trades, in the thousands of glasshouses, potters' kilns, blacksmiths' and gunsmiths' shops and dyers' yards that choked the backstreets. Wheezing visitors were shocked by the smuts that dirtied buildings and even the horses. 'Everything in the streets ... seemed dark even to blackness,' remarked the Prussian Pastor Moritz. 'This smoke,' commented the French traveller Pierre-Jean Grosley, 'forms a cloud which envelops London like a mantle; a cloud which ... suffers the sun to break out only now and then, which casual appearance procures the Londoners a few of what they call *glorious days*.' Lichtenberg had to agree, finding himself 'writing by the light of a candle (at half-past ten in the morning)'. Even Americans were appalled by foggy days in London town: 'It is difficult to form an idea of the kind of winter days in London,' confessed Louis Simond in 1810; 'the smoke of fossil coals forms an atmosphere, perceivable for many miles.'

The City – 'this sinfull Sea Cole Town', according to Lady Mary Wortley Montagu – thus had its minuses as a residence. After the Fire, not everyone returned. Dissenting tradesmen relocated to villages like Hackney and Stoke Newington, where they could worship without legal impediment, and the fashionable fled for ever. New houses stood empty for years. To tempt recruits, the Mayor relaxed conditions governing citizenship, but, even so, the City never again really became crowded. Estimated at around 80,000 by Gregory King in 1695, the population of the intramural City had risen to 87,000 by 1750, but by 1801 it was dipping back. The well-to-do started living away from their businesses, and aldermen were opting for country seats or sophisticated squares. 'Oh, how I long to be transported to the dear regions of Grosvenor-square!' sighed Miss Sterling in George Colman's popular comedy *The Clandestine Marriage* (1766), 'far, far from the dull districts of Aldersgate, Cheap, Candlewick, and Farringdon Without and Within.'

Among the deserters were many capitalists like the fictional Sterlings, no longer the

Whittingtons of old – worthy citizens with livery-company loyalties – but stockjobbing financiers, Georgian yuppies. Merchant princes now found City office a chore to escape rather than a privilege to enjoy – indeed, the Mansion House was largely paid for by fines collected from those dodging service. Over the next two centuries the City changed from a residence into a forest of offices, a nocturnal ghost town.

Meanwhile the metropolis swelled: no longer at the former breakneck pace, but swiftly enough to turn it into a monster city by world standards. In 1600 it had housed around 200,000; by the Restoration there were twice that number. In 1700 London's population was around 575,000, about the same as Paris's. By 1750 it had hit 675,000, while by 1880 it was 900,000, a third as large again as Paris, and London was the world's biggest city, with the possible exception of Edo (Tokyo). Heylin's nightmare ('monstrous growth') had become a reality. London towered like no other capital. In 1750, for example, one in ten of all English and Welsh people was resident in London, whereas only one Frenchman in forty lived in Paris.

The City had been dwarfed. 'London as a city only, and as its walls and liberties line it out, might, indeed, be viewed in a small compass,' Defoe explained:

but, when I speak of London, now in the modern acceptation, you expect I shall take in all that vast mass of buildings, reaching from Black-Wall in the east, to Tot-Hill Fields in the west ... to Islington north ... to Cavendish Square, and all the new buildings by, and beyond, Hanover Square, by which the city of London, for so it is still to be called, is extended to Hide Park Corner in the Brentford Road, and almost to Marylebone in the Acton Road; and how much farther it may spread, who knows?

Disapproving of this 'straggling, confus'd' growth – 'out of all shape, uncompact, and unequal' – Defoe guessed London's perimeter stretched for thirty-six miles, enclosing such villages as Deptford and Islington. As yet Chelsea, Knightsbridge, Marylebone, Poplar and Greenwich lay outside his mental map – but not for long, for 'Westminster is in a fair way to shake hands with Chelsea, as St Gyles's is with Marylebone; and Great Russell Street by Montague House, with Tottenham-Court'. 'Whither,' he inquired, 'will this monstrous city then extend?'

Time told. By the 1760s the green gaps within Defoe's 'line of circumvallation' had been infilled: Shadwell and Bethnal Green had dissolved into the sea of bricks; to the south, the Borough was spreading to Newington Butts; south-west, Tothill Fields in Westminster was edging into Chelsea and Knightsbridge; and Hammersmith, Chelsea, Paddington, Marylebone and St Pancras – the 'five villages beyond the Bills' (i.e. beyond the 109 parishes covered by the Bills of Mortality) – were joining the metropolitan orbit. Chelsea rose from 350 houses in 1717 to 1,350 in 1795; Marylebone from 317 to 7,764.

Instrumental in this spread were the building of Westminster Bridge in 1750 and

Blackfriars Bridge in 1769, opening up south London. So too was the construction in 1756–7 of the New Road (the present Marylebone, Euston and Pentonville Roads), running north of Marylebone, across Tottenham Court into St Pancras, and east to the Angel at Islington; this New Road chalked out Marylebone and Bloomsbury for development. London responded by shooting north from Tyburn Road (Oxford Street). Writing from Berkeley Square in 1791, Horace Walpole, who loved his comforts, observed that dispersion was killing the sedan-chair trade, 'for Hercules and Atlas could not carry anybody from one end of this enormous capital to the other'. 'The town cannot hold all its inhabitants,' he reflected,

so prodigiously the population is augmented. I have twice been going to stop my coach in Piccadilly, thinking there was a mob; and it was only nymphs and swains sauntering or trudging. T'other morning, i.e. at two o'clock, I went to see Mrs Garrick and Miss Hannah More at the Adelphi [off the Strand], and was stopped five times before I reached Northumberland House; for the tides of coaches, chariots, curricles, phaetons, &c., are endless.

The first national Census (1801) spoke in more august tones. 'The Metropolis of England,' it boasted, 'is at once the Seat of Government and the greatest Emporium in the known world.'

Walpole kept harping on at his theme: 'There will soon be one street from London to Brentford; ay, and from London to every village ten miles round!' His next morsel of gossip pinpointed the cause: 'Lord Camden has just let ground at Kentish Town for building fourteen hundred houses.' Aristocratic development explains the West End's unique character. The trend, of course, had begun much earlier. Lord Salisbury's St Martin's Lane and the Earl of Bedford's Covent Garden Piazza dated from early Stuart times. For half a century Covent Garden remained the meridian of fashion, the ecclesiastical historian John Strype observing around 1700 that it was 'well inhabited by a mixture of nobility, gentry and wealthy tradesmen … scarce admitting of any poor, not being pestered with mean courts and alleys'. This was not to last: it grew raffish and disreputable, pockmarked with taverns and brothels. The gentry fled west: by the Regency, Beau Brummell was mortified to be discovered one night *as far east as* the Strand (he had got lost, he explained).

In better days Covent Garden had triggered adjacent developments. Two pro-tagonists – worlds apart from each other – were crucial. They were Dr Nicholas Barbon, the Adam of all speculative builders, and the Earl of Southampton, a mighty landowner. The partnership of speculative builder and estate-owner was the making of the West End. Barbon was not alone, however: many spied profit in property, building west of Holborn, around St Giles, St Martin's Lane, Soho and Piccadilly. Sir Thomas Bond invested rather unsuccessfully in what became Bond Street. The disreputable gambler Colonel Thomas Panton erected Panton Square and Panton Street around 1674, with coach-houses and stabling yards. In the 1680s King's Square (later Soho Square) was developed, partly by the bricklayer/builder Richard Frith, immortalized in Frith Street.

But if he was one of many developers, Barbon was the most resourceful and unscrupulous. Son of Praise-God Barbon, the Puritan divine – what more suggestive link between Calvinism and capitalism? – he was an MD, an MP, a pioneer of fire insurance and a writer on economics; a jack of all trades, he was master of speculative building. Ambitious and audacious, he protested he had no time for small ventures – 'that a bricklayer could do'. The gain *he* expected was of great undertakings which would 'rise lustily in the whole'.

Barbon specialized in doing up or knocking down dilapidated properties. He leased the Tudor palaces along the Strand – Essex House from the Earl of Essex, York House from the Duke of Buckingham, and Devonshire House from the Earl of Devonshire – pulled them down, and filled the sites and their ample gardens with affordable housing. York House, for example, made way for Buckingham and Villiers Streets, Exeter House for Exeter Street and Exeter Change. Critics complained that his Strand redevelopments soon became riddled with 'taverns, alehouses, cookshops and vaulting schools'; Barbon did not care – his aim was profit.

His fingers dipped in many pies – Mincing Lane, St James's Square, Newport Street, and Bedford Row in Holborn: he built here a square, there a market, elsewhere lawyers' chambers. To shave costs he standardized, repeating the same simple but stylish ornamentations, creating a veneer of gentility. He was guilty of jerry-building and, like all great developers, utterly ruthless, riding roughshod over objectors and the law. In 1684 he launched a big scheme, Red Lion Square. In retaliation, the Gray's Inn attorneys beat up his workmen, but he overrode opposition, the representations of Wren, and writs from the Middlesex JPs: 'Such was the force of private enterprise,' commented Sir John Summerson, 'at long last freed by liberating itself from the tyranny of Royal Proclamations.'

Post-Restoration years saw *ad hoc* development north of the Strand and Fleet Street. Thomas Neale started building the area that was to become Seven Dials. Leicester Square took shape. Back in 1631 Robert Sidney, 2nd Earl of Leicester, had gained a licence to build a mansion north of the Royal Mews (now Trafalgar Square), in return for laying out land (Leicester Fields) with walks for parish benefit. These gardens were gradually encroached on by the Earl, however, until in 1670 he received a further licence to build south, east and west of the Fields and Leicester Square took shape. Residing at Penshurst in Kent, the Sidneys treated their London property as an investment; so they carved up the Leicester House garden to create Lisle Street (after the Earl's second title), and many profitable blocks followed as Soho (once hunting-

Soho Square, 1731. Open fields separate Oxford Street from Hampstead Heath

fields: 'So-ho!' was a hunting-cry) rose as an attractive but never august neighbourhood. Gerrard Street was built from the 1670s on land belonging to Charles, Lord Gerrard, and was developed by the ubiquitous Barbon. Some big houses were run up, including one for the Earl of Devonshire. Artists and writers moved in: John Dryden lived at 44 Gerrard Street and James Gibbs, the architect, later moved to No. 18. Like the rest of the neighbourhood, Gerrard Street lost its glamour, soon being known mainly for coffee-houses and taverns – No. 9 was the famous Turk's Head, where Johnson and Reynolds founded The Club.

Paralleling Gerrard Street to the north, Old Compton Street was built from the 1670s, becoming a shopping street and, like much of the area, a favourite of Huguenot refugees from France. Greek Street too was laid out then, developing the usual mix of fashionable tenants, artists and musicians, taverns and superior tradesmen's workshops. Greek Street afforded lodgings for visitors in an age when hotels were as yet unknown: Casanova stayed there in 1764, as did the teenage Thomas De Quincey, later author of *Confessions of an English Opium-Eater*. Josiah Wedgwood had his London warehouse and showrooms there, before moving in 1797 to the very superior St James's Square.

Frith Street also rose; among its visitors were Mozart and later John Constable. Adjacent Dean Street became a favourite with French immigrants. Joseph Nollekens, the sculptor, was born at No. 29, and George Cruikshank, the cartoonist, also lived there; later it provided lodgings for Karl Marx. The Leicester Square and Soho precinct thus became the haunt of artists, writers, bohemians, rakes and revolutionaries. Sir Isaac Newton occupied a house just off Leicester Square; Sir Joshua Reynolds lived in Great Newport Street and Leicester Square; Hogarth also lived there for several years, as did the surgeon and naturalist John Hunter – though he kept his menagerie of ostriches and leopards on a farm at Earl's Court.

The area west of Leicester Square and south of Tyburn Road was run up in a rather bitty way (alleys and courts still abound off Dean Street and north of Brewer Street). Carnaby Street was laid out in 1683 by Richard Tyler, a bricklayer. Its initial inhabitants were Huguenot craftsmen. Speculative builders were thus creating a West End by fits and starts, mingling the superior, the satisfactory and the shoddy. Scores of streets knocked up in this way survive in whole or part, sandwiched between Charing Cross Road and Tottenham Court Road in the east and Regent Street in the west – for instance, around D'Arblay Street and Newburgh Street, or by Rathbone Place, another artists' haunt.

But something altogether nobler arose further west: the squares and places of Mayfair and Marylebone, a tribute to the business strategies of great proprietors. Such developments reveal new standards of aristocratic elegance, shifts in taste, and hard-headed realism about urban design. West End estates were erected on the rule of optimal ground use, involving concentrations of the most compact dwellings the beau monde would be dying to occupy.

From medieval times grandees had, of course, preferred spacious piles somewhat akin to the *hôtels* of Henri IV's Paris – detached structures in their own grounds, safely behind walls. The requisitioned palaces lining the Strand – Somerset House, Russell House, York House and Northumberland House, with their great halls – gratified Elizabethan grandees. Private palaces continued to be put up after the Restoration – Buckingham House in Pall Mall, named after the 1st Marquess of Buckingham, Arlington House in St James's, built by the Secretary of State Lord Arlington, and Clarendon House in Piccadilly, erected by Lord Chancellor Clarendon.

Clarendon House significantly proved short-lived, however, being demolished in 1683 and its site redeveloped as Bond Street, Dover Street and Albemarle Street by speculators headed by Sir Thomas Bond. 'I went to advise and give directions about the building of two streets in Berkeley Gardens,' recorded John Evelyn in 1684, caught in two minds about development:

I could not but deplore the sweete place (by far the most noble gardens, courts, and accommodations, stately porticos, &c., any where about the towne) should be so much straighten'd and turn'd into tenements. But that magnificent pile and gardens contiguous to it, built by the late Lord Chancellor Clarendon, being all demolish'd, and design'd for Piazzas and buildings, was some excuse for my Lady Berkeley's resolution of letting out her ground also for so excessive a price as was offer'd, advancing neere £.1000 per ann. in mere ground-rents; to such a mad intemperance was the age coming of building about a citty, by far too disproportionate already to the nation; I having in my time seene it almost as large again as it was within my memory.

Mansions like Buckingham House, commissioned by leading peers, bore close family resemblance to their country cousins, the stately homes – not surprisingly, because those were all that top architects knew how to design. Architects' style books, like James Gibbs's *Book of Architecture* (1728), traditionally concentrated on country seats, paying little attention to town-house design. But change was afoot, and new ideals of urban living utilized space more artfully and profitably, by way of squares and terraces. And here lies the Earl of Southampton's importance.

Thomas Wriothesley, 4th Earl of Southampton, laid the foundations of modern Bloomsbury by creating Bloomsbury Square, the first London plot called a square, erecting a mansion somewhat in Inigo Jones's style with a square in front. The first Bloomsbury Square leases, granted in 1661, were of a kind destined to become crucial in the economics of the West End.

Southampton parcelled out plots to builders on forty-two-year leases at low ground rents, on condition that the lessee built substantial houses which would ultimately become the ground landlord's property. For the landlord, this minimized outlay while guaranteeing quality control and a regular income. The first tenants were mainly speculators. The builder could act as middleman, leasing plots to lesser speculators; or he could lease plots to tenants, building to order; or he could build on spec and then seek tenants. The builder was thus an entrepreneur, borrowing money, shouldering risks, raking in profits.

The building-lease system met London's needs to a T. The landlord got his estate developed without tying up capital, and the property remained his own – an essential arrangement because London estates were generally entailed or held in trust: they could not be sold. For his part, the speculative builder acquired a prime site. Master carpenters, plasterers and plumbers pooled resources to reduce costs; a speculative builder needed just sufficient capital or credit to buy materials. The building-lease system shared risks and got things moving.

Bloomsbury Square launched a new town-house style destined to dominate London: the narrow-fronted terrace. Each dwelling had a simple rectangular plan, rising to four storeys, constructed in brick with thick dividing walls to curb fire risks. Great ingenuity was devoted to packing accommodation into dwellings built on deep narrow sites. Houses were erected on a service basement ('area'), used for the kitchen and servants' hall. Above, there would be three floors for the family and an attic for the servants. The front door was imposing, with a semicircular arch. The sash windows were tallest on the first floor, smallest on the top.

Vertical living was a novelty. Attending the Duke of Ormonde's house in St James's Square, Jonathan Swift bantered about the experience to his friend Stella:

Today in the morning I visited upwards; first I saw the Duke of Ormond below stairs ... then I went up one pair of stairs and sate with the Duchess; then I went up another pair of stairs and paid a visit to Lady Betty; and desired her woman to go up to the garret, that I might pass half an hour with her, but she was young and handsome and would not.

Terraces were often boxed into squares, the central area compensating for the fact that residences had little land of their own. Side-streets accommodated essential tradesmen. Southampton realized that dwellings alone were not enough: a square had to form the focus of an eligible residential unit, a kind of village, comprising a grid of more modest streets, shops and services and creating a living-unit with cachet of its own. Evelyn latched on to this: 'Dined at my Lord Treasurer's, the Earl of Southampton in Bloomsbury, where he was building a noble square, or piazza, a little town.' Starting with the Grosvenor estate in the 1720s, the mews made its appearance, keeping stables and services close but hidden, and providing a back way for garbage to be carted off by the 'night-soil' men.

Streets on the new, elegant West End estates were up to sixty feet wide, with broad pavements. By urban standards this was handsome indeed – double the width of the widest traditional Paris streets. And of great importance was the London Building Act of 1774, which defined four 'rates'. The 'first rate' included big houses occupying not less than 900 square feet of area and four storeys high and valued at over £850; in the 'fourth rate' were two-storey houses. Each rate had its building rules. 'The real importance of the system', commented Sir John Summerson, was 'that it confirmed a degree of standardization in speculative building' – in other words, it curbed cowboys, and ensured that houses put up by builders rather than architects would not be a blot on the townscape.

*

Charles II had a fondness for St James's, by then an ageing palace built by Henry VIII out of the leper hospital of St James's. He planted his various mistresses nearby, and loved playing *palla a maglio* (a cross between croquet and bowls which gave its name to Pall Mall) and sauntering in the park. Open to the public, St James's Park allowed informal mixing of King and subjects. (George II's Queen Caroline later inquired of Sir Robert Walpole what it would cost to shut the royal parks to the public: 'Only three *Crowns*,' was the reply.)

The King and the park made St James's the heart of chic Restoration London. It was bound to attract speculative builders. The pioneer was Henry Jermyn, Earl of St Albans, who hatched the idea of a square to the far side of Pall Mall. One of the King's cronies, he cadged the land. St Albans envisaged St James's Square as an exclusive quarter of about ten grand houses, but he soon hit a snag: the aristocrats earmarked as neighbours were reluctant to fork out the sums needed to build such 'palaces'. So the Earl was compelled to scale his plans down and follow Southampton's lead in Bloomsbury. To reduce expenses he reduced the plots, and let them not just to the titled but to builders prepared to put up houses. The development remained splendid – Wren was commissioned to design a church, St James's Piccadilly, at the north end of Duke of York Street – but the work was no longer financed by the residents alone. At St James's, as everywhere else, speculators proved essential.

Thus transfigured, St James's Square became a template for the West End as a first-rate residential quarter, cramming much into compact spaces without sacrifice of elegance. St Albans's own house in the square boasted a frontage of some 120 feet; most had a width of around 50 feet, but some as little as half that. The message was clear: henceforth you could live *à la mode* in London in a shoebox: *multum in parvo*.

'I have been to see a very good house in St James's Square,' wrote Isabella, Lady Wentworth, to her son who in 1708 was looking for a place; she had taken a fancy to No. 31, a former residence of St Albans and the first house erected in the square:

It has thre large rooms forward and two little ons backward, closetts and marble chimney peicis, and harths to al the best rooms, and iron backs to the chimneys. Thear is twoe pretty clossets with chimneys and glas over them and picturs in the wenscoat over most of the chimneys, bras locks to all the doars, wescoat at bottom and top and slips of boards for the hangings. Thear will want little to be dun to it. Thear is back stairs, twoe coach housis, and stable for ii horses, rooms over for sarvents, very good offisis, a yard for the drying of cloaths, and leds for that purpus, a stable yard and a hors pond and back gate, which I forgot the street's name it goes into ... Tomorrow the man comes to tell me the prise.

St James's Square set the tone. When the Irish adventurer the Duke of Ormonde bought his house there in 1682, his son congratulated him: 'how ill it would look now you are an English duke to have no house there'. Rubbing shoulders with him were the 1st Earl of Conway; Sir John Ernley, the Chancellor of the Exchequer; the 4th Earl of Devonshire, Lord Steward of the Household; Lord Ossulston, Lieutenant of the Bodyguard; Lord Dartmouth, Master General of the Ordnance; the Earl of Ranelagh, Vice-Treasurer of Ireland; the 3rd Earl of Suffolk, Earl Marshal of England; the 1st Marquis of Halifax, the Lord Privy Seal; and the 1st Earl of Essex, First Lord of the Treasury. By 1721 no fewer than six dukes – Chandos, Dorset, Kent, Norfolk, Portland and Southampton – had their town residence there, as well as seven earls, a countess, a baron and a baronet. George III was born there. You no longer needed a palace: it was chic to live snug in a square with its highly visible comings and goings – by 1750 there were about 500 hackney cabs and 400 sedan chairs in London, and some 15,000 street lamps, lighting late-birds home.

Smart streets sprang up all around, such as Arlington Street, off Piccadilly, built up in the late 1680s. Barbara Castlemaine, Duchess of Cleveland – Charles II's mistress – lived there, and Sir Robert Walpole, Charles James Fox and Lord North were later residents. And fashionable developments spread north-west into Mayfair. Various free-standing aristocratic mansions were put up, including Burlington House (1713) in Piccadilly – now, ruined by Victorian improvements, home of the Royal Academy. Most of the rest – Isaac Ware's Chesterfield House, once in South Audley Street, Berkeley (later Devonshire) House (Piccadilly) and Grosvenor, Dorchester and Londonderry Houses (Park Lane) – have been demolished. Around 1760 Horace Walpole expressed his amazement at the transformation of a neighbourhood he could recall as rustic and full of stables. 'I started today at Piccadilly, like a country squire. There are twenty new stone houses. At first I concluded that all the grooms that used to live there had got estates and built palaces.' When Lord Chesterfield built his mansion, facing Hyde Park, the site was so rural he quipped he would need a dog to keep him company.

Around these aristocratic mansions, speculators were active. Beginning in 1701, Sir Henry Boyd sold freehold plots around Albemarle Street. The buyers included master craftsmen like Matthew Tomlinson, a carpenter of St Martin's parish, and Edward Buckingham, a mason of St Clement Danes, who ran up houses and then sold them off. *A New View of London* (1708) described Albemarle Street as 'a Street of excellent new Building, inhabited by Persons of Quality between the Fields and Portugal Street', while Dover Street was 'a street of very good Buildings, mostly inhabited by Gentry'.

And three great squares arose in Mayfair. First came Hanover Square – a topically patriotic name – laid out after 1714 with houses leased by a bunch of Whig generals, veterans of Marlborough's campaigns. Blessed by the fashionable church of St George, Hanover Square houses were spacious and inhabited by 'persons of distinction'. About half a dozen survive. The Hanover Square Rooms were long famed for their concerts, at which J. C. Bach, Haydn, Paganini and Liszt all performed.

Berkeley Square emerged a little later (1737), carved out of fields beyond the garden

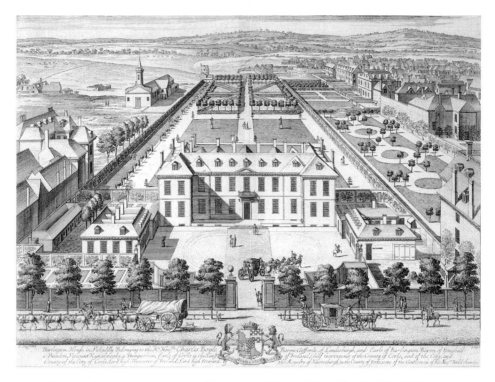

Eighteenth-century engraving of Burlington House, Piccadilly (Guildhall Library)

of Berkeley (later Devonshire) House, Piccadilly. It was to include what has been judged London's finest terraced house, No. 44, built in the 1740s by William Kent for Lady Isabella Finch. Together with the streets to the west – Hill Street, Chesterfield Street, Charles Street, Brook Street (where Handel wrote the *Messiah*), John Street (now Chesterfield Hill) and Farm Street – Berkeley Square became ultra-fashionable. Clive of India died in 1774 of an overdose of laudanum at No. 45. Berkeley Square was noble, yet it also housed some superior tradesmen. There was Gwynn's Coffee-House and, from 1760, the celebrated ice-cream- and pastry-maker Gunter's (which survived till the Second World War).

As its name suggests, Mayfair always remained a touch villagey, with cottages and even pockets of poverty in the backstreets and mews, whose tenants waited upon the upper crust. A survey of Mayfair's tradesmen listed fifty-five butchers, who would still drive livestock to their shops for slaughter (a Brook Street gentlewoman complained that she couldn't get her carriage 'aired' without being 'gored by bullocks'). And there were cowkeepers (to provide fresh cream), carpenters, masons, upholsterers, cabinet-makers, dressmakers, tailors, milliners and so on. The May Fair itself survived on the ground bounded by Tyburn Lane (Park Lane), Piccadilly, Curzon Street, and Half Moon Street, part of which was leased by Edward Shepherd, owner of Shepherd

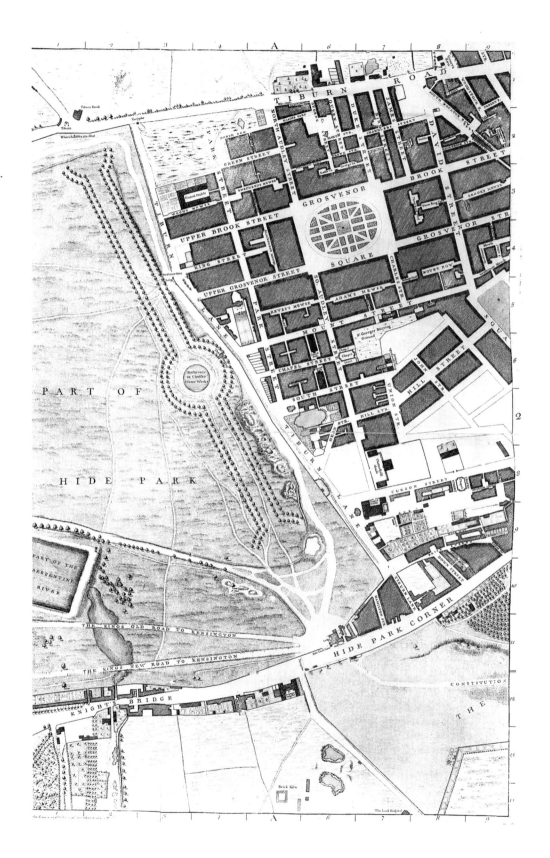

Market. There Londoners on a spree could enjoy fire-eating, prize-fights, juggling, tight-rope walkers and gingerbread sold by Tiddy Doll.

Grosvenor Square sprang up adjacent, on part of the vast Grosvenor estate, formed after the marriage in 1677 of Sir Thomas Grosvenor, a great Cheshire landowner, to Mary Davies, a twelve-year-old heiress. She brought to the marriage two gold-mines – 100 acres in Mayfair and more than half a square mile between Hyde Park and the Thames. Sir Thomas died in his mid-forties and Mary became deranged, but their three sons started building. Richard, the eldest, laid out a square with the family name. Six acres in extent, Grosvenor Square, London's largest, was completed in 1737, the Duchess of Kendal, George I's mistress, being among the earliest residents. Petronella Melusina, their daughter, married Lord Chesterfield, who built his magnificent house in South Audley Street. Alongside was Grosvenor Street, 'a spacious well built street, inhabited chiefly by People of Distinction'; about a third of its residents were titled. Top architects – Adam, Chambers, Soane, Wyatville, and James and Samuel Wyatt – all worked in Grosvenor Square, and many of its houses survive, though later stuccoed over.

To the east, Bond Street emerged as a mix of homes, shops and elegant lodgings. Laurence Sterne, author of *Tristram Shandy*, died at No. 41 in 1768. James Boswell had lodgings around the same time at the Piccadilly end. 'A genteel lodging in a good part of the town is absolutely necessary,' he judged: 'seeking a lodging was like seeking a wife. Sometimes I aimed at one or two guineas a week, like a rich lady of quality. Sometimes at one guinea, like a knight's daughter; and at last fixed on £22 a year, like the daughter of a good gentleman of moderate fortune.' Lord Nelson lived in Bond Street, and Byron stayed at Stevens's Hotel at No. 18. It was, after all, a grand place to see and be seen – close to Brooks's Club in St James's Street and to the Prince Regent's and Beau Brummell's tailors, Schweitzer & Davidson, in nearby Cork Street. Byron, who loved London – 'a damned place to be sure, but the only one in the world (at least in the English world) for fun' – was Mayfair man incarnate. 'Last night, *party* at Lansdowne House,' he wrote, recording the pain of West End pleasures; 'Tonight, *party* at Lady Charlotte Greville's – deplorable waste of time, and something of temper. Nothing imparted – nothing acquired – talking without ideas . . . Heigho! – and in this way half London pass what is called life.' The poet had lodged in St James's; in 1817 he moved into A2 Albany, a magnificent set of chambers rented from Lord Althorp, where, Byron noted with satisfaction, there was 'room for my books and sabres'. Mayfair offered a gentleman's every delight:

I have been boxing, for exercise, with Jackson for this last month daily. I have also been drinking, and, on one occasion, with three other friends at the Cocoa Tree, clareted and champagned till

Mayfair in 1746, by John Rocque. Knightsbridge is still open fields and duck ponds two – then supped, and finished with a kind of regency punch composed of madeira, brandy, and *green* tea, no *real* water being admitted therein. There was a night for you! ... I have also, more or less, been breaking a few of the favourite commandments.

St James's and Mayfair crowned the West End. Not all the beau monde could live there, however: they would not accommodate everyone; they were too dear. Other sites proved eligible, if not quite the tops. One was Marylebone. It was at least in the west; its drawback was that it lay on the wrong side of the disreputable Tyburn Road, described as 'a deep hollow road, and full of sloughs ... the lurking place of cut-throats'.

Cavendish Square arose first. It was the nucleus of the Harley–Cavendish estate, another child of a shrewd marriage alliance, between the 2nd Earl of Oxford (hence Oxford Street) and Henrietta Cavendish. The idea was to lay it out with noblemen's palaces designed by James Gibbs, architect of St Martin-in-the-Fields: Lord Chandos's house was to stand at the climax of a magnificent vista up Holles Street from Hanover Square. But the plan was stymied by a building slump. Chandos House – one of the finest surviving Adam houses, now the home of the Medical Society of London, on the corner of Queen Anne Street and Chandos Street – was eventually built in 1769–70 by Robert and James Adam for the 3rd Duke of Chandos. Further developments on the estate included Portland Place (named after William Bentinck, the 2nd Duke of Portland, who married the Cavendishes' daughter), Harley Street (after Edward Harley, 2nd Earl of Oxford – before the doctors dug in after 1800, it was a respectable residential street), Welbeck Street (after Welbeck Abbey, the Portland family home), and Wimpole Street (after the Harleys' Cambridgeshire seat).

The Cavendish development remained somewhat isolated. But after the Peace of Paris (1763) new blocks sprang up to its west, gradually filling the space defined by the New Road (Marylebone Road). Henry William Portman developed 200 acres of meadow passed down from a Tudor ancestor. He started in 1764 with a square, which was to owe its popularity to buildings by Robert Adam and James 'Athenian' Stuart, the architect of Montagu House. Built in the north-west corner of Portman Square for Mrs Montagu, 'Queen of the Blue Stockings', this housed ladylike female salons – and hosted a strange annual party for London chimney-sweeps. Home House, 20 Portman Square, was built in 1773–7 by Adam for Elizabeth, Countess of Home, with a splendid interior decorated by Antonio Zucchi and (perhaps) Angelica Kauffmann.

Tottenham Court Road and Oxford Street, 1746, by John Rocque. The New Road (later to become Marylebone Road and Euston Road) has not yet been built

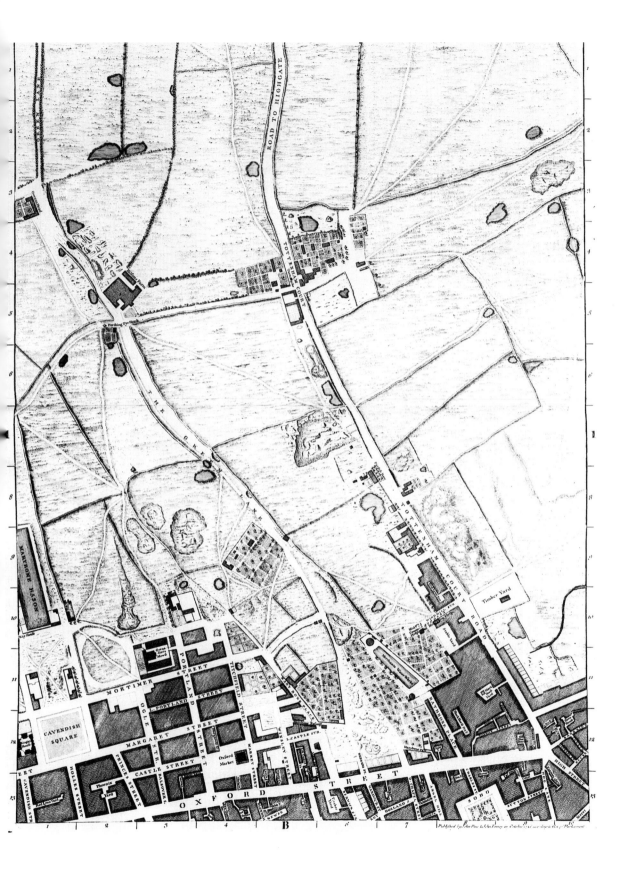

ROAD TO HIGHGATE

TOTTENHAM COURT

THE OKS

TOTTENHAM COURT ROAD

Timber Yard

MARYBONE HAY ON

CAVENDISH SQUARE

MORTIMER   STREET
PORTLAND   STREET
Grass Acre Mead

MARGARET   STREET
OGLE   STREET
PORTLAND   STREET
FITCHFIELD STREET
MARKET STREET
L. CASTLE STR.

Oxford
Market

CASTLE   STREET
PRINCE'S STREET
Phoenix
HOLLES STREET
CAVENDISH ST.

OXFORD   STREET

SOHO
HIGH STREET

B

Published by John Pine & John Tinney in October 1746 according to Act of Parliament

The Portman estate had its mews for tradesmen and retainers. One of these was Cato Street (Homer and Virgil Streets were its fellows), where, in the stable loft of No. 6 (now No. 1A), the 'Cato Street conspirators' laid plans to murder the entire Cabinet as they dined in Grosvenor Square on 23 February 1820. Baker Street was laid out from 1755 by William Baker, on land leased from Portman. Before Sherlock Holmes, it was the home of William Pitt the Younger (once of Berkeley Square), of Sarah Siddons, of Edward Bulwer-Lytton, and of Sir Richard Burton, the explorer and orientalist. Further east, the wide streets and elegant places of the Portland estate reached the New Road in 1775.

Just beyond St Marylebone's eastern edge, Fitzroy Square, designed by Adam, was begun in 1790, though in 1807 it was reported that 'the remainder has been a dreary chasm at least fifteen years'. ('Marylebone bankruptcies' had been quite a catch-phrase since the 1770s.) Charlotte Street was erected about 1791, later attracting artists like Constable, and Bloomsbury resumed in the 1770s the development originated a century earlier by the Earl of Southampton.

The Bedford family owned the vast tract north of Bloomsbury Square, acquired in the seventeenth century through a judicious marriage between the 3rd Earl and the Earl of Southampton's heiress. The cautious 3rd Earl was slow to build, and he missed the fashion, which migrated west. So while Bloomsbury remained choice – its eligibility upheld by a ducal iron grip over development – it did not gain aristocratic éclat, being solid rather than scintillating. So concerned were the Bedfords to uphold the tone that they rationed shops, banned taverns, and gated the entrances. Some gates survived until the twentieth century, and Bloomsbury is still short of shops and pubs.

Bedford Square and Gower Street were begun in 1776, becoming desirable quarters for lawyers and other professionals. Bedford Square – the first triumph of the 1774 Building Act, built entirely of 'first-rate' houses – is now Bloomsbury's only complete Georgian square. The central house on each side is pilastered and stuccoed; the rest are of brick with doors decorated with Coade stone. Until 1893 the square was gated, and trusty tradesmen had to deliver goods in person.

Building crept northward to the Euston Road early in the nineteenth century. In 1800 James Burton was commissioned to work to the east on Russell Square. A Scot who had set himself up in Southwark, Burton proved energetic and capable. In 1807 he built Tavistock Square, Burton Street and Burton Crescent (now renamed Cartwright Gardens after Major John Cartwright, the political reformer, who lived at No. 37). North-east of Queen Square lay the Foundling Hospital, possessing extensive grounds. Its governors commissioned Brunswick Square and Guilford Street, and Burton built almost 600 houses on the hospital's estate. The centre-piece, erected in 1795–1802, was Brunswick Square, with Mecklenburgh Square balancing it on the far side. Jane Austen has Emma's sister-in-law, Isabella, very full of it:

Our part of London is so very superior to most others! – You must not confound us with London in general, my dear sir. The neighbourhood of Brunswick Square is very different from all the rest. We are so very airy! ... Mr Wingfield thinks the neighbourhood of Brunswick Square decidedly the most favourable as to air.

Burton was the first captain of the building industry. He virtually mass-produced the joinery and ironwork for his houses. Like Thomas Cubitt after him, he helped give Bloomsbury its exceptional uniformity.

The town thus grew south in St James's, west to Marylebone, and centrally in Bloomsbury. High society was lured by many factors: Parliament and politics, shops and the season, marriages, money and mortgages. The Quality became convinced of the indispensability of owning, or at least renting, a town house. Yet, obvious though this development may seem to us now, it involved no mean persuasion, for cities had always had a mixed press. Babel was associated with pride, Babylon with corruption, Sodom and Gomorrah with perversion, Rome (in Protestant eyes) with the Beast. For Christians, the city represented both heaven and hell, *civitas Dei* and *civitas Diaboli*. Bucolic myths portrayed the countryside as innocent and virtuous. Pastoral visions were particularly potent because England's grandees gloried in a country-house culture linking land with liberty, by contrast to the sycophancy of court.

Restoration wits, of course, presented St James's as civilization itself, mocking Mummerset clodhoppers. Mistress Sullen in Farquhar's *The Beaux' Stratagem* calls country pleasures 'racks and torments'. Yet critics could always depict town as loose and lecherous and idealize Squire Honesty. 'I have got the London disease, they call Love, I am sick of my Husband, and for my Gallant,' William Wycherley's Mrs Pinchwife ominously declares. Compromises were needed. Town would be acceptable so long as it retained a rural touch. Beyond St James's Palace, on the northern front of Buckingham House, were inscribed the words '*Rus in Urbe*': 'The Country in the City'. There was a touch of truth to it. Open country stretched north to the Hampstead skyline, and the view led southward to the Thames. Though, by 1700, becoming the most populous city in Europe, London was still, by our standards, staggeringly compact.

Attempts were made to bring Wiltshire to the West End. Sheep were imported into Cavendish Square, where they safely grazed behind railings, almost prefiguring the fact that the rustic Regent's Park would have its zoo. Originally given a formal layout, Grosvenor Square sprouted sylvan clumps; spurred by the vogue for the picturesque, Portman Square was similarly landscaped, and Russell Square followed suit, landscaped by Repton. Late in his career the redoubtable John Nash jumped on the bandwagon by building two whole villages of *cottages ornées* on the east flank of Regent's Park, judged by Sir John Summerson the 'ancestors of all picturesque suburbia'. Yet such smuggling of country into town, like Marie Antoinette playing the milkmaid *à la mode*, was also lampooned. The author of *Critical Observations on the Buildings and Improvements of London* (1771) judged sheep browsing in Cavendish Square plain silly. 'To see the poor things starting at every coach, and hurrying round their narrow bounds, required a warm imagination indeed, to convert the scene into that of flocks ranging fields, with all the concomitant ideas of innocence and a pastoral life.' Almost all London squares, this critic concluded, were 'tinctured with the same absurdity ... they are parks, they are sheep walks; in short, they are everything but what they should be. The *rus in urbe* is a preposterous idea at best.'

Architectural styles had to be created to woo the eye and mind away from the country estate. Crucial in this were the more intimate designs and decorations created after 1760 by the Adam brothers, Robert and James, who imparted a fresh face to London buildings.

The glory of the Adam brothers was the Adelphi. In 1768 they leased the site of Durham House on the Strand, east of Charing Cross, and erected a magnificent terrace on a vaulted embankment overlooking the river. The Adelphi (Greek for 'brothers') was London's finest riverside building, incorporating catacombs and vaults, but it proved a commercial blunder – fashion had quit the river, which had become a dirty, cluttered commercial highway, and the brothers had to resort to a public lottery to save their skins. Though the Adelphi was demolished in 1936, traces of its elegance are still visible along John Adam Street.

Thanks to Adam brilliance, town living became stylish: smart, classy and exhilarating. The new Quality town houses may have been comparatively cramped – there was far less space than in the country or in a Parisian nobleman's *hôtel* – but overcrowding in town was a trivial sacrifice for grandees because they had their country parks. 'Englishmen of rank continue to consider their estates their real residences,' observed a foreigner, 'and their houses in London as a kind of pied-à-terre. Many who have revenues of £20,000 and more live in London with hardly a dozen rooms. Consequently, they and their numerous servants are rather crowded.' In town, Horace Walpole observed, the nobility lived in 'a dining room, a dark back room ... and a closet'. 'Very few persons of rank have what we on the Continent call a palace in London,' noted a traveller: 'their palaces, their luxury and grandeur are to be seen in the country.'

The art of London living was to make a virtue of necessity. Public spaces – streets, squares, shops, theatres, arcades and the club – were created where social life could flourish, and space was used to advantage at home. To aid this, Adam interiors created the illusion of spaciousness. Top-lit staircases secured the light and airy feel the Georgians valued. They excelled in designing reception rooms *en suite* to provide vistas, and in varying the height and shape of rooms to create diversity – domed rotundas, oval and recessed rooms, the curves suggesting depth. And the social round changed too. New fashions prized a sociability that was informal and flexible, with much casual visiting and paying of respects. West End homes were set up to cope with streams of callers. 'In the morning,' wrote Madame du Bocage, a mid-century French visitor,

breakfasts ... agreeably bring together both the people of the country and strangers. We breakfasted in this manner today at Lady Montagu's ... A long table covered with the finest linen, presented to the view a thousand glittering cups, which contained coffee, chocolate, biscuits, cream, butter, toasts, and exquisite tea. You must understand that there is no good tea to be had but at London. The Mistress of the house ... poured it out herself.

As a machine for entertaining, Norfolk House led the field. On the east side of St James's Square, its unpretentious façade led an observer to comment, 'Would any foreigner, beholding an insipid length of wall broken into regular rows of windows ... ever figure from thence the residence of the first Duke of England?' But the interior dazzled. 'Everyone who was there,' Captain William Farington wrote, back from the first-night party, 'agreed that Norfolk House was infinitely superior to anything in this Kingdom ... and to most things they had seen in Europe.' 'There were in all,' he told his sisters, 'eleven rooms open, three below, the rest above, every room was furnished with a different colour, which used to be reckoned absurd, but this I suppose is to be the Standard.'

A new town architecture catered for a vivacious social calendar, whose climax was the rout, a party that made overcrowding titillating. 'One of the social pleasures of London is a rout,' wrote the German visitor Christian Goede in 1802, rebounding from the crush:

nothing is presented to the view but a vast crowd of elegantly dressed ladies and gentlemen, many of whom are so overpowered by the heat, noise and confusion, as to be in danger of fainting. Everyone complains of the pressure of the company, yet all rejoice at being so divinely squeezed.

Man about town James Malcolm told the same tale. At the rout, he wrote, 'there is pleasure, there is amusement, and the inexpressible delight of languor, even fainting through exertion, heat and suffocation; the company endeavours to compress themselves for obtaining a space to dance in'. 'No cards, no music, only elbowing,' was Louis Simond's sour verdict on such metropolitan madness.

Edward Gibbon caught the West End bug. Born in Putney and trapped as a teenager in darkest Hampshire, he passed a year in town in his early twenties, and was enchanted: 'The metropolis affords many amusements, which are open to all,' he wrote: 'it is itself a perpetual and astonishing spectacle to the curious eye; and each taste, every sense, may be gratified by the variety of objects that will occur in the long circuit of a morning walk.' His throw-away conclusion – 'The pleasures of a town life, the daily round from the tavern to the play, from the play to the coffee-house, from the coffee-house to the Bagnio, are within the reach of every man who is regardless of his health, his money, and his company' – masked the fact that, on his father's death, he sold off the family estate and rented a bijou bachelor residence in Bentinck Street, drooling over the fine shag flock-paper he had chosen, light blue with a gold border, and purring at his good fortune:

I had now attained the solid comforts of life, a convenient well-furnished house, a domestic table, half a dozen chosen servants, my own carriage, and all those decent luxuries whose value is the more sensibly felt the longer they are enjoyed ... To a lover of books the shops and sales in London present irresistible temptations ... By my own choice I passed in town the greatest part of the year.

There, by Cavendish Square, together with a lapdog and a parrot, he composed *The Decline and Fall of the Roman Empire*.

Towards 1600 John Stow had been grousing about the 'small and base' tenements, 'filthy' cottages and lanes 'pestered with tenements' proliferating beyond the walls to the east. The pace of growth increased: east London rose from about 21,000 souls in 1600 to over 91,000 by 1700. Overcrowding worsened. But the area was not entirely a smelly slum. Occupationally and residentially, it was a mixed bag.

Development was densest along the riverside, a strip half a mile wide extending from Wapping Wall and Ratcliff Highway to Limehouse and Blackwall. 'The East end,' noted the German von Archenholz around 1780, 'especially along the shore of the Thames, consists of old houses, the streets there are narrow, dark and ill-paved, inhabited by sailors and other workmen who are employed in the construction of ships and by a great part of the Jews. The contrast between this and the West End is astonishing.'

And not just the West End. For, ten minutes' ride north, Mile End, Bow, Hoxton and Hackney were respectably bourgeois, and, at least early in the century, even Spitalfields, around Hawksmoor's Christ Church, wore a comely air. Born in 1660, Daniel Defoe remembered Spitalfields as *fields*: 'the part now called Spittlefields-market, was a field of grass with cows feeding on it'. Yet it was changing fast. By the time he wrote his *Tour through England and Wales* (1724), 320 acres of ground were 'all close built, and well-inhabited ... above two hundred thousand inhabitants'. 'Numberless ranges of building' had gone up, 'called Spittle Fields, reaching from Spittle-

---

The Mile End Road and Bethnal Green, 1746, by John Rocque

Published by John Pine & John Tinney in October 1746 ...

yard, at Northern Fallgate, and from Artillery Lane in Bishopsgate Street ... to Brick Lane, and the end of Hare Street, on the way to Bethnal Green'. Part consisted in smart housing for master weavers: what remains of Fournier Street and Wilkes Street recalls the wealth of the silk-masters living there.

Shacklewell and Stoke Newington, too, were popular as residential suburbs settled by City tradesmen. Hackney was a favourite Sunday resort. On 11 June 1664 Pepys recorded, 'With my wife only to take ayre, it being very warm and pleasant, to Bowe and Old Ford; and thence to Hackney. There light and played at shuffle board, eat cream and good cherries; and so with good refreshment home.'

About 100 prosperous Hackney and Clapton merchants kept carriages, Defoe reckoned, while within half a mile of Hackney church lived three former Lord Mayors, two East India Company directors, and several City liverymen and lawyers. There, too, was the home of Richard Ryder, a Cheapside linen-draper, whose law-student son Dudley recorded the highlights of village life in a charming diary, fooling around the coffee-houses with gentlefolks' daughters attending the finishing-schools for which Hackney was growing famous. For his health, Dudley Ryder took the waters at Islington. At home he made music with his friends, performing on flute and bass viol. In winter there were dances in Mrs Wallis's schoolroom, and in the great frost in January 1716 he went skating on Hackney Marsh. On summer days he rode out to leafy Edmonton and breezy Highgate, where he had a girlfriend.

Hackney long remained a village, its single church large enough to take the whole congregation – a new church was not begun until 1791. But even then the area was still largely rural, with a population of 12,730 – it quadrupled by 1851 – and its occupations remained rather genteel, with a host of classy schools (in 1830, fourteen private boys' schools and twenty girls' schools, and two grammar schools on top), to say nothing of five private lunatic asylums.

Poplar, Old Ford, Clapton, Stratford and Leyton – all these also remained picturesque villages. Bow stretched over the Lea bridge towards Stratford, and Bromley's main street hugged the River Lea. To the south, the Isle of Dogs remained the rough pasture it had been since medieval times. Along Millwall embankment stood the seven windmills that gave the place its name.

Closer in, things were changing rapidly. Mile End was still somewhat genteel (Captain Cook had a house there), but Bethnal Green was sprawling. Becoming a separate parish in 1743, its western end was packed by poor weavers, the Spitalfields overspill; the east part, still 'green', was settled by market gardeners and a sprinkling of comfortable suburbanites. It leapt from 15,000 inhabitants around 1750 to 85,000 in 1851, turning from attractive semi-rurality into London's poorest parish.

Thames-ward from Bethnal Green, it was the riverside developments that really repelled, especially the jungle of courts beyond the wall in St Katharine's, just east of the Tower. Ratcliff Highway was linked to Cable Street by mazes of alleys, notorious for bawds and seamen's lodgings; off Wellclose Square lay one of London's foulest precincts; and Lower Ratcliff was a knot of cramped courts branching off the main streets, the very names evoking chaos. North of St Katharine's, between Rosemary Lane and East Smithfield, there were Harebrain Court, Money Bag Alley, Hog Yard, Black Jack Alley, Black Dog Alley, Black Boy Alley and Holyday Court, occupied by sailors, lightermen, secondhand-clothes dealers, pawnbrokers, pothouse boys and porters. Off Butcher Row lay Sugarhouse Yard, Dolphin Yard, Shipwrights Hall, Mermaid Yard, Shoulder of Mutton Alley, Little Pump Yard, George Yard, Brew House. Much of Ratcliff waterfront was, perhaps mercifully, razed by a great fire in 1794. Wharves and boatyards, swarming with seafarers and shipwrights, caulkers and coopers, scavelmen, joiners, boatmakers, plumbers, pump-makers and pitchbeaters gave the East End its higgledy-piggledy appearance – and the south bank too, where shipping boomed from Southwark down to Deptford. Riverside Bermondsey and Rotherhithe had bad reputations. '*Gravesend,*' according to one guide, 'is a detestable exhibition of the worst out-skirts of London. – It is *Wapping* in miniature.'

But eligible residential areas were sprouting beyond the waterfront south of the river, especially after the opening of Westminster Bridge in 1750 and Blackfriars Bridge in 1769. Around 1750 Camberwell was still a straggling village of orchards and smallholdings, and the only settlements beyond it were a clump of houses at Peckham Rye (where the young William Blake saw a tree filled with angels), Goose Green, None Head and Dulwich Wells, whither citizens strolled on Sundays to take the air and the waters. Things were changing. Walter Harrison's *New and Universal History ... of London and Westminster*, published in 1776 – a year marked by Camberwell's first Act for lighting the parish – noted 'the spirit of building': 'between Newington Butts and Camberwell several new streets have been formed and a prodigious number of buildings erected'. St Giles church had to be extended in 1786, and by 1825 the new 'Waterloo church' of St George's went up in Wells Way alongside the canal. Suburban development put paid to local fairs – having outlived their market functions, they survived as suburban sprees until respectable residents closed them down. Peckham Fair was banned in 1827, but Camberwell's lingered another forty years. The country-side was in retreat.

Nor was Camberwell alone in this oozing of town. Defoe noted in 1724 how 'from Richmond to London, the river sides are full of villages, and those villages are so full of beautiful buildings, charming gardens and rich habitations of gentlemen of quality that nothing in the world can imitate it'. Richmond, Putney, Hammersmith, Fulham and Chelsea all found favour with him, often given cachet by some nearby lordly mansion. The Bishops of Winchester had a palace in Cheyne Walk, Chelsea; the Earl of Peterborough owned a 'stately' house at Parsons Green; Lord Burlington built at Chiswick. Surveying London's outskirts, Defoe guessed at 3,000 substantial houses within a radius of twenty miles, mainly built since the Restoration, many of which 'would pass for palaces'.

Favoured villages attracted a stream of citizens, and suburban living became a conversation point, as did the commuter. 'The greater part of his family,' observed John Howlett of this strange breed, 'are chiefly in the rural mansion, where he himself passes his nights, and only repairs to the city for the transaction of his commercial affairs by day.' Evidently a novelty, the commuter amused Robert Lloyd in 1757:

> Some three or four miles out of town,
> (An hour's ride will bring you down),
> He fixes on his choice abode,
> Not half a furlong from the road:
> And so convenient does it lay,
> The stages pass it ev'ry day:
> And then so snugg, so mighty pretty,
> To have an house so near the city!

There were even weekenders, with a residence in Carshalton or Barnet, Windsor or Ware. In Edward Kimber's *The Life and Adventures of Joe Thompson* (1750), Mr Diaper spent half the week in London, leaving his wife in his country 'box' to supervise the garden and artificial fountains. 'Every little clerk in office must have his villa, and every tradesman his country-house,' chuckled the novelist Richard Graves:

A cheesemonger retreats to his little pasteboard edifice on Turnham Green, and when smoking his pipe under his codling-hedge on his gravel walk rude with coal-ashes, fancies himself a Scipio or Cincinnatus in his retreat; and returns with reluctance to town on Monday night, or perhaps defers it till Tuesday morning, regardless of his shop, and his inquisitive and disgusted customers.

Suburban development was dense only along the river. Greenwich and Blackheath, Brentford, Chiswick, Richmond, Twickenham, Kew and Chelsea all became populous, families seeking country calm close to town. Once the home of Sir Thomas More and sporting many fine Queen Anne houses, Chelsea grew thanks to the Cadogan estate. On marrying Elizabeth Sloane in 1771, the Earl of Cadogan came into an extensive property left by his father in law, Sir Hans Sloane. This was laid out as Cadogan Place, with Sloane Street running through it, culminating in Sloane Square. Hans Town was built in the next ten years, separated from Westminster until Belgravia was developed. In nearby Ebury Street, Mozart composed his first symphony in 1764.

North of Chelsea, Kensington stirred, particularly after 1690, when William and Mary's court arrived at Nottingham House, later called Kensington Palace. Kensington

Square had taken shape back in 1685, incongruously in a rural setting, as the brainchild of Thomas Young, an enterprising wood-carver who envisaged 'a large square of large and substantial Houses fit for ye Habitacion of persons of good Worth and Quality'. The idea had dawned upon him while fitting up Soho Square. Young built six houses in the square, with a garden and a bowling-green to attract the Quality; but, like many a later speculator, his efforts proved unavailing and in 1687 he was imprisoned for debt, the bowling-green reverting to a strawberry patch.

The King's coming led to other changes. 'The Old Church then much ruin'd and decay'd, was thought not commodious enough for the Reception of so many Noble Inhabitants', and so it was 'Rebuilt, Pav'd, Pew'd, and made very Regular and Convenient'. The High Street emerged, as did Church Street and Holland Street. Settlements grew in the adjacent hamlets of Earl's Court and Brompton, and up the hill to Kensington Gravel Pits (now Notting Hill Gate). Wrights Lane developed from houses built in the 1770s for Gregory Wright, and nearby Edwardes Square was begun in 1811 on Lord Kensington's estate, taking his family name. North of Kensington High Street, villas were rising on the hillside dominated by the quaint Jacobean Holland House. One, Holly Lodge, was to be occupied by the historian Thomas Babington Macaulay.

Kensington became a burgeoning village suburb, a charming mixture of old and new, town and country. The 'delightful fruit gardens of Brompton, Earl's Court, and other parts of this parish' long remained celebrated; by 1851, however, Leigh Hunt lamented that the nursery was 'giving up its last green ghost before the rise of new buildings'.

To the north, Hampstead blossomed as a fashionable village, thanks to its elevation and its chalybeate spring water ('of the same nature and equal in virtue with Tunbridge Wells' – that is, it gave a good purge). In 1701 a pump room was built in Well Walk, and Dorothy Pippin sold water there. Fashionable society flocked in; a race course and bowling-green were opened near Jack Straw's Castle; teashops thrived, a concert hall opened, the fashionable Kit-Kat Club met at the Upper Flask Tavern in Heath Street. And smart people began to acquire residences there, Church Row, extending from Frognal, being built just after 1700. 'Hampstead indeed is risen from a little country village, to a city,' commented Defoe, continuing apprehensively:

On the top of the hill indeed, there is a very pleasant plain, called the Heath, which on the very summit, is a plain of about a mile every way; and in good weather 'tis pleasant airing upon it, and some of the streets are extended so far, as that they begin to build, even on the highest part of the hill. But it must be confest, 'tis so near heaven, that I dare not say it can be a proper situation, for any but a race of mountaineers, whose lungs have been so used to a rarify'd air, nearer the second region, than any ground for 30 miles round it.

By 1750, Hampstead was five times larger than Paddington, and it assumed an arty, intellectual air, its first literary circle being run by the dramatist and poet Joanna Baillie. The 'cockney poet' Leigh Hunt settled in the West End and later in the Vale of Health. His circle included John Keats, who lodged in Well Walk and then in Lawn Bank in John Street (later renamed Keats Grove), writing his finest poetry there between 1817 and 1820. Downshire Hill became a chic Regency address. John Constable claimed that Well Walk 'commands a view unequalled in Europe'.

To the east was Highgate, which in the seventeenth century became the site of aristocratic mansions: Arundel, Cromwell, Fitzroy and Lauderdale Houses. The Grove, stretching from West Hill towards Hampstead Lane, became its most elegant street, later known as Quality Walk. The opium-soaked Coleridge later dried out at No. 3, the home of his friend the surgeon James Gillman. But Highgate stayed small: by 1793 there were still only 200-odd houses.

Just south, Kentish Town was a pleasant village with gentlemen's residences. One, the Revd Dr Stukeley, rector of the fashionable St George the Martyr, Queen Square, and an antiquarian fascinated by Stonehenge, bought a 'Hermitage' there:

To compleat my felicity after 9 years assiduous enquiry, I found a most agreeable rural retreat at Kentish Town . . . extremely convenient for keeping my horses and for my own amusement . . . an half-hour's walk over sweet fields. 'Tis absolutely and clearly out of the influence of the London smoak, the dry gravelly soil and air remarkably wholesome.

Further east lay the first City suburb to be truly built-up. On high ground commanding a 'magnificent panorama' over London, Islington had a well which was credited with health-giving properties. (Sadler's Wells commemorates one of the 'spaws' so popular with the Georgians.) It was 'a pretty neat town, mostly built of brick, with a church and bells; it has a small lake, or rather pond in the midst, though at present much neglected', thought Goldsmith. But Islington became the butt of satire rather like Neasden today. George Colman mocked its denizens in *The Spleen; or, Islington Spa*, the tale of a tailor who retired to the 'country' and found it deadly dull:

> Would not he Islington's fine air forego
> Could he again be choak'd in Butcher-Row?

inquired the Prologue. High Street and Upper Street were house-lined by 1735; Colebrooke Row was completed by 1768. From 1760 building proceeded rapidly, peaking after Waterloo, when the New River Company ran up Georgian streets and squares.

Development stretched to Canonbury. In 1770 John Dawes, a stockbroker, built the new Canonbury House, and around 1800 Jacob Leroux erected Canonbury Square and Compton Terrace facing Upper Street; Canonbury developed as a pretty suburb, enhanced by the winding New River. Liverpool Road became a ribbon from the 1790s. On the west, Cloudesley Square was laid out around 1820. On its east, the Gibson estate was developed about 1840, with the routine Gibson Square and the astonishing Milner Square.

From the 1790s, Camden Town emerged in the no man's land between Islington and Hampstead, on the property of Charles Pratt, Lord Camden and Lord Chief Justice. It was too far from town to attract the Quality, and war halted building – by 1804 little more than Camden High Street was built-up. Camden Town was to prove a nineteenth-century, lower-middle-class development, activated but spoiled by the Regent's Canal and the railways.

Central London had its great developers, from Barbon to Burton. Suburban entrepreneurs had to invent allure for areas that had long been nondescript villages, scrubby piggeries or brick-fields. The secret of successful development lay in the naming. The royal family were always winners. 'George' and 'Hanover' were ubiquitous; 'Brunswick' came in with the Prince of Wales's marriage to Caroline of Brunswick in 1795; 'Regent' and 'Regency' date from 1811; Prinny's brothers provided 'York', 'Albany', 'Clarence', 'Kent', 'Cumberland', 'Sussex' and 'Cambridge'.

From the seventeenth century, when the titles of George Villiers, Duke of Buckingham, were attached to streets off the Strand, landlords' names were also popular – especially when aristocratic. The Cavendish–Harley estate exploited family names like Wimpole and Welbeck; likewise the Bedford estate. Street names all around Bloomsbury point to the Bedfords. Cardington Street, Goldington Street and Crescent, and Woburn Square all stem from their Bedfordshire lands; their Devon estates are marked by Taviton Street, Tavistock Square, Endsleigh Gardens and Endsleigh Street; Thornhaugh Street evokes their Northamptonshire property. Marriage connections with other noble families are enshrined in such names as Torrington Place (from Lord Torrington, father-in-law of the 6th Duke of Bedford) and Gordon Square and Huntley Street, alluding to the Dukes of Gordon, the Marquesses of Huntley. Builders' names sometimes occur: female Christian names attest their desire to flatter wives or daughters.

Fame sold sites. 'Wellington' is the most common, with 'Nelson', 'Chatham', 'Pitt' and 'Rodney' runners-up. With famous men went noble victories: 'Waterloo', 'Copenhagen', 'Trafalgar' (this belongs to 1805–6, though the Square came a quarter of a century later). Patriotism was popular: 'Albion' and 'Britannia' are common after Trafalgar, and 'Patriot' occurs in the East End.

'Prospect', 'Bellevue', 'Grove' or 'Oak' advertised the siting of the development. Sometimes charm is conjured up, as in Paradise Row, Bethnal Green. Naturally, the sites for which such names were selected were those where the amenities advertised were least obvious. What became promoted as the Vale of Health in Hampstead had long been notorious as a malarial marsh, traditionally known as Gangmoor or, scarcely more attractively, as Hatches (or Hatchett's) Bottom, after a Samuel Hatch who owned a cottage there.

Some names indicated architectural topography: Squares, Crescents, and Circuses. London has had four Paragons (at Richmond, the New Kent Road, Blackheath, and Hackney); two Polygons (Somers Town and Clapham), and two Ovals (one on the Duchy of Cornwall estate at Kennington, the other, later, north-east of Hackney Road).

'Unfortunately for the city and suburbs of London right lines have hardly ever been considered,' grumbled the architect John Gwynn in *London and Westminster Improved* (1766):

Such a vast city as London ought to have had at least three capital streets which should have run through the whole, and at convenient distances have been intersected by other capital streets at right angles, by which means all the inferior streets would have an easy and convenient communication with them.

The architect whined, but he had a point. For all London's energy and vivacity, there was little that was truly capital, and its public face remained largely disorganized. 'What is London? Clean, commodious, neat; but, a very few things indeed excepted, an endless addition of littleness to littleness, extending itself over a great tract of land,' commented Edmund Burke. Unlike baroque Dresden or St Petersburg, London's public buildings were unimpressive, the royal palaces made a poor show, and London Bridge, with its tottering skyline, was a medieval survival. True, Westminster Bridge had been erected (designed, to the chagrin of English architects, by a Swiss, Charles Labelye), but even that took nine years to build.

Critics complained that, after what we might call the 'Wrenaissance', ecclesiastical architecture had almost expired, though the Church Building Act of 1711 was responsible for six marvellous Hawksmoor churches – St Alfege in Greenwich, St Anne Limehouse, Christ Church Spitalfields, St George-in-the-East (Stepney), St George's Bloomsbury and the City church of St Mary Woolnoth. Other churches built under the Act included St Mary-le-Strand by James Gibbs and St Giles-in-the-Fields by Henry Flitcroft. Even then, London's pews could hold only a quarter of the population.

Gwynn deplored the failure of urban grandeur. Where were 'taste and elegance'? Sensing that growth had outrun grace, Glynn demanded 'that proper bounds may be set to that fury which seems to possess the fraternity of builders and to prevent them from extending the town in the enormous manner they have done and still continue to do'. He wanted a scenic London, with boulevards pointing to noble buildings. He was not alone. Where, demanded 'Athenian' Stuart, were the radial avenues, fountains, statues and gardens essential for setting off elegant West End terraces? Where was the grand vision that had transformed Berlin and Nancy? Many grumbled about the ill-kept streets and unsafe alleys of old London, its labyrinth rendered offensive by cattle markets and shambles. Ancient gates and narrow streets created bottlenecks, Charing Cross and Temple Bar were notoriously congested. Thoroughfares were dangerous and ill-maintained: the road beyond Aldgate 'resembled a stagnant lake of deep mud'. Refuse piled up at street corners, and the Fleet became an open sewer. In 1741 Lord Tyrconnel denounced the 'neglect of cleanliness of which, perhaps, no part of the world affords more proof than the streets of London, a city famous for wealth, commerce, and plenty, and for every other kind of civility and politeness; but which abounds with such heaps of filth, as a savage would look on with amazement'. Gwynn condemned 'nuisances' like ordure in the streets and ways blocked with sheds and stalls.

Not everyone was as critical as the undeniably self-interested architects. 'The stranger will be astonished at the improvements which have been introduced during the last 35 years and how money could be procured to complete them,' observed the Midlander William Hutton, down on a visit in 1785:

He will find every street and passage in the whole city, and its environs, has been paved in one regular and convenient stile; [as] the people of Birmingham ... must observe the conveniency arising from open streets, the centers of which are regularly paved and the sides, from one foot to sixteen, according to the width of the street, laid with flat stones, for the benefit of the passenger, it is surprizing they do not, at a humble distance, wish to imitate the Metropolis.

Physicians believed the town was growing more salubrious. 'In the airy parts of this city and in large, open streets,' commented Dr John Coakley Lettsom in 1773, 'fevers of a putrid tendency rarely arise.' (They continued in 'narrow courts and alleys'.)

The turning-point in urban improvement was the first Westminster Paving Act of 1762, followed by other Acts for the City and elsewhere. Hitherto it had been the obligation of householders to keep the street in front of their houses in good repair. Now paving commissioners were appointed, with paid staffs; gutters were built on either side of the road, and in main streets Purbeck paving-stones replaced pebbles. Combined with a convex carriageway, gutters and underground drains, pavements transformed street use, for pedestrians could now stroll along the sidewalks undisturbed by vehicles and animals. (Visitors noted, by contrast, how dangerous it was to saunter in Paris.) The Acts also provided for scavenging and cleansing, and for the removal of obstructions – open coal-holes, sheds and projecting balconies. Old shop signs were taken down, sewers and drains were deepened, and drainpipes were installed.

Amelioration was generally the joint work of parish élites and private companies.

Lighting improvements started in the 1680s with new oil-burning street lamps, supplied with reflectors. In 1694 the Convex Lights Company contracted for the City, and in 1704 the Conic Lights Company for Westminster. From 1736, lights were to be lit each night of the year. Traditionally they had been lit until midnight; from 1736 they were lit until sunrise. Lighting encouraged night-life – and made for safety. Foreigners were impressed. Moritz was 'astonished at the unusually good lighting of the streets, compared with which Berlin makes a pretty poor show'. Gas lighting arrived in 1807; but long before that travellers retailed the oft-told anecdote of the German princeling who on arrival in London was convinced the streets had been illuminated just for him.

Water provision was in the hands of numerous private companies. One fine supply had long before been secured. In 1609 Hugh Myddelton, a Welsh businessman, designed a channel stretching nearly forty miles from springs at Amwell in Hertfordshire to Islington and thence to the City. Money ran out, but help came from James I, who split the costs and profits. The New River Company proved an excellent source of water for central London and the City.

Most water, however, was pumped up from the Thames by outfits like the Chelsea Waterworks Company, incorporated in 1723 'for the better supplying the City and Liberties of Westminster and parts adjacent with water'. Its tide-mill works were established near the Thames on a site now covered by the Churchill Gardens estate, and it was also authorized to draw the overflow from the Serpentine in Hyde Park. The company was responsible for introducing the first iron main in London, in 1746; by 1767, with the introduction of steam pumps, 1,750 tons of water were pumped daily. Supplies of household water increased, representing an improvement so long as the Thames did not become excessively polluted.

Other improvements were in train. In the 1760s the City pulled down its overhanging street signs. Repaired in 1757–9, London Bridge was stripped of its decaying houses and shops. The Fleet problem was solved: in 1733 it was arched over from Holborn Bridge to Fleet Bridge; this ultimately became Farringdon Road. House numbering became normal in new districts. Hatton's *New View of London* (1708) remarked as a novelty that 'in Prescott Street, Goodman's Fields, instead of signs the houses are distinguished by numbers, as the staircases in the Inns of Court and Chancery'. In the 1760s the remaining City gates – Aldgate, Moorgate, Ludgate and Bishopsgate – were taken down to improve traffic flow. Temple Bar lasted longer, separating London from Westminster. Its persistence till 1878 marked a divided metropolis.

The West End aristocratic capitalists built a mosaic of elegant squares and terraces. It was left to the Prince of Wales to impose some form. The Regent had designs for the capital, not primarily out of public spirit but in pursuit of taste and to enhance his own prospects and properties, including the royal estates beyond Oxford Street. He envisaged an elegant connection between these estates and his residence, Carlton House in Pall Mall, which he was having improved at enormous expense to the taxpayer.

The true hero, however, was John Nash – a 'thick, squat, dwarf figure, with round head, snub nose and little eyes' (his own description). A millwright's son who trained as an architect under Sir Robert Taylor, Nash set up on his own, went bankrupt, and then bounced back. Gossip had it that he had the foresight to marry the Prince of Wales's mistress. A man of flair, Nash was a shrewd businessman, willing to take a risk but careless of strict accounting.

Princes' vices have public benefits. To meet his master's dreams, Nash envisaged one long, majestic south–north street, leading up from Carlton House through Lower Regent Street to a Quadrant (just north of the present Piccadilly Circus), and then along Regent Street and into Portland Place. This route was determined by ownership of the land: it was cheaper to plant the road on Crown property than to go as the crow flies. But Nash's path was not just cheap: it had another advantage. Between Piccadilly and Oxford Street it followed Swallow Street. It thus created a frontier between crowded, confused Soho on the east and elegant Hanover Square and Cavendish Square on the west. By restricting eastern access to Regent Street, Nash's route succeeded, in Sir John Summerson's phrase, in 'damming up Soho', and London's grandest thoroughfare thereby became its social barrier, with Portland Place and Regent Street screening the fashionable West End from *déclassé* quarters. 'No family of ton can breathe eastward of Berkeley Square,' remarked the *World* magazine in 1787: Regent Street embodied that observation.

At the far end, Nash created a royal park out of farm land. The spot was ideal – directly north of the finest Marylebone property, between Baker Street and Great Portland Street. Escaping from the routine grid of squares, the park – Regent's Park – was to be picturesque and surrounded by palatial terraces and a host of villas, so that 'the attraction of open Space, free air and the scenery of Nature ... shall be preserved or created in Mary-le-bone Park, as allurements or motives for the wealthy part of the Public to establish themselves there'. Almost creating the first garden city, Nash revivified the old ideal of *rus in urbe*. Retaining Georgian terraces, Nash added stucco and decoration, reminiscent of an Italian *palazzo*.

The park even had its canal. The idea of linking the Grand Junction Canal at Paddington with the Thames at Limehouse had been advanced earlier by the entre-preneur Thomas Homer. He first suggested driving a canal straight through London, but the land costs were prohibitive, so the scheme was dropped until 1811, when he approached Nash and suggested bending the canal north through Regent's Park. A company was formed in the Prince Regent's name, a quarter of a million pounds was raised, and six acres of park land were granted for £2,347 17s 6d.

Park Crescent and Regent Street were finished and Cornwall Terrace begun by

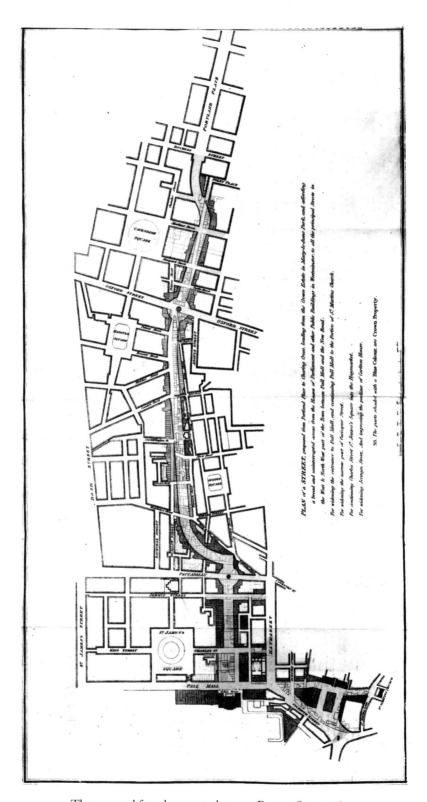

The proposal for what was to become Regent Street, 1813

The sweep of the Quadrant at what is now the Piccadilly Circus end of Regent Street,
designed by John Nash

1820; York Terrace, Sussex Place, Clarence Terrace, Park Square and Hanover Terrace
were soon built, and Gloucester, Cumberland and Chester Gates were up by 1828. It
was London's most beautiful estate, combining Georgian orderliness with the countryside, palace with terrace:

> Augustus at Rome was for building renown'd
> And of marble he left what but brick he had found:
> But is not our Nash, too, a very great master
> He found London Brick and he leaves it all plaster.

The Nash terraces were hated by the Victorians: stucco was like bad make-up. Indeed,
behind the glittering frontage, the construction was sometimes suspect. But Nash
profoundly affected the area. He secured the exclusiveness of the West End; he
facilitated future Primrose Hill and St John's Wood developments, soon to be festooned

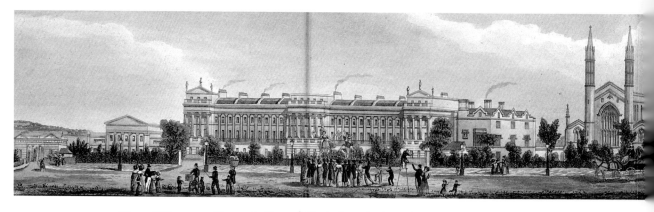

View of Gloucester Terrace by Regent's Park. Aquatint by Ackerman, *c.* 1810 (Guildhall Library)

with villas and stuccoed terraces for the affluent; and these in turn enhanced properties in Belsize Park and Hampstead.

Regent Street was built between 1817 and 1823. Sites were let to building speculators, including James Burton, but Nash himself built the Quadrant. With its shops and exclusive bachelor lodgings above, Regent Street became ultra-fashionable, rivalling Bond Street. Butchers and bakers were kept out. Regent Street was not a main road but a parade and shopping centre, ladies popping into drapers' before tea, while their carriages waited outside. It proved a great success, John Tallis's guidebook describing it in 1838 as a 'noble street', with 'palace-like shops, in whose broad showy windows are displayed articles of the most splendid description, such as the neighbouring world of wealth and fashion are daily in want of . . . it should be visited on a summer's day in the afternoon, when the splendid carriages, and elegantly attired pedestrians, evince the opulence and taste of our magnificent metropolis'. '*Was für Plunder!*' Field Marshal von Blücher supposedly exclaimed on viewing Regent Street after the peace banquet in 1814. This does not mean, however, as is commonly assumed, 'What a place to plunder!' but 'What a lot of stuff!'

CHAPTER SIX

Commercial City:
1650–1800

... a kind of Emporium for the whole Earth

JOSEPH ADDISON, *Spectator* (1711)

London became the wonder city. In 1500 its population equalled that of the six largest provincial towns put together; by 1680 it exceeded the *sixty* largest. If the seventeenth-century statistician Gregory King can be believed, by 1680 two out of every three English townsfolk lived in this colossus twenty times bigger than any of its rivals – the next largest town, Norwich, had only 30,000 people, and places like Manchester, Liverpool and Birmingham around 10,000.

London became a European marvel, too. In the sixteenth century many European towns had boomed; amidst widespread stagnation and even decline, however, London was one of the few whose expansion continued unchecked, even accelerating. Europe's boom cities were those enjoying the stimulus of centralizing administrations or inter-continental trade. London cashed in on both, and it was a major manufacturing centre too. This brew of government, trade and industry invigorated the metropolis, which surpassed even Paris. Paris's population, 400,00 in 1600, was nearing half a million towards 1700, but thereafter it grew little for a century. London, by contrast, continued to swell, rising, in round figures, from 200,000 in 1600 to 400,000 in 1650, 575,000 by the end of the century, 675,000 in 1750 and 900,000 by 1801, when the first Census provides a definite figure.

London dominated the nation like no other capital. In 1650 some 2·5 per cent of Frenchmen lived in Paris; by 1750 that figure had changed little. London, on the other hand, housed about 7 per cent of England's population in 1650, and as many as 10 per cent in 1750. With its 200,000 inhabitants, Amsterdam never accounted for more than about 8 per cent of the Dutch Republic. Amsterdam impressed – or horrified – contemporaries, who viewed it as entirely given over to Mammon. London was somewhat comparable, though it was the blend of its commercial and national roles that made the metropolis tick. Almost unique in uniting court and port, London benefited from England's exceptional political and economic centralization.

The capital's growth is all the more remarkable as its mortality rates worsened after 1670, the early eighteenth century bringing some of the worst death rates since records began in the 1540s. With its mass of migrants and intercontinental trade, the metropolis became an infection reservoir, its lethal reputation borne out by the Bills of Mortality, which tabled the great excess of deaths over births. Expansion remained entirely fuelled by migration. 'Not above one in twenty of shop and alehouse keepers, journeymen and labourers … were either born or served their apprenticeships in town,' it was observed, with some exaggeration; 'London will not feel any want of recruits,' judged the customs commissioner Corbyn Morris in 1751, 'till there are no people in the country.'

Some hailed from far afield. London was a magnet for the Scots – baited by Dr Johnson, himself from Lichfield. An Irish colony, known as 'little Dublin', grew in St Giles-in-the-Fields; another in the East End. The London Welsh were largely engaged in cattle-droving, livestock-dealing, and the dairy trade. Other foreign communities included some 20,000 Jews, chiefly in the East End. Sephardic Jews from Spain and Portugal established themselves from Cromwell's time, many becoming wealthy citizens. Continental anti-Semitism encouraged Jews to flee to London, though Jew-baiting was not unknown in England, fed by fears that immigrants would undercut labour – anxieties rising with the influx from around 1700 of poor Ashkenazim from Poland and Germany. Hats piled on his head and his arms draped with cloth, the bearded Jewish old-clothes man became a conspicuous figure in street-selling. While Whitechapel and the Petticoat Lane area became the hub of the Jewish community, in nearby Spitalfields congregated Huguenot migrants – French refugees fleeing religious persecution after the revocation of the Edict of Nantes (1685). They formed the core of the East End silk-weaving community, specializing too in watchmaking and engraving, and thriving as merchants and financiers. Spitalfields Huguenots, like the Jewish community, maintained strong cultural and religious traditions, establishing schools, churches and charities for their brethren. There were also around 5,000 to 10,000 blacks in Georgian London: some were seamen on ships on the North American run; others had arrived as slaves or to gratify tastes for black servants. Another exotic group were the Lascars, Orientals manning East India Company vessels.

Most of London's recruits came, however, from within England, particularly from the Home Counties and East Anglia. The lure of London, agrarian change and crises in rural cottage industries brought thousands to town. Migrants were attracted by good wages – as much as 50 per cent higher than provincial ones:

> O London is a dainty place,
> A great and gallant city!
> For all the Streets are pav'd with gold,
> And all the folks are witty.

London above all drew youths looking for employment: by 1700 perhaps 8,000 youngsters a year were arriving to seek their fortune. 'Young men and women in the country fix their eye on London,' rued the agrarian writer Arthur Young in 1771:

they enter into service in the country for little else but to raise money enough to go to London, which was no easy matter when a stage coach was four or five days creeping an hundred miles; and the fare and the expenses ran high. But now! a country fellow one hundred miles from London jumps on to a coach-box in the morning and for eight or ten shillings gets to town by night, which makes a material difference; [they] quit their clean healthy fields for a region of dirt, stink and noise.

People were sucked into London. And those who remained in the country increasingly had their lives shaped by the demands of the metropolis. 'This whole kingdom,' observed Daniel Defoe,

are employed to furnish something, and I may add, the best of everything, to supply the city of London with provisions; I mean by provisions, corn, flesh, fish, butter, cheese, salt, fewel, timber etc, and cloths also; with every thing necessary for building, and furniture for their own use, and for trade.

Defoe had the journalist's flair for exaggerations containing a kernel of truth. London, in his eyes, was the guts of the system. London's insatiable demands galvanized competitive agriculture, long-distance credit, and corn-badgers (i.e. dealers), chapmen, wholesale butchers, graziers, drovers, cattle-fatteners and other middlemen. Unlike Parisians, Londoners did not fear the provinces would squeeze and starve them.

Capital and hinterland synergized, creating what Defoe called the 'general dependence of the whole country upon the city of London ... for the consumption of its produce'. London, of course, was no less dependent upon the nation, but the capital called the tune. Above all, London spelt demand. It paid good prices for provincial produce, while its tiptop wage rates attracted hands and supported top craftsmen. Its hordes of workers boosted consumption, pushing up prices. 'Every thing there is exceeding dear,' griped Pierre-Jean Grosley, while La Rochefoucauld guessed that 'everything costs twice as much here as in France'. 'Nothing is certain in London but expense,' remarked Isaac d'Israeli. Yet, so long as London was growing, high wages and costs energized, rather than proving a dead weight.

London's unquenchable appetite for country produce stimulated dairying, market gardening, local specialization and new business chains among graziers, fruiterers and poulterers. Its pull spread. Market gardening flourished in the riverside parishes around Fulham, Hammersmith and Battersea; around 1600 the capital was said still to be fed 'principallie ... from some fewe shires neare adioyninge'. In the seventeenth century, more distant counties got sucked in, with eggs and geese coming from North-amptonshire and Bedfordshire. London's sheep were driven in from Gloucestershire; Midlands cattle and grain, east-coast malt and grains, Yarmouth herrings, Norfolk turkeys, Colchester oysters, Kentish apples, Cheddar cheese, Portland stone and Devonshire cider – all and more came to London by road, river and sea. Georgian London was said to consume each year 2,957,000 bushels of flour, 100,000 oxen, 700,000 sheep and lambs, 238,000 pigs, 115,000 bushels of oysters, 14,000,000 mack-erel, 160,000 pounds of butter and 21,000 pounds of cheese.

Leading provincial manufacturers also penetrated the London market. Recognizing 'Fashion is infinitely superior to merit' in securing sales, in 1765 the Stoke potter Josiah Wedgwood opened a showroom in Grosvenor Square, aimed at the nobility and gentry. Trade proved so brisk that in two years he moved to Portland House in Greek Street, and later to St James's Square. The watchword was lavish display and showmanship. Dinner services were set out on tables 'as if to do the needful for the Ladys in the neatest, genteelest and best method'. Wedgwood realized the worth of a London showroom, his high-quality goods needing 'fine prices' that he could not get among countryfolk haggling over a pedlar's basket at the annual Black Country fairs.

As the nation's only dynamo of fashion, London attracted provincials to come and spend on clothes and finery, pictures, objets d'art, books and the theatre. A season developed: from Stuart times London always contained, from October to June, a herd of rural landowners, down for pleasure or to draw on the services of doctors, architects, face-painters, barristers, attorneys and scriveners, bankers, brokers and other pro-fessionals. Its legal predominance increased after the abolition in 1650 of the regional councils at Ludlow and York that had served Wales and the North. In a fiercely litigious age, no gentleman was without a satchel of lawsuits that detained him in town, often for weeks at a time. He might at the same time be looking after his pecuniary interests, as London emerged as the financial and credit capital, where mortgages were raised and investments negotiated. In 1700 stockjobbing was cited 'as one of the principal causes of the prodigious conflux of the nobility and gentry from all parts of England to London, more than ever in former years'

Parliament's increasing workload drew the ruling class to London from November to April, creating demand for superior accommodation and services. And all the while, in the rambling Whitehall Palace complex, the court and administration grew. Tax revenues mounted, the army and bureaucracy expanded, and government dispensed ever more lucrative patronage: court lobbying was vital for those seeking loaves and fishes.

Communications improved between capital and countryside. Domestic trade was largely conducted by river and by coastal shipping between London and provincial ports – London had nineteen quays specializing in provincial traffic. But networks of road carriers appeared – by the mid seventeenth century they were advertising scheduled freight services to places as far away as York, Manchester and Exeter. The capital's carriers trebled between 1637 and 1715. Passenger facilities improved too, with scheduled stagecoaches appearing after 1650. By 1681 London was linked to 88 towns, and by 1705 to 180. 'Flying coaches' clipped times: by 1670 a stagecoach would get you from Oxford to London in a day. London and Manchester stood three days apart in 1750 but a mere eighteen hours in 1836; Bristol, two days' journey from town in 1754, could be reached by 1800 in under twelve hours. Travel between the major towns was four or five times faster in 1830 than in 1750.

Coaching became big business, with specialist coaching inns: the Bull and Mouth at St Martin's-le-Grand, the Belle Sauvage on Ludgate Hill, the Spread Eagle in Gracechurch Street, and many others with that quaint comfortableness familiar from *The Pickwick Papers*. Coaching firms boomed, the leviathan among them being run during the Regency by William Chaplin, who bought the Swan With Two Necks and then acquired the White Horse, the Spread Eagle and the Cross Keys. Chaplin's coaches went everywhere. In the 1830s he was employing 2,000 people, owning 68 coaches and 1,800 horses, and his annual turnover was half a million pounds.

Chaplin's rival, Edward Sherman, established himself in 1823 at the Bull and Mouth. Marrying three rich elderly women in rapid succession enabled him to rebuild his seventeenth-century galleried inn with a courtyard large enough for thirty coaches. In the great age of coaching, before the iron horse, Sherman pioneered long-distance day coaches to Liverpool, Manchester, Holyhead and North Wales. His pride was the Manchester Telegraph; starting from London at 5 a.m., it reached Manchester the same day, covering 186 miles in eighteen hours. 'Nobody is provincial in this country,' judged Louis Simond, noting the difference travel made:

You meet nowhere with those persons who never were out of their native place, and whose habits are wholly local – nobody above poverty who has not visited London once in his life; and most of those who can, visit it once a year. To go up to town from 100 or 200 miles distance, is a thing done on a sudden, and without any previous deliberation. In France the people of the provinces used to make their will before they undertook such an expedition.

Coaches carried the mails. Improvements in the mail shot London news, gossip and fashions into the shires. By 1700 there were three deliveries a week from and into London. From the General Post Office in Lombard Street – and, from 1829, a new building in St Martin's-le-Grand – mail coaches rattled off every evening at eight o'clock, having first loaded up their passengers from the inns.

All such developments enhanced London's dominance. What was to be made of it? Grumbletonians like Laurence Sterne's character Walter Shandy were sure that it was all a '*distemper*', threatening the nation's lifeblood. But boosters saw the benefits. Was there any truth, asked the early economist Edward Davenant, 'in this common and received notion that the growth of the city is pernicious to England; that the kingdom is like a rickety body with a head too big for the other members'? On the contrary: Davenant believed that 'the growth of the city is advantageous to the nation'. The bullish Defoe generally agreed. 'Those people are greatly mistaken,' he maintained in *The Complete English Tradesman* (1726), 'who pretend the growing greatness of [London] is too much for the whole country; alleging ... that the city draws away the nourishment from the country, like a dropsy, which swells the body, but draws the nourishment away from the extreme parts.' Defoe was adamant the truth was the opposite:

as every part of the kingdom sends up hither the best of their produce, so they carry back a return of wealth; the money flows from the city into the remotest parts, and furnishes them again to increase that produce, to improve the lands, pay rent to their landlords, taxes to their governors, and supply their families with necessaries; and this is Trade.

London's position peaked around 1750. It could not, of course, be indefinitely sustained. By 1800, mining and textile factories were creating independent growth-centres in the Midlands and the North, in South Wales and Scotland. London's share of the national population never again outweighed the provincial towns. All the same, its proportionate size continued to increase: in 1851 metropolitan London accounted for 13.2 per cent of the people of England and Wales, and for 16.4 per cent in 1901.

> Then commerce brought into the public walk
> The busy merchant; the big warehouse built;
> Raised the strong crane, choked up the loaded street
> With foreign plenty; and thy stream, O Thames,
> Large, gentle, deep, majestic, king of floods!
> Chose for his grand resort. On either hand,
> Like a long wintry forest, groves of masts
> Shot up their spires.

Thus sang James Thomson in *The Seasons* (1730). Commerce was London's precious lifeblood. Overseas trade and empire built England's economic muscle, and the heart of the exchange network was the Port. Around 1700, London's quays were handling a staggering 80 per cent of the country's imports, 69 per cent of its exports and 86 per cent of its re-exports, notably tobacco, sugar, silks and spices. Everything came to London. From the East Indies, noted Patrick Colquhoun in his *Treatise on the Commerce and Police of the River Thames* (1796), came 'tea, china, drugs, nankeens, muslins,

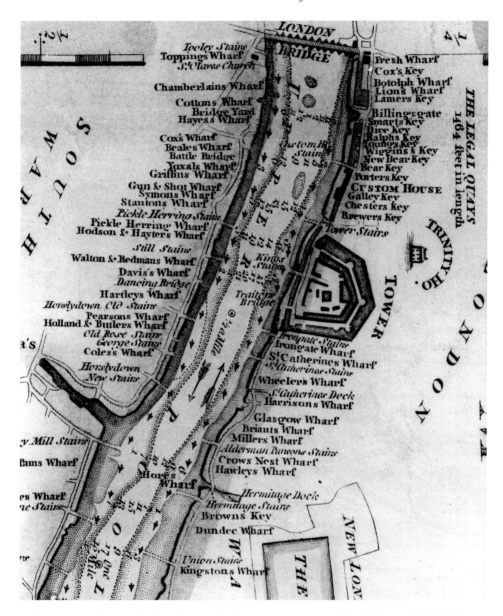

The riverside wharves (the 'legal quays') before the construction of the docks (Guildhall Library)

calicoes, long cloths, cotton yarn, pepper and spices, salt-petre, indigo, raw and manufactured silks, sugars etc.'; from the West, 'sugar, rum, coffee, cocoa, pimento, ginger'; Africa supplied 'fruit, wax, gums, elephants' teeth, palm oil, wine'; North America sent 'tobacco, rice, indigo, cotton, corn, oil, skins, and naval stores', while thriving Baltic networks brought 'hemp, linens, tallow, ashes, iron, masts, deals'. Thanks to the power

137

of the Royal Navy, the continuing expansion of the colonies – India and Canada were secured by the Seven Years War (1756–63) – and the effects of the monopolistic Navigation Acts, London was also the entrepôt *par excellence*. Silk, tea, sugar and tobacco warehouses lined the Pool of London; and commodity exchanges sprang up, like the tea exchange near East India House in Leadenhall Street. Imports rose over fourfold in the seventeenth century, and by a similar amount in the eighteenth; by 1797 exports totalled £17,721,441 – more than all the other ports combined. Eventually, of course, with the growth of American trade, Liverpool, Glasgow, Bristol and Whitehaven rose in relative importance, but London continued to hog trade with mainland Europe, and with India and the Far East, not least because of the privileges enjoyed by the chartered companies.

Since medieval times London's dominance had been due to the Thames – 'a broad slippery fellow', wrote Donald Lupton in 1632:

rest he affects not, for he is always in motion: he seems something like a carrier, for he is still either going or coming, and once in six or eight hours salutes the sea his mother . . . Merchandise he likes and loves; and therefore sends forth ships and traffic to most parts of the earth; his subjects and inhabitants live by oppression like hard landlords at land, the greater rule, and many times devour the less; the city is wondrously beholden to it, for she is furnished with almost all necessaries by it.

That 'beholdenness' grew – shipping activity on the Thames was so great that no writer (judged Defoe in the 1720s) could 'bring it into any reasonable compass'. The river was log-jammed – 'almost hidden by merchant vessels from every country', gasped César de Saussure.

Expansion continued, all manner of commodities passing through the Port. By 1600 Londoners were routinely burning coal for fuel; between 1650 and 1750 the quantity brought from Newcastle doubled, to about 650,000 tons – hence the fogs. Visiting Newcastle, Defoe described 'the inexhaustible store of coals and coal pits, from whence not London only, but all the south part of England is continually supplied; and whereas we are at London and see the prodigious fleet of ships which come constantly in with coals for this increasing city'. Steam pumps for draining northern mines were, tellingly, manufactured in the capital. 'All Proprietors of Mines and Collieries which are incumbered with Water,' announced the inventor Thomas Savery in 1702, 'may be furnished with Engines to drain the same at his Workhouse in Salisbury Court, London,' just off Fleet Street.

London's imperial position and the tripling of trade between 1720 and 1800 resulted in dire congestion, especially in the Upper Pool, where up to 1,800 vessels packed into mooring space for 500. Below London Bridge a few small docks had been constructed, a basin at Blackwall and the Howland Great Dock at Rotherhithe. This last, extending over twelve acres, could accommodate the greatest ships of the time; because of

London's riverside showing the Tower in the background, 1757. Engraving by L. P. Boitard

customs difficulties, however, it was never used to discharge cargo but only as a repair depot. Those early docks thus did not reduce congestion. Coasters berthed in the Upper Pool (from London Bridge to Union Hole), middling vessels in the Middle Pool (Union Hole to Wapping New Stairs), larger ships in the Lower Pool (Wapping New Stairs), while 450- and 500-tonners stuck to the Limehouse and Greenwich reaches, by Woolwich, Blackwall and Deptford, where they offloaded their cargoes into thousands of hoys and barges that exacerbated the jam. But all the Port's merchandise had to be funnelled through the legal quays on the north bank between London Bridge and the Tower, before being warehoused in adjoining streets. This archaic legal arrangement persisted despite the trade explosion. By the 1790s, overcrowding, delays and alarming theft levels threatened the Port itself.

Parliament investigated remedies. A palliative was the setting up in 1798 of the Marine Police, but the major change lay in dock-building, undertaken by chartered companies under special Acts of Parliament: the West India Docks on the Isle of Dogs opened in 1802, the London Docks at Wapping in 1805, the East India Docks at

Blackwall in 1806, and the Surrey Docks at Rotherhithe in 1807. Around the same time, the Admiralty opened the Royal Victualling Yard at Deptford to service the fleet.

Thames-side trade fuelled London's industries, not least shipbuilding itself, which required large yards with auxiliary trades – rope-, sail- and mast-makers and repair facilities. The will of a certain Edward Arlibeare of Wapping gives a glimpse of the varied ship-related enterprises in the 1660s. A mast-maker, Arlibeare left a mastyard on the water front. Nearby he owned another yard and wharf, rented to Guildford Elvey, a shipwright, adjoining the house of John Moore, another shipwright, and a mastyard occupied by Edward Grey. Arlibeare bequeathed a third piece of land (occupied by John Wright, a shipwright), on which stood a mastyard and two tenements. Droves of such craftsmen were operating around the congested alleyways of riverside Wapping.

Prominent among East End industries were distilling, sugar-refining and brewing. Big distillers, such as Booth's, Gordon's and Nicholson's, settled in Clerkenwell to take advantage of the high-quality well-water. St Katharine's and East Smithfield, east of the Tower, had many breweries, including the Red Lion, the Hart's Horn and the Three Kings. Further north in Spitalfields, Joseph Truman established himself around 1680 in Brick Lane, and began building up the Black Eagle, one of the great Georgian breweries. Other major concerns sprang up, including Meux, Perkins & Thrale's (in Park Street, Southwark), and Whitbread's. In 1786 Whitbread's alone produced 150,000 barrels of strong beer, while the London breweries between them made nearly 5 million barrels of porter, 1.5 million barrels of small beer, and over 0.5 million barrels of table beer. 'The sight of a great London brewhouse exhibits a magnificence unspeakable,' enthused the thirsty antiquarian Thomas Pennant.

London was proud of its quality trades: its cutlery was preferred to Sheffield's; its clocks and watches were renowned. Silk-weaving thrived at Spitalfields under Huguenot management. Though vulnerable to the whirligig of fashion, the industry expanded behind protective tariffs against imported silks, employing at its peak some 12,000 weavers. By 1750 there were 500 master weavers around Spital Square, about 15,000 looms at work, and 50,000 locals dependent on the trade. The industry soon faced severe difficulties, however. Trade down-swings created unemployment, leading to riots. 'Several thousand journeymen weavers assembled in Spitalfields,' a newspaper reported on 3 October 1763,

and in a riotous and violent manner broke open the house of one of their masters, destroyed his looms, and cut a great quantity of rich silk to pieces, after which they placed his effigy in a cart, with a halter about his neck, an executioner on one side and a coffin on the other. They then drove it through several streets, hung it on a gibbet and burnt it to ashes.

Disturbances continued. In 1769 fourteen ringleaders were apprehended, two being hanged outside a Bethnal Green tavern. The Spitalfields Act of 1772 attempted to rationalize the industry by curtailing recruitment of apprentices and forbidding weavers' unions, but problems continued, and the less skilled branches of the industry collapsed and moved to Macclesfield and other provincial centres where labour was cheap.

From the 1740s London had porcelain factories at Bow (Stratford High Street) and Chelsea, inspired by the Chinese porcelain the East India Company was shipping from the East. In Whitechapel stood the long-established bell foundry, which was sending church bells as far afield as Cologne and Carolina. (It later made 'Big Ben'.) Another superior trade was cabinet-making, boosted by the introduction of mahogany, replacing walnut veneer and oak.

Thomas Chippendale opened his workshops in Long Acre about 1745, later moving to St Martin's Lane. Hepplewhite set up shop in Cripplegate, and Thomas Sheraton arrived in 1790. And there were scores of other skilful cabinet-makers, many around Covent Garden but others in the City – in Lombard Street, Fenchurch Street, the Barbican, St Paul's Churchyard and St John Street, Smithfield. *The Gentleman and the Cabinet-maker's Director* (1754), Chippendale's elaborate catalogue with 160 engraved plates, marked him as the top of the tree. David Garrick ordered furniture from him for his house in the Adelphi, Lord Mansfield for Kenwood, and Lord Shelburne for Lansdowne House, Berkeley Square. 'He employs four hundred apprentices on any work connected with the making of household furniture, joiners, carvers, gilders, mirror-workers, upholsterers, girdlers – who mould the bronze into graceful patterns – and locksmiths,' remarked Sophie von La Roche in 1786, visiting the workshops of the Aldersgate cabinet-maker Thomas Seddon, with whom the Prince Regent later ran up debts reaching into hundreds of thousands of pounds.

The cabinet trade ranged from exquisite items to household stuff. Chippendale supplied Sir Rowland Winn with fine mahogany pieces, but also a deal stool for fifteen pence and a 'Large strong Elm Chopping block for the kitchen'. Hundreds of humbler joiners made boxes, sea-chests in deal or 'wainscot', shop furniture and bedsteads.

And scores of other crafts bloomed – a *Directory* of 1792 named 492. Weaving might be in decline, but the metropolis was Britain's most diversified craft centre. There were expert furnishers, house-painters and decorators, basket-makers, box-makers, watchmakers, printers and engravers and dozens more. Many precision crafts had connections with shipping: maps, globes, telescopes, barometers, scientific and surgical instruments, clocks, spectacles, plate and jewellery – all were made in London.

Well over 5,000 people were involved in watchmaking alone. The trade was minutely subdivided; the everyday trade located itself in Clerkenwell and St Luke's without Cripplegate, but the top watchmakers were to be found in the main shopping streets – Cornhill, Cheapside and the Strand. There were also London makers who supplied the provinces; Bayley's of Red Lion Street were making around 4,000 watches a year, employing over 100 workmen.

London also had its share of dirty trades. Scattered through the East End and in the poorer Surrey suburbs were bone-boilers, grease-makers, glue-makers, paint-makers and the dyeworks of Southwark ('an odious stinking business'). Trades such as tallow-making consumed the offal of Smithfield, poisoning the atmosphere. Industries formed zones. Sugar-houses crystallized in Ratcliff and St Katharine's, and starch-works in East Smithfield, Whitechapel and Poplar; Ratcliff specialized in glass and gunpowder. The metal trades, engravers and printers converged in Clerkenwell, lime-burning kilns were established in Bethnal Green and Mile End, and brickmaking developed around Brick Lane. The lower reaches of the River Lea were famous for milling. Today's St Leonard's Street, halfway to Poplar, was called 'Four Mill Street'; Three Mill Bridge led to the Three Mills Distillery. The Lea formed an important transport artery, Bromley's mills grinding corn barged down from Hertfordshire. Lea traffic grew with the digging of Limehouse Cut in 1770. Flemish dyeworks and copperas works were set up in Poplar. Across the river in Rotherhithe and Deptford there were ropewalks, coopers' and boat-builders' yards, and oil, colour and soap works.

London trades were labour-intensive. Stepney and Whitechapel housed wharfside workers, dockers and porters. The riverside community had its superior mariners too, including East India Company and Navy officers and masters, but they were heavily outnumbered by the able seamen who made Ratcliff Highway the sailors' haunt.

In time, some threats arose to London's manufacturing supremacy. Other trades as well as silk migrated to provincial centres where labour was cheaper. 'A practice hath lately prevailed by working in the country, manufactures for sale in London, which formerly employed great numbers of journeymen in this city,' Corbyn Morris wrote in 1751:

This is visible in the article of shoes, in which there are fewer by many hundreds retained at work than there were twenty years ago ... and this method will probably be followed in many other branches of consumption – especially as the carriage from the country to London, by the improvement of the roads, becomes easier.

Framework knitting shifted to Nottinghamshire, while by 1833 it was reported, 'there is little cutlery made in London ... it is not unusual for the word "London" to be stamped on many articles made in Sheffield' – London still retained prestige for the finest wares. A geographical division of labour was arising: simple processes would be performed in the provinces, half-completed goods then being carted to London for finishing and marketing.

Indeed, London's supremacy in retailing grew more visible. London's goods had traditionally been sold by hawkers, with their time-honoured cries, and above all vended in the twelve old retail markets: Leadenhall for hardware, leather, cloth, poultry, meat and dairy produce; Billingsgate for fish; Queenhithe for grain; Smithfield for cattle; Covent Garden for fruit and vegetables; and so forth. New markets opened with the expansion of the west, including the Haymarket by the Royal Mews (modern Trafalgar Square), where Charles II granted his old friend the Earl of St Albans the right to hold a twice-weekly sheep and cattle market. That area continued to be bothered by wagons carting hay and straw (over 26,000 loads in 1827) until 1830, when the market was finally removed to the new Cumberland Market east of Regent's Park. (There were also hay markets in Whitechapel, Smithfield and the Borough, and, from 1800, at Paddington.)

But high-grade retailing was becoming the province of stylish shops. Superior streets in both the West End and the City gloried in all manner of quality suppliers: upholsterers, glovers, goldsmiths, stationers, cartographers, mathematical-instrument-makers, music publishers, tailors, milliners, perfumiers, jewellers, chemists, druggists, tea and coffee merchants, wine and spirit merchants, pastrycooks, porcelain, china and glass shops, woollen- and linen-drapers, boot- and shoemakers, tobacconists, gold and silver lacemen, carpet manufacturers, parasol-makers, furriers, seedsmen and florists, lamp-makers – and scores more. Top shopkeepers became household names. Along Fleet Street at No. 16 was Bernard Lintot, the publisher of Pope's *Homer*; at No. 32 John Murray opened his publishing business in 1768; at No. 67, on the corner of Whitefriars Street, was Thomas Tompion's clock- and watchmaker's shop; and Samuel Richardson's printing office was on the corner of Salisbury Square.

Mayfair developed chic shops, particularly around Bond Street, and Burlington Arcade opened in the Regency (supposedly at the request of Lord George Cavendish of Burlington House, to prevent passers-by throwing rubbish into his garden). Lock, the hatter, was already flourishing by the 1760s: his chief suppliers were Thomas and William Bowler in Southwark Bridge Road. Regency bucks bought their military hats and uniforms at Hawkes of Piccadilly. A former footman in Queen Anne's household, William Fortnum opened a grocery shop close to the present site with his friend Hugh Mason. John Jackson was trading as a chandler and oil-man as early as 1604. From the 1680s the Jackson family was in business in the Piccadilly area, finally consolidating under Richard Jackson, wax and tallow chandler of 190 Piccadilly. In 1797 John Hatchard opened a bookseller's and publisher's in Piccadilly that quickly became a fashionable rendezvous.

Other famous names appeared. William Hamley founded in 1760 a toy shop at 231 High Holborn called 'Noah's Ark'. Business booming, his descendants opened a Regent Street branch. In 1766 James Christie, a former Navy midshipman, opened an auction house. His Pall Mall salerooms soon became the choice place for art sales, doubtless thanks to his acquaintance with Reynolds and Gainsborough. William Asprey, a descendant of Huguenot craftsmen, was working in Mitcham in 1781, specializing in fitted dressing-cases, silverware and *objets d'art*. In the 1830s his son Charles Asprey moved to 49 New Bond Street, and then in 1848 to the present premises at 165–6 New Bond Street.

Light, lofty and theatrically designed, London's shops induced awe. 'Oh, the lamps of a night!' exclaimed Shelley, 'her rich goldsmiths, print-shops, toy-shops, mercers, hardware men, pastry cooks, St Paul's Churchyard, the Strand, Exeter Change, Charing Cross, with a man upon a black horse! These are thy gods, O London!' Tourists were bedazzled. 'It is almost impossible to express how well everything is organized in London, every article is made more attractive to the eye than in Paris or in any other town,' crooned Sophie von La Roche about London's shops:

We especially noticed a cunning device for showing women's materials. Whether they are silks, chintzes or muslins, they hang down in folds behind the fine high windows so that the effect of this or that material, as it would be in the ordinary folds of a woman's dress, can be studied. Amongst the muslins all colours are on view, and so one can judge how the frock would look in company with its fellows . . . Behind great glass windows absolutely everything one can think of is neatly, attractively displayed, and in such abundance of choice as almost to make one greedy.

Both the display and the cornucopia astounded her. 'What an immense stock, containing heaps and heaps of articles!' she exclaimed, visiting Boydell's, London's biggest print-dealer:

Here again I was struck by the excellent arrangements and system which the love of gain and the national good taste have combined in producing, particularly in the elegant dressing of large shop-windows, not merely in order to ornament the streets and lure purchasers, but to make known the thousands of inventions and ideas, and spread good taste about, for the excellent pavements made for pedestrians enable crowds of people to stop and inspect the new exhibits.

She was given to gushing, but she had spied a dramatic transformation that Defoe had earlier noted. 'It is a modern custom, and wholly unknown to our ancestors to have tradesmen lay out two-thirds of their fortune in fitting up their shops. By fitting up,' he explained,

I do not mean furnishing their shops with wares and goods to sell . . . but in painting and gilding, fine shelves, shutters, boxes, glass-doors, sashes and the like, in which they tell us now, 'tis a small matter to lay out two or three hundred pounds, nay, five hundred pounds, to fit up a pastry-cook's, or a toy shop ['toy' here meant hardware].

London seemed designed to cater for the 'born-to-shop' mentality. 'A hasty sketch of an evening in the streets of London' that Lichtenberg offered a German friend described a saunter from Cheapside to Fleet Street:

On both sides tall houses with plate-glass windows. The lower floors consist of shops and seem to be made entirely of glass; many thousand candles light up silverware, engravings, books, clocks, glass, pewter, paintings, women's finery, modish and otherwise, gold, precious stones, steel-work, and endless coffee-rooms and lottery offices. The street looks as though it were illuminated for some festivity: the apothecaries and druggists display glasses filled with gay-coloured spirits; the confectioners dazzle your eyes with their candelabra and tickle your nose.

Jane Austen loved shopping expeditions while staying with her brother, Henry, who lived above the offices of his banking-house in Henrietta Street, Covent Garden. She often went to Layton & Shear's, the fashionable mercers in that street, sampling the silks, satins and brocades, Indian muslins, fur tippets, feather plumes, ribbons and fancy trimmings. On one occasion she allowed the milliner 'to go as far as *36s*' for a white-flowered cap, but then became far more extravagant when her other brother, Edward, gave her five pounds to spend, hurrying back to Layton & Shear's to treat herself to twenty yards of striped poplin. Later she spoiled herself 'in sattin ribbon with propre perl edge' from a shop in Cranbourn Alley. Shopping was the highspot of her visits. 'If I were to pass the remainder of my life in London,' commented Robert

Harding, Howell & Co., a fashionable draper's shop in Pall Mall, 1796–1820

Southey, 'I think the shops would always continue to amuse me. Something extra-ordinary or beautiful is for ever to be seen in them.'

As an essayist noted in 1749, Britain's world role in overseas and entrepôt trades demanded a rapid growth of 'Agents, Factors, Brokers, Insurers, Bankers, Negotiators, Discounters, Subscribers, Contractors, Remitters, Ticket-Mongers, Stock-Jobbers, and of a great Variety of other Dealers in Money'. The City in modern parlance – a financial centre – emerged after the Restoration. Until 1698 dealers in the trading companies met in the Royal Exchange. This growing 'vexatiously thronged', they moved to Jonathan's Coffee-House in Change Alley, where the London Stock Exchange came into being. Stockbrokers later moved to Capel Court, by the side of the Bank of England. The Baltic Exchange originated in 1744 at the Virginia and Baltick Coffee House in Threadneedle Street.

Banks developed. The earliest of the City's private bankers had been Sir Thomas Gresham, the founder of the Royal Exchange. He had been followed in the 1670s by Sir Josiah Child, and further banks – Stone's, Hoare's and Martin's – had sprung up by Queen Anne's time, alongside goldsmiths who engaged in banking as a sideline. Child's Bank alone had assets of over £175,000 in 1704, and £734,000 fifty years later. These private bankers began by discounting commercial bills for London merchants, but they later extended their business to the provinces, acting among other things as agents for country banks, of which there were 150 by 1776. Concentrated on Lombard Street, London's banks grew from around forty in the 1760s to nearly twice as many by 1800.

The financial vertigo after the Restoration revealed the need for sound money, especially after Charles II, faced with bankruptcy, 'stopped' the Exchequer in 1672 – that is, in effect appropriated the goldsmiths' money, ruining bankers and clients alike. A new system of public finance was urgently required. At war with France in the early 1690s, William III was desperate for funds. A national bank proved the answer. In July 1694 the *London Gazette* announced that commissioners would meet at the Mercers' Hall, Cheapside, to receive subscriptions of £500 or more for a Bank of England. Within ten days the sum had been advanced, the subscribers becoming members of the Company of the Bank of England, based on the revolutionary concept of a National Debt.

Operating in the Grocers' Hall in the Poultry, the Bank's business was restricted to dealing in bills of exchange and in gold and silver; it was to take no part in trade. Its deposits and influence growing, in 1723 the Bank moved to a new building in Threadneedle Street, designed by George Sampson, on the site of the house of Sir John Houblon, one of its first directors. Sir John Soane was responsible for a later magnificent building by Threadneedle Street.

Alongside banking, insurance also developed. Several companies had been formed after the Great Fire. Nicholas Barbon founded a Fire Office around 1680, charging

2·5 per cent per annum on brick houses and double that on timber-framed ones. His business flourished, insuring over 5,000 houses. The Fire Office later became the Phoenix. Alongside there grew up the Friendly Society (1684), the General Insurance Office (1685), the Amicable Contributors (later known as the Hand-in-Hand, because of the clasped-hands logo on their badge) and Lombard House (1694). The first London fire brigades were run by the insurance companies, and fire-engines became more efficient, with pumps with continuous jets.

Until the Fire, marine insurers had met in the Royal Exchange, then they moved to a room in Cornhill; but when Edward Lloyd opened his Tower Street coffee-house in the 1680s, moving to the corner of Lombard Street in 1692, the assurers became his most important customers and Lloyd's the centre of shipping news. Lloyd distributed information in *Lloyd's News*, which first appeared in 1696; changing its name in 1734 to *Lloyd's List and Shipping Gazette*, it is the oldest continuously published London newspaper.

London society was many-layered. The *bon ton* basked in St James's and Grosvenor Squares, the world of Chesterfield and Byron. There were also the labouring masses – street sellers of milk, coal, pastry, pickles, powder and washballs, brickdust, apples and gingerbread, as well as bellows-menders, tinkers and knife-grinders. The river demanded thousands of watermen and lightermen, and then there were porters, carmen, sedan chairmen and all those who worked with London's tens of thousands of horses – and coal-heavers, laystall-men (refuse-collectors), scavengers, drovers, men in the building trades, paviors, rag-pickers and ballad-sellers. Domestic service was by far the biggest occupation for females; the needle offered more permanent work, occupying about a quarter of all working women. At every level, labour had its own ranking of honour: the actress Mrs Charke admitted that when down on her luck she had hawked sausages, but indignantly refuted the aspersion that she had sold flowers. Around 1800 Robert Southey drew attention to London's forgotten masses, the 'people that cry fish, fruit, herbs, roots, news, etc. about town'; their stock, he explained, 'perhaps does not amount to more than 40 or 50s. and part of this they take up (many of them) on their clothes at a pawnbroker's on a Monday morning, which they make shift to redeem on a Saturday night, that they may appear in a proper habit at their parish churches on a Sunday'.

Between the lords and the labourers, however, between Westminster and White-chapel, lay Holborn, Hoxton and Hackney, the large metropolitan midriff inhabited by a couple of hundred thousand solid citizens: master craftsmen, genteel merchants, tutors, apothecaries, clothiers, skinners, brewers, ironmongers, salters, drapers, haberdashers, vintners, confectioners, chandlers, coalmen, joiners, cutlers, candlemakers, hatters and tailors – professional men, established artisans, journeymen and their families; apprentices and servants: thrifty, cautious, but comfortable. Around 1700 a successful master craftsman might own a few hundred pounds' worth of property. Wealthier manufacturers, retailers and wholesalers – timber merchants, yarn dealers, coachbuilders, silk manufacturers, coal merchants, brewers, coopers, printers, sugar-refiners, cheesemongers and leather-sellers – might be worth a few thousand pounds. Such men followed the traditions of the prosperous burgesses of Tudor and Stuart times.

Upon the next rung were the professionals. Around 1750 Sir John Fielding averred to the 'vast Multitude of Attorneys, Petty-foggers and Understrappers of the Law'. London had over a quarter of the nation's stock of solicitors, and more than six times as many attorneys as Liverpool, Bristol, Manchester, Norwich, Chester, Newcastle and Leeds all told. The medical profession also congregated in the capital, as did teachers and tutors. Although the proposal for a university of London advanced in Defoe's *Augusta Triumphans; Or, the Way to make London the Most Flourishing City in the Universe* (1728) came to nothing, London housed scores of schools, including four of the country's nine major public schools, and Gresham College, which offered public lectures on scientific and mathematical subjects. Experimental scientific lectures were offered, and private anatomy schools provided first-rate medical education.

The organization of work was decisively changing. So strong for three centuries or so, guilds were undergoing precipitous decline. They had long policed entry into trade, regulating apprenticeships, conditions of work and standards of behaviour, but London's economy had spread far beyond the walls, regulation was yielding to market forces, and livery companies were turning into the chummy dining-clubs with charitable functions familiar today. Some, like the Apothecaries, continued to exercise effective quality control. But company membership became irrelevant for the smaller masters of many trades, involving rising expenses and diminishing benefits.

The restrictive, collectivist ethos of the livery companies was at odds with capitalist realities. Law courts grew less inclined to uphold their privileges, especially the crucial right of search, essential if companies were to maintain a closed shop. The mushrooming of the metropolis had long made such procedures difficult to enforce outside the walls: were they even legal? And, even within the City, companies grew reluctant to act for fear of prosecution for trespass. Many abandoned searches altogether, and concentrated instead on property management, charity and junketings.

Nevertheless, company membership remained a popular way for burgesses to affirm their social identity; church or chapel was similarly important. Respectable sorts went to church on Sunday, some even twice. Certain Dissenters attended church as well as chapel – for occasional church attendance and parish service were essential for getting on. Indeed, the parish grew more important as the ward weakened. The court of wardmote was still held in each ward, presided over by the alderman and open to ratepayers. It elected officers, collected for the poor, and policed bawdy-houses and alehouses. These duties began to be whittled away, however, as authority passed from the rank and file to the Common Council of the ward (the alderman, his deputy and the resident common councilmen). With the rise of more oligarchic local committees, City wardmotes were in decline.

The parish retained its old significance. Parish membership could involve onerous responsibilities. Every middle-class householder had either to pay a fine or to serve in various offices on his 'parishioner's progress' from constable up to churchwarden. Parishes were responsible for law and order and care of the aged, sick, disabled and unemployed. The poor were becoming a growing problem, and from 1722 parishes were permitted to build workhouses. In theory designed to put the able-bodied to work, in reality workhouses became doss-houses for the old, the sick and single-parent families. They were often a disgrace: in the 1770s the workhouse of St Martin-in-the-Fields was 'very ruinous and in Danger of falling'. Workhouse mortality was a scandal. The philanthropist Jonas Hanway described the workhouse of St Giles-in-the-Fields and St George Bloomsbury as 'the greatest sink of mortality in these kingdoms, if not on the face of the whole earth'; a parliamentary inquiry in 1767 showed that only seven in a hundred toddlers under twelve months of age survived for more than three years in workhouses.

St Marylebone provides a cameo of a vestry at work. Three or four meetings a year, held at the church, were attended by about a dozen parishioners. Officers were chosen – two churchwardens, two overseers of the poor, two surveyors of the highways, and one constable. The poor ate up funds: items recorded include provision of a midwife, examination of unmarried mothers and a search for the father ('paid information of Lettice Julf lying-in of a bastard child, and going several times after ye father who at last gave security . . . 10/6'), and interminable business respecting Poor Law settlements ('paid Smithers [the Beadle] for enquiring after the settlement of two children at the parish nurse, 1/-'). Medicine was provided and death cost money ('Mr Bradley, grave-digger, for four burials, 4/-'); and there was always the end-of-the-year binge: 'at the Queen's Head, at our going out, 5/-'.

Faced with the swelling ranks of the poor, the St Marylebone vestry eventually built a workhouse, opened in 1752. At the north-east corner of the burial-ground facing Paddington Street, it consisted of a block surrounded by high iron railings. A board of governors was set up, consisting of the ministers, churchwardens, overseers and a dozen other parishioners. A workhouse master was appointed, to be paid eighteen pence a week for every poor person in his charge; he was to feed them and put them to work, promising 'to teach the children to read and write and cast accounts . . . and instruct them in the principles of religion, and also to employ the children and young people in spinning jersey'.

The lives of the middling sort in Fetter Lane or Finsbury were thus still bound up with church and chapel, and with the minutiae of ward and parish business. But new social activities were growing, perhaps the offshoots of greater wealth and leisure, and marking a shift away from religious preoccupations (though the more sober supported the various Societies for the Reformation of Manners that sought to bring drunks, profaners of the Sabbath and prostitutes to book). Freemasonry became popular, to some degree providing the trade contacts and access to credit necessary in an age when guilds were dissolving. And multitudes of clubs sprang up, catering for hobbies, sports, and interests in music, the arts, debating and self-improvement. The Society of Gardeners was formed, for instance, consisting of twenty working nurserymen who met at Newhall's Coffee-House in Chelsea. One of them, Thomas Fairchild, wrote a book called *The City Gardener*, published in 1722. A tavern yard edged with flowering currants, he suggested, would attract customers, and sweet peas, sweet williams, candy-tuft and love-in-a-mist would give city gardens a rustic quality. Here was *rus in urbe* bourgeois-style. Famous too was the Spitalfields Mathematical Society, founded in 1717 by a retired sailor, John Middleton, who kept the Monmouth Head Tavern in Monmouth Street. It lent out books and instruments like air-pumps and electrical machines. The membership was not to exceed the square of seven. They met on Saturday evenings, when everyone present was to employ himself on some mathematical puzzle. The Society eventually accumulated a library of nearly 3,000 volumes.

Spitalfield weavers were famed for their singing, forming the nucleus of the Madrigal Society founded in 1741 by the eccentric attorney John Immyns, who 'looked upon Mr Handel and Bononcini as the great corruptors of the science'. The snobbish Sir John Hawkins recorded the numerous musical clubs held at 'many places of vulgar resort in the villages adjacent to London', and in particular at 'sundry ale-houses in Spitalfields, frequented by journeyman weavers'. Bourgeois London was settling into a domestic, consumption-orientated culture; but its radical past had not yet been forgotten.

London's government grew more quirky. The City was ruled by an entrenched Corporation, but it was fast shrinking relative to the metropolis at large, which, though housing the vast majority of Londoners, was presided over by a crazy-paving of jurisdictions whose rationale lay in historical accident rather than efficiency. In some respects the City's writ ranged far beyond its wards and precincts: it held a legal monopoly of markets; it levied coal duties in a radius of twelve miles; it administered and taxed the Port of London, and it formed the governing authority for the Thames from Staines Bridge to the Medway (rendering William Blake's phrase about the 'charter'd Thames' particularly apt). Southwark was administered by the City ward of Bridge Without – though its adjoining parishes came under Surrey. But the 'five villages beyond the Bills' – Hammersmith, Chelsea, Paddington, Marylebone and St Pancras – were ruled by their diverse vestries, and some 200 parish vestries enjoyed greater or lesser authority within the metropolis.

Parish set-ups varied widely. The vestries of Marylebone and St Pancras, like certain of the 'close' (oligarchic) vestries of Westminster, had extensive powers over highways, poor relief and the rates. Further out, responsibility for poor relief and highways fell on the county justices. Overall, parochial power was gathering in the hands of 'the better sort', while the mass of ratepayers were losing their share in government. In about a quarter of the 200 metropolitan parishes, 'select' vestries superseded the old 'open' vestry, traditionally open to all ratepayers. The open vestry remained fairly common, however, as in Whitechapel, and some, like St Leonard Shoreditch, were 'mixed'. Bethnal Green was a law unto itself. In 1743 it became a separate parish with a population of 15,000. The vestry was open to all ratepayers with premises rated at £15 a year – about 2,000 householders. Joseph Merceron, a Brick Lane JP, established himself as a local political boss, controlling many beer-shops and public houses, and winning popularity by keeping the taverns open all night and organizing dog-fights and bull-baiting – meanwhile diverting parish money into his own pocket. In 1818 justice caught up with him, and Bethnal Green's 'turbulent democracy' was replaced by a sober 'close' vestry.

The fifty or sixty close vestries in London by 1800 included several City parishes, such as St Bartholomew-the-Great; most Westminster parishes; Marylebone and St Pancras among the 'five villages'; and various parishes in metropolitan Middlesex and Surrey. Authority in these was vested in self-perpetuating oligarchies of thirty or fifty persons. On the vestry of the posh parish of St George Hanover Square there were seven dukes, fourteen earls, two viscounts, seven barons and twenty-six other titled persons. St James's Piccadilly created a vestry quaintly divided between the 'estates': one-third noblemen, one-third gentlemen and one-third tradesmen.

Westminster was *sui generis*. Though called a city, it had never become a municipality with corporate status and a Lord Mayor or a Court of Aldermen. From 1585 it had been governed by a Court of Twelve Burgesses, appointed for life. Collectively, the burgesses tried petty offences and appointed constables, scavengers and jurymen. From the 1720s their authority was transferred to the 'close' vestries of the local parishes and the Middlesex justices who sat on the Westminster bench. Ordinary citizens – unlike their City fellows – thus played little part in Westminster government, but Westminster had an extraordinarily democratic parliamentary franchise open to all 'pot-wallopers' (resident householders). Westminster electors – victuallers, tailors, carpenters, peruke-makers, shoemakers, butchers, chandlers and bakers – played a major role in 1760s radicalism.

Further out, parishes lay under the vestries and the JPs meeting in quarter sessions.

In Surrey and Middlesex JPs appointed and directed the constables, overseers and surveyors of the highways; they were responsible for the poor; they regulated rates and prices; maintained workhouses, roads and bridges; licensed alehouses; administered houses of correction; and sat at petty and quarter sessions. The top dog was the chairman of quarter sessions.

As the metropolis thus approached a million inhabitants, its government was a fragmented historical relic, divided between hundreds of bodies, mutually distrustful and antagonistic. Small wonder that commentators often pictured it as a stormy sea. Some swam, others sank, and all were at the mercy of chance, fate and trade, and the vagaries of self-interest. Where was good government? Could anybody feel safe? Fears rose about a crime wave. In his *Enquiry into the Causes of the late Increase of Robbers* (1751), Henry Fielding – not just a novelist but a leading magistrate – argued that

Whoever indeed considers the Cities of London and Westminster, with the late vast Addition of their Suburbs, the great Irregularity of their Buildings, the immense Number of Lanes, Alleys, Courts and Bye-places; must think, that, had they been intended for the very Purpose of Concealment, they could scarce have been better contrived. Upon such a View, the whole appears as a vast Wood or Forest, in which a Thief may harbour with as great Security, as wild Beasts do in the Deserts of Africa or Arabia.

In 1782 Horace Walpole put Fielding's abstract anxieties about London's 'forest' into more urgent, concrete terms:

I am perfectly ignorant of the state of the war abroad ... but I know we are in a state of war at home that is shocking. I mean, from the enormous profusion of housebreakers, highwaymen, and footpads; and, what is worse, from the savage barbarities of the two latter, who commit the most wanton cruelties ... one dare not stir out after dinner but well-armed.

The gossipy Walpole loved to exaggerate; but he was not alone in his fears. To many, the metropolitan law-and-order machinery – all those antiquated constables, beadles and 'charlies' (watchmen) – had grown quite inadequate. 'London is really dangerous at this time,' reflected the poet William Shenstone in mid-century: 'the pickpockets, formerly contented with mere filching, make no scruple to knock people down with bludgeons in Fleet Street and the Strand, and that at no later hour than eight o'clock.' Not for the first time, journalists circulated tales of a fiendish criminal underworld.

In truth, however, those committing crimes – notably the 1,200 Londoners hanged in the eighteenth century – were less hardened professionals than servants and seamstresses and the labouring poor, down on their luck or out of work, starving, or just fatally tempted. Much crime arose out of the ambiguities of capitalism itself, involving mishandling of property. Many were executed, and thousands more whipped or transported, for workplace crime: for making off with oddments of cloth from master tailors, nails and plank-ends from shipyards, pocketfuls of tea or sugar from Thames lighters. Custom had traditionally allowed journeymen their rags, spillage and left-overs: such perks topped up meagre wages. But these customary entitlements were becoming criminalized through statutes like the Bugging Act of 1749, which penalized 'stealing the beaver' – switching fabrics in the hatters' trade. One rich source of loot was the ships and quaysides around London Bridge. In 1800 the magistrate Patrick Colquhoun estimated that river pirates plundered the West Indian merchants of an estimated £250,000 annually, watermen working in collusion with watchmen stealing hogsheads of sugar, coffee and tallow. In his *Treatise on the Police of the Metropolis* Colquhoun pointed out the 'chain by which these criminal people extend and facilitate their trade'. Half the hackney coachmen in London were said to be 'flashmen' in league with thieves.

Policing London long remained the task of beadles and constables and the parish watch and ward – a total force, amateur and professional, of a little over 3,000 unarmed men. A French visitor was contemptuous:

London is guarded at night by old men chosen from the dregs of the people who have no other arms but a lantern and a pole, crying the hour every time the clock strikes ... and whom it is the custom of young rakes to beat and use ill when they come reeling out of the taverns where they have passed the night.

Such men at least had the advantage of being firmly rooted among the citizens. Any attempt to impose a *metropolitan* system, under central government, would have been sternly resisted as an invasion of liberty. The old system worked reasonably well so long as crime was local, but its parochial character impeded magistrates in tracking down offenders across administrative frontiers, including those separating the City from Westminster or the Bills of Mortality parishes from the rural hinterland. It also proved quite incapable of dealing with major civil disorders, such as the Gordon Riots of 1780 – prompting Lord Shelburne to complain that 'the police of Westminster was an imperfect, inadequate, and wretched system ... a fit object of reformation'.

Amidst such dangers and defects the theatrical *symbols* of justice assumed colossal significance. Though few were actually hanged, the gallows overshadowed all. The first permanent gallows had been set up at Tyburn in 1571, though Smithfield and Newgate Prisons, Tower Hill and Execution Dock had also been execution sites, and the riverside marshes had their gibbets. Public executions were intended to act as a deterrent; but apprentices, allowed a 'Tyburn Fair' holiday, regarded victims as heroes, especially when they exited with a swagger. The procession from prison to gallows, Newgate to Tyburn (Marble Arch), would last about two hours; the carts stopped at taverns, and many condemned men were drunk by the time they reached their end – they would promise to pay for their drink 'when they came back'. Enormous crowds gathered, accommodated near the 'fatal tree' in a stand known as 'Mother Proctor's Pews'. 'The Executioner stops the Cart under one of the Cross Beams of the Gibbet,' noted a French observer, Henri Misson,

and fastens to that ill-favour'd Beam one End of the Rope, while the other is round the Wretches Neck; This done, he gives the Horse a Lash with his Whip, away goes the Cart, and there swing my Gentlemen kicking in the Air: The Hangman does not give himself the Trouble to put them out of their Pain; but some of their Friends or Relations do it for them: They pull the dying Person by the Legs, and beat his breast, to dispatch him as soon as possible.

Sometimes friends tried to support the hanged in hopes of reviving them. In 1709 John ('half-hanged') Smith was cut down and successfully revived. Battles broke out between the surgeons, who were allowed ten bodies a year for dissection, and the prisoner's friends, who judged 'anatomization' a crime.

To stamp out disorders, Tyburn gallows were demolished in 1783 and executions moved to Newgate itself, while the last beheading on Tower Hill was that of the Jacobite Lord Lovat, who had the last laugh as a stand collapsed, killing twelve. Britain's very last beheadings took place outside Newgate in 1820, when the five Cato Street conspirators had their heads taken off with a surgeon's knife.

Public hangings proved counter-productive. 'On Monday last eleven wretches were executed at Tyburn,' commented Henry Fielding,

and the very next night one of the most impudent street-robberies was committed near St James's Square, an instance of the little force which such examples have on the minds of the populace.

In real truth, the executions of criminals, as at present conducted, serve, I apprehend, a purpose diametrically opposite to that for which they were designed; and tend rather to inspire the vulgar with a contempt of the gallows rather than a fear of it.

Like Tyburn, London's prisons loomed large in the public imagination. By 1800 there were eighteen, including the Fleet, King's Bench, Bridewell and Newgate, rebuilt to designs by Charles Dance. They made a powerful statement. 'Newgate was an extraordinary building,' wrote Sir John Summerson:

Far from being a mere dump for felons, a gigantic lock-up, it was splendid and costly architecture, a great Palace of Retribution. To the street it presented a façade of magnificent gloom, hung with chains and enriched with carved figures of horrible appropriateness, writhing in constructed, boulder-like niches. Inside, though less theatrical, it was no less designedly grim.

In reality, jails were no more effective than the noose. Moreover, they encouraged crime by being so corrupt, full of extortion and fiddles. In 1691 Moses Pitt revealed that he was charged 8s every week (instead of the regulation 2s 4d) for his cell at the Fleet, and when his money ran out he was sent to the dungeon, where he slept on the floor with companions 'so lowsie that … you might have pick'd lice off from the outward garments'. In 1729 a parliamentary inquiry found the Fleet's Keeper, Thomas Bambridge, guilty 'of great extortions, and the highest crimes and misdemeanours in the execution of his said office'. He had 'arbitrarily and unlawfully loaded with irons, put into dungeons, and destroyed prisoners for debt, under his charge, treating them in the most barbarous and cruel manner'. In 1780 the Gordon Rioters wrecked the prison. Though it was rebuilt in 1781, the self-appointed inspector of prisons John Howard still found it 'riotous and dirty'. Many prisoners were drunk, men and women mixed freely, and there was no medical attention. 'The prisoners play in the courtyard at skittles, mississippi, fives, tennis etc.,' he complained, and outsiders would drop in for a drink:

The same may be seen in many other prisons where the gaoler keeps or lets the taps … On Monday night there was a wine club; on Thursday night a beer club; each lasting usually till one or two in the morning. I need not say how much riot these occasion, and how the sober prisoners, and those that are sick, are annoyed by them.

Howard found conditions no better. Dickens graphically described it in *The Pickwick Papers*, before it closed in 1842.

Hesitant steps were taken to improve public order. An expedient tried early in the century was the professional thief-taker, notably the self-styled 'Thief-taker-General of Great Britain and Ireland', Jonathan Wild, who turned out to be in cahoots with the criminal fraternity and was finally hanged in 1725. Some professional magistrates were employed, but these won little respect – Edmund Burke denounced the Middlesex JPs as 'generally the scum of the earth – carpenters, brickmakers and shoemakers'. Innovations in policing came with the Bow Street Office, founded by Henry Fielding in 1749. Fielding and his brother John, magistrates at Bow Street, recognized that many appearing before them were 'guilty of no crime but poverty'. They created a team of constables, known as the Bow Street Runners, paid one guinea a week and a share in the rewards for successful prosecutions. In 1798 the Thames Police Office was promoted by Patrick Colquhoun. But no metropolitan police force was set up to cope with what had, in many respects, become a metropolitan or even a national problem. By 1800 London had hardly begun to address the problem of public order in a world city.

This situation was exacerbated by sporadic political tensions between the government and the City – tensions unresolved since the Civil War. London threatened to be the cuckoo in the national nest, the overmighty subject. Citizens liked to shake their fist at Westminster, insisting on their rights and independence, yet such truculence may have confused rhetoric and reality.

The City's constitution had come through the Civil War, the Restoration and the Glorious Revolution extraordinarily unscathed. An oligarchic aldermanic bench still dominated, exercising growing patronage – there were over 150 official posts or sinecures. The Court of Aldermen still consisted of the Lord Mayor and the twenty-five other aldermen, elected for life by the freeman ratepayers in their various wards, and serving as magistrates and collectively as a City cabinet. After 1689 they exercised a veto on all legislative acts brought forward by the Court of Common Council. This sparked discord.

Aldermen were the City's fat cats. Of the forty-three aldermen holding office between 1768 and 1774, a dozen were bankers (two directors of the Bank of England), one a governor of the Hudson's Bay Company, two were West India merchants, and only a handful followed City trades. Friction grew between the oligarchic bench and the Court of Common Council, elected by all ratepaying citizens, which saw itself as representing the crafts and voicing grass-roots views. In 1739 its 210 members included twenty-six haberdashers and linen-drapers, fourteen druggists and apothecaries, eight carpenters, cabinet-makers, masons and bricklayers, six bakers and confectioners, and about eighty other tradesmen and craftsmen.

Battles ensued between bench and council, the aldermen tending to be Whig and Latitudinarian and the Common Council Tory and High Church. Supported by Walpole's Whig ministry, an Act of 1725 limited the freeman franchise to £10 house-holders, thus disqualifying less well-to-do voters and creating an aldermanic veto over Common Council acts. This situation lasted for two decades, until the Act was repealed and aldermen and Common Council once more joined forces to assume an opposition stance.

The City was proud of its privileges and precedents. In the 1640s it had led opposition to the 'tyranny' of Laud and Charles I; a generation later, at the Exclusion Crisis of 1681, when Parliament attempted to exclude Charles II's younger brother (later James II) from the succession, Shaftesbury's 'country party' and London's mob had formed a powerful pressure group. James II had revised London's charters, but the Glorious Revolution had restored its fortunes, so that by Anne's time it was re-emerging as a powerful political force, and under the Hanoverians it recovered its old independence. The City welcomed George I, and for a while the court and the Corporation saw eye to eye, till relations became strained with the South Sea Bubble financial scandal. Thereafter, tensions rose between the City and St James's, and not till Pitt the Younger did the City find a Prime Minister to its taste.

The City exercised an influence on national politics in various ways. Voters used Common Council to give 'instructions' to MPs they elected: in 1774 all four City

MPs were made to promise not to accept from Lord North's administration 'any place, pension, contract, title, gratuity, or emolument of any kind'. Since a high proportion of City and Westminster inhabitants had the vote, these constituencies often returned radical members. City political opposition peaked after Lord Chatham's resignation in 1763, when merchants shared his sympathies towards the American colonies. Mayor Crosby seized a House of Commons messenger sent to the City to arrest some printers accused of publishing Commons debates – shades of the arrest of five MPs before the start of the Civil War. For this he was cast into the Tower – but on his release accorded a triumphal procession. In 1770 Chatham's henchman Mayor Beckford told the King that enemies of the City were enemies of the people; his reward was a statue in the Guildhall. In 1774 City opposition culminated with the election as Mayor of the notorious John Wilkes, plague of King and governments alike during the previous decade.

The City loved playing the role of defender of liberties, a David against the ministerial Goliath. But in truth it was protecting its privileges, and its refusal to take responsibility for the rest of the town was reactionary. By 1800 nine-tenths of Londoners were living outside the City, but the Corporation persisted in regarding itself as London's sole authority, offering pig-headed resistance to reforms.

Since the Civil War, citizens had been independent and unruly, sometimes taking to the streets. The volatile mob was of particular concern, because protesters were politically intelligent. Foreigners found popular participation in politics astonishing. 'In general nothing is more difficult than to make an Englishman speak,' observed von Archenholz, 'he answers to everything by *yes* or *no*; address him, however, on some political subject and he is suddenly animated; he opens his mouth and becomes eloquent; for this seems to be connected from his infancy with his very existence.'

Londoners were used to expressing their loyalties on the streets, through processions, demonstrations and other forms of street theatre, in which traditional values were epitomized in emotive icons like the loaf, the noose and Magna Carta. The tensions of the last years of Charles II and the reign of James II led to violent street politics, notably the savage torchlit pope-burning processions of 1673–80, involving 'a most costly Pope … his ears, his belly filled full of live cats who squawled most hideously as soon as they felt the fire'. Under Anne, Whig pope-burnings and fireworks were countered by rival Tory displays, celebrating the anniversary of Charles I's martyrdom.

To stifle street politics, the Riot Act was passed in 1715. It had little effect. In 1719 there were London riots led by weavers. In the Rag Fair Riots of July 1736 the Irish found themselves the target. The 1743 Gin Act provoked riots in defence of cheap liquor, while elections proved occasions for riot. Londoners voted for only ten members of Parliament – four for the City and two each for Westminster, Southwark and the county of Middlesex – but they were notorious for their independence. 'The countrys always take the rule from hence,' observed Lord Halifax in 1705, 'and the true pulse of a nation is always felt at the heart.'

Popular power made itself felt in the 1760s, when supporters of John Wilkes engaged in a highly effective legal war against George III and his minister Lord Bute. Crowds repeatedly took to the streets in powerful yet disciplined riots, demanding justice and constitutional rights, and carrying out menacing but limited assaults on the property of opponents – smashing windows and the like. The essence was demonstration, not revolution. Wilkite rioters targeted the administration, not the metropolis.

The Gordon Riots, a few years later, were a different kettle of fish, with their blazing, bigoted anti-Catholicism. After the Jacobite rebellions of 1715 and 1745, Catholic harassment intensified. With the passing of the Catholic Relief Act of 1778, protests arose from anti-Catholics, supported by Common Council Whigs and radical shop-keepers, for whom Roman Catholicism represented France and Spain, despotism and Jesuits. A Protestant Association was formed in 1780. On 2 June its members marched to the House of Commons with Lord George Gordon, a fanatical anti-Papist, to demand the Act's repeal. Composed of the 'better sort of tradesmen', the deputation was joined by a rioting mob of 'upwards of 50,000 true Protestants'. For two days, they burnt the private chapels and houses of Roman Catholic gentry in Westminster and the City. Ministers were reluctant to summon troops, magistrates terrified to call on them to fire; the Lord Mayor informed a silk merchant whose house was under attack, 'I must be cautious what I do lest I bring the mob to my own house.' Firm action by the King finally decided the matter. A proclamation against the rioters was issued on Wednesday 7 June. The next morning the Riot Act was read, but rioters swarmed to Newgate, freed the prisoners and burnt the jail. Another crowd burnt down Lord Chief Justice Mansfield's house in Bloomsbury Square – he had aroused their wrath by favouring Catholic toleration.

Fires raged. The mob attacked the premises of a Roman Catholic distiller in Holborn, burning cellars containing 120,000 gallons of gin. They then attacked the Fleet, releasing the prisoners, before moving across the river to set fire to King's Bench, the New Gaol, the Marshalsea and the Surrey House of Correction. They burnt the Blackfriars Bridge toll-gates.

Their last attack was on the Bank of England. It was prepared: armed clerks and volunteers of the London Military Association were stationed on the roof, and guards waited outside and by the Royal Exchange. The rioters' first rush was greeted with a volley; the second charge was weaker; the rest fled, leaving behind their dead and wounded. The next day, despite skirmishing in the City, the military were in control and the riots petered out. Nearly 300 were killed, 450 prisoners were taken, and 160 were brought to trial, twenty-five being hanged and twelve imprisoned.

*

As so often before – for instance with the Plague or the Great Fire – a crisis found London's government hopelessly wanting, irresolute, impotent, paralysed. The Mayor and the aldermen were experts in money not men; theirs was a politics of property not people; they had no authority over the metropolis as a whole. But neither did anyone else, except ultimately the King and his ministers, who might have very mixed feelings about intervening to bale out the usually conceited and sniping Corporation.

At the dawn of the nineteenth century, the 'City within the Walls', with a population of around 70,000 – just a twentieth of the capital in 1821 – was far wealthier, per capita, than the metropolis as a whole. Westminster was growing, but the real nineteenth-century population explosion took place in new 'outer' London. The implications of this for London's government were long ignored by so-called practical men, though the dilemma had been addressed with exemplary, almost Benthamite, clarity by the pioneer statistician William Petty as early as the close of the Civil War.

From Blackwall to Vauxhall, Petty had argued, the metropolis formed one single political, economic and military unit. To allow it to persist under parish government, with the City and Westminster separated from it, was irrational. The whole should be subject to one Common Council, though subdivided into three smaller units (the City, Southwark and Westminster). What would later be called greater London should (Petty argued) return between eighty and ninety members to Parliament, as its population warranted. It was to form one diocese, one county, with a JP and a parson in every parish.

The problem Petty had confronted had not been tackled by 1800. In most respects London was then still, as Joseph Addison had seen it, a loose agglomeration of diverse elements, without any coordination beyond what market forces provided. How far, and for how much longer, could commerce supply the place of government? London was to provide a living experiment.

CHAPTER SEVEN

Culture City:
Life under the Georges

> When we came upon Highgate hill and had a
> view of London, I was all life and joy.
>
> JAMES BOSWELL (1763)

The capital had become a wonder, but was it a miracle or a monster? The thinkers of the Enlightenment saw that the future lay with cities, and generally approved: despite ancient anti-urban prejudices, the city now seemed to promise progress, peace, profit, pleasure and the erosion of ignorance; city man was civilized man. The Anglophile Voltaire considered London the cradle of social freedom and mobility by contrast to the rigid hierarchies of the fields. Yet cities had foes as well as friends; many still damned them as Babylon or Sodom – 'God made the country, and man made the town,' ran William Cowper's judgement. And, by a perverse logic, the greater the benefits metropolitan life conferred, the more the urban literati vilified it, idealizing Nature and lamenting the loss of rural innocence, in a movement culminating in Romanticism, that opium of the urban intelligentsia. Wordsworth thus presented urban alienation in *The Prelude*:

> . . . how men lived
> Even next-door neighbours, as we say, yet still
> Strangers, nor knowing each the other's name.

Himself a Londoner, William Blake anatomized the capital's squalor and crime, and the townsman's inhumanity to man:

> I wander thro' each charter'd street,
> Near where the charter'd Thames does flow,
> And mark in every face I meet
> Marks of weakness, marks of woe.

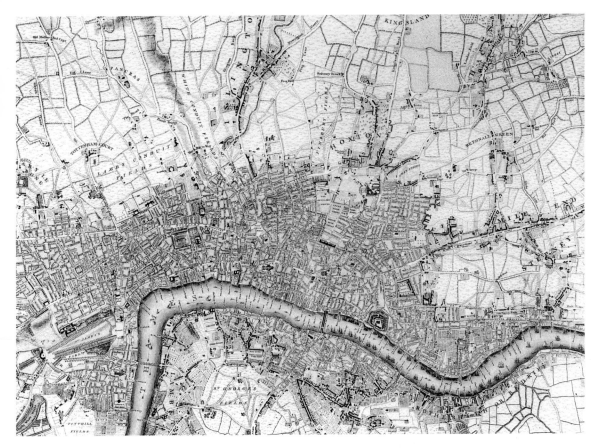

Ten miles around London, 1746, by John Rocque

In every cry of every Man,
In every Infant's cry of fear,
In every voice, in every ban,
The mind-forg'd manacles I hear.

How the Chimney-sweeper's cry
Every black'ning Church appals;
And the hapless Soldier's sigh
Runs in blood down Palace walls.

But most thro' midnight streets I hear
How the youthful harlot's curse
Blasts the new born Infant's tear
And blights with plagues the Marriage hearse.

And it wasn't only poets who vilified Georgian London. Defoe had dubbed it 'the monstrous city', Josiah Tucker found it 'no better than a wen', or wart; and it was William Cobbett, of course, who, damning all the nation's towns as 'wens', anathematized the capital as the 'great wen'.

Critics believed London tainted all it touched, sucking in the healthy from the countryside and, as the Bills of Mortality proved, devouring far more than it bred. 'The Capital is become an overgrown monster,' complained Smollett's character Matt Bramble, 'which, like a dropsical head, will in time leave the body and extremities without nourishment and support.' To luxury-lashing moralists, London seemed culprit-in-chief for the 'Waste of Mankind'.

Many doctors diagnosed London a hotbed of disease. In his influential *The English Malady* (1733), the Scottish physician George Cheyne credited the capital with being 'the greatest, most capacious, and close, and populous City of the *Globe*'; for those very reasons it was positively lethal:

The infinite Number of *Fires, Sulphurous and Bituminous*, the vast expense of Tallow and foetid Oil in Candles and Lamps, under and above the Ground, the clouds of Stinking Breathes and Perspirations, not to mention the ordure of so many diseas'd, both intelligent and unintelligent animals, the crouded *Churches, Church Yards* and *Burying Places*, with the putrifying *Bodies*, the *Sinks, Butchers Houses, Stables, Dunghills* etc. and the necessary Stagnation, Fermentation, and mixture of Variety of all Kinds of Atoms, and more than sufficient to putrefy, poison and infect the Air for Twenty Miles around it, and which in Time must alter, weaken and destroy the healthiest of Constitutions.

To such critics London was iniquity itself, the poisoned spring of fashion, the nursery of vice, crime, riot and all the other deformities and enormities unmasked in Samuel Johnson's satirical poem *London*. Its Grub Street – according to Johnson's *Dictionary*, 'the name of a street near Moorfields in London, much inhabited by writers of small histories, dictionaries, and temporary poems' – was the 'Temple of Dulness'. Not least, London was pestilential, as was all too evident to those who could see with their own eyes the rookeries of St Giles ('slum' was coined in Regency times to describe them) and sniff the stench of the Fleet ditch – that 'King of Dykes', in Pope's phrase. Indeed, William Cowper imagined the city itself as a sewer:

> ... thither flow
> As to a common and most noisome sewer,
> The dregs and feculence of every land.
> In cities foul example on most minds
> Begets its likeness. Rank abundance breeds
> In gross and pamper'd cities sloth and lust,
> And wantonness and gluttonous excess.

Hogarth's depiction of morning from the *Times of the Day* sequence

In cities, vice is hidden with most ease,
Or seen with least reproach; and virtue taught
By frequent lapse, can hope no triumph there
Beyond the achievement of succesful flight.
I do confess them nurseries of the arts,
In which they flourish most; where in the beams
Of warm encouragement, and in the eye
Of public note they reach their perfect size.
Such London is, by taste and wealth proclaim'd
The fairest capital of all the world,
By riot and incontinence the worst.

For some, the only consolation was that this Moloch could not endure but would be laid low in a grand apocalyptic fury. 'London will increase,' prophesied the radical Richard Phillips in 1813, but

the houses will become too numerous for the inhabitants, and certain districts will be occupied by beggary and vice, or become depopulated. This disease will spread like an atrophy in the human body, and ruin will follow ruin, till the entire city is disgusting to the remnant of the inhabitants; at length the whole becomes a heap of ruins: Such have been the causes of decay of all overgrown cities. Nineveh, Babylon, Antioch, and Thebes are become heaps of ruins. Rome, Delphi, and Alexandria are partaking the same inevitable fate; and London must some time, from similar causes, succumb under the destiny of every thing human.

Moralists lacerated London. Henry Fielding exposed its vanity, deceits and cheats, and William Hogarth's capital – Newgate, the Fleet, Tyburn, Bedlam – was all disease and violence, filth, noise, falling buildings and fallen women, chaos, poverty, drunkenness, suicide, distress, disarray, infidelity and insanity. In the moral contrasts drawn by Hogarth's *Industry and Idleness*, by Gay's *Beggar's Opera* and by Defoe's *Moll Flanders*, London's sordidness forbids any would-be idealization of the city as the cradle of refinement.

Despite such censure, contemporaries were invigorated by the urban experience: the metropolis was lively, energizing, an antidote to melancholy. London's diversity thrilled Boswell; he likened the city to a garden, to musical variations, to an exhibition. He would plan such treats as perambulating it in a day, beginning at Hyde Park Corner and climaxing at Covent Garden – 'the variety that we met with as we went along is amazing,' he marvelled: 'one end of London is like a different country from the other in look and manners'. From St Paul's dome he loved to gaze down at the city panorama. In 1763 he climbed the 311 stairs of the Monument:

When I was about halfway up, I grew frightened. I would have come down again, but I thought I would despise myself for my timidity. Thus does the spirit of pride get the better of fear. I mounted to the top and got upon the balcony. It was horrid to find myself so monstrous a way up in the air, so far above London and all its spires. I durst not look around me. There is no real danger, as there is a strong rail both on the stair and balcony. But I shuddered, and as every heavy wagon passed down Gracechurch Street, dreaded that the shaking of the earth would make the tremendous pile tumble to the foundation.

Boswell searched out London's nooks and crannies, like Mrs Salmon's waxworks and the rooms of the Sublime Society of Beefsteaks above the Bedford Coffee House, where 'almost everyone you meet is a polite scholar and a wit'. The streets, crowds and sights inspired him, affording an inexhaustible theatre in which to perform or spectate.

By way of literary exercise, Samuel Johnson sometimes maligned the metropolis:

> For who would leave, unbrib'd, *Hibernia*'s Land,
> Or change the Rocks of *Scotland* for the *Strand*?
> Here Malice, Rapine, Accident, conspire,
> And now a Rabble rages, now a Fire;
> Their Ambush here relentless Ruffians lay,
> And here the fell Attorney prowls for Prey;
> Here falling Houses thunder on your Head,
> And here a female Atheist talks you dead.

But Johnson fed Boswell's feeling that, tormented by the vacuity of human existence, London was a perennial tonic: 'when a man is tired of London, he is tired of life.'

Foreigners agreed. London had a thrill that, for all its shortcomings, elevated it far above Berlin or Turin. London's scale astonished. 'How great had seemed Berlin to me when first I saw it from the tower of St Mary's and looked down on it from the hill at Tempelhof,' reflected the Prussian Moritz; 'how insignificant it now seemed when I set it in my imagination against London!' London was not just big; it was incredibly *busy*, all crowds and clatter. 'The road from Greenwich to London was actually busier than the most popular streets in Berlin,' judged Moritz, 'so many people were to be encountered riding, driving or walking.' 'All is tumult and hurry,' growled Smollett's Matt Bramble:

one would imagine they were impelled by some disorder of the brain, that will not suffer them to be at rest. The foot-passengers run along as if they were pursued by bailiffs. The porters and chairmen trot with their burthens. People, who keep their own equipages, drive through the streets at full speed. Even citizens, physicians, and apothecaries, glide in their chariots like lightning. The hackney-coachmen make their horses smoke, and the pavement shakes under them; and I have actually seen a waggon pass through Piccadilly at the hand-gallop. In a word, the whole nation seems to be running out of their wits.

(Oscar Wilde would later say all Londoners looked as if they were rushing to catch a train.) Ever pressed for time, the city had even pioneered the fast-food take-away. 'I happened to go into a pastrycook's shop one morning,' Southey observed,

and inquired of the mistress why she kept her window open during this severe weather – which I observed most of the trade did. She told me, that were she to close it, her receipts would be lessened forty or fifty shillings a day – so many were the persons who took up buns or biscuits as they passed by and threw their pence in, not allowing themselves time to enter. Was there ever so indefatigable a people!

In our mind's eye, medieval London is dominated by St Paul's, 100 parish churches and a score of religious houses. Religion had orchestrated collective life in early

London. The Dissolution doubtless scarred the capital, yet the Reformation fired popular faith, and Puritan preachers later fortified citizens' morale in the Civil War, giving them an identity and a voice of their own.

During the Georgian century, by contrast, religion's role in daily life and urban ritual was on the wane. This had something to do with the growing discrepancy between population and parishes. Anglican churches lay packed in the City, but an ever-increasing majority of Londoners dwelt beyond the walls, where church distribution was haphazard and increasingly inadequate, and it was natural for taverns, clubs and street corners to become new community focal points. Too little was done, too late, to match parishes to populations. The London Churches Act of 1711 earmarked money, but only ten new buildings out of a projected fifty were actually constructed, largely because the trustees opted to erect a few architectural gems rather than the full quota. The nineteenth century dawned with the Anglican Church possessing an *embarras de richesses* in the City but ill-equipped to serve Londoners at large. Not least, Anglican churches remained furnished for the Quality: space-eating box pews provided comforts for the rich, but marginalized the poor. Hogarth's engraving of the *Sleeping Congregation* captured a prevalent view of Establishment piety.

Nonconformity did not slumber. Chapels flourished, for Protestant Dissent had a greater flexibility in erecting meeting-houses wherever congregations might form. By 1812 there were 256 Dissenting places of worship in London, compared to just 186 Anglican churches. Methodism had a metropolitan root. In 1738 John Wesley began preaching in London churches, but he was soon forced out of doors. With George Whitefield, he addressed gatherings of thousands on Blackheath. In November 1739 he preached at a disused foundry near Moorfields, which he purchased for £115. This remained his headquarters until 1778, when a new chapel was opened on the City Road. Other chapels were built at Southwark (1743), Spitalfields (1750) and Wapping (1764). Wesley's Methodism appealed particularly to tradesfolk, while Whitefield attracted more radical congregations to his Moorfields and Tottenham Court Road tabernacles.

Protected by the Toleration Act, Old Dissent – Presbyterians, Baptists and Independents – increased its numbers but proved more staid and sober than the Methodists. Their lives guided by 'inner light', Quakers grew respected as business people of integrity. Roman Catholics were less secure, as Pope-baiting bigotry periodically threatened them. Many Catholics worshipped in chapels attached to foreign embassies, like the Sardinian Chapel in Duke Street, off the Strand, burnt by the mob during the Gordon Riots.

Religion's waning presence was not just a matter of parishes and pews. It involved shifts of ethos, personal mores and social habit. Public life was assuming a more secular air. One must be circumspect, however, before speaking of religious apathy, for practical piety found abundant expression in energetic philanthropy in a century notable for charitable foundations. Five great new London hospitals were founded through private philanthropy and bequests, stemming from motives both religious and humanitarian. Westminster General Infirmary in James Street, Westminster, was established in 1719 for the relief of the sick and needy. London's first subscription hospital, it stemmed from the endeavours of the banker Henry Hoare and a small group of associates. Guy's Hospital, on the south side of St Thomas's Street, Southwark, was established in 1725 by Thomas Guy, a Lombard Street bookseller who had made his fortune by printing Bibles and through astute investment in South Sea stock. Guy's had accommodation for 400 patients, including a wing for the insane. St George's Hospital, Hyde Park Corner, was opened in 1733. The London Hospital, Whitechapel, was completed in 1752, with thirty-five wards and 439 beds. And the Middlesex was founded in 1745 as the Middlesex Infirmary, in Windmill Street, in houses rented from Mr Goodge, opening 'for the sick and lame of Soho', with three beds set aside for women in labour. In 1754 a site of twenty-five acres just to the west was acquired from Mr Berners. Some of the money was raised by Garrick and Handel, who gave performances gratis. In 1791 the brewer Samuel Whitbread gave £3,000 to endow a ward for cancer patients, who could remain until 'relieved by art or released by death'.

Numerous other charities were set up for the sick, needy and incapacitated. St Luke's Hospital for the insane was founded in 1751. Maternity hospitals were an innovation. In 1749 the British Lying-In Hospital was set up in Long Acre, Covent Garden; the City of London Lying-In Hospital came one year later, and the General Lying-In Hospital (later Queen Charlotte's) in 1752. The Lock Hospital for venereal cases opened in 1746, its patients receiving moral and religious instruction as well as medical care. It was closely associated with Lady Huntingdon's 'genteel Methodists', and her preacher, Martin Madan, was its chaplain for many years, until indiscreet public advocacy of polygamy compelled his resignation.

Charitable institutions aimed at something more constructive than mere alms-giving. The Marine Society in Bishopsgate, established in 1765, prepared poor boys for sea service, fitting out a ship moored between Deptford and Greenwich to receive 100 boys with a schoolmaster and officers to teach naval duties. In St George's Fields there was a School for the Indigent Blind, whose pupils made basketware for sale, and the Philanthropic Society was also established there in 1788 for the rescue of young children. In Craven Street, off the Strand, lay the Society for the Relief and Discharge of Persons Confined for Small Debts. Established in 1772, within fifteen months it had discharged 986 prisoners. Parliament Street housed the Society for Bettering the Condition of the Poor. The Samaritan Society, attached to the London Hospital, aided discharged patients unable to find work. The Foundling Hospital, set up in 1739 by Captain Thomas Coram, achieved special prominence. At first in Hatton Garden, in

1745 it moved to Lamb's Conduit Fields. Unwanted babies could be left anonymously. They were sent to the country for nursing until they were five, and then returned to the hospital for education and training in humble occupations.

Religious impulses led above all to the foundation of dozens of charity schools, whose religious instruction was strictly Anglican. In 1704, 2,000 children from over fifty such schools crowded into St Andrew Holborn to attend the first anniversary meeting of the London and Westminster charity schools. By 1711 twice as many were being taught in more than 100 schools, and over £10,000 was being raised annually for them. 'The Charity-Schools which have been erected in late years,' observed the dramatist and politician Richard Steele, 'are the greatest Instances of publick Spirit the Age has produced.'

All these philanthropic enterprises were expressions of a practical Protestantism that stressed the duties of Christian goodness, valuing deeds over doctrine. Characteristically, Hogarth painted a huge 'Good Samaritan' scene for St Bartholomew's Hospital; like many citizens, he had little love for the clergy but applauded Christian charity and espoused a fierce Protestant anti-Catholicism. Such charities were also signs that traditional parish government could no longer cope with social problems.

Despite all these pious expressions, religion was becoming eclipsed. A culture of sociability – hedonism even – was emerging, increasingly secular in form and content, contributing to what has been called the commercialization of leisure. London life had traditionally centred on ward, parish and guild, and all their attendant collective and calendar ceremonials. These continued, though with diminishing significance, but Georgian public life increasingly revolved around the town itself, its streets, public spaces, and entertainments. For citizens and visitors alike the urban environment, enhanced by commercial facilities like taverns, shops and pleasure gardens, set the scene for passing the time: sauntering, shopping, sitting, strutting, staring.

Retaining medieval nuclei with labyrinthine narrow streets lacking pavements, many European cities were cramped, noisy and unsuitable for elegant strolling. For such reasons, old Paris was widely found uncongenial. London was more fortunate; its antiquated centre had been burnt down and replaced by wider streets and modern street furniture; while from Covent Garden through St James's to Mayfair, the West End was wide and handsome, built to please those with money to burn and time to kill. The capital was like a Disneyworld: 'London has been justly described as a world by itself, in which we may discover more new countries, and surprising singularities, than in all the universe besides,' argued the author of *Tricks of the Town* in 1747.

Certain purlieus – the Strand, Covent Garden, Leicester Square – sucked in sightseers and *flâneurs*. It was smart to stroll and lounge, enjoying the delights of anonymity in the city of strangers: 'here you have the Advantage of solitude without its Disadvantage,' reflected Henry Fielding, 'since you may be alone and in Company at the same time; and while you sit or walk unobserved, Noise, Hurry, and a constant Succession of Objects entertain the Mind'. London leisure seemed particularly eligible. 'The English,' observed the traveller von Archenholz – he meant, of course, English *gentlemen* – 'live in a very remarkable manner. They rise late, and spend most of the morning, either in walking about town or sitting in the coffee-house.' This lifestyle impressed La Rochefoucauld. 'The conduct of an Englishman's day in London leaves little time for work,' commented the Frenchman: 'He gets up at ten or eleven and has breakfast (always with tea). He then makes a tour of the town for about four hours until 5 o'clock, which is the dinner hour; at 9 o'clock in the evening he meets his friends in a tavern or a club and there the night is passed in play and drink.' Leisured London – that was what he was describing – kept its own clock, and fashion held ever later hours. 'The Hours of the Day and Night are taken up in the Cities of London and Westminster by people as different from each other as those who are born in different Centuries,' commented Richard Steele: 'Men of Six o'Clock give way to those of Nine, they of Nine to the Generation of Twelve, and they of Twelve disappear, and make Room for the fashionable World, who have made Two o'Clock the Noon of the Day.'

Georgian London, as can be seen, had a well-mapped topography of pleasure. The precincts around Fleet Street, the Strand, Covent Garden and Charing Cross – once very superior – were being taken over by inns and taverns, shops, shows and street performers. (It was in Davies's bookshop in Russell Street, Covent Garden, that Boswell first met Johnson.) The main corridor connecting Westminster and the City, Fleet Street and the Strand were perfect for watching the world go by. Charles Lamb loved Fleet Street ('The man must have a rare recipe for melancholy, who can be dull in Fleet Street'); Boswell praised its 'cheerfulness ... owing to the constant quick succession of people which we perceive passing through it', and Johnson agreed – 'Fleet Street has a very animated appearance' – but he had his own favourite: 'the full tide of human existence is at Charing Cross'.

From Restoration times Fleet Street sported theatres, and it was also associated with literary London – being up-market from Grub Street (Barbican), the classic home of hacks. Off Fleet Street, John Dryden lived in Salisbury Court and Fetter Lane, Samuel Richardson in Salisbury Square. Johnson had ten successive addresses within a stone's throw of Fleet Street.

Fleet Street developed seedier associations. Particularly notorious were its clandestine 'Fleet marriages', conducted mostly by clergymen imprisoned for debt in the Fleet but allowed the 'liberties of the Fleet'. Though an end was put to Fleet marriages by Lord Hardwicke's Marriage Act (1753), the local shenanigans in *Sweeney Todd* over

Joanna's nuptials suggest that the area long continued under a cloud of matrimonial ill-repute.

Street-life was lubricated by places of refreshment. The fashionable site for socializing was the coffee-house. The traveller John Macky fancied that he knew all about them:

If you would know our manner of Living, it is thus: . . . About Twelve the *Beau-Monde* assembles in several Chocolate and Coffee Houses: The best of which are the *Cocoa-Tree* and *White's* Chocolate-Houses, St *James's*, the *Smyrna*, and the *British* Coffee-Houses; and all these so near one another, that in less than an Hour you see the Company of them all. We are carried to these Places in Chairs (or Sedans) which are here very cheap, a Guinea a Week, or a Shilling *per* Hour, and your Chairmen serve you for Porters to run on Errands as your *Gondoliers* do at *Venice*.

If it be fine Weather, we take a Turn in the *Park* till two, when we go to Dinner; and if it be dirty, you are entertain'd at *Picket* or *Basset* at *White's*, or you may talk Politicks at the *Smyrna* and St *James's*.

The first coffee-house was opened in 1652 in St Michael's Alley, Cornhill; by Queen Anne's death in 1714 there were approximately 500, catering for specialized clienteles. Merchants, for example, frequented coffee-houses near the Royal Exchange, while the booksellers' coffee-houses were by Paternoster Row. The Cocoa Tree, Pall Mall, became the meeting-place for Tories – in the 1745 rebellion it was denounced as the Jacobite headquarters. The nearby St James's Coffee-House was a Whig rendezvous. Man's Coffee-House, behind Charing Cross, catered for stockjobbers; Will's Coffee-House, on the corner of Bow Street and Russell Street, Covent Garden, was where wits were to be found; lawyers met at the Grecian, close by the Temple, clergymen at Child's in St Paul's Churchyard, artists at Old Slaughter's in St Martin's Lane, authors at Button's in Bow Street, military men at the Little Devil in Goodman's Fields, fops at Ozinda's in Pall Mall, and marine insurers, of course, at Lloyd's in Lombard Street.

According to César de Saussure in the 1730s, coffee-houses were 'not over clean or well furnished, owing to the quantity of people who resort to these places and because of the smoke'. But a prime attraction lay in the newspapers kept there: 'All Englishmen are great newsmongers,' he observed: 'workmen habitually begin the day by going to coffee-rooms in order to read the latest news.' The rise of the coffee-house thus spurred the emergence of the metropolis as the media centre. The *Daily Courant* appeared in 1702, the *Evening Post* in 1706, the *London Journal* in 1723 and *The Craftsman* in 1727. Within the next forty years the *Daily Advertiser*, the *Westminster Journal*, *Lloyd's Evening Post*, the *St James's Chronicle*, the *Middlesex Journal* and the *Morning Chronicle* were launched. *The Times* followed in 1785. Newspapers were the daily mirror of London life, and, since early provincial papers mostly reprinted London copy, the capital's virtual monopoly of the news media reinforced metropolitan dominance over the regions. Small surprise that the French author the Abbé Prévost hailed coffee-houses – 'where you have the right to read all the papers for and against the government' – as the 'seats of English liberty'.

The coffee-house craze did not provoke any decline in serious drinking, which remained a male sacrament – 'a man is never happy in the present,' opined Johnson, 'unless he is drunk'. Public drunkenness was no disgrace, and hundreds of inns and taverns were there to quench a thirst – early eighteenth-century London was reckoned to have 207 inns, 447 taverns, 5,875 beer houses and 8,659 brandy shops. More dignified taverns like the Mitre in Fleet Street housed concerts, dinners, canvassing and clubs. In a town of lodging dwellers, they were used to entertain friends, to hear the news or to settle business. Always a busy and a moderately sober man, Samuel Pepys named no fewer than 105 London taverns he visited, mostly on business. At Westminster he often dined in a tavern with civil servants to pick up the news, or at the Temple with lawyers on navy business. Dr Johnson had a regular chair at the Turk's Head in Gerrard Street, where he presided over The Club, which he and Reynolds founded in 1764; but he was equally at home in the Devil, the Mitre, and the Crown and Anchor in the Strand, where he sometimes dined with Boswell. Fleet Street swarmed with eating-places, from superior chop-houses, like Dolly's Beefsteak House, to fast-food joints like Mrs Lovett's later notorious pie shop.

Drinking roused other male appetites. The precincts from Charing Cross to Drury Lane were the favourite haunt of streetwalkers, as Boswell's journals amply document. John Gay warned the stroller (or told him where to go):

> O may thy Virtue guard thee through the Roads
> Of *Drury*'s mazy Courts and dark Abodes!
> The Harlots' guileful paths, who nightly stand
> Where *Katherine-street* descends into the *Strand*.

Tourists needing help could purchase Harris's *New Atlantis*, a guidebook to London's harlots, detailing addresses, physical characteristics and specialities. Beds could be hired in the back rooms of taverns and 'bagnios' (genuine bagnios – 'hummums' – were Turkish baths). Gentlemen might indulge in more romantic erotic activities at the 'Folly', a pleasure boat moored at Cuper's Stairs, near the Savoy, which had an enclosed deck with curtained booths. Pepys visited it in April 1668. But, in free-market London, prostitutes were chiefly to be picked up on the streets, which, Lichtenberg enthused, were paradise for horny males – women were available, he wrote,

got up in any way you like, dressed, bound up, hitched up, tight-laced, loose, painted, done up or raw, scented, in silk or wool, with or without sugar, in short, what a man cannot obtain here, if he have money, upon my word, let him not look for it anywhere in this world of ours.

Another German visitor, Z. C. von Uffenbach, was disgusted in 1710 to find 'innumerable harlots' and that the prices were 'prodigious dear'.

The crowded, cheery streets around Covent Garden and up into Soho were a man's world. Another scene of somewhat disreputable fun was the fair. Southwark Fair, May Fair and Bartholomew Fair (Smithfield) remained extremely popular. Lasting two to six weeks, each featured sideshows, rope-dancers, wire-walkers, acrobats, puppets, freaks and sometimes wild animals. They were also heaven for pickpockets and prostitutes. 'To Bartholomew Fair, and there saw several sights,' Pepys recorded on 1 September 1668, 'among others the mare that tells money, and many things to admiration.' Bartholomew Fair originally took place on 24 and 25 August, but during Charles II's reign it spread over a fortnight, its commercial function declining as its entertainment role increased. Hogarth visited Bartholomew Fair in his youth and engraved Southwark Fair (1734), displaying acrobats and actors, showmen, musicians, prizefighters and conjurors. Outraged citizens agitated to curb the fairs: Southwark Fair was finally closed in the early 1760s, though Bartholomew Fair lingered till around 1850, when its site was earmarked for the new Smithfield meat market.

A rare treat was the frost fair, staged when the Thames froze over during the so-called 'little ice age'. The first was held in 1564, when Elizabeth visited stalls and saw oxen roasted. The next came at Christmas 1683, when so many booths selling food, drink and souvenirs were set up on the river that they were arranged in streets. Coaches plied for hire on the ice, and attractions included bull-baiting, puppets, horse-racing and football. Evelyn walked the Thames to dine at Lambeth with the Archbishop of Canterbury, and Charles II took part in fox-hunting on ice. The winter of 1788–9 brought another frost fair. 'This Booth to let,' declared the *Public Advertiser* on 5 January 1789. 'The present possessor of the premises is Mr Frost. His affairs, however, not being on a permanent footing, a dissolution or bankruptcy may soon be expected and a final settlement of the whole entrusted to Mr Thaw.' The winter of 1813–14 saw the greatest frost fair, with a grand mall running from Blackfriars Bridge and named 'City Road'. It was also the last, another victim of progress: once old London Bridge was demolished in 1831, the improved flow of the river prevented it freezing over.

Londoners enjoyed processions and celebrations punctuating the rhythms of the ceremonial year: the King's birthday, the anniversary of William of Orange's landing, Guy Fawkes Night. The City provided routes and sites for diversions, public spectacles, political parades, mayoral shows, civic pageantry and apprentice rallies. Other corners of town afforded more sedate pleasures. Strolling across the Thames bridges was popular – though the irrepressible Boswell had to go one better:

At the bottom of the Haymarket I picked up a strong jolly young damsel, and taking her under the arm I conducted her to Westminster Bridge, and then in armour complete [that is, wearing a condom] did I engage up in this noble edifice. The whim of doing it there with the Thames rolling below us amused me much.

The Pall Mall promenade was popular, and from there the parks were accessible – Green Park, Hyde Park, St James's Park, Kensington Gardens and (later) Regent's Park. St James's Park offered fresh milk served from the cow. Hyde Park, the largest, given to the people by Charles I in 1637, became a fashionable ride; on summer evenings the sand track of 'the Ring' was filled with coaches. 'To Hide Parke,' recorded Pepys, 'where great plenty of gallants. And pleasant it was, only for the dust.' The King's Old Road to Kensington, known as Rotten Row – a gravelled *route du roi* – and the Serpentine, a lake formed at Queen Caroline's suggestion, was the *bon ton*'s rendezvous. Kensington Gardens, however, became the most exclusive green, after Queen Caroline had it fenced around in 1774, with servants 'placed at the different entrances to prevent persons meanly clad from going into the garden'. If dossers were excluded, duellists sneaked in. Though the Duke of Wellington preferred Battersea, it was in Hyde Park that Lord Mohun and the Duke of Hamilton slew each other in 1712, and fifty years later John Wilkes fought the blackguard Samuel Martin there.

Londoners loved outings. The Quality went to Epsom and Tunbridge Wells – less, Defoe observed, for the medicinal waters than 'for the diversion of the season, for the mirth, and the company, for gaming, or intriguing, and the like'. Middle-class day-trippers made do with Dulwich and the 200 or so other pleasure resorts dotted among London's suburban villages, with their fishponds, fireworks, musicians and masquerades. Among the spas and watering-places perfect for Sunday jaunts were Sadlers Wells in Islington, Kilburn Wells (where at the Bell Tavern the 'politest companies could come to drink the water from a nearby spring'), Bermondsey Spa (now marked by Spa Road), and Hockley-in-the-Hole (Clerkenwell), where there were ornamental gardens, fishing, cream teas, grottoes, skittle alleys, fountains, purgative waters and sometimes bear-baiting. At English Castle, another Clerkenwell pleasure garden, the proprietor advertised a 'Grand Grotto Garden and Gold and Silver Fish Repository', with an enchanted fountain and a beautiful rainbow (admission only 6d).

Reputedly once the summer retreat of Nell Gwyn, Bagnigge Wells was popular. Its grounds contained honeysuckle-covered tea arbours, a bun house, a skittle alley, a bowling-green, a grotto, a flower garden, fish ponds and fountains. Concerts were held in the pump room. Jenny's Whim, Pimlico, was celebrated for the 'amusing deceptions' in the garden: hidden springs caused harlequins and monsters to jump up before the unsuspecting, while floating models on a lake gave the impression of mermaids and flying-fish.

Lambeth Wells had a vogue of more than fifty years, combining the pleasures of

Vauxhall Pleasure Gardens, *c.* 1765

purging waters and all-night music. In 1755 its licence was discontinued because of its numerous brawls. Various other gardens were suppressed because of their notoriety – the Temple of Flora's proprietor was given a prison sentence in 1796 for keeping a disorderly house.

Leisure entrepreneurs also created more elaborate pleasure gardens. Long famous were Cuper's (or Cupid's) Gardens in Lambeth. New Spring Gardens, later known as Vauxhall Gardens, opened in 1660 up-river on the south bank, with a romantic access by boat. Laid out with walks, statues and tableaux, Vauxhall became the most luxuriant resort. Orchestras played, the fireworks were dazzling, there was dancing, one could sup in gaily decorated alcoves in the gardens – and all for a shilling. Hogarth was commissioned to paint the rooms, and Roubiliac's statue of Handel was displayed. One high spot came in 1749, when 100 musicians played to an audience of 12,000 – gridlock set in around London Bridge. Another came in 1802, when a Frenchman made a parachute landing from a balloon.

Adjoining Chelsea Hospital, Ranelagh Gardens opened in 1742, vying with Vauxhall.

'Ranelagh looks like the enchanted palace of a genie,' commented Tobias Smollett in *Humphry Clinker*:

adorned with the most exquisite performance of painting, carving, and gilding, enlightened with a thousand golden lamps, that emulate the noon-day sun; crowded with the great, the rich, the gay, the happy, and the fair; glittering with cloth of gold and silver, lace, embroidery, and precious stones.

Its chief attraction was a Rotunda, 150 feet in diameter, with an orchestra in the centre and tiers of boxes all round. 'Every night I constantly go to Ranelagh, which has totally beat Vauxhall,' declared Horace Walpole, an aficionado of both. One of its most fêted events was the Thames regatta in June 1775, followed by a supper and fancy-dress ball. Twelve boats raced from Westminster to London Bridge and back. But confusion set in as barges clogged the competitors' path, and women and children, caught by a low tide, had to wade in the mud. Besides, it rained. It was all very English.

The regatta fiasco epitomized the strange mix that was Georgian London: it aspired to elegance, but in reality it was a bit chaotic, all manner and conditions of people managing to show their face and create their own fun. 'There is no distinction or subordination left,' Smollett's Matthew Bramble groused about the hurly-burly:

The different departments of life are jumbled together – the hodcarrier, the low mechanic, the tapster, the publican, the shop-keeper, the pettifogger, the citizen, and courtier, *all tread upon the kibes of one another*: actuated by the demons of profligacy and licentiousness, they are seen every where rambling, riding, rolling, rushing, justling, mixing, bouncing, cracking, and crashing in one vile ferment of stupidity and corruption.

What was on in London? Everything. London spawned commercial enjoyments galore, run by entertainment impresarios:

Assemblies, parks, coarse feasts in city-halls,
Lectures and trials, plays, committees, balls,
Wells, Bedlams, executions, Smithfield scenes,
And fortune-tellers' caves and lions' dens,
Taverns, Exchanges, Bridewells, drawing-rooms,
Instalments, pillories, coronations, tombs,
Tumblers and funerals, puppet-shows, reviews,
Sales, races, rabbits and (still stranger) pews.

Old sports were spruced up into new pleasures. Londoners had long enjoyed im-promptu shooting-competitions, sculling races on the Thames, football on St George's Fields and ball games on Lamb's Conduit Fields; bowling and skittle alleys adjoined London's taverns. From medieval times citizens had gone out to Moorfields, just north of the walls, to practise archery. In 1682 Charles II attended a grand meeting of the Finsbury bowmen, and a few years later Pepys 'walked over the fields to Kingsland and back again; a walk, I think, I have not taken these twenty years; but puts me in mind of my boy's time when I ... used to shoot with my bow and arrows in these fields'.

Bull- and bear-baiting were traditional Bankside sports. There were also bear-gardens in Marylebone Gardens and at Hockley-in-the-Hole, Clerkenwell (entrance: half a crown). Cock-fights ('mains') were held at both cockpits and inns. At the Royal Cockpit in St James's Park, bouts lasted for hours, with feverish betting. A special favourite, the Welsh main was an elimination match with thirty-two cocks, only one of which would survive. 'I then went to the Cockpit,' Boswell recorded in December 1762,

which is a circular room in the middle of which the cocks fight. It is seated round with rows gradually rising ... The cocks, nicely cut and dressed and armed with silver heels, are set down and fight with amazing bitterness and resolution ... One pair fought three quarters of an hour. The uproar and noise of betting is prodigious.

There were also scraps between humans, including cudgelling, backsword and single-stick, and bare-fisted boxing, and bouts between men and dogs. In 1747 John Brough-ton, self-styled boxing champion of England, opened an academy off Cockspur Street at which gloves were used for the first time. There were female boxers too, and Grosly observed a unisex boxing-match in Holborn. Boxing became commercialized, as did another traditional sport, cricket. The top team was the White Conduit Cricket Club, led by the Earl of Winchilsea; they played on a pitch superintended by Thomas Lord at what is now Dorset Square in Marylebone. In 1767 it changed its name to the Marylebone Cricket Club, and its ground eventually settled in 1814 in St John's Wood. Spectators paid 6d for admission; by the turn of the century crowds of 4,000 to 5,000 gathered – as much for the betting as for the cricket.

Leisure entrepreneurs also saw money in myriad other spectacles, open to the public at modest fees (low prices meant large audiences). The equestrianist Philip Astley – a man 'with the proportions of a Hercules and the voice of a Senator' – had been honourably discharged from the cavalry in 1768 and was given his horse as a leaving present. He set up an Amphitheatre near Westminster Bridge, where a troupe of horses performed amazing feats, and dramatic re-enactments were staged of news events like famous battles. Another craze was ballooning. 'Balloons occupy senators, philosophers, ladies, everybody,' remarked Horace Walpole in 1785. An Italian, Count Zambeccari, made the first small hydrogen balloons seen over London.

More traditional tastes were also catered for. Circulating libraries opened: by 1800, the capital sported some 122 of these 'evergreen trees of diabolical knowledge'. Picture galleries were also set up, showing scenes from Shakespeare, the Bible and English history. The Royal Academy, founded in 1768, staged art exhibitions. In 1711 Mrs Salmon opened a waxworks in Fleet Street, long before Madame Tussaud arrived from Paris. The capital possessed an effervescent musical life, orchestrated by composers and impresarios such as Handel, Heidegger and, later, Salomon. Mozart performed. In 1791 Salomon paid Joseph Haydn £50 for each of twenty performances, with a £200 benefit on top. Subscription concerts were pioneered. Carlisle House in Soho Square was a leading musical venue, where Mrs Cornelys ran operatic concerts and masquerades. Fanny Burney judged 'the magnificence of the rooms, splendour of the illuminations and embellishments, and the brilliant appearance of the company exceeded anything I ever before saw'.

Theatre thrived. Royal patents granted by Charles II to the 'King's Men' and the 'Duke's Men' made their two playhouses the only public places in which drama could legally be presented. Such rights were guarded jealously, though there were constant evasions by the so-called 'minor' theatres. Restoration playhouses introduced painted scenery and actresses (female parts had previously been played by boys). Restoration comedy cultivated risqué wit, while John Gay's immensely popular *Beggar's Opera* (1728), with its low-life story filled with street songs and traditional airs, brought a more common touch.

During the eighteenth century the playhouse developed a deep fore-stage, bringing the actor into close contact with the audience and aiding the rise of stars like David Garrick, James Quin, Peg Woffington and, later, Sarah Siddons, Philip Kemble and Edmund Kean. Garrick, who spent his working life at Drury Lane, relinquished formal rhetoric and developed a more emotional, naturalistic acting style. He gave the theatre a new éclat. 'In London,' commented Benjamin Franklin, 'you have plays performed by good actors. That, however, is, I think, the only advantage London has over Philadelphia.'

Wren's Drury Lane theatre saw a succession of great playwrights, managers and actors: Killigrew, Congreve, Vanbrugh, Betterton, Cibber, Macklin, Garrick and Sheridan. It was redesigned in 1773 by Robert Adam, and eighteen years later was demolished to make way for Henry Holland's new auditorium which seated 3,611 and cost £150,000. This was destroyed by fire in 1809 but speedily rebuilt. Having to appeal to huge audiences, Drury Lane presented light opera, farce, burlesque and 'burlettas'; its playwrights had to write for middle-brows and mixed audiences, their hits being simple and sentimental, with elements of pantomime, farce and music-hall. The audience was a social microcosm. 'We have three ... different and distinct Classes,' noted a London guide in 1747:

the first is called the *Boxes*, where there is one peculiar to the King and Royal Family, and the rest for the Persons of Quality, and for the Ladies and Gentlemen of the highest Rank, unless some Fools that have more Wit than Money, or perhaps more Impudence than both, crowd in among them. The second is call'd the *Pit*, where sit the *Judges*, *Wits* and *Censurers* . . . in common with these sit the *Squires*, *Sharpers*, *Beaus*, *Bullies* and *Whores*, and here and there an extravagant *Male* and *Female Cit*. The third is distinguished by the Title of the *Middle Gallery*, where the Citizens' Wives and Daughters, together with the *Abigails*, Serving-men, Journey-men and Apprentices commonly take their Places.

Around Leicester Square, down to the Strand and up through Soho to Piccadilly, were scores of spectacles and exhibitions – Robert Powell's puppet shows in the Little Piazza, Covent Garden, and the 'wonderful tall Essex woman' at the Rummer in Three King's Court, Fleet Street, who was 'seven feet high' – as well as 'Young Colossuses', 'Tall Saxon Women' and an 'Ethiopian Savage' ('of a different species from any ever seen in Europe, and seems to be a link between Rational and Brute Creation'). Also on show were 'the Orang Outang, or real Wild Man of the Woods . . . a Calf with eight legs, two tails, two heads, and only one body' – all this 'opposite the New Inn, Surrey side of Westminster Bridge at 1s. each person'. In Panton Street the quack doctor James Graham was giving his celebrated displays of medicinal mud bathing, aided by a bevy of belles. In 1779 Robert Barker built his Panorama in Leicester Place, and nearby, in Lisle Street, James Loutherbourg opened his Eidophusikon, or magic lantern. All formed part of a great archipelago of shows, galleries, theatres, cockpits and exhibitions, making up London's new world of leisure.

'I believe the parallelogram between Oxford-street, Piccadilly, Regent-street, and Hyde Park encloses more intelligence and human ability, to say nothing of wealth and beauty, than the world has ever collected in such a space before,' boasted the Revd Sydney Smith. Around these eligible acres, exclusive spaces were carved out for those seeking select company. The club, probably a child of the coffee-house, defined an all-male enclave. White's, established in St James's Street in 1736, became the acme of fashion, though later rivalled by Boodle's and Crockford's, both in St James's Street, and by Almack's in Pall Mall, founded in 1762 by William Almack. In 1764 that club split into two, Boodle's and Brooks's, while a further two clubs met on Almack's premises, the Macaroni (for 'travelled young men with long curls and spying glasses') and the Ladies' Coterie, a fashionable unisex club. Brooks's in James's Street became the greatest gambling-den of all, Lord Lauderdale speaking of £70,000 being lost in a single night. Himself a member, Horace Walpole called Brooks's a place 'where a thousand meadows and cornfields are staked at every throw, and as many villages lost as in the earthquakes that overwhelmed Herculaneum and Pompeii'.

Clubs also catered for more elevated interests. Alongside gambling-dens were learned societies like the Royal Society, while connoisseurs met at the Society of

Antiquaries. A devoted clubman was the art-dealer Arthur Pond. A fellow of both those societies, in the 1740s he regularly attended four different clubs – the Roman, the 'D', the Tobacco and the Pope's Head – as well as the Royal Society Club. Such gatherings consolidated friendships, supported professional ambitions, and became important patronage sources. 'The members of the clubs of London, many years since,' reminisced the German officer Count Gronow, 'were without exception belonging to the aristocratic world.'

Wealth bought exclusivity. But fashion favoured peacock display too for the beau monde. The nobs wanted to see and be seen, chic London loved holding the mirror up to itself, and social curiosity was fed by prints and scandal sheets like *LOW LIFE; or One half of the World knows not how the Other Half Live* (1752).

Mocking bumpkins, the Restoration man of mode had basked in exquisite metropolitan pleasures. His great grandson, the Regency buck, equally upheld the superiority of town, but invented a new art – trendy slumming. The truly smart ('flash' was the word) blade hobnobbed in exclusive circles, but also revelled in cockpits, gambling-dens, boxing-booths and shady locales. The fad was immortalized by the cartoonists Robert and George Cruikshank and the Irish-born journalist Pierce Egan. In September 1820 appeared the first number of *Life in London or The Day and Night Scenes of Jerry Hawthorn, Esq., and his elegant friend Corinthian Tom, accompanied by Bob Logic, the Oxonian, in their Rambles and Sprees through the Metropolis.* Its 'scenes from real life' showed the adventures of the original Tom and Jerry, Egan's racy commentary exploiting slang and low-life lingo.

Corinthian Tom, Jerry Hawthorn and Bob Logic set out to 'see life', from Westminster to Wapping. They mingled with the swells at the St James's clubs and rode in the '*Show-stop* of the Metropolis – HYDE PARK'. But they also ogled the girls in Burlington Arcade, resorted to fisticuffs in a brawl, and visited 'All Max' (Max, like 'partiality', 'blue ruin' and 'flashes of lightning', was cant for gin), a Whitechapel back-street gin shop where the charleys (the watch) did not go:

Lascars, blacks, jack tars, coal-heavers, dustmen, women of colour, old and young, and a sprinkling of the remnants of once fine girls, &c., were all *jigging* together, provided the *teazer of the catgut* was not *bilked* out of his *duce. Gloves* might have been laughed at, as dirty hands produced no *squeamishness* on the heroines in the dance, and the scene changed as often as the pantomime from the continual introduction of new characters. *Heavy wet* was the cooling beverage, but frequently overtaken by *flashes of lightning*. The *covey* was no scholar, as he asserted, and, therefore, he held the pot in one hand and took the *blunt* with the other, to prevent the trouble of *chalking*, or making mistakes.

On the sudden appearance of our 'swell TRIO', and the CORINTHIAN's friend, among these unsophisticated sons and daughters of Nature, their *ogles* were on the roll, under an apprehension that the *beaks* were out on the *nose*; but it was soon made 'all right', by one of the *mollishers* whispering, loud enough to be heard by most of the party, 'that she understood as how the *gemmen* had only dropped in for to have a *bit of spree*, and there was no doubt that they *voud* stand a *drap* of *summut* to make them all *comfurable*, and likewise prove good customers to the *crib*. On the *office* being given, the *stand-still* was instantly removed; and the *kidwys* and *kiddiesses* were footing the *double-shuffle* against each other with as much *gig* as the '*We we-e-ps*' exert themselves on the first of May.

Bond Street loungers thus had their own incomparable ways of talking, walking and dressing – style was now defined not by King, court, or country but by the manners of town, that is, the West End. George Colman the Younger put these outlandish habits – they did not look like traditional good breeding! – on the stage. In the *Heir-at-Law* (1797), Lord Duberly is shocked to find his son, Dick Dowlas, so ill-behaved ('The boy rolls about like a porpoise in a storm'). 'That's the fashion, father; that's modern ease,' responds Dick: 'A young fellow is nothing now without the Bond Street roll, a toothpick between his teeth, and his knuckles cramm'd into his coat-pocket. Then away you go, lounging lazily along.' Regency bucks thus forged an aesthetic of the urban, a worship of town as a temple of pleasure that culminated in the image of the dandy. The emergence of the West End gave urban lifestyles a glamour that became the envy, or amusement, of the rest of the nation.

There was another side. 'Great cities,' remarked the physician John Coakley Lettsom in 1774, 'are like painted sepulchres; their public avenues, and stately edifices seem to preclude the very possibility of distress and poverty: but if we pass beyond this superficial veil, the scene will be reversed.' Fashionable slumming *à la* Tom and Jerry marked and mocked the contrasts between high and low life – distinctions evidently so secure they could be temporarily transgressed with amusement.

Visitors were surprised by the extraordinary degree of social mixing and the ease of intercourse possible in a monster town presided over not by king, court or Church but by commerce, cultural entrepreneurship and public taste. They were bowled over to find ordinary people – laundresses and lightermen – sitting in the gods or the coffee-house or tripping off to Vauxhall. To French and Prussians, such intermingling seemed dangerous, though it was an inevitable consequence of a social sphere where money talked and most had something to spend. Ordinary folk participated in public commercial culture, in processions and pageantry, in political crowds, the hustings and the hubbub of the streets. But urban geography secured them low-life zones all of their own, notably in the East End. Ratcliff Highway was said in 1763 to be a whirl 'of dissolute sailors, blackmailing watermen, rowdy fishermen, stock-fish hawkers, quarrelsome chairmen, audacious highwaymen, sneak-thieves and professional cheats … footpads, deserters, prisoners of war on parole, bravos, bullies and river vultures'. Teeming with taverns, Wapping became legendary:

I fell in with a lady so modest and meek,
She eats thirteen faggots and nine pigs feet,
Three pounds of beef, and to finish the meal,
Ate eight pounds of tripe and an old cow-heel.

I met with another borne down with fear.
She guzzled down thirteen pots of beer.
She threw up her heels and played the deuce,
And broke her nose at Paddy's Goose.

You jovial sailors, one and all,
When you in the port of London call,
Mind Ratcliff Highway and the damsels loose,
The William, The Bear and Paddy's Goose.

In the 1730s and 1740s the gin craze created an urban subculture exclusive to the poor, comparable perhaps to crack in the American inner-city drug ghettoes nowadays. For thousands the only known means of escaping misery, gin was cheap ('drunk for a penny, dead drunk for two pence, straw for nothing'), and it was consumed in staggering quantities – by the 1740s averaging two pints a week for every man, woman and child in London. Gin, reported the Westminster justices, is 'the principal cause of the increase of the poor and of all the vice and debauchery among the inferior sort of people, as well as of the felonies and other disorders committed about this town'.

Dram-shops multiplied: in some quarters, it was said in 1743, every eighth house sold spirits. Gin was also sold in workhouses, prisons, brothels and barbers' shops, and by street hawkers, and the bodies of the paralytically drunk littered the streets of Bethnal Green, Tothill Fields, Westminster and St Giles, the rookery Hogarth chose for 'Gin Lane'. Warning that 'should the drinking of this poison be continued in its present height during the next twenty years, there will be by that time few of the common people left to drink it,' Henry Fielding observed that gin was

the principal sustenance (if it may be called so) of more than a hundred thousand people in the metropolis . . . The intoxicating draught itself disqualifies them from any honest means to acquire it, at the same time that it removes sense of fear and shame and emboldens them to commit every wicked and desperate enterprise.

Fielding was correct, and it was fortunate for London that a combination of legislation and rising prices put paid to the craze by mid-century.

But Fielding was also symptomatic of a trend in Georgian London: the habit of the better sort berating, while being fascinated by, the lives of the poor. The respectable loved to gawp at low-life excesses, but we should not be misled by their sensationalism. Most journeymen were respectable – the sort who, over the generations, enjoyed

181

patriotic ballad literature and chap-books with titles like *Pleasant Conceits of Old Hobson the Merry Londoner* (set in Cheapside) or *The Nine Worthies of London*, which presented heroes from the great livery companies. Seventeenth-century works like *The Prentice's Practice in Godliness* (dedicated to 'the religiously disposed and virtuous young men, the apprentices of the City of London') and the various renderings of Dick Whittington remained popular in the Georgian era, alongside Hogarth's images of the industrious and idle apprentices.

With its heady brew of the high and low, London afforded a people's theatre. Foreigners had mixed feelings about the boisterousness – or 'love of liberty' – they encountered in the streets. 'The populace on that day,' remarked de Saussure, caught up in a Lord Mayor's Day crowd,

is particularly insolent and rowdy, turning into lawless freedom for the great liberty it enjoys. At these times it is almost dangerous for an honest man, and more particularly for a foreigner, if at all well dressed, to walk in the streets, for he runs a great risk of being insulted by the vulgar populace, which is the most cursed brood in existence. He is sure of not only being jeered at and being bespattered with mud, but as likely as not dead dogs and cats will be thrown at him, for the mob makes a provision before hand of these playthings, so that they may amuse themselves with them on the great day.

This popular theatre fascinated Hogarth, who revelled in it and reviled it at the same time. Hogarth's progresses – the *Rake's Progress*, the *Harlot's Progress*, the careers of the industrious and idle apprentices – are allegories but also literal journeys through the capital. Hogarth's industrious apprentice, Goodchild, ends up heading the Lord Mayor's procession in Cheapside, whereas Tom Idle makes his Cavalry-like way to Tyburn Tree. In the *Rake's Progress*, Tom Rakewell goes to the bad: from drinking at the Rose Tavern in Covent Garden he is arrested for debt in fashionable Piccadilly; after recouping himself by marrying an old maid, he loses his fortune gambling, and ends up successively an inmate of those two terrible institutions just beyond the City walls, the Fleet Prison and Bethlem Hospital.

'Paris,' reflected the poet Samuel Rogers during the Regency, 'is the City of the Great King, London of the Great People.' And this London was two things at once. It was super-smart wealth, style, fashion, elegance; perhaps the best place on earth for males with money to enjoy an inexhaustible round of pleasures. Yet, as well as being the playground of the rich, it possessed a special demotic energy, which many affected to hate but in reality found a drug. '*Make way there*, says a gouty-legg'd chairman, that is carrying a punk of quality to a *Morning's exercise*; or a *Bartholomew* baby-beau, newly launch'd out of a chocolate-house, with his pockets as empty as his brains' – here is the comic writer Tom Brown conjuring up the addictive hubbub of street-life:

Some carry, others are carried: *Make room there*, says another fellow driving a wheel-barrow of nuts, that spoil the lungs of the city prentices, and make them wheeze over *their mistresses* as bad as the phlegmatick cuckolds *their masters* do, when called to *family duty*. One draws, another drives. *Stand up there, you blind dog*, says a carman, *will you have the cart squeeze your guts out?* One tinker knocks, another bawls, *Have you brass-pot, iron-kettle, skillet or a frying pan to mend?* Whilst another son of a whore yelps louder than *Homer's* stentor, *Two a groat, and four for six-pence, mackerel.* One draws his mouth up to his ears, and howls out, *Buy my flounders*, and is followed by an old burly drab, that screams out the sale of her *maids* and her *soul* at the same instant.

This clattering London street-life astounded foreigners. Most had never seen such crowds, such noise, such energies. 'You stop, and bump! a porter runs against you shouting "By your leave" after he has knocked you down,' noted Lichtenberg, re-creating a London street scene:

In the road itself chaise after chaise, coach after coach, cart after cart. Through all this din and clamour, and the noise of thousands of tongues and feet, you hear the bells from the church-steeples, postmen's bells, the street-organs, fiddles and tambourines of itinerant musicians, and the cries of the vendors of hot and cold food at the street corners. A rocket blazes up stories high amidst a yelling crowd of beggars, sailors and urchins. Some one shouts 'Stop, thief,' his handkerchief is gone. Every one runs and presses forward, some less concerned to catch the thief than to steal a watch or purse for themselves. Before you are aware of it a young, well-dressed girl has seized your hand. 'Come, my lord, come along, let us drink a glass together,' or 'I'll go with you if you please.' An accident happens not forty paces away. 'God bless me,' calls one. 'Poor fellow,' cries another. A stoppage ensues and you look to your pockets. Every one is intent on helping the victim. Then there is laughter again: some one has fallen into the gutter. 'Look there, damn me,' cries a third, and the crowd passes on. Next comes a yell from a hundred throats as if fire had broken out, or a house was falling, or a patriot had looked out of a window. In Göttingen you can go anywhere and get within forty paces to see what is happening. Here, that is at night and in the City, you are lucky to escape with a whole skin down a side alley until the tumult is over. Even in the wider streets all the world rushes headlong without looking, as if summoned to the bedside of the dying. That is Cheapside and Fleet Street on a December evening.

What made Georgian London so special was the alchemy of money and the masses, its popular commercialism, run by capitalists great and small, from shareholders in Drury Lane theatre, through widows with their chop-houses, to gingerbread-vendors. Some made fortunes, others lost; but always there were plenty to take their place. This enterprise culture produced variety and change. If London did not beget a Mozart, it staged concerts in which he starred. Handel chose to work in London, as did Canaletto.

Crown and Parliament did little to mould London's public culture. Take painting. Commercial galleries opened in Georgian London, but there was no national collection to compare with those in Florence and France, and London had to wait till the nineteenth century for the National Gallery. Museums provide a similar story. London had various privately owned museums, open to the public for a fee. Cox's Museum included mechanical works of art in precious and semiprecious stones, a peacock which screeched and spread its tail when the hour struck, and a silver swan that dipped its beak and appeared to glide over water. Boswell visited the museum in 1772 on Samuel Johnson's recommendation and was impressed. But the British Museum – deriving from the will of Sir Hans Sloane – remained ill-managed and inaccessible. Only in the nineteenth century was it put on a better footing. What King and Parliament failed to provide – and what the Corporation of the City never even dreamt might fall within its duties – market forces brought into being. 'There is no place in the world,' thought the German traveller Pastor Wendeborn, 'where a man may lie more according to his own mind, or even his whim, than in London.' 'In London,' remarked Casanova, 'everything is easy to him who has money and is not afraid of spending it.' Overall it was a place of infinite variety and contrast. 'I have passed all my days in London until I have formed as many and intense local attachments, as any of you mountaineers can have done with dead nature,' Charles Lamb told Dorothy and William Wordsworth:

The Lighted shops of the Strand and Fleet Street, the innumerable trades, tradesmen and customers, coaches, waggons, playhouses, all the bustle and wickedness round about Covent Garden, the very women of the Town, the Watchmen, drunken scenes, rattles, – life awake, if you awake, at all hours of the night, the impossibility of being dull in Fleet Street, the crowds, the very dirt & mud, the Sun shining upon houses and pavements, the print shops, the old book stalls, parsons cheap'ning books, coffee houses, steams of soups from kitchens, the pantomimes, London itself a pantomime and a masquerade, – all these things work themselves into my mind and feed me ... and I often shed tears in the motley Strand from fullness of joy at so much in life.

– 'have I not enough,' he asked, 'without your mountains?'

Georgian Londoners became city-watchers, self-referential. They relished art and novels, journalism and theatre about themselves and their world. If they were still fascinated by Rome, Jerusalem and Byzantium, they were preoccupied with the challenge of superimposing those mythic cities on the London they knew, of which they were proud and by which they were puzzled. Londoners lapped up Ned Ward's *The London Spy* and Gay's *The Beggar's Opera*, they relished the local writings of Defoe and Fielding, and they loved George Lillo's tragedy *The London Merchant, or the History of George Barnwell*, produced at Drury Lane in 1731, which elevated apprentices and harlots into tragic figures. The metropolis, Raymond Williams has emphasized, was a new moral arena: 'As London grew, dramatically, in the eighteenth century, it was being intensely observed, as a new kind of landscape, a new kind of society.' Londoners fell in love with themselves.

Capitalism in the Capital: The Victorian Age

A mighty mass of brick, and smoke, and shipping
    Dirty and dusky, but as wide as eye
Could reach, with here and there a sail just skipping
    In sight, then lost amidst the forestry
Of masts; a wilderness of steeples peeping
    On tiptoe through their sea-coal canopy;
A huge, dun cupola, like a foolscap crown
    On a fool's head – and there is London Town!

LORD BYRON, *Don Juan*, 1822

The nineteenth century acknowledged London as the centre of things: the creation in 1884 of the Greenwich Meridian, marked by a brass rail inlaid in concrete, crowned it as the prime meridian – zero degrees longitude – whence all the continents spread out east and west. London thus put the world in its place – a development which confirmed, on a global scale, a similar symbolic status already achieved within the nation. Towns had traditionally had their own individual time: there had, for instance, been about ten minutes' difference between Bristol and London. With the advent of the railway, national time had to be created, and this was standardized by the timetable-makers upon London time, which, after 1852, was pulsed out by hourly telegraph signals. 'London Time is kept at all stations on the Railway,' the Great Western Railway helpfully announced in 1841 on the opening of the London to Bridgewater line, 'which is about 4 minutes earlier than READING time; $5\frac{1}{2}$ minutes before STEVENTON time; $7\frac{1}{2}$ minutes before CIRENCESTER time; 11 minutes before BATH and BRISTOL time; and 14 minutes before BRIDGEWATER time.'

By 1800 London was the grandest city in the West and probably in the world, with almost a million inhabitants. The succeeding decades brought unparalleled urban expansion worldwide, with trade and industry creating astonishing population nuclei. Between 1800 and 1850 the total of 'world cities' (over 100,000 inhabitants) jumped from 65 to 106, and nearly treble again by 1900. Whereas in 1800 London was the only 'million city', by the 1850s it had been joined by Paris and New York, and by 1900 there were 16 such cities, and another 27 of over 500,000, mainly in Europe and North America. 'The most remarkable social phenomenon of the present century is the concentration of population in cities,' observed the statistician Adna Weber in 1899, a concentration caused by technological change. 'All the agencies of modern civilization have worked together to abolish ... rural isolation,' Weber noted; 'the railways, the newspaper press, freedom of migration and settlement ... cause the spread of the ideas originating in the cities.'

Rising between 1800 and 1900 from just under a million inhabitants to some 4·5 million, London was the super-city *de luxe*. Driven by market forces, it 'just growed', without central command. A patchwork of dozens of autonomous districts, unevenly governed by often unrepresentative vestries, the metropolis sprawled on. It suffered from its administrative fault lines; but it also benefited, for confusion permitted diversity and interstitial growth.

It became difficult to envisage the whole. The journalist Henry Mayhew tried gazing down from a balloon, but even then it was impossible 'to tell where the monster city began or ended, for the buildings stretched not only to the horizon on either side, but far away into the distance ... where the town seemed to blend into the sky'. 'This vast bricken mass of churches and hospitals, banks and prisons, palaces and workhouses, docks and refuges for the destitute, parks and squares, and courts and alleys, which make up London' thrilled and horrified him all at once.

Economic expansion gained momentum. High concentrations of craft skills had established the capital as the supreme manufacturer, notably of quality wares. With colonial expansion the Port brought boundless business, creating riverside handling and processing industries – timber, sugar, tobacco, rum, molasses. The City profited immensely from the monopolies held by the East India Company and other chartered bodies. Imperial conquests in India, the Caribbean and the Pacific reinforced the capital's commercial dominance.

London's high-wage economy sucked in thousands, creating further spirals of demand. Its role as a residence and playground for the rich generated buoyant employment in retailing, porterage and transport, and many other services. Baronets, brokers and Bayswater ex-colonials required armies of shop assistants and crossing-sweepers, seamstresses and liveried footmen. Some indication of how far prosperity derived from servicing the rich was offered by the 1841 Census, which found that London had

168,701 domestic servants, 29,780 dressmakers and milliners, 16,220 laundry-keepers, washers and manglers, and 13,103 private messengers and errand boys.

Commercial and imperial success created platoons of middle-class jobs in shipping, banking, investment and insurance. Bourgeois affluence in turn required workers in construction, railways and transportation, in the distributive trades, in tailoring and dressmaking, in food and drink and retailing. London's service economy exploited casual, cheap and part-time labour, but there was at least employment for all, down to Covent Garden flower-sellers, match-girls, the thousands of streetwalkers, and all the weird and wonderful trades Mayhew documented. London avoided the over-dependence on any particular industry – like cotton in Lancashire or coal in South Wales – that made prosperity precarious elsewhere.

Yet challenges were looming. Rivals emerged with the Industrial Revolution, which has been called 'a storm that passed over London and broke elsewhere'. In Lancashire, the West Riding and the Midlands, a new economic order was being forged, based upon fossil fuels, iron and steel, textile factories, and heavy industries like engineering and shipbuilding. The new age, it has often been said, belonged to the factory not the workshop, to steam not handicrafts. 'The capital cities,' wrote Fernand Braudel, 'would be present at the forthcoming industrial revolution, but in the role of spectators. Not London but Manchester, Birmingham, Leeds, Glasgow and innumerable small proletarian towns launched the new era.'

This is too crude, however. For one thing, Industrial Revolution or not, the capital hardly lagged in technology and innovation. Late eighteenth-century London had more steam engines than Lancashire – they were used not in textile mills but in flour-mills and for pumping London's water supply. As late as 1850 London's manufacturing output was still unrivalled in Britain, for the obvious reason that the capital's vast population created unsurpassed demand. And the nation's industrial economy was profoundly dependent upon the capital's imports, transport and communications, wholesale and retail networks, finance skills and its service sector more generally. Historians have sometimes written about London's reliance upon 'service' employment as if that meant the capital were somehow less 'productive' than other regions – parasitic in fact. But this is a false assumption. The truth is that in the Victorian era jobs in services accounted for over half the *national* increase in employment, and the service sector contributed no less to economic activity than manufacturing: witness the high proportion of millionaires owing their fortunes to brewing and retailing. Leading historians today are reiterating the prime role of international trade in Britain's nineteenth-century economic miracle: the Port and the City were no less crucial to this than the factories of Lancashire or the coal pits of South Wales.

It is nevertheless true that industries planted elsewhere, on coal and iron deposits, in due course poached manufacturing and engineering business away from London. High costs were becoming a drawback; business began to leave London because outlays were lower elsewhere and labour cheaper. London experienced a slow but ominous decline as a manufacturing centre. Thames shipbuilding, for instance, was unable in the long run to compete with Tyneside and Clydeside. 'Transitions to the factory system are unfavourable to London,' noted the social analyst Charles Booth in the 1890s, 'except perhaps when the factory is content to supply the parts of the prepared materials used by the individual worker or the small workshop, as is done by the saw mills in the furniture trades; or when much of the labour appropriate to the machinery used is low paid and abundant.'

Clouds were thus gathering on the horizon. Yet in terms of production and employment Victorian London thrived, retaining prime place in all major sectors except metals and textiles. A seventh of the total population of England and Wales was living in London in 1871; a sixth of all the manufacturing workers lived there. One out of every three London workers was in manufacturing. According to the 1861 Census, London employed 25,000 in clothing and dressmaking, 95,000 in food-processing, 92,000 as builders, 59,000 in shopkeeping, 35,000 metalworkers, 25,000 furniture-makers, and so forth. The Census revealed large numbers in skilled, specialized trades – 13,000 machine- and tool-makers, 6,000 carriage-makers, and 5,000 musical-instrument-makers, for instance, to say nothing of numerous occupations found chiefly in a capital, including 26,000 people engaged in government, 61,000 in the learned professions or literature, art or science, and 23,000 in the hotel and catering industry. In all there were 469,000 workers engaged in manufacturing industry – 15 per cent of all those so employed in the whole of England and Wales.

Presiding over the empire upon which the sun never set, London lived by its river. Britain was at least as much the market of the world as the workshop of the world. Early in the nineteenth century, commercial expansion received a fillip from massive capital investment in docks. In 1799 the West India Company, which had suffered most from pilfering on the open Thames-side wharves, began building a dock complex on the Isle of Dogs: half a mile long, twenty-four acres in extent, and large enough to berth over 600 big ships, the West India Docks also provided vast warehousing facilities, the whole being surrounded by a twenty-foot-high brick wall as protection against theft. Further docks came one after the other: the London Docks at Wapping (1805), and the East India at Blackwall (1806), specializing in the tea trade, its buildings designed by Rennie. Surrey Docks followed on the south bank, and, by the Tower, St Katharine's Dock opened in 1828. By 1811 more than £5 million had been invested in these artificial lakes, all from private sources.

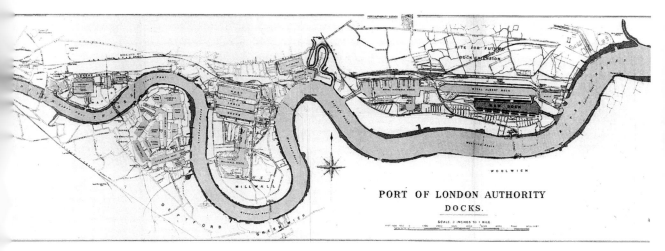

Plan of dockland development

In time, booming trade and the substitution of steam for sail required further construction, housing larger vessels. The Royal Victoria Dock opened in 1855 and the Millwall Dock in 1868. The London and St Katharine's Company then built the Albert Dock at West Ham in 1880, the East and West India Company retaliating in 1886 with Tilbury, twenty-six miles downstream. Some proved a lasting financial success, especially the Victoria Docks. Overall, however, this competitive leap-frogging down the river proved destructive, supply far outstripping demand. Tilbury Docks long remained semi-idle, reducing the East and West India Company to bankruptcy in 1888; the London and St Katharine's Company narrowly escaped ruin. London had become overdocked, and financial losses led to the Port of London Authority being constituted by Act of Parliament in 1908, the PLA assuming control over the entire Port.

The docks were, nevertheless, a wonder of engineering, and their warehouses were singled out by Baedeker as one of the sights of the city: 'Nothing will convey to the stranger a better idea of the vast activity and stupendous wealth of London than a visit to the warehouses, filled to overflowing with interminable stores of every kind of foreign and colonial products.' In *London Labour and the London Poor*, Mayhew voiced his admiration:

As you enter the dock, the sight of the forest of masts in the distance, and the tall chimneys vomiting clouds of black smoke, and the many coloured flags flying in the air, has a most peculiar effect ... The sailors are singing boisterous nigger songs from the Yankee ship just entering; the cooper is hammering at the casts on the quay; the chains of the cranes, loosed of their weight, rattle as they fly up again; the ropes splash in the water; some captain shouts his orders through his hands; a goat bleats from some ship in the basin; and empty casks roll along the stones with a heavy drum-like sound. Here the heavily laden ships are down far below the quay, and you descend to them by ladders; whilst in another basin they are high up out of the water, so that their green copper sheathing is almost level with the eye of the passenger; while above his head a long line of bowsprits stretches far over the quay; and from them hang spars and planks as a gangway to each ship.

Docks created enormous demand for riverside labour. Some was skilled: coopers, rope-makers, carpenters and stevedores (who worked on the ships' holds) established relatively regular work. But these were a minority: two-thirds of dock labour was low-paid and casual, hired on a day-to-day basis. And work was seasonal: China tea came in July and November; wool arrived in February and July; sugar and grain in September and April. Excessive capacity perpetuated the casual system. It was, recorded Mayhew, 'a sight to sadden the most callous, to see thousands of men struggling for only one day's hire'. A dockers' strike at the West India Docks in 1872 led to the employers being forced to agree to pay 5d an hour. By the famous strike of 1889, unions increased this by another penny, to 'the docker's tanner'.

The docks gave a boost to an already flourishing riverside (which, until pollution became too bad around 1820, harboured a flourishing fishing industry). Iron-founding had long been established, associated around 1700 with Ambrose Crowley, ironmonger and alderman. Shipbuilding prospered, and in 1850 London still boasted the nation's most prosperous yards. The trade had long been the pride of Poplar and Deptford, sustaining foundries, coopers' yards, sailyards, ropewalks, and block-and-tackle workshops – and making London shipyard workers a proud aristocracy of labour. London played a leading part in the switch from wood to iron: in 1822 the *Aaron Manby*, the first iron steamboat, was assembled at Rotherhithe. The millwright and engineer William Fairbairn opened his Millwall yards in 1833, building for the East India Company, and from the 1840s iron shipbuilding boomed at Millwall and Blackwall. The climax came in 1857, when Millwall saw the launch of Isambard Kingdom Brunel's iron ship the *Great Eastern*, then the world's largest vessel. The launch was bungled, however, and the ship remained high and dry. She proved a financial failure, and the fiasco was an omen of the demise of the London shipbuilding industry. Soon the great Poplar shipbuilding firm of Ditchburn & Mare, which built vessels for the Admiralty, went broke. The industry lurched through successive crises, dying just before the First World War. Distance from iron deposits, strong unions, high wages, and the metropolis's high overheads – all

View of the docks and warehouses on the Isle of Dogs, built to accommodate trade
with the West Indies, 1802

these factors combined spelt its downfall.

Around the docks and the boatyards, many activities developed on the waterfront, making use of coal brought by coaster. Newcastle coal was unloaded by man-power before the 1850s, but, with the increasing use of large steam colliers, handling became mechanized. On the Silvertown foreshore Cory & Son built a battery of hydraulic cranes and a floating derrick unloading coal directly into barges. Cory's were soon unloading two-thirds of the 2,750,000 tons of coal transported by sea, reducing prices. Meanwhile the railways were trimming costs to undercut the sea trade. Cheap coal and the North Woolwich railway encouraged the siting of industries and utilities in the Silvertown and Canning Town areas.

Among them were gasworks. In 1812, the Gas-Light and Coke Company had become the first gas company chartered to light the City, Westminster and Southwark. Rival companies followed, including the City of London, the Imperial and the Independent north of the river, and the South London, South Metropolitan and Phoenix south of the river. For cheapness, London's eighteen gasworks were mainly sited on the river, or on the Regent's and Grand Surrey Canals. In 1867, the Gas-Light and Coke Company bought a site at East Ham by the Thames, allowing coal to be landed straight from barges. The up-to-date plant was named Beckton, after Simon Adams Beck, governor of the company. The rival Imperial Company attempted a similar enterprise at Bromley-by-Bow, but its inland position proved no rival.

Ready coal, coke and gas supplies stimulated subsidiary industries dependent upon coal by-products. In 1856 Burt, Boulton & Haywood, tar distillers, set up in Silvertown, manufacturing naphtha, pitch, creosote, and disinfectants: they led the world in gas distilling. With the advent of aniline dyes, Burt's bought up Perkin's aniline-dye factory and transferred it to Silvertown; the British Alizarine Works was set up nearby; and in 1879 the Gas-Light and Coke Company built an ammonium-sulphate plant, making nitrogenous fertilizer. Numerous sulphuric-acid works sprouted in West Ham.

Riverside areas thus teemed with distilling, boiling, refining and chemical industries: the Isle of Dogs was 'covered with steam factories'. Chemicals, soap, confectionery, rubber, dye, engineering, rope-making, printing, tin-canister- and sack-making were all prominent. The river, the docks, the North Woolwich railway line and the availability of cheap land together ensured prosperity.

Canals also made their contribution to London's economy. In 1801 the Grand Junction Canal was extended from Uxbridge to Paddington, thereby providing a direct link between London and the Midlands, and bringing business to its terminus at the Paddington Basin. From 1820 the Regent's Canal joined with the Grand Junction Canal at Paddington, going eastward through a tunnel under Edgware Road, Maida Hill and St John's Wood and on, via Regent's Park, through Camden Town and Islington, thence through another tunnel and by way of Hackney to join the Thames at Limehouse, where another basin was constructed. Much used for coal and timber shipment, it linked all of North London to the national canal network and brought trade to Hackney, Hoxton (where Pickford's planted their depot), St Pancras and Camden Town.

By far the world's biggest food importer and consumer, the metropolis generated huge processing industries to feed its millions. Supplying its daily bread, corn-mills hugged the Thames, Wandle and Lea. Wandsworth's mills were the largest, using both steam and water power, but John Rennie's Albion Mills at Blackfriars were the world's first flour-mills to use steam power (till burnt down in 1791) – a mark of the metropolis's insatiable demand for bread. Sugar-refining grew up in Whitechapel and St George-in-the-East adjoining the Suffrance Wharves. Distilling and brewing were vast business, dominated by a dozen great firms, of which Barclay, Perkins' brewery in Southwark was the largest. Other giants included Charrington's in Mile End Road, Truman, Hanbury & Buxton in Spitalfields, Meux in Tottenham Court Road, Whitbread's in Chiswell Street and Watney's in Pimlico.

Pressures of business finally forced changes upon London's food markets – generally against opposition by the Corporation, which feared that removal of markets from the centre would cut revenues. The principal centres of the meat trade – Leadenhall Market, specializing in poultry and hides, Newgate and Farringdon Markets (dead meat) and Smithfield (live cattle) – were all owned by the City Corporation. With increased business they had become insufferable; in the early Victorian era cattle were still being driven through the streets to Smithfield, causing traffic chaos. The huge central slaughterhouse offended urban sensibilities. 'To-day I chanced to pass thro' Smithfield,' noted Thomas Carlyle:

Smithfield meat market, mid nineteenth century

I mounted the steps of a door, and looked abroad upon the area, an irregular space of perhaps thirty acres in extent, encircled with old dingy brick-built houses, and intersected with wooden pens for the cattle. What a scene! Innumerable herds of fat oxen, tied in long rows, or passing at a trot to their several shambles; and thousands of graziers, drovers, butchers, cattle-brokers with their quilted frocks and long goads pushing on the hapless beasts; hurrying to and fro in confused parties, shouting, jostling, cursing, in the midst of rain and *shairn* [dung], and braying discord such as the imagination cannot figure.

Smithfield became a favourite target for sanitary reformers. The City Corporation blocked reform, but in 1855 the live-cattle market was finally moved to new slaughterhouses in Islington (Market Road), and the Central Meat Market was built on the Smithfield site, in design echoing Paxton's Crystal Palace, a gigantic shed, its wide arcade supported by slender iron columns. With frozen meat arriving from the Argentine from 1876, cold stores were built beneath the market.

The principal fruit and vegetable markets remained the Borough market in Southwark, Spitalfields and Covent Garden; others were in decline and Hungerford market was closed in 1862 to make way for Charing Cross station. Owned by the Dukes of Bedford, Covent Garden was so lucrative that in 1828 the 6th Duke erected the famous graceful buildings in the centre of the Piazza. In the 1880s business grew greater as refrigeration brought produce from the Canaries and California, Australia and South Africa. Congestion worsened, as did public demand for the removal of the market. But little happened.

Food-processing became one of London's great growth industries, especially by the river. Alongside its candle and toilet-soap works, printing firms and laundries, Lambeth had beer and vinegar breweries, flour-mills, and factories for sauces and meat essences: by London Bridge were Brand's, Pearce Duff's, and Crosse & Blackwell. Tinned food began in Bermondsey, when in 1811 Bryan Donkin's Grange Road factory began tinning meat. Samples of his tinned beef were sent to royalty, and a letter of thanks returned ('your patent beef was tasted by the Queen, Prince Regent and several distinguished personages and highly approved'). Peek Frean's of Drummond Road was founded in 1857 by a City tea merchant, Mr Peek, who supplied the money, and a ship's biscuit-maker, Mr Frean, who provided the know-how.

In mid-Victorian times London had six major fields of industrial employment – the building trades, clothing and footwear, wood and furniture, metals and engineering, printing and stationery, and precision manufacture (watches, scientific instruments, surgical apparatus, etc.). The accent had long been on high-grade wares. Clerkenwell, known as 'a second edition of Birmingham', specialized in tinplate, barometers, thermometers, engraving and printing machinery; its makers of clocks, watches and scien-

Billingsgate fish market, 1858. From M'Connell/Sala's
Twice Round the London Clock

tific instruments were renowned. Around Hatton Garden, jewellers and diamond-dealers congregated.

Across the river, Bermondsey and Southwark formed the centre of the leather trade, especially around Tanner, Morocco and Leathermarket Streets. One Bermondsey tannery treated 350,000 skins a year. Hat-making flourished in the same area. Christy's of Bermondsey Street, with 500 employees in 1841, claimed to be the world's largest hat manufacturers. The hair and wool by-products of the leather trades provided the bodies for stuff hats, and Bermondsey leather met the demands of shoemakers, cabinet- and chair-makers, bookbinders and coachbuilders.

Silk remained significant. In 1851 there were some 5,500 silk-weavers in Bethnal Green and Whitechapel, and Spitalfields still led Lancashire and Cheshire in fine silk manufacture. But the industry was dying after the coming of free trade left it uncompetitive. Already by the 1830s tens of thousands of Spitalfields weavers were unemployed. '1,100 are crammed into the poor house, five or six in a bed; 6,000 receive parochial relief,' reported the politician Charles Greville in 1832:

The parish is in debt; every day adds to the number of paupers and diminishes that of ratepayers. These are principally small shopkeepers, who are beggared by the rates. The district is in a complete state of insolvency and hopeless poverty ... Government is ready to interpose with assistance, but what can Government do? We asked the man who came what could be done for them. He said 'employment', and employment is impossible.

The furniture trade fared better. Cabinet-makers clustered on an axis running north-east from St Paul's, along Cheapside towards Finsbury Square and Shoreditch, and also in the West End. Many high-class establishments employed between 80 and 100 artisans. And a ready-made trade was emerging alongside, aided by steam-powered sawmilling, the opening of the Regent's Canal, and the establishment of new timber yards convenient for Shoreditch and Finsbury. 'From Finsbury-pavement through Moorfields, by Finsbury-market, along the Curtain-road through Shoreditch' to Bethnal Green,' it was said in 1858, 'may be looked upon as one great emporium for the manufacture of household furniture.' Curtain Road became the heart of the ready-made trade, with hosts of associated carvers, turners, wood-merchants and upholsterers, and dealers in iron, steel, brass, silver, ivory and wood mountings. The typical business was small: a pound's worth of tools and a second pound in cash, it was said, started a cabinet-maker off. Child labour was crucial. Mayhew calculated that the 2,500 small masters in cabinet-making were employing 12,000 children.

London was also the nucleus of the printing industry, around Fleet Street and the Strand, Long Acre and St Paul's. Jobbing printing – of handbills, cards, illustrated fashion books and circulars – clustered around the Barbican and Bishopsgate; Clerkenwell was the growth area for colour printing.

Meanwhile, heavy engineering and the metallurgical industries continued to expand. Around 1820 there were 300 or 400 masters in 'various branches of machinery' concentrated along the south bank in Southwark and Lambeth (also the home of Doulton's pottery). The biggest works was owned by John Rennie, a Scot who learned his trade with Boulton and Watt in Birmingham before setting up in Holland Street near Blackfriars Road – Southwark, Waterloo and London Bridges were all his work. After his death, his younger son, John, carried on the trade, while his elder son, George, specialized in marine engines for the Admiralty – in 1840, he built the *Dwarf*, the first naval vessel with screw propulsion.

Among London's greatest engineers was Joseph Bramah. A Yorkshireman who trained as a cabinet-maker, Bramah developed an improved water-closet and the beer engine, for pulling a pint. He is primarily remembered, however, for precision locks. His protégé Henry Maudslay began at Woolwich Arsenal. For eight years they worked together, making machine tools and Bramah's patent hydraulic press, which provided engineers with a steady continuous pressure of practically unlimited power. James

Nasmyth and Joseph Whitworth also helped ensure London's engineering supremacy. In the 1840s Maudslay's and Rennie's were employing about 1,000 and 400 men respectively.

Down-river, another great engineer was long engaged upon a prodigious feat of engineering. The Rotherhithe-to-Wapping Thames tunnel was built by Marc Isambard Brunel and his son, Isambard Kingdom Brunel, the mastermind of the Great Western Railway. The elder Brunel ran saw-mills at Battersea and experimented with steamboats. John Penn made marine engines at Greenwich, while Stevens's of Southwark pioneered railway signal equipment.

Industries clustered locally: boot- and shoemaking in Bethnal Green, Shoreditch, Stepney, Hackney; leather and hatting in Bermondsey; jewellery in Clerkenwell. Decentralization became more common after 1850, costs being lower. Dye, glue and chemical works and jute, soap, match and rubber manufactures moved away from Bethnal Green and Whitechapel towards Bow, Old Ford and Hackney Wick. A celluloid factory opened in the late 1860s at Hackney, while Bryant & May's match factory was established by the River Lea, the river acquiring a 'urinous smell'. By 1850 West Ham, beyond the Lea, was becoming the home of soap, rubber, chemical, bonemeal, paint, glue and tarpaulin manufacture. Soon it could boast a major sugar-refinery, manure factory, creosote factory, vitriol factory, lampblack factory, varnish factory, tar factory, and the Chemical Light Company. West Ham became London's late Victorian industrial success story: it was ideally situated; its water-frontage cut transport costs; it was well provided with docks and railways; and, beyond the super-vision of the Metropolitan Board of Works and later the London County Council, its vestry was lax in the enforcement of building, factory and smoke regulations. East Ham, an agricultural village till the last quarter of the nineteenth century, also developed, stimulated by the Beckton gasworks.

In 1850 inner London's industries had been second to none: 'There are many establishments in or near London,' stated the guidebook writer George Dodd in 1841, 'such as water-works, gas-works, ship-yards, tan-yards, brewhouses, distilleries, glass-works, &c., the extent of which would excite no little surprise in those who for the first time visited them.' But thereafter problems multiplied. Space was comparatively costly in the capital. In the 1870s an acre in the City cost about twenty times as much as its suburban equivalent. Charles Booth noted that industry was moving out because of 'the double necessity of avoiding high rentals and of securing the early command of cheap means of transport'.

From the 1890s relocations occurred with increasing frequency. In 1895 the printers Ward Lock moved out of Fleet Street to Stoke Newington. Stratford, like West Ham a growth suburb, prospered largely thanks to the railway. In 1847 the Eastern County Railway had moved its locomotive and carriage works there, creating a spaghetti junction of lines and sidings. Stratford's works turned out a carriage a day and a locomotive a week. By 1900 they were employing nearly 7,000 people.

Yet this was the exception. London's industries were typically small. According to the 1851 Census, only seven firms employed over 350 men, and out of 24,323 employers only eighty employed over 100. There were 3,182 masters who employed just one man. Small workshops predominated. Petty capitalism had its advantages, notably affordable start-up costs. 'The experience of London,' Charles Booth observed, 'affords practical proof of the persistent vitality of small methods of business.'

With technological change, and especially mass production, London's manufactures faced challenges. Under stiffer competition, some collapsed. The leather industry underwent decline, and by the 1880s the Bermondsey tan-yards were depressed. The collapse of traditional heavy engineering was slow but sure after 1850, one firm following another to the industrial north. Innovations, however, still happened in the capital. It was in a laboratory in St Pancras that Henry Bessemer devised his revolutionary process for making steel, and in a little Clerkenwell workshop Hiram Maxim constructed his first machine-gun.

'At mid-century most clothing goods (including boots and shoes) were produced under what was called "honourable" conditions by masters and journeymen in the master's shop,' observed a nostalgic Bethnal Green shoemaker in the 1840s, describing the old trade:

Hours and wages were regulated by custom, not competition, and most goods were 'bespoke' goods, that is, they were produced to fill the order of a specific customer and contracted directly by the customer from the retailer and not produced for what was becoming known as the 'ready-made' trade. The middle and upper classes purchased their clothing and footwear in this manner, more likely than not in shops on the West End streets of Savile Row, Conduit Street, New Bond Street, Sackville Street, Maddox Street, and the like. The lower classes traditionally acquired the cast-off clothing of their betters, either purchased in used clothing stores or handed down from master to servant, or they made do with clothing made at home.

If the situation this evokes was ever other than a 'golden-age' myth, things certainly changed rapidly. Especially from 1870, the footwear and clothing industries were transformed through the advent of a new 'ready-made' trade. Prominent also in boot-making and furniture, 'sweating' was most conspicuous in clothing. Producing cheap ready mades, the slop trades exploited a flexible and extensive division of labour. Skilled labour processes were broken down into simple component parts, using an inexhaustible supply of cheap unskilled labour, notably East London Jewish immigrants. Different pairs of hands cut, sewed, buttonholed, ironed and packed. Craftsmen could not compete, especially after the invention of hand-driven machinery like the sewing-machine and the bandsaw. Work was done at home or in overcrowded work-shops, thus minimizing rent. Women and children formed the basis of this labour force. Scamping methods shortened the time it took to produce an article, and long hours, irregular employment and rock-bottom wages were ubiquitous.

Sweating sped production and minimized costs. The system was controlled by small wholesalers. With the rise of provincial factory production in footwear and clothing, the sweating system was the only answer to the problems of the traditional London manufacturer (high rents and high wages), being peculiarly well-suited to the fashion trade, where the erratic nature of demand, rush orders, sudden gluts, and rapid style changes gave the entrepreneur employing outworkers flexibility in production at little risk. In footwear, London abandoned competing with the provinces in the production of heavy boots, where styles were fixed and demand constant, but specialized in the superior trade – and in sending footwear to the Empire. It was sweating that made the fortune of men like Moses Moses. His two youngest sons, Alfred and George, opened a little shop in King Street, Covent Garden, later extending it to Bedford Street; by 1917 they had bought up other small shops till the firm occupied the whole corner site. They called themselves Moss Bros.

Sweating was a major source of women's work in days when women were excluded from heavy industry and transport, and from the professions, the civil service and clerical work. In 1851 140,000 women over twenty were employed in domestic service and 125,000 were in clothing and shoemaking; the bulk of the remainder were employed as shopkeepers, innkeepers and lodging-house keepers – or of course as housewives and mothers. Women's work fell into five main categories: household labour – washing, cooking, charring, sewing, mending, laundry work, mangling, ironing; child care; food distribution and retail; manufacturing; and prostitution. Laundries created labour for some 60,000 women by 1900 – they were such a landmark that Kensal New Town became known as 'Soap Suds Island', while 'Laundry Land' replaced 'Piggeries and Potteries' as the nickname for Notting Dale.

The eighteenth century brought the emergence of high-class shops, in the City, in Piccadilly and Mayfair. 'There are two sets of streets, running nearly parallel, almost from the Eastern extremity of the town to the Western, forming (with the exception of a very few houses), a line of shops,' an 1803 guidebook helpfully informed readers:

One, lying to the South, nearer the river, extends from Mile End to Parliament Street, including Whitechapel, Leadenhall Street, Cornhill, Cheapside, St Paul's Churchyard, Ludgate Street, Fleet Street, the Strand, and Charing Cross. The other, to the North, reaches from Shoreditch Church almost to the end of Oxford Street, including Shoreditch, Bishopsgate Street, Thread-needle Street, Cheapside, Newgate Street, Snow-hill, Holborn, Broad Street, St Giles, and Oxford Street.

The Southern line, which is the most splendid, is more than three miles in length; the other is about four miles. There are several large streets also occupied by retail trade, that run parallel to parts of the two grand lines, or intersect them, among the most remarkable of which are Fenchurch Street and Gracechurch Street in the City of London; and Cockspur Street, Pall Mall, St James's Street, Piccadilly, King Street Covent Garden, and New Bond Street, at the West end of the town.

With the additions of Knightsbridge and Westbourne Grove, these remained the key Victorian shopping zones; indeed Disraeli could judge the Strand 'perhaps the first street in Europe'.

The eighteenth century had designed the seductive shop-front. All that was lacking was brilliant lighting, but the early Victorian era changed that. 'Six or eight years ago the epidemic began to display itself among the linen drapers and haberdashers,' recorded Dickens in *Sketches by Boz*:

The primary symptoms were an inordinate love of plate-glass, and a passion for gas-lights and gilding. The disease gradually progressed, and at last attained a fearful height. Quiet, dusty old shops in different parts of town were pulled down: spacious premises with stuccoed fronts and gold letters were erected instead.

Really fashionable trade was moving from the City and Fleet Street to the West End, particularly to Oxford Street and Regent Street, where there was space for giant shops like Swan & Edgar's, with their great gaslit plate-glass windows. One of the most beautiful sights he had seen in London, recalled the journalist Henry Colman, was 'a ride down Regent Street, on a box-seat of an omnibus, in the evening, when the streets are crowded with people elegantly dressed, and the shops in long ranges, with their illuminated windows of immense length, and their interior exhibiting an almost indefinite perspective, are in all their glory'.

Drapers led the way. At 54 Oxford Street, Dickins & Smith opened in 1790 at the sign of the Golden Lion. In 1835 they moved to Regent Street, where from the 1890s the shop was known as Dickins & Jones. In 1833 Peter Robinson, a Yorkshireman, opened a linen-draper's shop at 103 Oxford Street, between Oxford Circus and Great Portland Street. It had a dressmaking department, and its lace department became famous. A 'Court and General Mourning House' was also opened in Regent Street, which became known as 'Black Peter Robinson's'. A brougham was always ready-harnessed to hurry off to a house of mourning.

A galaxy of Oxford Street shops catered for women's clothing and adornment – 'the whim-whams and fribble-frabble of fashion'. *Johnstone's London Commercial Guide* (1817) noted for that street 33 linen-drapers, 2 silk and satin dressers and dyers, 10 straw-hat manufactories, 2 drapers and tailors, 6 bonnet warehouses, 1 India-muslin warehouse, 5 woollen-drapers, 3 fancy trimmings and fringes manufactories, 5 lace warehouses, 3 plumassiers, 1 button manufactory, 24 boot- and shoemakers, and numerous others. Later developments included Liberty's, whose customers soon included William Morris (who founded Morris & Co. in 1861), John Ruskin, Burne-Jones and other members of the Aesthetic Movement. Bond Street long remained a man's street, with hatters, tailors, hairdressers and other expensive tradesmen catering for dandies.

The great Victorian innovation was the department store, beginning with William Whiteley. Whiteley daringly set up in Westbourne Grove. The first underground, the Metropolitan Railway, had just opened from Paddington to Farringdon, and fashion was heading west. Beginning in 1863 as a draper, Whiteley extended into a grander retailing style, with nineteen different departments under one roof by 1900. Aiming to make Westbourne Grove the 'Bond Street of the West', he gobbled up adjoining buildings and moved into books and ironmongery and installed a restaurant, a cleaning department (*nettoyage à sec* had been invented in 1849), a hairdressers and an estate agency. By 1872 he had departments for dressmaking, gentlemen's outfitting, tailoring, boots and hats, stationery, furniture, china and glass – styling himself 'The Universal Provider'. Whiteley's became a place where you could buy and furnish a house and feed and outfit yourself until you died, whereupon his funeral department was at your service.

Whiteley was a stern master, keeping men assistants in one set of lodgings and women in another; they had to sleep two or three to a bedroom and to obey 176 rules. Whiteley did, however, provide various clubs and societies, and a library, paid for by deductions from salaries.

His one-time employee John Barker expanded in Kensington. Combining grocery and drapery, by the 1880s Barker was already employing 400. Charles Digby Harrod meanwhile was turning his Knightsbridge grocer's into an emporium dealing in carpets, drapery and fashion goods, household merchandise and furniture, to say nothing of providing 'elegant and restful waiting and retiring-rooms for both sexes, writing rooms with dainty stationery, a club room, fitting rooms, smoking rooms, etc., free of charge or question'. No wonder Harrod adopted the telegraphic address of EVERYTHING, LONDON. Yet he too had started small. Henry Charles Harrod, a wholesale tea merchant of Eastcheap, ran a grocer's shop in Knightsbridge village. His son took it over. By 1867 he had five assistants, by 1870 sixteen. A two-storey extension was soon built, and further premises were acquired. By 1880 nearly 100 assistants were employed.

Big stores emerged around Tottenham Court Road, including Shoolbred's, Maple's and Heal's, catering for Bloomsbury. John Harris Heal came to London in 1805 and in 1810 set up at 33 Rathbone Place. His widow, Fanny, carried on the business, and in 1840 their son took control, moving to 196 Tottenham Court Road, in partnership with John Maple. Maple later broke away, and by 1884 Maple's were offering 'ten thousand Bedsteads in 6000 styles for immediate delivery'. The store was rebuilt in 1896, by when the firm supplied furniture for everyone from the modest middle classes to the Tsar of Russia. By 1930 it was said to be 'the largest furniture establishment in the world'.

All such department stores were notably less aristocratic than the traditional Bond Street and Regent Street shops. They dealt in cash purchases and they had a multitude of services to offer, including restaurants and 'retiring rooms' (lavatories) for ladies.

Multiples sprang up too. By the early 1890s Thomas Lipton, a close friend of Whiteley, had opened seventy grocery shops in London alone. He was soon emulated by the International Tea Company's stores, Maypole Dairies, the Home and Colonial, and Freeman, Hardy & Willis; Sainsbury's had begun business in 1869.

Around 1800 the City was still a busy shopping area, with that buzz of tradesmen, small works, shopkeepers and merchants inimitably evoked in Dickens's early fiction. It was to turn into a square mile of commerce, and increasingly of finance (though that was long the junior partner – till 1900 the City's principal role was trade).

In 1800 the Bank of England held a monopoly of joint-stock banking. Until 1826 all other banks were forbidden to have more than six partners, and so they remained small. The only giant, the Bank of England acted as the government's banker, and possessed the only large gold reserve. Private banks were, however, well established, some of the oldest firms having evolved from the goldsmiths' trade. Richard Hoare, goldsmith, the son of a horse-dealer, had established a bank in Cheapside in 1672, removing in 1690 to Fleet Street (where Hoare's remains).

The modern bill market, dealing mostly in short-term loans, was also securely established by 1800. The fixed capital of the Industrial Revolution – factory buildings and equipment – was financed by the industrialists themselves, not by the City. Until almost 1900, when limited-liability companies first became widespread, the London money market played little part in financing industry *per se*; but oiled the wheels of commerce, where liquid funds were constantly required to facilitate trade with the entire world.

After the South Sea Bubble, an Act of 1720 had forbidden the formation of companies except by royal charter or Act of Parliament. The Stock Exchange had therefore been confined to government stock. In the 1790s dealings in canal-company shares began, and soon afterwards water-, gas- and dock-company stocks were created. But before the railway era the Stock Exchange remained mainly concerned with public funds.

With the gradual dismantling of the restrictive eighteenth-century legislation on joint-stock companies, merchant bankers rose in London, specializing in raising money for overseas investments and for government. Following Baring's, established in 1763, eleven were founded between 1804 and 1839. Rothschild's outstripped all. As well as several great town houses in Piccadilly, the Rothschilds owned 30,000 acres of land around the Vale of Aylesbury, their country headquarters. When Baron Lionel Rothschild died in 1879, his personal estate was valued at some £2,700,000.

After the Napoleonic wars, foreign governments increasingly resorted to the City for their loans. Baring's organized the payment of French reparations, while Rothschild's floated loans for Russia, Prussia, Greece, and the new South American republics. Between 1822 and 1825 £40 million of loans for foreign states were issued in London, and numerous others besides for joint-stock companies operating abroad. London-based imperial and international banks specialized in financing international commerce. By 1900, there were over forty British overseas banks controlling a network of 1,156 branches in Asia, Latin America, Australia, Canada and South Africa. The Midland Bank, for example, had 132 foreign and colonial branches. The strength of the Bank of England gave foreigners confidence in the merchant banks.

The City thus became financier to the world. In the mid-1860s Bagehot described Lombard Street as 'by far the greatest combination of economical power and economical delicacy that the world has ever seen'. Total deposits in London banks were three times as great as in New York, and nearly ten times higher than in Paris. Investment leapt with imperial expansion, funding prairie development in Canada, public works in Australia, the Cape and the West Indies, and railways in India; between 1858 and 1867 India absorbed over £61 million of British capital. Nathan Rothschild stated in 1897 that Britain was 'in general the Bank for the whole world ... all transactions in India, in China, in Russia and in the whole world are guided here and settled through this country'. London became a honeypot for merchant-banking houses of foreign origin – George Peabody from Baltimore (later J. S. Morgan & Co.), Hambro's from Copenhagen, and Speyer's from New York – further extending the City's foreign networks. Imperial and Continental banks opened London branches: the Ottoman Bank (1863), Comptoir d'Escompte de Paris (1867), Crédit Lyonnais (1870), Société Générale (1871), the Swiss Bank Corporation (1898), and the major German, Italian, Belgian and Russian banks. These were followed by American banks – Chase Manhattan (1887), Morgan Garanty (1892) and Citibank (1902) – and the Bank of Japan arrived in 1898.

With the coming of the railways, large numbers of small investors became involved for the first time, and the Stock Exchange came into its own; but the Victorian city operated chiefly not by raising funds for domestic industry but by servicing trade, through exporting wealth in overseas investments.

Individual exchanges were built. The Metal Exchange, setting world prices, remained in the Royal Exchange until 1869. The Coal Exchange opened in 1849 in a building near the Billingsgate fish market that made experimental use of iron and a glass dome. The Old Corn Exchange handled grain and flour, the New Corn Exchange agricultural seeds. London gained a Wool Exchange in 1821, once Australian imports were influencing the market. The Baltic Exchange specialized in shipping grain, oilseeds, tallow and timber.

Insurance expanded. In the eighteenth century a number of provincial companies had been formed – notably the Norwich Union (1797) – but half a dozen London companies engrossed most of the business. The main new London firms were the Phoenix (1782), the County (1807), the Guardian (1821), and the Alliance (1824), whose backers included Alexander Baring, Samuel Gurney and Nathan Rothschild. In fire insurance, business was dominated by the big five – the Sun, the Phoenix, the Protector, the Royal Exchange and the County.

Overall, military and imperial expansion, maritime supremacy and the policy of free trade combined to make the Victorian City what David Kynaston in an expressive phrase has called 'a world of its own' – a world of big money. And this changed the very face of the City. From 1850 the great growth of clerical work demanded extensive rebuilding; imposing buildings on important sites would have the ground and first floors occupied by the building-owner and the upper floors parcelled out for offices. With the vogue for Italian *palazzi*, City architecture became a matter of prestigious façades, with offices behind to accommodate battalions of businessmen and pen-pushers. In 1851 there were 16,420 clerks in London; by 1891 five times that number. Rising demand led to clerical work being opened to women: in 1881 there were about 7,000 female clerks in London; by 1911 146,000 – changes stemming from the typewriter (1867) and the telephone (1876).

The City meanwhile declined as a residential district. Until 1850 the population of the wards was stable at around 130,000 inhabitants; thereafter it suffered rapid reduction as a result of the building of railway stations, warehouses and office blocks. By 1901 there were just 27,000 inhabitants. A double rhythm developed – daily pandemonium followed by night-time silence, broken by the bells: 'Oranges and lemons' was an audible reminder that London was a city of money.

CHAPTER NINE

'The Contagion of Numbers':
The Building of the Victorian Capital
1820–1890

It was a natural growth ... There are wide regions of London, miles of streets of houses, that appear to have been originally designed for prosperous middle-class homes of the early Victorian type. There must have been a perfect fury of such building in the thirties, forties, and fifties. Street after street must have been rushed into being, Camden Town way, Pentonville way, Brompton way, West Kensington way, in the Victoria region and all over the minor suburbs of the south side.

H. G. WELLS, Tono-Bungay (1909)

London grew astonishingly in the nineteenth century, with its hordes of labourers and landlords, its pen-pushers and porters. Between 1841 and 1851 alone, some 330,000 migrants flooded into the capital, representing a staggering 17 per cent of London's total population. Of these, 46,000 came from Ireland, fleeing famine and swelling the London Irish community to around 130,000. In the 1850s a further 286,000 migrants arrived; in the 1860s 331,000. Before 1840 the majority came from the south-east, but by the 1860s, with agriculture in crisis, the net widened; all were drawn by the hope of work, but they were also bewitched by what H. Llewellyn Smith was to call

the contagion of numbers, the sense of something going on, the theatres and the music halls, the brightly lighted streets and busy crowds – all, in short, that makes the difference between the Mile End fair on a Saturday night and a dark muddy land, with no glimmer of gas and with nothing to do. Who could wonder that men are drawn into such a vortex?

Figures speak for themselves. In 1800 London's population had been around a million. By 1881 it had soared to 4.5 million, and by 1911 to over 7 million. In 1800 around one in ten inhabitants of England and Wales dwelt in the metropolis; by 1900 it was a breathtaking one in five. The boom towns of the industrial revolution remained dwarfed – Manchester, Liverpool, Birmingham, Leeds and Glasgow had populations of between 50,000 and 100,000 in 1800, and none was to rise above a million or so.

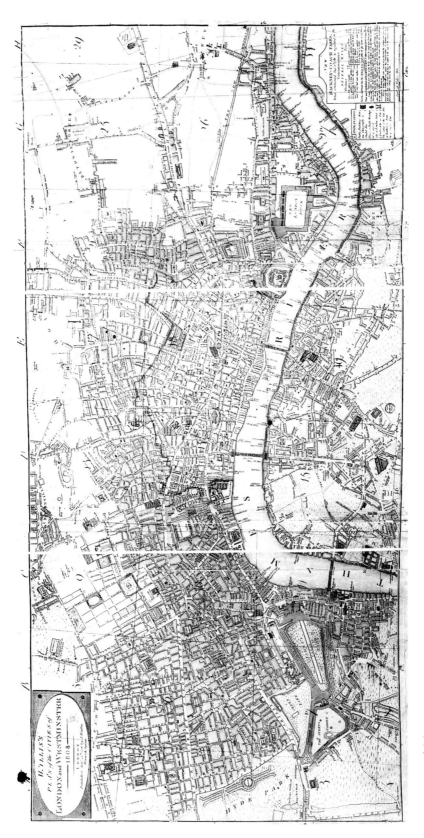

London and
Westminster, 1808

London thus formed a classic example of what has been labelled the 'primate city', one disproportionately vaster than all the others in the kingdom, a city relating not just to the nation but to the world. 'London is more than a city: it is a whole kingdom in itself,' judged Sidney Webb in 1891,

with revenues exceeding those of mighty principalities. With its suburbs it exceeds all Ireland in population: if it were emptied tomorrow the whole of the inhabitants of Scotland and Wales together could do no more than refill it: the three next largest cities in the world could almost be combined without out-numbering its millions.

It far exceeded Switzerland and Australia; it had twice the numbers of Norway or Greece. In London there were more Scotsmen than in Aberdeen, more Irishmen than in Dublin, and more Roman Catholics than in Rome. It was thus the capital of capitals: 'LONDON,' ran the opening sentence of a visitors' guide to the Great Exhibition of 1851, 'is the largest and wealthiest, as well as the most populous of the cities in the world.' 'London is unique,' reflected Friedrich Engels; 'immensity was the great fact', Henry James recalled.

The pace of expansion accelerated. The making of central districts like Holborn had been the work of centuries. The West End had emerged in the Georgian era, but that had involved but a few square miles, self-limited by the desire to maintain exclusivity. Victorian development, by contrast, was London unbound, a free-for-all, or (as Wells suggested) 'natural growth'. Unlike the Duke of Bedford in Bloomsbury, few Victorian landlords could afford to be choosy about precisely when and how their plots were developed. With numerous areas competing for capital and clients all at once – Kentish Town and Kilburn, Camberwell and Clapham, Herne Hill and Tulse Hill – property development was cut-throat. Every prudent freeholder, every speculative builder, every lessee knew that ripeness was all, that there was a moment for their field in Highbury or Hornsey, Brixton or Balham. Move prematurely and there would be no buyers; hesitate, and fashion would already have leap-frogged into the fields beyond, superior settlers would be pitching camp elsewhere, and the site would irreversibly plunge in prestige.

Development continued to rely on the tried and tested building-lease system. Plots belonging to landlords, to the Church Commissioners, to City companies and other institutions were pegged out into streets and then let off to builders on ninety-nine-year leases. The system was energized by mortgaging on a massive scale. Before 1850 it brought into being huge middle-class quarters – Barnsbury, St John's Wood, Paddington, Kensington, Chelsea, Clapham, Camberwell, Kennington. With its classical creamy terraces, crescents and squares, all such 'stuccovia' was, architecturally speaking, Nash's child, though often it spawned residences more ostentatious than their Georgian prototypes, with pilasters and porches. For, aiming to combine prestige and profit, Victorian builders dreamed of producing houses for superior clients – the carriage trade; or, a bit down the scale, businessmen and bank clerks; or, at least, master craftsmen. But there were never enough desirable buyers to go round. Demand rarely matched supply at the better end of the market, London was periodically overbuilt, and within the ceaseless trade cycles of boom and bust there were often more plots and properties than purchasers – Bloomsbury and Bayswater long had rows of ghost houses, awaiting completion or occupation, and in 1881 two in five of the 4,800 houses recently built for the petty bourgeoisie in East Dulwich couldn't find a buyer – though this was cold comfort to inner-city slum-dwellers, for whose needs no houses were ever built. The house glut, lamented *Building News*, would be revealed by 'a cursory inspection of any residential locality such as Richmond where agents' boards are sadly thick on the field'. The landlord's nightmare was to be left with unlet properties, for these were bound to fall to undesirable tenants, who would sublet, take in boarders, create 'lodging-house rot', lower the tone, and turn a potentially lucrative estate into a liability.

In the long run, however, builders' prospects remained bright, for population climbed and London was ringed by abundant cheap land – market gardens, rough grazing and piggeries – inviting development. This contributed to a feature decisively differentiating London from Paris and other Continental capitals: low urban density. Able to spread, London did. Big cities (classically New York) often involve high densities, but Victorian London had a residential density only half that of Paris, where apartment living became the norm, while London saw the proliferation of the family house, even the detached villa, as the residential ideal for those for whom the roof over their head was a matter of choice.

Aspirant folk were always moving somewhere new, more modish, seeking a villa (or at least a semi), or a house in sight of fields, further from the brickyards, the fog and the riff-raff. The coming of omnibuses and trams, overground and underground railways, meant development was never paralysed by inaccessibility or insupportably long journeys to work. The providential logic of the market kept population rise, housing demand, transport improvements and building capacity broadly abreast of each other – which is not to deny that many builders went broke, railway investors lost their savings in some of the City's more spectacular crashes, and tens of thousands ended up evicted to make way for the iron horse or found themselves at the bottom of the housing heap.

A giant thus arose, without planning or parliamentary direction, and without any overarching representative government, at least before the founding of the London County Council in 1888 – the City disclaimed responsibility for the town beyond its limits, while no ministry risked antagonizing the Corporation through creating rival popular metropolitan authorities. The strengths and shortcomings of Victorian

London were thus those of private capital. In H. G. Wells's *Tono-Bungay* the hero is shown round by his uncle: 'London, George, takes a lot of understanding,' explained the avuncular guide:

It's a great place. Immense. The richest town in the world, the biggest port, the greatest manufacturing town, the Imperial city – the centre of civilization, the heart of the world! . . . It's a wonderful place, George – a whirlpool, a maelstrom! whirls you up and whirls you down.

A scattered city – unlike Paris, which remained within the walls (converted into its great ring road, the *Péripherique*) – London was not a coherent development, dictated by government, given form by a rational road grid. In the century of Darwin – himself living beyond Bromley on London's outskirts – it was likened to some natural phenomenon, evolving spontaneously. Some saw it as confusion – 'this mighty mess the city – no! not the city, but the nation – of London', exclaimed Thomas De Quincey – but others preferred to think in terms of the organic evolution of inter-locking communities. Yet here we must avoid nostalgia. 'Village London' conjures up a myth of local identity, solid, rooted, stable, duckponds and all; in reality, London's districts were ever in flux, turbulent eddies of change, as citizens ceaselessly moved on, to avoid going down in the world.

Mobility was spurred by great material transformations, not least railways. From the 1830s the cuttings ploughed into the northern suburban areas on their routes into Euston, then King's Cross and St Pancras, reinforcing east/west social divides, devastating some areas while bettering others. By 1850 they were carving up vast swathes of south London. Everywhere, with such brutal invasions, developments were uneven: one man's convenience was another's calamity. In the disarray, some parts even became depopulated. The City suffered headlong residential decline as a result of middle-class out-migration to more salubrious quarters and the building of railway termini, warehouses and offices. The Strand, Holborn, Soho and other parts of the historic heartlands were also affected. Between 1851 and 1881, central districts shed 135,000 people in a new segregation of urban space accentuating contrasts between business and residential areas, the rough and the respectable, and involving long-distance commuting.

Dislocation and relocation were always occurring – nothing ever stood still, nothing was constant except mobility itself, as Romantics rediscovered the country and sani-tarians stressed the hazards of inner-city miasmata. First the plutocrats, then the professionals and lesser businessmen, and finally the shopkeepers quit Cheapside and Clerkenwell for suburbs like Primrose Hill and Herne Hill, or later Muswell Hill and Beulah Hill, while, pushed and shoved by central overcrowding, the poor wormed themselves into erstwhile middle-class strongholds, precipitating neighbourhood depreciation. Once-imposing niches of stuccovia such as Westbourne Park quickly became seedy or even slummy. In the 1820s the site of gracious villa-building and then long the outpost of respectable clerks, Holloway was run-down by 1900; the building of the jail in 1852 had not helped (and in 1910 Hilldrop Crescent was the scene of the Crippen case). Once-elegant Islington followed. And the same process was evident in working-class districts too. Silvertown, by the 'Royal' docks, was built for the better sort of carpenters, stevedores and dock gaffers. Yet they were soon moving out to East Ham, Upton Park and other newer, nicer neighbourhoods, their place being taken by costermongers and casual dock labourers.

Around 1800, London's informal border ran from Vauxhall Bridge to Park Lane, then up the Edgware Road, along Marylebone Road and City Road and southwards past Mile End, reaching the Thames at Shadwell. Apart from the capsules of Greenwich and Woolwich, London south of the river formed an arc from Lambeth to Rotherhithe. By 1850 the metropolitan tentacles had reached further out, and the spaces in between were being transformed into stuccovia, into goods and marshalling yards, and into wastelands where, as Dickens observed of parts of Holloway, 'tiles and bricks were burnt, bones were boiled, carpets were beat, rubbish was shot, dogs were fought, and dust was heaped by contractors'. In time these abandoned areas ('a suburban Sahara') were themselves built upon. In view of this changing picture of teeming local mutation, it makes sense to tour developments area by area.

Because the West End was so fashionable, town inevitably spread further westward still. Hyde Park and Kensington Gardens of course cut a great sacred wedge, a 'green belt', into the area – 'Within the memory of many now living,' Henry Fielding had noted as early as 1752,

the circle of the people of Fascination included the whole parish of Covent Garden and a great part of St Giles in the Fields and Golden Square. Hence the People of Fashion again retreated before the foe to Hanover Square; whence they were once more driven to Grosvenor Square and even beyond it, and that with so much precipitation, that had they not been stopped by the walls of Hyde Park, it is more than probable they would by this time have arrived at Kensington.

Development therefore had to be south, north and west of the inviolable parks.

To the south there was a pair of prime movers: a landowner, the Marquess of Westminster, and his builder, Thomas Cubitt, who between them were jointly responsible for Belgravia and its poor relation Pimlico, lying in the elbow of the Thames between Chelsea and Westminster. Cubitt was the age's greatest builder, the man who out-Burtoned Burton. Whereas James Burton had subcontracted work to specialist craftsmen, Cubitt gathered the entire business under his belt, organizing the first large-scale building firm, with some 2,000 employees, and hiring all craftsmen from plumbers to painters. Only a man combining vision with resourcefulness could have developed Belgravia.

Cubitt began with the Calthorpe estate, close to his Gray's Inn Road workshops, and then laid out Barnsbury, where he established his brick-fields. From 1821 he completed Burton's work in Bloomsbury, building Endsleigh Street, Tavistock Square, Gordon Square, Woburn Place and Woburn Walk, designed as a bijou shopping centre with bow-fronted shops. He dabbled simultaneously in Stoke Newington, Clapham and Camden Town; he also built Cubitt Town on the Isle of Dogs, a complex of brick-fields, sawmills, timber wharves, and cement and iron works that secured his supplies; and he had a hand in erecting the east front of Buckingham Palace – to say nothing of assisting Prince Albert with Osborne, the Italianate villa on the Isle of Wight destined to become Queen Victoria's great love.

Cubitt's prime enterprise lay to the west, however. Back in the 1780s Knightsbridge had been linked to Chelsea by the Hans Town development, Sloane Street forming its spine. East of Sloane Street, however, the Grosvenor estate, lacking the underlying gravel vital for drainage, had long been regarded as too boggy for building. Just as the Grosvenors had made their fortune out of Mayfair in the eighteenth century, Cubitt turned this quagmire into a gold-field for them.

The rebuilding nearby of Buckingham Palace by George IV provided the signal for development. From 1825 Cubitt raised the level, using spoil barged up the river from St Katharine's Dock (which he was also building), and laid out the most prestigious development yet attempted in London, with the ten-acre Belgrave Square as its *pièce de résistance*. 'This extensive area,' reported a contemporary, 'is now covering with mansions and handsome houses, laid out with beautiful plantations destined ... to be the future residences of the highest class of the fashionable world.' (Lady Bracknell's subsequent dark hint about the unfashionable side of Belgrave Square may have been a touch overstated.) Included in the development were Eaton Square and Eaton Place, taking their name from Eaton Hall, Cheshire, the Grosvenors' country seat. Chopin gave his first London recital at 99 Eaton Place, in 1848.

Long a patchwork of market gardens supplying Westminster, Pimlico was designed by Cubitt to serve as Belgravia's cheaper outer buffer, and it opened up the north bank of the Thames for building. By mid-century, development stretched west up to Chelsea village, an outlying retreat with a picturesque air. Fulham was still a market-gardening village, but by the 1870s it had 'become a portion of the outer fringe of the great city'. Hammersmith was to become an industrial as well as a dormitory suburb, boasting engineering works, distilleries, mills, boatyards and pumping works.

Meanwhile, abutting Pimlico, Millbank also developed on the Grosvenor estate, west of Horseferry Road and east of the awesome New Penitentiary (erected in 1821, where the Tate Gallery now stands). The key figure here was the energetic builder

John Johnson, a man who, though lacking Cubitt's genius, got a lot done. By the early 1820s streets had been built as far as Vincent Square (one modestly being called Johnson Street), and there were commercial developments too: in 1825 a site in Little Holywell Street adjoining the Gas-Light and Coke Company premises included industrial workshops and stables. Like all big builders, Johnson received leases from Earl Grosvenor, and laid out sites, drains, cellars and vaults in Holywell, Earl, Market and Peter Streets and Vincent Street (later called Wilton Street) adjacent to the penitentiary. Plain Millbanks were always needed to service palatial Belgravias.

North of Hyde Park, the West End spread beyond Marble Arch and the Edgware Road into Tyburnia (Paddington), after public executions had ended at Tyburn in 1783. Long a quaint clump of houses around the village green – it was one of the haunts of the weird prophetess Joanna Southcott – Paddington was energized by the cutting in 1801 of the Grand Junction Canal, with its wharf just west of the Edgware Road. The Bishop of London then embarked on a high-class building scheme on part of the 600-acre Church estates in the parish. After stops and starts and building failures, by the 1830s a handsome thoroughfare, Sussex Gardens, was completed, with carriage roads and a communal garden. Thereafter building accelerated, and within a decade Paddington had become a fashionable residential colony. In turn it stimulated development farther west: tea gardens, bowling-greens and even a suburban race course (the Hippodrome at Notting Hill) were set up as amenities, and speculators began to plant building estates.

Bayswater was the grandest of these smart neighbourhoods. It began modestly in the 1840s, with villas lining the curving Westbourne Park; larger town houses followed in the 1850s in Lancaster Gate, by Kensington Gardens, and in long terraces linking Westbourne Grove with the Bayswater Road. The moneyed paid £2,000 or more for them, maintaining half a dozen servants per family. By the 1860s Bayswater was attracting majors returning from India and was becoming a symbol of Imperial London. Commerce followed: fashionable drapers moved into Westbourne Grove, and William Whiteley's new department store drew the carriage trade. Bayswater's social character grew mixed, as some residential streets were taken over for hotels and shops, drawing a working population of milliners and shop assistants. Jewish and Greek families moved in, and Bayswater Road developed a cosmopolitan glitter (some said nasty vulgarity).

On the opposite side of Hyde Park, South Kensington – also formerly market gardens – developed with handsome terraces and squares built for illustrious Victorians around the museums arising after 1856 on land bought with the profits of the Great Exhibition. Three splendid new roads were laid out: Queen's Gate and Exhibition Road, leading south from Hyde Park, and Cromwell Road (named after a house supposedly lived in by the Protector) running west. Ornate five-storey Italianate stuccoed terraces were built, attracting top-notch residents – the Duke of Rutland lived in Cromwell Road, and Exhibition Road later housed Joseph Chamberlain. Onslow Gardens and Square formed a principal residential area – William Thackeray occupied 36 Onslow Square – as did the Boltons, with its double crescents of stuccoed houses with gardens and a church between.

The post-1850 decades saw the systematic building-up of Kensington south and west towards Fulham and Hammersmith, hitherto market gardens. With the advent of the District Railway, it was said in 1873 of West Kensington that building was

rapidly carried on where speculative builders had money or credit; the tall houses, detached or semi-detached, or in closed lines improperly called 'terraces' which ultimately became the sides of streets, rose up in a few months, roofed and windowed and calling for tenants.

In West Kensington, houses erected by the builders Gibbs & Flew Ltd sold well because they contained all the latest fittings, being provided with 'hot and cold water … while the encaustic tiles, stained glass and marble fenders give them an attractive appearance not often to be found in houses of this class'. West Kensington actually attracted the smart inhabitants for whom the district was intended.

Such could not be said of all of London's westerly development. Some was too close to patches of the poor; other zones became sullied by commerce and railways. Paddington, for instance, became allied westwards to Notting Hill via smart, Italianate Westbourne Terrace, Leinster and Princes Squares, and Hyde Park Gardens. Yet Paddington was always precarious, because rookeries lay nearby – north-west Kensington was notorious for its rough and migratory population, mainly of pig-keepers – and Paddington itself had a poor community round the canal basin, north-east of the Great Western Railway terminus. The railway and the Kensal Green gasworks attracted smiths, stokers and labourers, for whom housing was run up around the Harrow Road. By the 1860s the Metropolitan Railway intensified the need for cheap lodgings, and the 'respectable' working class began an exodus from the streets by the canal and railway, condemning the area to become a classic slum. Rags and riches thus eyed each other in Paddington, and social frontiers shifted as streets filled up with hosts of people dependent upon West End casual work.

Similar chequered development occurred further west. Tall rows of superior houses spread round Earl's Court Road and, to the south, the Redcliffe estate was genteel. Earl's Court itself, however, adjoined earlier developments to the east, where back in the 1820s the irrepressible John Johnson had built the factory of the wax-bleachers Freeman & Child at what became Child's Place, Child's Walk and Child's Street. Local bricklayers constructed houses, workyards and stables, while Johnson himself ran up (no surprise) Johnson's Place. Another Johnson development involved ten acres

London at the end of
the eighteenth century

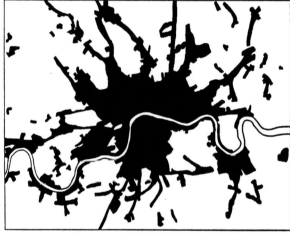

London in the 1830s

London in the 1870s

at Kensington Gravel Pits, near today's Notting Hill tube station. In the mid-1820s Johnson Street (yet another! – now Hillgate Street), Uxbridge Street and Kensington and Durham Places were erected by small builders around the old brick-field.

Every neighbourhood acquired a flavour of its own. East of Wormwood Scrubs, Notting Dale was popularly known as the 'piggeries and potteries' (there were said to be over 3,000 pigs and 1,000 humans). Conditions were described by the sanitary reformer Edwin Chadwick as 'filthy in the extreme', while Dickens portrayed it as 'a plague spot scarcely equalled in insalubrity by any other part of London'. Its largely Irish inhabitants (many settling there after eviction from slums knocked down to make way for railways) squeezed a living from pig-keeping, brickmaking, street selling and laundry. Squalid lodging-houses and furnished rooms abounded, with one public house for every twenty-five dwellings. As late as the 1890s, half the children born in the district died in their first year.

Yet but a mile to the south-east, Notting Hill scored. The Hippodrome racecourse built there in 1837, north of the Portobello Road, proving a flop, it was replaced by the striking Ladbroke estate, its axis being Ladbroke Grove, its centre St John's church. The superior gardens and squares constructed west of Kensington Park Road and north as far as Elgin Crescent attracted paired villas set in picturesque crescents. 'Leafy Ladbroke' spread east towards Bayswater and south of Westbourne Grove to include by the 1860s Chepstow Villas, Pembridge Villas and Pembridge Square. 'Kensington Park' became a district of handsome houses.

The development petered out towards the north, however. By the mid-1860s house-building for the wealthy had outrun demand, and Ladbroke Grove stopped short south of where the Hammersmith and City line was soon to run. Buildings off the beaten track, around Colville and Powis Squares, were unlucky from the start, being among the first in Kensington to be sliced up into multiple occupancy, declining by the 1870s into lodgings and bedsits.

Just to the south, however, Holland Park established itself as highly stylish, helped by the rising ground of Campden Hill and by Holland House, with its classy Whig salons. Turner painted sunsets from Campden Hill Square, while avant-garde architects and sculptors settled where Holland Park merges into Kensington, in Melbury Road, Holland Park Road and Addison Road – the architect William Burges designing 29 Melbury Road for himself as 'a model residence of the fifteenth century'. Holland Park's most exotic building was, however, 8 Addison Road. Built in 1906 for the store tycoon Sir Ernest Debenham, the walls, roof and interior of 'the Peacock House' were clad in dazzling blue and green tiles.

London washed westward to Hammersmith village – like Fulham, long known for its spinach and strawberries. Development brought no glory to Hammersmith, which became the terminal of the omnibus routes, and later trains, to the City – *Punch* liked to satirize the pretentious but much put-upon Hammersmith commuter. Cottages went up on boggy lands near Brook Green, mainly for Irish labourers drawn by brickmaking and work on the West London Railway. As late as 1856 only 2,000 houses had piped water, for (unlike Paddington or Kensington) Hammersmith had few landowners willing or able to invest in 'improvements' and thus attract ambitious speculators. Shepherd's Bush became plastered with two- and three-storey houses and small shops, bought up by traders and clerks with building-society mortgages. (By 1854 there were well over sixty freehold land societies operating in London and its suburbs, almost all locally based.) The penetration of the Metropolitan Railway to Hammersmith in 1864 accelerated development, the planting of stations in the open fields (Latimer Road, Goldhawk Road) encouraging speculators to buy up small-holdings. Hammersmith developers met the demands of the respectable lower middle class for solid but affordable homes.

Beyond Hammersmith, Chiswick had long been a rural retreat of farms and market gardens sprinkled with country houses. It was hardly urbanized until the railway. The first station was opened in 1849; in 1869 Turnham Green Station and Brentford Road (now Gunnersbury) followed. Horse trams, started in 1882 between Hammersmith and Kew Bridge and succeeded in 1901 by electric trams, further opened up Chiswick, Gunnersbury, Brentford and Kew.

Ealing too had long been renowned for its 200-odd market gardens. Its emergence as a middle-class suburb dates from the 1850s, when prosperous Londoners began installing themselves in villas: at the 1861 Census a sixth of Ealing households were classified as professional and managerial, compared with less than a twentieth in nearby Acton. (In 1911 Ealing still had a larger proportion of professional people and merchants than any other west-London locality; the 'Queen of the Suburbs' was famed for its healthy environment, superior villas and good amenities.) Industrial blight was avoided, and working-class accommodation was largely confined to West Ealing (Stevens Town). Commuting was improved by the construction in 1879 of the Ealing extension of the Metropolitan District Railway, with stations at Ealing Broadway and Ealing Common, followed by Northfields, South Ealing and North Ealing. In 1901 trams started running along the Uxbridge Road from Shepherd's Bush west to Southall, paving the way for cheaper estates.

Ealing long remained a middle-class dormitory, but centres of employment grew nearby. Like Notting Dale, Acton became a laundry centre. With budding factory employment, working people moved into the western suburbs after 1900, especially once the LCC began building in Hammersmith and Acton and transport was improved with electrification and the 'Twopenny Tube' (Central London Railway) from Shepherd's Bush to the City. Acton and Hammersmith became 'suburbs of production'.

*

The building story just told in some detail for west London applies, with different names and local twists, to many other districts. There is no room here to repeat it at length for St John's Wood, Maida Vale and Kilburn, or for Hampstead and West Hampstead, or Wandsworth and Wimbledon. Some districts became refined, others scruffy slums, as any Sunday stroll across the inner suburbs will show. A walk north-west from the Georgian elegance of Highbury Place (1774–9) or Highbury Terrace (1789), through the majestic Gothic glories of mid-Victorian Highbury New Park, rapidly leads into the cluttered misnomer of Drayton Park, all railway sidings and industrial odds and ends and jumbled neglect. Development was occurring every-where, and whether a particular zone rose or slid down-market depended upon hosts of local eventualities: the lie of the land (high ground was always superior, proving invulnerable to canals and railway tracks), the savvy of landlords, the proximity of transport and industry – to say nothing of timing and luck. Superb historical studies of districts such as Hampstead, Kentish Town, St Pancras and Camberwell have traced such developments street by street and decade by decade. Hence the rest of the tale of the bricking over of Victorian London will be broad-brush.

Like the contrasting South and North Kensington, or Notting Hill and Dale, north London developed its own adjacent yet intensely divergent communities: plebeian Somers Town, east of Hampstead Road, was within twenty minutes' walk of noble Regent's Park. Indeed, the park served as a great wall of London, demarcating the superior west from inferior parts eastward, John Nash keeping the barbarians at bay with the Albany Street barrier, preserving 'that best-built part of the town from the annoyance and disgrace which threaten it on either side'. East of the park, as Nash well knew, lay Lord Southampton's estate, where inferior houses were shooting up around the Hampstead Road owing to slack estate management and development beyond demand. 'Houses of such a mean sort as have been built at Somers Town,' complained Nash, 'and are now building on Lord Southampton's should disgrace this apex of the Metropolis, particularly as there is sufficient space on the lower grounds for any increase of buildings required for the lower classes.' East of the Southampton estate, still inferior development was started by Sir Charles Cocks, Bart, made Baron Somers in 1784. And east of Somers Town arose what early Victorians saw as the foulest north London development of all, Agar Town – or 'Ague Town' as it was dubbed. 'The place, in its present state, is a disgrace to the metropolis,' wrote W. M. Thomas in 1851 in an article for Charles Dickens's *Household Words*, entitled 'A Suburban Connemara':

It has sprung up in about ten years. Old haunts of dirt and misery, suffered to exist in times when the public paid no attention to such matters, are difficult to deal with; but this is a new evil, which only began to come into existence about the time when Mr Chadwick's Report first brought before the public a picture of the filthy homes and habits of the labouring classes, and of the frightful amount of crime and misery resulting therefrom. In Agar Town we have, within a short walk of the City, . . . a perfect reproduction of one of the worst towns in Ireland.

Fortunately, this shanty town with no proper drainage did not long survive, being taken over by the Midland Railway Company and demolished to make way for the St Pancras line (though not before Dan Leno, the great pantomime dame, was born there, in 1861).

Lower-class in character, Somers Town was yet another scheme of the ubiquitous John Johnson. In the 1820s he put up Seymour Street (now Eversholt Street) and its backstreets, using a number of local builders – for instance, a certain Thomas Ridyard, who built ten houses in Clarendon Street and nineteen in Little Clarendon Street and Johnson Street (yet another – now Cranleigh Street).

Just beyond, Camden Town developed, slowly at first but rapidly after 1820, when the Regent's Canal traversed the area, bringing coal wharves, builders' yards and industry. Charles Dickens lived as a boy in 15 Bayham Street, a small house of four rooms, basement and garret rented for £22 a year. (Bob Cratchit lived there too.) Dickens captured the scruffy, unfinished state of the neighbourhood in *Dombey and Son*:

There were frowzy fields, and cow-houses, and dung hills, and dust-heaps, and ditches, and gardens, and summer-houses, and carpet-beating grounds . . . little tumuli of oyster shells in the oyster season, and of lobster shells in the lobster season, and of broken crockery and faded cabbage leaves in all seasons . . . posts, and rails, and old cautions to trespassers, and backs of mean houses, and patches of wretched vegetation.

The area north of the New Road was transformed by the Regent's Canal into an industrial suburb. By the canalside in Somers Town arose the vast Imperial Company gasworks, built in 1822, still so conspicuous from trains leaving St Pancras; the canal also brought timber and building materials to Battle Bridge Wharf (King's Cross), numerous works and warehouses there supplying the building trade. Timber brought up by canal led to furniture and piano manufacturing in the St Pancras and Tottenham Court Road areas. Huge railway yards later completed the area's industrial make-up, still highly visible today.

Industry drew people. Thanks to the canal, St Pancras's population zoomed to 104,000 in the decade after 1821. Severe overcrowding resulted, particularly around Hampden Street, Brill Crescent and Brill Terrace, which became notorious slums. The terraces around Chalton and Ossulston Streets, all dingy courts and backyard

George Cruikshank's 1829 cartoon of the horrors of urban development, 'London Going out of Town'. This particular satire refers to plans for Camden Town

industries, were demolished under the Housing of the Working Classes Act of 1890, leading to one of the capital's first large-scale public-housing schemes. By the 1930s many of Johnson's houses, long bug-infested slums, were demolished (though a few can still be seen).

Somers Town scandalized the Duke of Bedford, anxious to maintain the tone of his Bloomsbury estates immediately to the south. He reacted by erecting a cordon sanitaire. 'There had always been a privilege of crossing the fields on the Bedford Estate uninterrupted in the memory of man,' it was observed, 'but when that street [Seymour Street: today's Eversholt Street] was nearly completed and a road across the fields really necessary; it was suddenly stopped and the fields barricaded to the general dismay of the holders of property.' Not content with blocking off Seymour Street, the Duke also cut off Union Street (now Chalton Street). Finally he completed his insulation of his estate from Somers Town by erecting gates at the entrance south of the Euston Road – these remained in place until the 1890s.

Having completed Woburn and Torrington Squares, the Duke himself began to develop north of Euston Road on Figs Mead, the fields north-west of Somers Town (now Mornington Crescent, Ampthill Estate and Harrington Square). His Figs Mead scheme was intended as a model middle-class suburb containing second- and third-rate houses; to ensure respectability, it was to be free of the backstreets that inevitably turned into industrial yards. This development, like so many, was wrecked by the railway – the building of Euston station proceeding despite objections from the Duke of Bedford and the Marquis of Camden.

Meanwhile, just east of the Duke's Bloomsbury properties arose a mixed development. Land owned by the Skinners' Company, including Judd Street, built between 1808 and 1816, was developed by James Burton. Thanet Street, behind Judd Street, still has some handsome two-storey workmen's cottages, built in 1812–22, showing that homes for artisans did not have to become slums.

Inner north London arose from the fields in a swathe from Kensal Rise through Kentish Town and Newington to Shacklewell, Haggerston, Dalston and Hackney. By 1850 this terrain lay in the shadow of the railway, an equivocal power that might bring accessibility and prosperity – or environmental havoc. For centuries Gospel Oak had been a hamlet off the beaten track between Hampstead and Highgate Roads, with pastures and watercress-beds irrigated by a tributary of the Fleet. Gordon House Road was created in 1806, but Gospel Oak Fields remained, and a fair was held there until the 1850s. Lords Mansfield, Southampton and Lismore all held land in the area (today remembered in street names). Developments were planned with elegant semi-detached villas, but, as happened elsewhere, everything deteriorated with the railways. The North London Railway, the Tottenham and Hampstead Junction Railway and, above all, the Midland Railway, St-Pancras-bound, violated the fields of Kentish Town, Gospel Oak and Chalk Farm with acre upon acre of shunting-yards; by 1867 the area designated for Lismore Circus was still only a 'mud island'. But around the railways less ambitious terraces appeared. Grafton and Malden Roads were built for artisans and clerks; while the fields north of Mansfield Road, whose potential had been spoiled once the railway had cut them off from Hampstead Heath, still obtained some superior housing.

South End, Hampstead, was a similar story. Land was owned by the Dean and Chapter of Westminster. One of the leaseholders was William Lund, with forty-five acres off Haverstock Hill. He tried for a 'St John's Wood'-style development, calling his estate St John's Park. With Hampstead station newly opened on the North London line, he hoped to attract City people, and within ten years he had built sixty semi-detached villas. But elements beyond his control wrecked his plans. The adjacent River

Fleet became an open sewer by the 1850s. A branch of the Midland Railway into St Pancras was tunnelled under the estate. And, to cap it all, a fever hospital was put up nearby to cope with smallpox epidemics. Poor Lund was left with unlet houses. A distraught resident of Upper Park Road grumbled about the blight, in all too familiar tones: 'The older houses are already greatly deteriorated in value ... after expending a large sum of money in purchasing, furnishing and fitting up this house it will be very annoying to be driven away.'

Change everywhere. Surveying suburban progress in the early 1860s from the heights of Primrose Hill, the journalist George Rose Emerson recalled that within living memory 'at its feet were swamps intersected by green lanes, leading from Marylebone fields and Tottenham Court':

Sixty years ago even the hill was as secluded and rural, as completely removed from the hum and bustle of a great city, as any Sussex or Devonshire hillock. Now, as we look Londonwards, we find that the metropolis has thrown out its arms and embraced us, not yet with a stifling clutch, but with ominous closeness ... St. John's Wood, spruce and trim, invades us on the right, and on the opposite side are huge railway stations, circular engine-factories, house upon house, and street upon street ... A huge cutting [the Euston Railway] traverses the valley at our feet, and pierces the bowels of the green hill ... But the tall trees crowning the ridge of Hampstead Hill are yet untouched ... and we willingly forget, that farther eastward, the once green slopes of Holloway are crowded with houses, and that castellated prisons rear their dismal and defiant towers.

Gospel Oak, he noted, was becoming 'covered with terraces and crescents; and Kentish Town is throwing out lines of bricks and mortar to meet its neighbours, Hampstead Heath and Downshire Hill'.

Emerson also gazed east. Hackney, Clapton and Dalston comprised, he believed – it may surprise us nowadays – 'one of the handsomest suburbs of London'. Hackney still wore 'an old-fashioned air'; 'Dalston has thrown out long lines of handsome villas across the fields and orchards on the south-west; Clapton has developed itself on the north-east ... and down in the Marshes ... are now large hives of manufacturing industry.' The creation of Victoria Park had enhanced nearby holdings.

This early Victorian image is worth recalling, since modern notions of the 'East End' all too readily exclude everything except dockland. That east London was, of course, real enough. At its heart, with its warehouses, docks, industry and tumbledown tenements, lay Stepney, with a quarter of a million people by 1850, no public drainage but a name for cholera. To the north lay Bethnal Green, by then infamous for slums.

*

In the post-1815 boom, the area was built over with small weavers' houses, with attic workrooms, but the trade folded. Farther east, the new West India and East India Docks, with the handsome new Commercial Road to the City, filled Poplar with dockers and local industrial workers. Beyond Poplar, Cubitt Town was meant to have a promontory, facing Greenwich, that would become the nucleus of a villa colony; but middle-class residents – then as now – were not attracted, and its population remained plebeian. 'They are for the most part countrymen imported some years back to break a combination of corn porters,' observed Beatrice Webb somewhat later of the Millwall dockers: 'cut off by their residence in the interior of the Isle of Dogs from the social influences of the East-end, they have retained many traits of provincial life.'

East London was a quilt of contrasts. North of the City, Shoreditch had become urbanized in the eighteenth century. After 1800, the timber and furniture industry around the canal provoked middle-class emigration; then, after 1850, some of the 100,000 largely working-class inhabitants were in their turn levered out by the overspill of City offices. Adjacent Hoxton and Finsbury saw in the 1820s and 1830s the building of pleasant residences for clerks and minor professionals; and Dalston and Stoke Newington, earlier a Quaker centre, filled in from the south. Islington conferred a certain dignity upon its borders. De Beauvoir Town, Hackney, was planned and in part built as a coordinated grid of streets and squares. The land had been inherited by a clergyman called Benyon who adopted the name of de Beauvoir and planned a superior estate, with, as its centre-piece, a large piazza from which diagonal roads would radiate to four smaller corner gardens. Only the south-east garden – today's De Beauvoir Square – was built, but the unusual diagonal roads nearby – Stamford, Ardleigh and Enfield – stem from the plan.

East London's population went up by leaps and bounds. Under Victoria, Poplar soared from 31,000 to 169,000 and Stepney by 100,000. Its position near the river and the availability of unskilled labour made it a magnet for the destitute and the displaced from all over Britain and the world.

Perhaps the most sensational transformation of the century lay to the south. London south of the river had always amounted to little more than Southwark (the Borough) and a ribbon of riverside industry up to Deptford, with the enclaves of Greenwich and Woolwich beyond.

Around 1800, Southwark was dominated by a tangle of works and warehouses and infilled with slums: one location, Jacob's Island (now Jacob Street, Bermondsey), was made notorious by *Oliver Twist*. But up-river there were Battersea's market gardens and what Dickens called 'cow fields, mud ditches, river embankments, [and] a waste expanse of what attempted to pass for country', though in 1842 Gideon Mantell wrote more charitably that Battersea Fields were covered on Sundays with 'tens of thousands of mechanics, little tradesmen, apprentices, and their wives and sweethearts'. Down-river the Surrey Commercial Dock Company chose Rotherhithe for its site, begun in 1809: warehouses and cheap housing followed. To the east, Deptford Creek had industry, boatyards and ship-repairing. Beyond Deptford the tone rose. With its palace and the Royal Naval Hospital and nearby picturesque Blackheath, Greenwich had

Southwark, 1799, from *Horwood's Map*

always been fashionable. It was absorbed into the built-up area only around mid-century. Woolwich crept westward, with its Royal Arsenal, Dockyard, Royal Military Academy and Royal Artillery Barracks, and its extensive riverside trade; and Charlton swelled.

South London began inexorable expansion after 1750 thanks to the building of Westminster and Blackfriars Bridges, and the new toll-roads radiating from St George's Circus. Improved access made south London an attractive, or at least affordable, place to live. Clapham was classy. As early as 1690 a stagecoach service had been established to Gracechurch Street, and handsome Queen Anne houses were built. Late in life, John Evelyn recorded, Samuel Pepys lived at Clapham 'in a very noble house and sweate place where he enjoyed the fruit of his labour in great prosperity'. Clapham Marsh was drained in 1760 to become Clapham Common, and 'the Saints', the Clapham Sect of wealthy evangelical Anglicans, became a presence. Camberwell too developed a genteel reputation, especially around The Grove, where the eminent physician John Coakley Lettsom set up residence. According to the Quaker philanthropist Priscilla Wakefield, Camberwell was 'a pleasant retreat of those citizens who have a taste for the country whilst their avocations daily call them to town'. Towards the Old Kent Road, however, Walworth and North Peckham grew industrialized after the digging of the Grand Surrey Canal. The opening of Vauxhall Bridge in 1816 led to the cutting of the Camberwell New Road direct from Kennington to Camberwell Green, replacing the ominous Cut Throat Lane. Thanks to further bridges (Waterloo in 1817, Southwark in 1819), when Victoria came to the throne Camberwell was already part of greater London.

Between Clapham and Camberwell, Brixton emerged after 1800 as an eligible suburb, especially Angell Town, with its wide curving streets opening off Wiltshire Road (including the significantly named Villa Road). City businessmen set up in spacious villas on the slopes of Denmark Hill and Herne Hill. It riled William Cobbett to find 'two entire miles of stock jobbers' houses on this one road'. Among those condemned by Cobbett would certainly have been the Ruskin family. John Ruskin's father, a City wine merchant, initially lived in Hunter Street, off Brunswick Square, Bloomsbury – though each summer the family moved to Hampstead or Dulwich. In 1823 he took a three-storey semi-detached at Herne Hill, continuing to travel daily to his office. By 1842 he could afford a detached house on Denmark Hill.

The Ruskins formed part of a more general exodus; the gradual expansion of residences and terraces along the main roads, accelerating since 1750, was giving way to something altogether more systematic, to what the *Builder* (the leading trade paper) at mid-century called the 'immense speculations in building which now give life and activity to the metropolis and its environs':

Kennington-common, Stockwell, Brixton, South Lambeth, Wandsworth-road, Vauxhall, and the more remote parts of the parish, are formed into streets and rows of first, second and third-rate buildings. Several squares have been formed and churches erected. Much taste is displayed in the architectural style of the suburban villas and cottages; but amidst this mass of buildings which strike the eye in almost every direction, hundreds of houses remain unoccupied. How so many private residences can find occupants is a question not easily solved.

The creation after 1800 of inner suburbs – Kensington and Kentish Town, Stockwell and Shacklewell – encouraged changing forms of mobility, which in turn resulted in further transformations of the urban landscape. After centuries that had brought little alteration in ways of getting about, the Victorians created a transportation revolution that changed not just the face of town but the status map of the metropolis.

London could expand as just described thanks to certain minor improvements in conveyance, allowing merchants and clerks to live three, four or five miles away from the City. The rich, of course, had their own carriages; hackneys were available, and hansom cabs were introduced in 1834. Some got to work by short-stage coaches (four or six passengers inside and a handful outside), plying from suburban Kew, Belsize Park, Clapham or Islington. And the middle class was still in the habit of walking.

But the omnibus began the commuter revolution. The first service was set up in July 1829 by George Shillibeer, running from the Stingo public house, Paddington, to the Bank, along the New Road (today's Marylebone, Euston and Pentonville Roads). Shillibeer's omnibuses were long, three-horse vehicles with benches for twenty passengers. Each held more than a short-stage coach, and fares were lower. His venture failed, however, and he was bankrupt by March 1831. The future of omnibuses was assured by the Stage Carriages Act of 1832, which abolished the hackney carriages' monopoly, thus allowing omnibuses into the central area. The omnibus companies grew, especially the London General Omnibus Company, which in the 1850s started buying out other concerns; by 1900 it owned nearly half the 3,000 horse-drawn buses and trams, carrying some 500 million passengers a year.

Horse-drawn buses remained middle-class, starting at eight, long after the working classes were at work. They proved effective, however, in permitting suburban living among tradesmen and clerks unable to afford a private carriage, with all the costly stabling, coachmen and horses that involved. The omnibus gave the inner suburbs a crucial boost.

It led, some thirty years later, to the horse tram, which made inner-suburb living easier for those lower on the social ladder. The tram was a cheap conveyance designed for respectable working folks. Being lower-class, the tram was from the start kept out of central London. Horse trams ran from working-class suburbs such as Poplar or

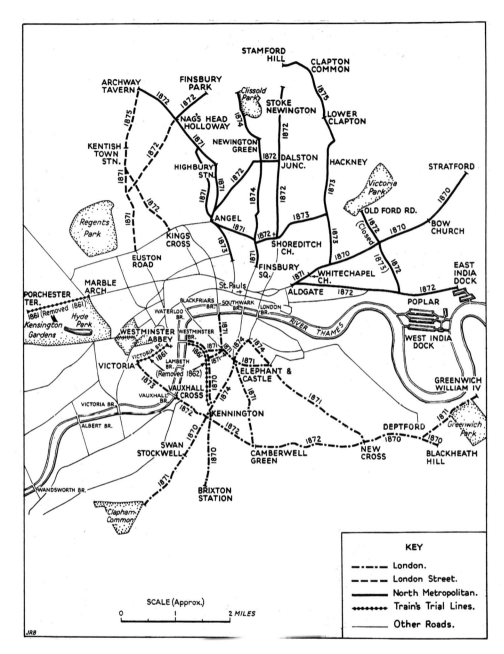

London's horse-drawn tram system in 1875

THE CONTAGION OF NUMBERS': THE BUILDING OF THE VICTORIAN CAPITAL

Deptford only to the central fringes. 'The bringing of these lines to the centre of London has always been . . . rigorously and successfully opposed . . . on the plea that it lowers the character of the thoroughfare,' observed the journalist A. H. Beavan as late as 1901.

Three tram companies received parliamentary authorization in 1869. The Metropolitan Company began running from Brixton to Kennington, and the North Metropolitan from Bow to Whitechapel – in the first six months this route carried a million passengers. Another service went from Blackheath to New Cross. Early horse trams carried forty-six passengers and charged 1d a mile: companies were also compelled to operate workmen's trams at $\frac{1}{2}$d a mile before 7 a.m. and after 6 p.m. Trams flourished; by 1898 there were 147 miles of lines, served by 1,451 trams with 14,000 horses.

These improvements in road transport increased mobility and filled the streets. By 1900 a staggering 690 omnibuses per hour were passing the Bank, and nearly as many crossed Piccadilly Circus. Bus and tram journeys per Londoner increased fivefold between 1881 and 1913. This presumably represented greater freedom; it also shows that changing domiciles were forcing people to travel more.

Swelling traffic – phaetons, hansoms, tilburies, growlers, dogcarts, gigs, broughams, landaus – problems with horses, and livestock being driven to Smithfield led to the appalling traffic jams about which so many Victorians griped and which Doré evoked in his famous view of Ludgate Hill. But, because London lacked unified municipal government, little was done to tackle traffic problems. With few policemen on point-duty, no traffic-lights (before 1929) and no one-way systems, jams could be grim, especially round Snow Hill and the foot of the steep Ludgate Hill (Holborn Viaduct was not open until 1869).

Some road improvements were made, however. Beyond the central area, turnpike roads were constructed like the New North Road (1812) and Archway Road (1813), carved out of Highgate Hill to reduce the gradient. A turnpike was built from Marylebone to Tottenham, now forming Albany Street, Parkway, Camden Road and Seven Sisters Road, though the plan to turn this into a north-east exit, Epping-bound, came to little. The new Caledonian Road provided a quick route into the City from Highgate, Hornsey and Holloway. Most ambitious of all, the Finchley Road (1826–35) provided a direct six-mile link from the West End to the North Road passing west of London's northern heights.

In 1826 the fourteen north-London turnpike trusts were amalgamated under one body of commissioners. But tolls remained – being payable not just on roads but on bridges too. Only London, Blackfriars and Westminster Bridges were free of toll until the Metropolitan Board of Works bought out the owners of nine major road bridges. Further in, traffic was hampered by dozens of gates, bars and tolls, notably in Notting Hill, Kentish Town, Holloway, Stamford Hill, Hackney, Peckham and Camberwell.

Little inner-city road improvement was undertaken before 1850, though Commercial Road, built around 1810, sped transport to the docks. In the late 1820s the City Corporation built King William Street, and Princes Street was added in the early 1850s. New Oxford Street was bulldozed through the St Giles slum in 1847, relieving west–east traffic, though the through-route it promised via Newgate, Cheapside, Cornhill and Aldgate to Whitechapel was hindered by the steep crossing of the Fleet valley, until Holborn Viaduct was opened in 1869. Overall, however, London's traffic problems were becoming ominous, as a result of the vast increase of traffic and the absence of any policy. For these reasons, the coming of rail transport, overground and underground, was critical in keeping the metropolis moving and in permitting the city to expand. But if the railway brought benefits, these were purchased at a high cost.

London's first railway, from Bricklayer's Arms, in Southwark, to Deptford, began operating in December 1836; it soon extended to London Bridge and to Greenwich. The London and Croydon Railway opened in 1839, and the London and Brighton in 1841. The Greenwich line grew into the South Eastern Railway, the others became part of the London, Brighton and South Coast Railway, and all brought passengers into London Bridge station, the first real terminus. The London and Birmingham Railway opened at Euston station in 1837, and the London and South Western extended inwards from Nine Elms to Waterloo in 1848. The Blackwall Railway was opened from Blackwall to the Minories in 1840, reaching to Fenchurch Street in 1841. The Eastern Counties Railway (later the Great Eastern), extended from Mile End to Shoreditch in 1840 and to Liverpool Street station in 1874. In 1853 the North London Railway was authorized, linking the western suburbs with the docks; a spur was run from Dalston to Broad Street in the City.

Thus a skeleton was created; but overall the impact of the railway was patchy and tardy. For railways were initially viewed mainly as inter-city (rather than intra-city) conveyances. The great companies built their London termini – Paddington (Great Western, 1838), King's Cross (Great Northern, 1852), St Pancras (London Midland, 1868) – with an eye to long-distance freight and passenger traffic. By 1850 a national network had been built, connecting Birmingham, the Midlands and the North with East Anglia, the south coast, Bristol and Holyhead. In this early burst, railway companies did not anticipate much commuter traffic, and so the first stop on the London Birmingham line was at Harrow, eleven miles from Euston, and on the Great Western at Ealing, six miles from Paddington. Targeting long-distance traffic, they did not fret when their termini were kept out of the central area by aristocratic landlords and City interests resisting the social disaster railways would bring. (Visionary planners, however, deplored this irrational fragmentation of termini, which wasted land and made inter-station transport slow; they demanded the Hauptbahnhof and encircling ring railway that became typical on the Continent. In truth, however, so long as there were numerous railway companies, termini were sure to multiply.)

Hence railways did not make an immediately explosive impact upon the life of the city. Commuting came late. There were only around 27,000 daily rail commuters entering London in the mid-1850s – a tenth of the number of foot and omnibus passengers. In 1873 the *Workman's Magazine* stated that many of the working classes never travelled by train.

Early rail termini were not well sited for work centres, with the exception of Fenchurch Street and London Bridge. Fenchurch Street was opened in 1841 by the London and Blackwall Railway, the first City terminus. Until 1849, however, no steam locomotives were used; trains were dragged from Blackwall to Minories by cables; they left by gravity, needing 'only a slight push from the platform staff'.

London Bridge was the first station carrying droves of commuters, developing out of the Greenwich line, whose success proved railways had a passenger potential: a fifteen-minute service at a minimum fare of 6d brought in nearly three-quarters of a million passengers in the first fifteen months of operation. The London and Greenwich Company then allowed London Bridge station to be used by other companies – the London to Croydon in 1839, the London and Brighton in 1841 (these later merged to become the London, Brighton and South Coast Railway), and in 1849 the South Eastern line to Gravesend via Lewisham. 'There is the enormous Greenwich trade, employing sixty trains a day in each direction,' noted Charles Knight, explaining in 1851 the success of the London Bridge terminus:

There is the rapidly growing North Kent traffic, which commanding such stations as Woolwich, Gravesend and Charlton, cannot be otherwise but extensive. There is the South Eastern Railway proper, whose seaside termini now comprise Whitstable, Ramsgate, ... Dover and Hastings. There is the South Coast which grasps Hastings at one end, Brighton at the centre, and Portsmouth at the other end ... And lastly the Croydon and Epsom branch which has about sixteen stations to accommodate 'short traffic' passengers.

By then, commuters were growing. The Eastern Counties Company line from Romford to Shoreditch prospered. South of the river, a line from Wimbledon to Nine Elms was pioneered in 1838 by the London and South Western Railway. Extended to Waterloo in 1848, it became part of the London, Brighton and South Coast railway.

Competition intensified between the companies. Railway bridges were built across the Thames to bring trains nearer the West End and City. In 1860 the London, Chatham and Dover got to Victoria, and in 1861 its route to Dover was complete, twelve miles shorter than the South Eastern's, which wound through Redhill up to London Bridge. The South Eastern retaliated with a line (opened in 1864) from

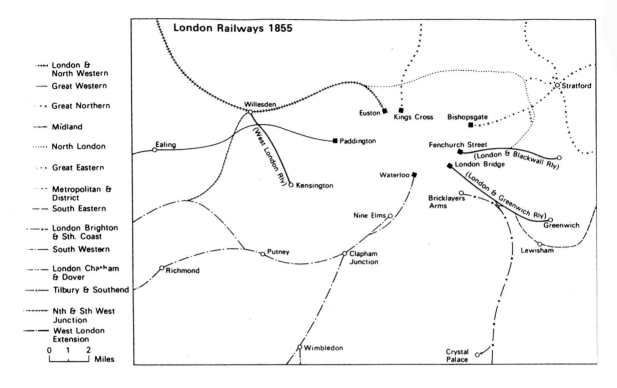

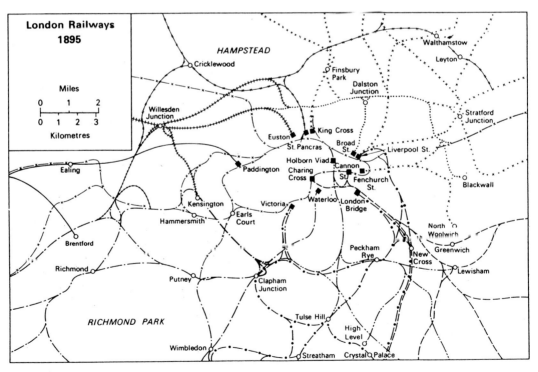

The London railways in 1855 and 1895

London Bridge across the river to the site of the old Hungerford Market at Charing Cross – this entailed the demolition of St Thomas's Hospital, for which vast compensation was paid. The London, Chatham and Dover struck back with a line north through the Elephant and Castle, joining the Metropolitan at Farringdon Street, involving colossal viaducts through the inner suburbs. (The Holborn Viaduct terminus was added in 1874.) The South Eastern trumped this with a line across the river to Cannon Street, opened in 1866.

To serve these four termini across the river, the southern suburbs were criss-crossed with approach lines. The Chatham and the Brighton companies threaded more trains into Victoria by building a new Peckham and Brixton loop; and a second terminus was built there for the Chatham trains, the wall down the centre of the station still marking this division. The South Western linked with the Chatham at Battersea, enabling it to run trains from the south-western suburbs into Ludgate Hill; the opening of Waterloo Junction gave a new approach to Charing Cross or Cannon Street.

Furious mid-Victorian competition thus created multiple termini serving the South East; vast intersections blighted Battersea, Balham, Brixton and New Cross (and, north of the river, Willesden, Acton, Kentish Town, Camden Town, Bethnal Green and Stratford) in pursuit of promoters' rivalries – and all with government approval. It was all possible because, especially south of the river, land was cheap in working-class districts and there were few blue-blooded landowners and posh residents to protest.

The railway mania had diverse effects. A staggering quantity of working-class housing was destroyed. In 1836, 2,850 homes were flattened by the building of the London and Blackwall railway; in 1845–8 the London and South Western's Nine Elms to Waterloo extension involved the demolition of 700 houses. By 1866 the North London Railway Company had destroyed 900 houses in building two miles of track from Kingsland to Finsbury. Demolitions in Somers, Camden, and Agar Towns for the London Midland Railway Company totalled 4,000 houses, containing 32,000 persons. In the 1860s the extensions into Charing Cross and Broad Street, and the Shoreditch to New Cross line, left 16,875 people homeless. Late in the century the Marylebone line destroyed yet more housing. Overall, between 1850 and 1900 about 100,000 people in central and inner suburbia had their homes destroyed by the railways. Railway companies had no obligation to rehouse. *Punch's* facetious 1845 prospectus for a 'Grand Railway from England to China', with its terminus on the site of a demolished St Paul's, struck home.

Railway-building dramatically exacerbated central overcrowding. Yet, while destroying, the railway also created – new life, new areas. 'The miserable waste ground, where the refuse-matter had been heaped of yore, was swallowed up and gone,' observed Dickens in *Dombey and Son* on the impact of railways:

and in its frowsy stead were tiers of warehouses, crammed with rich goods and costly merchandise. The old by-streets now swarmed with passengers and vehicles of every kind; the new streets that had stopped disheartened in the mud and waggon-ruts, formed towns within themselves, originating wholesome comforts and conveniences belonging to themselves, and never tried nor thought of until they sprung into existence. Bridges that had led to nothing, led to villas, gardens, churches, healthy public walks. The carcasses of houses, and beginnings of new thoroughfares, had started off upon the line at steam's own speed, and shot away into the country in a monster train.

Night and day the conquering engines rumbled at their distant work, or, advancing smoothly to their journey's end, and gliding like tame dragons into the allotted corners grooved out to the inch for their reception, stood bubbling and trembling there, making the walls quake, as if they were dilating with the secret knowledge of great powers yet unsuspected in them, and strong purposes not yet achieved.

But railways generally made things worse before they made them better. The tangle of lines into the capital appropriated over 5 per cent of London's built-up area. South London was permanently scarred, only the higher ground around Sydenham and Norwood escaped. The argument that the dispossessed would be able to occupy new railway suburbs was, in the short run, a pipedream: the labouring poor needed to live where they worked. 'The poor are displaced,' thundered *The Times* in 1861:

but they are not removed. They are shovelled out of one side of the parish, only to render more overcrowded the stifling apartments in another part ... But the dock and wharf labourer, the porter and the costermonger cannot remove. You may pull down their wretched homes; they must find others, and make their own dwellings more crowded and wretched than their old one. The tailor, shoemaker and other workmen are in much the same position. It is mockery to speak of the suburbs to them.

Railways did, however, encourage new housing for the middle classes. From the 1840s, stations shot up a few miles out from the centre – in Battersea, Wandsworth, Brixton and Balham; in Peckham, Dulwich, New Cross, Brockley, Forest Hill and Lewisham; in Kentish Town and Kilburn, Crouch End, Stroud Green, Hornsey and Wood Green – sparking the construction of middle-class villas and respectable terraces. All such areas underwent flux. Before the arrival of the railways, inner suburbs served by omnibuses had generally been rather elegant and moderately populated. Once railways invaded, street after street went up, row upon row of houses. Much development was still large and spacious, three- and four-storey houses for families with maids; but the density and monotony of it all robbed Brixton and Brockley and all such places of any pretensions to gentility, and made them hopelessly vulnerable, within a couple of decades, to multiple-occupation and the slide into slumdom. In 1890 *Building News* commented:

We find suburbs, once delightful retreats for the busy man, fast losing their ... reputation. Putney, Fulham, Richmond, Kew in the West, Hampstead, Highgate, Hornsey, Finsbury in the North; Clapham, Brixton, Dulwich in the South, are already being irretrievably spoiled ... while every acre of land is allowed to be crowded with 50 to 60 houses ... the higher class suburbs being brought down to the levels of the poorer districts.

The railway made a district, then marred it; the line moved on, and those who could afford to had to move on with it, in search of another desirable address. Families thus moved out from Camberwell to Streatham or Sydenham, Norwood or Beckenham; Peckhamites fled perhaps to Hither Green, whose Corbett Estate was advertised as a 'modern Hygeia', a 'Garden of Eden'. Balham was abandoned for Wimbledon or Surbiton, Battersea for Barnes. All such places – between five and ten miles from the centre – enjoyed a brief summer when the opening of a station brought superior villa housing, followed in due course by smaller, cheaper properties for petty clerks and shop assistants. Bromley, for instance, became drawn into London's orbit thanks to the railway which opened in 1858, ushering in rapid growth – though commuting was no more pleasurable in those early days than it is now. 'Sir,' opened an irate letter to *The Times* on 15 January 1864:

I live with thousands of others down the Mid Kent Railway below Beckenham, ten miles from London Bridge, all of us requiring to be in town more or less punctually every morning. The recent 'facilities of new lines', as the phrase goes, have only woefully obstructed our business journeyings, and made our homes practically now twenty miles off London. I arrived at the London Bridge Station this evening to go home by the train appointed in the railway bills to start at 6.15; and found our train had taken a trip to Charing Cross, leaving 200 or 300 of us waiting about 15 or 20 minutes on a very unsafe, cold, exposed, narrow platform, kicking our heels about while engines and trains passed to and fro, like Cheapside omnibuses, in dangerous proximity; and after undergoing one hour and five minutes from the time our train should have started, in making a journey of ten miles. And this is no solitary instance, and far from being one of our worst Mid Kent grievances.

No amount of inconvenience, however, could halt the mushroom growth of a commuter area immortalized by one of its residents, the finest commentator on turn-of-the-century suburbia, H. G. Wells. 'The roads came ... the houses followed,' Wells wrote in *The New Machiavelli* (1911), describing the changes railways brought to Bromley in the 1870s. 'They seemed to arise in the night. People moved into them as soon as the roofs were on ... already in a year some of these raw houses stood empty again from defaulting tenants with windows broken and woodwork warping and rotting.' Wells had no love of Bromley, but even he could accept that, for all its drabness, the new suburbia was more alive than the former sleepy market towns of Kent; town was but a ticket away.

And from the 1870s the railway brought something quite new: the working-class suburb, thanks to the 1864 Cheap Trains Act, with the idea of the workmen's fare. The London, Chatham and Dover Railway was required to run one train daily from Loughborough and Peckham Junction to Ludgate Hill, the up-journey before 7 a.m. and the return before 6 p.m., fare 1d. The London, Brighton and South Coast Railway had to put on a daily train between New Cross and Liverpool Street; from 1868 the South Eastern Railway issued workmen's tickets on the Woolwich line; from 1872 the Great Eastern Railway did likewise from Bethnal Green to Stoke Newington. By 1882, 25,000 workmen's tickets were sold daily, the Great Eastern Railway Company playing a major role.

All this encouraged speculative builders to provide housing for the respectable working classes in railway suburbs in districts unlikely to attract a better class of commuter. North-east and east London were particularly affected. From the 1870s, stations in Tottenham, Walthamstow, Leyton, West Ham, Plaistow, Upton Park, Manor Park and similar districts became surrounded by endless files of regimented, plain, two- and three-storey terraces, whose occupants were typically skilled artisans, policemen and firemen, railway engineers or gaffers in the gasworks, men with the security and income to allow them to rent or even buy a place of their own a half-hour train ride from work.

In the 1880s the four places with the highest rates of population increase in the whole nation were new working- and lower-middle-class railway suburbs: Leyton, Willesden, Tottenham, and West Ham. They doubled in a decade. Willesden had been mainly rural up to 1875, with clumps of villas occupied by City merchants at Willesden Green and Brondesbury. But, with the coming of the Metropolitan Railway in 1880, people stampeded in, at the rate of 100 a week. The merchants fled, but by 1895 Kilburn and Willesden had almost 80,000 inhabitants.

The impact of railways upon Victorian London was complex and spread over many decades; it involved a dialectic of property, transport and housing. In crude terms, however, the railways kept central London viable as a commercial centre, while blighting the inner suburbs – South Bermondsey, Bricklayer's Arms, Nine Elms, Kentish Town and so forth – a scarring from which such districts never recovered, although in time railway blight assumed a charm that appeals to some.

Above all, the railway made outer suburbs possible. No other form of transportation could have allowed tens of thousands to live in Bromley, Croydon, Kingston, Harrow, Wanstead and Walthamstow, commuting to work daily. During the last decades of the century, such places were growing at a phenomenal rate. Outer suburbs changed the capital's aura. Paddington and Camden Town had felt like extensions of the old city – so perhaps did Shepherd's Bush and Earl's Court – but the attraction of Barnet or Beckenham was precisely that it was not urban but suburban. A new suburbia emerged with the railway, and with it a way of life. Incorporating the earlier ideals of Nash's Park Village West and East and St John's Wood, suburbia finally abandoned the Georgian terrace in favour of villas and semi-detached houses.

Architects had to invent new styles – fusions of the urban and the rural – fit for suburbia. An influential model appeared at Bedford Park, the first garden suburb, built from 1877 near Turnham Green station on the new Metropolitan Railway, following a plan by Norman Shaw. It got its own church, a mock-Tudor inn and carefully placed trees. 'Queen Anne' houses were built in long rows, individualized with gables, elongated chimneys and windows. Hot water was plumbed to all houses. Rooms were spacious, light and informal. A remarkably imaginative architect, Shaw dreamt up a new town style, incorporating a country-house element, that was destined to run and run.

Suburbia affronted many. 'A modern suburb,' fumed a contributor to *The Architect* in 1876, 'is a place which is neither one thing nor the other; it has neither the advantage of the town nor the open freedom of the country, but manages to combine in nice equality of proportion the disadvantages of both.' It was easy to be snobbish about suburbanites. 'Once seen, they cannot be mistaken,' sneered J. F. Murray in the mid-Victorian era:

They are marvellously attached to gardening, and rejoice above all things in a tree in a tub. They delight in a uniformity of ugliness, staring you out of countenance with five windows in front, and a little green hall-door at one side, giving to each house the appearance of having had a paralytic stroke; they stand upon their dignity at a distance from the road, and are carefully defended from intrusion by a bodyguard of spikes bristling on a low wall.

'The life of the suburb', declared one of London's historians, Sir Walter Besant, half a century later, was life 'without any society; no social gatherings or institutions; as dull a life as mankind ever tolerated'. Suburbia was widely diagnosed as a social disaster and an aesthetic desert. Yet suburbia offered much the Victorians cherished: home sweet home, safe streets, a nest for children. It had solidity, respectability, residentiality. The games developers played provided status symbols in places like Muswell Hill or Raynes Park where the very name implied something superior or rustic.

Suburbia marked the end of the old London and the birth of the new. It was a radical departure, the moment when, for hundreds of thousands, the allure of urban living finally faded. Suburbia became a civilization of its own. In 1909 C. F. G. Masterman spoke of suburbans as 'practically the product of the past half century':

They form a homogeneous civilization – detached, self-centred, unostentatious – covering the hills along the northern and southern boundaries of the city, and spreading their conquests over the quiet fields beyond. It is a life of Security; a life of Sedentary occupation; a life of Respectability ... Its male population is engaged in all its working hours in small, crowded offices, under artificial light, doing immense sums, adding up other men's accounts, writing other men's letters. It is sucked into the City at daybreak and scattered again as darkness falls. It finds itself towards evening in its own territory in the miles and miles of little red houses in little, silent streets, in numbers defying imagination. Each boasts its pleasant drawing-room, its bow-window, its little front garden, its high-sounding title – 'Acacia Villa' or 'Camperdown Lodge' – attesting unconquered human aspiration ... The women, with their single domestic servants ... find time hangs rather heavy on their hands. But there are excursions to shopping centres in the West End, and pious sociabilities, and occasional theatre visits, and the interests of home.

Many factors, not just the railways, had got the suburban ball rolling, and, once started, the centrifugal tendency would not stop, for it was propelled by the pressure of private capital seeking profitable outlets. It afforded new business opportunities – for landowners, railway and tram promoters, shareholders in utilities, land companies, speculative builders, property dealers, solicitors, house agents, shopkeepers and publicans. With abundant supplies of cheap land, labour and capital, suburban development became a bonanza, especially for the petty capitalists who dominated the building trade (80 per cent of building firms had six or fewer houses under construction in 1872). 'Yesterday', it was observed in 1901, the solution 'lay in West Ham, in Streatham, Hackney and Tottenham: today it lies in East Ham, in Croydon, in Harrow: tomorrow it will be the belt of country lying beyond.' It was the pragmatic solution to London's problems: suburbia as safety-valve – a bit like the American frontier. It allowed continued expansion, demographically and economically, by decanting the affluent out of inner-city areas, many of which were being blighted by the very technology that permitted suburbia to develop. For the poor left behind, things usually became worse.

Ironically, the last decades of the Victorian era also brought a new inner-city development for the wealthy. With the erection of Belgravia and Kensington there was no more eligible central land upon which to build, and once-fashionable residential quarters like Soho or Fitzrovia had ceased to be acceptable addresses. The only resort for the rich lay in accepting a foreign solution: flats, or, as they were called, mansion blocks – desirably modern residences, in desirable parts, that did not require huge ground plots. It was the old Georgian solution (vertical living in terraces) taken to its logical conclusion.

In 1879 the versatile Shaw tried an innovative housing venture: Albert Hall Mansions, a giant block overlooking Kensington Gardens, complete with lifts, recessed balconies, Dutch gables, and some flats ingeniously planned on two levels. Many similar blocks followed in Mayfair, Regent's Park, St John's Wood and Kensington, where St George's Terrace was erected in Gloucester Road and Alexandra Court in Queen's Gate. Success depended on a high-status site. Investment in flats meant seizing central spots and building as high as the Building Acts would permit. In the 1890s Cavendish Square, Hanover Square, Berkeley Square and Kensington Square were all invaded by flats: the destruction of Georgian London was under way.

The shame was that the Victorian era never developed coherent styles of inner-city architecture to replace the ubiquitous Georgian. Neither did Victorian London acquire many splendid new townscapes – Trafalgar Square, developed in the 1830s, was one, which might have been all the more impressive had Colonel Trench's proposal to build a pyramid, taller than St Paul's, in the Square been adopted. Trench was one of several cranky would-be redesigners of the capital on the truly monumental scale that many found missing.

Nineteenth-century public buildings in the metropolis are remarkable for their stylistic mishmash: Gothic in the Houses of Parliament, Grecian in the British Museum, Italian in the Foreign Office. Gothic, Classical, Romanesque, Moorish, Byzantine, Egyptian and Chinese styles were all absorbed into the Victorian architectural bazaar. In the absence of unified metropolitan government, architectural coherence suffered like so much else.

London extended to the horizon. In 1871 Jeanette Marshall, the daughter of a fashionable surgeon, wrote about her father's patients, 'they have taken to living in the four corners of the globe: St John's Wood, Hornsey & I don't know where'. Her father paid house calls to rich patients as distant as Barnet, Richmond and Blackheath. Gone were the days when the rich could be expected to live within a mile or two of Piccadilly. Marshall felt a bit apprehensive about the darkest suburbs: on a visit to Wood Green he armed himself with a revolver. He was not alone: many deplored the ugly and amorphous sprawl. But in an unplanned and (in major respects) ungoverned city where commerce was king, social order was always elusive and exclusivity precarious. From Belgravia to Bloomsbury, there was hardly a classy enclave that did not have a colony of the lumpenproletariat just a stone's throw away. 'Behind the mansion there is generally a stable,' it was pointed out,

and near the stable there is generally a maze of close streets, containing a small greengrocer's, a small dairy's, a quiet coachman's public house, and a number of houses let out in tenements. These houses shelter a large number of painters, bricklayers, carpenters, and similar labourers, with their families, and many laundresses and charwomen.

London could hardly have developed otherwise, since the City had washed its hands of developments beyond the Square Mile and Parliament had no mandate.

As is clear from even the most cursory comparison with the Paris of Napoleon III and Baron Haussmann, with its massive scenic boulevards and monumental public buildings, the built environment of Victorian London grew not because of any government planning but because of the mysteries of the market: population growth, change in transport technology, and profitable building speculation. Empire-based prosperity meant that London kept growing; and new expedients in living were devised to prevent the capital from seizing up. 'Where will London end?' inquired a reporter from *The Builder* in 1870, standing in West Hampstead. 'Goodness knows,' answered a bystander.

CHAPTER TEN

Bumbledom?
London's Politics
1800–1890

At Victoria's accession in 1837, the built-up area reached north to the Regent's Canal and south to Clapham and Camberwell; west to Paddington and east to Limehouse. It was six miles across. To many it already seemed amorphous, not one place but a heap of bits and pieces. 'London differs very widely from Manchester, and indeed, from every other place on the face of the earth,' remarked the Charing Cross radical tailor Francis Place:

It has no local or particular interest as a town, not even as to politics. Its several [parliamentary] boroughs in this respect are like so many very populous places at a distance from one another, and the inhabitants of any one of them know nothing, or next to nothing, of the proceedings in any other, and not much indeed of those of their own. London, in my time, and that is half a century, has never moved [revolted]. A few of the people in different parts have moved, and these, whenever they come together, make a considerable number – still, a very small number indeed when compared with the whole number – and when these are judiciously managed, i.e. when they are brought to act together, not only make a great noise, which is heard far and wide, but which has also considerable influence in many places. But, isolated as men are here, living as they do at considerable distance, many seven miles apart, and but seldom meeting together, except in small groups, to talk either absolute nonsense or miserable party politics, or to transact business exclusive of everything else, they will tell you they have no time to give to the Association to help repeal the Corn Laws, while the simple fact is that, with the exception of the men of business (and even they lose much time), four-fifths of the whole do nothing but lose their time.

Paradox of paradoxes: this diverse and complex sprawl, which above all demanded effective government, had an administrative system lacking rhyme or reason. 'The present condition of this huge metropolis exhibits the most extraordinary anomaly in England,' declared the local-government expert Joshua Toulmin Smith. 'Abounding in wealth and intelligence, by far the greater part of it is yet absolutely without any municipal government whatever.' In 1855 *The Times* noted that London had no logic, being 'rent into an affinity of divisions districts and areas ... Within the metropolitan limits, the local administration is carried on by no fewer than 300 different bodies deriving powers from about 150 different local Acts.'

Despite reform movements, these peculiarities persisted right up to the establishment of the London County Council (LCC) in 1888, perhaps the first unified government the settlement had enjoyed since it had been Londinium. The struggle to reform London's administration became embroiled with the ambiguities of London's place on the national political stage and with wider parliamentary reform, and further aspects of London's government will be surveyed in Chapter 11, which examines new administrative machinery, notably the Metropolitan Board of Works, tackling London's daunting environmental problems.

The saga of administrative reform in London may be read after the event as one of intolerable abuses generating mounting reform pressures, finally precipitating reform itself. Surely a metropolis with 1, 2, 3 or 4 million inhabitants could not for ever be governed by archaic institutions like vestries originally designed for a few hundred – though it is a nice question at what point 'intolerability' grew sufficient to detonate change. But it would be wrong to cast the story as a melodrama, in which die-hard aldermen, guzzling turtle soup, were finally vanquished by heroic reformers, committed to efficiency, expertise, democracy, accountability and the future.

We must avoid anachronistic judgements. The post-1945 Welfare State mentality expected government to provide comprehensive personal and social services from cradle to grave. Such notions would have appeared peculiar, even pernicious, to influential Victorians. The fact that, by our standards, public bodies provided few public amenities does not mean there were no services. Private bodies, both philanthropic and profit-making, compensated in large measure for what to us seem the inadequacies of public authorities. Capitalism created many utilities, bringing sanitation, lighting, transport and housing to those who could afford them. London's private water supply long remained hazardous, but tram companies were at least making travelling cheap and efficient by 1900. Charities proliferated, plugging gaps; philanthropy was widely praised as the best way of alleviating individual, family and social problems, being more personal and cost-effective than bureaucratic action, which was widely suspected as being a cloak for jobbery. Merely because they did not produce our favourite nos-trums does not mean that Victorian Londoners did not respond with some intelligence and compassion to the problems created by growth and change. Even Ebenezer Scrooge saw the light. The callousness and anomie of today's capital caution us not to cast stones.

Optimists believed that market forces and personal benevolence would combine to solve London's problems. There was a counter-argument: such solutions would be, at best, stop-gaps. In his *Lectures on Social Science* (1851), the Owenite and educational reformer James Hole crushingly refuted the *laissez-faire* argument:

That the people of London, or the major part of them, do somehow or other get fed, is true, – but that this is done in the *best* and *wisest* manner would be a pure assumption, were it not a downright falsehood. The real fact is, that in this large 'wen' – this sponge which sucks up so much of the wealth of the nation – there are tens of thousands who scarcely know from whence the next day's subsistence shall come, – multiplied thousands who lie upon beds inferior to those which the farmer gives to cattle, – and a thousand at least, who, night after night, have no shelter whatever! So wisely are they supplied with the means of subsistence, that vast numbers have no recourse save prostitution and plunder. If ... a band of commissaries had to provide for the material wants of two millions of people, we question whether they could make so great a bungle of it as in the present case. The genuine wants of the deserving are left unsupplied, while the un-'natural law' ministers to the factitious ones of the undeserving.

Private profit could not be trusted, Hole argued, to produce the institutional require-ments of an urban society – adequate railways, postal services and municipal baths, and so forth. Still less could one leave it to private profit to prevent cholera. Dickens remarked that all such calamities were always deemed 'Nobody's Fault'.

Debate thus raged about London's government, a whirlpool of principle and preju-dice, bias and belief. Many acknowledged shortcomings in the status quo but feared change. Would not expansion of municipal government spell more nepotism and peculation, more red tape and expense, more interference from Westminster and Whitehall? Would it not bring greater regulation, threatening Liberty, that great Victorian shibboleth, and stifling trade and prosperity? Many thought London's strength derived from its being a city where freedom of capital and labour excited enterprise and industry. Not only the proverbial if slightly mythical port-swilling aldermen dreaded that Reform would impose standardization, eroding historical com-munities and local allegiances. Monolithic 'centralism' was to be resisted, it was argued, and London ought to remain a loose federation of localities, trades and interests, the Many rather than the One; healthy heterogeneity must not be reduced to Prussian uniformity. The arch-localist Joshua Toulmin Smith asked, 'What commonness of interests and management can Whitechapel have with Paddington, or Lambeth with Hackney?' Not all arguments against change arose from dyed-in-the-wool back-woodsmen, protecting privilege and prejudice behind a mask of Freedom. Many believed that London was a 'special case'.

With the establishment of a Royal Commission to 'inquire into the existing state of the Municipal Corporations in England and Wales', the Corporation became a prime target for reform. When, however, the commissioners at last presented their report on London – in 1837, two years after all the other large municipal corporations throughout the country had been reformed – they pointed to the intractable difficulties arising from London's unique history. 'The present distinction of this particular district [i.e. the City] from the rest', they said, 'had ancient precedent in its favour. The commissioners pondered setting up a single municipality for the entire capital, but noted that would 'raise the difficult question of the relation between the Government and some new municipal body'. This was an invitation for Lord Melbourne's administration to do nothing, and the City of London, alone among the great municipal corporations, survived unreformed.

Many feared that reform would in any case mean expense. London's vestries, Poor Law guardians and boards of education were, as ward and parish bodies always had been, elected bodies responsible to ratepayers. As such they were keen to trim the rates. Cheapness was seen as a cardinal virtue. If myopic as an approach to the metropolis's social and sanitary needs, this pinpointed an important fact: the Victorian growth miracle depended on a low-cost, nil-inflation economy. The burden of local government was to be reduced wherever possible.

Looking back, it would be easy to presume that London's true bugbear when Victoria came to the throne was *ancien régime* corruption – what Cobbett called 'The Thing'. Aristocratic influence was inevitably present – for centuries the nobility had formed London's great landlords. As late as 1900 the 9th Duke of Bedford became first Mayor of Holborn, the 15th Duke of Norfolk became Mayor of Westminster, and the Earl of Cadogan served as Mayor of Chelsea. The first Chairman of the London County Council was none other than Lord Rosebery, soon to be Prime Minister.

But London was no pocket borough. The trouble with London's government lay not in aristocratic privilege but in the parish-pump narrowness and acrimonious penny-pinching that ratepayer democracy produced. Vestries spelt localism and irrational subdivision and duplication of jurisdiction and function, each district fiercely defending its turf, the net result being parochial pettiness.

Many wrung their hands and prophesied London was about to be engulfed in Jacobin, Chartist or Communist revolution; and at various times, with Chartism, Fenianism or Socialism, such predictions seemed about to come to pass. But in truth the apparently ill-ungoverned conurbation remained remarkably stable. Street disorders and crime rates were falling. In years when barricades went up in Paris, bombs exploded in St Petersburg, and princes lost their thrones if not their heads, London remained comparatively tranquil, providing a safe haven for political refugees of all complexions from Karl Marx to Louis Napoleon, from Kossuth to Lenin (who met Trotsky for the first time while living in 30 Holford Square, off the Pentonville Road, in 1902). Up to a point, the bellows of wealth provided the metropolis with the government it needed.

On the brink of the parliamentary Reform Act of 1832 over 1·5 million people resided in a metropolis whose affairs were managed, or mismanaged, by the ancient vestries of over ninety parishes in Middlesex, Kent and Surrey. These parish assemblies presided over districts great and small, ranging from the tiny Liberty of the Old Artillery Ground near Bishopsgate, with an 1801 population of under 1,500, to St George Hanover Square, inhabited by over 60,000. All discharged similar functions, chiefly street paving, cleaning and lighting, poor relief, and public order. In the suburbs, many vestries were 'open', all ratepayers being entitled to attend the often rowdy meetings. But in areas such as Marylebone 'close' or 'select' vestries were the rule, power being restricted to a few dozen of the 'principal inhabitants', originally specified in a local Act of Parliament, vacancies being filled by nomination.

The disorderly, or at least difficult to suborn, open assembly of a parish with a mushrooming population was sometimes converted, by an Act promoted by the élite, into a select vestry, as happened in 1819 in St Pancras. There the new 'close' vestry was composed of 122 vestrymen, of whom seven had to be noblemen and two-thirds householders owning parish properties valued at over £150 and estates worth over £3,000. The remainder were to be householders with property above the value of £56 in St Pancras and estates valued at over £1,000. Formally the vestry included the Duke of Bedford, the Marquis of Camden, and Lords Southampton, Calthorpe and Somers, as well as substantial landholders, merchants and clergymen, but only some couple of dozen persons ever attended meetings.

The select vestry gave power to property. Though vestrymen were supposed to have no 'stake or interest in any contract of work', builders were amply represented on the St Pancras vestry. Sniffing corruption, radicals criticized certain members for being hand in glove with building speculators and 'their extravagance in paving and lighting contracts'.

In 1822 the vestry was given extended powers over street widening, and it set about building a new parish church, in the Grecian style, on the Bedford estate at the corner of the New Road and Southampton Row. The effect of this prestige project was to treble the rates, from £12,600 in 1821 to £36,700 by 1827 – proof, in radical eyes, of the parish's extravagance in projects that might line the pockets of certain capitalist parishioners or serve their social ambitions.

The St Pancras select vestry certainly looked after landed and commercial interests, and barely represented the petty bourgeoisie who formed the majority of the population – to say nothing of the labouring class. But it energetically exercised its powers relating to arranging for 'lodging, keeping, maintaining, and employing all or any of the Poor of the said Parish', sending vagrants to the house of correction, and making children parish apprentices. St Pancras Workhouse became notorious for corrupt administration.

London's select vestries came under sustained attack on account of their exclusiveness, jobbery and unaccountability, and in 1831 John Cam Hobhouse, the radical MP for Westminster, promoted an Act designed to extend the vote to all ratepayers in select-vestry parishes. The Act was duly adopted in five of the largest select vestries, including St Pancras.

Local Acts of Parliament gave vestries all manner of special powers. They also created innumerable separate paving trusts – managed by commissioners and, legally, utterly separate from the local vestry – responsible for paving, cleaning, lighting, and policing. There were also seven independent Commissions of Sewers, nominated by the Crown; an eighth, responsible for the City, was appointed by the Corporation. (A 'sewer' was traditionally a channel for the removal of surface water, flowing into the Thames; the Commissions of Sewers were thus concerned with the urban environment.)

London's unreformed local government provoked widespread complaint, and the prime target was the City and its Corporation, which retained all its time-honoured powers. City administration continued to be shared between an upper court of twenty-six aldermen, elected for life, and the Court of Common Council, the decisive voice in City affairs, made up of 234 freemen elected annually from the livery companies. Against central government the Corporation jealously guarded its rights, including electing its sheriffs and commanding its private militia.

The political history of the nineteenth century Corporation is that of an institution dedicated to fighting change. From Stuart times, City fathers had chosen to remain sovereign within their own patch, essentially the square mile within the walls and in the wards beyond. The City had rejected its suburbs, and this policy was staunchly upheld, alongside resistance to all encroachments by Whitehall upon its traditional jurisdictions. Thus, when in the eighteenth century the decision was taken to build Westminster Bridge, the City had protested rigorously. Westminster was, of course, separate from the City of London, but the latter had long possessed rights over the whole of the Thames down to the Medway.

The City resisted interference as a knee-jerk reaction, and the inevitable consequence was that ministries, understandably seeking to avoid head-on collisions with such a privileged and well-connected body, fought shy of attempts to legislate for the metropolitan area as a whole. Only very gingerly were the City's ancient and archaic prerogatives whittled away. In 1857 control of the Thames below Staines, for the previous 700 years vested in the Corporation, was finally granted to the Thames Conservancy – upon which, however, the Mayor and aldermen were amply represented. In the eyes of many, the City was a prehistoric monster like those prowling in plaster at Crystal Palace. A. G. Gardiner, the great Liberal journalist, called it 'a sort of obsolete appendix at the centre'. A Member of Parliament described it as 'a sort of strange animal pickled in spirits of wine'. Yet the City was, ironically, well placed to mount perfectly rational defences of its privileges. If the aim of municipal reform was to end closed corporations and introduce ratepayer democracy, then wasn't that (apologists argued) what the City of London had possessed for centuries? Far from being an obstacle, London was thus a pioneer. For the Corporation *was*, in a fashion, popularly elected: it gave the franchise to freemen of the City, and after 1867 to all £10 ratepayers. In the 1870s the Common Council was returned by the electors of a population of about 75,000.

Things were more complex than that, however. Not least, the City's population was falling – some wards had very few voters – and so its metropolitan (and national) influence was quite disproportionate to its shrinking numerical base. Cornhill, for example, with a population of only 309 in 1871, returned six councilmen; by contrast Farringdon Without, with a population of nearly 20,000, sent only sixteen members.

The apparatus of City government was growing more outlandish. This was at bottom because the livery companies, traditionally the foundations of corporate existence, had become an irrelevance, though they retained considerable clout. Some were verging on extinction. Of the eighty-nine companies examined by the Municipal Corporations Commission of 1833–7, no fewer than thirteen were extinct by the 1880s – the Combmakers, Fishermen, Gardeners, Hatbandmakers, Longbowstringmakers, Paviors, Pinmakers, Silk Weavers, Silk Throwers, Soapmakers, Starchmakers, Tobacco-pipe Makers and Woodmongers. The mid-Victorian decades mark a nadir in company recruitment, the livery roll declining from 12,000 in 1832 to 5,500 in 1855. For example, in 1832 the liverymen of the Wax-chandlers' Company numbered 93 and the freemen 59; fifty years later totals had fallen to 41 and 25 respectively. Court attendances tell similar stories. In 1867 the Coachmakers were described as 'worn out', while the Master and Clerk were the sole individuals present at the Tinplateworkers' business meetings from 1872–5. As the city lost its residents, it ceased to represent anything but money, and was thus a sitting target for radicals, eager to end its privileges. Common councilmen, critics griped, had abandoned themselves to the 'Worship of Gammons', enjoying juicy perks of office for which the City was notorious, benefiting from 'a patronage which in extent and value has rarely been equalled by a public body'. The councilman would get, it was said, free dinners:

He has his pocket full of public gloves; wands to carry on public occasions; heavy medals to transmit as heirlooms to generations unborn ... schools at which to educate his own children, and rights of presentation at the City of London and other schools for the children of his friends; surely he is a man to be envied!

The City bobbed, weaved and perfected the arts of counter-attack. In 1848, for example, the government promoted a public-health bill for the metropolis. Faced by this threat to its autonomy, but apprehensive in the face of another cholera epidemic, the Corporation pre-empted it by shepherding a Bill of its own through Parliament; under this Act, the Corporation chose as its first Medical Officer of Health John Simon, acceptable to the City because he was the son of a rich City businessman and a surgeon at St Thomas's. Simon proved surprisingly go-ahead, yet superbly diplomatic. Gradually the City's 'dirty' party gave way. Aldermen Thomas Sidney and Henry Lowman Taylor – dubbed by *The Times* 'the Defender of the Filth' – abandoned opposition and were converted to sanitary reform. Led by Simon, the City rode out two cholera epidemics with conspicuous success – and emerged as a shining example of sanitary progress. More by luck than judgement, the Corporation could no longer be attacked as reactionary in its public-health administration.

The call for local-government reform echoed round the land. The Municipal Corporations Act of 1835 transformed centuries-old corporation and parish administration, and abolished ancient jurisdictions such as courts leet and manorial courts. Boroughs were henceforth to be run by elected bodies. London was, however, exempted from this legislation. Reformers were affronted. In 1843 the reforming Whig Lord Brougham thundered it was 'utterly impossible that many months should elapse before municipal reform should be extended to the City of London'. Months proved decades, however, for London was also excused from the Town Improvements Act of 1847, which encouraged local authorities elsewhere to improve drainage, water supply and paving.

Meanwhile the metropolis grew in extent, numbers and health hazards, and squalor worsened: 'These functions of local government ... which in other towns are performed by the municipal authorities,' commissioners remarked in 1854, 'are, in the metropolis, actually discharged by parochial functionaries, or by local boards created by local acts.' If possible, things were worse still in the suburbs: 'In the parishes on the outskirts of the metropolis,' the commissioners noted, 'they may, for want of powers in the general law, be left for a time altogether unprovided for, to the serious inconvenience of the inhabitants, and to permanent injury of owners of property within the district.'

This situation may be variously interpreted. Inertia played its part. Fearing the City, Parliament let sleeping dogs lie, but it was also apprehensive lest some new metropolitan body might assume excessive authority – a concern that was to surface again in the late twentieth century. In any case, localism and traditionalism had doughty defenders. It was always arguable that London's ancient vestries, like the Corporation, already embodied precisely what the 1835 Municipal Corporations Act had aimed to establish – a semblance of ratepayer democracy. However bizarrely distributed and constituted, vestries actually accomplished much necessary parochial work; they pegged the rates and grew more professional. The main vestry work was no longer being done by amateurs serving on an annual basis but by salaried professionals, above all the parish clerk. An elected officer, though his post was usually for life, the clerk's demanding job was full-time in larger parishes, and it was he who kept the machinery running while vestrymen blathered or bickered. Some were well rewarded. In 1872 the parish clerk in Islington received £650 – the clerk of St Luke's, Old Street, received £800 but had to pay his staff from this. And as the clerk became an indispensable figure in the modernization of parish administration, other parish-work – that of the parish doctor or surveyor – was gradually professionalized. Yet tensions and jealousies were profound. In 1841 Battersea took a progressive step when it 'resolved that a Surveyor with a Salary be appointed for the execution of the office for the Repairs of the Highways'. This appointment did not last, however: for reasons of economy, he was replaced four years later by a board of ratepayers.

Despite shortcomings and criticism, early Victorian vestries did much for the metropolis. Amenities improved. Legislation of 1855 made them responsible for paving the streets, constructing sewers, and enforcing a sanitary code. Within five years Lambeth had laid down fifty-three miles of sewers at a cost of nearly £200,000, and Camberwell had spent over £100,000 on drains. Between 1855 and 1870 St Pancras spent nearly £885,000 on sewerage, paving and other improvements; Lambeth over £700,000. Yet early Victorian vestry government had to balance such administration with the stringent requirements of ratepayer democracy. Ratepayers were ferocious, vocal and numerous – mid-century Lambeth had about 22,000 parochial voters. They would not be pushed around. Many a parish and vestry proved the arena of fierce contests: sometimes party-political, occasionally religious, and invariably budgetary. In Kensington, residents of the professional classes battled with the shopkeepers' oligarchy during the 1850s and 1860s over the cost of poor relief: they almost came to blows over a recommendation to build a new workhouse. Kensington was at least known as an efficient parish, with able vestry clerks; in nearby Fulham, mal-administration gave rise to prolonged parochial scandal.

London's local administration was deeply affected by the Poor Law Amendment Act of 1834. This replaced the old haphazard methods of poor relief by installing a central Poor Law Commission, from whose Somerset House offices the new local boards of guardians of the poor were to be directed. Its architect was Edwin Chadwick, a disciple of Jeremy Bentham and a staunch advocate of strict, scientific, centralized administration. As the salaried secretary of this Commission, Chadwick became the most hated man in England, detested alike by the poor, by vestrymen and by local boards of guardians for his 'Prussian' style of operation.

The new Poor Law established the exclusive reign of the workhouse: there was to be no relief outside the workhouse. Extensive workhouse construction was put in train. Yet the scheme was too rigid, and 'outdoor' relief widely survived in London (as elsewhere), though the Poor Law Commission sought to shave it as much as possible. In St Pancras in 1850, adult males constituted only 28 per cent of those asking for aid, and most of those were old and single. Those receiving weekly pensions had their doles cut. Average payments dropped in St George, Southwark, to 1s 3d per family per week in 1843, and the nonsettled poor received less. In the late 1830s Bermondsey guardians gave Irish families a maximum of 1s per child per week: officials were reluctant to relieve the swollen Irish population. By 1900 Bermondsey was giving outdoor relief in kind only, to supplement other resources; those needing complete maintenance had to enter the workhouse.

This disinclination of the Poor Law guardians to support the needy outside the workhouse – naturally a policy supported by ratepayers – grew after 1870, when the Local Government Board renewed its commitment to 'deterrent' forms of relief. Henry Longley, a Poor Law inspector for the metropolitan area, reiterated what was believed to be the character-building quality of the workhouse stigma. The community would benefit, he argued, from

the inducement to a struggle for independence which the discipline, if not the disgrace, incident to residence in the Workhouse will offer to the pauper himself, in a far greater degree than does a mere weekly pittance, the receipt of which cannot but sap the independence and self-reliance of all but the most active and energetic, the very class who are conspicuous by their absence from the ranks of pauperism.

Longley recommended denial of outdoor relief to able-bodied males: all outdoor aid should end after three months (and medical care after one), forcing the applicant to enter the workhouse. To those objecting to breaking up the households of the poor in the workhouse, where husbands, wives and children were separated (something that Charlie Chaplin recorded as having happened in his family), he responded that an applicant often didn't have 'such a home that its loss will be otherwise than to the ultimate benefit of himself and his family'.

Nevertheless, despite central policy, in reality many relieving officers recognized the need for flexibility, and the poor knew how to work the system. The workhouse was doubtless punitive, and hung as a threat over the respectable, but the Poor Law could also serve as a vital social safety-net for the old, the sick and the helpless.

The workhouse became a favoured official weapon for reinforcing social discipline in a metropolis increasingly vast, anonymous and threatening. So too did policing. Since Shakespeare's times, London's watch had been derided as amateurish. Starting with the creation of the Bow Street Runners in 1750, reformers campaigned for efficient, professional policing – while meeting fierce opposition from localists terrified that a new police would, like Paris's *gendarmes*, essentially be soldiery, at ministerial bidding.

The breakthrough came in 1829, with the creation of the Metropolitan Police by the Home Secretary, Sir Robert Peel, moved to action by the inadequacy of the army in handling political demonstrations in the previous decade. The Metropolitan Police District was created to cover all the parishes within twelve miles of Charing Cross and a few more besides, thereby effectively creating the region later known for all manner of administrative purposes as 'Greater London'.

The establishment of the 'Peelers' involved crucial concessions to popular and local sentiments. Policemen were not to look like soldiers. The initial idea had been to dress them in military red, but dark-blue uniforms were preferred as smacking less of the resented redcoats. Constables were also to carry truncheons rather than swords or firearms. They were enjoined to be 'civil and attentive to all persons, of every rank and class'. The Metropolitan Police were, furthermore, not to operate in the City. When a London-wide professional force was first mooted, the City had screamed it would be a 'violation of all the Chartered Rights of the City'. Compromise was reached (Peel had privately confessed that he would 'be afraid to meddle' with the City): the City was to have its separate brigade. Once again government yielded when the City dug in its heels.

The Metropolitan Police Bill became law on 29 September 1829. The force was under the control of two Commissioners, Colonel Charles Rowan, a Peninsular and Waterloo veteran, and the Irish barrister Richard Mayne. Their headquarters was at 4 Whitehall Place – entered from Scotland Yard. It had about 3,000 men. In 1839 the Thames police and the Bow Street Runners (who had become little more than a private detective agency) were absorbed into the new force, and the old watch system was finally abolished in the City – though a separate police force, the City of London Police, was formed to patrol the Square Mile. The wages were poor and Peel's 'Blue Devils' were initially unpopular – in 1831, after a police constable was stabbed to death during riots in Clerkenwell, the coroner's jury brought in a verdict of 'justifiable homicide' – but by mid-century the 'peelers' had won public respect, though this was somewhat jeopardized by the mishandling of the Hyde Park Riots (1866), the Clerkenwell explosion (1867), and the Jack the Ripper murders (1888).

Crime rates diminished. This may be a reflection of the growing effectiveness of the Metropolitan Police, whose presence contributed to the more orderly feel of the metropolis as the Victorian era proceeded, but the signs are that London was in any case becoming a more settled city. Slum schemes were breaking up traditional thieves' dens. Work was available; prosperity bred stability and conformity. London escaped the demobbed soldiers who had triggered crime in the Georgian era. Not least, from 1870, compulsory schooling tamed youth. Despite occasional sensational incidents, like the Whitechapel murders, London, for all its vast expansion, avoided the reputation of a city racked by crime.

*

Possessing high concentrations of articulate, politically aware artisans, organized into guilds and accustomed to parish and ward office, London had from the seventeenth century been the breeding-ground of radical politics. The metropolis also harboured disgruntled members of the petty bourgeoisie – to say nothing of a floating population of sailors, soldiers and other crowd fodder. London constituencies had large, volatile, uncontrollable electorates. In Westminster (with 17,000 voters) and Southwark (with 3,000) the electorate was, roughly, all the resident householders. In the City, where the franchise worked differently, enfranchising trades not property, the vote was the privilege of the 12,000 liverymen. From time to time politicians were not averse to whipping up hustings mobs in their own interest. London was the hope of every reformer. Westminster radicals such as Sir Francis Burdett could always be a thorn in the government's side.

From the Exclusion Crisis of 1681, through 'Wilkes and Liberty', to the Gordon riots, London was occasionally at the mercy of the mob. Though life, limb and property might be at risk, riots posed no fundamental threat to the capital's rulers, since the Georgian crowd clamoured for redress of grievances rather than overthrow of the ruling class or a revolutionary new start. In any case, unpopular ministers, not the Corporation, tended to be the target of street politics.

The French Revolutionary era spawned new political threats as radical supporters of the Rights of Man convened in the metropolis, launching the London Corresponding Society and similar organizations, publishing inflammatory pamphlets, and threatening a People's Convention. The next thirty years saw thousands of meetings and blizzards of pamphlets. In reality, however, public disorder from the 1790s to the 1820s remained remarkably slight – the most dangerous events of the age, from Luddism to the Peterloo Massacre, occurring in the Midlands and the North. Isolated metropolitan incidents – the 1794 'Pop Gun Plot' (a rumoured insurrection) and the 1820 Cato Street Conspiracy – lent some credence, however, to government fears that revolution was brewing.

The Revolutionary and Napoleonic Wars seriously disrupted trade, and the Corporation remained critical of Pitt's war against France. The bungling of the campaign of 1807–9 kindled familiar City condemnations of expense, mismanagement, evil advisers and waste. In 1812 Common Council was demanding the removal of ministers. Yet with the end of the war, in 1815, the City lapsed into long political quiescence, and, except during George IV's proceedings against his wife, Queen Caroline, in 1820, City radicalism dwindled and political agitation within the metropolis fell into the hands of new groups.

Despite the 1799 Combination Acts, outlawing unions, trade organizations flourished and shipwrights, printers, coopers, cabinet-makers and other skilled artisans carried on combinations and strikes, though always at risk of prosecution. Early in the nineteenth century London artisans engaged in political education and agitation under the leadership of Francis Place. William Cobbett's *Weekly Political Register* and *Two-penny Trash* and the publications of radical printers such as William Hone and Thomas Wooler provided a flood of radical literature. Their *Black Dwarf* and *Yellow Dwarf* campaigned for the freeing of the press from government restriction. Repeal of the Combination Laws in 1824 led to strikes and the participation of London artisans in Robert Owen's Utopian schemes.

Some were more extreme still. A small revolutionary group based on the Spenceans, led by Dr James Watson and Arthur Thistlewood, aimed to precipitate revolution by metropolitan insurrection. Acquitted of a charge of high treason for involvement in the Spa Fields Riots of 1816, Thistlewood fomented the Cato Street Conspiracy of 1820, when the assassination of the Cabinet was expected to spark revolution. Thistlewood was executed.

Such cliques were tiny, however, and mainstream London radicalism lay in the continued efforts to consolidate political consciousness by moderates like Francis Place, Major Cartwright, Henry ('Orator') Hunt, Sir Francis Burdett and others. Such Westminster radicals put their faith in political-education schemes or enlightening the poor. Agitation out of doors occasionally continued – for example against the Corn Laws in 1815, the Spa Fields demonstration of the same year, and the Queen Caroline demonstrations in 1820 – but it was generally peaceful, concerned to make a show of strength rather than to mobilize violence.

Radicalism sustained itself in the 1820s with local cells and local issues. The Working Men's Association and later Chartist organizations put down roots in St Pancras, Somers Town and elsewhere; meetings pressed for the national franchise while also campaigning against the evils of the select vestry. In 1825 a trades newspaper was founded by carpenters and sawyers, and political interest was maintained by political discussions in pubs and coffee-houses. In 1831, London carpenters were promoting demands for a property tax, manhood suffrage, the secret ballot and the abolition of the property qualification for MPs. The following year they denounced the Reform Bill, when it failed to deliver working people the franchise. Lord Liverpool had apparently remarked that 'one insurrection in London and all is lost', but London failed around 1830 to develop the revolutionary tumult associated with Continental cities like Paris.

The Reform Act (1832) created potential for further metropolitan radicalization, since it not only extended the franchise but also increased the number of London parliamentary seats, by setting up Finsbury, Lambeth, Greenwich, Marylebone and Tower Hamlets. Until 1885, however, London remained grossly underrepresented in the House of Commons, with only about one-thirtieth of the whole House – quite disproportionate to its population.

The Smithfield Meeting of 1819

Radicalism was given fresh impetus in the 1830s with Chartism. Yet, unlike Georgian radicalism, Chartism was never first and foremost a metropolitan movement: its centres lay in Birmingham, Yorkshire, Lancashire and South Wales. In any case, most Chartists were not revolutionary. But the wave of revolutions in European capitals in February and March of 1848 suddenly made the threat of metropolitan revolution seem real to the authorities, and they took remarkable steps to secure the capital against insurrection.

Chartist leaders announced a mass rally on Kennington Common for Monday 10 April 1848, to be followed by a procession to Westminster to present the Charter containing 5 million signatures of workers from all over Britain. This created consternation. Parliament decided the capital's defence could not be left to the Metropolitan Police – although 4,000 were to be stationed along the Thames bridges. Public buildings were to be guarded by 'special constables'. Paterfamiliases were sworn in as specials, with white armbands and truncheons as symbols of their authority; many also carried umbrellas. There may have been as many as 85,000 'specials' on duty that day; gentlemen brought their gamekeepers from the country with their guns. Troops were garrisoned around all public buildings, including the Royal Exchange; the Bank of

England was sandbagged and cannon were set on the roof – soldiers, however, were prudently mainly kept out of sight. The mass meeting was held on Kennington Common, and the Chartists then progressed as far as the Thames bridges. There, halted by the police, they dispersed while the petition was taken to Parliament in a cab – to be ridiculed, since some signatures were clumsy forgeries.

Chartism collapsed and London grew more quiescent, despite the Fenian outrages and minor disturbances at the time of the Second Reform Bill agitation (1866–7). The capital became a centre of militancy once again only in the 1880s, with the growth of the new trade unionism. On Monday 8 February 1886, during a bitterly cold winter that had caused widespread unemployment, a demonstration was organized for Trafalgar Square, and a crowd of about 20,000 formed ('their numbers ... increased', *The Times* snootily reported, 'by a very great many of the idle class – of that large body in London who are spoken of by workers themselves as the class who want no work to do'). Ben Tillett, the dockers' leader, and John Burns from the Social Democratic Federation made speeches demanding work. A breakaway group headed for Pall Mall, and stones were flung at the Carlton Club's windows (apparently in retaliation after Reform Club members had insolently tossed nailbrushes at the demonstrators). The windows of clubs were broken, and the rioters pilfered from carriages, looted shops, and terrorized the West End. During the next two days 'roughs' gathered in Trafalgar Square, and a foggy London buzzed with rumour of riot. Shop windows were boarded up, banks closed, troops stood by, while threatening meetings and clashes were reported from Norwich, Northampton, Birmingham, Sheffield and Manchester. For months tension remained high, with the unemployed camping out in the royal parks and staging marches and demonstrations.

In the autumn of 1887 a ban was slapped on assemblies in Trafalgar Square; a protest demonstration was called for 13 November. The resulting fracas ('Bloody Sunday') was marked by unusual brutality as the police broke up the throng, which moved on to Hyde Park, overturning carriages and smashing the windows of Marshall & Snelgrove and Peter Robinson. It was 'almost incredible that, for at least an hour, the most frequented streets in the West End of London should be entirely at the mercy of the mob', W. H. Smith, founder of the bookshop chain, complained to the Commons. It is a revealing statement, since such would have been a commonplace event a century previously or even then in many European capitals: London had evidently become exceptionally orderly. Though the crowd had never offered any real prospect of revolution, the West End felt menaced.

Unrest continued. In 1888 700 match-girls working for Bryant & May went on strike for better conditions, and won. In August 1889 Will Thorne, the gasworkers' leader, demanded an eight-hour day for gasworkers employed by the South Metropolitan Gas Company. They too won, and other gas companies capitulated. Before the month was out, Ben Tillett had organized a shut-down of the London docks and declared, with the aid of the stevedores' and lightermen's unions – dockland's labour aristocracy – the formation of a Dockers' Union: their chief demand was a minimum wage of sixpence an hour. Burns, Tom Mann and Tillett conducted mass meetings on Tower Hill, leading dockers' marches for the next fortnight. The employers brought in blackleg labour, but the dockers were saved at the eleventh hour by subscriptions from Australia, prompting a stream of donations from British sympathizers, including trades unions, football clubs and the Salvation Army, which contributed money from the proceeds of *War Cry*. The Lord Mayor set up a conciliation committee, and Cardinal Manning duly presented the strike committee with an unconditional employers' surrender.

Overall, threats to public order remained remarkably slight. Even in 1830 and 1848, when revolution shook numerous European capitals, London was fairly quiet; the great Chartist demonstration remained peaceful. How do we explain this placidity?

The working class was increasingly politically isolated: City interests and the bourgeoisie no longer shared radical sentiments with rioters on the street. And the sheer size of Victorian London and the internal differentiation of the labouring classes played their part: London had become too big to be agitated, and working people were said to constitute numerous little 'islands', localized and fragmented, with little coherence and homogeneity. It has been suggested that a city's 'riot potential' may vary inversely with its size. As its population grew from 1 million to over 2 million during the first half of the nineteenth century, London ceased to be riotous. 'Those who shudder at the idea of an outbreak in the metropolis containing two millions and a half of people and at least fifty thousand of the "dangerous classes",' it was observed in 1856, 'forget that the capital is so wide that its different sections are totally unknown to each other. A mob in London is wholly without cohesion, and the individuals composing it have but few feelings, thoughts or pursuits in common.'

London's diminishing propensity for riot signals the decline of traditional popular politics. Both Owenism and Chartism, so militant elsewhere, were hampered by London's inertia. In 1839 Thomas Attwood claimed that London had long been 'remarkable for its soporific character', while Francis Place, as we have seen, thought London working men were isolated, 'living as they do at considerable distances, many seven miles apart'. Agitation 'must be rolled up to London from the country', argued the *Northern Star*, a Leeds newspaper:

London is always the last to stir, or when it takes the initiative, such is its overwhelming bulk, and the consequent segregation of its parts, that no powerful and well compacted concentration of popular energy is produced ... When you do get a large meeting it is not London, but the friendly parties who reside in different parts of it that are brought together by a common feeling. The outer public is scarcely stirred.

With its tight-knit body of artisans and freemen, Stuart and Georgian London had been readily mobilized. By the nineteenth century, working people were dispersed and often pitted against each other. Craftsmen were challenged by semi-skilled and unskilled labour, navvies, and tens of thousands of immigrants from Ireland and Eastern Europe. Traditionally, workers had been crowded in and around the City; by 1860 they were dispersed to Bow and Bermondsey, to Walworth and West Ham. South London in particular had no focus for political agitation. 'It is a city without a municipality, without a centre, without a civic history,' remarked Sir Walter Besant rather archly of London south of the Thames:

it has no newspapers, magazines or journals; it has no university, it has no colleges, apart from medical; it has no intellectual, artistic, scientific, musical, literary centre – unless the Crystal Palace can be considered as a centre; its residents have no local patriotism or enthusiasm ... it has no theatres except of a very popular or humble kind; it has no clubs, it has no public buildings, it has no West End. Its central edifice, a Frenchman remarked, was a public house – the Elephant and Castle.

Victorian social theorists, not least Karl Marx, thought that workers would most easily be politicized when concentrated in vast workplaces, notably factories. But London was dominated by small works, sheds, sweated labour – a far cry from the mill-town factories of the north. In Bolton or Bury, labour was fixed; in London it was mobile, and work was rarely continuous. It was therefore doubly difficult for trade-union loyalties to take deep root. Everything was unpropitious for effective political action. London's masses had to grab what benefits they could from the capital's rather confused prosperity, while waiting to see what would emerge from the long overdue creation of the London County Council in 1888.

With financial scandals over jobbery and peculation rocking the Metropolitan Board of Works in the 1880s, pressure grew overwhelming for its replacement by some more representative body. In 1884 Sir William Harcourt introduced a London Government Bill to unify the capital's administration in the capital, and 120,000 gathered in Hyde Park to cheer it on. The advent of the LCC had become only a matter of time, for the capital was acknowledged to be municipally backward. With its police force under central-government control and its gas and water supply, markets, docks and tramways and even some of its bridges and parks in private hands, London's administration in the age of Gladstone and Disraeli looked archaic in contrast, for instance, to the go-ahead municipalism of Birmingham. The Metropolitan Board of Works was not without achievements – it built the Thames embankment, the main drainage system and some major new streets; it set up the Woolwich Free Ferry, and planned the Blackwall Tunnel – but, as an indirectly elected body, it became the target of growing public suspicion. In an age of mass franchise, only the LCC could meet the metro-politan mood.

The LCC was established by the Local Government Act of 1888, lasting until superseded by the Greater London Council in 1965. Possessing jurisdiction over some 117 square miles, it was composed of 126 councillors elected every three years, plus twenty-one aldermen elected by the councillors for periods of six years. There were triennial elections to the Council, besides numerous lesser elections for the vestries, boards of guardians and the London School Board, all these being fought along party lines. Though the City still remained outside, a law unto itself, the creation of the LCC opened a new epoch in metropolitan government.

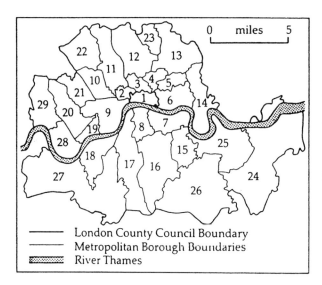

London County Council Boundary
Metropolitan Borough Boundaries
River Thames

The London County Council boundaries

1. City of London	16. Camberwell
2. Holborn	17. Lambeth
3. Finsbury	18. Battersea
4. Shoreditch	19. Chelsea
5. Bethnal Green	20. Kensington
6. Stepney	21. Paddington
7. Bermondsey	22. Hampstead
8. Southwark	23. Stoke Newington
9. City of Westminster	24. Woolwich
10. St Marylebone	25. Greenwich
11. St Pancras	26. Lewisham
12. Islington	27. Wandsworth
13. Hackney	28. Fulham
14. Poplar	29. Hammersmith
15. Deptford	

CHAPTER ELEVEN

Social Problems,
Social Improvement:
1820–1890

Hell is a city much like London –
A populous and a smoky city.
PERCY BYSSHE SHELLEY,
Peter Bell the Third (1819)

The monstrous city, the great wen, sin city – all such talk, building up over the years
from Heylin to Cobbett, was prophetic: its day was to come under Victoria. Population
rise had never been more explosive, industry never more polluting, disruption, demolition and building more frenzied. Air-, water- and bug-borne diseases multiplied, and
London was visited four times by Asiatic cholera. The teeming masses presented a
pandemonium of misery. 'Of this enormous Babel of a place I can give you no account
in writing,' Thomas Carlyle told his brother in 1824:

it is like the heart of all the universe; and the flood of human effort rolls out of it and into it
with a violence that almost appals one's very sense. Paris scarcely occupies a quarter of the
ground, and does not seem to have the twentieth part of the business. O that our father sey [*saw*]
Holborn in a fog! with the black vapour brooding over it, absolutely like fluid ink; and coaches
and wains and sheep and oxen and wild people rushing on with bellowings and shrieks and
thundering din, as if the earth in general were gone distracted ... No wonder Cobbett calls the
place a Wen. It is a monstrous Wen! The thick smoke of it beclouds a space of thirty square
miles; and a million of vehicles, from the dog-or-cuddy-barrow to the giant waggon, grind along
its streets for ever.

There is an excitement in all this, which is pleasant as a transitory feeling, but much against
my taste as a permanent one. I had much rather visit London from time to time, than live in it.
There is in fact no *right* life in it that I can find: the people are situated here like plants in a hot-
house, to which the quiet influences of sky and earth are never in their unadulterated state
admitted. It is the case with all ranks: the carman with his huge slouch-hat hanging half-way
down his back, consumes his breakfast of bread and tallow or hog's lard, sometimes as he swags

257

Panoramic view of London from the Monument by Carl Haag (1820–1915)

along the streets, always in a hurried and precarious fashion, and supplies the deficit by continual pipes, and pots of beer. The fashionable lady rises at three in the afternoon, and begins to live towards midnight. Between these two extremes, the same false and tumultuous manner of existence more or less infests all ranks. It seems as if you were for ever in 'an inn', the feeling of *home* in our acceptation of the term is not known to one of a thousand.

Carlyle saw London through traditional images of bedlam and hell. Another Scot, the journalist Robert Mudie, denounced it as *Babylon the Great; or, Men and Things in the British Capital*. London, for Mudie, was all 'desolation, where every street is a crowd ... and yet comfort from no lip, and pity from no eye'. The dissolute disported in gilded pleasure palaces, the poor avenged themselves through villainy. In similar tones, the author and politician G. W. M. Reynolds later wrote in his *Mysteries of London* of the 'lazar house, the prison, the brothel, and the dark alley ... rife with all kinds of enormity'. Terrifying catalogues of London's vices were hawked on the streets, telling of the decline of churchgoing, the increase in Sabbath-breaking the 100,000 London women who had slain their babies, the surge in savage crimes, the flood of pornography, the 80,000 prostitutes, the penny theatres, gambling, the 10,000 drinking-places – 'All this is in London!' proclaimed *The Masses Without! A Pamphlet for the Times on the Sanatory, Social, Moral and Heathen Condition of the Masses* (1857).

The larger London got, the worse the pollution. The sanitary reformer James Hole commented in 1866 on the fate of Kentish Town:

The inhabitant whose memory can carry him back thirty years recalls pictures of rural beauty, suburban mansions and farmsteads, green fields, waving trees and clear streams where fish could live – where now can be seen only streets, factories and workshops, and a river or brook black as the ink which now runs from our pen describing it.

London was spawning pauperism, misery, crime, disease: piecemeal attempts had long been made to combat these horrors with charities, infirmaries, Bible missions and anti-vice societies. But it was national events, political and epidemiological, that precipitated radical change. In 1834 Edwin Chadwick secured the Poor Law Amendment Act, formalizing the workhouse system. This had dramatic implications, and not just for paupers, as has already been seen, but for the wider community, as workhouses became the foci of further functions. For it became clear that the infirm, sick and dying formed a high percentage of paupers and hence of workhouse inmates. Infirmaries were built, with isolation wards and fever wings, and the Poor Law administration inevitably became intimately involved with sanitary reform, because of the high incidence of sickness among London's destitute. Smallpox, measles, whooping cough and scarlet fever felled labourers' families more than the affluent, as did the cholera epidemics of 1832 and 1848–9. Disease threatened social collapse. A letter appeared in *The Times* on 5 July 1849 above fifty-four signatures:

Sur,

May we beg and beseech your proteckshion and power. We are Sur, as it may be, living in a Wilderniss, so far as the rest of London knows anything of us, or as rich and great people care about. We live in muck and filthe. We aint got no privez, no dust bins, no drains, no water splies, and no drain or suer in the whole place. The Suer Company, in Greek Street, Soho Square, all great, rich and powerfool men, take no notice watsomedever of our complaints. The Stenche of a Gully-hole is disgustin. We al of us suffer, and numbers are ill, and if the Colera comes Lord help us.

Throughout the Victorian era the majority of able-bodied applicants for poor relief were sick. In poor districts like Shoreditch and Camberwell over a third of institutionalized paupers became infirmary patients. In London, as elsewhere, the workhouse became *faute de mieux* a hospital, hinting that the capital was but a gigantic sickhouse.

The new Poor Law authorized guardians to appoint medical officers, and by the late 1830s the larger London unions were each employing several doctors, seeing patients in the workhouse and even paying house calls. Demand for parish medical services soared. In 1853, when smallpox vaccination became compulsory, Poor Law doctors in effect became public-health officials.

A rationalist administrator, Edwin Chadwick expected to cure pauperism through the 'less eligibility' philosophy of the workhouse system, a self-operating mechanism for eliminating pauperism: the workhouse being intended as nastier than work. Yet destitution did not diminish. Why then was his pet workhouse system not working? Chadwick blamed disease. By preventing labour, sickness caused penury. The struggle against disease therefore fell, he argued, within the scope of government. Disease, in his view, was caused by miasmata, gases given off by putrefying organic matter. Smell was disease, and filthy environments were to blame. Though later contested by many medics, this miasmatism spurred Chadwick's sanitary reformism. He became evangelical for the sanitary idea.

Cholera concentrated the mind. Asiatic cholera spread across Europe, reaching England in 1831. Little was done by the government, beyond calling a day of national prayer and fasting. By autumn, 5,000 had died from the epidemic, but still no countermeasures were taken.

Awareness grew that public-health hazards were rising. The capital's death rate stood at 25.2 per thousand, compared with 22.5 for England as a whole. In poor districts, like St Giles-in-the-Fields, one in three children died before reaching the age of one. Symptomatic was the worsening condition of the Thames, as late as 1800 clean enough for salmon to be caught and for Lord Byron to go swimming by Westminster Bridge. 'He who drinks a tumbler of London Water,' Sydney Smith told Lady Grey in 1834, 'has literally in his stomach more animated beings than there are Men, Women and Children on the face of the Globe.' Pollution was, ironically, the offshoot of progress. Wider provision of piped water supplied by London's private water companies led to growing use of flushing water-closets. Instead of being deposited in cesspits, human waste was now gushing into sewers and so into the Thames. Yet most private water companies extracted their piped water from the river between Chelsea and London Bridge. London's sanitation thus became an increasing hazard – though the bacteriological explanation was still quite unknown to Chadwick and his generation.

Chadwick investigated disease. He appointed three physicians sympathetic to sanitary reform, Neil Arnott, James Phillips Kay (-Shuttleworth) and Thomas Southwood Smith, to survey the London districts with the worst epidemic mortality. In the *Appendix to the Fifth Annual Report of the Poor Law Commissioners* (1839), Southwood Smith documented the squalor of London rookeries. Noting that urban improvements had hitherto been confined to the rich – 'nothing whatever has been done to improve the condition of districts inhabited by the poor' – he argued:

These neglected places are out of view and not thought of; their condition is known only to the parish officers and the medical men whose duties oblige them to visit the inhabitants to relieve their necessities and to attend to the sick; and even these services are not to be performed without danger. During the last year, in several of the parishes, both relieving officers and medical men lost their lives in consequence of the brief stay in these places which they were obliged to make in the performances of their duties.

Southwood Smith was an inspiration to reformist groups like the Health of Towns Association and the London Epidemiological Society.

The key document, however, was Chadwick's massive *Sanitary Condition of the Labouring Population of Great Britain* (1842), which proposed the creation of a national public-health authority to direct local boards of health to provide clean water, drainage, cleansing and paving on the rates. Chadwick advocated comprehensive new sewage and drainage systems: traditional square, bricked, tunnel-like sewers, built for carrying off rainwater, should be replaced by small, glazed, egg-shaped sewers, to be flushed by water pressure. Liquid sewage could be recycled into fertilizer on sewage farms. Cesspits must be abolished, a pure water supply created.

Chadwick, who was soon to complain that Parliament had ignored 'the experience of evils arising from the want of unity in the metropolis', aimed to enforce his system in London through a single Crown-appointed Commission responsible for water, drainage, paving and street-cleaning. Such proposals were widely denounced as tyrannically centralizing. 'The principles of this Bill,' thundered opponents, 'would breed a revolution even in Russia, if attempted there.' In September 1847 the government stalled for time by setting up another Royal Commission to inquire 'what special means may be requisite for the Health of the Metropolis'. By then, however, cholera was again advancing from the East, and under this terrifying threat the Commission's first recommendation – that the seven Crown Commissions of Sewers should be replaced by a single Metropolitan Commission for the whole London area, except the City – was quickly put into effect. (The City Sewers Commission survived, because it was not a Crown appointment.)

The first British Public Health Act was passed in 1848. This created a central authority, the General Board of Health, and the town council became the sanitation authority, responsible for drainage, water supplies, and inspection, and permitted to raise rates. Councils were to appoint local medical officers of health, empowered to regulate offensive trades, to remove nuisances, to identify houses unfit for habitation, and to provide burial-grounds, public parks and baths. However, the act applied only to districts *outside* the metropolitan boroughs of London, deemed to be covered by the Metropolitan Commission of Sewers (1848), and *outside* the City of London, which obtained its own private Sewers Act 1848, outwith the jurisdiction of the General

Board, and appointed its own (part-time) Medical Officer of Health. Once again London's anomalous status led to it being left behind.

Medical officers of health did become compulsory in metropolitan districts from 1855, but their lot was not easy. Relations between energetic medical officers and niggardly vestries were often strained. The vestry of St James of Westminster, for example, *reduced* the salary of its medical officer from £200 to £150 to check his enthusiasm. Vestries often appointed part-timers. Despite its enormous area, Wandsworth provided seven medical officers at a miserly £25 a year.

To pre-empt the General Board, in October 1848 the City appointed as Medical Officer of Health John Simon, an eminent surgeon and a skilful diplomat with, it so happened, a deep commitment to the people's health. His reports were aimed to make complacent aldermen wriggle. 'Let the educated man devote an hour to visiting some very poor area in the metropolis,' he advised:

Let him fancy what it would be to himself to live there, in that beastly degradation of stink, fed with such bread, drinking such water ... Let him talk to the inmates, let him hear what is thought of the bone-boiler next door, or the slaughter-house behind; what of the sewer-grating before the door; what of the Irish basketmakers upstairs – twelve in a room; what of the artisan's dead body, stretched on his widow's one bed, beside her living children.

In the months between his appointment and the return of cholera, Simon forged a new local medico-sanitary administration for the City. He organized weekly returns of deaths; the City police were required to report on street nuisances, the four City inspectors of nuisances enforced cleansing of privies and suppression of cesspools. He persuaded the New River Company to supply water twice a day instead of once. His office became the spring of sanitary action, and he battled with his masters, the City commissioners, many of whom initially regarded his activities with suspicion.

In the 1849 outbreaks, Simon and the City seemed vindicated and Chadwick refuted, for cholera hit metropolitan London grievously but left the City largely unscathed. Perhaps in consequence, in October 1849 Chadwick was unceremoniously booted off the Metropolitan Commission of Sewers, leaving him with no direct London authority. A few years later there was a repeat story. When cholera again visited London, in 1854, the Corporation accounted for only 211 of the 10,738 victims in the capital as a whole. By a lucky stroke, the fogeyish Corporation had found itself, in Simon, with a superbly efficient head of sanitary administration.

The politicking surrounding Chadwick perhaps hindered metropolitan sanitary reform. Vilified as a centralizer, he was a sitting target for 'localists'. Yet amidst the Chadwickian tragicomedy the need for change became unarguable. It was primarily to deal with the sewage problem that, under the sponsorship of Chadwick's old enemy Sir Benjamin ('Big Ben') Hall – according to Chadwick, 'a huge impostor of a man' –

the Metropolitan Board of Works was founded in 1855 for 'the better management of the metropolis in respect of the sewerage and drainage and the paving, cleansing, lighting and improvements thereof'. Replacing the old tangle of commissioners, a new metropolitan administration was set up. In the twenty-three largest parishes – Kensington and Islington, for instance – the ancient vestries were retained. The remaining smaller parishes, such as St Paul Covent Garden, were yoked into fifteen boards, whose members were to be elected not directly by the electors but by the vestry. These thirty-eight bodies plus the Common Council of the City Corporation were, in turn, to elect the members of the new Metropolitan Board. This cumbersomely constituted Board operated for over thirty-years, often battling with vestries, the City Corporation and other vested interests. It was condemned by some as another dose of Chadwick – a 'system of centralization' that was repugnant 'to our principles and our taste, which have hitherto always encouraged local self-government'. Yet though widely unpopular, the Board succeeded, at long last, in giving some coordination to municipal administration.

The urgent task of the Metropolitan Board of Works was to construct 'a system of sewerage which should prevent all or any part of the sewage within the metropolis from passing into the Thames in or near the metropolis'. For three years little was done; then, on 30 June 1858, panic broke out in the House of Commons. The cause was 'the great stink', arising off the Thames (called by Disraeli 'a Stygian pool'). The windows of the Houses of Parliament had to be hung with sheets soaked in chloride of lime, and tons of lime were daily dumped into the river. The stench forced the House to adjourn. That settled matters.

Laissez-faire dogmatists hardened to 10,000 cholera cases in Whitechapel rushed a Bill through Parliament to confer the necessary powers upon the Metropolitan Board of Works. The Board's Chief Engineer, Sir Joseph Bazalgette, set about creating a grand scheme which, completed in 1875 at a cost of £6.5 million, still serves. His task was helped by the fact that, though the scientific causes of epidemics were still hotly disputed, consensus had emerged that poor sanitation – above all, contamination of drinking-water by sewage – was a deadly threat. In 1849 Dr John Snow had maintained that cholera was carried in water, and he dramatically confirmed his theory a few years later by proving that all the cholera victims around Broad (now Broadwick) Street, Soho, had drawn water from the same pump.

The son of a Navy man of French extraction, Bazalgette had been appointed Chief Engineer to the new Board of Works in 1855. He identified two great evils to be tackled. One was the open sewers that still disgraced the metropolis. In 1848 a committee described a Lambeth house whose window overlooked an open 'sewer whose stench was such that the family often could not eat'. All such offensive sewers had to go underground.

It was equally imperative to stop sewers flowing directly into the Thames in the central area, whence much of London's water supply was still drawn. A solution had already been offered long before by John Martin, a painter and planner, who had proposed draining London's sewage into large reservoirs along the river banks from which it could be distributed by canals to the countryside and used as manure. In his *Suggestions for Improving the State of the River Thames and the Drainage of London* (1843), Thomas Cubitt offered similar views. 'The best means of obviating this evil,' he opined,

would be to conduct the sewer drainage at once from west and north parts of London, by the shortest and straightest lines that can be found, to a place to the east of the town (and perhaps the low lands of Plaistow or Barking Level would be the best calculated for the purpose), and there, near to the river, to form one or more very large reservoirs to receive the discharge from the sewers, where it should remain during the flow of the tide, having gates or sluices to be opened as the tide goes down; so that it would only be allowed to mix with the river when on its passage to the sea ... By this plan none of the sewer water could travel back to London.

What Cubitt proposed, Bazalgette executed. Under his direction, eighty-three miles of main sewers were built, intercepting the old sewers at right angles. Rainwater and sewage were taken in underground pipes to the river's edge. Conduits then flowed into large sewers running west to east underneath a newly built Thames Embankment. North of the river, Bazalgette constructed a high-level sewer from Hampstead through Hackney down to Stratford, where it was joined by the middle-level sewer, running from Kensal Green. The low-level sewer began at Chiswick, being pumped up at Pimlico. From Abbey Mills, Stratford, its contents flowed by gravity to the Northern Outfall Works at Barking Creek, where the sewage was discharged.

South of the river, only two intercepting sewers had to be built, a high-level from Balham and a low-level from Putney; they met at Deptford, where they were pumped into the outfall sewer down to the Southern Outfall Works at Crossness on the Erith Marshes. At both outfalls, discharge took place only at high water, and the untreated sewage was carried downstream on the ebb. The Prince of Wales opened Crossness in 1864.

Bazalgette's scheme – 1,300 miles of sewers in all – involved constructing the Victoria and Chelsea Embankments, with a total length of three and a half miles, reclaiming in the process thirty-two acres of mud and producing new public gardens at Charing Cross and Cheyne Walk. With their sturdy parapets, handsome thoroughfares, plane trees and cast-iron dolphin lamps, the Embankments are a tribute to Victorian engineering at its best, impressing even the tetchy Carlyle. The Victoria Embankment attracted the baronial New Scotland Yard. And underneath ran the Circle and District lines.

A huge success, Bazalgette's engineering won credit for the Metropolitan Board of Works: sewage schemes infringed few private property rights. It was a very different

The construction of the Thames Embankment at Lambeth, 1866

story with London's water supply, where plans for change came to nothing. London's water was largely provided by interests such as the Chelsea Waterworks Company, incorporated in 1723 'for the better supplying the City and Liberties of Westminster and parts adjacent with water'. Fears arose about the purity of its water. In 1827 a petition to the House of Commons by Sir Francis Burdett alleged that

the water taken from the River Thames at Chelsea, for the use of the inhabitants of the western part of the metropolis, being charged with the contents of the great common sewers, the drainings from dunghills, and laystalls, the refuse of hospitals, slaughter houses, colour, lead and soap works, drug mills and manufactories, and with all sorts of decomposed animal and vegetable substances, rendering the said water offensive and destructive to health, ought no longer to be taken up by any of the water companies from so foul a source.

Chadwick advanced a grandiose alternative. In 1850 he demanded an end to the use of Thames water, recommending water be piped from Farnham in Surrey. The eight existing private companies must be amalgamated, and 'the whole works for the supply of water, and for the drainage of the metropolis' should be consolidated 'under one and the same management'. This Utopian scheme was a non-starter. But the private water companies were in due course forced to introduce filtration systems, and an Act of 1856 forbade them to draw supplies from the Thames below Teddington – though this was little enforced, and even in 1868, long after cholera's water-borne nature had been established, one company was still drawing water in Battersea. After decades of resistance, the water companies were municipalized in 1902.

Complementing sanitation, the Metropolitan Board of Works became active in road improvements. New Oxford Street had been built in 1847 as a clearing through the St Giles slums – though by driving people into the remaining rookeries it made matters worse. The City also initiated road improvements. New Cannon Street, costing about £540,000, was completed in 1854; in the 1860s came the new Blackfriars Bridge,

'Monster Soup', a satire from 1827 aimed at official complacency about London's water supply

266

costing nearly £400,000; and the City's monumental improvement, Holborn Viaduct, 1,400 feet long and 80 feet wide, was constructed between 1864 and 1869, costing over £2.4 million. Bronze statues on the Viaduct celebrated Commerce, Agriculture, Science and the Fine Arts, and four houses stood at the corners, with statues of Henry FitzAilwin, the first Mayor; Sir Thomas Gresham, founder of the Royal Exchange; Sir William Walworth, the Lord Mayor who killed Wat Tyler; and Sir Hugh Myddelton, pioneer of the New River Company.

In the 1860s came Garrick Street – the Duke of Bedford was anxious to improve access to his Covent Garden market – Southwark Street, the widening of High Street, Kensington, and the extension of Commercial Road, Whitechapel. The Board also rebuilt Northumberland Avenue, linking the Embankment with Trafalgar Square. Clerkenwell Road was driven through the Clerkenwell slums between Gray's Inn Road and Goswell Road at a cost of £1.6 million, linking New Oxford Street to Old Street, traversing the Italian quarter round Saffron Hill, bridging the Fleet valley by Farringdon Road, and cutting through St John's Square. Farringdon Road itself had been built in 1845–6, following the Fleet down from Coldbath Fields Prison (King's Cross) through the Saffron Hill rookeries towards Smithfield and Fleet Street.

In 1877 Parliament granted the Metropolitan Board of Works powers to construct Shaftesbury Avenue and Charing Cross Road, their route planned by Bazalgette and the Board's Architect, George Vulliamy. Charing Cross Road was essentially a widening of Crown Street and Castle Street; the east end of Shaftesbury Avenue hacked through the notorious St Giles rookery, which was, according to the urban reformer Thomas Beames, 'like a honeycomb, perforated by a number of courts and blind alleys, cul-de-sacs without any outlet other than the entrance ... In the centre of the hive was the famous thieves' public house called Rat's Castle.'

Architecturally Charing Cross Road was a disaster, with ugly tenements designed to house 900 people. Shaftesbury Avenue was marginally better, and at its west end Piccadilly Circus was created. That too was in part an exercise in clearance. 'Walked round by Piccadilly Circus,' wrote Jeannette Marshall who lived in nearby Savile Row: 'the pulling down of the small poky houses opposite the "Cri." is a great improvement. It is really a fine open space now, and leaves plenty of room for circulation. It will be rather a trap for the unwary in crossing' (one of the greatest understatements in London history). In the middle, Eros, cast in aluminium, was erected by public donations in memory of the philanthropic 7th Earl of Shaftesbury, representing not the god of love but Christian Charity. Piccadilly Circus soon grew commercialized: by 1910 the famous Bovril and Schweppes' signs had been erected.

The Metropolitan Board of Works also acquired or tended London's parks, including Hampstead Heath, Clapham Common and Finsbury Park. Blackheath came to the Board at no expense, the Earl of Dartmouth waiving manorial rights. Buying out the ancient feudal rights of Hackney commons, however, cost the Board £90,000, Tooting Bec cost £10,200 and Clapham Common £18,000. Many thought this quite scandalous. It was not the last time that pots of public money went into the pockets of private landlords.

If successful with sewers, streets and commons, the Metropolitan Board of Works was far less effectual with slums – though no more unsuccessful than any other agency in tackling a problem that was insoluble given Victorian beliefs about the sanctity of private property. London's vast population rise brought no provision of central accommodation for the central poor – the half a million who had to be 'on the spot at the lucky time' for work in Covent Garden market or the docks, and their wives, who had to char.

Catastrophic overcrowding was commonplace. In Goodge Place, for instance, off Tottenham Court Road – by no means one of the classic slums – the 1841 Census found 27 houses occupied by 485 souls (125 families and 64 single people). Each contained an average of 18 people, one contained 32, and many occupants carried on trades in the same room, littering the space with materials, tools and barrows.

Overcrowding was getting worse. Twenty-seven dwellings, averaging five rooms, in Church Lane, Westminster, housed 655 people in 1841, but 1,095 in 1847, a density increase in six years from 24 to 40 persons per house. The cause was 'improvements': demolition of nearby properties to widen streets, which forced the population into the remaining ones – a phenomenon repeated throughout central London with commercial development and railway construction.

Lodging-houses were reckoned a particular disgrace, their overcrowding encouraging 'immorality'. 'All the beds were occupied, single men being mixed with the couples of the two sexes,' a report noted in 1850:

The question was never asked, when a man and woman go to a lodging house, whether they are man and wife ... I have known the bedding to be unchanged for three months ... They are all infested with vermin, I never met with an exception ...

The people who slept in the rooms I am describing were chiefly young men, almost all accompanied by young females. I have seen girls of fifteen sleep with 'their chaps' – in some places with youths of from sixteen to twenty.

Subdivided houses lacked water supplies, privies, proper sanitation and refuse removal. Their absentee landlords saw little need to repair property in high demand. For the owner, a tenement was an admirable investment. Small landlords, Thomas Cubitt reflected, belonged to 'a little, shop-keeping class of persons who have saved a little money in business'. Many rookeries were the ultimate property of magnates, livery companies, or the Church; but (as George Bernard Shaw's play *Widowers' Houses* later showed) they were run by seedy middlemen who pocketed the profit. 'The houses are let out, and under-let again and again, so that there are several links between the owner and occupier – the latter perhaps not knowing the name of the former.'

People lived chicken-coop-style because they could afford nothing better. Renting a whole house would cost 7s 6d a week: that might just about be affordable by a successful craftsman, but many families had only 1s 6d or 2s a week to spare. That would still buy a room in mid-century, though 2s 6d a week was more normal in central London.

Excess demand led to the creation of slums wherever the better-off vacated ageing properties. According to Thomas Beames, writing in 1850, there were rookeries which had been so almost from first building – such as Agar Town, where new houses were 'mere lath and plaster' occupied by a 'band of settlers who seem ... to have squatted there'. However, most rookeries, he observed, had once been the homes of the prosperous:

In the dingiest streets of the metropolis are found houses, the rooms of which are lofty, the walls panelled, the ceilings beautifully ornamented ... the chimney-pieces models for the sculptor. The names of the courts remind you of decayed glory – Villiers, Dorset, Buckingham, Norfolk, telling of the stately edifices which once stood where you bow beneath the impure atmosphere of a thickly-peopled court ... The most aristocratic parishes, as they are termed, have a background of wretchedness, and are too often so many screens for misery.

In St Giles, by New Oxford Street, the natives were mainly costermongers, street-sweepers, herring-hawkers, thieves, tramps and vagrants, with, in addition, many Irish 'who annually seem to come in and go out with the flies and the fruit'. In one house it was twelve to a room, in another seventeen. Even so, in many rooms there was but a single bed, and that only straw. As late as 1901, more than a third of families in many of London's inner boroughs were living in one or two rooms; in Finsbury the figure was over 45 per cent. In St George-in-the-East half the families existed in single rooms; in suburban Battersea, by contrast, two-thirds of all families earned more than 25s a week and rented three rooms or more.

Subletting was a universal response to rising rents. By 1885, 4s was being paid for a single room in St Pancras, and 5s off Tottenham Court Road. Remedial legislation was passed. The Shaftesbury Act (1851) helped local authorities erect working-class lodging-houses. The Torrens Act (1868) provided for the improvement or demolition of slums and the building of new dwellings. The Home Secretary Richard Cross's Artisans' and Labourers' Dwelling Improvement Act (1875) extended this, adding compensation clauses. But, since no funds were to be centrally provided, the tendency was to demolish but to leave the site vacant – substantial compensation having been funnelled into the pockets of slum landlords, who were the real beneficiaries of all such legislation. An amendment to the Torrens Act stipulated that, if a local authority condemned a property as insanitary, the owner could require the authority to purchase it from him. This was an incentive to landlords to keep their properties slumlike. In 1881 even the Chairman of the City Commissioners of Sewers, a pillar of the Establishment, could remark that the compensation provisions worked as 'a premium on evil-doing; a man gets a reward for letting his property be condemned'. Housing legislation got a bad name. 'The Torrens and Cross Acts,' opined Joseph Chamberlain in 1885, 'are tainted and paralysed by the incurable timidity with which Parliament is accustomed to deal with the sacred rights of property.' The Acts theoretically gave local authorities wide housing powers, but in practice they were dead letters.

In such circumstances the Metropolitan Board of Works had little success with housing. It possessed the power to demolish but not to build – it was required to dispose of compulsorily purchased land to capitalists prepared to build for the poor. But little success was achieved in obtaining tenders for the sites it cleared, and losses were run up, because of the generous compensation awarded to slum landlords. Fourteen sites, comprising forty-two acres, were taken over by the Board at a cost of £1,661,372 but were sold with losses of over £1,100,000. Goulston Street, Whitechapel, for instance, was acquired at £371,600 but sold for £87,600. Legislation was thus counter-productive, intensifying instead of alleviating overcrowding, and rewarding slum landlords in the bargain.

Further legislation was passed, including the 1890 Housing of the Working Classes Act, but little was achieved before the twentieth century, when the newly formed London County Council proved more favourable to council housing. Though starting slowly, by 1914 the LCC had housed about 25,000 people under the 1890 Act; but public provision of housing for the poor was for long an uphill fight that made little headway in the face of what Henry Jephson's *The Sanitary Evolution of London* (1907) called 'the all-powerful, the all-impelling motive and unceasing desire' for 'commercial prosperity and success' – that is, the profit motive.

Victorians offered various diagnoses and remedies for urban problems. An eccentric minority judged that nothing short of concerted public action would suffice. 'The wretched lodgings of the poor are the cause of more than half the misery now existing,' claimed a correspondent to the *Builder* in 1855:

It is of no use preaching religion, or making education cheap, or founding ragged schools, while the present state of things in this respect exists. Give to the poor man a cleanly and cheerful home at a price his means will bear, and then order and sobriety will ensue.

Most demurred. Evils stemmed from poverty, some suggested, and poverty in turn from the sovereign laws of supply and demand. Hence there was no magic solution. A further gloomy view found favour late in the century: urban evils would never go away, some maintained, because they stemmed from the degenerate stock of the lumpenproletariat.

Pessimistic viewpoints – bad characters created bad environments – could, however, be given a more hopeful twist through the notion of moral amelioration. Things would improve not by coercive legislation but by moralizing the poor – teaching thrift, sobriety, industry and housewifery – and through judicious channelling of charity to deserving cases. We have been accustomed to think in terms of state benefits; the Victorians put their faith in charity.

A constellation of charities grew up, and, as documented in Mrs Pember Reeves's pioneering study of working-class household management, *Round About a Pound a Week* (1913), most working folk had recourse to them. Soup-kitchens were provided; borough sanitary officers offered whitewash; mothers' meetings ran clothing and coal clubs. Midwives and nurses were employed by the maternity charities attached to major hospitals. For children, there were Sunday-school treats, Band of Hope events, and summer outings – in 1899 nearly 34,000 London schoolchildren got two weeks at the farm or seaside. Charitable activities operating in Lambeth around 1900 included 36 temperance societies for children, 36 literary or debating societies for young men, 27 Bible classes, 27 girls' or young women's clubs, 25 savings banks or penny banks, 24 Christian Endeavour societies, 21 boot, coal, blanket, or clothing clubs, 17 branches of the Boys' Brigade or Church Lads' Brigade, a day nursery, a 'prostitutes' institute', several libraries, dozens of Sunday Schools, and scores of others.

Housing reform was seen as crucial. The Society for Improving the Condition of the Labouring Classes, founded by Lord Shaftesbury, aimed to uphold morality by keeping families together. 'The strength of the people rests upon the purity and firmness of the domestic system,' the Earl maintained in the 1860s, with a characteristic mix of idealism and realism: 'If the working man has his own house, I have no fear of revolution.' In 1844 the Society erected Model Buildings off Bagnigge Wells Road (now King's Cross Road). These formed 'a double row of two-storey houses, facing each other, and on three distinct plans, to accommodate in the whole twenty-three families, and thirty single females'. This was followed, in 1847, by the now destroyed Metropolitan Dwellings off Pancras Road. In 1848 the Society promoted the block of 'Model Houses for Families' still standing in Streatham Street, off New Oxford Street. It contained fifty-four flats – each with a living-room, two bedrooms and scullery off which was a water-closet – to be let at 4s a week. The Society also erected cottage flats in Hyde Park for the Great Exhibition of 1851, re-erected in Kennington Park after it closed.

Another initiative came from Octavia Hill, who disapproved of barrack-like dwellings (they lacked light and air) and preferred doing up cottages for the labouring poor.

Supervision by philanthropic lady rent-collectors would help improve the morals of their occupants.

Later efforts to rehouse the poor were largely undertaken by *commercial* philanthropies, which provided a dividend to investors ('five per cent philanthropy'). This movement began with the Metropolitan Association for Improving the Dwellings of the Industrious Classes. Founded in 1841, its aim was to provide 'the labouring man with an increase of the comforts and conveniences of life, with full compensation to the capitalist'. By 1850 it had housed 216 families in three tenement blocks, two in Spitalfields and one in St Pancras, its rent-roll yielding over £3,000. This philanthropico-commercial approach was later followed by the wealthy printer and stationer Alderman Sydney Waterlow. He began in 1862 by building, at his own expense, four dwelling-blocks in Mark Street, Finsbury, going on in 1863 to establish the Improved Industrial Dwellings Company, with a capital eventually reaching £500,000.

Also active were George Peabody, an American merchant resident in London, and Angela Burdett-Coutts, the millionaire daughter of Sir Francis Burdett and granddaughter of Thomas Coutts of Coutts' Bank. In 1860–62 Burdett-Coutts built four Gothic blocks, known as Columbia Square Buildings, in Bethnal Green, at a personal cost of £43,000; the project housed 183 families and yielded a return of 2·5 per cent. Her aim was to make homes for '*the very poorest of the industrious classes*'. Rents varied from 5s a week for three rooms to half a crown for one, and families with more than a week's arrears were evicted. A resident superintendent policed the community of 600. Burdett-Coutts also set up the Columbia market, Bethnal Green. An attempt to wean the costermongers from the streets, it was an open quadrangle surrounded by elaborate market buildings including a galleried Gothic hall. The costers preferred the streets, and the market failed.

Peabody made a donation of £150,000, for working-class housing. Tenancies were to be let to respectable people; the aim was to help the deserving poor to help themselves. London sprouted numerous 'Peabody Buildings', the first in Commercial Street, Spitalfields. By 1897 they were housing nearly 20,000. Peabody estates were strictly managed, with model rules reinforcing the sanitary idea. It was stipulated that:

No applicants for rooms will be entertained unless every member of the applicant's family has been vaccinated or agrees to comply with the Vaccination Act, and further agrees to have every case of infectious disease removed to the proper hospital ... The passages, steps, closets, and lavatory windows must be washed every Saturday and swept every morning before 10 o'clock. This must be done by the tenants in turn. Washing must be done only in the laundry ... Refuse must not be thrown out of the windows ... Tenants are required to report to the superintendent any births, deaths, or infectious diseases occurring in their rooms. Any tenant not complying with this rule will receive notice to quit.

Peabody dwellings thus aimed to forge a more respectable working class.

To meet the needs of 'the poorest class of self-supporting labourers', the East End Dwellings Company was founded in 1882, to build sanitary tenement blocks. An example survives off Cromer Street in King's Cross, with galleries overlooking an internal court. Such courtyard blocks of tenements looked grim; the poor were given solidity but no frills. George Gissing called them 'barracks ... for the army of industrialism'. And meanwhile the poorest were neglected. 'They have done nothing for the worst class in Somers Town and Agar Town,' John Hollingshead fumed about philanthropists:

and they have wasted their means on a class who are well able to help themselves ... The costermongers, the street hawkers – the industrious poor – are still rotting up their filthy, ill-drained, ill-ventilated courts, while well-paid mechanics, clerks and porters, willing to sacrifice a certain portion of their self-respect, are the constant tenants of all these model dwellings.

Other metropolitan improvements were meanwhile being undertaken, not by Downing Street, not by the Metropolitan Board of Works or by the vestries, but by joint-stock organizations. One was the provision of cemeteries. The dangers of overcrowded churchyards were exposed by Chadwick in the 1830s. 'On spaces of ground which do not exceed 203 acres, closely surrounded by the abodes of the living, 20,000 adults and nearly 30,000 youths and children are every year imperfectly interred,' he claimed. His report included gruesome details such as the Bermondsey woman who had seen four green and putrefying heads sticking up from St Olave's churchyard. In Russell Court, off Drury Lane, the whole burial-ground, raised several feet by constant use, was 'a mass of corruption'. Partly as a result of Chadwick's exposés, legislation was passed in 1850 and 1852 to prevent further burials in such places, new cemeteries being constructed instead.

Several joint-stock companies established cemeteries outside the built-up areas – well-drained, enclosed, properly managed and with landscaped grounds. The first, inspired by Père-Lachaise in Paris, was All Souls, Kensal Green, consecrated in 1833. The South Metropolitan cemetery at Norwood, opened in 1837, was also laid out as an English landscaped park. The London Cemetery Company established two cemeteries: Highgate (1839) and Nunhead (1840). Highgate's most famous inhabitant is Karl Marx. Abney Park cemetery, Stoke Newington (1840), was unusual in being unconsecrated, and hence favoured by Nonconformists; an arboretum as well as a cemetery, each shrub was labelled for educational purposes.

Philanthropy blossomed in Victorian London. (Great was the need for it.) Gladstone tried a good Liberal approach, reforming individual prostitutes. The Society for the Rescue of Young Women and Children, the London by Moonlight Mission, the Society for the Suppression of Vice, the London Society for the Protection of Young Females, the Reformatory and Refuge Union, the Female Aid Society, the Association for the Aid and Benefit of Dressmakers and Milliners – these were but a fraction of London's more than 550 charitable agencies, dispensing aid to 'unfortunates'. Their income totalled nearly £2 million per year. A guide in the 1860s listed London charitable institutions as:

general medical hospitals, lunatic asylums, special medical hospitals, residential hospitals, general dispensaries, alms-houses, refuges for the destitute, asylums for orphans, homes for the aged or the outcast, societies for relieving general distress and destitution, societies for relieving specific distress, societies for aiding cases of emergency or for preserving life, institutions for reforming offenders or reclaiming the fallen, societies for the ameliorating of public morals, societies for aiding the resources of the industrious, provident societies, charitable pension societies, religious book societies, Bible societies, missionary societies, and many institutions or associations of mixed or miscellaneous character.

The belief was that missionary zeal would moralize the poor and lead them into the paths of respectability. Whether because this worked or thanks to improvements in material conditions, the signs are that, by the close of the century, the majority of London's poor were becoming better integrated into the mainstream of urban life.

By 1870 the sanitary infrastructure was improving, and morbidity and mortality from infectious diseases like typhus were declining. As drinking-water and drains improved, typhoid, dysentery and cholera retreated. In Southwark, as elsewhere, open privies had for centuries marked the backyards. By 1875 some 700 cesspools had been abolished there, water-closets had been provided, and, reported the Medical Officer of Health, 'immense numbers' of house drains had been constructed. Other factors contributed to a healthier urban environment. Asphalt was increasingly used for street paving, the LCC introduced new by-laws for storage of horse-manure, and the traditional fixed dust-holes for household refuse began to be replaced in the 1890s by modern covered dustbins. Flies were in retreat. In 1850–60 Whitechapel had a typhoid death rate of 116 per 100,000; by 1890–1900 it was down to 13. Similar improvements were experienced elsewhere.

Despite sanitary improvements, perceptions remained strong – perhaps even grew – of an inner rottenness in metropolitan society, marked by dirt and deprivation but involving something deeper – a terror of the 'great unwashed' living amidst urban blight. 'Of all the districts of that "inner ring" which surrounds the City, St George's-in-the-East is the most desolate,' wrote John Hollingshead in *Ragged London* (1861); it 'appears to stagnate with a squalor peculiar to itself'. Andrew Mearns's *Bitter Cry of Outcast London* (1883) provided the most devastating blast. Offering 'a plain recital of plain facts', Mearns denounced London's evils in apocalyptic cadences:

How long then must the little hands toil before they can earn the price of the scantiest meal! Women, for the work of trousers finishing [i.e. sewing in linings, making button-holes and stitching on the buttons] receive 2½d. a pair, and have to find their own thread. We ask a woman who is making tweed trousers, how much she can earn in a day, and are told one shilling. But what does a day mean to this poor soul? *Seventeen hours*! from five in the morning to ten at night – no pause for meals. She eats her crust and drinks a little tea as she works, making in very truth, with her needle and thread, not her living only, but her shroud.

Few outsiders, Mearns insisted, had 'any conception of what these pestilential human rookeries are, where tens of thousands are crowded together amidst horrors which call to mind what we have heard of the middle passage of the slave ship'. He tugged and tugged at the heart-strings, shocking his reader:

To get to them you have to penetrate courts reeking with poisonous and malodorous gases arising from accumulations of sewage and refuse scattered in all directions and often flowing beneath your feet; courts, many of them which the sun never penetrates, which are never visited by a breath of fresh air, and which rarely know the virtues of a drop of cleansing water. You have to ascend rotten staircases, which threaten to give way beneath every step, and which, in some cases, have already broken down, leaving gaps that imperil the limbs and lives of the unwary. You have to grope your way along dark and filthy passages swarming with vermin. Then, if you are not driven back by the intolerable stench, you may gain admittance to the dens in which these thousands of beings who belong, as much as you, to the race for whom Christ died, herd together.

Mearns bared London's soul; he offered few solutions.

The journalist W. T. Stead likewise protested against working-class ills in his popular *Pall Mall Gazette*, notorious for its exposés of child prostitution. Arguing that 'the crying scandal of our age' was 'the excessive overcrowding of enormous multitudes of the very poor in pestilential rookeries where it is a matter of physical impossibility to live a human life', Stead deplored 'the stunted squalid savages of civilization' and exposed 'the foul ulcer of London'.

Such outcries are difficult to interpret. Were the living conditions of the huddled poor really reaching their nadir around the 1880s and 1890s? That is possible, since most of the central housing stock was ageing fast, and overcrowding had been exacerbated by the railways, by office building, and (ironically) by slum clearance. But the wail from journalists and philanthropists may, in fact, mainly reveal new tensions between haves and have-nots, new anxieties among the rich, a new social conscience, or simply a heightened interest in how the other half lived.

Certainly it became the done thing among the liberal intelligentsia to inspect the poor – for West End to observe East End, with the inevitable blend of prurience, fear, conscience, breast-beating and voyeuristic slumming. Outcast London was another country. A witness before the Select Committee on the Health of Towns in 1840 stated of East End social conditions that 'they are as much unknown as the condition of a district in Otaheite'. Fifteen years later the London Diocesan Building Society called the East End 'as unexplored as Timbuctoo'. 'It is not in country,' wrote Charles Booth,

but in town that 'terra incognita' needs to be written on our social map. In the country the machinery of human life is plainly to be seen and easily recognized: personal relations bind the whole together ... It is far otherwise with cities, where as to these questions we live in darkness.

Men like Booth aimed to make sure 'darkest London' became very well known indeed.

The first volume of his vast *Life and Labour of the People*, published in 1889, was entirely on East London. A second volume (1891) included the rest. These volumes were reissued between 1892 and 1902 as *Life and Labour of the People in London*. Booth's work differed from earlier shock-horror accounts by offering, on the basis of ample data, an exact social profile and a classification of poverty, developing the notion of the 'line of poverty'. For the first time ever, social statistics and social description of Londoners rich and poor were spelt out in great detail with some semblance of scientific accuracy. For this reason it is worth taking stock and examining Booth's findings – while not losing sight of his own prejudices (he was heir to a shipping-line).

Booth divided London into eight social classes, four below and four above the poverty line:

H. Upper middle class.
G. Lower middle class.
F. Higher-class labour.
E. Regular standard earnings – above the line of poverty.

D. Small regular earnings ⎫
                             ⎬ together the 'poor'.
C. Intermittent earnings ⎭
B. Casual earnings – 'very poor'.
A. The lowest class of occasional labourers, loafers
    and semi-criminals.

Booth anatomized the sources and structure of poverty, developing an idea akin to a 'poverty trap' – some could not, or would not, escape, and they tended to pull the rest down. The four poorest groups were:

Class A – *The lowest class*, consists of some occasional labourers, street sellers, loafers and semi criminals, together with the inmates of common lodging houses, and the lowest order of the streets. With these ought to be counted the homeless outcasts who on any given night might find shelter where they can.

Class B – *Casual earnings – very poor*. In East London the largest field for casual labourers is at the Docks ... [They] do not, on the average, get as much as three days work a week.

Class C – *Intermittent earnings*: – Stevedores and waterside porters may secure only one or two days' work in a week, labourers in the building trade only eight or nine months' work in a year.

- In this class the women usually work or seek for work when the men have none, they do charring, or washing, or needlework for very little money.

Class D – *Small regular earnings*. The men are the better end of the casual dock and waterside labour ... the rest are in regular work all the year round at a wage not exceeding 21s. a week, including factory, dock, and warehouse labourers, carmen, messengers, porters, etc.

Booth thus differentiated London's poor. Some were victims of circumstances; others were inferior of stock or character, doomed to destitution. 'Many good enough men are walking about idle,' he wrote, but 'the unemployed are, as a class, a selection of the unfit, and on the whole those most in want are the most unfit.' Using the imperial analogy that so readily sprang to mind, he asked, 'As there is a darkest Africa, is there not also a darkest England?':

Civilization, which can breed its own barbarians, does it not also breed its own pygmies? May we not find a parallel at our own doors, and discover within a stone's throw of our cathedrals and palaces similar horrors to those which Stanley has found existing in the great Equatorial forest?

The English slum resembled the African jungle in 'its dwarfish de-humanized inhabitants, the slavery to which they are subjected, their privations and their misery'. For such problem classes Booth offered drastic solutions: work colonies on farms or overseas, and the Army. The respectable poor had to be protected from their taint.

Despite such dark thoughts, it was Booth's contention that grinding poverty was diminishing. A survey like his conducted in earlier decades 'would have shown a greater proportion of depravity and misery than now exists, and a lower general standard of life'. Even in East London, the lowest of the low amounted to only 1 per cent. 'The hordes of barbarians of whom we have heard,' Booth commented, alluding to Mearns's emotional excesses – 'who, issuing from their slums, will one day overwhelm modern civilisation, do not exist. There are barbarians, but they are a handful, a small and decreasing percentage: a disgrace but not a danger.'

Booth was less concerned about the degenerate than about those whose poverty was not personal but structural. For 'Class B', the 'very poor' – 100,000 people, or 11.25

per cent of the city's total population – the source of penury was irregular and seasonal work, in the docks and the great markets:

The labourers of Class B do not, on the average, get as much as three days work a week, but it is doubtful if many of them could or would work full time for long together if they had the opportunity ... there will be found many of them who from shiftlessness, helplessness, idleness or drink, are inevitably poor ... these it is who are rightly called the 'leisure class' among the poor ... They cannot stand the regularity and dullness of civilised existence, and find the excitement they need in the life of the street.

Above Class B, the labouring poor with more regular employment were, Booth believed, on the road to improvement.

He was right. For all London's evils and iniquities, by the close of the Victorian era 'outcast London' was in the process of being integrated, thanks to a combination of sanitary improvement, mass education, widespread charitable intervention, the gradual growth of public-authority welfare services, the availability of employment, and, not least, rock-bottom food prices. Recent research has been showing that, despite popular stereotypes, London children around 1900 were bigger, stronger and sturdier than they had been half a century earlier. A solid, improving, self-respecting and often patriotic working class was establishing itself, which, for the next two or three generations, was to enhance the metropolis's socio-political stability and prosperity.

CHAPTER TWELVE

Victorian Life

The bigger London grew and the faster it changed, the more it astonished.

Three million five hundred thousand inhabitants; it adds up to twelve cities the size of Marseilles, ten as big as Lyons, two the size of Paris, in a single mass. But words on paper are no substitute for the effect on the eyes. You have to spend several days in succession in a cab, driving out north, south, east and west, for a whole morning, as far as those vague limits where houses grow scarcer and the country has room to begin.

Thus the French observer Hippolyte Taine in his *Notes sur l'Angleterre*, written in the 1860s. Taine found Victorian London a culinary and cultural wilderness, its atmosphere forbidding, disagreeable, deadening:

A wet Sunday in London: shops closed, streets almost empty; the aspect of a vast and well-kept graveyard. The few people in this desert of squares and streets, hurrying beneath their umbrellas, look like unquiet ghosts; it is horrible. A thick yellow fog fills the air, sinks, crawls on the very ground; at thirty paces a house or a steam-ship look like ink-stains on blotting paper ... after an hour's walking one ... can understand suicide.

Numerous foreigners were of a similar mind. London's remorseless business was more conspicuous than its gaiety; its greyness was insufferable. And yet it was endlessly eye-opening. 'The vast town,' commented Dostoevsky in 1862 – vastness was on everyone's mind – is

always in movement night and day, wide as an ocean, with the grind and howl of machinery, railways shooting above houses and soon to be beneath them, commercial adventure, disorder superficially unrestrained though in reality controlled by the strictest bourgeois discipline, the Thames befouled, the atmosphere packed with coal dust; the superb squares and parks ... Whitechapel with a populace half-naked, brutal and famished, the city with its vast moneybags.

The metropolis was too big, it had no soul: thus thought some. Dickens remarked, 'it is strange with how little notice, good, bad or indifferent, a man may live and die in London'. For others that very anonymity was a relief, a liberation. Henry James quit his native Boston for Europe. Leaving France, his first foreign home, he came to England in 1876, and stayed until his death. Oxford charmed, the Cotswolds tempted, and in 1896 he acquired a house in Rye, But, though admitting it was 'difficult to speak adequately or justly of London', it was in the capital that he settled:

It is not a pleasant place; it is not agreeable or cheerful or easy or exempt from reproach. It is only magnificent. You can draw up a tremendous list of reasons why it should be insupportable. The fogs, the smoke, the darkness, the wet ... the ugliness, the brutal size of the place ... the manner in which this senseless bigness is fatal to ... convenience, to conversation, to good manners ... You may call it dreary, heavy, stupid, dull, inhuman, vulgar at heart and tiresome in form ... But these are occasional moods and for one who takes it as I take it, London is on the whole the most possible form of life. It is the biggest aggregation of human life – the most complete compendium of the world.

An Englishman by election – he accepted British citizenship late in life – James took a somewhat perverse pride in London's situation: 'It is a real stroke of luck for a particular country that the capital of the human race happens to be British.'

Yet London was a capital that wasn't a capital. Even Londoners and London-lovers had to admit it was all fragments. 'London is like a newspaper,' ventured Walter Bagehot: 'everything is there and everything is disconnected ... there is no more connection between the houses than between the neighbours in the list of "births, marriages and deaths".' All could be accommodated somewhere. Émigrés invented Londons of their own – Karl Marx became the British Museum's greatest fan; van Gogh spent the happiest year of his wretched life working in Southampton Street, off the Strand, and living in Lambeth; Pissarro preferred Penge – and London was the home of artists, intellectuals, literati and England's Bohemians, in so far as the nation possessed an avant-garde. 'Town life nourishes and perfects all the civilized elements in man,' declared Oscar Wilde in 1891: 'Shakespeare wrote nothing but doggerel verse before he came to London and never penned a line after he left.'

London aroused love and hate. 'That great foul city of London,' exploded Ruskin, 'rattling, growling, smoking, stinking – a ghastly heap of fermenting brickwork, pouring out poison at every pore.' But all agreed it was unique: 'This is a London particular ... A fog, miss,' was Charles Dickens's way of expressing that quality.

For some, London spelt luxury. 'London has become a pleasure lounge for the idlers of the globe,' judged the author of *London of To-day* (1888): 'Americans, Frenchmen,

Germans, Indians, Colonials and persons of leisure and wealth from all parts of the world flock to the capital city during the season.' Its social machinery was well oiled. Lavish shops and plush hotels pampered the rich. Its clubs were exclusive: Taine judged the Athenaeum 'the last word of a high civilization', while Arthur Hayward cited 'the improvement and multiplication of Clubs' as 'the grand feature of metropolitan progress'. In their hallowed halls, Hayward observed,

a man of moderate habits can dine more comfortably for three or four shillings (including half a pint of wine) than he could have dined for four or five times that amount at the coffee houses and hotels, which were the habitual resort of the bachelor class . . . during the first quarter of the century.

It was not only bachelors who used the clubs. Their popularity among the married, foreigners observed, called into question the truth of 'home, sweet home'. By their superb comforts, critics jibed, clubs encouraged 'the cult of egoism, the abandonment of family virtues, the exclusive taste for material pleasures, and a deplorable laxity of morals of which the whole nation will someday feel the baneful consequences'.

The Victorian club had its own atmosphere. Georgian precursors like White's were gambling-dens. The new models were solid, sober, even stuffy; they kept up appearances. Indeed, they *had* impressive appearances. The United Service Club of 1827, designed by Nash and sited at the corner of Waterloo Place and Pall Mall East, was the first of a series of grand club houses to sprout in the area (it now, rather fittingly, houses the Institute of Directors). Designed by Decimus Burton, the Athenaeum arose in 1830, its Grecian flavour reflecting the fashion. The Travellers' Club (1829–32) was styled by Barry to resemble an Italian *palazzo*. The grandest was the Reform (1837–41), originally associated with supporters of the Great Reform Bill of 1830–32, its distinguished façade based on the Farnese Palace in Rome. The huge National Liberal Club, with its riverside site in Whitehall Place, was designed by Alfred Waterhouse. Conservatives, by contrast, congregated in the Carlton in St James's.

In a capital where, after George IV, the royal court lacked presence and there were few prestigious institutions of state comparable, for instance, to the Académie Française, clubs spanned the private and the public spheres, while upholding rank and gender exclusivity. 'These impregnable fortresses play a most important part in an Englishman's life,' wrote Monsieur Wey, a sour Frenchman, after dining at the Reform in the 1850s. An Englishman could not bear the vivacity of a Parisian café, he judged:

It is probably this fear that everyone has of compromising himself with a person of a rank too inferior to his own . . . that has made almost impossible the organization of those places of public meeting so common in France, where the natural gaiety of the inhabitants manifests itself almost without restraint, and where the presence of women prompts . . . grace and proverbial politeness.

Clubs helped keep London a masculine city, and St James's, with its bachelor chambers around King and Jermyn Streets, was its inner sanctum. The reign of the private club did not yield to the social fluidity of restaurants and hotels until the Edwardian era, by when Victorian reserve was turning into a more swaggering lifestyle among patricians and plutocrats, partly through the influence of American and colonial millionaires holidaying in town.

Meanwhile, out in the suburbs, Victorian London acquired its representative middle-class mascot, Charles Pooter, comic hero of George and Weedon Grossmith's *Diary of a Nobody*. A City clerk, Pooter lived with his wife and solitary servant in a semi-detached villa:

My dear wife Carrie and I have just been a week in our new house, 'The Laurels', Brickfield Terrace, Holloway – a nice six-roomed residence, not counting basement, with a front breakfast-parlour. We have a little front garden; and there is a flight of ten steps up to the front door, which, by-the-by, we keep locked with the chain up.

Pooter was funny but true because of his harmlessly snobbish unavailing attempts to keep up appearances in shabby-genteel surroundings. The air of social success was essential, though his circumstances were strained and tradesmen were always duping him. To make the best of a dreary social round, he wove fantasies around life at 'The Laurels'. 'We have a nice little back garden which runs down to the railway,' the opening page of his diary bravely proclaimed:

We were rather afraid of the noise of the trains at first, but the landlord said we should not notice them after a bit, and took £2 off the rent. He was certainly right; and beyond the cracking of the garden wall at the bottom, we have suffered no inconvenience.

Pooter represented City man. Like a hundred thousand of his fellows, he suffered a stifling, taxing working atmosphere requiring punctuality, formal dress, conformity and deference to his betters – all for a pittance, but with the compensation of feeling a cut above the manual workers from whose more vulgar lifestyles the Pooters so carefully distanced themselves. Suburbs like Holloway and Hornsey, or later Penge and Putney, built to cater for Pooters, created scaled-down versions of Paddington or Primrose Hill. The bourgeoisie aped their betters in their pursuit of taste, decorum and anxious gentility.

Pooterish sorts – decent fellows living in the inner, and later the outer, suburbs – were targeted by improving literature, works like *How I Managed My House on £200 a Year* (1864), in which the Victorian clerk and paterfamilias informs his wife that he has found a residence in an expanding suburb 'near Islington':

The house at thirty pounds, which stands in the open space of garden ground, close to the field of forty acres, will be just the thing for us. I should think it would be some years before the now pretty view can be built out. It is only three miles from London, perhaps a little more to the office, but that does not signify. We shall have no neighbours yet, and I have observed very common people do not live in semi-detached houses; they like to congregate near a market, and so ought we, as a matter of economy, but I think fresh air better than very cheap food. So, little wife, it is settled.

The capital's Pooters were attempting to put a chasm between themselves and the swarms of Londoners inimitably depicted (a generation earlier) by the supreme metropolitan journalist Henry Mayhew. He made the city his own. He so loved it, he felt impelled to ascend in a balloon and see the whole at once:

It was a wonderful sight to behold that vast bricken mass of churches and hospitals, banks and prisons, palaces and workhouses, docks and refuges for the destitute, parks and squares, and courts and alleys, which make up London – all blent into one immense black spot – to look down upon the whole as the birds of the air look down upon it, and see it dwindled into a mere rubbish heap – to contemplate from afar that strange conglomeration of vice and avarice and low cunning, of noble aspirations and human heroism, and to grasp it in the eye, in all its incongruous integrity, at a single glance – to take, as it were, an angel's view of that huge town where, perhaps, there is more virtue and more iniquity, more wealth and more want, brought together into one dense focus than in any other part of the earth.

But Mayhew always descended, and mingled with the masses. In a vast outpouring of magazine articles and books, notably *London Labour and the London Poor* (1851–62), he conveyed, like no one before him, save Dickens, the flavour, smells and the very expressions of teeming London. 'All are bawling together – salesmen and hucksters of provisions, capes, hardware, and newspapers, – till the place is a perfect Babel of competition' – this was his word picture of Billingsgate:

'Ha-a-ansome cod! best in the market! All alive! alive! alive O!' 'Ye-o-o! Ye-o-o! here's your fine Yarmouth bloaters! Who's the buyer?' ... 'Oy! oy! oy! Now's your time! fine grizzling sprats! good and cheap! fine cock crabs all alive O!' 'Five brill and one turbot – have that lot for a pound! Come and look at 'em, governor; you won't see a better sample in the market' ... 'O ho! O ho! this way – this way! Fish alive! alive! alive O!'

With his mental tape-recorder, Mayhew thus conveyed the sounds of London. But he also evoked its textures, colours and business:

In the darkness of the shed, the white bellies of the turbots, strung up bow-fashion, shine like mother-of-pearl, while, the lobsters, lying upon them, look intensely scarlet, from the contrast.

Brown baskets piled up on one another, and with the herring-scales glittering like spangles all over them, block up the narrow paths. Men in coarse canvas jackets, and bending under huge hampers, push past, shouting 'Move on! move on, there!' and women, with the long limp tails of cod-fish dangling from their aprons elbow their way through the crowd . . .

As you walk back from the shore to the market, you see small groups of men and women dividing the lot of fish they have bought together. At one basket, a coster, as you pass, calls to you, and says, 'Here, master, just put these three half-pence on these three cod, and obleege a party'. The coins are placed, and each one takes the fish his coin is on; and so there is no dispute.

At length nearly all the busy marketing has finished, and the costers hurry to breakfast. At one house, known as 'Rodway's Coffee-house', a man can have a meal for 1d, – a mug of hot coffee and two slices of bread and butter, while for two-pence what is elegantly termed 'a tightner', that is to say, a most plentiful repast, may be obtained. Here was a large room, with tables all round, and so extremely silent, that the smacking of lips and sipping of coffee were alone heard.

No mere impressionist, Mayhew was an anatomist of the poor, presenting uniquely detailed analyses of their diet and purchasing habits, their involvement with pawnshops and alcohol, and their streetwise ways with charities. He was an adroit observer of the petty capitalism pervading the metropolis from top to bottom, explaining piece-work, lump-work and contract-work and the domestic system.

London, Mayhew thought, had upwards of 40,000 street people, many extremely poor, making a little from a little. Barefoot children would buy a few pennyworth of watercress at Farringdon, wetting it at the Hatton Garden pump, bunching and selling it for a few pennies. Some had a tray of oranges. Flower-sellers were more suspect: bunches of violets were often a cover for 'immoral purposes'.

Most prominent were the costermongers (from costard, a type of apple). They cried their wares in the streets: 'Strawberries ripe and cherries in the rise', 'Rushes green' (for floors), 'Small coals', 'Old chairs to mend'. Street traders sold larks, sparrows and nightingales, roast chestnuts, baked potatoes, hot eels, muffins and ginger beer, and ink – anything portable. 'Duffers' sold fakes – imitation perfumes and antiques, and falsely painted birds. What distinguished them was their cockney slang, often turning words back to front. Yenep meant a penny, a top of reeb a pot of beer. 'There is the "Cagers' (beggars') cant", as it is called,' Mayhew wrote with John Binny in *The Criminal Prisons of London* (1862):

a style of language which is distinct from the slang of the thieves, being arranged on the principle of using words that are similar in sound to the ordinary expressions for the same idea. 'S-pose now, your honour', said a 'shallow cove', who was giving us a lesson in the St Giles' classics, 'I wanted to ask a codger to come and have a *glass* of *rum* with me, and smoke a *pipe* of *baccer* over a game of *cards* with some *blokes* at *home* – I should say, *Splodger*, will you have a Jack-sur*pass* of finger-and-*thumb*, and blow your yard of *tripe* of nosey-me-*knacker*, while we have a touch of the *broads* with some other heaps of *coke* at my *drum*?'

Lastly comes the veritable slang, or English '*Argot*', *i.e.*, the secret language used by the London thieves. This is made up, in a great degree, of the mediaeval Latin, in which the Church service was formerly chanted, and which indeed gave rise to the term *cant* (from the Latin *cantare*), it having been the custom of the ancient beggars to 'intone' their prayers when asking for alms. 'Can you roker Romany (can you speak cant)?' one individual 'on the cross' will say to another who is not exactly 'on the square'; and if the reply be in the affirmative, he will probably add 'What is your monekeer (name)? – Where do you stall to in the huey (where do you lodge in the town)?' 'Oh, I drop the main toper (get out of the high-road),' would doubtless be the answer, 'and slink into the ken (lodging-house) in the back drum (street).' 'Will you have a shant o'gatter (pot of beer) after all this dowry of parny (lot of rain)? I've got a teviss (shilling) left in my clinic (pocket).'

The four volumes of *London Labour and the London Poor* offer a panorama of street traders, street performers and prostitutes, while among the more skilled workers there are descriptions of tailors, shoemakers, hatters, cabinet-makers, toymakers, turners, carpenters, coopers, joiners, sawyers, shipbuilders and weavers. Mayhew chronicled their stories with a Dickensian ear – 'My informant, who is also dignified with a title, or as he calls it a "handle to his name", gave me the following account of himself,' he recorded of a Birmingham-born lad:

The first thing I remembers is being down on the shore at Cuckold's P'int when the tide was out and up to my knees in mud, and a gitting down deeper and deeper every minute till I was picked up by one of the shore-workers. I used to git down there every day, to look at the ships and boats a sailing up and down; I'd niver be tired a looking at them at that time. At last father 'prenticed me to a blacksmith in Bermondsey, *and than I couldn't git down to the river when I like, so I got to hate the forge and the fire, and blowing the bellows, and couldn't stand the confinement no how, – at last I cuts and runs.* After some time they gits me back ag'in, but I cuts ag'in. I was determined not to stand it. I wouldn't go home for fear I'd be sent back, so I goes down to Cuckold's P'int and there I sits near half the day, when who should I see but the old un as had picked me up out of the mud when I was a sinking. I tells him all about it, and he takes me home along with hisself, and gits me a bag and an o, and takes me out next day, and shows me what to do, and shows me the dangerous places, and the places what are safe, and how to rake-in the mud for rope, and bones, and iron, and that's the way I comed to be a shore-worker. Lor' bless you, I've worked Cuckold's P'int for more no twenty year. I know places where you'd go over head and ears in the mud, and jist alongside on 'em you may walks as safe as you can on this floor. But it don't do for a stranger to try it, he'd wery soon git in, and it's not so easy to git out agin, I can tell you. I stay'd with the old un a long time, and we used to git lots o' tins, specially when we'd go to work the sewers. I liked that well enough. I could git into small places where

Sewer hunting in the 1850s. Engraving by Mayhew

the old un couldn't and when I'd got near the grating in the street, I'd search about in the bottom of the sewer; I'd put down my arm to my shoulder in the mud and bring up shillings and half-crowns, and lots of coppers, and plenty other things. I once found a silver jug as big as a quart pot, and often found spoons and knives and forks and every thing you can think of ... There's some places, 'specially in the old sewers, where they say there's foul air, and they tells me the foul air 'ill cause instantious death, but I niver met with anythink about it, for I've worked the sewers, off and on, for twenty year. When we comes to a narrow-place as we don't know, we takes the candle out of the lantern and fastens it on the hend of the o, and then runs it up the sewer, and the light stays in, we knows as there a'n't no danger. We used to go up the city sewer at Blackfriars-bridge, but that's stopped up now; its boarded across inside. The city wouldn't let us up if they knew it, 'cause of the danger, they say, but they don't care if we hav'n't got nothink to eat nor a place to put our heads in, while there's plenty of money lying there and good for nobody. If you was caught up it and brought afore the Lord Mayor, he'd give you fourteen days on it, as safe as the bellows, so a good many on us now is afraid to wenture in. We don't wenture as we used to, but still it's done at times. There's a many places as I knows on where the bricks has fallen down, and that there's dangerous; it's so delaberated that if you touches with your head or with the hend of the o, it 'ill all come down atop o' you. I've often seed as many as a hundred rats at once, and they're woppers in the sewers, I can tell you; them there water rats, too, is far more ferociouser than any other rats, and they'd think nothing of taking a man, if they found that couldn't get away no how, but if they can why they runs by and gits out o' the road. I knows a chap as the rats tackled in the sewers; they bit him hawfully: you must ha' heard on it; it was him as the water-men went in arter when they heard him a shouting as they was a rowin' by. Only for the watermen the rats would ha' done for him, safe enough. Do you recollect hearing on the man as was found in the sewers about twelve years ago? – oh you must – the rats eat every bit of him, and left nothing but his bones. I knowed him well, he was a rig'lar shore-worker.

The rats is wery dangerous, that's sartain, but we always goes three or four on us together, and the varmint's too wide awake to tackle us then, for they know they'd git off second best. You can go a long way in the sewers if you like; I don't know how far. I niver was at the end on them myself; for a cove can't stop in longer than six or seven hous, 'cause of the tide, you must be out before that's up. There's a many branches on ivery side, but we don't go into all, we go where we know, and where we're always sure to find somethink. I know a place now where there's more than two or three hundredweight of metal all rusted together, and plenty of money among it too; but its too heavy to carry it out, so it'll stop there I s'pose till the world comes to an end. I often brought out a piece of metal half a hundred in weight, and took it under the harch of the bridge, and broke it up with a large stone to pick out the money. I've found sovereigns and half sovereigns over and over ag'in, and three on us has often cleared a couple of pound apiece in one day out of the sewers. But we no sooner got the money than the publican had it. I only wish I'd back all the money I've guv to the publican, and I wouldn't care how the wind blew for the rest of my life.

Life was tough, and the street people's work exotic. But most were self-sufficient, law-abiding, and fiercely independent. 'Bless your heart the smell's nothink,' Mayhew was told by the man who searched the sewers for anything saleable, 'it's a roughish smell at first, but nothink near so bad as you thinks, 'cause, you see, there's sich lots o' water always a-coming down the sewer. The reason I likes this sort of life is, 'cause I can sit down when I likes, and nobody can't order me about.'

Thanks to Mayhew, and to Thomas Wright's classic *The Great Unwashed* (1868), the complex layerings and status gradations of London's masses are recorded. Alongside the gross distinctions between St Giles and St James, there were also 'aristocracies of rags' – 'how great is the distinction between the layers of straw'!

The streets gave great pleasure. 'I am in very good health,' Mendelssohn wrote home to his family in 1829:

London life suits me excellently. I think the town and the streets are beautiful. Again I was struck with awe when I drove in an open cabriolet yesterday to the City, along a different road, and everywhere found the same flow of life, everywhere green, yellow, red bills stuck on the houses from top to bottom, or gigantic letters painted on them, everywhere noise and smoke, everywhere the ends of the streets lost in fog. Every few moments I passed a church, or a market-place, or a green square, or a theatre, or caught a glimpse of the Thames, on which the steamers can now go right through the town under all the bridges, because a mechanism has been invented for lowering the large funnels like masts. To see, besides, the masts from the West India Docks looking across, and to see a harbour as large as Hamburg's treated like a pond, with sluices, and the ships arranged not singly but in rows, like regiments – all that makes one's heart rejoice over the great world.

No native recorded the pleasures of strolling better than Arthur Munby, the civil servant who got a sexual kick out of working-class women and found unquenchable joy in the toings and froings of street-life. 'I walked up to the New Road [Euston Road], and had a long talk with the old ballad seller opposite S. Pancras church,' he recalled one day:

A very respectable intelligent man, of some education: said he had been there twenty years and brought up a family of nine children on the proceeds of his stall. The trade, he said, was never so good as now: the public concert rooms have created a large demand for popular songs of the day, and the old fashioned ballads sell well too. Has customers of all classes, but mostly young men, shopmen and artisans, who buy sentimental parlour ditties, and servantmaids. These when they first come to London buy the old ballads they've heard at home in the country; but afterwards they choose rather the songs – from English operas and so on – which they hear young missis a playing upstair.

London's streets saw occasional public pageantry, and Victoria's reign culminated in three exceptional state occasions in which Londoners participated: the Golden Jubilee of 1887, the Diamond Jubilee of 1897 and, in 1901, the Queen's funeral. Of these, the 1887 Jubilee was the most brilliant, involving a great gathering of European royalty, a thanksgiving service at Westminster Abbey, and a review of the Volunteers in Hyde Park, which was also the scene of a gigantic party for poor children, each being given a bun and a Jubilee mug. Charity dinners marked the occasion in the East End.

Victorian London saw the Indian summer of that eighteenth-century phenomenon the pleasure garden. The high spot was Cremorne Gardens in Chelsea, opened in 1832 by a man styling himself the Baron de Beaufain. First conceived as a sports club, it was soon offering all kinds of other diversions – pony races, evening dances and ballooning: Charles Green ('the intrepid aeronaut') made an ascent accompanied by a lady and a leopard. But most of the Georgian pleasure gardens disappeared because their sites became engulfed in housing developments and were killed off by residents' objections. The popular Highbury Barn, which drew crowds to its large lamp-lit open-air dance floor, lost its licence owing to local objectors and was closed down in 1876. Vauxhall Gardens were built over in 1859 by the main-line railway into Victoria.

The Metropolitan Fairs Act of 1871 stated that 'fairs are unnecessary, are the cause of grievous immorality and are very injurious to the inhabitants of the towns where they are held'. Hampstead Heath and Blackheath, however, continued the fun of the fair as popular cockney bank-holiday resorts, with sports and slides and donkey rides. More distant fairs in places like Epping Forest attracted day-trippers, and the Derby Day excursion to Epsom was as much for the roundabouts as the races.

Semi-rustic sports continued, including cricket. In 1811 a three-day county match for a purse of 500 guineas was staged between the ladies of Surrey and the ladies of Hampshire. 'The combatants were dressed in loose trousers,' Richard Phillips's *Monthly Magazine* reported, 'with short-fringed petticoats descending to the knee, and light flannel waistcoats with sashes round the waist.' Hampshire won. From mid-century, sport grew more professional and better organized. Football, rugby and cricket gradually assumed familiar forms, the creation of teams like Arsenal giving cultural expression to works and local loyalties.

London Zoo flourished. Established in 1828 on the north side of Regent's Park, it boasted the world's largest animal collection. Decimus Burton planned the layout, and the animals were augmented by those of the Tower menagerie. In August 1851 a staggering 145,000 visitors – most up for the Exhibition – went to the Zoo, the chief attraction being a four-ton hippopotamus, judged by Macaulay 'the ugliest of the works of God'.

Though squeezed by propriety and the police, many traditional amusements survived. Under George IV cock-fighting, dog-fights and ratting were all in vogue, attracting, like horse-racing, wide clienteles, from the criminal to the cream. Cock-fighting was banned in 1849. Public hangings remained a popular spectacle: more than 30,000 people would assemble at Newgate, and up to £25 might be paid for a room with a good view. After 1868 the hangings took place behind prison walls. Newgate had a 'horrible fascination' for Dickens. It crops up in *Barnaby Rudge*; in *Oliver Twist*, in which Fagin waits for the end, in the Condemned Hold, behind 'those dreadful walls';

and in *Great Expectations*, in which Pip is taken inside 'the grim stone building', to view the yard where the gallows are kept and 'the Debtors' Door, out of which culprits come to be hanged'. It was finally demolished in 1902 to make way for the Central Criminal Court.

Commercial leisure culture spawned shows and events. A great 'orama' craze began with panoramas, moving on to dioramas, cycloramas, cosmoramas and kineoramas. An early peep-show was the St James's Street Cosmorama. This possessed fourteen peep-holes set in the walls and fitted with convex lenses to magnify different scenic effects dramatized by special lighting. Jacques Daguerre, inventor of photography, ran a Diorama in Park Square East, one of Nash's fashionable new terraces. It opened with immense pictures of Canterbury Cathedral, eighty feet long and forty feet high, exhibited to spectators in a revolving chamber. You could also see 'Etna in Sicily under Three Effects, Evening, Sunrise and an Eruption', and 'Moving Pictures of the Bosphorus, the Dardanelles, and Constantinople'. The Colosseum, opened in 1826, was a huge circular building in Regent's Park by Decimus Burton. It offered a vast panoramic view of London as seen from the top of St Paul's and had, in addition, a Hall of Mirrors, a Gothic aviary, and a Swiss Chalet with a panorama of Mont Blanc. Then there were Burford's Panorama and Wyld's Globe, both in Leicester Square, providing exhibitions of the sights of the world, and the Egyptian Hall, Piccadilly, holding 'upwards of Fifteen Thousand Natural and Foreign Curiosities, Antiques, and Productions of the Fine Arts', belonging to William Bullock. In 1815–16 Bullock made £35,000 by a display of Napoleonic relics, including the Emperor's bullet-proof carriage.

Waxworks were firm favourites, especially Mrs Salmon's famous exhibition in Fleet Street. Madame Tussaud started in Paris in 1780, exhibited in the Lyceum Theatre in 1802, and then moved to the Baker Street Bazaar.

Scores of other shows attracted audiences. Perennially popular was Astley's Circus in Westminster Bridge Road. For concerts there were Covent Garden; the Italian Opera House, Haymarket, which became Her Majesty's Theatre; and the Hanover Square Rooms, where the Royal Academy of Music gave its first concert in 1823, and Liszt and Mendelssohn later performed.

All manner of other events had their day. In the 1870s roller-skating was all the rage; in the 1880s Cruft's Dog Show was born. Charles Cruft became James Spratt's assistant in 1860, selling dog food in Holborn. His 'First Great Terrier Show' at the Royal Aquarium, Westminster, in 1886, attracted 500 entries. From 1891 the name Cruft's Dog Show was used.

But amidst all these entertaining odds and ends – some spectacular, some tawdry – one spectacle stood out. To display Britain to the world, and vice versa, the Great Exhibition was staged in 1851. In a rather English way, it was designed not by a professional architect but by the Duke of Devonshire's gardener, Joseph Paxton, who had earlier erected a stupendous glass conservatory at Chatsworth. In July 1850 the *Illustrated London News* published his revolutionary design for an immense exhibition hall of iron and glass. Construction began in Hyde Park in September. By January 1851 the number of men employed rose to 2,112. They fixed 2,300 cast-iron girders on to 3,300 columns, and emplaced 900,000 square feet of glass, mass-produced in standard units, into 202 miles of wooden sash bars. Five hundred painters worked from cradles which ran along the building's thirty miles of gutters. The Crystal Palace was a high-tech triumph, with all its glass and its tubular iron pillars that doubled as drains. Above all, it was factory-made, prefabricated in standard sections. It was dazzling.

In February the doors were thrown open, at 1s a head (Friday 2s 6d and Saturday 5s). The average daily attendance was over 40,000. Queen Victoria made eight visits in the twelve weeks before the official opening and went thirty-four times afterwards – Dickens, by contrast, went just twice.

The 19,000 exhibits – Raw Materials; Machinery and Mechanical Inventions; Manufactures; and Sculpture and Plastic Art – formed the greatest array yet seen by men. There were the largest pearl ever found and the Koh-i-Noor diamond, engines of every description, carriages, china, glass and cutlery, including a knife with 300 blades. It was meant to be a showcase for Britain – though the quality of some French, Belgian and German goods was ominous.

Six million people visited this 'galaxy of splendour'. Thomas Cook conveyed some 165,000 of them – railway excursions made the Great Exhibition an astonishing triumph, and brought vast business to London. 'Thirty years ago,' *The Times* declared, 'not one countryman in one hundred had seen the metropolis. There is now scarcely one in the same number who has not spent a day there.' As usual, *The Times* got its figures all wrong, but the general point was true.

Everyone made money – business people, the government, and even the Exhibition Commissioners, who used the profits to turn South Kensington into a cultural quarter. The Exhibition attracted working-class and middle-class alike, and all the dire fears of vice and revolution proved unfounded. So popular was the Crystal Palace that resistance developed to its removal. A company was formed to re-erect it elsewhere, and Sydenham was chosen. Two railway stations, High Level and Low Level, were constructed to bring the millions. Destroyed by fire in 1936, little now remains but the life-size models of prehistoric monsters – the megalosaurus and the ichthyosaurus – looming amidst the foliage on an island in a lake.

A mini replica was the Alexandra Palace, north of Hornsey, named after the Princess of Wales. Gutted by a fire just after it opened, it was rebuilt in 1875. Equipped with one of the world's largest organs, the concert hall held 14,000 people.

A bold venture that flopped was the plan to build London's greatest pleasure grounds at Wembley. Served by the Metropolitan Railway, the site was intended to include an iron tower 1,000 feet high to dwarf the Eiffel Tower. It reached a paltry 200 feet before being demolished in 1907. But London acquired yet more monster halls and pleasure domes. Olympia was opened in 1886, and Earl's Court pleasure ground in 1894, with a Great Wheel and Buffalo Bill's Wild West Show. Olympia housed Barnum's circus in 1889, but in the next year it became a huge rink with the revival of roller-skating. Nearby the Royal Albert Hall went up, capable of holding 10,000 and destined to play a huge part in the musical life of London, particularly with the later Promenade Concerts.

Under Walpole's licensing act of 1737, London had two patent theatres, at Drury Lane and Covent Garden, and later acquired a third, Her Majesty's, in the Haymarket, which specialized in Italian opera. Around 1800 Drury Lane declined, but Covent Garden shone under the Kembles. Occasional Shakespeare, classic comedies, English opera, and some new plays dominated the bills; then in the 1830s Covent Garden led a Shakespeare revival.

In the free-trade spirit, the Theatres Act (1843) essentially de-licensed the theatre: henceforth the Lord Chamberlain was to withhold his licence only 'in the interest of good manners, decorum or the public peace'. This permitted the surge of the Victorian theatre, and the years after 1870 saw the building of the commercial West End familiar today. The cutting of Charing Cross Road and Shaftesbury Avenue in the late 1880s, and the formation of Piccadilly Circus, produced prestigious sites for the Lyric, the Royal English Opera House (now the Palace Theatre), the Duke of York's, Wyndham's, the New (now the Albery), the Apollo, the Globe, the Queen's, and the Prince's (now the Shaftesbury). The opening of Aldwych and Kingsway in 1905 resulted in a new Gaiety (now demolished) and the Aldwych and Strand theatres.

Theatre was hugely popular. The music-halls and theatres sprinkled round the West End and City could hold around 300,000 people – giving attendances of up to 100 million a year. Size spelt the heyday of the actor-manager, including the first stage knight, Sir Henry Irving, manager of the Lyceum from 1878 to 1902: Ellen Terry was his leading lady. Great actor-managers such as Harley Granville-Barker and Herbert Beerbohm Tree continued until the First World War, and, despite the cinema's challenge, theatre-building occurred in central London as late as the 1920s, including the Fortune, the Piccadilly, the Duchess, the Cambridge, the Phoenix and the Whitehall, and the reconstruction of the Adelphi and the Savoy.

Gilbert and Sullivan made the fortune of the impresario Richard D'Oyly Carte. He first produced *Trial by Jury* at the Royalty Theatre in Dean Street, Soho, going on to form a Comedy Opera Company which staged *The Sorcerer*, *H.M.S. Pinafore* and *The Pirates of Penzance*. In 1881 he opened the Savoy Theatre in the Strand with *Patience*.

He went on to build the ornate Royal English Opera House in Shaftesbury Avenue and the Savoy Hotel, naming suites after the Gilbert and Sullivan operas.

But not all the theatres were in the West End. In early Victorian times Shoreditch – the original home of London's theatre – was theatrically energetic. Popular at mid-century in the East End was the 'penny gaff', a makeshift theatre descended from the theatrical booths held at London's many fairs, staged in converted warehouses or similar premises, holding a couple of hundred rowdy young spectators. Performances were advertised by garish street posters, and a band would play to draw in the people. The usual offering consisted of two twenty-minute plays – usually melodramas, with titles like *Seven Steps to Tyburn* or the *Bloodstained Handkerchief* – with a song in the interval. The audience would throw missiles on to the stage – or halfpennies. In *A Hoxton Childhood*, A. S. Jasper described being taken to an East End theatre around 1900 by his sister Jo:

Sometimes on a Monday night she would come home from work and if she had a few coppers left over from the week-end she would say to Mum, 'Get yourself and the kids ready, we're going up to the Brit.' This was the old Britannia Theatre in Hoxton. Jo loved the dramas that were performed there. If Mum could afford it we had a bag of peanuts or a ha'penny bag of sweets. We went in the 'gallery' for two pence – half price for us kids. Among the dramas I remember was 'The Face at the Window' – real horrible. Others were 'Sweeny Todd', 'Maria Marten', 'Why Girls Leave Home' . . . Sometimes we went to Collins Music Hall or the Islington Empire. That was different. They always had variety shows. We saw Harry Champion, Vesta Tilley, the two Bobs, Hetty King, comedians of all sorts and stars of the day.

London had always abounded in inns and taverns, such as the Cock, specializing in steaks and chops, and the Cheshire Cheese, serving beefsteak pudding on Saturdays. Such hostelries had traditionally been for all. The Victorian era saw things change. With new snobberies and the emergence of restaurants and hotels, better people deserted the old drinking-haunts. The pub emerged for working men – and, alongside pubs, the gin-palaces. 'Gin drinking is a great vice in England,' observed Dickens in *Sketches by Boz*:

but wretchedness and dirt are greater and until you improve the homes of the poor, or persuade a half-famished wretch not to seek relief in the temporary oblivion of his own misery, with the pittance, which, divided among his family would furnish a morsel of bread for each, ginshops will increase in number and splendour.

Pubs generated an entertainment culture of their own. 'I went down to Tothill Street, Westminster, to examine a place there which advertises itself as "The Albert Saloon",' Arthur Munby recorded. He found thirty or forty people sitting on benches, drinking porter and smoking.

At the end of the room was a cracked square piano ... a young woman sat on a broken chair, with her back to the audience, strumming on the piano with unmeaning monotony. Three other young women, without bonnets and wearing cheap muslin gowns & jackets, sat among the people ... There was no curriculum of entertainment: every now & then one of the young women would say, 'I think I'll sing a song,' and would mount ... to the stage, and warble some 'Aunt Sally' or other harmless popular thing; the pianist strumming ever as usual. Sometimes the daubed canvas dropscene was raised, and a stage of about 6 feet by 10 was displayed, where one of the ladies performed a few conjuring tricks, or – on one occasion – a statuesque group of very mild & unexceptionable kind was represented by a woman and a child ... I came away ... much gratified with the rude picturesqueness and propriety of the place.

Out of such pub entertainments arose the music-hall. Its main ingredient was variety, a succession of individual turns – singers, conjurors, dancers, illusionists, acrobats, quick-change artists, strong men, monologue-reciters, eccentrics. Music was the mainstay. Singers appeared in character, and audiences joined in.

Enterprising publicans paid local singers to take part, and the master of ceremonies became an important ingredient, introducing the performers and exhorting patrons to fill their glasses. The catalyst was the new law of 1843 allowing concert rooms attached to pubs to be licensed for musical entertainment. Rapid developments followed, culminating in grand purpose-built music-halls. The Canterbury Hall in Lambeth, built by Charles Morton in 1854–7, is often called the first music-hall: it set the style for others such as the Old Mo in Drury Lane, the Panorama in Shoreditch, Wilton's in Wellclose Square, and the Cambridge in Bishopsgate. The Canterbury had brilliant gas lighting, lavish décor, vast chandeliers, an open platform stage, and rows of dining-tables with waiters serving food and drink. The chairman would lead the singing. Customers stood drinking at the bars, free to come and go. On stage, the singers wore evening dress.

Music-hall created the variety show, with star performers. Dan Leno's patter, Marie Lloyd's 'A Little of What You Fancy' and 'Oh Mr Porter', Charles Coborn's 'Two Lovely Black Eyes', Lottie Collins's 'Ta-ra-ra-boom-de-ay' – all became renowned. Sentimentality went down well, and so did jingoism: in 1897 Arthur Reece's 'Sons of the Sea' told the Germans that, though they might build a navy, they could not 'build the boys of the bulldog breed/Who made Old England's name'.

Centred on Hoxton, Shoreditch and Whitechapel, music-hall had become big business. In Hoxton Street stood the Britannia Theatre; MacDonald's, also in Hoxton Street, opened in 1864, and the Varieties, in Pitfield Street, in 1870. But by 1900 pub-based music-halls had been eclipsed by gorgeous variety palaces, with proscenium-arched stages and fixed seats in rows. Magnates like Oswald Stoll and Edward Moss were looking for family audiences to fill their giant West End Coliseums and Hippodromes, while the puritanical tendencies of the London County Council forced drink out of the auditorium. Battles were fought over the notorious promenades at the Empire Leicester Square and the Alhambra, both used as pick-up points for tarts. And, although the first London cinema was not opened until the new century, it was at the Alhambra that the first successful film was shown. Recording the 1896 Derby, won by the Prince of Wales's horse Persimmon, it was greeted with wild enthusiasm, the audience demanding the film be repeated over and over again.

London had always been Britain's beacon of learning and science. The Royal Society was chartered in 1662, while in 1778 the first specialist scientific society was created when James Smith bought the collections of the Swedish naturalist Carl Linnaeus and formed the Linnean Society to promote natural history. At Burlington House the Linnean rubbed shoulders with other learned societies: the Royal Astronomical Society, the Society of Antiquaries, the Royal Society of Chemistry and the Geological Society, most dating from the early years of the nineteenth century.

In 1754 the Society for the Encouragement of Arts, Manufactures and Commerce was founded: it has occupied its present home in John Adam Street ever since the house was built in 1774 as part of the Adelphi complex. It helped organize the Great Exhibition of 1851 – and the Festival of Britain a century later. Aiming at the popularization of science, the Royal Institution was founded in 1799 in Albemarle Street. First employed as assistant to Humphry Davy, its later Director Michael Faraday delivered popular Christmas lectures as well as making major discoveries in electromagnetism.

On the other side of the 'two cultures' divide, the Royal Academy had been founded in 1768 as a school of art and an exhibition centre. For nearly a century it was London's only public training-school for artists, although private establishments were also set up. What is now the Royal College of Art began in 1837 as a school of design and 'practical art' to serve industry.

With the Royal Academy developing a name for conservatism, the torch of change was taken up by the Slade School of Fine Art, opened as part of University College in 1871 and named after the art collector Felix Slade. Numbering among its pupils Walter Sickert, Augustus John and Stanley Spencer, its location contributed to the arty flavour of Bloomsbury, home of painters, writers and Bohemian intellectuals. Two schools founded in 1896 attest the Victorian interest in crafts: the Central School of Art and Design, established by the London County Council, and the Camberwell School of Arts and Crafts, founded by private philanthropy. The Royal Academy of Dramatic Art (RADA) was set up in 1904 by the actor-manager Sir Herbert Beerbohm Tree.

London had lacked a university. This was rectified when there opened in Bloomsbury in 1826 what became known as University College – or, as detractors styled it, 'that godless institution in Gower Street' – admitting non-Anglicans, who were excluded from Oxford and Cambridge. Anglicans retaliated with King's College a couple of years later. The University of London itself was created in 1836 to set examinations and grant degrees to students from both colleges. Other parts of the present London University came later. The London School of Economics and Political Science (LSE) was set up in 1895 on the instigation of Sidney Webb with money left by the Fabian Henry Hunt Hutchinson. Imperial College was formed out of three separate colleges in 1907, specializing in technological education.

The University of London's charter of 1858, allowing external students to sit its examinations, resulted in the rapid expansion of Birkbeck College, which had started life in 1824 as the London Mechanics' Institution, offering evening education to working men. Renamed in 1866 the Birkbeck Library and Scientific Institution, in recognition of its founder, the physician George Birkbeck, it became part of the university in 1920. In 1878 the University of London opened its examinations to women and thereafter admitted two women's colleges: Bedford College, founded in 1849 by Mrs Elizabeth Jesser Reid – convinced that we should never have better men till men had better mothers – and named after its original Bedford Square site, and Royal Holloway College, opened by Queen Victoria in 1886.

Part-time adult education expanded. Early moves were linked with religious movements, like Quintin Hogg's Youth's Christian Institute (1882). Arising at the same time as the City and Guilds Institute, Hogg's institute developed into the Polytechnic of Regent Street, offering full-time courses in practical and commercial education; the City and Guilds concentrated on part-time technical courses. 'Mutual improvement' societies, private schools and evening schools flourished, for instance the 'Camden Hall Evening School for Young Men', teaching book-keeping, arithmetic, reading and writing, etc.

Schools proliferated – elementary and advanced; religious and secular. In the 1860s there were reckoned to be 860 public day schools in the capital, some 1,700 private schools, about 700 Sunday schools and 100 evening schools. Girls' education had traditionally lagged: in the 1860s there were only three endowed secondary and nine proprietary schools for girls in the whole of London, containing fewer than 1,000 pupils. But girls' schools were improving. In 1848 F. D. Maurice founded Queen's College in Harley Street, for girls and mature women, a year before Mrs Reid opened her ladies' college in Bedford Square.

Miss Frances Buss set up her first school in her father's house in Camden Street in 1851. The syllabus included natural philosophy, Latin and branches of science, as well as more basic subjects. Twenty years later she established Camden School for Girls. Her forty pupils were the daughters of copy clerks, tailors, civil servants, builders and grocers; she found their ignorance of general knowledge 'beyond belief'. Her school was run on the lines of a boys' public school; discipline was strict, and the aim was to prepare girls for public examinations and acceptance at universities, for training as teachers, and for professional careers.

Education of the poor had traditionally been wretched, and in the hands of a hotchpotch of dame schools and Church and charity schools. In the 1840s in Bethnal Green there were 8,000 to 10,000 children without daily instruction. It was for children such as these – excluded from denominational schools by their 'rude habits, filthy condition and their want of shoes and stockings' – that the ragged schools were intended. In 1844 the Ragged School Union came into being under Lord Shaftesbury. By 1858 there were 128 ragged schools in Middlesex alone, with 11,632 pupils. Yet, even at school, children might learn little. In many of the schools of the National Society and the British and Foreign School Society one master was in charge of 200 or more boys. Because of demand for child labour, the average age for leaving school in East London in 1845 was ten. Thousands of parents were said to be 'either too indifferent, or too ignorant, or too vicious, or too little able to command their children, ever to avail themselves of such educational opportunities as existed'.

This changed after the 1870 Education Act, when elementary education became compulsory, to be provided by locally elected school boards. Hundreds of imposing school buildings were erected. They even caught the eye of Sherlock Holmes. 'It's a very cheering thing to come into London by any of these lines which run high and allow you to look down upon the houses like this,' he told Dr Watson:

I thought he was joking, for the view was sordid enough, but he soon explained himself. 'Look at those big, isolated clumps of buildings rising up above the slates, like brick islands in a lead-coloured sea.' 'The Board schools.' 'Light-houses, my boy! Beacons of the future! Capsules, with hundreds of bright little seeds in each, out of which will spring the wiser, better England of the future.'

Libraries too were lighthouses. Circulating libraries and private subscription libraries were popular. The London Library was founded in 1841 by men of letters including Thomas Carlyle and John Stuart Mill, aiming to provide members with 'good books in all departments of knowledge'. Provision of public libraries was made possible by the Public Libraries Act of 1850, but the vestries' response was so laggardly that, for thirty years after the Act, the parishes of St Margaret and St John in Westminster provided the only rate-aided library in the capital. Finally others followed, encouraged by benefactors such as the sugar tycoon Sir Henry Tate (also founder of the Tate Gallery) and the Scottish-born American steel magnate Andrew Carnegie.

Other institutions arose promising public edification. The National Gallery was founded in 1824 after George IV and Sir George Beaumont persuaded the government to buy the collection of the Russian-born merchant and philanthropist John Julius Angerstein. A gallery was built on the north side of Trafalgar Square. The National Portrait Gallery was added in 1856; the Tate Gallery was opened in 1897.

Above all, the profits of the Great Exhibition created the South Kensington museum-land. Eighty-eight acres facing Hyde Park were to house the four great museums and, in due course, the Royal Colleges of Art, Organists and Music, such learned societies as the Royal Geographical Society, and the Imperial College of Science and Technology. The Victoria and Albert, begun in the 1850s and first called the South Kensington Museum – the present name as well as façade came later – was the first to appear, followed by the Natural History (1873–81), Science (1907) and Geological (1933–5) Museums. (The Royal Albert Hall was a private development, though part of the same cultural movement.) South Kensington expresses High Victorian confidence in progress, the arts and sciences, and, perhaps above all, education. Opposite in Hyde Park, under a Gothic canopy, Victoria's Prince Consort sits in gilt bronze holding in his hands the catalogue of the Great Exhibition of 1851 and presiding over 178 marble statues of artists and four large statuary groups symbolizing Agriculture, Manufacture, Commerce and Engineering.

If Victorian London gloried in the arts and sciences, its growing irreligion shocked the godly. 'What is St Paul's?' Henry Mayhew asked a London costermonger: 'A church, sir, so I've heard, I never was in church.' Religion had no hold upon London's masses. The cleric William Walsham How remarked that East Enders thought of religion 'as belonging to a wholly different class from themselves', associated 'with a prosperity they envy, and a luxury which they resent'.

Three surveys (1851, 1886 and 1903) documented this popular paganism. East and South London had the nation's lowest church attendance. In working-class inner areas fewer than one in five attended a place of worship. London was no city of God: on Sunday 30 March 1851 only 874,339 of London's population of 2,362,236 attended any form of public worship.

The middle classes, of course, went to church religiously, but neither the Church of England nor any of the Protestant sects achieved much following among the masses. This drove William Booth to found the Salvation Army. Originally a Wesleyan lay preacher, he became convinced that only the poor could save the souls of the poor, and in 1865 he launched his 'Christian Mission for the Heathen of our own Country', from which the Army later evolved. By the 1880s the Salvation Army had achieved phenomenal growth – underlining the inability of the other Christian bodies to break through social barriers.

Eminent Victorians were shocked less by poverty than by prostitution and criminality.

Prostitution flaunted itself in Victorian London. In 1859 2,828 brothels were known to the police, though the *Lancet* thought London housed over twice that number and 80,000 prostitutes. The trade was high-profile because it mainly took the form of streetwalking. Near the Bank of England prostitutes were said to stand in rows like hackney coaches, while by the Ratcliff Highway and Shadwell High Street whores strolled about 'bare-headed, in dirty-white muslin and greasy, cheap blue silks with originally ugly faces horribly seamed with small-pox, and disfigured by vice'. The Haymarket was known as 'Hell Corner'. After a walk down the Haymarket and the Strand in the 1860s, Hippolyte Taine reported that

every hundred steps one jostles twenty harlots; some of them ask for a glass of gin; others say, 'Sir, it is to pay my lodging.' This is not debauchery which flaunts itself, but destitution – and such destitution! The deplorable procession in the shade of the monumental streets is sickening; it seems to me a march of the dead. That is a plague-spot – the real plague-spot of English society.

Child prostitution was a scandal. Indeed, a high proportion of the capital's criminals were children – neglected, prowling the streets, begging and stealing. 'They are to be found,' Mayhew observed, 'in Westminster, Whitechapel, Shoreditch, St Giles's, New Cut, Lambeth, the Borough, and other localities. Hundreds of them may be seen leaving their parents' homes and low lodging-houses every morning, sallying forth in search of food and plunder.' As they grew up, they grew more skilful; some turned to picking pockets, house-breaking and burglary, or to prostitution. A girl with a pretty face might count herself lucky if she landed a toff, who might set her up in a St John's Wood villa or some leafy neighbourhood and see that she was educated. 'As for their virtue, they lose it as one loses his watch who is robbed by the highway thief,' wrote such a woman to *The Times* in 1858, on a working woman's life: 'Their virtue is the watch and society is the thief. These poor women toil on starvation wages, while penury, misery, and famine clutch them by the throat and say "Render up your body or die."'

Pooter's London loved hearing about crime scares from the newspapers. In 1867 a new dimension was added with the bombing of Clerkenwell prison and the attempted rescue of Fenian prisoners, while a garrotting outbreak hit the headlines, it being reported that the 'more brutal and inexpert thieves press the fingers of both hands into the victim's throat, others use a short stick, which is passed across the throat from behind, and hauled back at both ends'.

But most notorious were the 'Ripper' murders. The first took place in the early hours of 31 August 1888 in Buck's Row (now Durward Street), Whitechapel. Polly Nicholls, a gin-soaked doss-house inmate, was found with her throat cut. The second victim, Annie Chapman, was killed a week later half a mile away in Hanbury Street. Then one night, 30 September, two more unfortunates (Elizabeth Stride and Catherine Eddowes) were carved up with a knife. Finally, Mary Kelly met the most violent end of them all after taking a man back to her dingy room in Miller's Court, off Dorset (now Duval) Street. These murders created hysteria. More than 600 plain-clothes policemen were called in. Their failure to catch the culprit led to the resignation of Sir Charles Warren, the ineffectual Police Commissioner, who at one point was pursued across Tooting Common by bloodhounds he was training to track the Ripper.

Statistical shortcomings leave it unclear whether Victorian fears about crime waves had the slightest substance. Mayhew's vivid accounts of London's underworld – with characters such as 'Swindling Sall' and 'Lushing Loo' – suggest what was probably true: there were few hardened criminals but thousands routinely needing to bend the law in order to survive. Steal or starve was the law for the poor.

Many took it on themselves to redeem rogues and rescue fallen women. Missions were set up, like the London City Mission, established in 1835, and the Open-Air Mission. Members toured London preaching temperance and salvation. Yet London was undergoing a notable transformation, becoming sober and orderly. The spread of gas lighting made the streets safer by night. Pall Mall had been illuminated as early as 1807; by 1841, it was claimed, 'the metropolis now burns gas in every square, street, alley, lane, passage, and court', and thereby 'half the work of prevention of crime was accomplished'. The establishing of the Metropolitan Police created a comprehensive system of official regulation. The early Victorian capital affords us pictures of a culture of despair, poverty and punishment: Fagin, Bill Sikes, Oliver Twist in the workhouse, and the boy Dickens himself toiling in Warren's blacking-factory while his father languished in the Marshalsea for debt. By the dawn of the twentieth century photographs of slumland are telling a different story: poverty, privation and poor health are everywhere present, but a new domestic orderliness is suggestive of the transformation of outcast London into an integrated proletariat.

Events like the Ripper murders fixed the gaze on one particular quarter: the East End. Between St Katharine's and the London Docks, the desperately unfortunate sought refuge in the narrow, rotten houses behind the main streets. Their occupants pursued vile and grotesquely unsavoury trades. Mudlarks and juvenile thieves infested the river and the violent jungle around the Ratcliff Highway. Women sieved a livelihood from refuse mountains piled up on waste ground, sorting out rags and bones. The most disgusting of these occupations was the pure-finder. 'Pure', or dog-shit, was used in dressing leather, and old men and women gathered it as a final resort, rather than enter the workhouse. A bucketful bought a day's lodging and food. Images like these – half true, half exaggerated – dominated the travellers' tales or anthropological findings of those who ventured east to the dark continent beyond Aldgate.

Gustave Doré's evocation of Whitechapel, from *London*, 1872

The East End had the worst slums, the worst overcrowding, the worst death rates. It also housed London's immigrants. From the eighteenth century London's Jewish population expanded. Wealthy immigrants from Spain and Portugal (Sephardim) had settled in the City under the later Stuarts, and they were joined under William III and

Anne by Ashkenazim from Germany, Poland and the Netherlands. In Duke's Place, close to Houndsditch and Aldgate, the Ashkenazim established their first Great Synagogue. By 1850 London's Jewish population had increased to about 20,000, and in the following thirty years it more than doubled, peaking in the 1880s as refugees poured in from central Europe, Poland and Russia – some of them fleeing pogroms. Many accepted wretched earnings in the sweatshops. Tailoring, however, was only one of the trades followed by the immigrant Jews: many were employed by furriers, jewellers, or the furniture trade; they made cigars, umbrellas and coconut matting; and thousands were engaged in street trading from stalls and barrows.

In May 1884 an investigation into the sanitary conditions of 'the Polish colony of Jew tailors' found 'close upon 30,000 Russo-Polish Jews huddled together in districts that were already overcrowded':

In Emily Place ... we found five persons living in one room, while in another house we came upon a Jewish potato dealer who kept his wife, five children and huge stock of potatoes all in one room measuring 5 yds by 6. There was one bed in the room and probably some of the family slept on the floor.

By 1901, 42,032 Russians and Poles were resident in Stepney – a figure exceeded by only five towns in Poland itself. Among these exiles were radicals such as the cooperativist Prince Peter Kropotkin and Rudolf Rocker, the intriguing German anarchist who (though a Gentile) edited the Yiddish *Arbeiter Fraint* from Stepney Green. But for most, economic survival and success were paramount. The teenaged Montague Burton passed through Whitechapel in 1900 on his way from Lithuania to Leeds, to become the world's largest men's clothing distributor. Lew and Bernard Winogradsky, who arrived in Brick Lane in 1912 from Odessa, ended up as Baron Grade and Baron Delfont of Bethnal Green. The property tycoon Charles Clore attended the same elementary school as the Winogradsky boys in Spitalfields. The young Jacob Bronowski discovered science in Whitechapel Library. Jewish communities spread outwards: synagogues were established in Dalston (1885), Stoke Newington (1903), Finsbury Park (1912), Stamford Hill (1915) and Golders Green (1922).

The East End had other immigrants too. The Chinese began settling in Limehouse before 1850, arriving as seamen or ships' launderers. By 1890 sailors from Shanghai were colonizing Pennyfields, Amoy Place and Ming Street, while those from Canton and southern China chose Gill Street and Limehouse Causeway, slightly further west. The Irish also crowded into dockland.

But the East End became principally associated with the cockney. Derived from the middle English *cokeney*, meaning cock's egg, a misshapen egg, the word had originally meant a townee; banteringly it came to mean a Londoner. The cockney had not always been an *East Ender*: he was originally a Londoner in general. Not necessarily working-class, the true cockney was smart, wearing flash attire, perhaps a battered silk hat – the image of the London lad: bright, sharp, never-say-die, streetwise. 'The cockney ... is the supreme type of Englishman,' observed Edwin Pugh in 1912,

in his sturdy optimism, in his unwavering determination not only to make the best of things as they are, but to make them seem actually better than they are by adapting his mood to the exigencies of the occasion, and in his supreme disdain of all outside influences.

By Pugh's time the working-class East Ender had become the cockney, often quite jingoistic about London. Just as the Jewish community had its novelists – notably Israel Zangwill, whose *Children of the Ghetto* (1892), subtitled *A Study of a Peculiar People*, documented life in the Petticoat Lane neighbourhood, with its street sellers and owners of sweat shops, rabbis and scholars, old and young, beautiful and ugly – Arthur Morrison chronicled the cockney. 'Who knows the East End?' asked Morrison in his *Tales of Mean Streets* (1894). His *A Child of the Jago* (1896) centred on a famous slum clearance of the 1890s, when Nicol Street and its courts and alleys around Arnold Circus, Stepney, were destroyed and replaced by blocks of flats. 'This street is in the East End,' opens *Tales of Mean Streets*:

There is no need to say in the East End of what. The East End is a vast city, as famous in its way as any the hand of man has made. But who knows the East End? It is down through Cornhill and out beyond Leadenhall Street and Aldgate Pump, one will say: a shocking place, where he once went with a curate; an evil plexus of slums that hide human, creeping things; where filthy men and women live on penn'orths of gin, where collars and clean shirts are decencies unknown, where every citizen wears a black eye, and none ever combs his hair.

The classic East Ender was rebellious, irreverent, brazen – 'bolshie'. But he was not conventionally 'political'. Some became socialists, but many were xenophobes, or simply cynical. 'In Farringdon Road, you will run across the more traditional Cockney,' reflected H. J. Massingham, surveying the *London Scene* in 1933:

whose astuteness, nonchalance, easy indifferent fellowship, tolerance, casual endurance, grumbling gusto, shallowness, unconcern for anything but the passing moment, jackdaw love of glitter, picaresque adaptability and jesting spirit make up a unique individual.

By then, the cliché cockney was primarily associated with street markets, or with certain speech habits (including the famous rhyming slang noted by Mayhew) – Eliza Doolittle was phonetically pinned down to Lisson Grove by Professor Higgins in the first act of Shaw's *Pygmalion*. As the East End grew more integrated – through trams and buses and commuting – life and art grew confused. The true cockney became the music-hall cockney, the stage cockney, the film cockney, harking back to a previous generation – that of George Robey and Albert Chevalier, of 'Knocked 'em in the Old

Kent Road' and 'The Coster's Serenade' fame. Recently cockneys live only in nostalgia: 'Fings ain't what they used to be.'

The East End came under intense scrutiny. The moneyed, the educated and the holy came from the West End, from Oxford, from the pulpits, to gaze, explore, deplore, reform, redeem. Samuel Barnett pioneered the idea of 'settlements'. The idealistic young Arnold Toynbee begged the forgiveness of the poor of London for the remissness of the élite. 'We – the middle classes, I mean, not merely the rich – we have neglected you,' Arnold Toynbee confessed to the working men who attended his East End lectures in the 1870s:

instead of justice we have offered you charity, and instead of sympathy, we have offered you hard and unreal advice; but I think we are changing ... I think that many of us would spend our lives in your service. You have – I say it clearly and advisedly – you have to forgive us, for we have wronged you; we have sinned against you grievously – not knowing always; but still we have sinned, and let us confess it; but if you will forgive us – nay, whether you will forgive us or not – we will serve you, we will devote our lives to your service, and we cannot do more.

Toynbee turned guilt into institutions – the Whitechapel Library, the Whitechapel Art Gallery, and Toynbee Hall itself, that mission to the poor, symbol of the white man's burden in darkest Stepney. The success of Toynbee encouraged others. In 1884 the Warden of Keble College, Oxford, established Oxford House in Bethnal Green, run on Church of England lines. The Canning Town Women's Settlement (1892); St Mildred's House, Isle of Dogs (1897); St Hilda's East, Bethnal Green (1889); St Margaret's House, Bethnal Green (1889) all followed.

Movements like Toynbee Hall show the paradoxes of late-Victorian London, a world of two cities in which the poor were described as degenerate while being sentimentalized as cockneys. It is easy to sneer at the do-gooders, yet the work of discovery was an important moment in London's coming to know itself. 'It is flat, it is ancient, dirty and degraded' – here is a mid-century view of Bethnal Green, as recorded by William Cotton, the indefatigable banker and philanthropist, Bishop Blomfield's 'lay adjutant':

its courts and alleys are almost countless, and overwhelming with men, women, boys, dogs, cats, pigeons, and birds. Its children are ragged, sharp, weasel-like; brought up from their cradle – which is often an old box or an egg chest – to hard living and habits of bodily activity. Its men are mainly poor dock labourers, poor costermongers, poor silk weavers, clinging hopelessly to a withering handicraft, the lowest kind of thieves, with a sprinkling of box and toy makers, shoe makers, and cheap cabinet makers. Its women are mainly hawkers, sempstresses, the coarsest order of prostitutes, and aged stall keepers. On Sundays the whole neighbourhood is like a fair.

Dirty men in their sooty shirt-sleeves, are on the house-tops, peeping out of little rough wooden structures, built on the roofs to keep their pigeons in. They suck their short pipes, fly their fancy birds, whistle shrilly with their forefingers placed in their mouths, beat the sides of the wooden building with a long stick like a fishing rod, and use all their ingenuity to snare their neighbour's stray birds.

Thanks to such works of exploration, it became possible for London to discover that it possessed a single identity, and to set about the communal endeavour of public improvement. The generations from Victoria's Jubilee to the affluent 1960s were to witness a remarkable breaking-down of traditional barriers, an equalizing process, and a new mobility both physical and social.

CHAPTER THIRTEEN

'A Fungus-Like Growth': Expansion 1890–1945

Fearful observers of former centuries had labelled London a cancer, a monster, a disease. In the wake of Darwin they tended to term it a force of nature, an evolving organism. Shelley called it 'that great sea, whose ebb and flow at once is deaf and blind'. London was a 'polypus … a vast irregular growth', thought the pioneering urban planner Patrick Geddes, 'perhaps likest to the spreading of a great coral reef'. In *Life in West London* (1901), Arthur Sherwell painted it as 'a great, hungry sea, which flows on and on, filling up every creek, and then overspreads its borders, flooding the plains beyond'. 'Go where we will – north, south, east or west of this huge over-grown Metropolis,' reported *Building News*:

the fungus like growth of houses manifests itself stretching from town to suburb and village – as from the southern suburbs to Herne Hill and Dulwich, and from Streatham to Croydon. In every direction we see the same outward growth of dwelling houses of a small and unpretending class – generally a repetition of a type of house that has been found to meet the requirements of the middle class and artisan. The larger and more commodious residence of fifty years ago is being pulled down, or swamped by this tide of small houses: where a large house existed ten, or a hundred or more have been built, absorbing the acres of gardens and private park lands. This is one of the social revolutions of the age.

Indeed it was, and the flood, or fungus, surged relentlessly on: between 1890 and 1940 Greater London grew by 3 million, from 5,638,000 to 8,700,000. By global standards, however, it was no longer unique: other world cities were now growing faster and bigger. In that period the Paris region grew from 4,128,000 to 6,598,000; Greater Berlin rose from 1,579,000 to 4,332,000; by 1942 the Tokyo region had 7,358,000 inhabitants, while greater New York zoomed to 11,691,000. In Europe alone, 'million cities' leapt from five in 1890 – London, Paris, Berlin, Vienna, Moscow – to fourteen in 1940, and there were eleven in the United States.

London's expansion was taking a new direction. Growth till around 1850 was essentially urban. Thereafter development became radically, even aggressively sub-urban – it was meant to be a new beginning, a new way of organizing domestic living: not rural, admittedly, but not like the city of Johnson, Nash, Chadwick or Mayhew.

So long as so much of the centre remained a city of dreadful night, barely fit for human habitation, suburbanization would always be attractive. Pockets of property survived from the seventeenth century, and acre upon acre from the eighteenth, long quit by better-class tenants and abandoned to those who could not afford anywhere better. Certain nineteenth-century developments, for instance Somers Town, had rapidly sunk into shocking slums. And some of the areas most disreputable in the early twentieth century involved properties run up under Queen Victoria. Off the Hornsey Road, the Seven Sisters Estate had been developed piecemeal from the 1850s. With the market glutted and rents low, building was slow, chaotic and substandard. By the early twentieth century Campbell Road, in its midst, had a reputation of being almost a prize exhibit in run-downness.

Exacerbated by railway development and later by slum clearances, overcrowding remained inveterate. The 1901 Census showed that 45 per cent of families in Finsbury still lived in one or two rooms; in neighbouring boroughs the proportion exceeded a third. As late as the 1930s the social observer Margery Spring Rice reported a Battersea woman living in two rooms with a family of seven:

I have a bed in the back for the two girls, and a bed for the boy which I take down every day ... to make more room. We have our own food in this room, I do all my cooking here; in the other room is my bed, one bed I make up for the little boy on the settee, and the pram the baby sleeps in.

The LCC set a standard of twelve houses per acre. In 1931 Drysdale Street, Shoreditch, was a narrow wedge containing some 120 houses, with culs-de-sac and constricted passages, enclosed on three sides by a railway and industrial buildings. At eighty houses per acre it was a classic example of the 'narrowness, closeness and bad arrangement' that created slums. Stepney vied with Shoreditch in awfulness, largely due to low wages and unemployment. In 1933 it was noted of Stepney that the 'amount of property which is hopelessly defective and altogether deplorable is very large. Damp, dilapidation of every kind, obsolete design and construction, vermin ... abound throughout the whole borough, and impart to much of it a character of unrelieved defectiveness.' There were said to be so many unfit, dilapidated, damp, defective houses and slums that the 'only real remedy would seem to be the reconstruction of the whole borough'. 'It is only because the thing was spread over a hundred years and not concentrated into a few weeks,' fumed H. G. Wells, 'that history fails to realize what sustained disaster, how much massacre, degeneration and disablement of lives was due to the housing of people in the nineteenth century.'

The Victorians built next to no houses in central London for the poor; some ended up in the new tenement barracks, the rest were forced to squeeze into housing abandoned by others. Attempts were belatedly made to tackle the problem. The Housing of the Working Classes Act (1890) gave councils compulsory-purchase powers for land for housing. About twenty local authorities adopted the Act, notably Battersea and the outer boroughs of West Ham and Hornsey. Other councils – Croydon, East Ham and Woolwich – used the Act to build around the fringes of London. Certain charitable initiatives were taken. In Somers Town the Church of England played an important role, Basil Jellicoe, Vicar of St Mary's Somers Town, founding the St Pancras House Improvement Society in 1924. 'Somers Town,' he wrote, 'is really gigantic theft. Overcrowding and poverty are here being used by the Devil in order to steal from the children of God the health and happiness which are their right.' The London County Council had already started the Churchway Estate in the area; the St Pancras House Improvement Society reconditioned eight houses and began building blocks of flats in Drummond Crescent, Werrington Street, Bridgeway Street, Aldenham Street and Chalton Street.

But planned and systematic rehousing on a significant scale became a reality through the activities of the LCC's early 'Progressive' leadership. Fired by vocal Fabian elements, the LCC Housing Committee became committed to an energetic housing policy, using the 1890 Act. After gaining a parliamentary amendment in 1900, allowing it to erect 'working class tenements' on green-field sites beyond its boundaries, it began rehousing Londoners into new perimeter estates. (Progressives believed in decentralizing problem people.) There were four in particular.

One, Totterdown Fields at Tooting, was a logical development, thanks to the electrification of the local tramway acquired by the LCC a few years earlier. In May 1903 the Prince of Wales opened the line from Embankment to Totterdown Street and visited the first cottages, solidly built and containing indoor toilet and bathroom facilities. A second estate, at Norbury outside the LCC area, was slightly more problematic, for the trams terminated at the LCC boundary half a mile short. A third, White Hart Lane in Tottenham, was a bigger challenge, as the hoped-for Underground line failed to materialize. At the fourth site, Old Oak in west London, they were luckier: the estate was planned around an extension of the Central Line, and East Acton station was finally opened in 1920. The Old Oak Estate remains a particularly good example of the 'cottage' ideal.

Impetus for further LCC development came from a 1920 government report which noted that the capital still had 184,000 people in the LCC area living in 'unhealthy' districts, and over half a million in 'unsatisfactory' conditions. One possibility –

building upwards – was rejected as 'quite unsuitable for a working-class population who are dependent on their own services for domestic services and care of their children'; medical officers of health emphasized that the 'self-contained house is what appeals to working people'. The LCC commitment to building houses not flats was given a boost by the Addison Act. 'What is our task?' Lloyd George had asked at the end of the war: 'To make Britain a fit country for heroes to live in.' With that end in mind, in 1919 Dr Christopher Addison, Minister of Health in the coalition government, introduced a Housing and Town Planning Act which encouraged local authorities to build subsidized housing. (Less idealistically, the Parliamentary Secretary to the Local Government Board stated that 'the money we are going to spend on housing is an insurance against Bolshevism and Revolution.') Costs above a penny rate would be met by the Exchequer: this was *carte blanche* for local-authority expenditure. The LCC, then under Conservative control, enthusiastically extended its existing pre-war estates on the fringes and bought land for new ones.

Armed with government cash and some garden-city ideals, the LCC set to work. In 1920 an estate was begun in Roehampton, and in the same year building began at Bellingham (Downham) near Catford and at Becontree. Of these, Becontree was to become the world's single biggest council development, despite the fact that in 1921 the Addison dream ended abruptly, as economic crisis precipitated public-spending cuts.

It took eighteen years to complete the vast Becontree Estate, with its own railway line carrying building materials up from the Thames and fifty miles of roads. Becontree grew bigger than many English provincial towns – Oxford for example – experiencing between 1921 and 1931 almost tenfold increase (from 9,127 to 89,362). Like other LCC estates, Becontree had its shortcomings. The housing was drab. Amenities were lacking: no school was built until September 1923, and there was only one doctor to every 8,300 inhabitants and no hospital – though eventually a social centre was built and four cinemas. In central London there was one pub for every few hundred people, but in Becontree just six pubs were provided – one per 20,000 – while at Downham there was just one pub for the entire estate of 35,000 – and LCC pubs themselves were designed to deter hard drinking, promoting lemonade and family areas. To create an image far different from the old snug, smoky, packed bars, they weren't actually called pubs at all but 'refreshment houses'. The Downham Tavern initially had no stand-up bars – an LCC member denounced 'perpendicular drinking'. 'As for pubs,' commented George Orwell,

they are banished from the housing estates almost completely, and the few that remain are dismal sham-Tudor places fitted out by the big brewery companies and very expensive. For a middle-class population this would be a nuisance, it might mean walking a mile to get a glass of beer; for a working-class population, which uses the pub as a kind of club, it is a serious blow at communal life.

It was not easy for working-class families, decanted to the periphery, to adapt. Men missed the local and the street-corner bookie; their wives found the shops distant, prices higher, and credit hard to come by. Becontree long had no pawnbroker. Stories circulated about families keeping coal in the bath. Strong pressure had to be exerted on many to leave Bethnal Green for Becontree. Nevertheless, the sheer quantity of building was impressive. Between 1919 and 1938, 76,877 dwellings were completed for the LCC and as many for the other councils. The LCC housed 19,000 at Watling in north-west London, 30,000 at Downham in south-east London, and 40,000 in St Helier around the new Morden tube station. These 'model estates' brought immense improvement in housing standards, though more for the artisan than for the really poor, who could not afford the burden of rent and fares. Estates like Becontree began to put an end to the traditional 'mean streets', and contributed to the disappearance of the bare-foot urchin.

Complementing the LCC effort, certain boroughs also built cottage houses and flats. Using direct labour, Labour-controlled Woolwich erected 4,500 houses by 1939 on three large estates. North of Eltham Green, the 334-acre Page Estate, started in 1920, eventually contained 2,306 dwellings, four primary schools, three churches, two clubs, a shopping centre, a welfare centre and a children's playground. It was served by an LCC tram.

Public housing in Greater London peaked at just over 16,000 units in 1927. (At the time of writing it is about 300 a year.) Construction then fell to fewer than 10,000, but picked up after 1936. The 1930s saw a switch of focus from great peripheral estates to blocks of flats in inner London. Whereas cottages comprised over 85 per cent of the output between 1919 and 1927, by 1939 something like 90 per cent were flats.

Public housing was unevenly distributed. Almost half the LCC's new tenement blocks were put up in only four boroughs: Southwark, Lewisham, Wandsworth and Lambeth, where land was cheap and local Labour majorities sympathetic. Radical boroughs like Bermondsey, Finsbury, Fulham and Woolwich had housing programmes of their own; but little was done in some districts where housing was sorely needed. Boroughs dominated by the Conservative Municipal Reform Party would not allow the LCC in, and did little themselves. Whereas Labour-controlled Bermondsey built 2,700 dwellings between 1929 and 1938, the Conservative boroughs of Paddington, Kensington, Holborn and St Marylebone built only a few hundred dwellings between them.

The LCC and the boroughs built soundly and solidly. Real inroads were made into London's housing problems, and the quality of both houses and flats was such that the interwar estates have resisted slummification better than many postwar developments. This forms one of the more remarkable achievements in London government, and contributed much to the marked improvement of conditions between the wars for the capital's working classes.

Developments in public housing were at least matched by a mushrooming of private house-building in the outer suburbs. These depended heavily upon better transportation. In the Victorian age, improvements in mobility had been largely piecemeal and uncoordinated. The twentieth century pioneered more integrated approaches to housing, work and transportation. Attempts were made to anticipate commuter needs and coordinate transport policy. Twentieth-century suburbia spawned analysts and planners – yet the most perceptive and prescient commentator was a novelist. 'We are … in the early phase of a great development of centrifugal possibilities,' H. G. Wells argued at the dawn of the new century:

the available area of a city which can offer a cheap suburban journey of thirty miles an hour is a circle with a radius of thirty miles. And is it too much … to expect that the available area for even the common daily toilers of the great city of the year 2000, or earlier, will have a radius very much larger even than that? … Indeed, it is not too much to say that the London citizen of the year 2000 A.D. may have a choice of nearly all England and Wales south of Nottingham and east of Exeter as his suburb … And so, though the [city] centre will probably still remain the centre and 'Town', it will be essentially a bazaar, a great gallery of shops and places of concourse and rendezvous, a pedestrian place … and altogether a very spacious, brilliant, and entertaining agglomeration.

Enough now has been said to determine the general nature of the expansion of the great cities in the future, so far as the more prosperous classes are concerned. It will not be a regular diffusion … but a process of throwing out the 'homes' and of segregating various types of people. The omens seem to point … to a wide and quite unprecedented diversity in the various suburban townships and suburban districts …

But the diffusion of the prosperous, independent, and managing classes involves in itself a very considerable diffusion of the purely 'working' classes also. Their centres of occupation will be distributed, and their freedom to live at some little distance from their work will be increased.

For these reasons, the very notion of 'town' had to be thought afresh. 'Enough has been said to demonstrate that old "town" and "city" will be, in truth, terms as obsolete as "mail coach" …' Wells concluded, aware of what he termed London's 'vast endlessness'. 'We may for our present purposes call these coming town provinces "urban regions".' He was right.

The technological breakthrough that permitted town to move out of town was electricity – and, at a later stage, the internal-combustion engine. Cheap, readily available electricity sparked three major innovations. One was the electric tram. The old horse-tram network was electrified bit by bit, starting when an American-backed group, Imperial Tramways, bought out West Metropolitan Tramways in Hammersmith and created in 1901 the capital's first electric tramway, the London United, running from Shepherd's Bush to Acton via Hammersmith. The LUT went on to build tramways to Hounslow (1901) and Uxbridge (1904), and then lines to Twickenham, Hampton, Teddington, Kingston-on-Thames and Surbiton. Kingston was then linked in 1907 with the LCC boundary at Merton via New Malden, Raynes Park and Wimbledon. East Ham Council ran its first electric service in 1901, while the LCC, for its part, electrified more slowly, partly because it rejected the overhead wires that were acceptable in outer suburbs.

The northern and southern halves of the tramway system were initially unconnected, as lines had never been allowed to cross the Thames. The LCC eventually overcame this obstacle by cutting a tunnel under Kingsway as part of the Aldwych slum-clearance scheme. In 1906 the LCC started running trams alongside the Embankment and across Westminster Bridge. Within Greater London, however, the tram system remained fragmented, boroughs to the east launching services of their own, private operators running trams in the west, and the LCC active in the middle. Electric trams were, nevertheless, a great boon, being cheaper than buses and holding more passengers, and running faster than horse-drawn trams.

Penetrating further and further, trams quickened the distant suburbs. Before 1914, Metropolitan Electric Tramways established services along the main roads through north London, terminating almost in open country, and so staking out future development: they went to Edgware; to Edmonton, and then on to Ponders End and Waltham Cross; to Whetstone, Barnet, Wood Green, Palmers Green, Winchmore Hill, Enfield, Stonebridge Park, Wembley and Sudbury. They linked up with the LCC tramways at Harlesden, Manor House, Stamford Hill and Finsbury Park. In east London, local authorities operated trams in East Ham, Ilford, Barking, West Ham, Walthamstow and Leyton. In the south-east, Erith, Dartford and Bexley councils created lines, and Croydon Corporation's system ran from the LCC boundary at Norbury to rural Purley, with lines to Thornton Heath, Selhurst, Anerley and Addiscombe. By the 1930s the trolley bus had also arrived.

Railways also began to be electrified – a boon for passengers, as steam locomotives were ill-suited to the constant stop-and-start inevitable on suburban lines. Additional stations were planted on old lines, and commuter routes were extended as the railway companies cultivated middle-class traffic from five to twenty miles from town. In 1907 the London and South Western Railway started advertising the joys of Epsom, just twenty-five minutes from Waterloo; the Great Western was promoting Windsor, Datchet and the Thames Valley, and the Great Eastern extolled Bishops Stortford. A

Great Northern Railway inquiry bureau promoted the 'Northern Heights', trying to sell Potters Bar and Hatfield. In the 1920s and 1930s developers' subsidies helped to build new stations like Byfleet, Brookman's Park, Petts Wood, Hinchley Wood, Woodmansterne, Stoneleigh, Berrylands and Hersham. Most flourished: by 1934 Petts Wood was issuing 320,000 tickets a year.

Railway commuting in outer suburbia was encouraged by the amalgamation of three railways in 1923 to produce Southern Railways, running all the lines in Kent, Surrey, Sussex and Hampshire except the Morden line, built in 1928 by the Underground. Electrification on the Southern encouraged new railway suburbs at Raynes Park, Motspur Park, Worcester Park, Stoneleigh, New Malden and similar settlements in Kentish London that all enjoyed mushroom growth. Between the wars, Malden and Coombe, Epsom and Ewell, Sutton and Cheam, Coulsdon and Purley, Surbiton and Banstead were doubling in population by the decade.

Electrification throughout the London railway system encouraged long-distance commuting. The electrification of the Liverpool Street line to Shenfield in 1949, extended in 1956 to Southend, increased commuting from Romford, Gidea Park, Shenfield and Brentwood, where house prices were still low. Though south Essex lacked the charm of Cheam or Chertsey, postwar affluence meant more working-class people could afford their own homes, and builders knocked up cheap estates in places like Thundersley, Billericay and Rayleigh, their owner-occupiers commuting in droves to the City. By the late 1950s south Essex had more commuters than anywhere else in the Home Counties.

Electrification also transformed the Underground network. Underground railways had begun as early as 1863 with the opening of the Metropolitan Railway from Paddington to Farringdon. To save demolition of costly properties, the line had followed the New Road, before snaking south-east at King's Cross under the newly built Farringdon Road. Costs were kept down by 'cut-and-cover' construction. Instead of tunnelling, a trench was cut, the line was inserted and arched over, and the road was replaced. The initial Marylebone Road route meant that little housing had to be demolished. By contrast the extension through Bayswater to Kensington High Street, opened in 1868, ran under squares and terraces. Dummy houses had to be built at 23/24 Leinster Gardens to preserve the façade. A major problem was ridding the tunnels of smoke from the steam engines. The Metropolitan reassured passengers that the atmosphere in the tunnels was usually clear enough to enable the drivers to see the signals – and that the smoke was beneficial for TB sufferers!

The Metropolitan was an immediate success. In the first six months 26,500 people used it daily. With a 3d fare for the eighteen-minute Paddington–City journey, it beat the horse-bus hands down. And there were cheap fares for workmen, too.

The next big project was to turn the Metropolitan Railway into the Circle. The

The Metropolitan Railway. Opened in 1863, it ran from Paddington to Farringdon and was designed to ease traffic congestion above. From Gustave Doré's *London*, 1872

Metropolitan built the section from Paddington to South Kensington, opened in 1868, and the Metropolitan District Railway (later called the District) built the stretch east from South Kensington. By 1868 this was open as far as Westminster, with a subway for MPs to the House of Commons. Thence the District moved eastwards, via the Victoria Embankment, to Blackfriars, opened in 1870. In 1871 it reached Mansion House; but the plan to complete the Circle to Moorgate under the costly City was delayed until 1884, when the Metropolitan and District lines met at last at Mark Lane station (now Tower Hill) – and then they burrowed eastward to Whitechapel on the East London Railway from Shoreditch to New Cross. Electrification of the Circle was completed in September 1905, the round trip being reduced from seventy to fifty minutes.

Other Underground lines were being built meanwhile. The District line extended eastwards to Earl's Court in 1868, to Hammersmith in 1874, to Richmond in 1877, and from Turnham Green to Ealing Broadway in 1879. The West Brompton to Putney Bridge extension was opened in 1880, and in 1889 the District began running to Wimbledon. The Whitechapel to Bow extension was opened in 1902.

All these early lines – the Metropolitan, District and Circle – had been steam-powered, using shallow tracks with frequent cuttings. Central London was ill-suited for any further extension of such 'cut-and-cover' lines. This explains the enthusiasm for deep-hole boring – the 'tube' – which had freedom to carve out routes without disturbing the townscape. The problem was traction: in deep holes, steam was impossible. Initially cable-cars were planned, but these were plagued by technical difficulties. Introduced in the USA in 1888, electric locomotion made all the difference.

The first deep tube, between the City and Stockwell (now part of the Northern Line), had been planned without electric traction. Only when it was nearly complete were cable-cars abandoned in favour of electric engines. The line opened in 1890. But what *Punch* called the 'sardine-can' railway attracted too many passengers. To counter overload, the City and South London reduced fares to 1d before 8 a.m. (for workmen), raising them to 3d between 8 and 10 a.m. for middle-class commuters. The City and South London failed to make a profit, but others benefited from its experience. There followed the Waterloo and City Line, built in 1898, early dubbed 'the Drain', and promoted by the London and South Eastern mainline railway company, anxious to siphon its passengers direct from Waterloo to the commuters' mecca, the City.

The next venture was the Central London Railway. Because British investors were cautious about putting up money for another tube, international finance was brought in to raise the £3.7 million required for the Bank to Shepherd's Bush line, which opened in 1900, with an extension to White City added shortly after, to serve the Anglo-French exhibition and the 1908 Olympic Games. The Central Line was a fully electrified tube, with tunnels 60 to 110 feet below the surface, electric lifts, and a flat fare of 2d. The 'Twopenny Tube' proved a huge success. Although originally intended as a city line and not as a trunk line, in 1920 it was extended westward to Ealing Broadway; later branches were made west to Ruislip and east to Leyton, and then to Epping and Ongar.

Tube proposals abounded around 1900, at a time when, with the population growing and spreading, London's old horse-drawn and steam-driven transport was increasingly obsolete. Two schemes were supported by mainline railway companies: the Baker Street to Waterloo, and the Great Northern and City Railway from Finsbury Park to Moorgate. Another was a proposed Hampstead to Charing Cross line, with a King's Cross branch. The key figure in post-1900 developments was the American 'robber baron' Charles Tyson Yerkes, whose philosophy was to 'buy up old junk, fix it up a little and unload it upon other fellows'. Having succeeded in Chicago, Yerkes bought himself into the loss-making District Railway and the proposed Hampstead tube. Though dying in December 1905 before any of his schemes were completed, during his London years the tycoon laid the foundations for the modern Underground system. Mergers between a number of lines – the District, Bakerloo, Piccadilly and Hampstead – helped to create the great combine, the Underground Group.

The 'Yerkes' parts of the Underground – the Bakerloo, Piccadilly and Hampstead lines, and the electrified District – were completed by 1907, their stations distinctive through their red glazed tiles. His triumph was the Piccadilly Line, opened in 1906

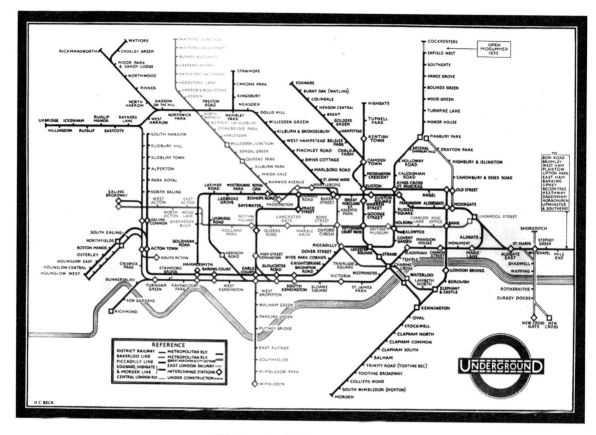

The London Underground, 1932

from Finsbury Park to Hammersmith. It was then the longest tube railway in London, and it soon boasted London's first railway escalator. (To counter the public mistrust, a man with a wooden leg was hired to travel up and down all day to reassure passengers.) In the 1930s the Piccadilly Line was extended north to Cockfosters and west to Uxbridge.

The tube was ripe for further development. Following the American example, where tramway promoters built into open country beyond city limits, making a killing on land values in streetcar suburbs, Yerkes made sure that the tube ceased to be just another form of inner-city transport, like trams and buses beneath the pavements, and began the drive deep into commuterland. The original scheme for the Hampstead tube had been traditional, but Yerkes had the business vision to insist upon an extension into the fields of Golders Green. (A famous Underground poster would later sell Golders Green as *rus in urbe* twentieth-century style.)

And, after the First World War, further extensions were sped by government aid, when in the 1921 depression Lloyd George pumped money into unemployment schemes. Treasury finance of £5 million was secured to extend the Hampstead Line to Hendon in 1923 and to Edgware in 1924. Burnt Oak station remained in the fields until the LCC built its cottage estate at Watling. Thanks to government subsidies, the Hampstead Line was then connected with a modernized City and South London tube at Euston and Camden Town, to form the twin branches of the present Northern Line. The contractors, Mowlem, brought in Welsh miners to excavate the tunnels. Unlike in the Thatcher and Major years, interwar governments, listening to Keynes, tried to put the unemployed to work, and under the 1935–40 New Works Programme the Northern Line was extended to High Barnet and Mill Hill East, bringing its length to forty miles, including the world's longest continuous land tunnel, 17 miles 528 yards between East Finchley and Morden. The Underground Group also pushed into Southern Region territory, with the line from Clapham Common to Morden, opened in 1926, carrying south of the Thames the expansionist policy of driving lines out into open country, to pick up traffic at station suburbs. It proved a great focal point; from 17,532 in 1921, the population of Merton and Morden leapt to 68,980 in 1938 – a 223 per cent increase.

But the development that caught the public imagination was the construction by the Metropolitan Railway of two new electric lines: to Watford, Amersham and Uxbridge (1925) and to Stanmore (1932). As far back as the 1880s the Metropolitan had leased land at Wembley, promoting an amusement park with, as its centre-piece, a grander Eiffel Tower – unfinished and abandoned. This was demolished to make way for Wembley Stadium. The Metropolitan promoted other forms of property development along its lines, setting up a new company, Metropolitan Country Estates Ltd, which acted as a housing developer in places around Pinner and Harrow, adopting for publicity purposes the term 'Metroland'.

> Hearts are light, eyes are brighter,
> In Metroland, Metroland

according to a ditty composed by the journalist George R. Simms.

A veritable Metroland soap opera was launched, through a booklet called *Metroland*, issued annually from 1919, with space devoted to housing development. 'My Little Metro-land Home', a song and dance, was published in 1920. 'Stake your claim at Edgware,' the Underground instructed:

Omar Khay-yam's recipe for turning the wilderness into paradise hardly fits an English climate, but provision has been made at Edgware of an alternative recipe which at least will convert pleasant, undulating fields into happy homes. The loaf of bread, the jug of wine and the book of verse may be got there cheaply and easily, and, apart from what is said by the illustration, a

The new underground system promised to transport the public from cramped terraced houses to leafy suburbs

shelter which comprises all the latest labour-saving and sanitary conveniences. We moderns ask much more before we are content than the ancients, and Edgware is designed to give us that much more.

Abutting the railway, estates were developed at Neasden, Wembley, Pinner, Rickmansworth and Chorley Wood, and along the Uxbridge branch at Rayners Lane, Eastcote, Ruislip and Hillingdon. Metroland mushroomed. Between the wars, Harrow gained 134,480 new residents, the largest influx of any local authority in Greater London; Wembley grew by 552 per cent; Ruislip–Northwood leapt from 9,112 in 1921 to 47,760 in 1939. Thanks to the tube, north-west London's outer suburbs –

Dollis Hill, Barnet, Hendon, Mill Hill, Finchley, Kenton, Edgware and so forth – grew phenomenally.

Road improvements also played their part in suburbanization. Severe postwar unemployment prompted government subsidies for the construction of new roads. The Ministry of Transport programme for 1920–4 involved 190 miles of construction, including Eastern Avenue (Wanstead to Romford and Ilford to Woodford), Sidcup to Wrotham, the Watford Bypass, the Barnet Bypass, the Great West Road (Gunnersbury to Hounslow to Hanwell), Western Avenue (East Acton to Greenford), part of the North Circular, and so forth. Roads brought homes and jobs.

In 1933 the capital's tubes, trams and buses were first yoked under a common public authority, the London Passenger Transport Board. Till then developments had had a piecemeal air, often with meagre results for investors. But rationalization and the new power sources – electricity and petrol – made the decades from the 1930s the peak of London's public transport, helped in part by Frank Pick's modernistic Underground maps and posters that imparted a pride in the network. Londoners were using buses, tubes, trams and trolley-buses more than ever before or since; the average Londoner took 210 rides a year on tubes, buses and trams in 1911, but almost twice as many by 1939. Not until around 1950 did the motor car seriously lure commuters away from public transport.

Improved communication links helped solve the problem of inner-city and inner-suburb overcrowding, but not as the visionaries imagined. Assorted urban reformers had been analysing the Victorian city, finding it wanting, and coming up with fundamental new solutions. The most radical scheme was Ebenezer Howard's garden-city idea, brought to fruition in two prototypes, Letchworth and Welwyn, founded by Howard and built by the Garden Cities and Town Planning Association.

The dream of a green and pleasant town away from city smoke, din and dirt, was unfolded in Howard's *Garden Cities of Tomorrow* (1902). Towns offered jobs and the country offered health. Howard's garden city grafted the best of both worlds in a unified planned environment keeping home and work somewhat apart – but not too far, to lessen commuting. Rejecting further suburban expansion – the dormitory suburb was no solution – Howard proposed new towns around London, with a population limited to 30,000, surrounded by a 'Green Belt' separating them from London itself. Any increase in population would be met by the creation of additional satellites, at least four miles away. Howard's imagined city was circular with factories and houses set on open ground, to combine town and country advantages. The garden city allowed space for nature: not more than a sixth of the area should be covered by buildings. Within the town, the distribution of boulevards, buildings and factories was to be rigidly controlled. Howard hoped for government finance, but initially the state provided none, so he found private backing for Letchworth, begun in 1903, and Welwyn Garden City (1920).

The garden-city vision dominated interwar planning. With the passing of the Town and Country Planning Act of 1932, the LCC prepared a London-wide plan which received government approval, though before the outbreak of war in 1939 little was achieved apart from the creation of the Green Belt. This was conceived as a band of farmland, parkland and recreation ground around London, some five to ten miles wide, in which any building development was to be carefully controlled. Its aim was to provide amenities within easy access of the city-dweller and to prevent the tentacle-like spread of the metropolis. During the war Sir Patrick Abercrombie, Professor of Town Planning at University College, London, was appointed to prepare plans, and the *County of London Plan* and *Greater London Plan* were drawn up in 1943 and 1944 respectively.

In the meantime, however, while new towns and 'the green girdle' (Raymond Unwin's phrase) were being imagined by urban reformers, London was independently undergoing its greatest ever centrifugal migration, often into distant suburbs ten or fifteen miles from the central workplace, but in large degree heedless of Howard's ideals. By 1931 Westminster had lost over half its 1861 population, Marylebone nearly a third, and Southwark, Shoreditch and Bethnal Green had begun to thin. Battersea, Chelsea, Islington, Camberwell, Fulham and Hackney all lost population between the wars, with people pouring out into the distant suburbs. Suburbia thus spread, eating up the fields.

While the population of the County of London (the LCC area) grew gently between 1881 and 1911, that of the 'outer ring' shot up from 936,000 to 2,730,000, notably in places like Walthamstow and Tottenham, where in 1905 Henrietta Barnett described 'small villas side by side ... the monotony of mediocrity unbroken by fine public buildings or large open spaces'. The great transformation, however, came after the First World War. Middlesex's population grew by almost a third between 1921 and 1931, five times the national increase and the highest of any county. Between those dates the *population* of Greater London increased by 9.7 per cent but the built-up *area* virtually doubled.

This astonishing growth stemmed from the private-housing boom, fed by developers large and small, the annual output reaching a peak of 72,700 in 1934. Of the astonishing 700,000 new houses built around London between the wars, three-quarters were put up by private builders. Railways and the Underground provided the seed-bed and water for suburbs to shoot up. On the Surrey claylands between Sutton and Kingston new semis were under £1,000; property over £1,000 appeared on the Downs round

Epsom; the appealing Esher and Weybridge heathlands were preferred sites for pricey housing, while Croydon, Waddon and Mitcham were all cheaper. Similar developments took place all round the rim. Attracting owner-occupiers, Chingford expanded from 9,506 in 1921 to 39,460 in 1939, Hornchurch grew by 335 per cent between 1921 and 1938.

The outer suburbs had many attractions. Transport improvements made long-distance commuting feasible; agricultural depression created cheap building land; standardization and mass production enabled big building companies – latter-day Cubitts – to create agreeable dwellings at affordable prices. Between them, a handful of big firms – Costain, Crouch, Davis, Laing, Nash, New Ideal Homesteads, Taylor Woodrow, Wates, and Wimpey – built over 100,000 homes. Nash began at Kenton in about 1925, and Wates were building small houses from the early 1920s; but the real pioneers of large-scale estate development were Richard Costain & Sons Ltd, originally a Liverpool firm. Their first venture, at leafy Kingswood, Surrey, opened in 1923. They went on to plant new estates at Selsdon, Addington, Caterham, Croham Heights and Brent Water. The last, on the North Circular Road near Cricklewood, was a new departure, its cut-price residences designed for affluent manual workers in the local electrical and engineering industries. Further developments for the lower-income group followed, like Rylandes Farm (1931) and Elm Park, Hornchurch (1934) – both soon occupied by Ford workers from Dagenham.

The most prolific London developers were New Ideal Homesteads, formed by Leo P. Meyer and opening their first estate in 1930 at Dartford. By 1932 they were offering a three-bedroom semi for just £395, and an agreement with the Halifax Building Society enabled them to sell for a deposit of only 5 per cent (£20). In 1934 sixteen New Ideal Homestead estates were in operation around the suburbs, and some 5,700 houses were sold that year. Wates Brothers were selling on fifteen estates in 1935 and twenty in 1939, by when they had erected some 30,000 houses.

Suburban properties were dreams come true. All post-1919 housing had electricity, a bathroom and an inside WC, and at least a half-tiled kitchen. Most were fitted with a back-boiler for hot water (central heating was still widely thought unhealthy and un-English). Though standardization kept prices down, gestures towards individuality attracted buyers. 'No pair of houses alike in road,' boasted a 1927 billboard in Purley; 'Every house different,' claimed Berg's all-detached Hinchley Wood estate of 1931. On Glock's Catford estate, you could take your pick of 'Queen Anne, Jacobean, Georgian or Tudor' styles. Osbert Lancaster mocked the spate of 'By-pass Variegated', the clutter of mock-Tudor and modernism:

here are some quaint gables culled from *Art Nouveau* surmounting a façade that is plainly modernistic in inspiration; there the twisted beams and leaded panes of Stockbrokers' Tudor are happily contrasted with bright green tiles of obviously Pseudish origin; next door some terra-cotta plaques, Pont Street Dutch in character, enliven a white wood Wimbledon Transitional porch, making it a splendid foil to a red-brick garage that is vaguely Romanesque in feeling.

Demand was buoyant, for, despite the slump, London was prospering. Clerks and skilled workers galore were desperate to leave run-down central London and were enticed by the prospect of 'all mod cons'. Electricity was a great selling-point, particularly with irons, vacuum cleaners, cookers and other labour-saving appliances flooding the market – many of them made in west London's new electricals factories. Few of those delights were available to housewives trapped in subdivided gas-lit Victorian inner-suburban houses in Peckham, Walworth or Finsbury Park, rented from landlords who had no incentive to improve property. No wonder Londoners migrated, as cheap and cheerful suburban developments in Hanwell or Hounslow, Hayes or Harlington, could be afforded by skilled manual workers earning as little as £3 or £4 a week. Teachers, clerks and civil servants could invest in bigger houses, perhaps detached.

The private-house boom was made possible by low interest rates and cheap mortgages. Building societies became big business. The Abbey Road Building Society was formed in 1874, taking its name from its first address (in NW10), the founders being members of the Free Church. By 1914 its assets stood at £750,000; by 1925 they were £3.5 million, and it was developing rapidly into a familiar modern building society. In 1927 it moved to new headquarters in Baker Street, amalgamating in 1944 with the National to become Abbey National. The Woolwich, founded in 1847, began with contributions from workers in Woolwich Arsenal. It rocketed after the First World War, its assets reaching £27.1 million by 1934.

The London house-buyer had never had it so good, and never would again. Not everyone approved: 'semi-detached' implied for some a weary, dreary way of life, hemmed in by net curtains and propriety. Critics dubbed suburbia 'Subtopia'. The author of *The Suburbans*, published in 1904, thought that in the suburbs

you will understand, as it were, intuitively, and without further ado, the cheapness and out-of-jointness of the times; you will comprehend the why and wherefore and *raison d'être* of halfpenny journalism ... you will perceive the whizzers, penny buses, gramophones, bamboo furniture, pleasant Sunday afternoons, Glory Songs, modern language teas, golf, tennis, high school education, dubious fiction, shilling's worth of comic writing, picture postcards, miraculous hair-restorers, prize competitions, and all other sorts of twentieth-century clap-trap have got a market and a use, and black masses of supporters.

'Morningside Park ... a suburb that had not altogether, as people say, come off' was mocked, in a most arch manner, by H. G. Wells:

It consisted, like pre-Roman Gaul, of three parts. There was first the Avenue, which ran in a consciously elegant curve from the railway station into an undeveloped wilderness of agriculture, with big yellow brick villas on either side, and then there was the Pavement, the little clump of shops about the post office, and under the railway arch was a congestion of workmen's dwellings. The road from Surbiton and Epsom ran under the arch, and like a bright fungoid growth in the ditch there was now appearing a sort of fourth estate of little red-and-white rough-cast villas, with meretricious gables and very brassy window blinds.

The middle-class housewife's Ideal Home supposedly spawned suburban neurosis at the kitchen sinks of Kingsbury and Kingston, Sidcup and Sudbury. Yet those with the deposit money voted with their feet: for millions, the new suburbs proved overdue liberation from central districts that grew dingier by the year, and perhaps a new start, away from the class strait-jackets of town.

Yet, on a good day, central London might still gleam in all its glory, and send shivers up the spine. 'London is enchanting,' thrilled Virginia Woolf:

I step out upon a tawny coloured magic carpet, it seems, and get carried into beauty without raising a finger. The nights are amazing, with all the white porticos and broad silent avenues. And people pop in and out, lightly, divertingly like rabbits; and I look down Southampton Row, wet as a seal's back or red and yellow with sunshine, and watch the omnibuses going and coming and hear the old crazy organs. One of these days I will write about London, and how it takes up the private life and carries it on, without any effort.

Virginia Woolf captured in *Mrs Dalloway* what Thomas De Quincey, a century earlier, had called 'the roar of unresting London'. London certainly became busier and noisier. Yet, in all kinds of ways, traditional central London was ossifying. The Strand, Fleet Street, Holborn, all the haunts of commerce and City men, became more antiquated. The Edwardian era brought puffed-up hotels and banks, swollen with imperial grandeur, and the 1920s and 1930s produced more of the same. Central London became a playground for plutocrats, or, as Conan Doyle put it, 'a great cesspit into which all the loungers of the Empire are irresistibly drained'.

For better or worse, London missed out on the daring departures in urban architecture springing up in the United States, France and Germany. Change was slow. Apart from the coming of the motor car, on the outbreak of war in 1939 huge tracts of the City, Holborn, Clerkenwell, Soho and the West End still looked remarkably as they had at Victoria's death. The development of outer London had 'spared' the centre – or left it behind.

Yet something was new: from Edwardian days a new mass-market commercial culture sprang up, energized and funded by the more modern, democratic culture on the other side of the Atlantic. Pitched between the traditional plebeian world of the pub and the upper-class milieu of the club, the new metropolitan culture catered for the burgeoning multitudes, the better class of council-house dwellers, the new people with mortgages in Metroland, the many, not just the millionaires. Not least, commercial culture wooed couples and women: the male grip on town was finally loosened. The area around Piccadilly Circus and Leicester Square became something new: a pleasure zone for respectable people in their millions.

Ironically, war contributed much to relaxing the rigid social protocols of old London. The strains of the First World War created a more ebullient night-life. Soho emerged as a popular restaurant area. Young women, increasingly employed as clerks and civil ser-vants, felt freer to meet soldier friends in the West End. Nightclubs developed; sex-ual inhibitions were relaxed. The *Daily Mail* noted a new breed of 'Dining Out Girls':

The war-time business girl is to be seen any night dining out alone or with a friend in the moderate-price restaurants in London. Formerly she would never have had her evening meal in town unless in the company of a man friend. But now, with money and without men, she is more and more beginning to dine out.

After the war, the return of the Season and the example of the flapper and the 'bright young thing' encouraged younger Londoners to enjoy themselves, taking advantage of the better transport facilities offered by buses and tubes. The cinema caught on. There had been ninety cinemas in London before the war, offering luxury to the little man, and London's suburbs became the sites of film studios – Ealing, Pinewood, Elstree. In the 1920s the age of the London super-cinema now dawned, with the Tooting Granada (constructed in a Hispano-Moorish style inspired by the Alhambra Palace in Granada), the Finsbury Park Astoria, the Elephant and Castle Trocadero, and other giants housing 'mighty Wurlitzers'. There were scores of smaller local cinemas too – in Bermondsey alone the Stork in Storks Road, the Trocette in Tower Bridge Road, the Grand in Grange Road, the Rialto in St James' Road and the Palace in Southwark Park Road.

Other forms of popular entertainment flourished, including amusement arcades with pinball machines. The 'roaring twenties' gave way to the age of dance bands – Jack Hylton, Billy Cotton and Ambrose, who played at the Mayfair Hotel. London theatre between the wars was stylish, with Noël Coward and Ivor Novello and the famous Aldwych farces by Ben Travers. Jack Hulbert and Cicely Courtneidge enjoyed great popularity, as did Fay Compton, Gladys Cooper and Sybil Thorndyke.

The cinema encouraged popular eating-places. The capital had traditionally been poorly served with cafés, partly because of the hold of gentlemen's clubs. Around 1890 the Aerated Bread Company (ABC) and the Express Dairy opened hundreds of milk-and-bun shops, but the breakthrough came with J. Lyons & Co. Ltd, who started their first teashop in 1894, at 213 Piccadilly. The firm was founded by Salmon and

Gluckstein, tobacconists; the name came from Joseph Lyons, a relatively minor figure. The first Lyons Corner House was established in 1909 on the corner of Coventry Street. By the 1920s Lyons had three Corner Houses, each seating up to 3,000 and providing music, inexpensive food and a taste of luxury for common folk.

Seeing the potential of the leisure industry, in 1895 Lyons opened the Trocadero, a high-class Piccadilly Circus restaurant; they built the Strand Palace Hotel in 1909; the Regent Palace, at the back of Regent Street, in 1915; and in 1933 the Cumberland Hotel, at the junction of Oxford Street and Park Lane. Above all they became leaders in the mass production of tea, ice-cream, cakes and sticky buns at their factory at Cadby Hall, near Olympia: in 1931 500,000 rolls were daily dispatched from the bakery, while 160 million meals were served a year, providing 'luxury catering for the little man'.

All this brought an Americanization of the capital. The cinema in particular promoted an American culture accessible to London's masses. It opened up the West End to many more people. So, too, did chain stores, like Woolworth's – another American import – which arrived in London with an Oxford Street store in 1924.

Such developments were not confined to the West End. A new economy of leisure was springing up elsewhere. Streatham got the Streatham Hill Theatre in 1929, and two cinemas were opened in the 1930s. Then the Locarno dancehall and the Streatham Ice Rink consolidated Streatham's reputation of being the entertainment centre of south London. Of his youth in Raynes Park in the 1930s, the broadcaster Paul Vaughan remembers:

There were three cinemas within easy reach of our house and we became regular customers at both local Odeons, one at Tolworth, one at Worcester Park, or the shabbier Plaza at New Malden. If my father was in the mood, and if we had gone to the Odeon at Tolworth, we would cross the road and dine out at the Toby Jug, where the Grill Room, smelling enticingly of steak dinners, had a small dance orchestra and a space for couples to perform the fox-trot or the waltz. There was a Master of Ceremonies, in black tie, with lapel badge bearing the letters 'MC', who would announce the sets with a repertoire of jokey remarks. The food was straightforward: steak or fish. My mother would have a gin and It or a sweet sherry, my father a pint of bitter.

Toby Jug dinners were rare events, but rarer were visits to the theatre. My mother favoured Streatham Hill, but if my father were the instigator, it would be the Kingston Empire for a variety bill. This was much like old-style music hall, with the number of the act flashing up in electric lights at the side of the stage and a bar at the back of the stalls from which you could watch the performance.

Slowly London was adapting to the new century: an age of mobility, growing affluence, leisure and the family. The new suburbs provided environments in which these could flourish.

CHAPTER FOURTEEN

Modern Growth, Modern Government: 1890–1945

The new patterns in housing, the new consumer orientation, had, of course, an economic basis. It was built upon London's role as the 'clearing-house of the world' (the phrase was Joseph Chamberlain's). Late Victorian, Edwardian, and post-First World War London basked in imperial glory. In 1901 the intellectual Charles Masterman edited a book called *The Heart of the Empire: Discussions of Problems of Modern City Life in England*. 'We can hardly foresee any causes, apart from the decay of Britain itself, which shall lead to a failure ... of London,' declared Sir Halford Mackinder, geographer and statesman, in 1902. Mackinder was spot-on. In a world of international maritime services, London cashed in so long as the Empire thrived. What he failed to perceive was how quickly the Empire would decline and dissolve. The intimate links between the metropolis and the Empire were symbolized in Niels Lund's 1904 painting *The Heart of the Empire*. Donated by Lord Mayor Sir William Treloar to the Corporation of London, it displayed a glorious, confident City crowned by St Paul's. Mackinder spelt out the ideas behind that picture:

The life of the great metropolis at the beginning of the twentieth century exhibits the daily throb of a huge pulsating heart. Every evening half a million men are sent in quick streams, like corpuscles of blood through the arteries, along the railways and the trunk roads outward to the suburbs. Every morning they return, crowding into the square mile or two wherein the exchanges of the world are finally adjusted.

Empire was written in so many ways on the very topography of the capital. The arrival of a British force in Ethiopia in 1868 was duly recorded in Abyssinia Road, Battersea. The fortress there destroyed is named in Magdala Avenue, Archway – streets of the same name are also found in Isleworth and in South Croydon, where Magdala Road adjoins Napier Road, commemorating the British leader. Clapham streets allude to the second Afghan War (1879–80): Afghan Road and Khyber Road run to Candahar

326

Road, which leads to Cabul Road. Berber Road, Clapham, refers to Gordon's expedition in 1884. There are Khartoum Roads in Tooting, Ilford and Plaistow. The Boer War is remembered, through Tugela River, in Tugela Road (Selhurst) and Tugela Street (Catford). Colenso Road, Clapton, refers to a disaster; another street bears that name in Ilford, in a quartet including Ladysmith Avenue, Kimberley Avenue and Mafeking Avenue. Pretoria Road occurs in Tooting, in Ilford (near Natal Road), Romford and Chingford. In Canning Town, Pretoria Road adjoins Ladysmith Road, Kimberley Road and Mafeking Road.

The *Pax Britannica* brought business – shipping, imports, investments – that even the First World War failed to destroy. London continued to grow; between 1911 and 1939 its population increased from 7.25 to 8.73 million, entirely in the outer ring beyond the LCC boundaries. Massive suburban growth was made possible by dramatic communications improvements. Between 1902 and 1928 there was a 352 per cent rise in the number of passengers carried by public transport, while by 1938 London and the Home Counties sported about half a million private cars. This stunning expansion had a solid economic grounding.

As the new century dawned, London's position at the hub of the world's largest empire gave work to half a million in the docks and in import-related occupations. It also guaranteed middle-class employment in Whitehall but above all in the City, where tens of thousands of Pooterish clerks meticulously documented the transactions of the thousands of companies, great and small, involved in worldwide mercantile and shipping enterprises. In turn, London's wealthy created demand for labour galore in the transport, food and retail industries and in domestic service. Building, catering, clothing, shops, restaurants and hotels expanded as Victorian prosperity became Edwardian conspicuous consumption. London was long the world's biggest consumer. Even in the dark days of the 1930s unemployment barely bit, because London, unlike the industrial North, had never become dangerously overdependent upon a single staple such as coal, textiles or shipbuilding. London was dependent on the Empire, but the Empire was intact.

Inner London's economy continued broadly as before. Commerce and manufacturers big and small upheld riverside prosperity, and the railways generated employment. At its Stratford works, the Great Eastern Railway was east London's largest single employer, with over 7,000 workers. Long-established breweries expanded, such as Truman, Hanbury & Buxton in Brick Lane, Mann, Crossman & Paulin in the Mile End Road, and Taylor Walker's Barley Mow Brewery in Limehouse. Mineral-water and soft-drinks factories sparkled in West Ham. Flour-mills, margarine factories, jam, sweets and sugar factories flourished along the Silvertown riverfront, involving such familiar names as Henry Tate, Abram Lyle and Keiller & Sons. By the mid-1950s Tate and Lyle's sugar-refinery employed almost 8,000.

The Port of London, easily the largest in the world, was still growing. The Greenland Dock was opened in 1904 on the Surrey side, and in 1921 King George V named a dock after himself in East Ham, south of the Royal Albert Dock, near Beckton's gasholders. Its three miles of quays held huge liners; in August 1939 the 35,655-ton *Mauretania* berthed there. Dock development by then received government sponsorship, and homes were provided for displaced families.

The Port of London Authority had been created in 1908 to administer the Port, the City Corporation thereby finally relinquishing its control of the river. All the docks were busy: the London and St Katharine handling fruit and wine; the Surrey Commercial timber; down-river, the India and Millwall Docks; farther east again the three huge basins of the 'Royal' docks – the Royal Albert, the Royal Victoria and the King George V – between them providing fifty-three deep-water berths and eleven miles of quays; and, twenty-six miles from London Bridge, the Tilbury Docks began serving liners.

Stepney and its neighbourhood housed the clothing industry and other sweated trades supplied by petty capital and casual labour. The rag trade was flourishing in the City and Finsbury – wholesale millinery in Golden Lane, necktie-makers in Wood Street, merchant tailors and uniform manufacturers in Stepney and Bethnal Green. Baby-clothes establishments sprang up in budding Walthamstow, while Mortimer Street became the hub of West End fashion wholesalers.

Inner London continued to excel in high-quality products. In Clerkenwell, Cossor's, manufacturers of scientific glassware, began specializing in radio components. In 1902 they made the first British Braun-type cathode ray tube, going on to lead the field in wireless receivers and valves. London pioneered telephone and radio equipment. Traditional manufacturing, however, was leaving the core for the outer suburbs. Long-established inner-city manufacturing areas – Holborn, Finsbury, Shoreditch, Clerkenwell – were hideously overcrowded: businesses had no room to grow; rates and labour costs were high; stringent LCC regulations led capitalists to seek districts with fewer controls and less inspection. The growth of late Victorian dormitory suburbs meant that areas like Southall and Acton, Willesden and Harlesden, Tottenham and Edmonton, and, to the south, Wandsworth, Balham and Tooting already possessed large labour forces ripe for local employment. They generally had ample cheap land for expansion. Situated on or near the main railway lines, outer suburbs could build railway sidings, while the Grand Union Canal threaded through the north-west. The switch to electric power also facilitated suburban industry. Previously much industry had needed to be next to the Thames or a canal for vital coal supplies. Centrally generated electrical power overcame this restriction. Once the North Metropolitan Electric Supply Company's Brimsdown power station was built, nearby Ponder's End and Enfield were perfectly situated for works like the Edison Swan United Electric Light Company (1886).

Not least, arterial road-building programmes, initiated to combat postwar unemployment, gave suburbs superb routes at precisely the moment when road haulage was expanding. Western Avenue, the Great West Road and the North Circular attracted factories and plant. The Great West Road was opened by King George V in 1925. Originally planned as a Brentford bypass, it was soon dubbed 'the Golden Mile', thanks to the scores of new factories built along it – Smith's Crisps, Curry's cycles and radios, Maclean's toothpaste, and various American companies such as Trico-Folbert (windscreen manufacturers), Firestone tyres, Gillette and Hoover. Opened in 1933 on Western Avenue (the A40) near Perivale station, the Hoover building was designed in the art-deco style by Wallis Gilbert & Partners, famous for several Great West Road factories. It was floodlit from the beginning. The 'Golden Mile' was a roadshow of modern architecture, as each firm exploited its site to project its image. The majority of American firms setting up in Britain between the wars settled in the area. Southall, Osterley, Heston, Isleworth and Hanwell all blossomed. In 1919 the first civil airport in the country opened on Hounslow Heath, with a daily London to Paris service. Further development took place around Hounslow, particularly after the Piccadilly Line arrived in 1932. Thanks to Western Avenue, J. Lyons & Co. Ltd, Rockware Glass, Glaxo and Aladdin all planted themselves in Greenford. Speculative housing throughout the 1930s meant that the area was largely built up by 1940. At the end of 1936 it was reckoned 'practically impossible to obtain a site of any size on the Great West Road, Kingston By-Pass Road and Western Avenue'. North-west London enjoyed a gold-rush boom. 'The extraordinary growth of Willesden Green and Harlesden, and the likelihood of new suburbs and commercial property continually expanding, generally inspires investors to favour these districts,' trumpeted the *Estates Gazette* in 1923.

A key innovation was the industrial estate, on which a development company would provide factories for sale or lease, or would sell the land in plots. Park Royal, between Acton and Wembley, led the field. Handily situated just west of the railway yards of Willesden Junction, it started as a Royal Agricultural Society showground, then was taken over during the First World War for munitions factories. Served by the Great Western Railway, the Grand Union Canal and (from 1920) by Western Avenue and the North Circular, it was ripe for postwar development. Major Allnatt, a Reading businessman, took over the disused sheds to cater for visitors during the Empire Exhibition in 1924. When the exhibition closed, he built units for lease. By the 1930s he was completing a factory every two weeks. Standard Road, Minerva Road and Sunbeam Road commemorate some of the cars manufactured there. Biscuits, tinned foods, electrical goods, car components, pharmaceuticals and Guinness were all manufactured in the district. North Acton station on the Central Line made it accessible.

Wembley itself was developed at the same time, assisted by the infrastructure laid for the Empire Exhibition. Alperton also expanded, spurred by the opening of the Metropolitan Line service beyond Acton and the coming of the Piccadilly Line to South Harrow in 1932. The Glacier Metal Company made bearings for Morris Motors there, and during the 1930s industry expanded eastwards on to the purpose-built Abbey Manufacturing Estate.

The outer suburbs benefited from industrial relocation – that is, decentralization. The gas-cooker firm Glover & Main, for instance, migrated in 1900 from Clerkenwell to the Angel Road, Edmonton. Shortly afterwards Eley Bros. shifted their cartridge manufacturing from Grays Inn Road to Edmonton. But the suburbs, especially the swathe from Hendon down to Brentford, Isleworth and Southall – became the seed-bed for new industries. Three were particularly prominent: aircraft, electricals and motor vehicles. Aircraft firms needed space for flying-grounds. Handley Page moved to Cricklewood in 1912, where an airfield was attached to the work. Airco (later De Havilland's) shifted to Hendon just before the First World War, taking over a bus garage and leasing Hendon Aerodrome. De Havilland's also acquired an aerodrome in Edgware, close to Airco's Hendon wind-tunnel and to Napier's, who, established since the 1830s as machine engineers in Lambeth, had moved in 1903 to Acton, employing more than 500 men and soon abandoning cars for aero-engines. Vickers began manu-facturing aircraft before 1914 among its gun factories at Erith, Dartford and Crayford, which had developed fast after Hiram Maxim chose in 1888 to make his machine-guns there. Vickers made Wolseley cars during slumps in the armaments business. Hawker aircraft, succeeding Sopwith at Kingston after 1918, used Brooklands to test engines and aircraft. As aircraft manufactures expanded, firms had to migrate further. In the early 1930s Handley Page left Cricklewood for Radlett, Herts.

The aircraft and engineering industries thrived, creating confidence. Automobiles developed too. 'The chief development in West London is I think the motor-car industry,' reported a factory inspector in 1903, noting the tendency 'for the larger factories to move out of London into the country westward to Hayes, Southall, and even so far as Reading'.

Other new industries also sprang up in the outer suburbs. The British film industry became established in Elstree, Croydon, Surbiton, Pinewood, Cricklewood and Ealing. Sir Alexander Korda's Denham Studios in Buckinghamshire had its own power plant.

Similar developments were going on to the east. From the 1870s cheap rail fares had enticed workers into Tottenham, Edmonton and Walthamstow. In due course, firms involved in traditional east-London trades – clothing, metal and engineering, and furniture – followed the workers, attracted by plentiful labour, transport facilities and cheap Leaside land. Between 1900 and 1914 the Lea valley attracted thirty-seven factor-ies, nineteen from inner London. Chemicals and electrical-engineering works followed.

East London's real coup was the arrival of Ford's at Dagenham. Henry Ford was operating in Britain before 1914, building his original factory in Old Trafford, Manchester. But in the 1920s, planning a European sales drive, he decided on a site near London. He built on marshy Thames-side land, using enormous concrete piles, and set up his own foundry – during the 1930s it was fuelled partly by LCC rubbish formerly dumped on the site. Nearby was the mass of labour recently exported by the LCC to the vast Becontree Estate. Dagenham also profited by the removal there of May & Baker Ltd pharmaceuticals in 1934.

Overall, London's new industries proved hugely successful. In the 1930s, during the Slump, 1,055 factories closed in London but 1,573 were opened – 43 per cent of the nation's total. About two-thirds of the new jobs created in Great Britain between the wars lay in Greater London. Nine hundred new firms employing twenty-five or more people were set up between 1932 and 1938 – half the national total. This stunning success hinged entirely on outer-ring growth – between 1934 and 1938 the LCC area suffered a net loss of 191 factories while outer London gained over twice as many new plants. London proved a good host for new industries, such as electronics. In 1951 Greater London provided half of England and Wales's jobs in wireless valves, electric lamps, wireless and telephone apparatus. While the old smoke-stack industries of Wales and the North East were being ravaged by foreign competition, new London-based consumer industries grew: Gillette razor blades, Marconi radios, Hoover vacuum cleaners, nylons, Horlicks, Heinz canned foods and gramophone records – all targeted at the mass market, promoted by press and cinema advertising, and benefiting from American capital and business methods. In a time of recession, London tightened its ancient grip on national wealth.

Meanwhile, decline was accelerating in the inner-city industrial base and in some traditional trades. East London's footwear industry was on its uppers by 1914 – big Midlands factories were forcing it out of business. Yet central London had its successes, thriving as a centre for consumption, tourism, leisure and pleasure. The very rich made London their playground. Department stores blossomed. In 1909 Debenham & Freebody's opened their reconstructed store in Wigmore Street, just north of Oxford Street, with a historic telephone number: Mayfair One. And the same year witnessed the opening of the grandest store of all, the creation of an American who had made his fortune in Chicago. In his fifties, Gordon Selfridge came to London and built a super-store designed to shake the capital up. Like other American businessmen, Selfridge saw London as commercially fuddy-duddy. Perceiving how the entrenched establishments were still emulating 'the subdued and disciplined atmosphere of the gentleman's mansion', Selfridge sought a different image. His vision was less a conventional shop than a multi-media experience: 'I want them to enjoy the warmth and light, the colours and styles, the feel of fine fabrics.' He installed a soda fountain and a bargain basement, a library, a first-aid room, a *bureau de change*, a theatre booking-office, a luncheon hall, a tea garden. Selfridge's – somewhere between a shop and a hotel – was one of many marks of new American influence in London. Not all approved: his emporium, critics complained, presented 'the appearance of a fair'. That description, however, applied much better to Walter Gamage's longer-established store in High Holborn, with its 'People's Popular Emporium' tag, crammed with garden tools, toys, kitchen gadgets, camping equipment and lawn mowers, and supplying the Boy Scouts' movement.

Both Harrods and Whiteley's were also rebuilt at this time – Whiteley's opening a purpose-built palace in Queensway in 1911. All such stores proved a breath of fresh air: 'The atmosphere is better,' it was said:

There is more space and more air to breathe. There is more display, or perhaps exhibitionism is the truer word. There is less servility and more actual service ... there is much more varied and fresher stock, and articles which formerly could be had only by the well-to-do are now available to the many.

The Edwardian era saw London stores at their apogee, almost as grand as royalty. Attendance was equally essential: 'I got up to London just before twelve,' recorded Cynthia Asquith in 1915, struggling with the crowds, 'and had a hellish morning in pursuit of my summer tweeds from Harrods.'

Travel, glitter and ostentation among the rich also led to a golden age of hotels. In 1903 the Savoy spent a million pounds, doubling its size, adding 200 rooms. A rubber roadway was laid for the benefit of sleeping guests. In Piccadilly two hotels were demolished to make way for Monsieur Ritz's 'small house', which also cost a million. Grosvenor House Hotel was completed in 1929, and two years later the Dorchester went up on the site of the old Dorchester House. Park Lane was beginning to resemble Fifth Avenue, only without skyscrapers – a regulation of 1894 prohibited buildings higher than eighty feet. Though inner London's manufactures began to falter, the metropolis's magnet ensured its services thrived.

Such growing and broad-based prosperity, grounded on plentiful employment, provides the background for the puzzles of London politics in the first half of the twentieth century. What the City and die-hard localists had long dreaded came about: a central governing body for London was installed. Yet the expected dire, even revolutionary, consequences did not follow.

In operation from 1889, the London County Council began with great expectations, for the Liberal/Radical Progressives who controlled the Council for its first eighteen years regarded municipal activity as the best solution for social problems. Their achievements, however, were less than glorious, a fact echoed by the saga of its premises.

Beginning its rule on 21 March 1889, the LCC inherited inadequate offices in Spring Gardens, Trafalgar Square. In 1905 it acquired a riverside site on the far side of Westminster Bridge, then a tangle of wharves, timber-yards and factories. Building began, then ceased in 1916 owing to the war, and County Hall was not opened until 1922: not auspicious progress, and indicative of a lumbering quality that was to dog the LCC bureaucracy.

The Council's standing was not helped by the creation of borough councils. To ensure the Progressives could not grow too powerful, the Conservative ministry of Lord Salisbury conceived the idea of building up countervailing authorities on the basis of the existing vestries. The London Government Act (1899) therefore created twenty-eight borough councils, giving them independent powers likely to conflict with the LCC. In the event, the ruse backfired, in that certain boroughs, notably Poplar, later fell into left-wing hands, whereas Conservatives enjoyed perhaps surprising success on the LCC.

The LCC's political history is intricate. The wrangles of the LCC with central government and with the boroughs, and the struggles of political cliques on the Council, would fill volumes. It was dreadfully subject to factionalism and localism, and was not entirely helped by certain dominant personalities, notably Herbert Morrison. In simple terms, however, its history falls into three periods of dominance: by Progressives – that is, by Liberals and others on the left – (1889–1907); by Municipal Reformers – the name the Conservatives used – (1907–34); and by Labour (1934–65). The Council's apogee lay in the long reign, from 1934, of Morrison and his successors with what may loosely be called a Fabian dream of municipal socialism run by experts for Londoners' good. Such a vision had been put forward in the 1890s, when Sidney Webb drafted the influential *The London Programme*. This included demands for abolition of the vestries and district boards, the equalization of London's rates and the creation of a 'municipal common fund', the taking-over by the Council of the monopoly of water, gas, markets, trams and docks, the 'municipalization of hospitals', and a large-scale municipal housing programme: 'London's poor,' Webb stressed, 'can only be rehoused by London's collective effort.'

Under the LCC many services were municipalized, paralleling earlier developments elsewhere (in Birmingham, for instance) as a result of the 1835 Municipal Corporations Act. Successive Acts of Parliament conferred ever wider functions on the Council, and ultimately its powers were very considerable. It became responsible *inter alia* for main drainage, the control of building, the fire service, and, with the twenty-eight metropolitan borough councils, for housing. It bought out all the London tramway companies and ran the trams until the formation of the London Passenger Transport

Board in 1933. It built Blackwall and Rotherhithe tunnels, rebuilt six bridges (its demolition of old Waterloo Bridge in 1937 drew fierce opposition), and laid out Kingsway. In 1938 it initiated the London Green Belt, and by 1939 it had doubled the acreage of parks and open spaces which it had inherited from the Metropolitan Board of Works. In 1905 it started a steamboat service on the Thames, making huge losses. Of far greater consequence, when the Education Acts of 1902 and 1903 abolished the old school boards, their schools and those of the voluntary agencies (mostly denominational) were placed under the Council. In 1930 the LCC took over all the Poor Law infirmaries, turning them into a municipal hospital service, with 40,000 beds and 20,000 staff. Three out of every four hospital beds for Londoners were provided by the LCC.

The LCC took pride in its housing record – and with good reason, as indicated in the previous chapter, providing some 86,000 new dwellings by 1938. Its administrative responsibilities were mind-boggling. In 1925, for instance, it licensed 239 lodging-houses (with accommodation for 20,300 persons), 166 slaughterhouses, 130 cow-houses and 355 offensive businesses. It also maintained 966 public elementary schools, with 700,000 pupils; it supported 67 secondary schools, attended by 27,000 boys and girls, and 259 technical and evening schools with 193,000 pupils. It employed some 23,500 teachers. It ran 160 miles of tramways, with a staff of 15,000, carrying more than 700,000,000 passengers a year. It looked after the upkeep of 10 bridges over the Thames, 4 tunnels under it, and the Woolwich free ferry. It ran 115 parks and open spaces in and near London. It maintained the London Fire Brigade, with 66 stations, and also the London Ambulance Service. It supervised public safety at 655 theatres, music-halls, cinemas, and other places of entertainment. It registered more than 800 employment agencies and 720 massage establishments. It issued about 200,000 establishment, dog, gun, game and carriage licences. It maintained 10 mental hospitals, where nearly 18,000 patients were treated, including the Maudsley Hospital, Denmark Hill, and the Manor Hospital, Epsom, for mental defectives. It provided 347 cricket pitches and 436 football pitches (140 on Hackney Marshes alone), and 713 tennis-courts. In 1925 the Council's net income was about £23 million, of which nearly £12 million came from the rates and over £7 million from government grants.

This administrative achievement was, by any standards, phenomenal. But in certain respects the LCC proved surprisingly passive. Housing apart, it had only slight influence on the town's physical surroundings, with far fewer street schemes to its credit than the maligned Metropolitan Board of Works. The creation of Kingsway and Aldwych – opened in 1905, handsomely 100-feet wide, though with inferior flanking architecture – remained the sole significant twentieth-century road improvement in central London until the Hyde Park Corner underpass in 1962.

The Progressives drove through only a fraction of their vaunted municipalization programme. When they were voted out of office in 1907, the LCC had only a toe-hold in the tramway system, and had made little ground over local taxation and rates. As might be expected, the Municipal Reformers (that is, Conservatives) who came to power in 1907 were cautious from the start, pegging expenditure in the ratepayer's interest and preserving boroughs' prerogatives. Nevertheless it was, perhaps ironically, the Conservatives who launched the vast LCC housing estates: Becontree, St Helier, Watling, Downham, Bellingham and Mottingham, which, for all their monotony, set the standard for decent working-class housing on an unprecedented scale. Conservatives were happy to build on the rim; they were far less willing to make encroachments upon property and the environment in central London. They were also unwilling to intervene in London's economy. This was most obvious in the case of Becontree, where the LCC built houses but provided no work. The arrival of Ford's at Dagenham prevented what might otherwise have been a disaster – or, one might say, demonstrated the soundness of Conservative economics.

After 1934 Morrison and his Labour successors at County Hall behaved in a slow-and-steady way, despite widespread expectations of Socialist radicalism. He recognized he had to appeal to middle-class as well as working-class voters. There were always fears of left-wing firebrands in the boroughs, in trade unions and on trades councils: hence the first priority, in Morrison's view, was to uphold discipline and unity and create confidence. Morrison had a perception of the LCC's vulnerability. With the vast growth of Greater London the LCC area was losing population and wealth, and might ultimately lose its very rationale and mandate. Hence a certain protectiveness was in order. Under Labour the LCC was not in an expansive mood; it concentrated upon functions it knew it could fulfil.

The LCC's relationship to borough activism was ambiguous. Local Labour Party branches were founded in various boroughs in the early years of the century, and by 1914 most London districts were covered by a local Labour Party or by a trades council serving the same purpose. In that year there was, unsurprisingly, no Labour Party in Chelsea or the City – wealthy districts, politically hopeless for Labour. But Bethnal Green, Stepney and Camberwell – all working-class boroughs – had no Labour Party either. Ethnic and religious divisions, large-scale migration, chronic poverty – factors such as these bred over the years a mixture of party-political apathy and erratic factionalism. In Hoxton and Bethnal Green small-scale industry assisted the survival of an old-fashioned radicalism. In Stepney an Irish colony and a Jewish group with their traditional attachments to Liberalism proved additional complications. In Hampstead, St Marylebone, Westminster, Wandsworth, Greenwich and Lewisham Labour Parties were founded but predictably failed to make headway. Overall, despite heavy working-class domination of many inner-city areas, coherent and powerful Labour followings were slow to form.

In the 1919 LCC elections, however, Labour made striking gains, notably in Hackney, Bethnal Green and Poplar. The left dominated many borough councils and Poor Law boards of guardians (responsible for the welfare of the old, sick, poor and unemployed), and battles to improve welfare services and living standards were fought by rebellious borough Labour Parties in the 1920s. Complaints in 1922 that wealthy boroughs such as Kensington and Westminster were not contributing their fair share towards relief in the poorer boroughs led Poplar council to refuse to disburse its quota to the LCC or to central-government agencies like the Metropolitan Police. Poplar councillors fixed a low rate, using most of that to relieve local poor. Such direct action brought the councillors into conflict with the law, with the LCC and with Westminster. The Poplar guardians started to pay relief rates above the maximum fixed by the government orders; after twelve months they faced a surcharge of £110,000. They also made illegal unemployment-benefit payments to dockers involved in the unofficial London dock strikes of 1923. The Bermondsey, Battersea, Bethnal Green, Poplar and Woolwich Labour councils all resisted Whitehall pressure to reduce council workers' wages. In 1925, however, after five years of 'overpayments', the councils were forced by the courts to lower their wage rates. Eventually, from 1929, central government began to remove Poor Law boards' powers, creating a new system of public-assistance committees.

The most spectacular clash between a borough and central authority between the wars, 'Poplarism' also created tensions within the Labour Party. The decision of Bermondsey and Poplar in the mid-1920s to pay a minimum wage of £4 to their employees irked Morrison, for he believed that borough councils ought to fall in line with the LCC. He sought a middle way between unilateral borough action over public assistance and the regime of the Municipal Reformers.

London's politics remained local, factional and confused. The clear-cut class conflicts of mining and shipbuilding areas during the Slump did not surface. The Labour Party did not quickly or lastingly win working-class loyalties even in the East End, to say nothing of mixed areas like Lambeth or Lewisham. Casual labour and workshop production persisted in the inner-London economy, and the impact of the factory was slight. Hence trade unionism remained precarious in industrial Poplar, Shoreditch, Stepney, Bethnal Green and Hackney; the new mass unions blossoming during the First World War soon collapsed with the postwar slump. Union organization was fitful in the cabinet-making, tailoring and sweated trades dominating the East End economy.

Conditions during the First World War brought about decisive advances of labour organization in the docks, and hopes were raised for the decasualization of dock labour. Yet neither employers nor dockers were prepared for the sacrifice of freedom of action that decasualization would entail. A limited registration scheme implemented from 1919 reduced the numbers competing for dock work. Registered dockers still greatly outnumbered work available, however, providing employers with a large reserve pool of labour and thereby prolonging the insecurity of casual labour.

With the shop-floor unpropitious, some looked to local government itself to create Socialism on Stepney Green, with visions of upright communities of working people – ragged-trousered philanthropists – almost on the model of William Morris. 'We must turn the local councils into so many forts from which to assail the Capitalist order,' declared Theodore Rothstein, one of the founding members of the British Communist Party. Clement Attlee, the first Labour Mayor of Stepney and a supporter of Poplarism, could agree that 'municipal work is part of the means of changing the basis of society from profit-making to Life'; while George Lansbury, a later Mayor of Stepney, described his fellow councillors as 'all clear class-conscious socialists working together, using the whole machinery of local government and Parliament for the transformation of Capitalist Society into Socialism'. But only fitful collaboration followed between borough councils and County Hall.

In the 1930s London politics were further muddled by the rise of Fascism. From the mid-1930s Sir Oswald Mosley's paramilitary jackbooted blackshirts of the British Union of Fascists began stirring up anti-Semitic feeling in the East End. In July 1936 Mosley addressed 5,000 followers in Victoria Park, Hackney; rioting followed. Mosley then announced that on 4 October he would lead his blackshirts on a march through the East End. When Sir John Simon, the Home Secretary, did nothing, a clash inevitably resulted. Disobeying Labour Party advice to stay at home, by mid-afternoon 100,000 anti-Fascist demonstrators were massed in Whitechapel Road and Commercial Road by the junction of Cable Street. Over 2,000 blackshirts assembled. Their route was blocked in Cable Street by an overturned brick lorry, its load serving as an improvised barricade. In the 'Battle of Cable Street', anti-Fascists fought the police, to prevent them from clearing the barricade to let the BUF through. Belatedly, the Home Secretary ordered Mosley to call off the march.

This was seen as a decisive victory by the Jewish People's Council against Fascism and Anti-Semitism, by Labour Party workers, and by the Independent Labour Party and the Communist Party. But Fascist youths were soon out again, smashing shop windows along Mile End Road and beating up Jews. From New Year's Day in 1937 a Public Order Act banned political uniforms and tightened the law on provocation and marches, and never again was there so serious a confrontation, but the BUF retained a considerable East End following. In 1937 it contested the LCC elections for the first time, polling 23 per cent in Bethnal Green North-East, 19 per cent in Limehouse and 14 per cent in Shoreditch (one candidate was William Joyce, subsequently known as 'Lord Haw-Haw' for his wartime pro-Hitler broadcasts from Berlin). No Fascist was elected to the LCC, but in Stepney the Communists secured their first electoral success.

*

Such battles with the Fascists heralded the descent into Hitler's war. London's first taste of Total War had come earlier, in the First World War. Near midnight on 31 May 1915, a Zeppelin dropped incendiaries from Stoke Newington down to Hackney and Stepney on its route back to Germany. Six were killed and thirty-five injured. Vigilance was improved and a warning system developed, with maroon rockets being fired when a Zeppelin was detected, and policemen cycling around carrying 'Take Cover' signs. Boy scouts bugled the all-clear.

The Second World War was of a different order, though it proved far less destructive of London than many had feared. 'London,' wrote Bertrand Russell, predicting the impact of war, '... will be one vast raving bedlam, the hospitals will be stormed, traffic will cease, the homeless will shriek for help, the city will be a pandemonium.' In an 'avalanche of terror', chaos would reign and the enemy would dictate its terms. The philosopher's expectation that London would be 'levelled to the ground on the outbreak of war' was widespread. The Air Ministry warned that 'one week's bombing will involve 18,750 casualties' in London.

On the declaration of war, on 3 September 1939, a mass evacuation of schoolchildren, toddlers and expectant mothers was carried out and the capital's wartime defences were activated by the Army and the Home Guard. Three defence lines were prepared. The first two, on the outskirts, were anti-tank lines with deep trenches, pillboxes and roadblocks. The outermost circled the suburbs, linking Rickmansworth, Potters Bar and Epping Forest in the north with Hounslow, Kingston-upon-Thames and Bromley in the south. The middle line linked Enfield, Harrow, Wanstead and West Norwood. The inner defence line was bounded to the south by the River Thames and to the east and west by the Lea and Brent. This crucial inner line was to be wholly manned by the regular Army. Crack troops like the Royal Marines were, if necessary, to make a last stand in Whitehall. Machine-guns were placed on strategic buildings, and pillboxes were disguised as tea kiosks. If London looked doomed, the royal family and the Prime Minister were to be airlifted out.

After a year's phoney war, the Blitz began on 7 September 1940 ('Black Saturday'). Bombs fell first on Woolwich Arsenal, then on the Victoria and Albert, East India and Surrey Commercial Docks, setting them ablaze, along with whole dockland communities. Over 1,400 incendiary canisters fell on dockland in the second week of September, and almost a thousand tons of high-explosive.

Citizens improvised defences, including sheltering under railway arches. Officials had rejected the use of the Underground as shelters, wishing to keep it clear to speed the movement of troops, the injured and the evacuated, and fearing that, once down the tube, people would turn troglodite. But the people saw safe refuge in the tubes, and within five days of the start of the Blitz there was a stampede to the stations. People camped on platforms, in corridors, on the stairs; within days more than 150,000 were sleeping in the tubes. 'I bore my way through darkness and descend into the Tube,' wrote G. W. Stonier in his *Shaving Through the Blitz*:

People are everywhere, draped about staircases, along corridors, on platforms. My beloved Rats, but how your cage smells. Lively people in the attitudes of dying; fat ones sleeping, the thin propped up before a newspaper. Children frisk. A block of air moves in from the tunnel. Somewhere at the other end of the line a train has moved.

The danger here is not bombs, or even burial or typhus, but of going native and not coming up again till after the war, when you will emerge with a large family and speaking another language.

In the face of official dithering, the people's take-over of the Underground system signalled self-reliance, community initiative and a new spirit of resistance.

On 12 October, Hitler, confronted with the success of the RAF and the resistance of Londoners, abandoned his invasion plan; but the Blitz continued, nightly till early November and then more intermittently. On 8 December 1940 the Luftwaffe dropped over 3,000 incendiary bombs – eight times more than on the first day of the Blitz. On 29 December the commercial heart of the capital was wrecked by hundreds of incendiaries. Churches, banks, offices and houses caught fire, creating a massive conflagration. On the south bank a strip of houses and warehouses a mile long and a quarter of a mile wide was destroyed. But though streets around St Paul's were ruined, the cathedral itself had been saved, majestic above the ruins, symbolizing defiance.

The severest bombing raid of the whole Blitz came on 10 May 1941, creating fires from Romford to Hammersmith. More civilians were killed than in any other single raid on Britain: 1,436. The House of Commons, Westminster Abbey, the Law Courts, the Royal Mint and the Tower of London were all hit.

London was both well- and ill-prepared for the Blitz. One plan was mass evacuation: 89,000 mothers and children were evacuated under the official scheme. For those left behind, there were gas masks and domestic bomb shelters, the most effective being the Anderson shelter, a tunnel-like structure made of corrugated steel, sunk three feet into the back garden and covered with earth. It could withstand anything but a direct hit. Two and a quarter million Andersons had been provided free by the government before the Blitz. The problem was that many Londoners had no garden.

Local government did not respond particularly effectively, especially to the problem of homelessness. Empty houses were only slowly requisitioned for the displaced – much was left to the Women's Voluntary Service. The worst-hit boroughs failed to cope. Stepney, for example, was, according to government inspectors, in 'unbelievable chaos', still having set up no rehousing department after two months of bombing. The emergency machinery of some boroughs cracked, and the crisis in many of them grew

St Paul's, 1942, by Dennis Flanders

so deep that the War Cabinet considered transferring rehousing responsibility from local councils to a special commissioner.

However, the Blitz produced far fewer deaths and casualties than had been feared. Between September 1940 and May 1941 nearly 20,000 tons of bombs were dropped on the capital. Altogether about 20,000 died and another 25,000 were hurt. During the six years of the war the total number of casualties in the LCC area was around 50,000 – only two and a half times the number of casualties initially expected in a single week. Hindsight diminishes the ordeal, however, for in May 1941 it must have seemed likely that the bombing would go on until London was flattened, though in fact London's trial was then over until the rocket attacks of 1944–5.

Hitler's intention had been to terrorize the population into surrender; in the event, the bombardment proved counter-productive. Morale generally remained high – despite resentment of inept officialdom – and crisis brought Londoners, traditionally deeply divided by class and district, closer together. 'It is not the walls that make the city, but the people who live within them,' George VI told London in 1940. 'The walls of London may be battered, but the spirit of the Londoner stands resolute and undismayed.'

Londoners were expected to 'dig for victory'; self-sufficiency was the thing. Allotments sprouted in bomb-sites, parks, and even the Tower of London moat. Keeping chickens and rabbits became popular, and the swimming-bath of the Ladies Carlton Club in Pall Mall was converted into a giant pigsty. A new spirit of cooperation emerged, with a greater emphasis on equality. The rich sacrificed some privileges. Wrought-iron railings were removed from West End squares for munitions use. In 1942 the government restricted petrol supplies for pleasure motoring and placed a 5s limit on restaurant meals. Displays of extravagance faded, and social levelling was welcomed by Londoners prepared to tighten belts if all mucked in. 'Now we can look the East End in the face,' exclaimed Elizabeth, the wife of George VI, surveying the bomb damage to Buckingham Palace.

A terrifying assault was renewed in 1944. On Tuesday 13 June, Londoners became the target for the v1 – a pilotless plane that exploded on impact, launched from across the Channel. More sophisticated v2s attained an altitude of sixty miles, taking only four minutes before they reached their target, exploding on impact. There was no defence. And because the Germans were launching the 'doodle-bugs' from camouflaged mobile trailers in the Netherlands, the RAF found it impossible to locate and destroy them before they were airborne.

The doodle-bugs brought devastation. Whereas destruction during the Blitz had been caused largely by incendiary bombs and fire, now it resulted from bomb blast, the warheads damaging houses within a quarter of a mile radius. The first catastrophic rocket attack was the New Cross disaster of 25 November, when a missile scored a direct hit on a Woolworth's packed with Saturday shoppers, killing 160. Flying-bomb attacks damaged more than 1.25 million London houses – almost half of the capital's housing stock. By the last months of the war 130,000 houses had been destroyed or utterly damaged. Mass evacuation and the temporary patching-up of 750,000 houses staved off calamity, but the v2 attacks produced a desperate shortage of accommodation during the winter of 1944–5. Some districts began to look like shanty towns.

Killing only 20,000 civilians, the Blitz destroyed or damaged 3.5 million homes in metropolitan London. London's wartime toll was thus less in deaths or social breakdown than in destruction to property. Within the City itself 225 acres – about a third of its area – were devastated; this was little more than half the acreage that had been destroyed in the Great Fire of 1666. But the damage covered a far wider area: much of Stepney, Poplar and Bermondsey had been laid waste, and the total reconstruction required was greater than after the Fire.

The war effort and the devastation allowed the planners to come into their own. An

Act of 1944 gave local authorities the right of compulsory purchase over blitzed areas, and the City acquired 115 acres, including much of the present Barbican site. The LCC and the boroughs were additionally given comprehensive powers over all private redevelopment in their areas. Meanwhile, the two reports produced in 1943–4 by Patrick Abercrombie laid down planning guidelines for the capital's future.

The war rendered London a less rooted place. It did little to alter land tenure, but it altered the bonds tying owners and tenants to their buildings. With some 9 million square feet of office space destroyed in the Blitz, and London's economy picking up again after 1945, a lively property market ensued. Communities were disrupted. Many born and bred in Bermondsey, Bow or Bethnal Green had gone to the outer suburbs. They often put down roots in the areas where they now worked. Bombing created mobility. The war made homeless at least 1.5 million Londoners, mainly from the inner boroughs. Out of 8 million people, about 40 per cent had moved from their neighbourhood for some period of the war. In many cases the move proved permanent. For long, numbers in London's poorest boroughs had been falling, but the impact of the war years was vast: Stepney's population, for example, was declining during the 1930s by about 2 per cent a year; during the war it dropped by over 40 per cent. Some moved back; most never did.

Such upheavals changed expectations. Young women in particular made a far wider range of friends, thanks to war work and opportunities to go out on their own. Such independence would have been widely regarded as immoral in the pre-war years. They met servicemen; American GIs, in particular, offered friendship uninhibited by English conventions of class and respectability. The chance to meet people from different backgrounds broadened horizons.

London survived. The war loosened the capital's hierarchies and snobberies, and gave promises of a freer life in the offing. It created new aspirations. The Luftwaffe had left old London in ruins. If it were not transformed in the postwar years, why would people wish to stay?

The price had been enormous. So many pieces had to be picked up. 'Long ago in 1945 all the nice people in England were poor, allowing for exceptions,' recalled Muriel Spark in her novel *The Girls of Slender Means*:

The streets of the cities were lined with buildings in bad repair or in no repair at all, bomb-sites piled with stony rubble, houses like giant teeth in which decay had been drilled like the ruins of ancient castles until, at a closer view, the wallpapers of various quite normal rooms would be visible, room above room, exposed, as on a stage, with one wall missing; sometimes a lavatory chain would dangle over nothing from a fourth- or fifth-floor ceiling; most of all the staircases survived like a new art-form, leading up and up to an unspecified destination that made unusual demands on the mind's eye. All the nice people were poor; at least, that was a general axiom, the best of the rich being poor in spirit.

There was absolutely no point in feeling depressed about the scene; it would have been like feeling depressed about the Grand Canyon or some event of the earth outside everybody's scope. People continued to exchange assurances of depressed feelings about the weather or the news, of the Albert Memorial which had not been hit, not even shaken, by any bomb from first to last.

CHAPTER FIFTEEN

Swinging London, Dangling Economy: 1945–1975

Postwar London presents an enigma. After the doodle-bugs the sigh was for 'business as usual', for peace and quiet and cosy, familiar routines, and Londoners resumed their old lifestyles as if the clock could be turned back. Demobbed majors dusted down their brollies; wives left munitions work and went back to the kitchen sink; cricket enjoyed the golden age of the Comptons and Bedsers; the Olympic Games came to London in 1948. The late 1940s and early 1950s were old London's Indian summer, when the docks still thrived and the trams sailed majestically through pea-soupers; East Enders had their knees-up at the pub and went hop-picking in August; contented commuters in Chessington tended their herbaceous borders; before it was finally killed by television, variety enjoyed its swansong at the Hackney and Deptford Empires, or Collins' at Islington. The coronation of Elizabeth II in 1953, when chummy neighbourhood parties were staged in bunting-festooned streets, was the high spot of London as a prosperous, well-integrated, secure, safe city.

The postwar years proved difficult, of course, with their fuel shortages, power cuts and ubiquitous queuing. Rebuilding proceeded slowly. With money short and a certain LCC puritanism in the air, reconstruction was cautious and vision rationed. If the post-1666 rebuilding was a chance missed, that judgement applies all the more to the post-1945 era. London's fabric was patched up, but no fresh start was made with respect to street plans, transport or the siting of employment. And there was no Wren.

As a pick-me-up after five years of austerity, the Festival of Britain was staged in 1951 on derelict land by Waterloo Bridge. It included the Royal Festival Hall, the Skylon obelisk and the Dome of Discovery. The South Bank was launched as an arts centre further concert halls followed in the 1960s and the National Theatre in the 1970s – but the Festival's half-cock modernism underlined London's loss of both opulence and confidence since the Great Exhibition a century before. The event proved less a festival than a fumble.

*

The postwar decades restored an economic even keel. Office work grew; engineering, electricals and vehicle-building – those huge interwar successes – prospered in particular. Conspicuous was the Associated Equipment Company (AEC) chassis works at Southall, which, with the Park Royal Body Builders, led the field in buses and trucks, exporting London's traditional double-deckers by the hundred to the Commonwealth. Demand for cars surged, and, with the European motor industry initially war-ravaged, British companies had a field-day with exports. Ford's enjoyed astonishing success: in the 1950s Dagenham was turning out a quarter of a million vehicles each year – Populars, Prefects, Consuls and Zodiacs, mostly for export. A new foundry was opened in 1957, and, thanks to the Cortina, in the 1960s Dagenham's workforce increased to 30,000.

Aided by Whitehall subsidies for BOAC and BEA, London's aircraft industry also boomed in the 1950s. Vickers at Weybridge and De Havilland at Colindale and Hatfield won government research-and-development money. The Vickers Viscount became the most successful British airliner ever. This was partly because Londoners could increasingly afford to go abroad and to fly. The 1950s saw the birth of the package holiday. Given official government status under the Ministry of Civil Aviation in 1946, London Airport (Heathrow) boomed, starting regular scheduled flights to America from 1946, and opening new terminals in the 1960s, 1970s and 1980s. Gatwick airport was meanwhile opened in 1958, acquiring its second terminal twenty years later. By the late 1970s Heathrow was handling over 100,000 passengers a day. Gatwick became a major employment source for the new town of Crawley, as Heathrow did for west London.

Postwar recovery and full employment led to rising wages, making the 1960s the decade of the affluent worker, with Londoners' disposable incomes almost double pre-war levels. In Leyton and Lewisham the working class was now able to afford washing-machines, refrigerators, radiograms, TVs and even a Ford. A high proportion of these consumer durables were manufactured in the London area. This was the age of consumerism; Londoners had never had it so good.

Yet, despite affluence which sustained the buoyant 'Swinging London' mood of the 1960s, underlying trends were treacherous, and soon many began to feel the pinch. After centuries of being in the right place at the right time, the metropolis now had the cards stacked against it. London's proud role as world commercial capital had stemmed from Britain's ruling the waves. With the postwar sterling crises and with imperial decline accelerating after Indian independence in 1947, and wars following in Malaysia, Kenya, Cyprus, Aden and so forth, London could no longer count on jobs and riches galore simply through being the Empire's port.

Population leakage was both a cause and a symptom of emergent postwar economic troubles. Inner London had long been thinning, but now even Greater London was becoming less great. Greater London contained about 6.25 million people in 1938. Exodus was becoming a stampede by the 1960s: in the decade after 1961 Greater London lost over half a million people or fully 7 per cent of its population; between 1971 and 1981 three-quarters of a million (10 per cent) moved out. By 1981 Greater London had nearly 2 million people fewer than in 1938.

From the early 1960s major traditional employers began to contract: in the decade after 1966 Greater London was to lose some half a million factory jobs – a full 40 per cent. Manufacturing employment in inner London in fact plummeted by almost a third during the five years from 1971 to 1976 alone. By the mid-1970s, 70 per cent of London's jobs were in services.

Globally Britain became a loser, as her industries – overmanned, undercapitalized and obsolete, their success long dependent upon imperial preference and soft markets – failed to meet the challenge of the USA and the reborn postwar economies of Germany, France, Italy and the Low Countries. Exports faltered, and imports began pouring in from Japan and the Pacific Rim, from Eastern Europe and China. The UK's failure to join the European Economic Community until 1971 impeded Continental trade.

With the decline of protected imperial markets and with hot world competition, many of London's traditional employers collapsed. Others – some thriving, some gasping – decided their best bet was to move out of central or Greater London and relocate in the 'Outer Metropolitan Area' or still further afield, some thirty to forty miles from the centre, where traditional towns such as Basingstoke, Luton, Dunstable, Aylesbury and Hemel Hempstead became light-industry boom centres and where around 1950 the LCC planted new towns such as Crawley. The beyond-the-belt Outer Metropolitan area grew by almost a million in the 1950s – representing two-fifths of the net growth of the British population; it went up by another 650,000 in the 1960s and by a further quarter of a million by 1981. In 1971 over half a million were commuting daily into London from Reading, Dartford, Gillingham, Maidstone and similar towns in the Outer Metropolitan Area.

Familiar firms came under great pressure. Many underwent take-overs, becoming minor cogs in national or international machines; their new directors often had no residential or sentimental links with London. To thrive, or just survive, they had to relocate to sites where there were lower rates, space to expand, better communications, weaker trades unions and lower pay. And, odd as it seems in retrospect, relocation was positively encouraged by the government: to implement the 'new-town' policy promoted by the planners, a Location of Offices Bureau was set up in the 1960s, helping 2,000 firms and 150,000 people to decentralize to places in the outer suburbs like Watford, Slough and Croydon, and further out still. The aim was to relieve overloaded services; the effect was a brain drain and a loss of enterprise and confidence.

After 1960, industry after industry shrank, collapsed or moved. Postwar prosperity among aircraft manufacturers proved brief; from the Comet fiasco onwards, numerous projects foundered, government investment was axed, retrenchment followed. In the early 1960s Vickers and De Havilland disappeared, swallowed up into BAC and Hawker Siddeley, whose production centres mainly lay outside London. By the 1990s Hawker's works at Kingston, there for over seventy years, had finally closed. London's once-proud bus industry proved a spectacular casualty. In 1962 AEC and Park Royal were taken over by Leyland, which, struggling with world competition, became part of British Leyland in 1968. Eight years later the London works shut their gates.

The significance of the disintegration of London's manufacturing base was masked in the 1960s, since general prosperity afforded work in various fields – retailing, tourism, construction. Men who lost work making buses became minicab drivers, opened betting-shops, repaired TVs, or sold used cars or double-glazing. Things were different by the 1970s, when recession bit deep. Employment in manufacturing was almost halved, falling from a million in 1973 to just over 500,000 ten years later. Hardest hit was the once-glorious west-London industrial belt, where Hounslow's and Ealing's engineering and electrical industries collapsed. Those two sectors alone lost 150,000 jobs in the decade after 1973; in the 1970s Ealing was shedding jobs at over 2,000 a year. Pears had made soap in Isleworth ever since 1862: in its centennial year the factory closed. British Aerospace cut 2,000 jobs in helicopter production from Hayes (Middlesex), moving to Yeovil in Somerset; Lucas sacked 1,500 car-component workers in Acton; the General Electric Company (GEC) cut 6,000 from their Willesden electrical factories; and Thorn-EMI shed 2,000 jobs in Hayes and Ilford. Many such companies shifted to new plants around Stevenage, Romford, Basingstoke or Southampton, or down the Western Corridor by the side of the new M4, near Reading, Swindon, Bath or Bristol. ICI, Rank Xerox and British Aluminium all went west in the 1970s, building new plant and electronic offices on green-field sites, complete with state-of-the-art computer technology. This 'Sunrise Belt' – soon, with the microchip revolution, dubbed England's 'Silicon Valley' – offered superior communications and cleaner, safer, cheaper environments where aspirant families could bring up children away from London's grime and crime.

Not just factories but commerce too began moving out of central London to avoid spiralling rents, inflated wages and transport snarls. Blaming bad commuter conditions, traffic congestion, and rising office costs, the Sun Alliance insurance group, the sixth biggest in Britain, quit London in the 1960s for a new field-side building in Horsham: the world's oldest insurance company, the Sun had been in the City since 1710. Government offices moved out too; much of the Inland Revenue quit London, to stimulate regional development, to slash costs, and to relieve inner-city overcrowding. Millions of Londoners currently send their monthly credit-card payments to North-

347

ampton (Barclays), Westcliff-on-Sea (NatWest) or Brighton (American Express), and haggle with tax offices in Bradford or Wrexham.

Unemployment, unknown in London in the 1950s, was unstoppable by the 1970s, particularly among the unskilled and semi-skilled, as refineries, flour-mills and processing plants connected with dockland industries closed and railway goods yards and coal depots dwindled. Between 1971 and 1982, manufacturing jobs fell from 1.09 million to 0.63 million – a drop of 42 per cent. This followed national trends, but London was particularly hard hit. Thus employment in clothing and footwear declined nationally by 10 per cent between 1966 and 1974, but by nearly 40 per cent in the capital. Inner London suffered disproportionately, where obsolescent plant occupied cramped sites. A deprived inner-city area was emerging, for between 1971 and 1981 three-quarters of the capital's losses were concentrated there – its job fall was exceeded only by Liverpool's. In 1976 the Environment Secretary, Peter Shore, admitted that the unbalanced nature of migration from the inner cities was leaving them with 'a disproportionate share of unskilled and semi-skilled workers, of unemployment, of one-parent families, of concentrations of immigrant communities and overcrowded and inadequate housing'.

Certain collapses were spectacular and psychologically damaging. 'Fleet Street' disappeared almost overnight. Still dominated in 1970 by the national and many provincial newspapers, by journalists and news agencies, Fleet Street experienced in the next fifteen years the departure of all its national newspapers. Of course they did not move far, and in the process of relocation to new works in Wapping, Battersea and so forth overall job losses proved small, but Fleet Street had been the hub of publishing since Caxton; its demise set a huge question mark over the economic future of central London.

Most drastic was the death of the docks. London docks had flourished immediately after the war – indeed, Port of London tonnages hit record levels: in 1956, 1,000 ships were docking each week, and the Port was handling 70 million tons of goods. But world trade patterns were changing profoundly. The Empire and Commonwealth had long ensured London's position as the world's premier port and entrepôt. Independence, however, loosened old trading ties; no longer was trade automatically routed through London, and new nations created trading preferences of their own, selling direct to America, Germany and Japan. During the 1960s Commonwealth trade was halved, and London shrank as an entrepôt.

Moreover, whereas the Port had merely been patched up after the war, Rotterdam, Hamburg and Dunkirk had enjoyed huge investment and could provide superior facilities, becoming ports of choice for world traders dealing with a burgeoning Europe. With Britain's entry into the EEC, Channel and North Sea ports such as Dover, Harwich and Felixstowe benefited, equipped to deal with containerized traffic and

controls to stop further mixtures of homes and industry, action to remove factories from residential streets, and redevelopment of housing. Some 1,033,000 Londoners and their workplaces were to be shifted beyond the Green Belt in a massive overspill operation.

Abercrombie's *Greater London Plan* specified how this overspill was to be handled. Ten new towns were to be built beyond the Green Belt. By 1946 one of them, Stevenage, was already under way, and within four years seven more were begun. Abercrombie urged a ban on new industry in London. Like many planners, he regarded city industry as synonymous with grime, muddle and pollution, and saw inner-city communities as slums. Population and employment were to be expelled from inner London; development was to be encouraged beyond the Green Belt. Hemel Hempstead, Watford, Hatfield, Harlow, Bletchley, Dunstable and dozens of other centres, including Milton Keynes, received hundreds of thousands of former Londoners, some commuting to London, others forming local centres of employment.

Established after the war, the Green Belt has remained remarkably stringently enforced: London's suburbs suddenly stop, frozen at the point they had reached in 1939. In the era of rapid building from the mid-1950s it became the target of acute commercial pressures, aiming to nibble it away, but successive governments almost fetishistically ensured its preservation.

Movement out of town eased but could not solve the housing problem within the LCC area and in Greater London. The Blitz had deprived over 100,000 families of their homes; bomb-sites and prefabs abounded. In reconstruction plans, priority was given to rehousing. By the end of 1949 around 50,000 new homes had been provided by either the boroughs or the LCC, and a further 64,000 were in the pipeline. Camberwell, Stockwell, Walworth, Peckham, Deptford, Camden Town, Kentish Town, Kensal Rise, Shepherd's Bush, Hammersmith, Fulham, Stoke Newington, Woodberry Down, Tottenham and all the East End boroughs saw the rise from the late 1940s of countless blocks of flats, dull but decent.

But aggregate housing supply never remotely matched demand, especially as so much of London's housing stock was ancient and severely dilapidated and expectations were rising – families wanted inside toilets and bathrooms, and individual bedrooms.

Postwar housing problems were exacerbated by the decline of rented accommodation. In central London and the inner suburbs, low-grade but affordable housing had traditionally been provided by private landlords. With pressure on accommodation mounting, especially with soaring Commonwealth immigration, profiteering landlords enjoyed a bonanza. The Rachman case became notorious. Using incentives provided by the 1957 Rent Act, Peter Rachman and similar landlords would impose monster rent increases or harass occupants to winkle out sitting tenants in order to obtain lucrative vacant possession. Rachman was exposed by the press and brought to justice, public rage turned against private landlords, the Labour government elected in 1964 introduced legislation to control rents and establish rent tribunals, landlords' profits declined, many sold out, and the private sector dwindled. Areas like Islington and Holloway, Notting Hill and Shepherd's Bush, long the bailiwicks of private landlords, were from the late 1950s taken over by owner-occupiers, while prosperity resulted in fewer taking in lodgers. Demand for accommodation became acute from young people and newly-weds, immigrants and the worse off.

For some, the withering away of rented accommodation was a step in the right direction. Bureaucrats in Labour-controlled boroughs shed no tears over the decline of private landlordism, accepting it as a sign of social progress that town halls should be assuming primary responsibility for housing locals – the more public housing the better. 'The proportion of privately rented flats must be expected to fall,' remarked Camden's Director of Housing in 1971, 'and, with a vigorous housing programme the number of Council dwellings must be expected to increase.' Yet residents felt less happy than officials, as council waiting-lists lengthened, allocations rarely seemed fair, and town halls built hated high-rise blocks on wilderness estates. Caught between dingy and expensive rented accommodation or the trials of living on 'rough' council estates, affluent workers saved for a deposit on a semi in Streatham or Southfields, Edgware or Wembley, or further out in Hornchurch or Harlow. In inner-London communities polarization followed between huge estates of poorer working-class and immigrant council tenants and, on the other hand, affluent owner-occupiers. Islington, Kentish Town, Camden Town, Kilburn, Lewisham, Sydenham, Wandsworth and adjoining districts were becoming parcelled up between estate ghettos and expensive enclaves of owner-occupation.

Gentrification spread as the middle classes infiltrated and recaptured central and inner-suburb precincts abandoned by their grandparents, and then indulged in an orgy of improvements. In Highbury, Notting Hill, Paddington and Camberwell, and later in Bethnal Green, Mile End, Bow and Stepney, once proud squares and terraces and shabby mews were restored into elegant, spacious family residences or swish bachelor pads. Late Georgian cottages – so recently condemned as fit only for the bulldozer – became, once tastefully refurbished, enticing and profitable properties, quaint, full of character, and close to transport and to town. Victorian villas in Holloway and Kennington, long debased by use as lodging-houses, were transformed into luxury flats for young professionals or snips for first-time buyers – or were repossessed by the class of family for whom they had first been built, unable to bear any longer the frustrations of Southern Region commuting, bored by suburbia, or quick to spot a bargain: in a property boom, doing up old houses in Fulham or Greenwich became a congenial way to make a fast buck. A Property Letter ('circulated privately to businessmen') had this to say about Barnsbury in February 1970:

Lonsdale Square sets the hottest standards for others to follow. It is undoubtedly one of the most attractive in the whole of London. But you'd need a rich man's money to get in there now. Latest prices we've heard of are £15,000 for an unsweetened 11-room terraced property and £20,000 for its adjacent sister that has had the full improvement treatment. That is about £5,000 up on 1968 levels and a cool £7,000 up on 1966 margins.

For a cheaper alternative, look at the eastern end of Richmond Avenue. The property is not in the same class as that in Lonsdale Square. But at least one side backs on to the Square. You would expect to pay £10,000 for three stories plus basement. For that you'd get roughly eight rooms, still in unsweetened condition.

Poorer people were edged out of pockets of Hackney, Camden Town, Tufnell Park, Willesden, Clapham, Battersea, and adjoining areas. The opening of the Victoria Line speeded gentrification around Highbury and Finsbury Park, Pimlico, Vauxhall and Stockwell.

Meanwhile the evangelical commitment of the LCC and certain boroughs to planning doctrines brought problems of its own, as 'slum clearance' came to entail the ritual flattening of old communities and their replacement with tower-block estates. The LCC's celebrated Architect's Department, under Leslie Martin, led with its great Le Corbusier-style slabs in Roehampton. Boroughs chipped in with their own contributions to shoebox skylines, like Southwark's north-Peckham slabs, which quickly became some of London's most troubled blocks, as did the tall towers of the LCC's Elgin Estate in North Paddington. The high-rise heyday between 1964 and 1974 saw 384 tower blocks being built.

Planners' Utopias proved tenants' nightmares, as streets in the sky turned to slums in the sky. High-rise architecture killed traditional street-life, atomized communities, and produced disaffection, delinquency and crime. Rebuilding replaced substandard housing with social problems that have proved far more intractable.

Lifts and central heating failed, children vandalized the launderettes, rubbish chutes became nests of rats, old people were terrorized – all was disaster. Aided by the sensational collapse after a gas explosion in 1968 of Ronan Point, a Canning Town state-of-the-art tower block, denunciation of the boxes became deafening. Local authorities had to halt their pet programmes, shifting the accent to refurbishing older properties. By the 1970s the era of town-hall big-spending was over. Housing programmes were cut and cut again, public properties deteriorated, private house prices in Greater London zoomed, and more people quit London altogether.

Founded by immigrants, London has had a ceaseless history of immigration. After 1850, Jewish immigration into the East End was especially spectacular, but many other districts of the Victorian metropolis gained high migrant concentrations. Finsbury was

LONDON: A SOCIAL HISTORY

Little Italy, and there were large German communities in Fitzrovia, Camden Town and Kentish Town – quarters infiltrated after 1960 by Greek Cypriots, at the same time as the dominant culture of enclaves of the East End was changing from Jewish to Islamic.

Britain's imperial chickens came home to roost with the flaring of racial tensions from the 1950s, associated with New Commonwealth immigration. What precipitated violence was the impending introduction in 1961 of strict immigration controls, provoking a deluge to beat the ban. Indian and Pakistani arrivals in Britain, running at a mere 3,000 in 1959, leapt to 48,000 in 1961; West Indian immigration, around 16,000 in 1959, jumped to 66,000 in 1961; Cypriot immigration quadrupled in 1960–61. The great majority of immigrants initially settled in London, and a few areas – Brixton, Notting Hill, Camden Town and Southall – bore the brunt. London's first race riot erupted in Notting Hill in late August 1958, when white mobs attacked the homes of blacks, smashing windows and throwing petrol bombs. In the next fortnight attacks spread.

Racial tensions simmered through the 1960s and 1970s, associated with poverty, unemployment, rotten housing and a growing bush war between blacks and the police. In 1981 rioting, burning and looting resulted in an orgy of damage in Brixton. London's worst race riots, resulting in the death of a policeman and the conviction of three blacks, took place in October 1985 at Broadwater Farm in Tottenham (the Court of Appeal later quashed the conviction, finding that the police had fabricated the evidence). Broadwater Farm was, unsurprisingly, a prize-winning estate built in 1970 that declined into a housing hell and a nursery of crime. Built on stilts, its ground-floor levels were given over to parking not people (cars became vandalized); its pedestrian walkways were tailor-made for gangs to learn the arts of mugging. It had no community hall, no social centre, no pub, no youth club, no sports facilities, no surgery for a doctor. By 1980, the estate was more than half black and had become a no-go area for the police.

Given the scale of immigration, it is remarkable that such incidents have been so few. The New Commonwealth immigrant community totalled 631,000 in 1981. Of London's 1981 population of 6.6 million, more than one in six was born outside the UK: 382,000 in Europe, 296,000 in Asia, 170,000 in Africa, 168,000 in the Caribbean, 69,000 in the Mediterranean. Afro-Caribbean and Asian migrants have clustered in the inner suburbs. In inner London they account for almost one in five, in the outer suburbs around one in ten. By 1981 Brent's population was a third brown and black, and Ealing had wards with over 85 per cent coloured. Blacks have tended to settle near the centre (Notting Hill, Lambeth), while Asians, setting up shops and small businesses, have headed for suburbia, especially west and north-west London. Cheap owner-occupied property developed in and around Southall, where Asian families became prominent on manufacturing and industrial estates, and especially in services connected with Heathrow Airport.

Tensions have arisen over cultural differences, language, religion, schooling and so forth. Racial hatred and violence have been fomented by white neo-Nazi groups and tolerated by police insensitivity. Over the last decade nine blacks have died in questionable circumstances in Stoke Newington police station alone; no one has ever been brought to account for their deaths. Poverty, deprivation, unemployment and poor police practices have fostered ghetto and criminal subcultures.

Victorian and early twentieth-century London was an experiment in the laws of supply and demand; government took a back seat, and the market led. After Hitler's war the philosophy changed: London's mess and muddle had become unbearable, the sprawl was offensive, and traffic stalled. What was needed, all agreed, was rational planning. Strategies poured from architects, bureaucrats and academics. The golden rules of the planners stated that industrial, commercial and residential zones should be segregated; a radical highway structure and orbital ring roads should be erected; building densities should be regulated; and so forth.

After the war, the LCC had earmarked reconstruction areas in badly bombed Poplar, Stepney, the City and Bermondsey. Its ambitious Stepney–Poplar scheme laid down precise changes in land use, residential density, industrial relocation and the provision of community services. A comprehensive London Development Plan was finally submitted in 1951 for ministerial approval. Public inquiries lasted two years, and it was finally sanctioned two years later. By then financial stringency had resulted in the shelving of Abercrombie's ambitious ring-road proposals and the curtailment of the East End scheme. The early history of London's first development programme was thus not happy; it proved a melancholy overture to every subsequent attempt to replan London. The metropolis was, however, undergoing modernization willy-nilly, the energy coming from a brew of private money, public works and the planning ethos.

Speculative development was nothing new – legally there had never been anything to stop it. 'If there is any beautiful object of the past, some house, perhaps, that could be utilised for library, club, museum, school, or parish purposes,' howled the architect C. R. Ashbee in 1900, 'it is torn down and sold to the wreckers.' Not till the 1932 Planning Act could local authorities prevent historic buildings from being destroyed, and then, with habitual English tenderness towards private property, they were required to pay full compensation for the lost development. When Norfolk House was endangered in 1936, the LCC declined to preserve it because of the expense. The following year the Adam brothers' Thames-side Adelphi was demolished.

With the introduction of death duties in 1893, great aristocratic estates had begun to be broken up. After the First World War, Mayfair's great mansions nearly all fell victim. In 1919 the Marquess of Salisbury sold his Arlington Street house; Dorchester

House and Grosvenor House (the Duke of Westminster's town house) in Park Lane were pulled down in the 1920s, to be replaced by hotels of the same name. Nash's Regent Street shop fronts were pulled down. Chesterfield House in South Audley Street gave way in the 1930s to flats. Protests arose against the commercialization and vulgarization of dignified London by rapacious developers. 'Greed moulds the landscape of London,' deplored E. M. Forster.

But the pace quickened greatly after the war. The death of Lord Portman led to the disposal of 150 acres of his Marylebone estate. The Bedford estate sold much of north Bloomsbury, including Gordon, Tollington and Woburn Squares, to London University, which soon erected buildings of unique hideousness, such as Denys Lasdun's Institute of Education (which ruined the elegant Woburn Square). On the death of the 2nd Duke of Westminster in 1953, the Grosvenors met death duties of £20 million through having prudently sold off much of Pimlico three years previously.

Property development accelerated in the 1950s. Park Lane underwent further change. In 1956 the property developer Charles Clore bought a Regency terrace facing Hyde Park and replaced it with the twenty-eight-storey London Hilton – the tallest building in London. The Macmillan government overruled the protests of the LCC. Soon afterwards the Marquess of Londonderry sold his great, gloomy Park Lane mansion to the developer Isaac Klug for £500,000; it was replaced by the ugly Londonderry House Hotel.

Crucial to the development boom was the ending of office controls. Statutes authorized developers to do no more than restore pre-war office levels, recouping the 9 million square feet lost in the Blitz; yet loopholes were legion. Under the Third Schedule of the 1947 Town and Country Planning Act, 10 per cent could be added to the pre-war volume of any building. In 1954 Harold Macmillan extended this provision to cover postwar buildings. Offices for export businesses could dodge most planning controls. Macmillan thus issued a licence to build; developers had never had it so good, and between 1958 and 1962 the share value of property companies rose eightfold. Concrete colossuses soared above the skyline – the Bowater Building in Knightsbridge, the Thorn Building in Upper St Martin's Lane. Giant office blocks were actually illegal – the 1939 London Building Act had limited buildings to 100 feet, 'unless the Council otherwise consent' – but in 1960 the government encouraged permissiveness by allowing Basil Spence to design a tower block at Knightsbridge Barracks. Thereafter blocks grew and grew, and abundance of bomb-sites speeded City redevelopment: a third of the area was rebuilt between 1945 and 1972.

Profits were equally sky-high, especially before capital gains tax (1962). Borrowing short-term for site acquisition, tycoons could turn derelict plots into gold. In 1958 Max Rayne built Eastbourne Terrace, adjoining Paddington Station, for the Church of England, pocketing £3.9 million from a project in which he invested a mere £1,000. Harold Samuel built his Land Securities Investment Trust from nothing in 1944 to £204 million in 1968; it became the world's biggest property company. With office blocks generating rent out of all proportion to costs, speculators had a bonanza.

Public authorities proved remarkably obliging to developers. All the great office blocks flanking London Wall by the Barbican were built by property men on land leased from the City. The government itself brought in developers to erect offices – aristocratic landowners were usually too conservative to exploit their lands without assistance – and the LCC was compliant. The need to acquire land for traffic schemes put the LCC in the developers' power. Developers bought up the land required and made it over to the LCC; the Council in return granted planning permission on adjoining land owned by their benefactors. The most notorious case was Centre Point. In the late 1950s the LCC decided to construct a roundabout at the junction of St Giles's Circus; the plan was thwarted by the Pearlmans, directors of the property company owning the land, who fended off compulsory purchase. Harry Hyams, the duke of developers, came to the LCC's rescue. He bought out the Pearlmans for £0.5 million, amassed adjacent properties, handed over £1.5 million worth of land to the Council, and took it back on a 150-year lease at the risible rent of £18,500 per annum. Part of this plot was reserved for the traffic scheme, but Hyams received permission to erect the thirty-five-storey Centre Point. Construction costs amounted to £3.5 million, but by 1968 the building was worth £17 million and Hyams's profit was over £11 million. The only good news is that the roundabout was never built.

Similar deals spawned other tower blocks, equally insensitive to their surroundings, including the arid Euston Centre (where the LCC received £2 million worth of land and Joe Levy's Stock Conversion and Investment Trust cleared £22 million profit), the oppressive Stag Place in Victoria, and the nondescript Camden Towers in Notting Hill Gate. The developers' most popular architect was Richard Seifert, who, with his 400 London blocks, has had more influence over the London skyline than any man since Wren – though Wren's was positive. A practitioner of conveyor-belt modernism, Seifert's main aim was to realize a site's bulk potential. (Bulk, comments Simon Jenkins, was money.) London thus slipped out of the hands of aristocratic landlords into the clutches of the Metropolitan Estates Property Company, Town and City, Great Portland Estates, Amalgamated Investment and Property Company, and other development companies. From Shepherd's Bush to Shoreditch, the developments of the 1960s are not a pretty sight: witness Victoria Street, with its Monsanto House, Ashdown House, British Petroleum House and Esso House – all, like hundreds of look-alikes, characterless boxes that rapidly became eyesores. Eventually, however, after the erection of scores of slabs like these that cocked a snook at Londoners, curbs were placed on speculators. In 1964 the new Labour government created the 'Brown Ban' – George Brown's limiting of office-development permits to users essential to the capital's economy. This ham-fisted measure, however, succeeded only in driving up rents and so still further enhancing developers' profits. Brought into disrepute, controls were relaxed in 1970 under City pressure.

The 1960s created what might prima facie seem a paradoxical liaison between speculators and County Hall bureaucrats. The explanation is simple. Well aware of London's genuine problems – ageing buildings and infrastructure, desperately needing rational and efficient solutions to its housing and traffic problems – planners were modernizers with a mission. Despairing of the existing street plan – crumbling, laby-rinthine, narrow, and seemingly conceived by a drunken, deranged cartographer – they were eager to experiment with modernism, with clean, direct lines, with wide motorways and flyovers, with superhighways and freeways, with tower blocks, high-rise buildings and multi-level precincts, to drag London kicking and screaming into the twentieth century. 'Ask any self-respecting planner of 1963 how to renew London's outworn fabric,' the urban geographer Peter Hall has commented,

and the answer would come straight back: bring in the bulldozers. Tear it all down. Rebuild from the ground up. Segregate the traffic from the people, preferably on different levels: put the pedestrians on decks, put the flats in the air above them. Elsewhere, leave the people on the ground, but segregate different kinds of traffic: put fast through traffic on to new urban motorways; distribute local traffic via appropriate local streets to parking spaces between or below flats and offices and shops; leave pedestrians in full charge of busy shopping streets.

The planners' equivalent of doing the crossword was rethinking London's road system. Boldness was in the air. 'Because of the sporadic nature of war damage, many of the road improvements schemes so far achieved have produced a piecemeal effect,' complained the City's Improvements and Town Planning Committee in 1963:

The time has now arrived when, with the added impetus of greatly accelerated expenditure on road improvements, the Corporation must take decisive measures to secure within the next 10 years the completion, if possible, of the Southern through road and substantial completion of the Northern through route.

Plans were two-a-penny, and no landmark was sacred: schemes were floated for the demolition of St Pancras station, the Foreign Office and Whitehall, Tower Bridge, and even the Houses of Parliament. One totemic figure in the landscape was actually annihilated, the triumphal arch at Euston station – a symbol of classicism yielding to modernism, the past to the present, the ornate to the functional. There was a desperate fight in 1962 to save the arch:

Its destruction is wanton and unnecessary – connived at by the British Transport Commission, its guardians, and by the London County Council and the Government, who are jointly responsible for safeguarding architectural creations of the early nineteenth century and the most important – and visually satisfying – monument to the railway age which Britain pioneered.

Thus the *Architectural Review*, doyen of English architectural journals, began a denunciation of the 'long drawn out history of bureaucratic dilatoriness and evasion' which led up to the demolition of the arch. The new concrete piazza erected by British Railways in front of Euston Station to show they were 'with it' became a nasty, inhospitable wind-trap.

In road schemes, the City Corporation proved energetic. It constructed the Blackfriars underpass and widened Upper and Lower Thames Streets, affecting in the process many historic churches as well as Billingsgate Market and the famous Coal Exchange. When, however, the entire riverfront became scheduled for redevelopment, howls went up from conservation groups and the press about the hideousness of the planning proposals, the vandalism they entailed, and the vast profits coming the way of various City enterprises. Critics condemned the City's philistine destructiveness and rejected the dystopic prospect of a City overshadowed by monoliths and dominated by traffic.

LCC development was even less popular than that of the City or the speculators. The LCC's two key central development areas were the South Bank and the Elephant and Castle. With its great grey, arid, howling spaces, the South Bank 'cultural complex' has seemingly been designed to be as unwelcoming as possible. A large part of this area, between Hungerford Bridge and County Hall, has remained a car park since it was vacated by the Festival of Britain. At the Elephant and Castle, once the heart of south London's cockney life, the LCC aimed to create a 'Piccadilly Circus of South London'. Its planners destroyed what had survived the Blitz, and redeveloped around two mega-roundabouts, following the style popularly known as the 'new brutalism'. The shopping area included a warren of bleak walkways and tunnels, tailor-made for drunks, dossers and drug addicts. At Piccadilly Circus itself the LCC was saved from its own folly. In 1959 the Council approved Jack Cotton's Monico office block as part of a new Circus traffic layout; this, however, was stopped in its tracks when Cotton so riled public opinion in boasting of his coup that the government was forced to veto it.

The ruling orthodoxy of the 1960s was that traffic problems could be solved by building more and bigger roads (an elementary fallacy: traffic expands to fill the road space available). Following this dogma, the most startling attempt to grapple with London's traffic problems was the gargantuan urban-motorway scheme concocted by the new-born Greater London Council. The Ringways were envisaged as a spider's web of orbitals and radials, intended to give London its first new communications network since the Underground. Eight hundred miles of roads, costed at £2,000 million, or £800 per head for every Londoner, they were the vastest investment ever proposed in London's fabric. Some 100,000 people would lose their homes to make way for the motorways – about the same total as displaced by all the railways in the whole of the Victorian era.

Londoners were just becoming familiar with such structures. The Hammersmith Flyover was built in 1961 to relieve Hammersmith Broadway. And Westway, carved through working-class North Kensington, had given a glimpse of an urban motorway. Environmentally brutal, with no attempt at landscaping, Westway turned locals against similar developments. The Ringways programme was subjected to mounting oppo-

An urban nightmare – the partially completed Hammersmith Flyover, designed to reduce traffic congestion from central London to the west

sition – people and homes before roads, was the rallying cry. After the Conservative GLC defeat in 1973, the new Labour administration, though earlier supporting the programme, abandoned its inner rings and placed greater emphasis on public transport and traffic management, including parking-meters and traffic wardens (who had first appeared in 1958).

The defeat of the Ringways was repeated on a smaller scale at Covent Garden. This densely populated Dickensian area was badly dilapidated. With the removal of Covent Garden fruit and vegetable market to Nine Elms, Battersea, scheduled for the early 1970s, the GLC planned to replace the obsolete buildings with high-rise offices, shops and dwellings for displaced residents. Rebuilt on split levels with pedestrian decks, and with a dual-carriageway Strand snaking through the side-streets to the south, this would be the London of the future. The locals demurred, the Covent Garden Community Association organizing vociferous media opposition denouncing the prioritizing of commerce over homes and the destructive character of the road proposals. Once again the government found it wise to intervene. In 1973 the Secretary of State, Geoffrey Rippon, announced the listing of over 100 properties as historic buildings, thereby sabotaging comprehensive development and demonstrating the GLC's impotence in its own house. The Labour victory in the 1973 GLC elections killed the scheme. Big was brutal.

The public thus turned against urban motorways, high-rise flats and comprehensive road development, and suspicions mounted against town-hall and County Hall planning departments. Urban plans became acceptable only if in someone else's backyard; redevelopment blueprints seemed insensitive to the urban fabric and the local community.

Significantly, the only major developments that actually went ahead were underground. In the 1960s the Victoria Line was built. It was followed in the 1970s by the Jubilee Line (originally styled the Fleet Line), the main construction work for this, a new tunnel between Charing Cross and Baker Street, being completed in 1979 at a cost of £87 million, met by the GLC and the government. The original plan to drive the line east from Charing Cross to the new south-east-London estate at Thamesmead was abandoned for reasons of cost, though, as of 1994, the go-ahead appears to have been given to extend it, via Bermondsey, to Canary Wharf on the Isle of Dogs, in the belated hope of improving connections between new dockland developments and central London.

Hitler's war had one beneficial effect: it dynamited some of the stuffiness of the capital's traditional cultural life. Post-Edwardian London had a chequered cultural identity. A largely male, loosely aristocratic and Establishmentarian literary world, with links to publishers and journalism, attached itself to West End clubs and select eating- and meeting-places. This was the milieu dominated by Arnold Bennett, T. S. Eliot, Compton Mackenzie and Evelyn Waugh. Bloomsbury flourished between the wars as a rather refined, raffish, risqué set. Chelsea harboured artists posh and penniless. Cosmopolitan cliques sprang up in Soho, associated with jazz, swing, the new poetry, and Black American culture; by the 1950s frustration was increasingly expressed against the exclusiveness of the cultural establishment. The 1960s brought a revolt, of sorts.

In spring 1966 *Time*'s front-cover headline read 'LONDON – THE SWING-ING CITY', against the background of a pop star and a long-haired girl wearing a mini-dress. 'In this century every decade has its city,' claimed *Time*'s London correspondent:

During the shell-shocked 1940s thrusting New York led the way, and in the un-easy 50s it was the heady Rome of *La Dolce Vita*. Today it is London, a city steeped in tradition, seized by change, liberated by affluence, graced by daffodils and anemones, so green with parks and squares that, as the saying goes, you can walk across it on the grass. In a decade dominated by youth, London has burst into bloom. It swings, it is the scene.

London's new international cultural trendiness was somewhat fortuitous – not least because the best pop culture came out of Liverpool – but the 1960s truly formed a time when special features of the capital interacted to produce creativity and optimism.

London had long nourished a welter of service industries involved in fashion and the media. As the 1960s brought new affluence, especially among the young, and with it tremendous yearnings for style, colour, exuberance, fun, after five years of war and long years of austerity, London was well placed to become a major international centre for fashion, design and music. These boom businesses interlinked with a galaxy of kindred industries – like photography, modelling, magazine publishing and advertising – which also clustered in the capital. Between them they created wealth and provided work for almost a quarter of a million Londoners, in the process giving London a new image and its people a fresh sense of identity and vitality. Barriers crumbled, and the old pin-stripe stuffiness was out. Blimpish notions of London as the heart of Empire were eclipsed by a new 1960s-style chauvinism, embraced by the younger generation, celebrating the capital's leading position in the popular arts and the permissiveness of the swinging city. London seemed a free-and-easy, happy, relaxed place, in days when way-out clothes were cheap and cheerful in Carnaby Street, the Christine Keeler affair gave glimpses of a smart or sleazy sexual underworld, and England was winning the World Cup at Wembley.

The dives and pubs of Soho formed the centre of cultural change. Soho had become an artistic Bohemia in the late 1930s, attracting literary figures like Dylan Thomas. By the early 1950s basement clubs honeycombed its streets, offering jazz, beat and later skiffle. In the 1960s the area supported a youth culture which for a while was remarkably successful in bringing together artists, art-school students, the radical intelligentsia and the young, but also go-ahead men and women in fashion, music, advertising, design, publicity, publishing, film, television, the media. A culture materialized that was irreverent, offbeat, creative, novel. Politically idealistic and undogmatically left-wing, it broke through class barriers and captured and transformed many of the better elements of traditional London: its cosmopolitanism and openness, its village quality, its closeness, its cocktail of talent, wealth and eccentricity. There was a rare alliance between youth culture and commerce, aristocratic style and a new populism. It was a breath of fresh air.

After decades of aesthetic barrenness, London acquired some flair. One mani-festation of the style revolution was Biba, in Kensington, launched in 1963 by Barbara Hulanicki and famous for its art-deco imagery and its 1930s-influenced clothes. Another was Habitat, founded by Terence Conran. A graduate of the Central School of Art and Design, Conran spent fourteen years persevering with his furniture designs in workshops in various parts of London before deciding in 1964 to open a shop in Fulham. Habitat sold contemporary well-designed furniture and household goods at prices the young and trendy middle classes could afford. 'I'd always believed that well-designed things should be available to the whole population, that it shouldn't be an élitist thing,' he maintained, in tune with the times:

And I think this coincided with a lot of people who'd had further education coming through who were discontented with the way things were. The fashion revolution was just beginning – certainly, music was well on its way – and we wanted to provide home furnishing in the widest sense of the word to this type of person. There was beginning to be a little bit of demand for it – not a great deal – but you could feel the atmosphere of discontent. Most of the other stores weren't sensitive to change in society and they thought it was only a flash in the pan.

The carefree atmosphere couldn't last. Not least, economic down-swings in the 1970s and above all the 1980s showed up Swinging London for what it was: a veneer of modernity on an ageing superstructure. Punks and skinheads became more in tune with the times, and 1960s innocence yielded to 1970s cultural cynicism, misanthropy and despair. And with reason. For times of hope gave way to the frustrations of a capital that seemingly lacked the resources and will to sustain a prosperous but people-friendly urban environment. Inactivity in the face of manufacturing collapse pointed to graver problems London still had not resolved. Who was to govern it? How was it to be governed? The setting-up of the Greater London Council in the thick of Swinging London in 1965 seemed to provide a fresh start.

CHAPTER SIXTEEN

Thatcher's London

We are too close to set recent changes in perspective, but we may have been living through a critical period in London's history. Rival forces – global, national and municipal – have been buffeting the capital since the 1960s. Britain's international economic plunge has accelerated, accentuated by particularly jarring events, such as dropping out of the European Exchange Rate Mechanism in 1992, which involved further economic toils and troubles for the capital and stupendous losses for the taxpayer. If, in the 1920s and 1930s, London could thrive while Depression gripped the nation, today the capital is going down with the national ship. Inveterate ambivalence towards Europe from both major political parties has tended, in the two decades since the UK belatedly joined the EEC, to sideline London from a Continent in which Brussels and Strasbourg have become the seats of European government, Paris boasts the most bubbling public culture (and even Euro-Disney), and Frankfurt is fast assuming the status of financial headquarters, while Berlin calls the political tune. Quirks of British politics – the idiosyncratic prescription of free-market economics and authoritarian political centralism championed by Mrs Thatcher while Prime Minister – have brought to the capital a witch's brew of blessings and curses. The 1980s resounded with clarion calls from the Tory administration for businessmen to revitalize the capital so that it could spearhead a new nationwide prosperity – such initiatives being interpreted by many as pretexts for the withholding of Treasury investment in a city towards which the administration entertained deeply ambivalent feelings. The mixed fate of such revitalization measures creates grave doubts about the future health of the aged and ailing patient.

The post-1960 decades have proved momentous for London politics. For three-quarters of a century after 1889 the capital's government, or rather the administration of the inner metropolitan area, lay in LCC hands. From 1934 that body was securely under Labour control. The London Labour Party had its paths to progress plotted out. Labour leaders were champions of municipal socialism, committed to 'Fabian' visions of beneficent supervision by County Hall experts. The LCC was to shield London from Whitehall, while exerting a fatherly watch over the boroughs. In services such as education and housing, the LCC's record was laudable, although its penchant for bureaucratic paternalism won it few bouquets.

In the early 1960s, weary of permanent Labour rule at County Hall, Harold Macmillan's Conservative government decided to abolish the LCC and replace it with the Greater London Council (GLC). Expectations of party-political advantage prompted this decision: incorporating the prosperous outer suburbs, the GLC was expected to return safe Conservative majorities. But there were also reputable administrative reasons for the change. The LCC area had long since ceased to be representative of the metropolis. As early as 1900 the actual built-up area ('Greater London') stretched well beyond the LCC boundaries. By the 1960s the LCC was resembling a latter-day City Corporation – an isle lapped by a vast metropolitan sea over which it exercised no control. A unified government for the 610 square miles of Greater London made far more economic, fiscal and demographic sense.

Born in 1965 – by which time Harold Wilson's Labour administration was ensconced in Westminster – the Greater London Council was composed of ninety-two members elected every four years, and was given responsibility for the broad administration of Greater London. Its duties included traffic management, maintenance of main roads, refuse disposal, and the running of the ambulance service and Fire Brigade. Within the inner London area (i.e. the old LCC fiefdom), education was to be handled by the Inner London Education Authority (ILEA), a committee of the GLC. There were also thirty-one boroughs – Camden, Tower Hamlets, Redbridge, Hillingdon and so forth – merging the previous borough councils, and the Cities of Westminster and London. New boroughs generally had populations of around a quarter of a million, and their councils were responsible for most roads, social and welfare services and amenities – and, in outer London, education. Other services remained in national hands. The Metropolitan Police were under the Home Secretary (the City of London *still* retained its own force), hospitals were provided by four regional health authorities, the docks were under the Port of London Authority, water and drainage were administered by the Thames Water Authority. In all this, turf disputes were inevitable, and councils quickly established the London Boroughs Association to boost their leverage.

The GLC thus involved a classic British political compromise, with an ambiguous division of obligations and other countervailing powers besides. Housing, for instance, was divided between the two strata of government, as were roads. The GLC was given overarching control of planning, and was empowered to prepare a new Development Plan, setting population and employment targets, making transport projections, and designating redevelopment zones.

The GLC thought big. Whereas the Labour LCC had protected its patch, the Tory GLC demonstrated its eagerness – as London's closest-ever approximation to a comprehensive governing body – to transform the capital, on the basis of coordinated programmes for transport, resources and growth. Planning was all the rage: with Harold Wilson's talk of the 'white heat of the technological revolution' ringing in its ears, a confident metropolis, experiencing new affluence, was readier for change than ever before – or since.

The Conservatives, as anticipated, won the early GLC elections and, as sketched in the previous chapter, the Council advanced plans for a highway revolution. These blueprints were vilified – their environmental impact was judged catastrophic, the outlay astronomical – and, following this fiasco, the Tories were routed at the 1973 GLC elections. Macmillan's scheme had backfired: what had been envisioned to be a Conservative poodle was about to become a mighty monster of the left.

From 1973 the Labour-controlled GLC pursued pet programmes of its own. Rejecting exorbitant redevelopment plans, Labour buried the freeways and instead gave priority to environmental protection and public transport. And, most conspicuously, from the late 1970s it promoted energetic social policies, of a kind that had never even been imagined to fall within the GLC's remit. Through its influence over employment, housing, licensing and education, and by funding new capital and community projects, Labour promoted socialist, anti-racist policies, championed ethnic and sexual minorities, and developed schemes to aid the disabled, the disadvantaged and the underprivileged. Alongside such affirmative action, by 1980 the GLC leapt on to the national political stage, registering opposition to nuclear power and weapons. Its leader, the populist and picturesque Ken Livingstone – runner-up to the Pope in the BBC's 1982 Man of the Year competition – used the GLC as a pulpit for attacking the Thatcher administration's military record and Ulster policies. What the Tory press and many Londoners saw as 'loony left' elements, associated with ideologically motivated and politically correct activists (often themselves prominent in local Labour parties) among a mushrooming GLC staff, were represented as squandering ratepayers' money on fringe projects – for instance, supplying schools with literature expounding liberal views on homosexuality – and all this at a time when unemployment was rising, key services were deteriorating, and rates were soaring. GLC policies aggravated London's economic plight and quickened the flight from the metropolis.

If its endeavours for minority causes were contentious, the GLC's transport policies proved popular. In 1981 its Labour leadership decided that a simple and environmentally sound way of reducing London's intractable traffic problems lay in generous subsidies for London Transport, enabling the slashing of bus and tube fares. The result was a considerable reduction of car traffic. 'Fares Fair' met public approval.

The Thatcher government was stung into vicious reprisal. The Prime Minister's doctrinaire *laissez-faire* private-enterprise policies for the nation – advanced in the name of realism ('there is no alternative') – could not afford the reproach of successful municipal socialism on her doorstep. Hence action was taken through the law courts to have the 'Fares Fair' policy declared illegal. While that was being accomplished – litigation proved protracted and resulted in a somewhat pyrrhic victory – the government determined to go the whole hog and abolish the GLC, as part of a nationwide strategy of sapping local-government independence and destroying traditional Labour bailiwicks. (There was some consistency here: as Mrs Thatcher believed that there was no such thing as society, only individuals and families, it was pretty logical to deny that there was any such thing as London.) The GLC fought resourcefully but unsuccessfully to preserve itself, winning popular affection for the first and only time in its history, and even gaining endorsement from the House of Lords. The final abolition of the GLC in 1986 left London as the only major city in the West without an elected government to speak on its behalf and run its affairs. GLC powers were split three ways, being divided between thirty-one boroughs, the City and Westminster, five government departments, and sixty quangos and committees. Responsibility for London Regional Transport and for major metropolitan roads was transferred to the Department of Transport.

Abolition was an act of Thatcherite spite – her henchman Norman Tebbit stated that the GLC was abolished because it was 'Labour-dominated, high-spending and at odds with the government's view of the world' – but it must also be seen in a wider perspective, as yet another episode in the perpetual tragicomic quarrel between central government and metropolitan powers, giving further expression to uncertainties as to what species of authority would truly meet the capital's needs. From time to time, from the setting-up of the mayoral office in the twelfth century, Westminster has judged the capital to require some unified ruling body: in due course this meant the supplementing (or counterbalancing) of the City Corporation with the Metropolitan Board of Works, the LCC, and the GLC. But Parliament has typically lived to regret establishing such bodies, once they proved overmighty subjects.

The spectre of GLC independence and opposition haunted the Thatcher administration; yet in reality the GLC was ineffective and accomplished astonishingly little in its twenty years. Its vision was Utopian, its achievements modest. Its abolition was widely viewed as wholly retrograde, and even some staunch Tories have found peculiar the continuing absence of a central controlling agency for London – hence the suggestion, touted by Lady Porter when leader of Westminster Council, for the appointment of a Minister for London. Yet in some ways the absence of an incorporated metropolitan assembly has allowed other, more effective, bodies to flourish: the new borough councils.

Although the junior partners in the scheme inaugurated in 1965, boroughs got on with the job of local government during the long-running war between Whitehall and County Hall, benefiting from an influx of new blood into local government – youthful individuals, often disillusioned with national politics and committed to grass-roots causes. For instance, councils quickly used the terms of the Civic Amenities Act of 1967 to establish conservation areas (defined as 'area[s] of special architectural or historic interest the character or appearance of which it is desirable to preserve or enhance'). The first London borough to declare such an area was Greenwich, so designating the zone surrounding the Royal Naval College. A third of Westminster and half of Kensington and Chelsea were soon chalked within designated conservation areas. By the mid-1980s there were nearly 30,000 listed buildings and over 300 conservation areas in Greater London. Kensington and Chelsea sponsored a parliamentary Bill to obtain new powers over hotels and shop premises; Westminster and Islington experimented with traffic-free 'environmental areas'; others have pioneered 'traffic-calming' programmes. Boroughs thus became champions of local interests.

The new boroughs discovered they possessed effective blocking and delaying powers against the ambitions of County Hall. In certain fields deadlock set in almost from the start. Land use, planning and transport were early bones of contention, not least because traditional outer-London county boroughs like Croydon had long histories of self-government and a strong sense of autonomy; they had no intention of meekly taking orders from County Hall.

Crucial in eroding the GLC's authority were the prolonged delays in the presentation of the Greater London Development Plan. This took four years to assemble, another three to steer through a public inquiry, and a further four to get the Secretary of State's signature for what proved a diluted version. There was, in effect, a decade's freeze, during which the boroughs were given a free hand. They became skilful at seizing opportunities to put pressure on governments – especially Conservative ones – to clip the GLC's wings.

Battles raged over everything from parking-meters and zebra crossings to public transport. Despite the 'Fares Fair' policy, the GLC had no responsibility for British Rail's commuter services, and no coordinated transport policy emerged. Since the mid-1980s, with the ending of the London Transport monopoly and the announced privatization of British Rail, transport *policy* receded into the past – or the indefinite future. It was Thatcherite dogma that public-transport improvements (new tube lines, the high-speed rail link to the Channel Tunnel) must not principally be financed by public funds. Public-transport improvements inevitably ceased: even the planned and desperately needed west–east Cross-Rail link was abandoned in May 1994 – though apparently revived in July 1994, yet more stop-go. As of 1994 average weekly public-transport costs in London are double those of Paris and five times higher than in Madrid.

The years following the abolition of the GLC saw a localization of London, with boroughs staking out distinct political programmes. Camden and Lambeth became entrenched Labour strongholds. In Brent, the ethnic-minority vote led to the emergence of ethnic power-brokers within the Labour Party. Conservative Wandsworth and Westminster enthusiastically embraced Thatcherism, cutting rates by slashing public services, privatizing others, and selling off public utilities like cemeteries and council houses – and being hailed as 'flagship councils' by Mrs Thatcher. Under the leadership of Lady Porter, the Tesco multimillionaire heiress, Westminster Council turned council-house sales to shameless party-political advantage, by systematically selling properties in marginal wards with a view to bolstering the number of Tory voters – an election-rigging policy that was exposed in 1994 by the district auditor as 'disgraceful, wilful, unlawful, unauthorized, improper'. Rehousings and discounts involved in the gerrymandering cost local ratepayers some £21 million. Meanwhile Labour-held Lambeth wasted millions corruptly through its direct-labour schemes, and in 1993 in Labour Hackney a headmistress, Jane Brown, banned an infant-school visit to see *Romeo and Juliet* on the grounds that it was politically incorrect – that is, it was 'blatantly heterosexual'. The balkanization of the metropolis encouraged rotten boroughs, political localism and extremism of all stripes.

The scrapping of the GLC roads scheme and the void since 1985 in County Hall – to lay the LCC/GLC ghost, the building has been disposed of to a Japanese company for refurbishment as a hotel – have meant the neglect of many of the capital's traffic and communications problems. The Conservative governments of Mrs Thatcher and John Major have been pleased to let London stew in its own juice. Traffic and pollution have increased – total car-miles in inner London were up 16 per cent between 1972 and 1986, in Greater London as a whole up 25 per cent; peak traffic went up 22 per cent from 1975 to 1985; by 1985 peak-period speeds were 11 per cent slower than in 1968. Public transport decayed. Deteriorating bus and tube services have prompted greater use of cars, causing worse congestion, and all in a downward spiral. British Rail and London Underground management requested government investment to maintain safety and services; such calls fell on deaf ears in a government implacably hostile to nationalized railways and desperate to keep taxes down. Little was done, beyond running repairs, to transform a traffic impasse that was appallingly wasteful of time and resources and remorselessly turning London into a less desirable place for working and living. In Paris, millions were poured into expanding the Metro; £400 million a year is currently invested in public transport there, compared with £60–70 million in London.

Gridlock is symptomatic of late twentieth-century London. Its traditional industrial base has collapsed – London manufactures serve chiefly local needs. The idea of London-made buses being shipped to Johannesburg, as was London's pride only forty years ago, is now quite unthinkable. If the essence of Thatcherism consisted in subjecting everything to the strict discipline and searching judgement of market forces, it at least proved negatively effective in demonstrating that large-scale, non-specialist manufacturing in Greater London had ample drawbacks and scant advantages. Unknown in the capital in 1950 but growing from the 1960s, unemployment rocketed in the 1980s: by 1990, 20 per cent of Hackney's and Haringey's population was out of work, as was 35 per cent in the King's Cross area of Camden. Central government believed that publicly funded job-creation schemes (such as built the tubes in the 1920s) were unwise. It is far from clear how or when – if ever – such unemployment plateaux will be significantly reduced, although long-term unemployment is seen as a prime component of mounting social problems, as well as being a bottomless budgetary drain.

De-industrialization has proved traumatic for London, with the capital suffering more severely than any other British city – even Liverpool. Aggravated by unemployment, the once tight-knit social fabric appears to be fraying – and disintegrating in worst-hit areas like Tower Hamlets, Hackney and parts of Haringey and Lambeth. Inner London has become the nation's capital for poverty, family breakdown, school truancy, delinquency, crime (against the person and against property), alcoholism, vandalism and violence; growing heroin and crack use has fuelled drugs-related, gang-based crime. A rising percentage of Londoners is dependent upon welfare services and benefits; 654,900 people in London – over 10 per cent – were on income support in 1992.

This amounts to more than a fleeting economic down-swing or a temporary social dislocation. Many indices of decline suggest a new urban order is emerging. In place of the employed, self-sufficient and respectable working classes who abounded from the time of the guilds to the 1960s 'affluent worker', a new outcast London is coming into being, poorly integrated into the disciplines of work, family and neighbourhood, into common values, and lacking expectations of a better economic future. Homelessness, family breakdown, classroom violence, unemployment, casual crime, poverty, sickness, racial attacks – all aggravate spirals of deprivation, alienation, despair, and antisocial activities among a proliferating lumpenproletariat. Poverty and deprivation deepen, and an underclass is emerging that is perceived as a threat by the respectable, law-abiding and integrated. Resentment intensifies polarization. Violence and fear stalk the metropolis to a degree unthinkable thirty or forty years ago. In 1985 the *Islington Crime Survey* found that

72 per cent of women feared for their safety after dark, as opposed to 27 per cent of men. Women generally, and particularly older women and black and Asian women who are subject to racial attack, feel they must restrict their behaviour as a precaution against crime. For example, 37 per cent of women in the borough *never* go out unaccompanied after dark, and 50 per cent usually or always went out with someone rather than alone. 60 per cent of young white women and 72 per cent of young black women experience street harassment – kerb crawling, lewd suggestions etc.

Crime and violence aside, in the eyes of many families much of the capital – notably run-down inner-city districts such as Walworth, Peckham, Hoxton, Dalston and Tower Hamlets – appears decaying and dangerous, an undesirable environment for bringing up children. Capable and aspirant workers continue to quit Greater London for cleaner, safer, greener pastures elsewhere – in new towns or in 'Silicon Valley': a 1991 survey found that 48 per cent of people said they would like to leave London. As a result, London is being left with a disproportionate population of 'problem people' – resource consumers rather than producers: the old, sick and disabled; broken and lone-parent families; the chronic unemployed; children in care; alcoholics; addicts; new immigrants (many illegal); vagrants and derelicts who have drifted to London as a place of escape, refuge or last resort. Such people are making growing demands upon overstretched social services at a time when Tory ministers have hamstrung local authorities through rate-capping and, in the light of unrelenting animosity towards public-sector housing, have forced councils into preposterously wasteful expedients such as housing the homeless in bed-and-breakfast accommodation. Falling aggregate population is used as a pretext for reducing school and hospital services, whereas the need for such services increases, since London has a population ill-educated and sick by national standards.

In confronting its crises, London has been constrained by the very factor that has, if not created, at least exacerbated many of these problems – namely, government determination to set ceilings on local-authority spending, irrespective of needs and the democratic wishes of voters. Centrally imposed expenditure cutbacks started in 1975, when Anthony Crosland, Labour Secretary of State for the Environment, announced that 'the party was over'. He and his successor, Peter Shore, cut central government's subsidy to local authorities from 66.5 per cent to 61.5 per cent of their rates income. Reduction of that Rate Support Grant, *ad hoc* under Labour, became policy under Mrs Thatcher, who chiselled away at local-authority expenditure partly to curb inflation, in the name of monetarism, and partly because neo-liberal Toryism was keen to prevent the use of rates for social-engineering purposes. During the 1980s the Rate Support Grant was cut to 42 per cent, and after 1983 other controls and penalties were enforced with growing stringency. The Inner London Education Authority, the GLC, and fourteen boroughs were rate- or poll-tax-capped under Mrs Thatcher; £7,900 million of Treasury support were lost to London boroughs in the 1980s, the government penalizing councils for possessing severe social problems within their boundaries and for having the temerity to propose spending money to tackle them.

Yet, while budgets were being trimmed to the bone, demand for social services rose, and the metropolis's social fabric showed worsening tears and holes. Reported crimes in the metropolis rose from 584,000 in 1979 to 834,000 in 1990. With a squeeze on educational expenditure, 148 schools were closed during the 1980s; by 1990 it was estimated that £1,000 million of repairs were required on London's school buildings, while staff turnover was running at over 20 per cent each year. Hospital wards closed; at the time of writing, it seems likely that major hospitals that have served London for centuries, including St Bartholomew's and Guy's, are also about to be closed. Homelessness became the most visible feature of social breakdown, rising from 16,579 households in 1980 to 37,740 households and 65,000 single homeless a decade later. The obligation to sell public housing denied councils the means to respond constructively to such problems. Borough building programmes fell from 9,131 new starts in 1979 to a wretched 302 in 1990.

Homelessness – eradicated by the mid twentieth century – became endemic again during the Thatcher years. Swarms of dossers and vagrants reappeared, cardboard cities sprouting in the luxuriance of yuppie affluence. An encampment of tramps and the homeless arose at the Waterloo Bridge roundabout, fifty yards from the Festival of Britain site and next to the National Theatre, while elegant Lincoln's Inn Fields became a Third World shanty town for scores of the homeless – a settlement tolerated for several years, since nobody wished to assume responsibility. As in Third World countries, thousands in London now beg by day ('homeless and hungry') and sleep rough in shop doorways and church porches, constituting 'eyesores', according to the Prime Minister, John Major. The sprouting of ghetto cultures of unemployed ethnic minorities, associated with drug-trafficking and attended by bush warfare with the police, signals a novel crisis for London; in previous centuries immigrants – Flemish weavers, Huguenot craftsmen, Irish navvies and Jewish refugees – were integrated fairly quickly into the community, because London was a city of economic opportunity. The availability of work always facilitated the integration of newcomers, the young and the poor.

The misery and waste, strife and demoralization threatening to engulf London cannot be viewed in isolation from the decrepitude of its infrastructure. Paying the price for being the first million city, London has ageing amenities. Old cities have attractions – period charm seduces affluent tourists. The human scale of the buildings and street plans laid down in the Georgian, Victorian and Edwardian eras renders London inhabitant-friendly. But ageing cities do not easily or cheaply meet modern needs – for rapid movement, for flexible buildings and convenient services. Old is expensive.

London has been tardy in renewing ageing facilities. Bazalgette's sewer system, which has proved its worth for well over a century, is collapsing. Investment in public transport – in track, signalling and safety equipment on railways and the Underground – has dwindled. After London pioneered both the Underground and the tube, boldly constructing lines until the Second World War, only one truly new line – the Victoria – was constructed in the subsequent half-century. Plans for a new cross-London tube from Chelsea to Hackney have been abandoned; the Jubilee Line extension into dockland has been repeatedly postponed. London remains scandalously without any high-speed link to Heathrow, one of the world's busiest airports. The high-speed link between London and the Channel Tunnel has been delayed so often as to be a joke – and partly for this reason the long-awaited redevelopment of the King's Cross area has remained totally paralysed.

Financial stringency and environmentalist opposition have frozen, perhaps terminally, any major innovations to the road system. Over the last twenty years, leaving aside the M25 orbital road – the world's longest bypass, which snarled up almost immediately it was opened – only minimal changes have been made to inner London's road layout and traffic patterns. Schemes for new roads have largely been abandoned, and innovations in traffic management – one-way streets, metered parking, etc. – have been timid. No bold attempts have been made to reduce traffic and parking on the streets or to exclude it from central London. Use of private vehicles rises unchecked. The social costs are high. Not least, worsening exhaust pollution is responsible for the rapid growth of respiratory disorders, notably asthma: one in seven London children is now a sufferer. The health costs may prove gargantuan.

Safety deteriorates. On 18 November 1987 the Underground suffered the King's Cross fire, in which thirty-five people died. The fire led to the uncovering of major safety hazards in the system. One year later British Rail suffered a crash with fifty-six fatalities at Clapham Junction, due to shortcomings in signalling. Investment in safety equipment could, a report found, have prevented the disaster. Government unwillingness to fund safety measures since then makes repetition of such disasters inescapable.

Such are the endemic problems of any large city. None is insoluble, but solutions depend upon three possibilities: the generation of wealth sufficient to settle problems as they arise, the provision of central finance, and the existence of appropriate agencies. Hostile to the latter two mechanisms, the Thatcher government abolished London's governing body and looked to market forces as the fairy godmother.

As 1970s inflation and inefficiency decimated the industrial base (manufacturing, processing, marketing) that had so long supported the capital, awareness of London's economic plight grew. Whence would recovery come? The administrations of Margaret Thatcher and John Major committed themselves to the view that London's regeneration must and would be market-led. Above all, the hope was that a booming financial sector would energize the capital, creating a new enterprise culture, buzzing with dynamic business people eager to seize golden opportunities to make their fortunes. Whittington would live again. City prosperity, the theory ran, would have knock-on effects, generating investment, property development, new businesses great and small, extensive service employment, and a consumer boom among an affluent yuppie generation – barrow-boy capitalists making big money in and around the Square Mile.

Such faith could feed on certain truths about the historical role of the City in stimulating Britain's economic success. From medieval times, London was the heart of the British trading economy. Even during the Industrial Revolution Britain's unbounded prosperity depended at least as much upon London-based trade and finance as upon the mines and mill-towns of the Midlands and the North. The Victorian success of the City was achieved with remarkably little direct government involvement. In the prevailing climate of *laissez-faire* liberalism, government set few restrictions upon the operation of private capital in the market.

There were thus historical precedents for the bold departure of Thatcherite Conservatism after 1979, with its abandonment of the view – shared by Labour and Tory leaders alike in the 'Butskellite' 1960s and 1970s – that business and the state would beneficially align. The Thatcher administration was willing to put its trust in an international trade and finance sector that had long brought London immense wealth and extensive employment through the nexus of banking, investment and currency-handling. Until the Second World War, the City of London's pre-eminence as a world financial centre derived almost entirely from its position as the capital of a great trading nation whose empire spanned the globe. Gold, backed by sterling, was the main trading currency in the nineteenth century, accounting for a quarter of world trade even in 1939.

Faith in the continuing role of the City was reinforced by post-1945 events. When Britain emerged crippled from two world wars and the golden eggs of Empire ceased, it might have been expected that the City would have entered genteel decline. Not so: the City grew impressively from the 1960s, thanks to a combination of accident, expertise, language and geography. And Thatcherism put its trust in the regenerative power of the international money markets. These were seen as akin to an electric generator and circuit: all that was needed was that Britain should be plugged in and turned on. The City was the socket; government had its finger on the switch.

From the late 1950s the City had been well placed to cash in on the general capitalist recovery. By the 1960s corporations and governments worldwide were desperate to borrow capital, for financing expansion. Americans regarded London favourably; it was English-speaking and little regulated, and it possessed financial experience. With a sophisticated and stable banking system and a geographical position conveniently midway between Asia and North America, in the 1960s London became the world's largest single borrowing source, attracting by the 1980s the offices of more than 450 foreign banks (more than twice as many as in 1960). In securing this pre-eminence the Bank of England played an important role, largely by interfering little but being a symbol of strength. The Bank did not insist on the level of regulation that impeded the formation of such international markets in New York.

Though the Stock Exchange acquired a new building in 1972, it became apparent to Tory policy-makers that its antiquated restrictive practices and fuddy-duddy gentlemen's club atmosphere were hampering expansion: capital flow was being checked at a time of huge international opportunity. Without reform, the Exchange would lose business to other financial centres. Hence government forced the Stock Exchange to open itself to overseas members in the so-called 'Big Bang' of October 1986. Initially hostile to change, brokers in the end accepted deregulation. The name was significantly changed to the International Stock Exchange. The bedlam of the trading floor yielded to computerized electronic trading in new headquarters throughout the City. Many firms were bought up by banks, which pumped in capital. With boom conditions in 1986 and early 1987, it looked as if the internationalization of money markets would generate business recovery in Britain after the downswing of the early Thatcher years. Credit was plentiful, money flowed – and not too many questions were asked about insider trading and other shady practices. The Thatcher dream appeared to be coming true. Prospects of turning into a Porsche-driving yuppie, making serious money, taking one's pick of new real estate in dockland, were dangled before the ambitious.

The bubble burst in October 1987. The stock market crashed and recession set in. By 1990 there were hundreds of millions of pounds of losses among dealers and thousands of redundancies had ensued. Yet stability returned; London's daily turnover continued higher than either New York's or Tokyo's; and, largely freed from international currency controls, by the early 1990s the City resumed a period of prosperity as a mighty engine of finance, banking and insurance. London remains one of the world's leading insurance centres, host to over 800 companies as well as Lloyd's. The City leads the international gold market, helped by traditional connections with gold-mining areas, especially South Africa, and by the Bank of England's expertise in bullion. The five biggest British banks have London headquarters. Many merchant banks, managing investments and trade bonds and shares, occupy the City.

The City thus remains an impressive financial empire. In 1987 the old London Commodity Exchange, renamed the London Futures and Options Exchange, moved to a new building near St Katharine's Dock. The Baltic Exchange, in St Mary Axe, dominates the shipping industry and air freight: its importance is perhaps indicated by its building being the target of a devastating IRA bomb attack in 1992. Lloyd's continues a central, if accident-prone, institution, occupying since 1986 Richard Rogers's high-tech building in Leadenhall Street, its losses and scandals offering a reminder of the underlying instabilities of cut-throat international capitalism.

The City remains intimately involved in international commerce. Physical trade – handling goods warehoused in the City – has declined. But paper trade, concerned with organizing the movement of goods which never pass through London, continues.

And the futures trade booms, involving trading in commodities in advance of production or demand. Despite the demise of the docks, international trade remains a key source of City transactions. And, aside from financial services, central London dominates retailing, property, advertising, hotels and leisure, while housing the offices of major national and international companies – BP, Shell, Exxon and Mobil in oil; firms such as Allied Lyons, BAT and Cadbury in food, drink and tobacco; Courtaulds in fibres; and News International in printing and publishing – to say nothing of huge holding companies such as Lonrho and Hanson.

With this welter of financial and commercial expertise and investment, there was clearly some plausibility in government hopes that the City – freed from the shackles and suspicions that had beset it under Labour governments – would breathe new life into the metropolis. It was, after all, one of the very few sectors of the UK economy with special, even unique, economic skills lastingly in international demand. In regard to Britain's world profile, the City's performance since the Second World War has been a striking success – not least in preserving in the short term the prestige of sterling. Net invisible earnings rose from £740 million in 1965 to £12,000 million in 1986 – easily compensating for a deficit of £9,000 million on visible trade.

The snag to this strategy of relying heavily upon international capitalist transactions is that it renders both London and the nation deeply vulnerable not just to market fluctuations but to the vagaries of multinational companies and financial conglomerates – indeed to the speculation, even caprice, of world capitalism. In a system of multinational companies, the great majority of them not British owned or based, there can be no guarantee that they will continue to bring substantial business (investment, employment) to Britain, or that they will operate in favour of wider British interests. City financiers may be party to lucrative take-overs resulting in the destruction of British industries, as with the buy-out in 1989 of the US foods corporation Nabisco, which led to the closure of London's largest biscuit manufacturer, Peek Frean's at Bermondsey. The growing manipulation of the City by foreign firms and the growing ownership of London's hotels, shops, business and property by foreign capital (signalled by the Fayed brothers' purchase of Harrods) carries perils. These risks were accepted – encouraged even – by Thatcherite policies. Beginning in 1979 with the abolition of foreign-exchange controls, of office-development permits and of the Location of Offices Bureau, the Thatcher government embraced greater international competition embodied in the freedom of capital. The expected benefit was, of course, that market freedom would bring capital and business to London; but the upshot was the inevitably growing presence in the City of non-British financial-services firms, particularly Japanese and United States banks. The biggest office development ever to take place in London, the building of Canary Wharf, was floated by a Canadian firm, Olympia & York.

Another hazard for those hoping finance would prove London's deliverance has lain in longstanding uncertainties about the level of Britain's participation in Europe. The UK has become sidelined from key financial institutions, such as the Exchange Rate Mechanism. Britain may choose not to join, or may defer or dither about entering, a single European currency and the other stages of monetary and political union. The decision has been taken to site the European Central Bank not in London but in Frankfurt. The consequences for the City may well be ominous – catastrophic even, if European banks choose to resite their international offices in Germany. Insecurity will grow about the future of sterling in a second-division economy, and North American and Asian investors will turn from London towards the Continent. Under such circumstances the erosion of London's *industrial* base in the 1960s could be followed by a parallel erosion of the City's *financial* base, as London pays the price for the persistent hallucination among its ruling élites that Britain still commands unique world status.

In any case, a further question remains problematic: to what degree does City prosperity truly dynamize the capital at large? This question used to have a simple answer. The imperial City kindled commerce; trade brought overwhelming quantities of goods to the Port, creating activity, employment and consumption. Despite this, it has ever been the grumble of moralists and analysts from William Cobbett to Tony Benn that the City creates wealth for itself, not for the nation – Victorians pointed out that the City was loaning vast quantities of capital to South America, Europe and the Empire, but little was invested in Britain. The notion that the City is parasitic upon the nation – or at best is 'a world of its own' – had underlain traditional Socialist policy of nationalizing, or at least controlling, the City, so as to channel capital into British industry.

How much business City finance currently creates for Londoners is debatable. City employment peaked at over 500,000 in the 1930s, in the days when physical trade was still king. Many factors – new technologies, relocation of staff – had reduced this to just over 304,000 in 1981. It has continued to fall; and, with the computer revolution, there is no longer good reason why commercial concerns should employ non-core staffs in central-London offices.

Culminating in 1987, the Thatcher ethos created *nouveaux riches* in the City and in certain fields of enterprise (the success of the advertising company Saatchi & Saatchi achieved great prominence). Yuppies helped generate a property boom in gentrifying districts, and employment grew in boutiques, restaurants, car showrooms and other forms of domestic and conspicuous consumption. But Square-Mile affluence never trickled down very far. London unemployment rose through the 1980s, and the rising unemployment associated with deep recession since 1987, with an epidemic of bankruptcies among the new small businesses seeded in the Thatcher years (now the *nouveaux pauvres*), suggests that London cannot expect settled prosperity if it is heavily

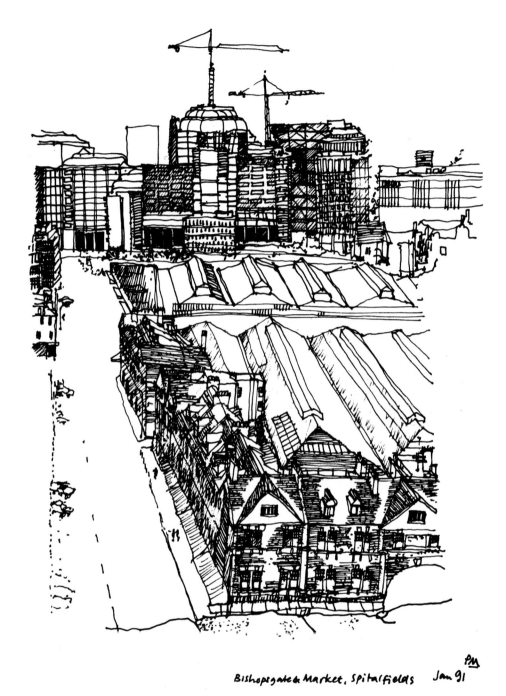

Bishopsgate Market, Spitalfields   Jan 91

A study in contrasts. Bishopsgate market with the rebuilding of the City in the
background. Drawing by Paul Middleton, 1991

dependent upon fluctuating money markets. These doubts are inseparable from the equivocal fate of enterprise culture since Mrs Thatcher came to power.

London's economic base (Thatcherism declared) was being eroded by bureaucrats, cumbersome social legislation, and strait-jackets upon capital. Freed from red tape and the dead hand of the trade unions, the entrepreneurial spirit would arise and regenerate the metropolis. This philosophy found its crucial experiment in dockland. When the Tories came to power in 1979, Michael Heseltine, as Secretary of State for the Environment, swiftly abolished the South East Economic Planning Council, on the grounds that planners stifled growth. The market would 'plan' more effectively than the planners. For the East End he established a London Docklands Development Corporation. Used also in Liverpool, this became the Tory device for inner-city regeneration; bypassing local government, the LDDC would speak the language of business.

The aim was to facilitate brisk development of run-down urban land, replicating the 1960s property boom. An opportunist style replaced the planning ethos of the 1960s. It was assumed that business knew best. As the Docklands Chief Executive explained:

The sheer scale of dereliction which the LDDC was charged with addressing was of such an order that the only way to tackle the problem without an enormous influx of public funds ... was to generate a kind of critical momentum, a 'development snowball' that would create a real credibility for Docklands early on amongst potential commercial and residential developers. Thus it was necessary to be opportunist with regard to proposals from developers.

In the docks the Development Corporation was given unprecedented powers, hitherto in the hands of local authorities. It lured the private developer partly through the device of the 'enterprise zone', within which, for ten years, no rates would be levied on commercial or industrial premises and all capital investment might be offset against tax. The idea was that, through this 'tax holiday', the LDDC would 'lever in' private capital. By mid-1986 it had used £279 million of public funds to bring in nearly six times that amount of private investment; it had attracted 400 new companies and provided sites for nearly 4,000 new homes, with 10,000 under construction or planned; and work had begun on a light rail system. It seemed to be succeeding. Yet the concrete results were discouraging: for, despite all this, only 8,000 new jobs were *created*, though a fair number of office jobs were relocated from central London – there was job transfer, not job creation.

Indeed, the tangible achievements of the first seven or eight years of the LDDC were rather paltry. In 1989 42 per cent of office space built in Docklands was unlet (the figure had risen to 50 per cent by 1992), and there were 3,000 empty houses or flats. In view of this, there was tremendous (if somewhat unthinking) enthusiasm for a

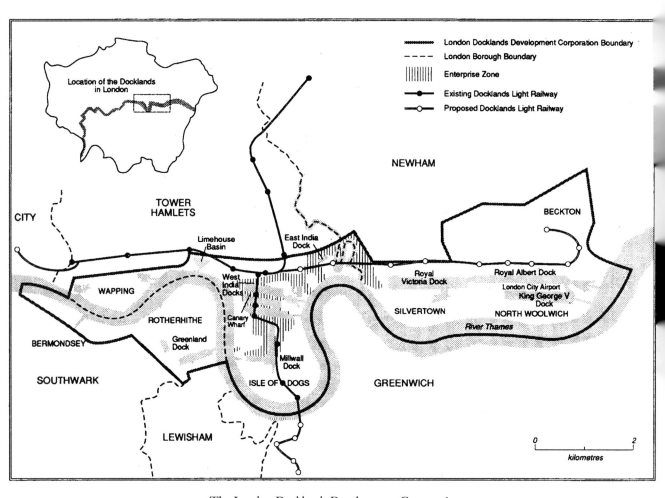

The London Docklands Development Corporation area

plan by a North American consortium for a huge office complex at Canary Wharf on the Isle of Dogs, at the heart of the LDDC area, capitalizing on its enterprise-zone status. This claimed to be about to provide an estimated 46,000 office jobs. Agreement was reached with a Canadian group, Olympia & York, in July 1987, amidst much drum-banging – the enterprise zone, it seemed, was at last about to produce a real employment bonanza, thanks to the influx of North American big bucks.

By March 1988 the Canadian developers submitted designs for Canary Wharf, notably an 800-foot skyscraper, surmounted by a pyramid, with fifty floors. Six years later, thanks to the recession and the bankruptcy of the company in May 1992 – it was at one point losing £38 million a day – the building is unoccupied. Despite plans to relocate parts of the civil service within it – plans that have met fierce opposition from the service – the venture looks like being a white elephant, and is jokily referred to as the Margaret Thatcher Memorial Tower.

The broader redevelopment of the Isle of Dogs has also made very patchy headway. That is hardly surprising, since the government, for both ideological and budgetary reasons, long refused to finance the investments in infrastructure – above all road improvements and a tube line – that would make the area attractive to employers, workers and residents.

Physical access has been a serious obstacle. In the 1970s planners envisaged a tube extension through the heart of dockland. This proposal was rejected by the LDDC in favour of a much cheaper alternative, the Docklands Light Railway. Seven and a half miles of the £77 million project were opened by the Queen in July 1987, between Tower Gateway, Island Gardens (the southern extremity of the Isle of Dogs) and Stratford. The cost of further extensions – downriver to Gallions Reach and, in the west, by tunnel to the Bank – was estimated at £137 million, half to be raised by Olympia & York and half government-funded. Eastward extension would help develop the 'Royal' docks district and unblock communications between the City and Beckton. The planned extension of the DLR was involved with the siting on the 'Royals' of a short-take-off-and-landing airport (STOLPORT) for business travel to European capitals. The London City Airport was opened by the Queen on 5 November 1987, by which time five newspaper groups had established their headquarters in Docklands. But airport traffic has been lower than projections, and the Docklands Light Railway has proved troublesome. Its value as a means of developing the area's amenities has been limited by the fact that, quite absurdly, it has a different gauge from the Underground and British Rail and so is incapable of being directly integrated within the transport system at large. It became widely known as the Mickey Mouse Railway.

Despite the LDDC's much-trumpeted hope of creating jobs for East Enders, unemployment actually continued to mount in the 'urban development area', going up by 50 per cent between 1981 and 1988 (and at the same time homelessness in the area has tripled). East End unemployment runs at twice the capital's average. All this is hardly surprising, since no efforts were made to attract business appropriate to traditional East End labour skills: the accent was always on high-prestige office development (which merely sucked employment away from elsewhere) rather than creating jobs for locals. Likewise, unlike traditional borough councils, the LDDC had no particular brief to look after the housing needs of local residents. They protested with slogans like 'People before Profits' and 'Kill the Canary'. It all looked like a repeat of the railway and office bonanza of the mid-Victorian age, when the working class was levered out of the inner city without any compensation. It is a terrible irony that the first London council seat ever won by a Fascist (British National Party) candidate was in a ward within the LDDC area, on the Isle of Dogs. Explaining his victory in

September 1993, the candidate cited mounting unemployment as the major cause of his support.

That councillor blamed Bangladeshi immigrants for the East End's troubles. That the area is deeply socially and racially divided is beyond doubt, though many would highlight the distressing divisions between impoverished traditional communities (for whom the LDDC did little) and the *nouveaux riches* who moved into smart new housing in the area. Docklands offered a region ripe for redevelopment, but success has been patchy and seems to have stalled partly because of international economic realities and partly because government refused to finance the infrastructure for regeneration. The bright idea of privatizing whole areas of the metropolis cannot, at the time of writing, be said to have brought much benefit to anyone.

More successful an enterprise has been the selling of London over the last thirty years as a Mecca of tourism – and as a residence for the international super-rich: the 1970s oil crisis brought London a vast increase of business generated by oil-rich Arabs. Tourism's importance was first officially recognized when Harold Wilson's first Labour government granted a £1,000-per-room subsidy to hotel developers. The policy was, however, ill-conceived, producing scores of characterless hotels in Kensington, Knightsbridge and Bloomsbury.

The tourist boom is, ironically, intimately linked with industrial decline, for it has arisen precisely because nations like Korea, to say nothing of Japan, have acquired the industrial wealth to finance mass tourism to places like London. By 1990 London was receiving up to 25 million tourists a year, many housed in the luxury West End high-rise hotels built during the late 1960s and early 1970s. Their presence is the ghost of the old aristocratic season. And just as the Victorian season required hordes of servants, so the new one demands legions of porters, cleaners, catering staff, chambermaids, shop assistants, coach-drivers and tourist guides to service their pleasures. One in ten jobs in London is tourism-linked, many filled by first-generation immigrants, receiving paltry wages.

London as a tourist playground creates mixed feelings. It is a source of employment, and it provides indispensable support to an ailing economy; but tourism creates low-wage, low-skill economies, appallingly dependent upon the vagaries of fashion, the world economy and international exchange rates. In any case, tourists are vultures. London can have no desire to be the Venice of the twenty-first century.

Besides, London may be unable to continue satisfying its tourists if it grows more dirty, run-down and violent, and if IRA terrorism continues. Tourism also requires public money only partly forthcoming. London's public arts are starved of funds. In 1990–91 the Royal Shakespeare Company at the Barbican ran out of cash and closed for four months. Lacking any central authority, London was so disorganized that it failed even to put in a bid for the 2000 Olympic Games. Though much of London's income is generated through culture, the financing of that culture is uncertain – and must remain so, as long as London has no government of its own.

Enterprise culture has had its successes since the late 1970s. There has been much new building, especially outside the central area. Shopping malls have multiplied, on the model of Brent Cross, a fully enclosed, air-conditioned, two-storey mall, opened in 1967, close to the intersection of the M1 and the North Circular, catering for shoppers in private cars. Wood Green is best known for its Shopping City, opened by the Queen on 13 May 1981. Croydon has become a major development centre. The pre-GLC Croydon County Borough began a vigorous campaign to attract new offices in the 1950s, the district being perceived as a prestige location by senior executives who could work within relatively short commuting distance of desirable residential areas like Coulsdon and Caterham. By the late 1960s 20,000 office workers were employed there, 50 per cent in offices that had moved from central London. An extensive shopping precinct was developed (the Whitgift Centre) and an entertainment complex (Fairfield Halls). During the 1980s Croydon continued its growth. The irony, of course, is that the success of the likes of Croydon (Bromley, Watford and Kingston are parallel cases) increases the problems of central London and the inner suburbs.

Each year 350,000 Londoners move out while only 250,000 provincials and immigrants move in. Moving out makes sense, since good jobs in London become harder to find. This haemorrhage of jobs and population is the fulfilment of the dreams of the planners. In 1943 Abercrombie recommended reducing inner London's population by a million; between 1951 and 1976 the number living there decreased by 850,000. Abercrombie laid down that industry should leave the centre of town, and it did. Abercrombie believed this would be progress. But was it? So long the nation's envy, London now has unemployment rates well above the national average. The planners failed to ponder what would happen to an inner city continually losing work and workers.

The early Thatcher years produced much upbeat boosterism. City wealth would produce jobs and regenerate the capital's fabric. Yuppies would prove the new, brash, aggressive, assertive streetwise cockneys; their drive would revitalize run-down areas, create demand, produce style; the 'greed is good' ethos would inject high voltage into London life and make new wealth respectable – not before time.

But the warning writing was always on the wall. Riots swept Brixton as early as 1981; Tottenham's Broadwater Farm riots occurred in 1985; from 1987 it was not only dockers but brokers who were out of work. In 1986 a group appointed by the Archbishop of Canterbury published *Faith in the City*, a report which triggered a political furore. The report echoed the 'darkest England' damned by the late Victorian preachers. 'There is a danger,' it noted, of many outer estates, in particular, becoming areas which have a quite different social and economic system, operating almost at a subsistence level, dependent entirely on the public sector, where the opportunities for improvement either through self-help, or through outside intervention are minimal ... the degeneration of many such areas has now gone so far that they are in effect 'separate territories' outside the mainstream of our social and economic life.

The group attacked the city of the planners, which thumbed its nose at inhabitants:

the architect-designed system-built slums of our post-war area ... poor design, defects in construction, poor upkeep of public areas, no 'defensible space' ... packs of dogs roaming around, filth in the stairwells, one or two shuttered shops, and main shopping centres a 20-minute expensive bus journey away ... unemployment rates are typically 30–40 per cent, and rising ... Bored out-of-work people turn to vandalism, drugs, and crime – the estate takes the brunt, and the spiral of decline is given a further twist.

They condemned the new Thatcherite indifference. They stated, italicizing, *'Too much emphasis is being given to individualism, and not enough to collective obligation.'* They condemned government policies: 'It is the poor who have borne the brunt of the recession, both the unemployed and the working poor. Yet it is the poor who are seen by some as "social security scroungers", or a burden on the country, preventing economic recovery. This is a cruel example of blaming the victim.'

What is fascinating is the report's resemblances to such tracts of a century earlier as Andrew Mearns's *Bitter Cry of Outcast London*. Anti-urbanism, like Luddism, is perennial; critics always condemn the city of dreadful night. It also highlights the trajectory that London has traced during the last century and a half. Around 1850 London was a shock-horror town: rapid expansion, the railways, the workhouse, the Irish, the Jews – all were creating chaos and confusion, poverty and fear of breakdown. Then generations followed when life grew more settled. London thrived, employment was for the taking, family life stabilized; confidence grew in urban living. This sense of integration, however, has latterly been yielding to disintegration. There is a new pessimism, a new anxiety about the future.

CHAPTER SEVENTEEN

Conclusion:
The London Marathon

Sweet Thames, run softly, till I end my song.

EDMUND SPENSER, *Prothalamion* (1596)

The temptation at the conclusion of a volume like this is to offer either a blueprint for metropolitan regeneration or a funeral oration. London has received many premature obituaries, and there is no shortage today of Cassandras of the capital, prophets of urban doom. Historians, however, make rotten physicians, worse planners and appalling prophets. I shall therefore resist the temptation to offer diagnoses and prescriptions.

The tenor of the analysis in the last few chapters has, nevertheless, been gloomy. London seems to be becoming one of the historic towns of Europe: a museum piece – even a dinosaur – and in some ways an irrelevance. In 1990, a gigantic exhibition called *London World City 1800–1840* was staged in Essen. Proposals that it should transfer from Germany to London came to nothing. It is touching that Europeans show more interest in Britain's capital than do its natives. It may be worrying, however, that the title of the exhibition appears to suggest that London's apogee came in the late Georgian and early Victorian eras, over 150 years ago. Historically and aesthetically, that reading is no doubt intelligible; but it might be taken to imply that London has been living on borrowed time and capital for a long while. Of course, such a judgement may apply to Europe as a whole, in an era when world economic and population growth have decisively shifted elsewhere. Once it was Europe that had most million cities: now the United States has 37, China 45, Latin America 21, Japan 10, and even Africa 21.

Not so long ago London stood for a rock-solid middle-class sense of security born of precisely those nineteenth-century decades, a comfortableness enhanced by 'London particulars'; by the City sheltered by a St Paul's that was to survive Hitler's worst; by glittering Regent Street and hectic Holborn Viaduct; by well-established inner suburbs, with their terraces, railway bridges, gasworks and church halls, Woolworth's and the Co-op, the friendly corner store and big red buses; by outer suburbs with their villas, shopping parades, tennis clubs and golf-courses; by urban spaces protective of privacy yet suffused with community.

John Betjeman was born in London, living most of his life in Highgate, the City and Chelsea, celebrating London in poetry and prose, and fighting to save it from what he called 'The Planster's Vision'. In his infancy his parents moved from Parliament Hill Mansions, Lissenden Gardens, up the road to West Hill, Highgate, where he grew up 'safe in a world of trains and buttered toast'. When he was eleven, however, his childhood cosiness was shattered by the family move to Chelsea:

> What is it first breeds insecurity?
> Perhaps a change of house? I missed the climb
> By garden walls and fences where a stick,
> Dragged in the palings, clattered to my steps.
> I missed the smell of trodden leaves and grass,
> Millfield and Merton Lanes and sheep-worn tracks
> Under the hawthorns west of Highgate Ponds.

For Betjeman, cities were reservoirs of memory. But, even in his lifetime, Betjeman's London – with its well-attended, well-tended churches and teashops – was fast fading into memory lane. Destruction and loss, rather than promise and prospects, dominate his outpourings. In a public poem celebrating the Lord Mayor's Parade, he could not resist a call to save old London from the developers:

> The many-steepled sky
> Which made our City fair,
> Buried in buildings high
> Is now no longer there.

The virtual disappearance of St Paul's behind the 1960s slabs spoke all too plainly of new priorities. Betjeman gloried in the London of ordinary citizens whose unsung, humdrum existence had been the backbone, and the lifeblood, of the city. He identified with Charles Pooter, turning that figure of fun into an object of envy. 'Thoughts on the *Diary of a Nobody*' imagined the Pooters snug in their Holloway home, with its long-lost footpath leading up to Muswell Hill:

> Dear Charles and Carrie, I am sure,
>   Despite that awkward Sunday dinner,
> Your lives were good and more secure
>   Than ours at cocktail time in Pinner.

Betjeman's London – Holloway *and* Pinner – is now in the melting-pot, and much else that the word 'London' has long evoked is becoming a thing of the past, like the 'cockney sparrer', or the pearlies with their spangled titfers, or 'Dock Green', or 'Albert Square'. How much longer will the bowler-hat brigade survive? Betjeman's London was a moment in the middle-class dream, and few tears are called for. The passing of other aspects of that tough, tenacious, bursting, bustling capital city would be more disquieting.

That London remains a habitat of wealth – fabulous, luxurious, ostentatious wealth – it is not hard to see. After a drive round Belgravia or Barnes, Holland Park or Hampstead, one is tempted to ask, How can there be such congregations of wealth? Yet, alongside, certain social phenomena grow more ominous: massive and endemic unemployment (at a rate worse than Belfast's), theft, violence, 'joy-riding', vandalism, truancy, the formation of criminal and ghetto subcultures, desolation, despair. For many, especially in the inner areas, family life as long understood is crumbling – or at least is in a state of transition whose outcome is obscure. Outside the dazzling enclaves, much of the urban environment suffers neglect and dereliction, shops are boarded up, amenities and public transport deteriorate, traffic stalls. One doesn't have to be nostalgic about the Bethnal Green of Young and Willmott's *Family and Kinship in East London* to see how in run-down central and inner-suburban districts the sense of roots and neighbourhood grows more tenuous. Stretched to the limit, social services cannot pick up the pieces; in any case, communities aren't built on welfare cheques alone.

Some might look to apocalyptic collapse, but one thing that London's history shows time and again is that the millennial mode is premature: London's crack-up has a long way to go before it bears mentioning in the same breath as many North American cities – Newark, Chicago, Detroit, Los Angeles, Washington and maybe these days Miami – where poverty, homelessness, hopelessness and appalling levels of violence have created anti-cities at the city's heart; where those who can have fled the inner city. By contrast, much of London – central, inner and outer suburbs alike – still radiates the deeply livable quality evoked by Betjeman, admired by Steen Eiler Rasmussen when he first wrote about *London: The Unique City* some fifty years ago, and readily recognizable from Mayhew, Samuel Johnson or Stow. It is not hard to head away from the abominations of slums old and new to be found around the Elephant and Castle or in South Hackney, and discover great swathes of town – not just expensive enclaves like Primrose Hill or Greenwich but mixed areas like Notting Hill or Denmark Hill – that still bear witness to the special quality of London as it grew over the centuries, from Defoe to Dickens, a customary urban texture, small-scale, cheek-by-jowl, with houses close to shops, small factories and schools, and open spaces, and centres of business and community life, and people who like the feel of the streets.

Over the centuries London was able to thrive – and avoid any devastating recession –

because of certain endowments and windfalls: its geographical site with respect to Europe and the Atlantic, its status as capital and court, its situation at the heart of the empire on which the sun never set. These factors brought populousness, business, prosperity and employment. In themselves, work and prosperity contribute greatly towards the familial structures and community fabrics that huge and restless cities need if they are to avoid degenerating into the atomized haunts of the dispossessed and the desperate, if they are to avoid being torn by silent civil wars between haves and have-nots, to avoid being held together only by compulsion (as perhaps in some South African townships today). Over the centuries, business and resources enabled London to buy its way out of difficulties. There was always private and public money around to build houses, transport and amenities, and (through parish government, welfare services and charity) to provide safety-nets for those poorly integrated into the regular social fabric. And there was always a moving frontier to which to escape and try again.

London was additionally fortunate. It avoided the horrors of religious persecution, ethnic pogroms, political violence and all-out war. Divisions between rich and poor remained bridgeable, particularly as London had the largest middle-class concentration in the world. The seismic shocks associated with the Industrial Revolution struck elsewhere. Continuities in social texture and governmental structures allowed change without disaster or mayhem. In this respect epitomizing the nation at large, London attests the benefits of gradualism. And all the time – this cannot be stressed too strongly – London's ever-rising position as a European and world trading city produced and reproduced the market effervescence that made its problems soluble, its hardships bearable, and which left rich and poor living in decent reciprocity (or at least tolerance) in Cheapside and Whitechapel, in Bedford Square and St Giles, in Notting Hill and Notting Dale; it always provided suburban frontiers on to which metropolitan problems could be displaced – be they (in different centuries) Shoreditch or Southwark, Croydon or Crawley, Shepherd's Bush or Stevenage. In any case, commerce civilizes. Over the centuries the commercial city became cosmopolitan, multi-racial, multi-religious, broad-minded, patient. Commerce absorbs and assimilates.

For deep-seated historical reasons, London's position as a making and trading city has been undergoing erosion during much of the twentieth century. No longer do wealth, ingenuity, and a smidgen of cockney cheek solve problems of their own accord. The safety-valve of the frontier may now be proving a disaster as young and ambitious Londoners flee beyond the Green Belt and end up not in London but in Bristol or Peterborough.

Perhaps for the first time, therefore, London's basic and ever-present fault line – the anomaly of its government – has come out into the open. Because of niggling petty jealousies and a failure of will, the predicament of London's governance is now further than ever from being solved, at precisely the time when effective government is most imperative. It is possible that it will (at least for a time) suit international capitalism to have London as a kind of free port – a Danzig or a Hong Kong. Only a blind believer in the benevolence of the free market would assume that will be good news for Londoners.

Over the centuries London's government was bumble and bungle: internal confusion on a day-to-day basis, and paralysis at times of crisis – the Plague, the Fire, the Gordon Riots, even the Blitz. In the past, the failures – structural and personal – of London's government have been neutralized by the socially redemptive power of its trading position and the cohesiveness of its population. It is hard to feel confident that this good fortune will continue. London was always a muddle that worked. Will it remain that way?

Further Reading

Any bibliography of London history, like its subject, risks suburban sprawl: there are thousands upon thousands of works about London's past. A browse round a secondhand bookshop or local library will turn up tons of books such as W. G. Bell's *Unknown London* (London: John Lane, 1920) or Geoffrey Fletcher's *The London Nobody Knows* (London: Hutchinson, 1962) with something or other of historical interest in them. There are scores of antiquarian and antiquated histories of London, which still make entertaining browses. Books such as Daniel Lyson's *The Environs of London: Being an Historical Account of the Towns, Villages and Hamlets, Within Twelve Miles of that Capital, etc.* (London: Thomas Caddel, 1792–7) and John Timbs's *The Curiosities of London: Exhibiting the Most Rare and Remarkable Objects of Interest in the Metropolis* (London: J. C. Hotten, 1865) have a charm of their own and convey much recondite information about London's old institutions and traditions. As Stanley Rubinstein shows in his entertaining *Historians of London: An Account of the Many Surveys, Histories, Perambulations, Maps and Engravings Made About the City and its Environs, and of the Dedicated Londoners Who Made Them* (London: Peter Owen, 1968), there is a long history to writing London's history. Some old historico-topographical works have been reprinted in paperback. The numerous works of Edward Walford are mines of information. See, for instance, his *London Recollected: Its History, Lore and Legend* (London: Alderman, 1987). Prolific historian-antiquarians active early this century include Sir Walter Besant, who produced works such as *East London* (London: Chatto & Windus, 1901) and *London in the Time of the Tudors* (London: A. & C. Black, 1904), and Edwin Beresford Chancellor, who wrote *Memorials of St James's Street, Together with the Annals of Almack's* (London: Grant Richards, 1922), *Pleasure Haunts of London During Four Centuries* (London: Constable, 1925) and lots more. All such works are dated, but most contain something of charm or curiosity; their nostalgia and London pride are themselves of historical interest.

Histories of towns and scholarship about London have grown vastly in recent years. I have therefore found it necessary to impose a bibliographical green belt in what follows. I will not list works relating to British history in general, or to architecture *per se*. For the first of these, the 'Further Reading' suggestions in Kenneth Morgan (ed.), *Oxford History of England* (Oxford University Press, 1988) should be followed up, as also those in F. M. L. Thompson (ed.), *The Cambridge Social History of Britain 1750–1950*: vol. 1, *Regions and Communities*, vol. 2, *People and Their Environment*, vol. 3, *Social Agencies and Institutions* (Cambridge: Cambridge University Press, 1990). For buildings, one should consult the phenomenally detailed *Survey of London* (currently being published by the Athlone Press), of which forty-two volumes have so far been published. Classic is Nikolaus Pevsner, *London*, vol. 1, *The Cities of London and Westminster* (Harmondsworth: Penguin, 1957), vol. 2, *Except the Cities of London and Westminster* (Harmondsworth: Penguin, 1952). These have so far been revised as follows: Nikolaus Pevsner and Bridget Cherry, *London*, vol. 1, *The Cities of London and Westminster*, 3rd edn (Harmondsworth: Penguin, 1973), vol. 2, *South* (Harmondsworth: Penguin, 1983), vol. 3, *North West* (Harmondsworth: Penguin, 1991). Elain Harwood and Andrew Saint's *Exploring England's Heritage London* (London: HMSO, 1991) and Ann Saunders's *The Art and Architecture of London: An Illustrated Guide* (London: Phaidon, 1988) are both first-rate architectural guidebooks – and much more besides. Steen Eiler Rasmussen's *London: The Unique City*, rev. edn (Cambridge, Mass.: MIT Press, 1967) is more than an architectural history, while delightfully personal is [Ian] *Nairn's London*, rev. Peter Gasson (Harmondsworth: Penguin, 1988).

What follows is also restricted to London's *history*. London's physical and urban geography, London life today, London's literary associations and all manner of similar subjects are beyond my reach: a brief, general introduction is Michael Leapman (ed.), *The Book of London* (London: Weidenfeld & Nicolson, 1989), which surveys London today with a historical dimension.

I have also made no attempt to begin to list the masses of works dealing with London's localities and their history. There are scores of old antiquarian studies, such as W. H. Blanch's *Ye Parish of Camberwell* (London: E. W. Allen, 1875); many local history societies (such as the Islington Archaeology and History Society or the Hornsey Historical Society) and borough libraries have issued brief district histories; and there are a few superb recent histories of particular areas, such as Gillian Tindall's *The Fields Beneath: The History of One London Village* (London: Temple Smith, 1977) – an account of Kentish Town – and F. M. L. Thompson's *Hampstead: Building a Borough, 1650–1964* (London: Routledge & Kegan Paul, 1974). A taste of the books and pamphlets likely to be found in local libraries might include: D. H. Allport, *Dulwich Village* (London: Cardcraft & Publishing Service, 1950); M. Boast, *The Story of Bermondsey* (London: Borough of Southwark, 1978); Mary Cathcart Borer, *Two Villages: The Story of Chelsea and Kensington* (London: W. H. Allen, 1973); Geoffrey Evans, *Kensington* (London: Hamish Hamilton, 1975); E. Clarke,

Clarke's History of Walthamstow (London: Walthamstow Antiquarian Society, 1980); J. M. M. Dalby, *Tottenham Parish Church and Parish: A Brief History and Guide* (London: J. M. M. Dalby, 1979); William Gaunt, *Chelsea* (London: Batsford, 1954) and *Kensington* (London: Batsford, 1958); G. Gower, *A Brief History of Streatham* (London: Streatham Society, 1980); V. Hart, R. Knight and L. Marshall, *Camden Town 1791–1991: A Pictorial Record* (London: London Borough of Camden, Leisure Services Department, 1991); L. Hasker, *The Place which is called Fulanham: An Outline History of Fulham from Roman Times until the Start of the Second World War* (London: Fulham and Hammersmith Historical Society, 1982); Colm Kerrigan, *A History of Tower Hamlets* (London: London Borough of Tower Hamlets, Libraries Department, 1982); Beryl Platts, *A History of Greenwich* (Newton Abbot: David & Charles, 1973); K. J. Valentine, *Neasden: A Historical Study* (London: Charles Skilton, 1989); Annabel Walker and Peter Jackson, *Kensington and Chelsea: A Social and Architectural History* (London: John Murray, 1987); Jack Whitehead, *The Growth of Stoke Newington: A Model for Other Local Studies* (London: Jack Whitehead, 1983); Charles Harris, *Islington* (London: Hamish Hamilton, 1974); and Pieter Zwart, *Islington: A History and Guide* (London: Sidgwick & Jackson, 1973). There are hundreds more; a good introduction is offered by P. Marcan, D. Payne, and L. Baker, *London's Local History* (High Wycombe: P. Marcan, 1983), which is an annotated catalogue of publications and resources.

What follows is highly selective and rather personal. Systematic listing and reviews of recent writings may be found in the *Urban History Yearbook* (since 1992 renamed *Urban History*); consult also the annual listings of periodical articles in *The London Journal*, which also carries extensive reviews, and P. L. Garside, 'The Development of London: A Classified List of Theses Presented to the Universities of Great Britain and Ireland and the CNAA, 1908–77', *Guildhall Studies on London History*, iii (1978), 175–194. There is a valuable interpretative survey in Patricia L. Garside, 'London and the Home Counties', in F. M. L. Thompson (ed.), *The Cambridge Social History of*

Britain, 1750–1950, vol. 1, *Regions and Communities* (Cambridge: Cambridge University Press, 1990), 471–574. A superb bibliography of earlier writings is Heather Creaton (ed.), *Bibliography of Printed Works on London History to 1939* (London: Library Association Publishings, 1994).

1 Introduction

Planners, geographers and social scientists have had much to say about the THEORY OF CITIES. Influential texts include Manuel Castells's *The Urban Question* (London: Edward Arnold, 1977). Readers who, like myself, find such works the literary analogue to the high-rise architecture of the 1960s should turn instead to feet-on-ground sociology – works such as Ruth Glass's *Clichés of Urban Doom, and Other Essays* (Oxford: Basil Blackwell, 1988).

There have been valuable INTERPRETATIONS OF THE CITY in history, in society and in the future. Pioneering and propagandistic were Sir Patrick Geddes's *Cities in Evolution: An Introduction to the Town Planning Movement and to the Study of Civics* (London: Williams & Norgate, 1915) and Lewis Mumford's *The Culture of Cities* (London: Secker & Warburg, 1940) and *The City in History: Its Origins, its Transformations and its Prospects* (Harmondsworth: Penguin, 1961). For discussion of Mumford's notions of megalopolis and necropolis, see Theo Barker and Anthony Sutcliffe (eds.), *The Giant City in History* (London: Macmillan, 1993). Other insightful works on the city include Leonardo Benevolo, *The History of the City*, trans. Geoffrey Culverwell (London: Scolar Press, 1980) and *The European City*, trans. Carl Ipsen (Oxford: Blackwell, 1993); Mark Girouard, *Cities and People: A Social and Architectural History* (New Haven and London: Yale University Press, 1985), and *The English Town* (New Haven and London: Yale University Press, 1990); Fernand Braudel, *Capitalism and Material Life, 1400–1800*, trans. Miriam Kochan (London: Weidenfeld & Nicolson, 1973); Peter Hall, *The World Cities*, 3rd edn (London: Weidenfeld & Nicolson, 1984); Emrys Jones, *Metropolis: The World's Great Cities*

(Oxford: Oxford University Press, 1990); Anthony D. King, *Global Cities: Post-Imperialism and the Internationalization of London* (London: Routledge, 1990) and *Urbanism, Colonialism and the World Economy: Cultural and Spatial Foundations of the World System* (London: Routledge, 1990) – both of these applying urban theory to history; Richard Lawton (ed.), *The Rise and Fall of Great Cities: Aspects of Urbanization in the Western World* (New York: Belhaven Press, 1989); Paul Hohenberg and Lynn Hollen Lees, *The Making of Urban Europe* (Cambridge, Mass.: Harvard University Press, 1985); Anthony Sutcliffe (ed.), *Metropolis 1890–1940* (London: Mansell, 1984); Jan de Vries, *European Urbanization 1500–1800* (London: Methuen, 1984); and Thomas Angotti, *Metropolis 2000: Planning, Poverty and Politics* (London: Routledge, 1993).

For a rather rare attempt at directly COMPARATIVE URBAN HISTORY, see Donald J. Olsen, *The City as a Work of Art: London, Paris, Vienna* (New Haven and London: Yale University Press, 1986). Attempts to create a discipline of 'urban history', with concepts of its own, can be sampled in a collection of H. J. Dyos's writings: *Exploring the Urban Past: Essays in Urban History*, ed. David Cannadine and David Reeder (Cambridge: Cambridge University Press, 1982); see also H. J. Dyos (ed.), *The Study of Urban History* (London: Edward Arnold, 1968); Derek Fraser and A. Sutcliffe (eds.), *The Pursuit of Urban History* (London: Edward Arnold, 1983); and Philip Abrams and E. A. Wrigley (eds.), *Towns in Societies* (Cambridge: Cambridge University Press, 1978).

There are various powerful SYNOPTIC HISTORIES of London with emphases different from mine. Felix Barker and Peter Jackson's *London: 2,000 Years of a City and its People* (London: Macmillan, 1974) combines a fine text with magnificent illustrations; Christopher Hibbert's *London: The Biography of a City* (Harmondsworth: Penguin Books, 1980) is richly evocative; Robert Gray's *A History of London* (London: Hutchinson, 1978) combines narrative and analysis with great skill. More offbeat histories are Felix Barker and Ralph Hyde's *London as It Might Have Been* (London: John Murray, 1982) and N. J. V. Barton's *The Lost Rivers of London* (Leicester: Leicester University Press, 1962). Highly traditional are works in the *Victoria County History* series, of which nine volumes relating to London have been published between 1909 and 1989, and others are in the pipeline.

Other sorts of books must be mentioned here. ANTHOLOGIES of writings about London and by Londoners include A. N. Wilson (ed.), *The Faber Book of London* (London: Faber, 1993); Andrew Saint and Gillian Darley, *The Chronicles of London* (London: Weidenfeld and Nicolson, 1994); Norman George Brett-James, *A London Anthology* (London: G. G. Harrap, 1928); and Christopher Logue (ed.), *London in Verse* (London: Secker & Warburg, 1982). For writers, see Peter Vansittart's *London: A Literary Companion* (London: John Murray, 1992), a quilt of quotes in poetry and prose; G. G. Williams's *Guide to Literary London* (London: Batsford, 1973); and Edwin Webb's *Literary London: An Illustrated Guide* (Tunbridge Wells: Spellmount, 1990) – an area-by-area account of who lived and is buried where. Among the thousands of impressionistic books about London by writers and novelists, I have got much out of V. S. Pritchett's *London Observed* (London: Hogarth Press, 1986).

ART featuring London is explored in David Piper's *Artists' London* (London: Weidenfeld & Nicolson, 1982); Malcolm Warner's *The Image of London: Views by Travellers and Emigrés 1550–1920* (London: Trefoil, 1987); and Celina Fox's *Londoners* (London: Thames and Hudson, 1987). See also John Hayes's *London: A Pictorial History* (London: Batsford, 1969).

The THAMES has attracted many authors: Eric Samuel De Mare, *London's River: The Story of a City* (London: Bodley Head, 1964); P. Burstall, *The Golden Age of the Thames* (Newton Abbot: David & Charles, 1981); Blake Ehrlich, *London on the Thames* (Boston: Little, Brown, 1966); Aytoun Ellis, *Three Hundred Years of London River* (London: Bodley Head, 1952); Mervyn Savill, *Tide of London: A Study of London and its River* (London: Britannicus Liber, 1951); and, best by far, Gavin Weightman, *London River: The Thames*

Story (London: Collins & Brown, 1990). Further titles can be accessed via B. Cohen, *The Thames, 1580–1980: A General Bibliography* (London: B. Cohen, 1985).

London is lucky in its WORKS OF REFERENCE. Truly magnificent in every way is Ben Weinreb and Christopher Hibbert (eds.), *The London Encyclopaedia*, 2nd edn (London: Macmillan, 1993); also useful is William Kent (ed.), *An Encyclopedia of London*, rev. edn (London: Dent, 1970).

London's history makes little sense without MAPS. Highly recommended are Hugh Clout (ed.), *The Times London History Atlas* (London: Times Books, 1991); Felix Barker and Peter Jackson, *The History of London in Maps* (London: Barrie & Jenkins, 1990); Ida Darlington and James Howgego, *Printed Maps of London, circa 1553–1850* (London: George Phillip, 1964); Andrew Davies, *The Map of London from 1746 to the Present Day* (London: Batsford, 1987) – this juxtaposes John Rocque's maps of London, published in 1746, against modern equivalents; J. Fisher (ed.), *A Collection of Early Maps of London 1553–1667* (Lympne Castle, Kent: Harry Margary in association with Guildhall Library, 1981); and Philippa Glanville, *London in Maps* (London: The Connoisseur, 1972). The huge TOPOGRAPHICAL LITERATURE produced from the eighteenth century contains plates and descriptions now of great historical value: see Bernard Adams, *London Illustrated 1604–1851: A Survey and Index of Topographical Books and their Plates* (London: Library Association, 1983).

London's history is revealed by a built environment. Hence the best supplement to a good book is a pair of eyes, and walking shoes, a bicycle, a taxi and an *A to Z*. Much of London's history is written on its walls, not least in the blue plaques to famous people. Oscar Wilde remarked, of the manner in which 'language is apt to degenerate into a system of almost algebraic symbols', that 'the modern city-man who takes a ticket for Blackfriars Bridge, naturally never thinks of the Dominican monks who once had their monastery by Thames-side, and after whom the spot is named'. London's history lies coded in its STREET

NAMES – Bread Street, Camomile Street, Clerkenwell, Threadneedle Street, Ropemakers Fields, Walbrook, Cornhill – and in pub names too. See F. H. Harben's *London Street Names: Their Origin, Signification, and Historic Value* (London: T. Fisher Unwin, 1896); Edgar Stewart Fay's *Why Piccadilly? The Story of the Names of London* (London: Methuen, 1935); Al Smith's *Dictionary of City of London Street Names* (Newton Abbot: David & Charles, 1970); and John Field's *Place-Names of Greater London* (London: Batsford, 1980).

2 Formation to Reformation

A guide to PRE-ROMAN LONDON is N. Merriman, *Prehistoric London* (London: HMSO, 1990). Early myths are discussed in Lewis Spence, *Legendary London: Early London in Tradition and History* (London: Robert Hale, 1937). For the ROMANS, see R. Merrifield, *The Roman City of London* (London: Ernest Benn, 1965), *Roman London* (London: Cassell, 1969), *The Archaeology of London* (London: Heinemann, 1975) and *London: City of the Romans* (London: Batsford, 1983); Jenny Hall and Ralph Merrifield, *Roman London* (London: Museum of London, 1986); and John Morris, *Londinium: London in the Roman Empire* (London: Weidenfeld & Nicolson, 1982). For an overview, see M. Lobel (ed.), *The British Atlas of Historic Towns*, vol. 3, *The City of London: From Prehistoric Times to c. 1520* (Oxford: Oxford University Press, 1989).

PRE-CONQUEST LONDON may be explored through John Clark, *Saxon and Norman London* (London: Museum of London, 1989); Tony Dyson, 'King Alfred and the Restoration of London', *The London Journal*, xv (1990), 99–110; and C. N. L. Brooke and G. Keir, *London 800–1216: The Shaping of a City* (London: Secker & Warburg, 1975). For the findings of recent early excavations, see Alan Vince, *Saxon London* (London: Seaby, 1990).

On the NORMANS, see Derek Brechin, *The Conqueror's London* (London: Macdonald, 1968). The Tower has attracted numerous historians: R. J. Minney, *The Tower of London* (London: Cassell, 1970); Christopher Hibbert, *Tower of London* (New York: *Newsweek*, 1971); J. Charlton (ed.), *The Tower of London: Its Buildings and Institutions* (London: Department of the Environment, 1978); P. Hammond, *Royal Fortress: The Tower of London through Nine Centuries* (London: HMSO, 1978); Derek A. Wilson, *The Tower: The Tumultuous History of the Tower of London from 1078* (New York: Scribners, 1979); and John Schofield, *The Building of London: From the Conquest to the Great Fire* (London: British Museum Publications, 1984).

For LATER MEDIEVAL TIMES see R. Bird, *The Turbulent London of Richard II* (London: Longmans Green, 1951); Caroline Barron, 'London and Parliament in the Lancastrian Period', *Parliamentary History*, ix (1990), 343–67; A. R. Myers, *London in the Age of Chaucer* (Norman: University of Oklahoma Press, 1972); and Gwyn A. Williams, *Medieval London: From Commune to Capital* (London: Athlone Press, 1963).

On GUILDS, see G. Unwin, *The Gilds and Companies of London* (London: Methuen, 1908); Robert James Blackham, *The Soul of the City: London's Livery Companies, their Storied Past, their Living Present* (London: Sampson Low, 1931); Arthur Henry Johnson, *The History of the Worshipful Company of the Drapers of London: Preceded by an Introduction on London and her Gilds up to the Close of the XVth Century*, 2 vols. (Oxford: Clarendon Press, 1914–22); Philip E. Jones, *The Butchers of London: A History of the Worshipful Company of Butchers of the City of London* (London: Secker & Warburg, 1976); and Thomas F. Reddaway, *The Early History of the Goldsmiths' Company, 1327–1509* (London: Edward Arnold, 1975).

For the MEDIEVAL ECONOMY, see Sylvia Lettice Thrupp, *The Merchant Class of Medieval London 1300–1500* (Chicago: University of Chicago Press, 1948; Michigan: University of Michigan Press, 1962); and Derek Keene, 'Medieval London and its Region', *The London Journal*, xiv (1989), 99–111.

3 Tudor London

Norman Lloyd Williams's *Tudor London Revisited*

(London: Cassell, 1991) offers a dramatized narrative, blending fact and fiction. The PHYSICAL AND DEMOGRAPHIC GROWTH of London are analysed with great scholarship in R. Finlay, *Population and Metropolis: The Demography of London, 1580–1650* (Cambridge: Cambridge University Press, 1981); A. L. Beier and Roger Finlay (eds.), *London 1500–1700: The Making of the Metropolis* (London: Longman, 1986), 37–59; and Vanessa Harding, 'The Population of London, 1550–1700: A Review of the Published Evidence', *The London Journal*, xv (1990), 111–28. Peter Burke's 'Some Reflections on the Pre-Industrial City', *Urban History Yearbook*, ii (1975), 13–21, is a think-piece.

On the ECONOMY, see G. Unwin, *Industrial Organization in the Sixteenth and Seventeenth Centuries* (Oxford: Clarendon Press, 1904), and F. J. Fisher, *London and the English Economy, 1500–1700*, ed. P. J. Corfield and N. B. Harte (London: Hambledon Press, 1990).

SOCIAL ORDER and CIVIC GOVERNMENT form the theme of Ian W. Archer, *The Pursuit of Stability: Social Relations in Elizabethan London* (Cambridge University Press, 1991); Jeremy Boulton, *Neighbourhood and Society: A London Suburb in the Seventeenth Century* (Cambridge: Cambridge University Press, 1987); F. F. Foster, *The Politics of Stability: A Portrait of the Rulers of Elizabethan London* (London: Royal Historical Society, 1977); and Steve Rappaport, *Worlds within Worlds: Structures of Life in Sixteenth-Century London* (Cambridge: Cambridge University Press, 1989).

RELIGIOUS CHANGE is brilliantly surveyed in Susan Brigden, *London and the Reformation* (Oxford: Clarendon Press, 1989), and Andrew Pettegree, *Foreign Protestant Communities in Sixteenth-Century London* (Oxford: Oxford University Press, 1986).

The extent of POVERTY, TURBULENCE AND CRIME are assessed in A. L. Beier, *Masterless Men: The Vagrancy Problem in England 1560–1640* (London: Methuen, 1985) and 'Social Problems in Elizabethan London', *Journal of Inter-*

disciplinary History, ix (1978), 203–21; Thomas R. Forbes, *Chronicle from Aldgate: Life and Death in Shakespeare's London* (New Haven and London: Yale University Press, 1971); and Steven R. Smith, 'The London Apprentices as Seventeenth Century Adolescents', *Past and Present*, lxi (1973), 146–61. On the disputed question of the UNDERWORLD, John McMullan's *The Canting Crew: London's Criminal Underworld, 1550–1700* (New Brunswick: Rutgers University Press, 1984) and Gamini Salgado's *The Elizabethan Underworld* (London: Dent, 1977) are to be used with caution, as are E. J. Burford's *In the Clink: England's Oldest Prison* (London: New English Library, 1977) and *Bawds and Lodgings: A History of the London Bankside Brothels, c. 100–1675* (London: Peter Owen, 1976).

Robert Ashton, 'Popular Entertainment and Social Control in Later Elizabethan and Early Stuart London', *The London Journal*, ix (1983), 3–19, examines the CULTURE OF THE PEOPLE, as do Sandra Billington, 'Butchers and Fishmongers: Their Historical Contribution to London's Festivity', *Folklore*, ci (1990), 97–103, and Peter Burke, 'Popular Culture in Seventeenth-Century London', *The London Journal*, iii (1977), 143–62. Lawrence Manley (ed.), *London in the Age of Shakespeare* (London: Croom Helm, 1986) is an anthology. On THEATRE, see Herbert Berry, *Shakespeare's Playhouses* (New York: AMS, 1987).

For a CONTEMPORARY OVERVIEW, see John Stow, *A Survay of London: Contayning the Originall, Antiquity, Increase, Moderne Estate, and Description of that Citie Etc.*, ed. C. L. Kingsford, 2 vols. (Oxford: Clarendon Press, 1908; first published 1598); Robert Ashton, 'Stow's London', *Transactions of the London and Middlesex Archaeological Society*, xxix (1978), 137–43; and Michael J. Power, 'John Stow and his London', *Journal of Historical Geography*, xi (1985), 1–20.

4 War, Plague and Fire

On the BUILDING OF EARLY STUART LONDON, consult Norman George Brett-James, *The Growth of Stuart London* (London: Allen &

Unwin, 1935); Malpas Pearse, *Stuart London* (London: Macdonald, 1969); and Sir John Summerson, *Inigo Jones* (Harmondsworth: Penguin, 1966). COVENT GARDEN is discussed in Mary Cathcart Borer, *Covent Garden* (London: Abelard-Schuman, 1967), and Robert Thorne, *Covent Garden Market: Its History and Restoration* (London: Duckworth, 1979).

For the CROWN, see E. S. Turner, *The Court of St. James* (London: Michael Joseph, 1959), and John Beattie, *The English Court in the Reign of George I* (Cambridge: Cambridge University Press, 1967).

On COMMERCIAL CHANGE and its political ramifications, see Robert Ashton, *The City and the Court, 1603–1643* (Cambridge: Cambridge University Press, 1979); K. N. Chaudhuri, *The English East India Company: the Study of an Early Joint-Stock Company, 1600–1640* (London: Frank Cass, 1965); Theodore K. Rabb, *Enterprise and Empire: Merchant and Gentry Investment in the Expansion of England, 1575–1630* (Cambridge, Mass.: Harvard University Press, 1967); Robert Brenner, *Merchants and Revolution: Commercial Change, Political Conflict and London's Overseas Traders, 1550–1653* (Cambridge: Cambridge University Press, 1993); and Valerie Pearl, *London and the Outbreak of the Puritan Revolution: City Government and National Politics, 1625–43* (Oxford: Oxford University Press, 1961). Pearl has also written major articles: 'Puritans and Poor Relief: The London Workhouse, 1649–1660', in D. Pennington and K. Thomas (eds.), *Puritans and Revolutionaries: Essays in Seventeenth-Century History Presented to Christopher Hill* (Oxford: Oxford University Press, 1978), 206–32; 'Change and Stability in Seventeenth-Century London', *The London Journal*, v (1979), 3–34; and 'Social Policy in Early Modern London', in H. Lloyd-Jones, V. Pearl and B. Worden (eds.), *History and Imagination: Essays in Honour of H. R. Trevor-Roper* (London: Duckworth, 1981), 115–31.

On the CIVIL WAR AND INTERREGNUM, see Tai Liu's *Puritan London: A Study of Religion and Society in the City Parishes* (London: Associated University Press, 1986). Paul Seaver's *Wallington's World: A Puritan Artisan in Seventeenth Century*

London (London: Methuen, 1985) gets under the skin of a Puritan.

On the PLAGUE, see Frank Percy Wilson, *The Plague in Shakespeare's London* (Oxford: Clarendon Press, 1927); Walter G. Bell, *The Great Plague in London in 1665* (London: Bodley Head, 1951); and, best of all, Paul Slack, *The Impact of Plague in Tudor and Stuart England* (London: Routledge & Kegan Paul, 1985).

On the FIRE, see Walter G. Bell, *The Great Fire of London in 1666*, rev. edn (London: Bodley Head, 1951), and John E. N. Hearsey, *London and the Great Fire* (London: John Murray, 1965). REBUILDING is covered in Thomas F. Reddaway, *The Rebuilding of London After the Great Fire* (London: Jonathan Cape, 1940); Martin S. Briggs, *Wren the Incomparable* (London: Allen & Unwin, 1953); and Sir John Summerson, *Sir Christopher Wren* (London: Collins, 1953).

Michael Power has written fascinatingly about the emergent EAST END: 'The Social Topography of Restoration London', in A. L. Beier and Roger Finlay (eds.), *London 1500–1700: The Making of the Metropolis* (London: Longman, 1986), 199–223; 'East London Housing in the Seventeenth Century', in Peter Clark and Paul Slack (eds.), *Crisis and Order in English Towns, 1500–1700: Essays in Urban History* (London: Routledge & Kegan Paul, 1972), 237–62; 'The East and West in Early-Modern London', in E. W. Ives, R. J. Knecht and J. J. Scarisbrick (eds.), *Wealth and Power in Tudor England: Essays Presented to S. T. Bindoff* (London: Athlone Press, 1978), 167–85; and 'Shadwell: The Development of a London Suburban Community in the Seventeenth Century', *London Journal*, iv (1978), 29–46.

For a taste of TOWN in the mid seventeenth century, nothing beats *The Diary of Samuel Pepys*, ed. Robert Latham and William Matthews, 11 vols. (London: George Bell, 1970–83); see also Robert Ashton, 'Samuel Pepys's London', *London Journal*, xi (1985), 75–87.

5 The Triumph of Town: From Restoration to Regency

Overviews of the SOCIAL LIFE of Georgian London include M. D. George, *London Life in the Eighteenth Century* (Harmondsworth: Penguin, 1966); Jack Lindsay, *The Monster City: Defoe's London, 1688–1730* (London: Hart-Davis–Mac-Gibbon, 1978); Richard B. Schwartz, *Daily Life in Johnson's London* (Madison: University of Wisconsin Press, 1983); André Parreaux, *Smollett's London* (Paris: A. G. Nizet, 1968); and George Rudé, *Hanoverian London, 1714–1808* (London: Secker & Warburg, 1971).

On the FINANCING OF THE WEST END (and on so much else), Simon Jenkins's *Landlords to London: The Story of a Capital and its Growth* (London: Constable, 1975) is extremely informative and witty as well; see also his *The Selling of Mary Davies and Other Writings* (London: John Murray, 1993). Also illuminating are David Cannadine, *Lords and Landlords: The Aristocracy and the Towns, 1774–1967* (Leicester: Leicester University Press, 1980); Andrew Byrne, *Bedford Square: An Architectural Study* (London: Athlone Press, 1990); and Lawrence Stone, 'The Residential Development of the West End of London in the Seventeenth Century', in Barbara C. Malament (ed.), *After the Reformation* (Manchester: Manchester University Press, 1980), 167–212. Sir John Summerson's *Georgian London*, rev. edn (London: Barrie & Jenkins, 1970) is a classic. Frank Banfield's denunciation of *The Great Landlords of London* (London: Spencer Blackett, 1890) is still worth reading.

On the DOMESTIC LIFE OF TOWN, see Christopher Simon Sykes, *Private Palaces: Life in the Great London Houses* (London: Chatto & Windus, 1986); Elizabeth Burton, *The Georgians at Home* (London: Longman, 1967); Dan Cruickshank and Peter Wyld, *London: The Art of Georgian Building* (London: Architectural Press, 1975); Dan Cruickshank and Neil Burton, *Life in the Georgian City* (London: Viking, 1990); and Andrew Byrne, *London's Georgian Houses* (London: Georgian Press, 1986). FASHIONABLE TOWN forms the subject of Sheila Birkenhead, *Peace in Piccadilly: The Story of Albany* (London: Hamish Hamilton, 1958); M. C. Borer, *Mayfair: The Years of Grandeur* (London: W. H. Allen, 1975) and *A History of Berkeley Square* (London: Berkeley Square Jubilee Association, 1978); Carol Kennedy, *Mayfair: A Social History* (London: Hutchinson, 1986); Arthur Irwin Dasent, *Piccadilly in Three Centuries: With Some Account of Berkeley Square and the Haymarket* (London: Macmillan, 1920) and *Grosvenor Square* (London: Macmillan, 1935); J. Desebrock, *The Book of Bond Street Old and New* (London: Tallis, 1978); and G. Mackenzie, *Marylebone: A Great City North of Oxford Street* (London: Macmillan, 1972). Fascinating on Bloomsbury is Gladys Scott Thompson, *The Russells in Bloomsbury, 1669–1771*, 2 vols. (London: Jonathan Cape, 1940).

Material on LONDON'S VILLAGES is contained in M. C. Borer, *Hampstead and Highgate: The Story of Two Hilltop Villages* (London: W. H. Allen, 1976), and Nerina Shute's *London Villages* (London: Robert Hale, 1977) and *More London Villages* (London: Robert Hale, 1981).

For an eighteenth-century view of LONDON AS IT SHOULD BE, see John Gwynn, *London and Westminster Improved, Illustrated Plans, to Which is Prefixed a Discourse on Public Magnificence, With Observations on the State of Arts and Artists in the Kingdom* (London: printed for the author, 1766).

And for the REGENCY see T. Davis, *John Nash* (Newton Abbot: David & Charles, 1973); Ann Saunders, *Regent's Park: A Study of the Development of the Area from 1086 to the Present Day* (Newton Abbot: David & Charles, 1969); Hermione Hobhouse, *A History of Regent Street* (London: Macdonald & Jane's, 1975); and, the classic, Sir John Summerson, *The Life and Work of John Nash Architect* (London: Allen & Unwin, 1980).

6 Commercial City: 1650–1800

Easily the best account of LONDON AS A LEADING SECTOR is E. A. Wrigley, 'A Simple Model of London's Importance in Changing English

Society and Economy, 1650–1750', *Past and Present*, xxxvii (1967), 44–70.

For POPULATION RISE, see E. A. Wrigley and R. S. Schofield, *The Population History of England, 1541–1871: A Reconstruction* (London: Edward Arnold, 1981), and John Landers, *Death and the Metropolis: Studies in the Demographic History of London 1670–1830* (Cambridge: Cambridge University Press, 1993).

On HOME TRADE see J. A. Chartres, 'Food Consumption and Internal Trade', in A. L. Beier and Roger Finlay (eds.), *London 1500–1700: The Making of the Metropolis* (London: Longman, 1986), 168–96; for overseas trade, Ralph Davis, *The Rise of the English Shipping Industry in the Seventeenth and Eighteenth Centuries* (London: Macmillan, 1962) is excellent. P. J. Cain and A. G. Hopkins's *British Imperialism*, vol. 1, *Innovation and Expansion 1688–1914*, vol. 2, *Crisis and Deconstruction 1914–1990* (London: Longman, 1993) stresses the significance of colonial development to London's capitalism in ways I find wholly convincing. Patrick Colquhoun's *A Treatise on the Commerce and Police of the River Thames* (London: Joseph Mawman, 1800) agrees.

Ways into FINANCE CAPITALISM are offered by James Alexander, 'The Economic Structure of the City of London at the End of the 17th Century', *Urban History Yearbook* (1989), 47–62; W. R. Bisschop, *The Rise of the London Money Market, 1640–1826* (New York: Augustus M. Kelley, 1968); Sir John Clapham, *The Bank of England: A History*, 2 vols. (Cambridge: Cambridge University Press, 1970); and Philip G. M. Dickson, *The Financial Revolution in England: A Study in the Development of Public Credit, 1688–1756* (London: Macmillan, 1967).

On LONDON'S TRADES, a splendid contemporary source is R. Campbell, *The London Tradesman* (1747: facsimile reprint, Newton Abbot: David & Charles, 1969). On SHOPS, see Dorothy Davis, *A History of Shopping* (London: Routledge & Kegan Paul, 1966).

Francis Sheppard, *Local Government in St Marylebone, 1688–1835: A Study of the Vestry and the Turnpike Trust* (London: Athlone Press, 1958) explains VESTRIES.

On the CITIZENRY, see Peter Earle, *The World of Defoe* (London: Weidenfeld & Nicolson, 1976), *The Making of the English Middle Class: Business, Society and Family Life in London, 1660–1730* (London: Methuen, 1989) and *A City Full of People: Men and Women of London 1650–1750* (London: Methuen, 1994).

DISORDER AND CRIME are easily sensationalized; thoughtful accounts are offered in Peter Clark, 'The "Mother Gin" Controversy in Early 18th-Century England', *Royal Historical Society Transactions*, xxxviii (1988), 63–84; J. S. Cockburn (ed.), *Crime in England, 1550–1800* (Princeton: Princeton University Press, 1977); the excellent essays in Lee Davison, Tim Hitchcock, Tim Keirn and Robert B. Shoemaker (eds.), *Stilling the Grumbling Hive: The Response to Social and Economic Problems in England, 1689–1750* (Stroud: Alan Sutton, 1992); Frank Martin, *Rogue's River: Crime on the River Thames in the Eighteenth Century* (Hornchurch: Henry, 1983); and Donald Rumbelow, *I Spy Blue: The Police and Crime in the City of London from Elizabeth I to Victoria* (London: Macmillan, 1971) and *The Triple Tree: Newgate, Tyburn, and Old Bailey* (London: Harrap, 1982). Peter Linebaugh's *The London Hanged: Crime and Civil Society in the Eighteenth Century* (London: Allen Lane, 1991) shows up Georgian callousness. A contemporary discussion is Patrick Colquhoun's *A Treatise on the Police of the Metropolis* (London: C. Dilly, 1796).

PRISONS are dealt with in A. Babington, *The English Bastille: A History of Newgate Gaol and Prison Conditions in Britain, 1188–1902* (London: Macdonald, 1971); C. W. Chalklin, 'The Reconstruction of London's Prisons, 1770–1799: An Aspect of the Growth of Georgian London', *The London Journal*, ix (1983), 21–34; and Joanna Innes, 'The King's Bench Prison in the Later Eighteenth Century: Law, Authority and Order in a London Debtor's Prison', in John Brewer and John Styles (eds.), *An Ungovernable People: The English and their Law in the Seventeenth and Eighteenth Centuries* (London: Hutchinson, 1980), 250–98.

For POLITICS AND DISORDER see Gary Stuart De Krey, *A Fractured Society: The Politics of London in the First Age of Party 1688–1715* (Oxford: Clarendon Press, 1985); Tim Harris, *London Crowds in the Reign of Charles II: Propaganda and Politics from the Restoration until the Exclusion Crisis* (Cambridge: Cambridge University Press, 1987); Nicholas Rogers, *Whigs and Cities: Popular Politics in the Age of Walpole and Pitt* (Oxford: Clarendon Press, 1989); George Rudé, *Paris and London in the Eighteenth Century* (London: Collins, 1952) and *Wilkes and Liberty* (Oxford: Oxford University Press, 1962); and J. Paul de Castro, *The Gordon Riots* (London: Oxford University Press, 1926).

7 Culture City: Life under the Georges

For contrasting attitudes to URBANISM, see M. Byrd, *London Transformed: Images of the City in the Eighteenth Century* (New Haven and London: Yale University Press, 1978); P. J. Corfield, *The Impact of English Towns 1700–1800* (Oxford: Oxford University Press, 1982); Ian Donaldson, 'The Satirists' London', *Essays in Criticism*, xxv (1975), 101–22; G. Pechey, 'The London Motif in Some Eighteenth Century Contexts: A Semiotic Study', *Literature and History*, iv (1976), 2–29; Pat Rogers, *Grub Street: Studies in a Subculture* (London: Methuen, 1972); Carl E. Schorske, 'The Idea of the City in European Thought: Voltaire to Spengler', in Oscar Handlin and John Burchard (eds.), *The Historian and the City* (Cambridge, Mass.: MIT Press and Harvard University Press, 1963); Arthur J. Weitzman, 'Eighteenth Century London: Urban Paradise or Fallen City?', *Journal of the History of Ideas*, xxxvi (1975), 469–80; and Raymond Williams, *The Country and the City* (London: Chatto & Windus, 1973).

On RELIGION and the Churches, see Elizabeth and Wayland Young, *London's Churches* (London: Grafton, 1986), and Tim Hitchcock, 'Paupers and Preachers: The SPCK and the Parochial Workhouse Movement', and Robert B. Shoemaker, 'Reforming the City: The Reformation of Manners Campaign in London, 1690–1738', in

Lee Davison, Tim Hitchcock, Tim Keirn and Robert B. Shoemaker (eds.), *Stilling the Grumbling Hive: The Response to Social and Economic Problems in England, 1689–1750* (Stroud: Alan Sutton, 1992), 145–66, 99–120. The SECTS are interestingly covered in C. Maurice Davies, *Unorthodox London or Phases of Religious Life in the Metropolis* (New York: Augustus M. Kelley, 1969).

Donna T. Andrew's *Philanthropy and Police: London Charity in the Eighteenth Century* (Princeton: Princeton University Press, 1990) is admirable on PHILANTHROPY; also see Ruth K. McClure, *Coram's Children: The London Foundling Hospital in the Eighteenth Century* (New Haven and London: Yale University Press, 1981), and Craig Rose, 'London's Charity Schools, 1690–1730', *History Today*, xl (1990), 17–23, and 'Evangelical Philanthropy and Anglican Revival: The Charity Schools of Augustan London, 1698–1740', *The London Journal*, xvi (1991), 35–66.

On HOSPITALS, see Archibald Edmund Clark-Kennedy, *London Pride: The Story of a Voluntary Hospital* (London: Hutchinson Benham, 1979), and James Bettley, 'Post Voluptatem Misericordia: The Rise and Fall of the London Lock Hospitals', *The London Journal*, x (1984), 167–75.

For METROPOLITAN AMUSEMENTS, see E. J. Burford, *Wits, Wenchers and Wantons: London's Low Life: Covent Garden in the Eighteenth Century* (London: Robert Hale, 1992); Penelope J. Corfield, 'Walking the City Streets: The Urban Odyssey in Eighteenth-Century England', *Journal of Urban History*, xvi (1990), 132–74; M. Willson Disher, *Pleasures of London* (London: Robert Hale, 1950); and Bryant Lillywhite, *London Coffee Houses* (London: Allen & Unwin, 1963).

For SEX, see Peter Wagner, *Eros Revived: Erotica in the Age of Enlightenment* (London: Secker & Warburg, 1986) and *Harris's List of Covent Garden Ladies: Or Man of Pleasure's Kalendar for the Year 1793* (facsimile reprint, Edinburgh: P. Harris Publishing, 1982).

On PLEASURE GARDENS, read William Biggs

Boulton, *The Amusements of Old London: Being a Survey of the Sports and Pastimes, Tea Gardens and Parks, Playhouses and Other Diversions of the People of London from the 17th to the Beginning of the 19th Century* (London: J. C. Nimmo, 1901); Mollie Sands, *Invitation to Ranelagh 1742–1803* (London: John Westhouse, 1946); James Granville Southworth, *Vauxhall Gardens* (New York: Columbia University Press, 1941); and Warwick William Wroth, *The London Pleasure Gardens of the Eighteenth Century* (London: Macmillan, 1896). Guy R. Williams's *The Royal Parks of London* (London: Constable, 1978) is helpful.

The PLEASURES OF THE RICH are examined in Robert Joseph Allen's *The Clubs of Augustan London* (Cambridge, Mass.: Harvard University Press, 1933), and Henry Blyth's *Hell and Hazard: Or, William Crockford versus the Gentlemen of England* (London: Weidenfeld & Nicolson, 1969). For SPECTACLES see Richard Daniel Altick, *The Shows of London: A Panoramic History of Exhibitions, 1600–1862* (Cambridge, Mass.: Harvard University Press, 1978), and for THEATRE Emmett L. Avery (ed.), *The London Stage 1600–1800*, 2 vols. (Carbondale: Southern Illinois University Press, 1968), and Sybil Rosenfeld, *The Theatres of the London Fairs in the 18th Century* (Cambridge: Cambridge University Press, 1960). CONCERT LIFE is covered in William Weber, *Music and the Middle Class: The Social Structure of Concert Life in London, Paris and Vienna* (London: Croom Helm, 1975). Stella Margetson's *Regency London* (London: Cassell, 1971) brings SMART LONDON to life.

The best CONTEMPORARY SOURCE for this period is James Boswell, *Boswell's London Journal, 1762–1763*, ed. Frederick A. Pottle (London: Heinemann, 1950); see also John Gay, *Trivia; or, The Art of Walking the Streets of London*, ed. W. H. Williams (London: Daniel O'Connor, 1922), and *Johnson's Juvenal: 'London' and 'The Vanity of Human Wishes'*, ed. Niall Rudd (Bristol: Bristol Classical Press, 1981).

8 Capitalism in the Capital: The Victorian Age

There are some excellent GENERAL WORKS about Victorian London: H. J. Dyos and Michael Wolff (eds.), *The Victorian City: Images and Realities*, 2 vols. (London: Routledge & Kegan Paul, 1973); Asa Briggs, *Victorian Cities* (Harmondsworth: Penguin, 1968); David Feldman and Gareth Stedman Jones (eds.), *Metropolis London: Histories and Representations since 1800* (London: Routledge, 1989); L. C. B. Seaman, *Life in Victorian London* (London: Batsford, 1973); Francis Sheppard, *London, 1808–1870: The Infernal Wen* (London: Secker & Warburg, 1971) and 'London and the Nation in the Nineteenth Century', *Transactions of the Royal Historical Society*, 5th ser., xxxv (1985), 51–74; and Gavin Weightman and Steve Humphries, *The Making of Modern London, 1815–1914* (London: Sidgwick & Jackson, 1983). *London – World City, 1800–1840*, ed. Celina Fox (New Haven and London: Yale University Press, 1992), has superb illustrations matched by an illuminating text.

INDUSTRIALIZATION is explored in T. Barker's 'Business as Usual: London and the Industrial Revolution', *History Today*, xxxix (1989), 45–51; the ROLE OF LABOUR in E. J. Hobsbawm's 'The Nineteenth-Century London Labour Market', in R. Glass (ed.), *London: Aspects of Change* (Centre for Urban Studies Report No. 3) (London: MacGibbon & Kee, 1964), 3–28, and his 'Labour in the Great City', *New Left Review*, clxvi (1987), 39–51; also consult L. D. Schwarz, *London in the Age of Industrialization: Entrepreneurs, Labour Force and Living Conditions, 1700–1850* (Cambridge: Cambridge University Press, 1992). Useful background is offered in Rex Pope (ed.), *Atlas of British Social and Economic History since c. 1700* (London: Routledge, 1989).

On the DOCKS, see Sir Joseph Guinness Brookbank, *A History of the Port of London*, 2 vols. (London: Daniel O'Connor, 1921), and Ivan S. Greeves, *London Docks, 1800–1980: A Civil Engineering History* (London: Thomas Telford, 1980). The economic importance of the CANALS and the THAMES is emphasized in Herbert Herbert, *London's Canal: The History of the Regent's Canal* (London: Putnam, 1961), and S. Pollard, 'The Decline of Shipbuilding on the Thames', *Economic History Review*, 2nd ser., iii (1950–51), 72–89.

MANUFACTURING is explored in Peter G. Hall, *The Industries of London since 1861* (London: Hutchinson, 1962); P. Kirkham, P. Mace and J. Parker, *Furnishing the World: The East London Furniture Trade, 1830–1980* (London: Journeyman Press, 1987); and James A. Schmiechen, *Sweated Industries and Sweated Labour: The London Clothing Trades, 1860–1914* (London: Croom Helm, 1984). See also Sally Alexander's *Women's Work in Nineteenth-Century London: A Study of the Years 1820–50* (London: Journeyman Press and London History Workshop Centre, 1983). RETAILING forms the theme of Alison Adburgham's *Shopping in Style: London from the Restoration to Edwardian Elegance* (London: Thames and Hudson, 1979) and her *Liberty's: A Biography of a Shop* (London: Allen & Unwin, 1975).

For BUSINESS AND THE CITY, David Kynaston's *The City of London*, vol. 1, *A World of Its Own, 1815–1890* (London: Chatto & Windus, 1994) is clear and convincing.

Sir John Summerson's 'The Victorian Rebuilding of the City of London', *The London Journal*, iii (1977), 163–85, investigates CITY ARCHITECTURE.

9 'The Contagion of Numbers': The Building of the Victorian Capital, 1820–1890

BUILDERS AND BUILDING now have an excellent coverage: see Linda Clarke, *Building Capitalism: Historical Change and the Labour Process in the Production of the Built Environment* (London: Routledge, 1992); H. J. Dyos, 'The Speculative Builders and Developers of Victorian London', *Victorian Studies*, xi (1968), 641–90; Hermione Hobhouse, *Thomas Cubitt, Master Builder* (London: Macmillan, 1971); and Donald J.

Olsen, *The Growth of Victorian London* (London: Batsford, 1976), *Town Planning in London: The Eighteenth and Nineteenth Centuries* (New Haven and London: Yale University Press, 1982) and *The Growth of Victorian London* (London: Edward Arnold, 1983).

For particular DISTRICTS, see (among many items) C. R. Clinker's *Paddington, 1854–1979* (Bristol: Avon–Anglia Publications, 1979); W. H. Draper's *Hammersmith: A Study in Town History* (London: Anne Bingley, 1989); H. J. Dyos's classic *Victorian Suburb: A Study of the Growth of Camberwell* (Leicester: Leicester University Press, 1966); Michael Hunter's *The Victorian Villas of Hackney* (London: Hackney Society, 1981); Isobel Watson's *Gentlemen in the Building Line: The Development of South Hackney* (London: Padfield Publications, 1989); and J. B. Wilson's *The Story of Norwood* (London: London Borough of Lambeth, 1973).

On TRANSPORTATION CHANGES, the authoritative work is T. C. Barker and R. M. Robbins, *A History of London Transport*, vol. 1, *The Nineteenth Century* (London: Allen & Unwin, 1963); also consult John Camp, *Discovering London Railway Stations* (Tring: Shire Publications, 1969); Edwin Course, *London Railways* (London: Batsford, 1962) and *London's Railways: Then and Now* (London: Batsford, 1987); and John Robert Day, *The Story of the London Bus: London and its Buses from the Horse Bus to the Present Day* (London: London Transport Executive, 1973).

The impact of RAILWAYS is assessed in H. J. Dyos's 'Railways and Housing in Victorian London', *Journal of Transport History*, ii (1955–6), 11–21, 90–100, and his 'Some Social Costs of Railway Building in London', *Journal of Transport History*, iii (1957–8), 23–30; and in J. R. Kellett's *The Impact of Railways on Victorian Cities* (London: Routledge & Kegan Paul, 1969).

For ARCHITECTURAL DEVELOPMENTS, see Sir John Summerson's *The Architecture of Victorian London* (Charlottesville: University Press of Virginia, 1976) and Mark Girouard's *Sweetness and Light: The 'Queen Anne' Movement 1860–1900*

(Oxford: Clarendon Press, 1977). On PUBLIC BUILDINGS, see Rodney Mace's *Trafalgar Square: Emblem of Empire* (London: Lawrence & Wishart, 1976). A COMPARATIVE PERSPECTIVE is presented in Anthony Sutcliffe's *London and Paris: Capitals of the Nineteenth Century* (Leicester: Victorian Studies Centre, University of Leicester, 1983).

10 Bumbledom? London's Politics 1800–1890

Admirable on ADMINISTRATIVE DEVELOPMENTS are Ken Young and Patricia L. Garside, *Metropolitan London: Politics and Urban Change, 1837–1981* (London: Edward Arnold, 1982), and John Davis, *Reforming London: The London Government Problem, 1855–1900* (Oxford: Clarendon Press, 1988). For what the VESTRIES did, see Janet Roebuck, *Urban Development in Nineteenth-Century London: Lambeth, Battersea and Wandsworth, 1838–1888* (London: Phillimore, 1979).

An astute assessment of the role of the POLICE is offered in Clive Emsley, *The English Police: A Political and Social History* (Hemel Hempstead: Harvester Wheatsheaf, 1991); also see Ruth Paley, ' "An Imperfect, Inadequate and Wretched System"?: Policing London Before Peel', *Criminal Justice History*, x (1989), 95–130; Wilbur R. Miller, *Cops and Bobbies: Police Authority in New York and London, 1830–1870* (Chicago: University of Chicago Press, 1977); Phillip Thurmond Smith, *Policing Victorian London: Political Policing, Public Order, and the London Metropolitan Police* (Westport, Conn.: Greenwood Press, 1985); and J. Wilkes, *London Police in the Nineteenth Century* (Cambridge: Cambridge University Press, 1977).

The role of THE CAPITAL IN POLITICS is assessed in J. Ann Hone, *For the Cause of Truth: Radicalism in London 1796–1821* (Oxford: Clarendon Press, 1982); Iain McCalman, *Radical Underworld: Prophets, Revolutionaries, and Pornographers in London, 1795–1840* (Cambridge: Cambridge University Press, 1988); I. Prothero, *Artisans and Politics in Early Nineteenth Century London* (Folkestone:

Dawson, 1978); and more broadly in John Stevenson (ed.), *London in the Age of Reform* (Oxford: Basil Blackwell, 1977). On the POOR LAW see Felix Driver, *Power and Pauperism. The Workhouse System, 1834–1884* (Cambridge: Cambridge University Press, 1993), and Lynn Hollen Lees, 'The Survival of the Unfit: Welfare Policies and Family Maintenance in Nineteenth Century London', in Peter Mandler (ed.), *The Uses of Charity: The Poor on Relief in the Nineteenth Century Metropolis* (Philadelphia: University of Pennsylvania Press, 1990), 68–122.

11 Social Problems, Social Improvement: 1820–1890

On DISEASE AND THE ENVIRONMENT see J. A. I. Champion (ed.), *Epidemic Disease in London* (London: Institute of Historical Research, University of London, 1993); Anne Hardy, *The Epidemic Streets* (Oxford: Oxford University Press, 1993); and W. E. Luckin, 'The Final Catastrophe: Cholera in London, 1866', *Medical History*, xxi (1977), 32–42. POOR LAW HOSPITALS are dealt with in Gwendoline M. Ayers, *England's First State Hospitals and the Metropolitan Asylums Board, 1867–1930* (London: Wellcome Institute, 1971).

On the METROPOLITAN BOARD OF WORKS, D. Owen's *The Government of Victorian London, 1855–1889*, ed. Roy MacLeod (Cambridge, Mass.: Harvard University Press, 1982), is definitive; and see Gloria Clifton's *Professionalism, Patronage, and Public Service in Victorian London: The Staff of the Metropolitan Board of Works, 1856–1889* (London Athlone Press, 1992).

Lively on STREET IMPROVEMENT is James Winter's *London's Teeming Streets, 1830–1914* (London: Routledge, 1993).

For WATER, see H. W. Dickinson's *Water Supply of Greater London* (London: Newcomen Society, 1954) and Bill Luckin's *Pollution and Control: A Social History of the Thames in the Nineteenth Century* (Bristol: Adam Hilger, 1986).

On POVERTY, see David R. Green's 'A Map for

Mayhew's London: the Geography of Poverty in the Mid-Nineteenth Century', *The London Journal*, xi (1985), 115–26; on HOUSING, J. A. Yelling's *Slums and Slum Clearance in Victorian London* (London: Allen & Unwin, 1986); Enid Gauldie's *Cruel Habitations: A History of Working-Class Housing, 1780–1918* (London: Allen & Unwin, 1974); and the first-rate works of Anthony S. Wohl: *The Eternal Slum: Housing and Social Policy in Victorian London* (London: Edward Arnold, 1977) and *Endangered Lives: Public Health in Victorian Britain* (London: Dent, 1983). For REHOUSING, see J. White's *Rothschild Buildings: Life in an East End Tenement Block, 1887–1920* (London: Routledge & Kegan Paul, 1980).

For CONTEMPORARY SHOCK-HORROR LITERATURE, see Thomas Archer, *The Terrible Sights of London* (London: S. Rivers, 1870); Thomas Beames, *The Rookeries of London: Past, Present and Prospective* (London: Thomas Bosworth, 1852); James Greenwood, *Low-Life Deeps* (London: Chatto & Windus, 1875) and *The Seven Curses of London* (London: S. Rivers, 1869; Oxford: Basil Blackwell, 1981); J. Hollingshead's *Ragged London in 1861* (London: Everyman, 1986); and Andrew Mearns, *The Bitter Cry of Outcast London* (Leicester: Leicester University Press, 1970; first published 1885).

For CONTEMPORARY INVESTIGATIONS, see Charles Booth (ed.), *Life and Labour of the People in London*, 17 vols. (London: Macmillan, 1892–1903); Albert Friend and Richard M. Elman (eds.), *Charles Booth's London: A Portrait of the Poor at the Turn of the Century, drawn from 'Life and Labour of the People in London'* (London: Hutchinson, 1969); Helen Dendy Bosanquet, *Social Work in London, 1869 to 1912: A History of the Charity Organization Society* (London: John Murray, 1914); Asa Briggs, *Toynbee Hall: The First Hundred Years* (London: Routledge & Kegan Paul, 1984); and S. Meacham, *Toynbee Hall and Social Reform: The Search for Community 1880–1914* (New Haven and London: Yale University Press, 1987).

12 Victorian Life

The FEEL of Victorian London is variously explored: see Aldon D. Bell, *London in the Age of Dickens* (Norman: University of Oklahoma Press, 1967); Alexandra Welsh, *The City of Dickens* (Oxford: Clarendon Press, 1971); F. S. Schwarzbach, *Dickens and the City* (London: Athlone Press, 1979); and Kellow Chesney, *The Victorian Underworld* (Harmondsworth: Penguin, 1979).

For the VISUAL DIMENSION, see Blanchard Jerrold and Gustave Doré, *The London of Gustave Doré* (New York: Dover, 1970); Alex Potts, 'Picturing the Modern Metropolis: Images of London in the Nineteenth Century', *History Workshop*, xxvi (1988), 28–56; and Gavin Stamp, *The Changing Metropolis: Earliest Photographs of London, 1839–1879* (Harmondsworth: Viking, 1984).

COSMOPOLITANISM is assessed in Rosemary Ashton, *Little Germany: Exile and Asylum in Victorian England* (Oxford: Oxford University Press, 1986); for FOG, see Peter Brimblecombe, *The Big Smoke: A History of Air Pollution in London Since Medieval Times* (London: Methuen, 1987).

On MIDDLE-CLASS LIFE, see the recollections of Mary V. Hughes, brought up in Canonbury in the 1870s: *A London Child of the 1870s* (Oxford: Oxford University Press, 1977), *A London Girl of the 1880s* (Oxford: Oxford University Press, 1978), *A London Home in the 1890s* (Oxford: Oxford University Press, 1978) and *A London Family Between the Wars* (Oxford: Oxford University Press, 1978). See also Zuzanna Shonfield, *The Precariously Privileged: A Professional Family in Victorian London* (Oxford: Oxford University Press, 1987). Helpful is Geoffrey Crossick, *An Artisan Elite in Victorian Society: Kentish London, 1840–1880* (London: Croom Helm, 1978).

On WORKING-CLASS LIFE AND MIDDLE-CLASS OBSERVERS, see Anne Humphreys, *Henry Mayhew* (Boston: Twayne Publishers, 1984); Gareth Stedman Jones, *Outcast London: A Study in the Relationships between the Classes in Victorian*

Society (Oxford: Clarendon Press, 1971; Harmondsworth: Penguin, 1976); and E. P. Thompson and Eileen Yeo, *The Unknown Mayhew: Selections from the Morning Chronicle 1849–50* (Harmondsworth: Penguin, 1973). Henry Mayhew's *London Labour and the London Poor*, 4 vols. (London: Griffen Bohn, 1851–62), is eternally fascinating.

Particular aspects of Victorian London discussed in this chapter can be followed up in Frank Richard Cowell, *The Athenaeum: Club and Social Life in London 1824–1974* (London: Heinemann, 1975); Alan William Ball, *The Public Libraries of Greater London: A Pictorial History, 1856–1914* (London: Library Association, 1977); Sir Charles Theodore Hagberg Wright, *The London Library: A Sketch of its History and Administration* (London: London Library, 1926); Bernard Henry Becker, *Scientific London* (London: H. S. King, 1874); Hugh Hale Bellot, *University College, London, 1826–1926* (London: University of London Press, 1929); Cecil Delisle Burns, *A Short History of Birkbeck College (University of London)* (London: University of London Press, 1924); Sir Sydney Caine, *The History of the Foundation of the London School of Economics and Political Science* (London: London School of Economics and Political Science, 1963); Negley B. Harte, *The University of London, 1836–1986: An Illustrated History* (London: Athlone Press, 1986); Gordon Huelin, *King's College London, 1828–1978* (London: King's College, 1978); Stuart Maclure, *One Hundred Years of London Education, 1870–1970* (London: Allen Lane, 1970); Ron Ringshall, Dame Margaret Miles and Frank Kelshall, *The Urban School: Buildings for Education in London 1870–1980* (London: Architectural Press, 1983); and Dame Margaret Janson Tuke, *A History of Bedford College for Women, 1849–1937* (London: Oxford University Press, 1939).

For RELIGION, consult Jeffrey Cox, *The English Churches in a Secular Society: Lambeth, 1870–1930* (Oxford: Oxford University Press, 1982), and, for a pastoral mission, H. Edgar Bonsall in collaboration with Edwin H. Robertson, *The Dream of an Ideal City: Westbourne Park, 1877–1977* (London: Westbourne Park Baptist Church; York: Sessions, 1978).

For SHOWS, see Ralph Hyde, *Panoramania! The Art and Entertainment of the 'All-Embracing' View* (London: Trefoil, 1988); for THEATRE, R. Booth, 'The Metropolis on Stage', in H. J. Dyos and Michael Wolff (eds.), *The Victorian City: Images and Realities*, vol. 1 (London: Routledge & Kegan Paul, 1973), 211–26; on DRINKING, see Mark Girouard, *Victorian Pubs* (London: Studio Vista, 1975), and Brian Harrison, 'Pubs', in H. J. Dyos and Michael Wolff (eds.), *The Victorian City: Images and Realities*, vol. 1 (London: Routledge & Kegan Paul, 1973), 161–90.

On the EAST END, see A. Davies, *The East End Nobody Knows* (London: Macmillan, 1990); Alan Palmer, *The East End: Four Centuries of London Life* (London: John Murray, 1989); and Millicent Rose, *The East End of London* (London: Cresset Press, 1951). The IRISH are discussed in Lynn Hollen Lees, *Exiles of Erin: Irish Migrants in Victorian London* (Manchester University Press, 1979). On the JEWISH COMMUNITY, see Chaim Bermant, *Point of Arrival: A Study of London's East End* (London: Eyre Methuen, 1975); David Feldman, 'The Importance of Being English: Jewish Immigration and the Decay of Liberal England', in David Feldman and Gareth Stedman Jones (eds.), *Metropolis London: Histories and Representations since 1800* (London: Routledge, 1989), 56–84; William Fishman, *The Streets of East London* (London: Duckworth, 1979); and Aubrey Newman (ed.), *The Jewish East End 1840–1939* (London: Jewish Historical Society of England, 1982). On the image of the CHINESE COMMUNITY, see Virginia Berridge, 'East End Opium Dens and Narcotic Use in Britain', *The London Journal*, iv (1978), 3–28. The archetypal East End image is JACK THE RIPPER: see D. Rumbelow, *The Complete Jack the Ripper* (London: W. H. Allen, 1975), and Judith R. Walkowitz, *City of Dreadful Delight: Narratives of Sexual Danger in Late-Victorian London* (London: Virago, 1992).

The COCKNEY is anatomized in Gareth Stedman Jones, 'The "Cockney" and the Nation, 1780–1988', in David Feldman and Gareth Stedman Jones (eds.), *Metropolis London: Histories and Representations since 1800* (London: Routledge, 1989), 272–324; also consult William Matthews, *Cockney Past and Present: A Short History of the*

Dialect of London (London: Routledge & Kegan Paul, 1972).

For a taste of CONTEMPORARY WRITINGS, see George and Weedon Grossmith, *The Diary of a Nobody* (Harmondsworth: Penguin, 1983; first published 1892); E. Hyams (ed.), *Taine's Notes on England* (London: Thames and Hudson, 1957); and Arthur Morison, *Tales of Mean Streets* (London: Methuen, 1895).

13 'A Fungus-Like Growth': Expansion 1890–1945

TRANSPORT IMPROVEMENTS are assessed in T. C. Barker and R. M. Robbins, *A History of London Transport*, vol. 2, *The Twentieth Century to 1970* (London: Allen & Unwin, 1974); also see F. Merton Atkins (comp.), *London's Tramways* (London: Shirley, 1954); James Graeme Bruce, *Tube Trains under London: An Illustrated History of London Transport Tube Rolling Stock, including Heathrow Airport and Jubilee Line Trains* (London: London Transport Executive, 1977); John Robert Day, *The Story of London's Underground* (London: London Transport, 1979); H. F. Howson, *London's Underground* (London: Ian Allan, 1981); and R. W. Kidner, *The Motor Bus in London 1904–8* (Blandford: Oakwood Press, 1975).

The PLANNING ideal is explained in W. Ashworth, *The Genesis of Modern British Town Planning: A Study in Economic and Social History of the Nineteenth and Twentieth Centuries* (London: Routledge & Kegan Paul, 1954); the basic text is Ebenezer Howard, *Garden Cities of Tomorrow* (London: Sonnenschein, 1902). See also Anthony Sutcliffe (ed.), *Planning and the Environment in the Modern World*, vol. 1, *The Rise of Modern Urban Planning, 1800–1914* (London: Mansell, 1980), and Anthony Sutcliffe (ed.), *British Town Planning: The Formative Years* (Leicester: Leicester University Press, 1981).

For the continuation of SLUMS, see Jim Yelling, 'The Metropolitan Slum: London 1918–51', in S. Martin Gaskell (ed.), *Slums* (Leicester: Leicester University Press, 1990), 186–233, and J. White,

The Worst Street in North London: Campbell Bunk, Islington, Between the Wars (London: Routledge & Kegan Paul, 1986).

For PRIVATE HOUSE-BUILDING see F. M. L. Thompson (ed.), *The Rise of Suburbia* (Leicester: Leicester University Press, 1982), and Alan A. Jackson, *Semi-Detached London: Suburban Development, Life and Transport, 1900–39* (London: Allen & Unwin, 1973). SUBURBAN DEVELOPMENTS are illuminated in Brigid Grafton Green, *Hampstead Garden Suburb, 1907–77* (London: Hampstead Garden Suburb Residents' Association, 1977); G. Hewlett, *A History of Wembley* (London: Brent Library Service, 1979); D. A. Reeder, 'A Theatre of Suburbs: Some Patterns of Development in West London, 1801–1911', in H. J. Dyos (ed.), *The Study of Urban History* (London: Edward Arnold, 1968), 253–71; *Then and Now: The Changing Scene of Surrey Life in Coulsdon & Purley* (Caterham: Bourne Society, 1989); S. Wallmann, *Living in South London: Perspectives on Battersea, 1871–1981* (Aldershot: Gower, 1983); and Alan R. Warwick, *The Phoenix Suburb: A South London Social History* (London: The Blue Boar Press, 1972). All these topics are illuminated by Gavin Weightman's *The Making of Modern London, 1914–1939* (London: Sidgwick & Jackson, 1984) and by Paul Vaughan's wonderful autobiographical account of growing up in the southern suburbs in the 1930s: *Something in Linoleum* (London: Sinclair-Stevenson, 1994).

London's changing CULTURAL PROFILE defies summary in a few books. See, however, Karl Beckson, *London in the 1890s: A Cultural History* (New York: Norton, 1992); Wolf Von Eckardt, Sander L. Gilman and J. Edward Chamberlin, *Oscar Wilde's London: A Scrapbook of Vices and Virtues, 1880–1900* (Garden City, N.Y.: Anchor Press, 1987); Patricia L. Garside, 'West End, East End: London, 1890–1940', in Anthony Sutcliffe (ed.), *Metropolis 1890–1940* (London: Mansell, 1984), 221–58; Alistair Service, *London, 1900* (St Albans: Crosby, Lockwood & Staples, 1979); G. Norton, *London Before the Blitz, 1906–40: From the Coming of the Motor Car to the Outbreak of War* (London: Macdonald, 1970); Philippa Pullar, *Gilded Butterflies: The Rise and Fall of the London*

Season (London: Hamish Hamilton, 1978); Gavin Weightman, *Bright Lights, Big City: London Entertainment, 1830–1950* (London: Collins and Brown, 1992); Doris M. Bailey, *Children of the Green: A True Story of Childhood in Bethnal Green, 1922–1937* (London: Stepney Books, 1981); Richard Trench, *London Before the Blitz* (London: Weidenfeld & Nicolson, 1989), a rich evocation of the physical environment on the EVE OF WAR; James L. Howgego, *London in the 20s and 30s from Old Photographs* (London: Fitzhouse Books, 1978), which documents the age of the flapper and the bright young things; and, for a more sombre photographic record, Bill Brandt, *London in the Thirties* (London: Gordon Fraser, 1983). For a slightly later period, see Daniel Farson, *Soho in the Fifties* (London: Michael Joseph, 1987), and the classic survey of life among the WORKING CLASSES: Michael Young and Peter Willmott, *Family and Kinship in East London* (London: Routledge & Kegan Paul, 1957; Harmondsworth: Penguin, 1962).

For WRITERS' LONDON, see Robert Crawford, *The Savage and the City in the Work of T. S. Eliot* (Oxford: Clarendon Press, 1987); Burton Pike, *The Image of the City in Modern Literature* (Princeton: Princeton University Press, 1981); Jean Moorcroft Wilson, *Virginia Woolf – Life and London: A Biography of Place* (London: Cecil Woolf, 1987); Robert Hewison, *Literary Life in London 1939–45* (London: Weidenfeld & Nicolson, 1977); and John Thompson, *Orwell's London* (London: Fourth Estate, 1984).

14 Modern Growth, Modern Government: 1890–1945

The feel of London as the heart of the EMPIRE is conveyed in Ford Madox Ford, *The Soul of London: A Survey of a Modern City* (London: Alston Rivers, 1905).

On the evolving ECONOMY, see David R. Green, 'The Metropolitan Economy: Continuity and Change 1800–1939', in Keith Hoggart and David R. Green (eds.), *London: A New Metropolitan Geography* (London: Edward Arnold, 1991), 8–

33; John Marriott, ' "West Ham: London's Industrial Centre and Gateway to the World" ', I, 'Stabilization and Decline 1910–1939', *London Journal*, xiv (1989), 43–58; Douglas H. Smith, *The Industries of Greater London* (London: P. S. King, 1933); and James Frederick Patrick Thornhill, *Greater London: A Social Geography* (London: Christopher's, 1935).

For the economics of LEISURE AND PLEASURE, see M. C. Borer's *The British Hotel Through the Ages* (Guildford: Lutterworth Press, 1972) and Hugh Montgomery-Massingberd and David Watkin's *The London Ritz: A Social and Architectural History* (London: Aurum Press, 1980). Gordon Honeycombe's *Selfridges. Seventy Five Years. The Story of the Store, 1909–1984* (London: Park Lane Press, 1984) is helpful on the AMERICANIZATION of early twentieth-century London.

The LCC has been well covered: see Paul Richard Thompson, *Socialists, Liberals and Labour: The Struggle for London, 1885–1914* (London: Routledge & Kegan Paul; 1967); Andrew Saint (ed.), *Politics and the People of London: The London County Council, 1889–1965* (London and Ronceverte: Hambledon Press, 1989); I. G. Gibbon and R. W. Bell, *History of London County Council, 1889–1939* (London: Macmillan, 1939); and William Eric Jackson, *Achievement: A Short History of the London County Council* (London: Longman, 1965).

On METROPOLITAN POLITICS and in particular the rise of LABOUR, consult Julia Bush, *Behind the Lines: East London Labour, 1914–1919* (London: Merlin Press, 1984); Mark Clapson, 'Localism, the London Labour Party and the LCC between the Wars', in Andrew Saint (ed.), *Politics and the People of London: The London County Council, 1889–1965* (London and Ronceverte, Hambledon Press, 1989), 127–46; Susan Goss, *Local Labour and Local Government: A Study of Changing Interests, Politics and Policy in Southwark 1919–1982* (Edinburgh: Edinburgh University Press, 1988); and John Marriott, *The Culture of Labourism: The East End Between the Wars* (Edinburgh: Edinburgh University Press, 1991); JEWISH POLITICS form the theme of Geoffrey Alderman's *London*

Jewry and London Politics, 1889–1986 (London: Routledge, 1989) and William Fishman's *East End Jewish Radicals 1875–1914* (London: Duckworth, 1975).

For the WAR, see Clive Hardy and Nigel Arthur, *London at War 1936–1945* (London: Quoin, 1989) – mainly a picture-book; David Johnson, *V-1, V-2: Hitler's Vengeance on London* (New York: Stein & Day, 1982); Joanna Mack and Steve Humphries, *London at War: The Making of Modern London, 1939–1945* (London: Sidgwick & Jackson, 1985); J. Neville, *The Blitz: London Then and Now* (London: Hodder & Stoughton, 1990); W. Sanson, *The Blitz: Westminster at War* (Oxford: Oxford University Press, 1990); Constantine Fitz Gibbon, *The Blitz* (London: Allan Wingate, 1957); and J. D. Stewart, *Bermondsey in War 1939–45* (London: Bermondsey and Rotherhithe Society, 1981).

15 Swinging London, Dangling Economy: 1945–1975

The PLANNERS' BLUEPRINT was Sir Patrick Abercrombie's *Greater London Plan: 1944* (London: HMSO, 1945); see also his *Town and Country Planning* (London: Butterworth, 1933). For the world of PLANNERS AND RELOCATION, see Donald Foley's *Controlling London's Growth, 1940–60* (Berkeley: University of California Press, 1963); Nicholas Deakin and Clare Ungerson's *Leaving London: Planned Mobility and the Inner City* (London: Heinemann, 1977); David Thomas's *London's Green Belt* (London: Faber, 1970); and Ray Thomas's *London's New Towns: A Study of Self Contained and Balanced Communities* (London: Political and Economic Planning, 1969).

SOCIAL CHANGE is surveyed in Ruth Glass (ed.), *London: Aspects of Change* (London: Mac-Gibbon & Kee, 1964); on GENTRIFICATION, see Chris Hamnett and Peter Williams, 'Social Change in London: A Study of Gentrification', *The London Journal*, vi (1980), 51–66.

ECONOMIC DEVELOPMENTS are analysed in J. T. Coppock and H. G. Prince (eds.), *Greater London* (London: Faber, 1964), and J. E. Martin, *Greater London: An Industrial Geography* (London: George Bell, 1966); on the DOCKS, see John Christopher Lovell, *Stevedores and Dockers: A Study of Trade Unionism in the Port of London* (New York: Augustus M. Kelley, 1969).

The HUMAN DIMENSIONS OF CHANGE are brought out in Steve Humphries and John Taylor's *The Making of Modern London, 1945–1985* (London: Sidgwick & Jackson, 1986), while Michael Young and Peter Willmott's *Family and Class in a London Suburb* (London: Routledge & Kegan Paul, 1960) discusses the new suburban affluent workers.

On REDEVELOPMENT, see O. Marriott, *The Property Boom* (London: Pan, 1967); Oliver Leigh Wood (comp.), *From Splendour to Banality: The Rebuilding of the City of London 1945–1983* (London: SAVE Britain's Heritage, 1983), whose title speaks for itself; and Christopher Booker and Candida Lycett Green, *Goodbye London* (London: Fontana, 1973). The account in Simon Jenkins's *Landlords to London: The Story of a Capital and its Growth* (London: Constable, 1975) is superb, and see also his splendid 'Seifert's Towers', in *The Selling of Mary Davies and Other Writings* (London: John Murray, 1993), 71–9. MODERN PROPERTY DEVELOPMENT is criticized in HRH The Prince of Wales's *A Vision of Britain: A Personal View of Architecture* (London: Doubleday, 1989).

On IMMIGRATION, see Nick Merriman (ed.), *The Peopling of London: Fifteen Thousand Years of Settlement from Overseas* (London: Reaktion Books, 1993); Edward Pilkington, *Beyond the Mother Country: West Indians and the Notting Hill White Riots* (London: I. B. Tauris, 1988); and Marianna Economou and Paul Halliday, *Here and There: The Greek Cypriot Community in London* (Salonica: Interpreter, 1988).

16 Thatcher's London

For the crisis of LONDON'S ECONOMY TODAY, see John M. Hall, *Metropolis Now: London and its Region* (Cambridge: Cambridge University Press,

1990); Hugh Clout and Peter Wood (eds.), *London: Problems of Change* (London: Longman, 1986); and Keith Hoggart and David R. Green (eds.), *London: A New Metropolitan Geography* (London: Edward Arnold, 1991). On the CITY, see R. Michie, *The City of London: Continuity and Change, 1850–1990* (London: Macmillan, 1992), and Derek R. Diamond, 'The City, the "Big Bang" and Office Development', in Keith Hoggart and David R. Green (eds.), *London: A New Metropolitan Geography* (London: Edward Arnold, 1991), 79–94.

For the GLC, see Gerald Rhodes and G. R. Ruck, *The Government of Greater London* (London: Allen & Unwin, 1970), and Ken Young and John Kramer, *Strategy and Conflict in Metropolitan Housing: Suburbia versus the Greater London Council, 1965–1975* (London: Heinemann, 1978).

For LONDON'S POLITICAL FUTURE, see Shirley Porter, *A Minister for London: A Capital Concept* (London: FPL Financial, 1990).

An issue of the *London Journal* (xvii, 1992) is given over to historical and sociological discussion of the redevelopment of DOCKLAND, with articles by Andrew Church and Martin Frost, Janet Foster, Patricia L. Garside and David R. Green,

Ray Hall and Philip E. Ogden, and Michael Hebbert. See also Sue Brownhill, *Developing London's Docklands: Another Great Planning Disaster* (London: Paul Chapman, 1990).

My reading of how THATCHERISM failed London owes much to the analysis offered by one of her own Cabinet ministers, Ian Gilmour, in his *Dancing with Dogma: Britain Under Thatcherism* (London: Simon & Schuster, 1992).

Where is London going? Various DIAGNOSES AND PRESCRIPTIONS are offered in Peter G. Hall, *London 2001* (London: Unwin Hyman, 1989) – highly stimulating; Andy Thornley (ed.), *The Crisis of London* (London: Routledge, 1992); Richard Rogers and Mark Fisher, *A New London* (London: Penguin, 1992) – which condemns Thatcherism and looks forward to a 'new urban culture'; and two books which highlight the contrasts between government ideology and inner-city realities: Paul Harrison, *Inside the Inner City: Life Under the Cutting Edge* (Harmondsworth: Penguin, 1992), and Patrick Wright, *A Journey Through Ruins: The Last Days of London* (London: Radius, 1991).

For NOSTALGIA, see Pennie Denton (ed.), *Betjeman's London* (London: John Murray, 1988).

Index

NOTE: page numbers in *italic* indicate illustrations